SO-AAK-000

The
# Official®
DIRECTORY TO
# U.S.
# FLEA
# MARKETS

The
# Official®
DIRECTORY TO
# U.S. FLEA
# MARKETS

### Edited by
### Kitty Werner

## SEVENTH EDITION

House of Collectibles
The Ballantine Publishing Group • New York

*Important Notice:* The publisher assumes no responsibility for any losses incurred as a result of consulting this directory, or for any objects or services bought, sold, or traded at any flea market listed in this publication. All information relating to specific flea markets has been obtained from the owner, manager, or promoter to the best of the publisher's knowledge and is accepted in good faith.

Copyright © 2000 by Random House, Inc.

This is a registered trademark of Random House, Inc.

All rights reserved under International and Pan-American Copyright Conventions.

Published by: House of Collectibles
The Ballantine Publishing Group
201 East 50th Street
New York, New York 10022

Distributed by The Ballantine Publishing Group, a division of Random House, Inc., New York, and simultaneously in Canada by Random House of Canada Limited, Toronto.

Cover design by Min Choi
Cover photo by George Kerrigan

Manufactured in the United States of America

ISSN: 1073-208X

ISBN: 0-676-60190-1

Seventh Edition: February 2000
10 9 8 7 6 5 4 3 2 1

# CONTENTS

# INTRODUCTION

When using the listing of markets at the end of each state keep in mind that I have not personally checked each of these markets and cannot guarantee that they exist after this book is printed. For the 1996 book, one market sent in their listing and closed within a month! If the market is new to you, please call first, just in case. Quite a few markets have closed—some burned down, others had their land bought from under them. And just as many have opened since the Sixth Edition.

I was in Spain for a winter week one January and there in gorgeous Segovia was a local flea market covering about two blocks in the old part of town—no doubt the same place vendors have been selling for centuries. My children and I traveled around Europe for two summers and found that even in tiny villages in Provence, France, the Saturday market in my grandfather's hometown was similiar to the markets in tiny villages in northern Germany, near my husband's hometown. So much of the new merchandise is exactly the same as that sold here in the States. What makes a market different are the people, the atmosphere and the local produce and crafts. When you find a market that suits you—frequent it. Get to know its dealers and learn about the old treasures. Most of the dealers I have met love to talk about their wares and the history behind them.

In writing this book, I have spoken to hundreds of strangers in as many cities and towns around this country. I learned a great deal about flea markets in general, and collected some terrific stories. In this edition, these stories have been added to their respective market's listing. If you have a market story to share, send it along to me; my address is in the back of this book.

What I have gleaned from many conversations with these markets are these two basic facts:

1.    The majority of people running flea markets are working for the fun of it, for the "family" a really good market becomes, and because they are, quite simply, dedicated to antiques, collectibles, and the treasures that may show up.

2.    Those markets opened up "just to make a buck" quickly fold. It takes a lot of work and dedication to make a market work and grow, and more important to the market's survival, a healthy, loyal following of customers and dealers.

In fact, some of these markets become so "family" to dealers and customers that weddings and other major events are planned around market days. In one case, an elderly gentleman who lived at "his other home" for twenty-some years of the market's existence, seated at a different dealer's booth each week, died just before the market reopened in April. His funeral happened to fall on opening day. As a tribute, his funeral procession drove slowly through the market in a final salute.

Two dealers we heard about, again, both elderly, died at their booth spaces, one while laughing with his customers, the other, an 87-year-old who had vowed to die on "his space," did so after having driven completely around the market, pulling into his accustomed space, and getting out of his car.

Another market, newly opened, became "family" so fast that when one dealer's husband required surgery, the other dealers kept her booth running for her so the family wouldn't go broke.

In a different vein, one market told me that one of their dealer spaces was lost/won (depending on your point of view) in a divorce settlement!

## So, What Do You Sell?

When it came to asking about the merchandise sold, I asked the same question: What sort of things does your market sell? The answer is invariably the same: "You name it, we've got it!" Perhaps we should rename this book.

Occasionally I encountered a nagging question, "Was this market really a flea market?" Some markets are, of course, flea markets by any definition of the phrase. But still, what is the *real* definition of today's flea market? Do they sell only "old" items—a former qualification? Or is new merchandise fair game? Some markets have grown so large they have turned themselves into "malls." Quite a few of the "real malls" were removed from the book. However, some one-person antique shops were included, kept or added, simply because I felt that if you are hunting for antiques and collectibles, and these places were highly recommended, then they should be here for you, the dealer, looking to buy treasures.

Recent changes in markets and what they sell stem from the simple fact that there are only a finite amount of antiques and collectibles available— period. Chippendale only lived about 61 years and could only create a finite amount of furniture. The same goes for other "names" in the business. There were only so many baseball cards printed in any one year. That is what makes one card more valuable than another.

Trends make a difference too. Where sports cards were the rave several years ago, now it's something entirely different. Beanie Babies are hot. Collectible Barbies are hot. Star Wars is hot. Cards aren't.

## More Is Less, or Is It More?

As more markets open for business, the fewer dealers there are to go around. If there are, in fact, more dealers (as more go into the business), there is still a "finite" amount of goods to spread even more thinly.

As a result many markets have opened their stalls to "new merchandise." Still, the die-hards hold out and you can still find markets that only deal in antiques and collectibles. They are mentioned in the description of each market. But remember, to keep the market doors open, many markets that may have been more selective are now forced to sell the products the dealers have to sell—namely new merchandise.

Many markets proudly boast about their size—"We are the largest in northeast Whatchamacallit!" Or "We are the largest Wednesday and Thursday market anywhere!" Sometimes you have to take such claims with a grain of sand. I had one man tell me he had the largest market in the business—"125,000 square feet!" I'm afraid I shattered his ego when I told him about a market that opened in an abandoned Ford factory (since gone out of business). Using only two of the six floors, they owned close to 750,000 square feet altogether. In fact, there are many markets in the 100,000-square-foot category. And just as many smaller ones—they seem to have the richest stories to tell. Bigger isn't always better. It simply depends on what you are looking for: a good time, your "other" family, a specific object, just to waste a day, a carnival atmosphere, whatever.

Many of the markets listed have turned into semi-carnivals to attract buyers, or to provide a more interesting place to visit as a get-away with the family. One market owner bought the contents of a former amusement park and has all the gnomes and creatures scattered around his property, including a 30-foot totem pole and twin pink elephants. Colonial Valley in Pennsylvania had a 26-inch-tall steer named Clyde (who unfortunately died). Mt. Sterling, Kentucky, celebrates the Third Monday Court Days, started in 1870 when the circuit court judge would pass through the towns of Maysville, Flemingsburg, and then Mt. Sterling doing his business—including the sentencing of some offenders to hang! The entire town shuts down and celebrates for three days (with over 2,000 dealers). Maysville and Flemingsburg joined in the act around 20 years ago restarting their "Court Days." Their markets start Sunday after church and continue until the dancing ends on Monday night.

Last edition I found the Texas Court Day markets and added most of them to my listings. Traditions die hard.

## Educate Yourself

A neighbor of mine has found the greatest antique treasures in the local flea market, not noted for anything grand. She says you just have to look carefully and know what you are getting. Her house is furnished with numerous pieces of furniture, from chests and beds to baby highchairs, mostly culled from this one market. She has collected complete sets of china and silverware in five different patterns for each of her five children—all from flea markets.

A caution about being sure of what you want and knowing its value. There are numerous stories sprinkled throughout this book of surprise finds— the dealer who sold a frame for $75 only to hear later that the savvy buyer sold the old master in it for $250,000, and so on. Look carefully. You never know.

Do educate yourself if you are a serious buyer of antiques and collectibles. It obviously pays off.

Public Broadcasting Service (PBS) has been showing the Antique Road Show this past year or so. It is a revelation to the uninitiated. If you haven't seen it, do try to see it. People bring in their curiosities, found stuff, and treasures to the show and expert antique appraisers and dealers tell the owner what their item is worth. Many times the owner doesn't realize that 1) it's a fake, 2) it is worthless, or more exciting, 3) it's a lost masterwork worth thousands upon thousands of dollars.

# FLEA MARKETS: THEN AND NOW

Look at the history and development of the phenomenon of flea markets as an alternative to *shopping*—that is, going to town and wandering from store to store. The term "flea market," a direct translation from the French phrase *marché aux puces*, has come to signify a specially designated occasion for the purpose of exchanging a wide variety of goods—anything from valuable antiques to backyard junk.

In France, where the term was coined, fleas were found to accompany old furniture and clothing drawn from attics or barns. Today, some flea markets in the United States maintain a curious tie to this tradition by demanding that all furniture be either fumigated or else banned from the sale area entirely.

The flea market in the United States, however, has taken on other European customs—customs found not only in France but throughout the Continent. One custom is Market Day, a regularly scheduled time when a portion of town, usually the main square, is closed off from traffic as farmers, itinerant tradesmen, butcher and bone-men, and other dealers sell their merchandise—anything from produce and clothing to fresh meats and kitchen appliances—to the people of the town and surrounding area. From early in the morning—6:00 AM, even earlier—to the middle of the afternoon, buyers and sellers get together in a particular place for the single purpose of striking bargains. In America, where so many ancestors came from rural Europe, small towns have since the first settlement conducted fairs, animal shows, and farmers' markets as means of distributing locally made products. For early farmers, tool makers, and other craftsmen, the local market could prove an effective gateway to the larger markets of other cities and large towns in the region, as buyers from nearby districts would frequently come looking for special deals. The flea market in the United States, then, is a bit of a mongrel, with its Old World mixed parentage combined with that peculiarly American flair for the entrepreneurial. The giant flea markets like the Rose Bowl Flea Market in Pasadena, California, and the First Monday Trade Days in Canton, Texas, are cousins, and not very distant, to that of the antique shows and sales that keep popping up with increasing frequency throughout the country. The current popularity of flea markets large or small around urban centers, as well as in the deep country, suggests that these events have become a welcome and permanent part of our day-to-day lives.

A flea market may range in size from just a few sellers standing on the side of a highway trying to clean out the unwanted contents of their homes to a complex, labyrinthine structure of dealers' booths sprawled out across acres of open space indoors or outdoors or both. In other words, a flea market is rather like beauty—it is all in the eye of the beholder.

Thinking another way, it is not so much a particular kind of event (whether it's a "swap meet" or an antique show and sale), but rather an alternative to shopping at the mall—a place where the individual buyer is on equal terms with the individual dealer, where no prices are fixed, and the fun comes in finding just what you want and buying or selling it for a price that feels right to *you*.

In this seventh edition, our directory has grown to include the listings for all the markets we could find in business directories. That should bring our total number of markets to well in the thousands. Just be reminded that we didn't contact any of them listed in those sections. There simply wasn't enough time and space to do so. We do include just about any conceivable flea market from the one-man market to the gigantic San Jose market in California. One of my criteria was courtesy and friendliness. I didn't find every market that exists. I've been told that between Kansas and Texas there must be 4,000 flea markets alone! But I did find some obscure markets that are fund-raisers for churches, schools, and firehouses. According to the people who run these markets, you wouldn't believe the treasures that can be found there. One Texas market is simply the local residents' once-a-year garage sale. There is another market in Maryland doing the same thing.

There are some newer markets that have opened and grown tremendously since the sixth edition was published and we've added them too.

I think you'll find this a wonderful mix. There are plenty of places that cater to families, providing rides, perhaps video arcades, games, petting zoos, and whatever they can think of that children might enjoy.

You could plan a vacation around many of the markets listed here. Don't be shy. The people I have talked with represent a rich cross-section of America, doing this because they loved the people who came as dealers and those who came as visitors. They are having fun and they want to share it. It's up to you.

# BUYING AND SELLING
# AT FLEA MARKETS

## Coming Prepared

When shopping at flea markets—and this is as true for the fine antique shows as for the markets that feature new merchandise—be sure to distinguish between the valuable and not so valuable articles offered for sale. Keep in mind that flea markets trade in all kinds of things, not only antiques and fine collectibles, but also brand new objects and some odds and ends that have ended up, somehow, in the dealer's hands. Notes promoter R. G. Canning of his early days organizing California's world-famous Pasadena Rose Bowl Flea Market and Swap Meet: "It was amazing to me that people would come to buy all that junk."

Of course, there is nothing wrong with your paying money for someone else's junk; it just depends on how much you value it. The flea market (in the most general sense of the term) is really not unlike a communal yard sale. It often provides the opportunity to sell things to other people who might be able to find a use for them—though they might be hard pressed to say what that is exactly at the moment of purchase.

But whether it is a fine antique show or something as manic as the Rose Bowl Swap Meet, it is advisable to subject *all* merchandise to careful scrutiny, and not just the antiques and collectibles either. When shopping for "brand-name" items, be especially careful to check for fakes—some imitations are so masterful that they can fool a seasoned shopper. While imitations of brand-names appear to match the originals in craftsmanship and quality of materials, there have been many disappointed shoppers who have watched their "once-in-a-lifetime" bargains disintegrate in a matter of weeks or even days under normal use. Most flea markets monitor and insist that their dealers represent their goods honestly and use fair business practices. Several listed herein make known their policy of having their dealers not only stand behind their merchandise, but also offer refunds if the merchandise fails to please. This serves the double purpose of protecting both the buyer and the reputation of the market. Be sure to report any unfair or dishonest practices to the owner or operator of the market where this occurs. It is always best to be an alert and educated shopper.

## Knowing When to Haggle

At flea markets, as with just about any kind of trade, a deal is made when both the seller and the buyer think they are getting a bargain.

Put a value on an item as soon as you can and stick to it, as best you can. Changing your mind in the middle of a sale is a sign of weakness and uncertainty—one that a hardened seller will be quick to take advantage of. The more sure you are in your initial assessments, the easier and more pleasant your overall shopping will be. And when you encounter an object that is not marked with a price, don't suggest one, but rather prompt the seller to give you one. After all, it is the obligation of the seller to have a price to quote for any item he sells.

And don't forget that a main activity at the flea market isn't so much shopping as bargaining. In other words, don't automatically assume that the first price you hear is final, whether offered by voice or by a price tag. In fact, you have a right as a potential buyer to ask for a "last price" before you make up your mind on an item. (Remember, though, that you can only ask for a last price once.) You are not necessarily being rude by passing up an object after hearing the final offer, so long as you are polite in your refusal and thank the seller for his/her offer.

Don't ever let a seller use intimidation to force you to buy an object. You alone can know whether you want an object and, if so, how much it is worth to you.

Carry lots of cash, best of all in small denominations. As a general rule, always be working toward a deal in your negotiations with flea market salespeople. After all, their business is to sell, not to talk. Do not ask for a price on an item unless you are genuinely interested.

If you want to haggle, be careful how you do it. Part of the trick is in knowing real value, of course. Even if something is already priced low, a deft haggler takes the position that it can be driven down further. If he's going to make an offer he'll make a considerably lower one, representing maybe 50 percent of the asking price or even less, figuring that the end result is likely to be a compromise.

The wrong way to ask for a discount is by deriding the merchandise or the price, by suggesting that the dealer does not know his business, or by doing anything which could trigger a negative reaction. For example, never say "The shop down the street is selling one just like this for $20 less." Or, worse, "You don't really expect to get $75 for this, do you?"

Remember that the sellers have heard every possible pitch for discounts. They hear them every day, the same ones over and over. After just a short time in business they get thoroughly turned off by most types of discount-seeking approaches, and by most of the typical "I-want-a-discount" customers.

The majority of such customers act as if the dealer owes them a favor. You need to be a little original in trying to obtain a discount and, above all, courteous. Be inventive, use your imagination, and, most important, make a good impression. As they say in show biz, always leave 'em laughing. You may want to return some day, and you will want to be welcome next time.

## Selling at Flea Markets

First of all, decide which markets you want to participate in. There may be several nearby. A beginner is apt to make his choice based on the wrong considerations, thinking in terms of which show offers the best rate on space, or how he can save $1.50 on gas by selling close to home. It's really useless to give much thought to these points. The important thing is, at which flea market are you likely to do the most selling? Visit different markets as a browser; look at what is going on. How many dealers are present? Are nearly all the spaces taken, or are the grounds half empty? Unless the flea market is a new one, or in some cases the season is winding down, empty ground space indicates an unsuccessful market. What are the sellers offering? What percentage of the sellers are offering collectors' items? If you're interested in collectibles, for example, it is unwise to take a space at a show where collectibles are seldom sold.

After deciding on the flea market at which to sell, make arrangements for a space well in advance. Talk to the manager and find out about the rules and regulations. They are more or less the same from one show to another but there could be some differences. Every show has restrictions on what can and cannot be sold. With collectibles, you are not likely to run afoul of any taboos, except with firearms. Most flea markets do not permit the sale of firearms, antique or modern. Knives are almost always okay, except switchblades—some states have laws against them. Markets listed as "family" markets generally don't allow pornography either.

Mostly you'll want to find out what you will be getting for your rental money. Does the management provide a table? What is the exact size of the space you'll get? Will you be required to collect sales tax? Is this show held rain or shine? If the show is canceled because of bad weather, do you get a refund or a raincheck for the next show?

Put some thought into what you are going to take to the show. It's always better to have a variety of merchandise than to go heavy on just a few kinds of items. Large items such as furniture will cut down your exhibit space. If you are going to show small things of moderate or high value, such as jewelry or scarce coins, try to get a display box with a glass top and a lock. This will reduce the risk of theft. Clean up merchandise before packing it off to the show. This does not mean an indiscriminate scrubbing that could lessen the value and desirability of an antique, but dusting and (where appropriate) polishing. It does not enhance sales value when items have a just-out-of-the-dustbin appearance. Try to arrange everything in a way that will make browsing as easy as possible. If you are selling magazines, stand them upright in a carton. That way customers can flip through them with a minimum of fuss. This will also help to keep the covers from tearing, which is sure to happen if they are just piled together in a heap. When selling magazines of high value, or old comic books, slip them into protective Mylar bags. Scarce coins should be displayed in 2" × 2" holders. Some items are, of course, more of a headache to display than others: with glassware and china you run the risk of breakage not only as a result of clumsy browsers but strong gusts of wind. If you are displaying a lot of breakables, you can take the precaution of making certain that your table is well anchored. One way of anchoring a table is by sinking the leg tips two or three inches into the ground, if this is feasible. Another is to place heavy stones or bricks on top for ballast. In any event, keep breakables toward the center of the table if you can, where they are not as likely to be swept away by an errant arm or sleeve.

Figure out how much you want to get for each item before the show and whether or not you are going to use price tags. Don't wait until somebody asks the price before you start thinking about it. Most flea market exhibitors mark prices on their merchandise, and this is probably the best course to follow, simply because many browsers just won't bother to ask the price, even if they are mildly interested. Of course the marked price need not necessarily be the actual sum for which you would sell the item; you can leave yourself some leeway for bargaining, and it is usually a good idea to do this. But don't set your marked prices too much higher than what you would be willing to accept.

# PERIODICALS OF INTEREST

Following is a selective list of periodicals with good coverage of flea markets. The approximate geographical scope of each publication is listed in parentheses after its name. The publications listed are produced either in tabloid newspaper or magazine format. This list, though far from complete, should help the reader find the most up-to-date listings for some of the many flea markets that, due to space limitations or our own oversight, have regrettably been omitted from this guide.

*Antique Review* (Midwest). PO Box 538, Worthington OH 43085-0538. Tel: (614) 885-9757. Monthly. Subscriptions are $20 per year. Email: subscriptions@antiquereviewohio.com. Web: www.antiquereviewohio.com.

*Antique Trader Weekly, The* (Midwest). PO Box 1050, Dubuque IA 52004-1050. Tel: (319) 588-2073. Weekly. Subscriptions are $37 per year. Email: Traderpubs@aol.com. Web: www.csmonline.com/antiquetrader.

*Antique Week* (Two editions: Eastern and Mid-Central). PO Box 90, Knightstown IN 46148-0090. Tel: (765) 345-5133. Weekly. Subscriptions are $28.45 per year each, and $54.60 for both; includes Antique Shop Guide issue.

*Antiques & Art Around Florida*, PO Box 2481, Ft Lauderdale FL 33303-2481. Subscriptions are $10 per year, 4 issues. Email: aarf@shadow.net. Web: www.aarf.com.

*Antiques & Auction News, Joel Sater's* (Pennsylvania/Northeastern US). PO Box 500, Mount Joy PA 17552-0500. Tel: (717) 492-2541. Weekly. Subscriptions are $17.50 per year, third class; $40 for 6 months or $70 per year, first class mail.

*Antiques & Collectibles* (New York City/Long Island, NY). PO Box 33, Westbury NY 11590-0033. Tel: (516) 334-9650. Monthly. Subscriptions are $18 per year. Email: savannah@slip.net.

*Antiques & The Arts Weekly* (New England/Northeastern US). c/o The Newtown Bee, 5 Churchill Rd, Newtown CT 06470. Tel: (203) 426-8036. Weekly. Subscriptions are $56 per year. Email: thebee@connix.com. Web: www.thebee.com/aweb/aa.htm.

*Arts & Antiques*, 2100 Powers Ferry Rd, Atlanta GA 30339. Tel: (770) 955-5656. Subscriptions are $24.95 for 11 months. Email: arts&antiques@billian.com. Web: www.artantiquesmag.com.

*Collector's Journal* (Midwest). PO Box 601, Vinton IA 52349-0601. Tel: 1-800-472-4006. Weekly (except last two weeks in December and first week in January). Subscriptions are $26.95 per year. Email: antiquescj@aol.com.

*Collectors Mart.* 700 E State St, Iola WI 54990-0001. Tel: 1-800-258-0929. Bi-monthly. Subscriptions are $23.98 a year, $45.98 for two. Web: www.krause.com.

*Collectors News* (National). PO Box 156, Grundy Center IA 50638-0156. Tel: 1-800-352-8039. Monthly. Subscriptions are regularly $28 per year. Email: collectors@collectors-news.com. Web: http://collectors-news.com.

*Hudson Valley Antiquer, The,* and *Western CT/Western MA Antiquer.* PO Box 640, Rhinebeck NY 12572. Tel: (914) 876-8766. Fax: (914) 876-8768. Distributed free at markets, antique shops and auctions.

*Maine Antiques Digest* (New England). PO Box 1429, Waldoboro ME 04572-1429. Tel: 1-800-752-8521. Monthly. Subscriptions are $43 per year, second class. Email: mad@maine.com. Web: www.maineantiquedigest.com.

*Mid-Atlantic Antiques Magazine* (Mid-Atlantic States). PO Box 908, Henderson NC 27536-0908. Tel: (919) 492-4001. Monthly. Subscriptions are $18 per year or $27 for two years.

*New England Antiques Journal.* 4 Church St, Ware MA 01082. Tel: (413) 967-3505. Monthly. Subscriptions are $12 per year or $20 for two years.

*New York Antique Almanac, The* (New York State). PO Box 2400, New York NY 10021-2400. Tel: (212) 988-2700. Published 9 times per year, including three bi-monthly issues. Subscriptions are $10 per year or $18 for two years.

*New York–Pennsylvania Collector, The* (Eastern and Mid-West US and Canada). 73 Buffalo St, Canandaigua NY 14424. Tel: (716) 394-0770 or 1-800-836-1868. Monthly. Subscriptions are $24 per year; Canadian subscriptions are US$36 for one year. Email: messenger@frontiernet.net.

*Renninger's Antique Guide* (Eastern US). PO Box 495, Lafayette Hill PA 19444-0495. Tel: (610) 828-4614. Bi-weekly. Subscriptions are $15 a year for 25 issues or $28 for two years.

*Today's Collector.* 700 E State St, Iola WI 54990-0001. Tel: 1-800-258-0929. Monthly. Subscriptions are $23.98 a year.

*Treasure Chest.* 564 Eddy St Ste 326, Providence RI 02903. 1-800-557-9662. Monthly. Subscriptions are $25 a year, first class.

*Upper Canadian, The.* PO Box 653, Smiths Falls, Ontario Canada K7A 4T6. Tel: (613) 283-1168. Bi-monthly. Subscriptions are US$27 for one year (C$26 in Canada), US$48 for two years (C$46 in Canada). Email: uppercanadian@recorder.ca. Web: www.uppercanadian.com.

# WEBSITES OF INTEREST

There are many new websites being developed for those interested in flea markets and antiques and collectibles. For those of you new to the Internet, if you type in the main word of what you are looking for in the long, blank white line, i.e. antiques, the "search engine" will promptly go looking for anything with the word "antiques" in it, which can lead to some rather interesting finds. However, to get you started, here are some links that should be of interest.

**www.collectors.org** — Collector's Organization. The official site of the National Association of Collectors. It has links to antique shows, flea markets, appraisers, and just about anything connected to the business.

**www.delmarweb.com** — Maryland and Delaware Markets

**www.fleacountryusa.com** — A flea market directory by state. Sketchy information, mostly names and addresses.

**www.fleamarketguide.com** — Flea Market Guide of US Flea Markets has listings of markets around the country as entered by the markets themselves, so the information is somewhat "puffy" or not necessarily accurate since the listings aren't always updated.

**www.fleamarketusa.com** — Another state-by-state listing of markets; mostly names and addresses.

**www.openair.org** — The World Wide Guide to Farmers' Markets, Street Markets, Flea Markets and Street Vendors. Scattered information from around the world.

**www.swapmeets.com** — The Unofficial Swapmeet & Flea Market Directory is essentially advertising space plus some listings of markets.

**zipmall.com** — A few markets in the South; essentially an advertising platform for markets.

# HOW TO USE THIS BOOK

The flea markets listed in this book vary from those having fewer than 5 dealers to more than 2,000 dealers in some cases. The markets are listed alphabetically by state, and by town within each state. Each listing is broken down into the following subheadings:

**DATES:** Market days are listed here, including specific dates for 2000 where applicable. Rain dates are noted where applicable.

**TIMES:** Hours during which the flea markets are held are listed.

**ADMISSION:** If there is a cost to enter a market, the fee will be listed. Information about the availability and cost of parking is also presented.

**LOCATION:** A street address for the market is supplied where available; brief directions are provided for those traveling from out of town by car.

**DESCRIPTION:** This section discusses the size of the market, its age, the types of merchandise available, whether food is served on the premises, and any other interesting facts pertaining to its operation. All markets listed have toilet facilities on the premises or nearby, unless otherwise noted.

**DEALER RATES:** This section provides the most complete information available at press time regarding costs of selling space at the market, and whether advance reservations are required.

**CONTACT:** Complete mailing address and telephone number of the market operator are supplied wherever possible for dealer or shopper inquiries.

*The Official Directory to U.S. Flea Markets* has been designed to provide essential information about flea markets across the country selected for variety of merchandise, number of dealers attending, or other information of interest to the bargain hunter. The at-a-glance format previously outlined aids in making this guide the easiest as well as the most up-to-date reference available on the subject.

# IMPORTANT NOTICE

While the editors have made every effort to obtain the most exhaustive and accurate information available on a selection of flea markets from coast to coast in the continental United States, the reader is advised that in a work of this scope, inaccuracies may occur. House of Collectibles assumes no responsibility for any misprints or other errors found in this directory; all show dates, admission fees, dealer rates, etc. listed herein are subject to change at any time without notice. It is recommended that users of this directory call ahead or consult local sources whenever possible when planning a visit to a flea market.

# FLEA MARKET LISTINGS

# ALABAMA

## ATTALLA
### Mountain Top Flea Market

**DATES:** Every Sunday, year round. Rain or shine.
**TIMES:** 5:00 AM-dark.
**ADMISSION:** Free. Parking is free.
**LOCATION:** 11301 US Hwy 278 W, 6 miles west of Attalla. Hwy 278 W at 101 mile marker.
**DESCRIPTION:** Located on a mountain top on 96 acres, this mostly outdoor flea market first started in 1971 and currently consists of approximately 1,000 dealers selling everything from antiques and collectibles to new merchandise (jewelry, clothing, shoes, tools, furniture), from handcrafted items from three states to fresh produce from local farmers. They describe themselves as "Alabama's longest market—with 2.6 miles of shopping." They average over 40,000 buyers every Sunday! Twelve snack bars are on the premises. Restrooms with handicap facilities are available.
**DEALER RATES:** $8 per 10' × 22' space outside per day, $10 for 10' × 10' booth inside (very limited inside space). Shed tops for rent at $2 per day. Call the toll-free number for the latest information. Overnight camping with showers and restrooms is available. Reservations taken Monday 12:30 PM-4:00 PM, Tuesday through Thursday 8:00 AM-4:00 PM, Saturday 9:00 AM-6:00 PM.
**CONTACT:** Janie Terrell, Mountain Top Flea Market, 11301 US Hwy 278 W, Attalla AL 35954. Tel: 1-800-535-2286. Email: mtopflea@hopper.net. Web: www.lesdeal.com/MTFM.

## BESSEMER
### Bessemer Flea Market

**DATES:** Every Friday, Saturday, and Sunday. Rain or shine.
**TIMES:** 8:00 AM-5:00 PM.
**ADMISSION:** Free. Parking is also free.
**LOCATION:** From Birmingham, take I-59 south to Bessemer Exit 112. Turn left under freeway, to Hwy 11, turn right and go 3 blocks to market on left behind McDonalds.
**DESCRIPTION:** Started in 1980, this indoor/outdoor market accommodates approximately 700 dealers on 16 acres. There are as many as 10-15,000 people attending these shows. A variety of goods from antiques to

new merchandise can be found. A snack bar serves a variety of concession foods. Restrooms are available.

**DEALER RATES:** $6 to $11 per day, depending on size. Weekend rates are $16-$33 per space. Prepayment is required to reserve indoor space, outside is always available. There are overnight parking and shower facilities for traveling dealers.

**CONTACT:** Bessemer Flea Market, 1013 8 Ave N, Bessemer AL 35020. Tel: (205) 425-8510.

---

### Just Buzzing Around

Warned of a bunch of wasps swarming, the intrepid owners grabbed some wasp spray and decided to play hero. Arriving at the scene of noise, they realized they were facing honeybees—albeit a volleyball-size nest worth of the little critters. As one of their dealers raises bees, he was called upon to remove them. With his special bee vacuum, he safely removed the bees to his hives, where they thrive today.

---

# BIRMINGHAM
## The Birmingham Fairgrounds Flea Market

**DATES:** First weekend of every month, year round, plus the second and third weekends in December.

**TIMES:** Friday, 3:00 PM-9:00 PM. Saturday and Sundays, 9:00 AM-6:00 PM.

**ADMISSION:** Free. Parking is free.

**LOCATION:** Alabama State Fairgrounds. Exit 120 off I-20/59, follow the signs to the Alabama State Fair Complex.

**DESCRIPTION:** Operating under its current management for 10 years, this market has 600 dealer spaces, mostly indoors. Billed as "Alabama's Largest Indoor Flea Market." Antiques; collectibles; furniture; oriental rugs; gold, silver, vintage and costume jewelry; gems; sterling silverware; glassware; vintage clothing; new clothing and accessories; purses; prints and framed art; gifts; ceramics; fishing gear; electronic equipment; golf clubs and accessories; automotive accessories; dolls; plants; tools; leather; toys; crafts; phones; make-up; bedding; coins; sport cards; comics; knives; books; CD's; cassettes; records; lamps; jewelry repair; crystal restoration; flowers; and "you name it!" There are concession stands and restrooms on the premises, all handicapped accessible.

**DEALER RATES:** $55-$65 per 10' × 10' indoor booth, per weekend; $25 for a "two-parking-space" size area outdoors. The fairgrounds provide camping facilities for a fee.

**CONTACT:** Cindy, The Flea Market, 621 Lorna Sq, Birmingham AL 35216. Tel: 1-800-3-MARKET (1-800-362-7538) or (205) 822-3348.

## Jefferson County Farmers' Market Flea Market
**DATES:** Daily.
**TIMES:** 8:00 AM-5:00 PM.
**ADMISSION:** Free. Parking is free.
**LOCATION:** 344 Finley Ave W.
**DESCRIPTION:** Now held on a field with 30 booths and open outdoor spaces, this flea market sells antiques, electronics, tools, belts, belt buckles, tapes, and assorted new and used merchandise. The Farmers' Market is open 24 hours a day next door, so there's plenty of produce at the market. Public restrooms, a snack bar and a store are on site; a restaurant is just down the road.
**DEALER RATES:** $7 per lock-up booth; $4.50 per open space. Reservations are not required for the open space, but there is a huge waiting list for the booths. Office hours are 6:30 AM-3:00 PM. Ask for Kathy.
**CONTACT:** Jefferson County Farmers' Market, 344 Finley Ave W, Birmingham AL 35204. Tel: (205) 251-8737. Fax: (205) 251-8106.

## COLLINSVILLE
### Collinsville Trade Day
**DATES:** Every Saturday. Rain, shine or the occasional snowflake.
**TIMES:** 4:30 AM-2:30 PM.
**ADMISSION:** Free. $.50 for parking.
**LOCATION:** Hwy 11, S.
**DESCRIPTION:** Started in 1955 by Mrs. Harris on 4 acres of land, this market has grown to 65 acres after her son took over 18 years ago. They were written up in *National Geographic* in 1972. About 1,000 vendors sell antiques, collectibles, books, jewelry, used and new clothing and tools, stamps, cookware, toys, fresh produce, and new merchandise. Up on Coon Dog Hill livestock is traded and sold. There are 15 concessions and snack bars selling "festival food" to the hungry. Handicapped-accessible restrooms are available.
**DEALER RATES:** $8 for covered space, $5 for open space. Reservations are suggested.

**CONTACT:** Charles Cook, Collinsville Trade Day, PO Box 256, Collinsville AL 35961-0256. Tel: (256) 524-2536 or 1-888-524-2536.

---

### Chopper Shoppers

In the '70s, before there were laws to prohibit such sales, a fellow from a dental lab brought a foot-tub loaded with rejected dentures to the market and set up shop. People crowded around the tub sampling and wriggling dentures for fit. By the end of the day, he had sold every piece.

---

# CULLMAN
## Cullman Flea Market

**DATES:** Saturday and Sunday.
**TIMES:** 8:00 AM-5:00 PM.
**ADMISSION:** Free. Parking is also free.
**LOCATION:** 415 Lincoln Ave SW. Next to I-65, on US Rt 278 at Exit 308.
**DESCRIPTION:** Opened in May 1989 and located on 40 acres of land with nine acres just for parking, this market has 300 dealer spaces indoors and more space outdoors. Their dealers sell a variety of antiques, collectibles, handmade and craft items, tools, hardware, jewelry, woodwork, handbags, glassware, baseball cards, coins, fresh produce, cheese and dairy products, and new merchandise. Three concession stands with seating areas provide food to hungry shoppers. Clean restrooms with handicapped facilities are on the premises. They have added two antique buildings since 1994, open Thursday through Monday. Also on the premises is Country Village, built of old barnboard, a collection of speciality shops selling mostly antiques.
**DEALER RATES:** $20 per 9' × 10' booth for two days; $30 per 10' × 10' booth for two days. Reservations are required. RV hookups for vendors.
**CONTACT:** Frances Kilgo, Cullman Flea Market, PO Box 921, Cullman AL 35056-0921. Tel: (256) 739-0910. Fax: (256) 739-5352.

# DOTHAN
## Sadie's Flea Market

**DATES:** Friday, Saturday and Sunday, year round.
**TIMES:** 8:00 AM-5:00 PM.
**ADMISSION:** Free. Parking is free.

**LOCATION:** On Rt 231 S, 5 miles south of Ross-Clark Circle in Dothan. From Rt 109, turn left on 231; market is a few hundred yards down the road.

**DESCRIPTION:** Open since May 1989, this market, located on 50 acres, has over 300 booths with 60 permanent dealers, but many times is full to capacity. Dealers sell a large variety of everything including antiques, collectibles, crafts, produce, new and used merchandise—"real flea market stuff." A large Peanut Festival is held in the area in late October through early November. There are many antique car shows held in the area throughout the year. One large snack bar quells hunger, and two large handicapped-accessible restrooms are on the premises. There is a small RV park as part of the market.

A local ultralight plane club has frequent fly-ins attracting much local attention. Occasionally a sponsored local gospel group or a country band will perform here.

**DEALER RATES:** Indoors: $6 per day for a 10' × 10' booth; outside: $3 per day for a 4' × 8' table. Reservations are preferred.

**CONTACT:** Sadie, Sadie's Flea Market, 7990 US 231 S, Dothan AL 36301. Tel: (334) 677-5138.

# FOLEY
## Foley Indoor Flea Market

**DATES:** Saturday and Sunday.

**TIMES:** 9:00 AM-5:00 PM.

**ADMISSION:** Free. Parking is free.

**LOCATION:** 14809 Hwy 59, 1½ miles south of Summerdale, 3 miles north of Hwy 98 on Hwy 59.

**DESCRIPTION:** This market opened in July 1997 and is quickly growing filling its 197 indoor booths, and because the dealers wanted it, they added outdoor space for yard sales. The 45,000-square-foot air-conditioned/heated building sits on 16 acres. There are 10 dealers who specialize in antiques and collectibles. The rest sell plants, coffee, ceramics, wood crafts, collectibles, garage sale drag-ins, whatever comes along. TJ's offers food, including barbecue, during market hours. Handicapped-accessible restrooms are available.

**DEALER RATES:** $35 per weekend inside space, $10 and up per day for a table under awnings. Reservations are not required. There are RV setups with full hookups for the vendors.

**CONTACT:** Foley Indoor Flea Market, PO Box 838, Foley AL 36536-0838. Tel: (334) 943-6349. Fax: (334) 943-6349.

# HARPERSVILLE
## Dixie Land Flea & Farmers Market

**DATES:** Saturday and Sunday, year round.

**TIMES:** 9:00 AM-5:00 PM.

**ADMISSION:** Free. Parking is also free.

**LOCATION:** I-280 E to Hwy 25 S, exit at Harpersville about 4 miles south of Harpersville. On SR 25 between Harpersville and Wilsonville.

**DESCRIPTION:** Opened in 1986 on 70 acres of land, this market has 400 booths inside a 70,000-square-foot building and acres of outside booths selling antiques, furniture, arts and crafts, jewelry, baseball cards, toys, evening gowns, fruits and vegetables, and plenty of new and used merchandise. Two hundred of the dealers are permanent and the market advertises heavily in newspapers, on radio and television and hosts "live remotes" for on-air promotions. They have "everything and anything" in this "country flea market." "Huge deer and wild turkeys" roam around this market "driving hunters crazy" during the appropriate seasons. This is a clean, well-run, friendly market. There is entertainment to keep the children busy. Plenty of food is available on the premises supplied by three restaurants and an ice cream parlor. There are clean restrooms with handicapped facilities.

**DEALER RATES:** $7 per day includes table, plus electricity outside, but covered. Open outside space is $5 per day. Inside it starts at $12 per day. Campers can camp and hookup for $3 per day. There is full-time security, showers for dealers, and special handicapped facilities. Each booth has its own entrance with parking behind it.

**CONTACT:** Dixie Land Flea Market, 33985 Hwy 25, Harpersville AL 35078. Tel: (205) 672-2022. Fax: (205) 672-2203.


# HIGHWAY 127
## Highway 127 Corridor Sale

**DATES:** August, from the Thursday before the 3rd Sunday through Sunday for 4 days.

**TIMES:** Whenever.

**ADMISSION:** Free. Parking is wherever you can find it—*off* the road.

**LOCATION:** All along US Hwy 127 through three states: Kentucky, Tennessee, and Alabama. When you see a collection of sellers, it's there.

**DESCRIPTION:** Started in 1987 as a way to get travelers off the interstate and back onto the country roads by Fentress County's former County Executive Mike Walker and some of his friends, this market of thousands of dealers in "oddities and antiques," yard sale unloaders, and whoever and whatever else shows up, sells everything old and/or crafty. If you wish to travel the entire 450-mile route, start in Covington KY and work your way down to around Gadsden AL. There are plenty of food vendors. This has to be "the World's Longest Outdoor Sale."

**Rules of the road:** 1) *Drive Cautiously*—then you won't hit pedestrians or miss that goody you've been looking for. 2) Be *extremely* careful crossing the road! 3) Use your turn signals and don't stop suddenly for that goody (have a lookout who can give you ample warning). Otherwise, you may be dealing with insurance companies and wreckers rather than rare Ming.

**DEALER RATES:** Whatever the local landowner charges. Check out the website for a list of contacts in each state (it's huge) or call.

**CONTACT:** Southern Segment Coordinator at (205) 549-0391 for AL. Or Wanda (head coordinator), Fentress County Chamber of Commerce, PO Box 1294, Jamestown TN 38556-1294. Tel: (800) 327-3945. Web: jamestowntn.org.

## JASPER
### Kelly's Flea Market

**DATES:** Wednesday, Saturday and Sunday, year round, and the occasional holiday Monday.

**TIMES:** Sunup on Saturday to sundown on Sunday, really. Wednesday 7:00 AM-3:00 PM.

**ADMISSION:** Free. Parking is free.

**LOCATION:** Hwy 78. Just 3 miles east of the city limits of Jasper, 6 miles from the city center or 25 NW of Birmingham on US 78.

**DESCRIPTION:** Opened in April 1978, this outdoor market has 43 booths outside and under sheds with dealers selling antiques, produce, farm and home needs—described as "yard sale heaven." It is a "very laid-back, friendly, popular, family market." The market started when June wanted to stay home with her small child, quit work and had a yard sale at Mom's. Mrs. Kelly was so friendly that soon others joined her. No problem, it still grew!

**DEALER RATES:** $4 in the shed with electric, $2 for a table. If you want to reserve, do so, but if you don't, grab your spot by 7:00 AM or it will be gone! There are others waiting to use it.

**CONTACT:** Ray and June Fowler, 10016 Hwy 78, Jasper AL 35504. Tel: (205) 483-6045.

# KILLEN
## Uncle Charlie's Flea Market

**DATES:** Every Saturday and Sunday.

**TIMES:** 9:00 AM-5:00 PM.

**ADMISSION:** Free. Ample free parking is available.

**LOCATION:** On Hwy 72 W, 5 miles east of Florence, in the Killen area.

**DESCRIPTION:** This indoor market started in 1982 and accommodates approximately 400 dealers. They exhibit a wide variety of items including antiques, collectibles, arts and crafts, new merchandise and fresh produce. For your convenience, there are food and restrooms (with handicapped facilities) available on the premises.

**DEALER RATES:** $25 for 10' × 10' space per weekend. Reservations are required.

**CONTACT:** Tom Mabry, PO Box 190, Killen AL 35645. Tel: 1-800-542-2848. Day of show call or fax (205) 757-1771.

# MADISON
## Limestone Flea Market

**DATES:** Saturday and Sunday.

**TIMES:** 9:00 AM-5:00 PM.

**ADMISSION:** Free. Parking is free.

**LOCATION:** Hwy 72 at Burgreen Rd between Athens and Huntsville.

**DESCRIPTION:** Opened in July 1991, this indoor market of 450 booths filled with over 200 dealers sells antiques, collectibles, some garage sale goodies, furniture (with a separate Furniture Mart), crafts, coins, pool tables, oriental rugs, household goods and accessories, and lots of new merchandise. As Rosa says, "If it's 'hot,' it's here." In case of need, there are five concession stands and handicapped-accessible restrooms.

**DEALER RATES:** $41 for 10' × 8' for the weekend. There are also 10' × 9' and 10' × 10' spaces, as well. Reservations are required. There are dealer showers and facilities, 2 camper hookups and overnight parking.

**CONTACT:** Limestone Flea Market Inc, 30030 US Hwy 72, Madison AL 35756. Tel: 256-233-5183. Fax: (256) 233-1415.

# MOBILE
## Flea Market Mobile

**DATES:** Saturday and Sunday, year round. Rain or shine.

**TIMES:** 9:00 AM-5:00 PM.

**ADMISSION:** Free. Parking is free.

**LOCATION:** 401 Schillingers Rd N. Take I-10 to I-65, get off at Airport Blvd, about 8 miles west of I-65 take a right turn on Schillingers Rd. Follow the signs!

**DESCRIPTION:** Opened in 1988, this outdoor market is considered the largest in Alabama with 700 dealers selling under cover. The goods run the gamut: antiques, collectibles, jewelry, new merchandise, "everything." There are three full-size concession stands serving the hungry.

**DEALER RATES:** $20-$25 per weekend for 8' × 10' space or $30-$35 for a larger size.

**CONTACT:** Flea Market Mobile, 401 Schillingers Rd N, Mobile AL 33608. Tel: (334) 633-7533. Fax: (334) 639-0570.

# SCOTTSBORO
## First Monday Flea Market

**DATES:** First Monday and preceding Sunday of each month.

**TIMES:** 8:00 AM until dark.

**ADMISSION:** Free. Parking is also free.

**LOCATION:** Courthouse Square in the center of downtown Scottsboro.

**DESCRIPTION:** Said to be the second oldest market in the southeast, this is another classic 100-plus-year-old outdoor market started when the hanging judge showed up, held court and dispatched the bad guys, which of course, brought all the locals to watch the show—and naturally, trade stuff. Although the court system has evolved somewhat, the market keeps going and going. From 250 dealers in winter to 300 dealers in the summer sell a variety of antiques, collectibles and secondhand items. For your convenience, food is served on the premises.

**DEALER RATES:** $15 per parking space. Availability of space is on a first-come, first-served basis.

**CONTACT:** Gayle Swafford, First Monday Flea Market, 23123 John T Reid Pkwy, Scottsboro AL 35768. Tel: (256) 574-4468. Fax: (256) 574-4339.

# SELMA
## Selma Flea Market

**DATES:** Every Saturday, year round. Rain or shine.

**TIMES:** 5:00 AM-until.

**ADMISSION:** Free. Parking is also free.

**LOCATION:** Selma By-Pass at River Rd.

**DESCRIPTION:** This market opened in 1986 in beautiful historic Selma. It attracts from 170 to 200 plus dealers in sheltered spaces selling about 50% antiques and collectibles; the rest is handmade crafts, fresh produce and meats, new merchandise, garage sale and household items. There is a snack bar on the premises, restrooms, as well as overnight parking and an RV park on site.

**DEALER RATES:** $8 per 10' × 10' booth. Reservations are requested.

**CONTACT:** Gary Maluda, Selma Flea Market, 606 River Rd, Selma AL 36703. Tel: (334) 875-0500.

# SUMMERDALE
## Highway 59 Flea Market

**DATES:** Saturday and Sunday, year round.

**TIMES:** 8:00 AM-4:00 PM.

**ADMISSION:** Free. Parking is also free.

**LOCATION:** On Hwy 59, between Foley and Robertdale, 13 miles north of Gulf Shores.

**DESCRIPTION:** This very busy market, "the best in this part of the country," has been in existence since the summer of 1985. Under new ownership since 1996, the market accommodates approximately 300 to 400 dealers outdoors but under cover, and 35 individual shops. They do not specialize in one particular area; instead they sell a wide variety of goods. Included are antiques, fine art, reproductions, and fresh produce, to name a few. The market is located on 33 acres which also includes a 10,000 square-foot air-conditioned/heated mall. There is a restaurant on the premises as well as a RV park with reasonable rates ($165/month for vendors) and full hookups.

**DEALER RATES:** $10 for 10' × 10' space per day, per table. Reservations are not required.

**CONTACT:** Jeff Smith, Highway 59 Flea Market, 804 S State Hwy 59, Summerdale AL 36580. Tel: (334) 989-6642. Fax: (334) 989-6809.

# OTHER FLEA MARKETS

We know or have heard about these markets, but have not personally contacted each one, as we have the markets with descriptions. If you plan to visit one of these markets listed below, *please call first* to make sure they are still open. Flea markets do come and go. While they were open when we went to press, they may not be later. We can't be responsible. *Call first!*

**Alabaster:** Buck Creek Flea Market, 1097 11 Ave SW. Tel: (205) 664-0022.

**Alexander City:** Flint Hill Flea Market, 4329 Dadeville Rd A. Tel: (256) 234-2950.

**Birmingham:** Ensley Flea Market, 1924 Ave E. Tel: (205) 595-2666.

**Birmingham:** North Birmingham Flea Market, 4650 Decatur Hwy. Tel: (205) 841-8946.

**Boaz:** Sammy's Flea Market, 15491 AL Hwy 168. Tel: (256) 561-4298.

**Camp Hill:** People's Flea Market, 161 S Main St. Tel: (256) 896-4006.

**Castleberry:** Castleberry Flea Market, Cleveland Ave. Tel: (334) 966-5888

**Centre:** Flea Market, 260 Cedar Bluff Rd. Tel: (256) 927-2117.

**Cherokee:** Cherokee Flea Market, Hwy 72. Tel: (256) 370-7858.

**Childersburg:** Cotney's Flea Market, 3160 Desoto Caverns Pkwy. Tel: (256) 378-5151.

**Enterprise:** Glover Avenue Flea Market, 723 Glover Ave. Tel: (334) 393-7878.

**Eufaula:** Corner Flea Market, 439 S Randolph Ave. Tel: (334) 687-0071.

**Fort Payne:** Hwy 35 Indoor Flea Market, 918 AL Hwy 35. Tel: (256) 997-9876.

**Glencoe:** Flamingo Flea Market, 1818 US Hwy 431 S. Tel: (256) 492-0200.

**Heflin:** I-20 Trade Day, 100 Cheaha State Park Dr. Tel: (256) 253-2286.

**Jasper:** Sandford & Mum Flea Market, 181 Red Bird Ln. Tel: (205) 387-2886.

**Killen:** Greenhill Flea Market, 363 Hwy 43. Tel: (256) 757-9247.

**Killen:** North Alabama Flea Market, 7730 Hwy 72. Tel: (256) 757-1040.

**Lanett:** Korner Flea Market, 1008 County Rd 299. Tel: (334) 576-6054.

**Leighton:** Galaxy Flea Market, 1895 1 St. Tel: (256) 446-5614.

**Leighton:** Galaxy Flea Market, 8910 2 St. Tel: (256) 446-5343.

**Letohatchee:** Country Squire Flea Market, Exit 151 IH 65 & Hwy 97. Tel: (334) 227-4000.

**Mobile:** Stokes Flea Market, 236 S Wilson Ave. Tel: (334) 457-8130.

**Montgomery:** Cloverland Flea Market, 3865 S Court St. Tel: (334) 834-0450.

**Montgomery:** Crystal Palace Flea Market, 2373 Cong W L Dickinson Dr. Tel: (334) 279-1417.

**Montgomery:** Fantasy Land Flea Market, 3620 Atlanta Hwy. Tel: (334) 272-8841.

**New Hope:** B & G Flea Market, 4248 Hwy 431 S. Tel: (256) 723-7919.

**Opelika:** Station Point Flea Market, 931 S Railroad Ave. Tel: (334) 745-4000.

**Phenix City:** Valley Flea & Farmers' Market, 3864 US Hwy 80 W. Tel: (334) 298-3728.

**Roanoke:** Hall's Flea Market, 33344 US Hwy 431. Tel: (334) 863-7775.

**Roanoke:** Joyce's Flea Market, 924 Main St. Tel: (334) 863-5810.

**Smiths:** Lee County Flea Market, Hwy 431 N and 280 W. Tel: (334) 291-7780.

**Sylacauga:** Coaling Road Flea Market, 1923 Coaling Rd. Tel: (256) 245-2867.

**Theodore:** Hwy 90 Flea Market, 5751 Hwy 90 W. Tel: (334) 653-6589.

**Tuscaloosa:** Tuscaloosa County Flea Market, 1033 19 Ave E. Tel: (205) 553-9206.

**Tuscumbia:** B & J Flea Market, 5910 Hwy 43. Tel: (256) 381-8506.

**Tuscumbia;** Gene's Grocery & Flea Market, 17250 Hwy 72. Tel: (256) 381-3632.

**Wetumpka:** Goolsby Farmers' & Flea Market, Hwy 231. Tel: (334) 567-5858.

**Wetumpka:** Hilltop Flea Market, Hwy 231 N. Tel: (334) 567-5417.

# ALASKA

## ANCHORAGE

### Anchorage Downtown Saturday Market

**DATES:** Every Saturday from mid-May through mid-September.

**TIMES:** 10:00 AM-6:00 PM.

**ADMISSION:** Free. Parking is free if you can find it, otherwise there are pay lots at $2 per day nearby.

**LOCATION:** In parking lot at 3rd and E Sts across from Hilton Hotel.

**DESCRIPTION:** This market, started in 1993, hosts approximately 285 vendors in 327 booths selling antiques and collectibles, new merchandise, jewelry, native arts, fine art (expensive stuff!), fancy feet (handmade and decorated footwear), crafts, and fresh produce. You can't possibly starve as there are 35 food vendors including the enormously popular Kettle Corn (popcorn popped with sugar, really), and fresh seafood (seriously fresh!). After all the food sampling, the port-a-potties may come in handy.

**DEALER RATES:** $55 per 9' × 15' space per day, $40 per day under longer contract. There is a huge waiting list for spaces, so reservations are mandatory. However, there are usually up to 20 standby spaces if you get there early (before 5:30 AM, they might get a bit perturbed).

**CONTACT:** Bill Webb, Saturday Markets, PO Box 102440, Anchorage AK 99510. Tel: (907) 272-5634. Fax: (907) 272-5635. Email: saturdaymarket@alaskalife.net.

### Anchorage Downtown Wednesday Market

**DATES:** Every Wednesday from Memorial Day through Labor Day Wednesday.

**TIMES:** 10:00 AM-6:00 PM.

**ADMISSION:** Free. Parking is free if you can find it, otherwise there are pay lots at $.50 per hour, maximum $5 per day nearby.

**LOCATION:** Covering 6 blocks along 4th Ave from C and F Sts, and along F and D Sts between 4th and 5th Sts.

**DESCRIPTION:** This market, started in 1999, hosts approximately 100-plus vendors in 150 booths selling antiques and collectibles, new merchandise, jewelry, native arts, fine art (expensive stuff!), fancy feet (handmade and decorated footwear), crafts, and fresh produce. You can't possibly starve as there are 35 food vendors including an open pit barbecue selling Huli Chicken and KC Ribs, the enormously popular Kettle Corn (popcorn popped with sugar), and fresh seafood (really fresh!). After all the food sampling, the port-a-potties may come in handy. (Yes, these are mostly the same vendors, same management, same almost everything, just different location.)

**DEALER RATES:** $95 per 10' × 10' space per day, $75 per day under longer contract. There is a huge waiting list for spaces, so reservations are mandatory. However, there are usually up to 20 standby spaces if you get there early (before 5:30 AM, they might get a bit perturbed).

**CONTACT:** Bill Webb, Wednesday Markets, PO Box 102440, Anchorage AK 99510. Tel: (907) 272-5634. Fax: (907) 272-5635. Email: saturdaymarket@alaskalife.net.

# SEWARD
## American Legion Flea Market

**DATES:** Winter: Thursday through Saturday.

**TIMES:** 12:00 PM-4:00 PM.

**ADMISSION:** Free. Parking is free.

**LOCATION:** 402 5th Ave. In the American Legion's big gray building. Can't miss it!

**DESCRIPTION:** This 12-year-old market is a non-profit run by the American Legion to raise money for local charities, scholarships, help for anyone in need, and the famous "Santa gifts to kiddies scramble" at Christmas (much like a similar scramble in Ross-On-Wye in Wales)—the kids "line up" to collect their gift from Santa, courtesy of the American Legion's donations. Everything is donated, period. However, the donations are incredible. Consider that anyone leaving Alaska tends to unload their worldly goods here so they don't have to transport it all down south. Therefore, antiques, collectibles, tons of clothes, dishes, furniture, and winter sports gear abound—the list is endless. People off cruise ships have been known to come in just for the buttons! Think of this as a huge garage sale in progress. This is the "home" of the famous Mt. Marathon foot races. Ask about the poor runners scrambling down the shale hillside during the downhill part of the race. Nasty!

**DEALER RATES:** None.

**CONTACT:** Joanne Winn or Helen Nelson, American Legion Flea Market, 402 5 Ave, Seward AK 99664. Tel: (907) 224-5440.

# ARIZONA

## APACHE JUNCTION
### American Park N Swap

**DATES:** Friday, Saturday and Sunday, October through April. Rain or shine.
**TIMES:** 7:00 AM-4:00 PM.
**ADMISSION:** Free. Parking is free.
**LOCATION:** 2651 W Apache Trail. US 60 to Signal Butte exit, north on Signal Butte to Apache Trail, turn east on Apache Trail. Park N Swap is on the south side of the road.
**DESCRIPTION:** This market, started in 1965, houses up to 300 dealers daily selling everything from desert gold and crystals, hair cuts, Indian artifacts, golf clubs, redwood signs, silk plants, pet supplies, De Grazia, nuts, sandpaintings, kachinas, ironwood carvings, housewares, tools, books, produce, antiques, collectibles, crafts and handmade items, wind chimes, toys and bicycles—the list is endless! There is a huge barbecue pit in the center of the market and several smaller concessions, and handicapped-accessible restrooms are scattered conveniently around the selling floor. They are close to Superstition Mountain and recreational lakes. They donate a lot of space and hold events for local charities.
**DEALER RATES:** $12-$16 per 18' × 21' space per day. First come, first served. There are contract prices available.
**CONTACT:** Steve Haskett, Manager, American Park N Swap, 2651 W Apache Trail, Apache Junction AZ 85220. Tel: (492) 288-0571 or 1-800-772-0852. Web: www.americanparknswap.com.

## CASA GRANDE
### Shoppers Barn and Swap Meet

**DATES:** Saturday and Sunday.
**TIMES:** 7:00 AM-4:00 PM.
**LOCATION:** Selma Rd and Hwy 84, off I10, Exit 198, between Tucson and Phoenix.
**ADMISSION:** Free. Parking is free.
**DESCRIPTION:** Open since 1983 under the same management, this outdoor market sells antiques, collectibles, new and used toys and merchandise, used auto parts, ceramics, and appliances. They are in town on a main road and next to many amenities. Restrooms are available.

**DEALER RATES:** $5 per day for center space, $7 per day for corner space, tables are $1 per day. First come, first served. There is security and the grounds are locked at night. Dealers can set up Friday night. There are RV spaces available Friday through Sunday at $29 with electric.
**CONTACT:** Bud Gray, 13480 W Hwy 84, Casa Grande AZ 85222. Tel: (520) 836-1934.

# GLENDALE
## Glendale 9 Swap Meet

**DATES:** Saturday and Sunday.
**TIMES:** 5:00 AM-until.
**LOCATION:** At 5650 N 55th Ave. South of Bethany Home Rd on 55th Ave. Northwest of Phoenix.
**ADMISSION:** $.50 per person, children 11 and under free.
**DESCRIPTION:** This outdoor market of 350-450 dealers sells about half new and half used merchandise including Indian crafts, antiques, collectibles and garage sale treasures. There is a snack bar, 3 concessions and some hot dog, soda and coffee carts roaming the market.
**DEALER RATES:** $10 for a 36' × 10' space. Reservations are available on a monthly or yearly basis. Vendors enter from 4:30 AM.
**CONTACT:** Nancy Crane, Glendale 9 Swap Meet, 5650 N 55 Ave, Glendale AZ 85301. Tel: (602) 931-0877. Fax: (602) 931-8135. Web: www.centurytheater.com.

# MESA
## Mesa Market Place Swap Meet

**DATES:** Friday, Saturday and Sunday
**TIMES:** 7:00 AM-4:00 PM.
**ADMISSION:** Free. Parking is free.
**LOCATION:** 10550 E Baseline. East on Hwy 60 to Exit 193-Signal Butte Rd. Make a right at light to Baseline Rd, then turn right, entrance is on right.
**DESCRIPTION:** This covered market at the base of the Superstition Mountains is spread over 55 acres. To keep shoppers comfortable in the summer while shopping their 1,600 booths, there is a mister system (outside air conditioning!). The dealers sell just about everything from antiques to new merchandise, food, furniture, clothing, used goodies, whatever. One restaurant and six snack bars recharge the shopping batteries, while handicapped-accessible restrooms deal with other issues. So family oriented is

this market that they hold special events to raise money for local non-profit organizations. Just in case you get bored (?), there is free entertainment.
**DEALER RATES:** $25 and up per space.
**CONTACT:** Mesa Market Place Swap Meet, 10550 E Baseline, Mesa AZ 85208. Tel: (602) 380-5572. Fax: (602) 380-5578. Email: mesamarke@aol.com. Web: www.fleaamerica.com/mesa.html.

# MOJAVE
## Mojave Swap Meet
**DATES:** Everyday but Monday.
**TIMES:** 7:30 AM-4:30 PM. Saturday till 10:00 PM.
**ADMISSION:** Free. Parking is free.
**LOCATION:** 5005 Hwy 95, 12 miles south of Laughlin, Nevada or 12 miles north of Needles, California. One mile south of the Safeway.
**DESCRIPTION:** Started in 1987, and now under new ownership (formerly Bud's), this indoor/outdoor market has 150 dealers in winter and 30 dealers in summer selling antiques, collectibles, produce, coins, stamps, cards, garage sale goodies, crafts, furniture, toys, gift items, jewelry (custom gold), flowers, a fix-it shop (the manager's), appliances, and new merchandise. There are 18 stores in 6 buildings. Roberto's Tacos Restaurant and handicapped-accessible restrooms round out the facilities. This market is undergoing a complete renovation under the new ownership. Aiming for newer merchandise to accommodate the locals needs, as there isn't any other shopping nearby.
**DEALER RATES:** $10 per 12' × 24' space daily; $65 monthly; or $125 monthly for shed with a 12' × 24' space. Reservations are not required.
**CONTACT:** Mojave Swap Meet, 5005 Hwy 95, Mojave AZ 86426. Tel: (520) 768-3103.

# PHOENIX
## American Park N Swap
**DATES:** Every Wednesday, Friday, Saturday, and Sunday. Rain or shine.
**TIMES:** Wednesday 4:00 PM-10:00 PM; Friday 6:00 AM-2:00 PM; Saturday and Sunday 6:00 AM-4:00 PM.
**ADMISSION:** Friday free, otherwise $1 per person, 12 and under free. Parking is free.
**LOCATION:** 3801 E Washington St at 40th and Washington. From Loop 202 go south on 40th St.

**DESCRIPTION:** This show first opened in 1961. It is both an indoor and an outdoor market that accommodates from 1,500 dealers in summer to 2,500 in winter. Billed as "the largest open air flea market in the southwest." Whatever you want, you will probably find at this market. There are dealers selling art, crystal, jewelry, musical instruments, toys, clothes, pictures, housewares, garage sale items, weight loss products, and tools. Finally, when you grow hungry from shopping, hit one of the many food courts, where there are many different types of foods available, from Mexican to Indian Fry Bread to American burgers and fries. Handicapped-accessible restrooms abound.

**DEALER RATES:** $15 and up per 9' × 21' booth per day, Saturday and Sunday. $10 and up per booth per day Wednesday, and $5 and up on Friday. Reservations are suggested.

**CONTACT:** Richard K Hogue, PO Box 61953, Phoenix AZ 85034-1953. Tel: (602) 273-1250 ext 46 or 1-800-772-0852 out of state. Email: kpw26@aol.com. Web: www.americanparknswap.com.

## Fairgrounds Antique Market

**DATES:** Third weekend of each month, except October (no show due to State Fair) and December when it is held on the second weekend. During the Summer months of June through August, the show is held Saturdays only.

**TIMES:** Saturday 9:00 AM-5:00 PM; Sunday 10:00 AM-4:00 PM except in summer.

**ADMISSION:** $2 for adults; children 14 and under free with parent.

**LOCATION:** 1826 W McDowell Rd, State Fairgrounds, at the intersection of Grand Ave, 19th Ave and McDowell Rd.

**DESCRIPTION:** This show started in June 1986. The indoor market currently draws over 200 dealers in summer and 500 in winter. Dealers set up to sell a variety of antiques and collectibles. Food is served on the premises and there is full overnight RV camping.

**DEALER RATES:** $75 for a 8' × 10½' space. Additional spaces cost $45. $85 for a corner 8' × 10½' space. Add on $30 for electricity. Tables and free-standing pegboards are $10. Reservations are strongly advised.

**CONTACT:** Arthur or Linda Schwartz, Artlin, Inc & Jack Black Enterprises, PO Box 61172, Phoenix AZ 85082-1172. Tel: (602) 943-1766 within AZ or 1-800-678-9987 nationwide. Email: phxantique@jackblack.com. Web: www.jackblack.com.

## Paradise Valley Swap Meet

**DATES:** Saturday and Sunday.

**TIMES:** 5:30 AM-3:30 PM.

**LOCATION:** 2414 E Union Hills Dr. Go 1 mile north of Bell Rd and Cave Creek Rd. On the northeast corner of Cave Creek Rd and Union Hills Rd.

**ADMISSION:** Free. Parking is free.

**DESCRIPTION:** This outdoor market, in operation for over 24 years, has 132 spaces and hosts from 40 dealers in summer to capacity in winter. They sell everything from antiques and collectibles to soaps, tools, jewelry, boxed foods, produce, t-shirts, garage sale, new merchandise, crafts, and the occasional reptile. There's a full concession stand to quell the munchies, and handicapped-accessible restrooms.

**DEALER RATES:** $10 per 10' × 10' or 10' × 29' space; corner space for $15; double space at $20 to $25 for 20' × 18' space; drop-off space at $10 for 10' × 10' or 10' × 15'. Reservations are a must in the winter, not required in the summer. Office is open Thursday and Friday 10:00 AM-1:00 PM.

**CONTACT:** Joseph Brudeau, Manager, Paradise Valley Swap Meet, 2414 E Union Hills Dr, Phoenix AZ 85050. Tel: (602) 569-0052.

# PRESCOTT VALLEY

## Peddler's Pass, Inc

**DATES:** Friday (except during January and February), Saturday, and Sunday, year round.

**TIMES:** Sunup to sundown.

**ADMISSION:** Free. Parking is free.

**LOCATION:** 6201 E Hwy 69, 6 miles east of Prescott on Hwy 69 in Prescott Valley.

**DESCRIPTION:** This market of 350 dealers in summer and 150 in winter started in 1987. The dealers feature a good mix of new and used merchandise and fresh produce with a strong market for antiques and collectibles. They even sell used cars! When the heat is too much in valley markets, dealers head up to the cooler mountains of Peddler's Pass. They are the "largest market in Northern Arizona," a clean, neat and well-organized "no hassle" market. They have added a 3,000-square-foot building to house a farmers' market pavilion. One big concession serves home-cooked food on the premises. There are handicapped-accessible restrooms on site.

**DEALER RATES:** $15 per 9' × 9' farmers' market space; $13 per 20' × 20'; $15-18 per 25' × 20' corner and $23 per 40' × 20' space. The largest space also comes with electric and water hookups. Reservations are suggested. Vendors can camp out on their site from Thursday noon until the market closes 5:30 PM on Sunday.

**CONTACT:** Suzy Arnold, Peddler's Pass Inc, 2201 Clubhouse Dr, Prescott Valley AZ 86314-2921. Tel: (520) 775-4117 Wednesday through Sunday.

---

### Versatility

Years ago, Ron, a dealer who painted pictures on trucks at the market, was approached by a neighboring dealer with a very sore tooth. Ron grabbed some pliers and removed the offending ivory. Later that same day, he married a young couple in the pavilion.

---

# QUARTZSITE
## The Main Event

**DATES:** The Big Show is held annually the last full two weeks in January. The area is open every day of the year with 14 hearty vendors in 7 shops.

**TIMES:** 8:00 AM-6:00 PM (essentially dawn to just before dark).

**ADMISSION:** Free. Some parking is free, some is paid.

**LOCATION:** On I-10 (Business 10), Mile Post 17.

**DESCRIPTION:** This Annual Gemboree first began in 1982. It is held on 100 acres of land with over 1,000 dealers from all corners of the globe and is well known as one of the largest gem sales in the country, as well as one of the most exciting flea markets. Dealers set up to sell a virtually limitless range of antiques and collectibles including bottles, coins, hobby crafts, etc., along with lapidary equipment and thousands of specimens of gems and minerals from as far away as Brazil, Australia and Hong Kong. Food is served on the premises. Camping facilities for buyers as well as dealers with a fee for overnight parking.

**DEALER RATES:** Starts at $464.10 including state sales tax for 18' × 32' space which includes electric, water and sewer hookups, depending on space size. Reservations are advised.

**CONTACT:** The Main Event, PO Box 2801, Quartzsite AZ 85346-2801. Tel: (520) 927-5213. Fax: (520) 927-4496. Email: mainevent@redrivernet.com. Web: www.quartzsite.com.

# SURPRISE
## Surprise Swap Meet

**DATES:** Every Thursday, Saturday, and Sunday.

**TIMES:** Thursday 3:00 PM-10:00 PM; Saturday and Sunday 6:30 AM-3:00 PM.

**ADMISSION:** Free. Parking is free.

**LOCATION:** 12910 Santa Fe Dr, east of Dysart Rd.

**DESCRIPTION:** This indoor/outdoor market, started in 1980, hosts 200 dealers on Thursday (the big day) and 45-50 during the summer on weekends. You can buy antiques, collectibles, books, used furniture, jewelry, crafts, produce, some garage sale goodies, junk, everything and new merchandise. A Spanish restaurant and a snack bar serve up the food, and when needed, there are handicapped-accessible restrooms.

**DEALER RATES:** Call. Reservations are necessary.

**CONTACT:** Surprise Convention Center & Swap Meet, 12912 W Santa Fe Dr, Surprise AZ 85374-4190. Tel: (623) 583-1616.

# TUCSON
## American Park N Swap

**DATES:** Saturday and Sunday.

**TIMES:** 7:00 AM-4:00 PM.

**ADMISSION:** Free. Parking is free.

**LOCATION:** 2601 S 3rd Ave. In the parking lot of the Greyhound Track.

**DESCRIPTION:** This new outdoor market opened in the fall of 1999. See the sister markets in Phoenix and Apache Junction for what to expect. There will be concession stands and handicapped-accessible restrooms on site as well as a huge variety of merchandise, local and otherwise.

**DEALER RATES:** Call for rates, but under $15 per space. First come, first served. There are contract prices available.

**CONTACT:** Richard Hogue, Tucson Park N Swap, 2601 S 3 Ave, Tucson AZ 85713. Tel: 1-800-772-0852. Email: ppns0010@aol.com. Web: www.americanparknswap.com.

## MarketPlace USA

**DATES:** Friday, Saturday, and Sunday.

**TIMES:** Friday 12:00 PM-9:00 PM; Saturday 10:00 AM-9:00 PM; Sunday 10:00 AM-6:00 PM.

**ADMISSION:** Free. Parking is free.

**LOCATION:** 3750 E Irvington Rd. Off I-10 at Palo Verde N Exit, east on Irvington Rd approximately 2 blocks.

**DESCRIPTION:** Opened in November 1990, this market currently has dealers selling antiques, collectibles, crafts, produce, and new merchandise. Housed in a 150,000-square-foot building, they offer everything from plants, electronics, grandfather clocks, dolls, and tools to chiropractors. Billed as "the largest indoor marketplace for independent retailers in the Southwest" this market has 505 spaces plus a 26,000-square-foot Exposition Center, 5 snack bars, and a supervised arcade. Their Expo Center is attracting more shows yearly including Gem & Jewelry, Coin, and Corvette Shows, Bridge tournaments, Junior League Rummage Sales and the like, all bringing in more shoppers.

**DEALER RATES:** $160-$360 for four weeks (12 selling days). Reservations are not required.

**CONTACT:** Joanne Moebus, Manager, MarketPlace USA, 3750 E Irvington Rd, Tucson AZ 85714-1958. Tel: (520) 745-5000. Fax: (520) 571-9163.

## Tanque Verde Swap Meet

**DATES:** Thursday, Friday, Saturday and Sunday, year round, weather permitting.

**TIMES:** Thursday and Friday 3:00 PM-11:00 PM; Saturday and Sunday two sessions: 7:00 AM-3:00 PM and 3:00 PM-11:00 PM.

**ADMISSION:** Free. Parking is free.

**LOCATION:** 4100 S Palo Verde Rd. Just south of Ajo Way. Or take I-10 to Palo Verde N Exit 264B, go north 1 mile.

**DESCRIPTION:** This large outdoor family owned market started in 1974 and is now considered a local tourist attraction as well as a city and county landmark. Its 800 dealers sell everything from antiques and collectibles to fresh produce, from unique Southwestern items to handcrafted treasures to new and used merchandise—"Everything from toothpicks to houses, except processed food." There are 12 restaurants and snack bars. A well-equipped cafeteria, The Food Mercado, creates homemade Mexican dishes and assorted specials every weekend, all at very reasonable prices.

**DEALER RATES:** $12 per 11' × 26' space; $14 per 11' × 35' space; $16 per corner space. Reservations are not required, unless for monthly reservations.

**CONTACT:** Tanque Verde Swap Meet, PO Box 19095, Tucson AZ 85731-9095. Tel: (520) 294-4252. Fax: (520) 294-2358. Email: tvsm@flash.net. Web: www.flash.net/~tvsm.

## Tohono O'Odham Swapmeet

**DATES:** Saturday and Sunday.

**TIMES:** 5:00 AM to whenever.

**ADMISSION:** Free. Parking is free.

**LOCATION:** 5721 S Westover Ave. On the corner of W Drexel and S Westover Aves.

**DESCRIPTION:** First started in the 1970s as the Westover Swap Meet and now under new management, this outdoor swap meet set on 185 acres attracts several hundred dealers in winter with 67 permanent monthly dealers and somewhat less in the hot summer. The only new items sold here are by one dealer in new furniture. The rest is garage sale goodies, storage buy-outs, tailgate goods, collectibles, some antiques, produce, fruits, birds, lumber, paint, swords, knives, Indian crafts, and whatever. There is a Mexican concession and handicapped-accessible restrooms on site as well as plenty of vendors selling prepared foods throughout the market.

**DEALER RATES:** $10 per 18' × 28' space, $12 for a corner space. There is plenty of room for RVs. Reservations are not required.

**CONTACT:** Tohono O'Odham Swapmeet, 5721 S Westover Ave, Tucson AZ 85746-3006. Tel: (520) 578-9183. Fax: (520) 578-1052.

# YUMA

## Arizona Avenue Swap Meet

**DATES:** Daily, October through May.

**TIMES:** 8:00 AM-5:00 PM.

**ADMISSION:** Free. Parking is also free.

**LOCATION:** 1749 Arizona Ave, 2 blocks south of 16th St on Arizona Ave.

**DESCRIPTION:** This outdoor show first began in 1976. Currently, approximately 50 to 100 dealers sell a wide range of goods, including antiques and collectibles, fine art, arts and crafts, books, tools, chalk, new merchandise, and fresh produce, to name a few. Food is served on the premises.

**DEALER RATES:** $5 per 18' × 20' space per day; $25 per 18' × 20' space per week. Tables available for $.50 per day.

**CONTACT:** Bob Butcher, 1749 Arizona Ave, Yuma AZ 85365. Tel: (520) 343-1837.

## Yuma Park 'N Swap

**DATES:** Winter: Thursday through Sunday. Summer: Saturday and Sunday

**TIMES:** Winter: 6:00 AM-4:00 PM. Summer: 6:00 AM-2:00 PM.

**ADMISSION:** Free. Parking is free.
**LOCATION:** 4000 S 4ᵗʰ Ave. Take 4ᵗʰ Ave to 40ᵗʰ St. Call for exact directions.
**DESCRIPTION:** This family oriented, friendly market is considered the "biggest and best flea market in Southwestern Arizona." In the busy winter months, when the weather is at its finest, this market is filled with over 1,000 vendors selling just about everything to an average of 15,000 buyers. Summers are quieter as the weather is hotter. However, the bargains are generally greater and the crowds are less large.
**DEALER RATES:** $10 and up per day.
**CONTACT:** Max Dunham, General Manager, Yuma Park 'N Swap, 4000 S 4 Ave, Yuma AZ 85365. Tel: (602)726-4655 or outside AZ (800) 722-6811. Fax: (602) 344-0115. Email: bill@gresser.com. Web: www.ypns.com.

## OTHER FLEA MARKETS

We know or have heard about these markets, but have not personally contacted each one, as we have the markets with descriptions. If you plan to visit one of these markets listed below, *please call first* to make sure they are still open. Flea markets do come and go. While they were open when we went to press, they may not be later. We can't be responsible. *Call first!*

**Eloy:** Eloy Indoor Swap Meet, 323 N Main St. Tel: (520) 466-3211.
**Flagstaff:** Big Tree Campground, 6500 N US Hwy 89. Tel: (520) 526-2583.
**Holbrook:** Holbrook Flea Market, 1251 W Hopi Dr. Tel: 520-524-9098.
**Kingman:** Historic Route 66 Swap Meet, Rte 66 & Thompson Ave. Tel: (520) 692-1428. Mon-Thurs. Near Kingman Airport. Every Fri, Sat & Sun. Admission free.
**Phoenix:** ABC Discount Center, 3410 W Van Buren St. Tel: (602) 272-6316.
**Phoenix:** Bargaintown, 6719 W Thomas Rd. Tel: (602) 849-8289.
**Phoenix:** Great Southwestern Swap Meet, 1820 S 35 Ave. Tel: 602-352-1228.
**Phoenix:** Indoor Swap Mart, 5115 N 27 Ave. Tel: 602-246-9600.
**Quartzsite:** Four Corners Swap Meet, Ironwood Dr. Tel: 520-927-5219.
**Tucson:** 6th Avenue Flea Market, 2310 S 6 Ave. Tel: (520) 628-2000.
**Yuma:** Yuma Greyhound Park, 4000 S 4 Ave. Tel: 520-726-4655.

# ARKANSAS

## BATESVILLE
### The Market

**DATES:** Every Friday, Saturday, and Sunday, year round. Rain or shine.
**TIMES:** Friday 9:30 AM-6:00 PM, Saturday 8:30 AM-6:00 PM, and Sunday 11:00 AM-6:00 PM.
**ADMISSION:** Free. Free parking is provided.
**LOCATION:** 310 W Main St, at the low end of downtown Batesville. On the site of the historical Ringold home.
**DESCRIPTION:** This indoor/outdoor market first opened in 1980 and now under new ownership currently accommodates over 140 dealers. Everything from antiques and collectibles to new merchandise, from fine art to fresh produce can be bought here. It is located on the historic home site of one of the founders of Batesville. Food served on the premises and handicapped-accessible restrooms round out the amenities.
**DEALER RATES:** Booth size is 10' × 10'; $10 per day, $25 per weekend, $60 for 4 weekends. Advance reservations are required during winter months.
**CONTACT:** Mark Davis, The Market, 310 W Main St, Batesville AR 72501. Tel: (870) 793-7508.

## HOT SPRINGS
### Higdon Ferry Flea Market

**DATES:** Daily.
**TIMES:** 10:00 AM-5:00 PM.
**ADMISSION:** Free. Parking is free.
**LOCATION:** 2138 Higdon Ferry Rd. Just off Rt 7 S. If you are coming from town, it's the first street on the right past and opposite the Hot Springs Mall and over the hill. If you are coming the other way, it's a left turn before the mall. Go behind the building, under the skating rink.
**DESCRIPTION:** Opened in 1986 on 11 acres, this market of over 70 dealers sells mostly antiques and collectibles, furniture, glassware, some reproductions and plenty of standard flea market fare. No food concessions, but two handicapped-accessible restrooms are on site.
**DEALER RATES:** $175 for a 12' × 24' single space per month. $75 a month for a 8' × 12' space, $125 for 8' × 20'. Reservations are requested. There are a few outdoor spaces for traveling dealers at $5 per day.

**CONTACT:** Higdon Ferry Flea Market, 2138 Higdon Ferry Rd, Hot Springs AR 71913. Tel: (501) 525-9927.

# JONESBORO
## Nettleton Flea Market

**DATES:** Daily, except Christmas.

**TIMES:** Weekdays 10:00 AM-5:00 PM, Saturday 10:00 AM-6:00 PM, Sunday 1:00 PM-5:00 PM.

**ADMISSION:** Free. Parking is free.

**LOCATION:** 3339 Nettleton Ave. From 63 take Stadium north, turn right onto Nettleton Ave, go 3 blocks. The market is next to Jami Bee Motel.

**DESCRIPTION:** Opened in 1996, this market houses 37 dealers selling antiques, collectibles, garage sale goodies, stamps, cards, coins, and new merchandise.

**DEALER RATES:** $7.50 a week for 3 shelves 6' long to $25 per week for a booth in the front window. Reservations are a must, in case anything opens.

**CONTACT:** John Hancock, Nettleton Flea Market, 3339 E Nettleton Ave, Jonesboro AR 72401-5521. Tel: (870) 931-9307. Email: johnh@bscn.com.

# JUDSONIA
## Thackerland Flea Market

**DATES:** Saturday and Sunday.

**TIMES:** 7:00 AM-5:00 PM.

**ADMISSION:** Free. Parking is free.

**LOCATION:** 666 Hwy 367. Only 50 miles north of Little Rock.

**DESCRIPTION:** Open for 12 years, this market is noted for its wonderful antiques collected and auctioned on the first and third Thursdays by the owner. Hundreds of dealers set up indoors in two long newly air-conditioned buildings, outdoors and under sheds selling glassware, more antiques, collectibles, tools, coins, and more. This is a haunt for dealers looking to replenish their supplies. During the summer it's more like a carnival with all the music and carryings on. A small restaurant is on site and serves the vendors during non-market hours. On summer weekends there is entertainment and dancing for everyone. Gary is always adding to the market. They used to have dealers selling ostriches, pot-bellied pigs and other "exotic" animals during the appropriate fads which was entertaining in itself. However, as the fads have fazed, the market has quietly enjoyed their newfound "peace and quiet." (There's still the awesome music!)

**DEALER RATES:** $12.50 inside space, $6 for outside space and it varies for the sheds depending on size. There is RV space with arrangements for vendors as well as bathing facilities. Reservations are suggested.

**CONTACT:** Gary Thacker, Thackerland Flea Market, PO Box 791, Judsonia AR 72081-0791. Tel: (501) 729-3063. Fax: (501) 729-3154.

# LITTLE ROCK
## Memphis Flea Market
## The BIG One at Little Rock Expo Center

**DATES:** Saturday and Sunday, the second weekend of the month.

**TIMES:** 8:00 AM-6:00 PM.

**ADMISSION:** $1 per person. Children 12 and under are free. Parking is free.

**LOCATION:** Little Rock Expo Center, 13000 I-30. From Memphis take I-40 to I-30 to Exit 128, then continue west 1 mile; market is on right.

**DESCRIPTION:** Over 500 vendors come to sell antiques, collectibles, clothing, garage sale goodies, books, crafts, furniture, used and new merchandise. There are concessions to feed you and handicapped-accessible restrooms when the time comes.

**DEALER RATES:** $40 per weekend for outside spaces, $60 for regular, $70 for premium. Reservations are required. Regular office hours are Monday through Friday 8:30 AM-5:00 PM. Also during the market week including Friday 9:00 AM-9:00 PM, Saturday and Sunday 7:00 AM-4:30 PM. Inside spaces are 10' × 10'. Outside spaces are available on a first-come, first-served basis. Tables are available for $6 each, per weekend, through the office.

**CONTACT:** Memphis Flea Market, Little Rock Expo Center, 13000 I-30, Little Rock AR 72209. Tel: (501) 455-1001 for tape, 455-1002 or fax: (501) 455-0162. Email: memflea@aol.com. Web: www.americanparknswap.com.

# PRAIRIE GROVE
## Battlefield Flea Market
## aka Daisies and Olives Antiques and Gifts

**DATES:** Daily, except Thanksgiving, Christmas and New Year's Day.

**TIMES:** 9:00 AM-5:00 PM, Sunday 10:00 AM-5:00 PM.

**ADMISSION:** Free. Plenty of free parking.

**LOCATION:** 129-135 E Buchanan St, on Hwy 62 W in Prairie Grove.

**DESCRIPTION:** Opened in 1990, and purchased by the Cooper-Ritchie family in 1997, this market's 50-plus dealers, located in two buildings (one an old livery stable, the other an old theater), are loaded with lots of antiques, collectibles, primitives, furniture, vintage clothing, and "dust collectibles." Restrooms are on site and if you get hungry there is a cafe a half block away or a fast-food place in the other direction a half block.

**DEALER RATES:** Call for rates. Reservations are required. There is a waiting list.

**CONTACT:** Steve and Martha Ritchie, Battlefield Flea Market, PO Box 688, Prairie Grove AR 72753-0688. Tel: (501) 846-1800.

---

**Historical Note**

The Battle of Prairie Grove was fought here during the Civil War. There is a state park next door commemorating the battlefield site.

---

## Oak Grove Flea Market

**DATES:** Saturday and Sunday, year round.

**TIMES:** 8:00 AM-4:00 PM.

**ADMISSION:** Free. Parking is also free.

**LOCATION:** Corner of Oak Grove and Elm Springs Rds.

**DESCRIPTION:** Considered one of the largest and oldest of northwest Arkansas's flea markets, having opened in 1977, this indoor/outdoor market hosts between 60 to 100 dealers depending on the season. They sell antiques, collectibles, furniture, fresh produce, crafts and new merchandise. Two concessions serve American or Mexican food. Restrooms are available.

**DEALER RATES:** $8 per 12' × 14' space per day, outside; $85 per month inside. Reservations are required for inside space; outside is first come, first served.

**CONTACT:** Ramona or Bob Wallis, 3 S Ethel Ave, Fayetteville AR 72701. Tel: (501) 756-0697 or (501) 521-5791.

# SPRINGHILL
## Springhill Flea Market

**DATES:** Daily.

**TIMES:** 8:00 AM-5:00 PM.

**ADMISSION:** Free. Parking is free.

**LOCATION:** 660 Hwy 65 N. Exactly 7 miles out of Conway going to Greenbrier, 5 miles from Pickle's Gap.

**DESCRIPTION:** This market averages 32 vendors selling "antiques to junctiques," including a vendor specializing in comics; one vendor with a collection of 30,000 books and "every variety of knife"; oil paintings, lamps and lampshades, clothing, cow skulls and hide, and antique tools. In warmer weather there are vendors outside, but they tend to vanish in the cold weather (wonder why?). Sodas, coffee and restrooms are available on premises.

**DEALER RATES:** $90 per month for a 16' × 20' inside booth; $35 per month for outside space plus electric, free outside setup otherwise; $3 per day for electric hook-up for dealers wishing to hang around awhile. Reservations are suggested, or at least a call, one week in advance for inside space; first come, first served for outside space.

**CONTACT:** Bill Wisler, Springhill Flea Market, 660 Hwy 65 N, Springhill AR 72058. Tel: (501) 679-9106.

# WEST MEMPHIS
## West Memphis Flea Market

**DATES:** Thursday through Sunday.

**TIMES:** Thursday through Saturday 10:00 AM-6:00 PM. Sunday 11:00 AM-5:00 PM.

**ADMISSION:** Free. Parking is free.

**LOCATION:** 512 E Broadway. Easy access from either I-40 or I-55 from Exit 7 (both interstates), go to Broadway, right, 2 blocks to market on your right.

**DESCRIPTION:** Located along the Mississippi River, this market of 45 permanent and up to a total of 75 dealers sells everything from antiques and collectibles to household goods, glassware, new and vintage clothing, jewelry, the latest fads, and new merchandise. Other dealers come here to shop because the deals and merchandise are so good. They are near a RV park, a dog track for the bold, and only 7 miles from Memphis.

**DEALER RATES:** Inside there is a waiting list, outside is $7 for a 12' × 20' space under canopy. Reservations for outside aren't really necessary.

**CONTACT:** Virginia McNeely, West Memphis Flea Market, 512 E Broadway, W Memphis AR 72301-3201. Tel: (870) 735-9332 (leave message) or (870) 735-1644.

# OTHER FLEA MARKETS

We know or have heard about these markets, but have not personally contacted each one, as we have the markets with descriptions. If you plan to visit one of these markets listed below, *please call first* to make sure they are still open. Flea markets do come and go. While they were open when we went to press, they may not be later. We can't be responsible. *Call first!*

**Alma:** Flea Market, 1727 Hwy 71 N. Tel: (501) 632-2551.

**Alma:** Red Dyer's Flea Market, 5101 N Hwy 71. Tel: (501) 632-5599

**Bella Vista:** Bella Vista Flea Market, 2878 Bella Vista Way. Tel: (501) 855-6999.

**Benton:** Benton Flea Market, 18325 I-30. Tel: (501) 778-9011.

**Benton:** South Street Flea Market, 1229 W South St. Tel: (501) 315-6185.

**Bryant:** Collectors' Flea Market, 22430 I-30. Tel: (501) 847-6899.

**Camden:** Camden Flea Market, 1945 California Ave SW. Tel: (870) 836-9836.

**Clarksville:** Westside Flea Market, 2006 W Main St. Tel: (501) 754-3484.

**Conway:** Gap Flea Market, 13 Gapview Rd. Tel: (501) 679-4347.

**Conway:** Kenny's 64 East Flea Market, 3 Foxmoor Cir. Tel: (501) 730-0203.

**Crossett:** North Crossett Flea Market, 4807 Hwy 82 W. Tel: (870) 364-4383.

**Crossett:** North Crossett Flea Market, 1027 Hwy 133 N. Tel: (870) 304-2524.

**De Queen:** M & B Flea Market, Hwy 70 E. Tel: (870) 642-3316.

**De Witt:** De Witt Flea Market, 204 S Main St. Tel: (870) 946-2008.

**Eureka Springs:** Hideaway Flea Market, 4527 Hwy 62 W. Tel: (501) 253-8269.

**Foreman:** Foreman Flea Market, 107 Shuman St. Tel: (870) 542-6606.

**Fort Smith:** Rainbow Country, 3715 Towson Ave. Tel: (501) 646-1502.

**Fort Smith:** Zero Flea Market, 71 S. Tel: (501) 648-9909.

**Gassville:** Poor Girls Flea Market, 315 E Main St. Tel: (870) 435-6634.

**Gravel Ridge:** Northside Flea Market, 18801 Hwy 107. Tel: (501-834-8060

**Gravette:** Gravette Flea Mart, 404 1 Ave NE. Tel: (501) 787-6170.

**Green Forest:** Green Forest Flea Market, 224 Public Sq. Tel: (870) 438-5801.

**Green Forest:** Hands Flea Market. Tel: (870) 438-5495.

**Harrisburg:** Downtown Flea Market, 404 E Jackson St. Tel: (870) 578-5490.

**Harrison:** Cherokee Flea Market, 108 N Walnut St. Tel: (870) 365-3917.

**Harrisburg:** Harrisburg Flea Market, 8142 Hwy 163. Tel: (870) 578-2598.

**Harrison:** Lake Harrison Flea Market, 112 E Stephenson Ave. Tel: (870) 743-4287.

**Harrison:** Mountain Mama's Flea Market, 716 E Stephenson Ave. Tel: (870) 741-0305.

**Hot Springs:** Central City Flea Mart, 3310 Central Ave. Tel: (501) 623-4484.

**Hot Springs:** Resort City Flea Market, 1239 Central Ave. Tel: (501) 624-0419.

**Hot Springs:** Snow Springs Flea Market, 3628 Park Ave. Tel: (501) 624-7469.

**Huntsville:** Flea Market, RR 2. Tel: (501) 665-2355.

**Jacksonville:** B & M Flea Market, 660 W Main St. Tel: (501) 985-1788.

**Jonesboro:** Forty Nine South Flea Market, 3202 Southwest Dr. Tel: (870) 932-4538.

**Judsonia:** Exit 48 Flea Market, 359 CW Rd. Tel: (501) 729-4769.

**Knoxville:** Highway Sixty Four Flea Mart, Hwy 64 W. Tel: (501) 885-6104.

**London:** London Flea Market, 10 Allen Way. Tel: (501) 293-4309.

**Malvern:** Cotten's Flea Market, Hwy 270 E. Tel: (501) 337-5772.

**Mountain Home:** Trade Days, 5089 Hwy 62 E. Tel: (870) 492-5229.

**Mountain View:** Jack's Flea Market, Hwy 14 E. Tel: (870) 269-4166.

**Mountain View:** Main Street Flea Market, 110 E Main. Tel: (870) 269-8986.

**Mountain View:** Rainbow Flea Market, W Main St. Tel: (870) 269-3261.

**Newport:** Campbell Station Flea Market, 6601 N Hwy 67. Tel: (870) 523-4466.

**N Little Rock:** Beech Street Flea Market, 902 N Beech St. Tel: (501) 372-7664.

**Osceola:** Osceola Flea Market, 213 W Hale Ave. Tel: (870) 563-7423.

**Paragould:** 7 Acres Flea Market, 2607 E Kingshighway. Tel: (870) 236-1922.

**Paragould:** Huffman's Flea Market, 207 N Pruett St. Tel: (870) 239-9613.

**Paragould:** Overpass Flea Market, 200 E Kingshighway. Tel: (870) 239-4478.

**Pea Ridge:** Snow's Ozark Craft & Flea Mart, 812 S Curtis Ave. Tel: (501) 451-8260.

**Pine Bluff:** 270 & 65 Flea Market, 8112 Sheridan Rd. Tel: (870) 247-9957.

**Pine Bluff:** Pine Crest Flea Market, 407 N Blake St. Tel: (870) 536-3532.

**Pleasant Plains:** Pleasant Plains Flea Market, 6830 Batesville Blvd. Tel: (501) 345-2720.

**Pocahontas:** D & D Flea Market, 1971 Hwy 67 N. Tel: (870) 892-1562.

**Rison:** Highway 15 Flea Market, Hwy 15. Tel: (870) 357-8777.

**Rogers:** Pioneer Flea Market, 1018 N 2 St. Tel: (501) 631-6150.

**Springdale:** 412 Flea Market, 2298 W Henri De Tonti Blvd. Tel: (501) 361-9118.

**Springdale:** 71 Plaza Flea Market, 1300 N Thompson St. Tel: (501) 751-8222.

**Springdale:** Best Yet Flea Market, 633 Sanders Ave. Tel: (501) 751-4642.

**Springdale:** Betty's Homestyle Flea Market, 4556 N Thompson St. Tel: (501) 872-0355.

**Springfield:** Birdtown Flea Market, 4456 Hwy 9. Tel: (501) 354-1200.

**Trumann:** Speedway Flea Market, 316 W Speedway St. Tel: (870) 483-5881.

**Walnut Ridge:** Ma & Pa's Flea Market, 712 Hwy 67 N. Tel: (870) 886-7737.

**Walnut Ridge:** Poor Boys Flea Market, 500 SW Front St. Tel: (870) 886-1513.

**West Memphis:** Eastern Arkansas Flea Market, 557 E Broadway St. Tel: (870) 735-9055.

**Wynne:** Wynne Flea Market, 100 Kennedy Ave W. Tel: (870) 238-8598.

# CALIFORNIA

## ANDERSON *Too Far North*
### Jolly Giant Flea Market

**DATES:** Saturday and Sunday, year round.

**TIMES:** 6:00 AM-4:00 PM.

**ADMISSION:** $1.25 for a family, $.50 general, 6 and under free.

**LOCATION:** 6719 Eastside Rd. Take I-5 to Anderson. At Junction 273, exit off I-5; the market is 4 miles north of Anderson. The cross street is Latona Rd.

**DESCRIPTION:** Started in 1979, this indoor/outdoor market has 90,000 square feet of merchandise for sale. As they describe it, "More fun than you can bargain for." Their 150-250 dealers sell antiques, produce, cards, coins, furniture, garage sale goodies, utility trailers, tools and new and used merchandise. When you wilt from hunger, try the bar, the snack bar, or one of three restaurants. When the need hits, there are handicapped-accessible restrooms too.

**DEALER RATES:** $6 for 10' × 10' space on Saturday; $8 on Sunday. Reservations are suggested.

**CONTACT:** Tim Roberts or Jim or Patti Smith, Jolly Giant Flea Market, 6719 Eastside Rd, Anderson CA 96007. Tel: (916) 365-6458 or fax: (916) 365-6450.

## BAKERSFIELD *N of L.A.*
### Bakersfield Fairground Swap Meet

**DATES:** Tuesday, Saturday and Sunday.

**TIMES:** Tuesday 6:00 AM-2:00 PM, Saturday 6:00 AM-3:00 PM, Sunday 5:00 AM-3:00 PM.

**ADMISSION:** Tuesday $.50, Saturday $.75, Sunday $1. Parking is free.

**LOCATION:** At the Kern County Fairgrounds, at the intersection of Ming and Union, right on the corner.

**DESCRIPTION:** This outdoor market, open since 1986, attracts 300 to 400 dealers year round selling antiques, collectibles, crafts, produce, new merchandise, farm tools, cars, boats, motor homes, used merchandise and "everything under the sun." Loads of snack bars and handicapped-accessible restrooms add to the amenities.

**DEALER RATES:** $10-$15 for a 20' × 20' space. Reservations are not required.

**CONTACT**: Ed Murphy, Bakersfield Fairgrounds Swap Meet, 312 Stable, Bakersfield CA 93307. Tel: (805) 397-1504 or 833-1733 (not during nap times).

## Pacific Theater Swap-O-Rama

**DATES**: Sundays. Rain or shine.
**TIMES**: 6:00 AM-4:00 PM.
**ADMISSION**: $.75, children under 12 free. Free parking is available. There is $1 parking as well.
**LOCATION**: 4501 Wible Rd. Take Fwy 99, Exit White Ln and Wible Rd, 2 blocks south.
**DESCRIPTION**: This show opened in 1971. It is an outdoor market accommodating anywhere from 450 to 550 dealers. The dealers sell approximately 90% new merchandise, modern clothes, etc. for the mostly Hispanic shoppers. There is also an assortment of secondhand goods. Fresh produce is available in season. For your convenience, there is Mexican food available (including menudo to help sober people up after too much time at the beer garden), the beer garden, picnicking under the trees, carnival rides, a barber shop, plenty to keep the kids happy, and live music. Handicapped-accessible restrooms are on site.
**DEALER RATES**: $15 reserved space, $20 for non-reserved. Reservations are suggested. The office is open Friday for reservations from 9:00 AM-3:00 PM and Saturday 8:00 AM-6:00 PM.
**CONTACT**: Pacific Theater Swap-O-Rama, 4501 Wible Rd, Bakersfield CA 93313. Tel: (661) 831-9342. Fax: (661) 831-2158.

# BERKELEY
## Berkeley Flea Market

**DATES**: Saturday and Sunday, year round.
**TIMES**: 7:00 AM-7:00 PM.
**ADMISSION**: Free. Parking is free.
**LOCATION**: Ashby Bart Station. Located off of Hwy 80, take the Ashby Ave Exit and go straight up. The market is located on Ashby Ave and Martin Luther King Way at the Ashby BART station.
**DESCRIPTION**: Open since 1973, this multi-cultural flea market is operated by Community Service United, a non-profit organization with proceeds shared by local charitable social service agencies. It accommodates up to 280 dealers (but hey, many take more than one, so average is 190) selling antiques, collectibles, used furniture, electronics/appliances, musical instru-

ments, tools, new and used clothing, books, international items, household goods, and ethnic products. They encourage used items. There is a produce section and a snack bar. They were voted "Best of the Bay '99" Flea Market by the *Bay Guardian*, as a truly classic flea market in the bay area.

**DEALER RATES:** $20 per day, $19 if paid in advance. Reservations can be made in the office Thursdays 5:00 PM-7:00 PM, Fridays 12:00 PM-3:00 PM, Saturday 7:00 AM-4:00 PM, Sundays 7:00 AM to 4:00 PM. Weekends, the office closes for lunch from 12:00-1:30 PM. Office closes at 2:30 on the second Saturday of each month. Reservations are not required, but are suggested.

**CONTACT:** Charisse Cronland, Berkeley Flea Market, 1937 Ashby Ave, Berkeley CA 94703. Tel: (510) 644-0744. Email: findme@communityonline.net. Web: www.berkeleyfleamarket.com.

# BLOOMINGTON
## Bel-Air Swap Meet

**DATES:** Wednesday, Friday, Saturday and Sunday.
**TIMES:** 6:00 AM-3:00 PM.
**ADMISSION:** $.50. Parking is free.
**LOCATION:** 17565 Valley Blvd.
**DESCRIPTION:** Open since 1986 and moved down the road in June 1997, this outdoor market averages 638 dealers year round selling antiques, collectibles, crafts, produce, furniture, coins, produce stamps, cards, garage sale goodies, and new merchandise. A snack bar and restrooms are on site.
**DEALER RATES:** Wednesday or Friday $15 and up, Saturday or Sunday $20 and up. Space size: 18' × 25'. Reservations are required with a sellers permit.
**CONTACT:** Bel-Air Swap Meet, 17565 Valley Blvd, Bloomington CA 92316. Tel: (909) 875-3000 or (323) 754-3000. Fax: (909) 877-1633.

# CAMPBELL
## Second Saturday Flea Market

**DATES:** Second Saturday of every month, weather permitting.
**TIMES:** 7:00 AM-dusk.
**ADMISSION:** Free. Parking is also free.
**LOCATION:** South from Santa Cruz on Hwy 17, turn west at Hamilton; then travel ½ mile to Winchester Blvd; then turn left and go ½ block to Campbell Center Shopping Center.

**DESCRIPTION**: This show started in 1971. The outdoor market accommodates 40-50 dealers. You can find almost anything here from antiques and collectibles to fine art and new merchandise—"whatever dealers bring that is legal to sell." Sometimes, fresh produce is available. Although it originally started as only a mini-market it has grown to a full-fledged flea market. John, a record dealer, has been here since anyone can remember. He has found or sold "any record you can imagine." There are several restaurants in the shopping center, and there is Jerseys, too, with "the best cheese steak this side of the Delaware River." This market is noted for the friendliness of people. "It's like a family. When one gets sick, the others help out." Some of the vendors have been here every weekend since the market opened.

**DEALER RATES**: $10 for 10' × 10' space. Reservations are not accepted—first come, first served.

**CONTACT**: Second Saturday Flea Market, c/o Jerseys Cheese Steak Co, 1781 S Winchester Blvd, Campbell CA 95008. Tel: (408) 374-1415.

# COLTON
## Maclin's Colton Open Air Market and Auction

**DATES**: Every Thursday and Saturday.

**TIMES**: 7:30 AM-3:00 PM. Antique auctions are held every Thursday at 10:00 AM.

**ADMISSION**: Free on Thursday. $.50 on Saturday, children 12 and under free. Parking is free.

**LOCATION**: 1920 W Valley Blvd. From points west, take I-10 east to Riverside Ave, then north to Valley East. From points east, take I-10 west to Pepper, then go north to Valley West. Look for a 2-story blue Auction Building.

**DESCRIPTION**: For over 50 years now, this market has grown to accommodate 150 to 300 dealers and between 1,000 to 3,000 buyers daily. While the grounds are completely paved and the spaces are covered, it is considered an open-air outdoor market. Their furniture/antique/collectible auction, however, is held indoors. Their merchandise selection is huge. They sell antiques, fine art, collectibles, arts and crafts, gold jewelry, clothing, home furnishings, and shoes, just to name a few! Snack bars, cantinas and other food outlets and handicapped-accessible restrooms deal with munchies and other necessaries. Live entertainment is provided by musicians invited to play and sell their recordings.

**DEALER RATES**: $7-$25 depending on size and location. Walk-ins are welcome and advised to be there between 7:00 AM-7:30 AM the morning of the market to get a good spot.

**CONTACT**: Maclin Markets Inc, 7407 Riverside Dr, Ontario CA 91761. Tel: (909) 877-3700 or toll-free in California 1-800-222-7467 for information about Colton. Fax: (909) 988-8041. Email: info@maclinmarkets.com. Web: maclinmarkets.com.

# CONCORD (near Berkly & S.F.)
## Solano Drive-In and Swap Meet

**DATES:** Saturday and Sunday.
**TIMES:** 6:00 AM-4:00 PM.
**ADMISSION:** Saturday $.25, Sunday $1. Free parking.
**LOCATION:** Solano Drive-In Theater, 1611 Solano Way. Just off Hwy 4.
**DESCRIPTION:** This 10-year-old outdoor market, one of the largest and oldest in the Northbay area, draws about 200 dealers on Saturday and up to 500 dealers on Sunday selling lots of garage sale goodies and household treasures, some antiques, collectibles, storage buyouts, bulk items, household stuff, new and used stuff, junk, produce, and whatever. There is a snack bar on site.
**DEALER RATES:** Saturday $5, Sunday $15; monthly and yearly rates available. Otherwise, first come, first served.
**CONTACT:** Anita Ahamdi, Solano Swap Meet, 1611 Solano Way, Concord CA 94520. Tel: (925) 687-6445. Web: www.centurytheater.com.

# COSTA MESA
## The Orange County Market Place

**DATES:** Saturday and Sunday except during the Orange County Fair (in late July).
**TIMES:** 7:00 AM-4:00 PM.
**ADMISSION:** $1; children under the age of 12 are admitted free.
**LOCATION:** Orange County Fairgrounds, 88 Fair Dr. Take 55 Fwy W Exit at Fair Dr and go right on Fair Dr, or 405 Fwy Exit at Fairview and follow the signs to the Orange County Fairgrounds.
**DESCRIPTION:** Since 1969, an average of 40,000 to 50,000 shoppers per week come to buy from their 1,000-plus vendors spread over 60 acres in this clean, outdoor market. Considered the largest outdoor market in Southern California, its emphasis is on family and fun. There are plenty of food concessions and handicapped-accessible restrooms on site.
**DEALER RATES:** Call for 15' × 27' space prices. Office hours Monday through Friday 9:00 AM-4:00 PM.

**CONTACT:** Orange County Fairgrounds, 88 Fair Dr, Costa Mesa CA 92627. Tel: (949) 723-6606 (for vendor info) or 723-6660 office or shopper's hot line: (949) 723-6616. Fax: (949) 723-6659. Email: telphil@earthlink.net. Web: www.ocmarketplace.com.

# CUPERTINO
## DeAnza College Flea Market

**DATES:** First Saturday of every month. Rain or shine.
**TIMES:** 8:00 AM-4:00 PM.
**ADMISSION:** Free. Parking is $3 on campus.
**LOCATION:** 21250 Stevens Creek Blvd. Take Hwy 280 north or south to Hwy 85 west, then to DeAnza College via Stevens Creek Blvd.
**DESCRIPTION:** This outdoor market began in 1972 and is operated by the student government and the student activities committee, with proceeds benefitting the student body. There are over 900 booths selling antiques, fine art, arts and crafts, collectibles, and new merchandise. From 10-15,000 people attend this event each day! Food is served on the premises.
**DEALER RATES:** $25 for two parking spaces approximately 18' × 20' as selling area; $50 for four spaces approximately 36' × 20'. Reservations must be made one month in advance.
**CONTACT:** DeAnza Flea Market, 21250 Stevens Creek Blvd, Cupertino, CA 95014. Tel: (408) 864-8946.

# ESCONDIDO
## Escondido Swap Meet

**DATES:** Wednesday through Sunday.
**TIMES:** Wednesday and Thursday 6:30 AM-4:00 PM; Friday 1:30 PM-9:30 PM; Saturday and Sunday 6:00 AM-4:00 PM.
**ADMISSION:** Wednesday $.50, Thursday $.35, Friday and Saturday $.75, Sunday $1.
**LOCATION:** 635 W Mission Ave. Take 78 east to Centre City Parkway South, take next left at Mission Ave, left at Quince St. Market is on the right side.
**DESCRIPTION:** Since 1970, on the site of a drive-in movie theater, this indoor/outdoor market is generally fixed stands and set prices. There is mostly new merchandise with a heavy Mexican accent and some used goods. Some of the merchandise seen for sale: tools, loads of clothes, dishes and books. Thirteen concessions include Mexican, pizza, ice cream, fish and chips, barbeque, standard snack bar, and a bakery. A farmer's market sells inexpensive fresh produce, cheeses and dairy products and meats.

**DEALER RATES**: Per 18' × 20' booth: Wednesday $10, Thursday $8, Friday and Saturday $15, Sunday $20. Reservations are not required, first come, first served.

**CONTACT**: Lee Porter, Escondido Swap Meet, 635 W Mission Ave, Escondido CA 92025. Tel: (760) 745-3100.

# EUREKA
## Flea Mart by the Bay

**DATES**: Every Friday, Saturday and Sunday.

**TIMES**: Friday 8:00 AM-4:00 PM, Saturday and Sunday 8:00 AM-5:00 PM.

**ADMISSION**: Free. Parking is free.

**LOCATION**: 1200 W Del Norte, off Hwy 101. They are next to the public fishing pier.

**DESCRIPTION**: Since 1981, this indoor market of 50-70 dealers has been selling collectibles, crafts, coins, cards, video games, tools, toys, garage sale goodies, furniture, and new merchandise. When the need hits, there is one snack bar and handicapped-accessible restrooms. During December, they hold drawings for prizes and giveaways. During Thanksgiving weekend, Santa pays a visit giving out candy.

**DEALER RATES**: $5 per 3' × 8' space daily. $10 for the weekend, $56 for the month. Reservations are suggested, but otherwise first come, first served.

**CONTACT**: Leah Patton, Flea Mart by the Bay, 1200 W Del Norte St #3, Eureka CA 95503. Tel: (707) 443-3103. Email: lindystar3@aol.com.

# FOLSOM
## Annual Peddlers' Faire and Antique Market

**DATES**: Antique Market (spring) is the third Sunday in April and Peddlers' Antique and Collectible Faire (fall) is third Sunday in September. Rain or shine.

**TIMES**: 8:00 AM-4:00 PM.

**ADMISSION**: Free. Some parking is free, some paid.

**LOCATION**: On Sutter St in historic Folsom. From Hwy 50, take Folsom Blvd Exit, turn left, 2.9 miles to Sutter St.

**DESCRIPTION**: Started in 1966, this outdoor market in the Sierra foothills now accommodates 300 dealers that sell antiques and collectibles. No new merchandise is allowed. More than 20,000 people attend this semi-annual fair. In the heart of "gold country," this fair is located in the middle of some fascinating history: the Folsom Powerhouse was the first commercial transporter of long-distance electricity; there are the logging and gold mining histories; Chinese diggings; special exhibits of early Indian life at the History Museum on Sutter Street and more. Food is plentiful.

**DEALER RATES**: $80 for 10' × 10' space. Reservations are required; set-up starts at 2:30 AM and dealers should take note that crowds may start appearing as early as 3:00 AM.

**CONTACT**: Attn: Pamela Dulyea, Sutter Street Merchants Association, PO Box 515, Folsom CA 95763-0515. Tel: (916) 985-7452 or Folsom Visitors Center at (916) 985-5555.

# FRESNO *( near Nev. Border, east of San Jose)*

## Cherry Avenue Auction, Inc

**DATES**: Open every Tuesday and Saturday.

**TIMES**: 6:30 AM-5:00 PM.

**ADMISSION**: Free. Parking is $1 per car, Tuesday; $2 per car on Saturday.

**LOCATION**: 4640 S Cherry Ave. Take Hwy 99 to Jensen Ave exit (Jensen is 2 miles south of downtown Fresno); then go west 1 block to Cherry; then go south to yard. Cherry Auction is on Cherry Ave between Central and American Aves.

**DESCRIPTION**: This show began over 60 years ago. Now there are over 3 acres of vendor spaces and walkways under sheds or canopy and 15 acres total vendor area. The 800-plus dealers who attend this market sell "1,000 + 1 items," from antiques and collectibles to new merchandise and fresh produce—it can all be bought. This is one of the oldest outdoor markets in the area. There is also a unique "Auction Line" where anything and everything is auctioned off. There is a variety of food available as well as clean restroom facilities on the premises.

**DEALER RATES**: Reservations are taken only by the month. The cost for dealer space is $10 per 10' × 20' space on Saturday; $8 per space on Tuesday (Tuesday is a 2 for 1 deal). Reservations are not required.

**CONTACT**: Cherry Avenue Auction Inc, 4640 S Cherry Ave, Fresno CA 93706. Tel: (556) 266-9856 or fax: (556) 266-9439.

# FULLERTON

## Troubleshooters Antiques and Collectibles Round-Up

**DATES**: The first Sunday in May and October. Rain or shine.

**TIMES**: 9:00 AM-2:00 PM.

**ADMISSION**: $5, children under 12 free with adult. Parking is free. Dealers can get in early (from 6:00 AM to 9:00 AM) to buy for $10.

**LOCATION**: Cal State University just off the 57 Fwy at Nutwood Ave exit. Turn west on Nutwood and at the first light into the Cal State Fullerton campus and follow the signs.

**DESCRIPTION**: This outdoor show, started in 1962 and recently moved to this location, is sponsored by the Register Charities (*Orange County Register* newspaper) with all profits going to charity. The 800 dealers sell antiques and collectibles. It is the largest antique-related event in Orange County. Food is available on the premises.

**DEALER RATES**: $50 for 8' × 18' booth. Reservations are recommended.

**CONTACT**: RG Canning, PO Box 400, Maywood CA 90270-0400. Tel: (323) 560-7469 ext 15. Email: rgc@rgcshows.com or website: www.rgcshows.com.

## GALT (S. of Sacramento)
### Galt Market

**DATES:** Every Tuesday and Wednesday, except Christmas Day.

**TIMES:** 6:00 AM until everyone packs up (usually around 3:00 PM).

**ADMISSION:** Free. Parking is free.

**LOCATION:** Approximately half way between Stockton and Sacramento on Hwy 99. From the south: take the Central Galt Exit, turn left across the bridge and at the bottom of the bridge, turn left at the stop light. From the north: take the Central Galt Exit, turn right at the stop sign, at the bottom of the bridge, turn left at the stop light. The Galt Market is located directly behind the Marion O Lawrence Library and parking is available to the left or right.

**DESCRIPTION:** This is two distinct outdoor markets with the Tuesday market specializing in new merchandise, crafts, clothing, home decor items, jewelry, statuary, wood products, pictures/frames, dried flowers, awnings, oriental rugs, and loads more. The Wednesday market is the "old" flea and produce market and deals in antiques, collectibles, crafts, garage sale goodies, and the like. The produce market is considered quite awesome with plenty of ethnic specialties. There are 860 dealer spaces on over 10 acres, with an average of 400-plus dealers. This market draws vendors from throughout California and the surrounding states as well as a number of foreign countries. Many of their vendors attend trade shows around the United States and some make regular buying trips to Europe, the Middle East and the Orient. Food vendors provide plenty of eatables. The entire market is handicapped accessible, right down to the restrooms. Market advice: "Wear good walking shoes and shop until you drop!" Grab a market guide as you enter. Customer carry-out services are offered to adjacent parking lots and

loading zones. The market is exceptionally busy during Spring Break and the summer, so get there before 9:30 AM for good parking and selections.
**DEALER RATES:** Tuesday: $30 for non-food vendors for a 10' × 30' space; food vendors pay $70 for a 20' × 30' space. Tuesday dealers must have a State of California Board of Equalization Seller's Permit and a City of Galt Business License to sell. Wednesday: $20 for non-food vendors for a regular space; food vendors pay $70 for a regular space. Wednesday vendors selling at the market more than two times per year are required to have a State of California Board of Equalization Seller's Permit. All vendors selling prepared or packaged food or plants on either day, and all Wednesday produce, are required to have Sacramento Country Environmental Health Permits. Please check their website, call or write for their vendor brochure.
**CONTACT:** Galt Market, c/o 380 Civic Dr, Galt CA 95632. Tel: (209) 745-2437 for a tape message, or if you want a human when the tape starts touch "0" during office hours—Monday through Wednesday. Or call (209) 745-4695. Fax: (209) 745-9794. Email: clerk@ci.galt.ca.us. Web: www.ci.galt.ca.us.

# ⚓ GLENDALE ( part of L.A.)
## Glendale Community College Swap Meet
**DATES:** Every third Sunday of the month.
**TIMES:** 8:00 AM-3:00 PM.
**ADMISSION:** Free. Parking is free.
**LOCATION:** Glendale Community College, upper parking lot. Take the Glendale 2 Fwy north, exit on Mountain St, take a left; it is on the right side of the road just behind the bridge.
**DESCRIPTION:** There are approximately 150-200 spaces. From a reader who visited this market and was impressed: only antiques and collectibles are sold here, no new stuff. Goodies include: stamps, coins, books, crystal, dishes, glasses, knickknacks, some clothing and fabric. You can still make a deal. Snacks are available and there are restrooms.
**DEALER RATES:** $35 for a 3-parking-stall space per Sunday. You must park your vehicle in that space. If you are not considered an occasional seller, you must get a "seller's permit" from any local State of California Board of Equalization office. Reservations are an excellent idea, although if any spaces are empty, they are let on a first-come, first-serve basis. Gates open for vendors at 6:00 AM.
**CONTACT:** Jon Harris, GCC Swap Meet Office, 1122 E Garfield Ave, Glendale CA 91205. Tel: (818) 240-1000 ext 5805, Monday through Thursday 8:00 AM-6:00 PM. Email: jharris@glendale.cc.ca.us.

# GOLETA
## Santa Barbara Swap Meet

**DATES:** Sunday.

**TIMES:** 7:00 AM-2:00 PM.

**ADMISSION:** $1. Children under 12 free. Parking is free.

**LOCATION:** 907 S Kellogg Blvd. Going south on Hwy 101, get off at Fairview, left on Hollister, right on S Kellogg, stay on S Kellogg until the end of the road. Going north on Hwy 101, get off on 217 Junction, right on Hollister, left on S Kellogg, stay on until the end of the road.

**DESCRIPTION:** This outdoor market, open since 1967, is crammed with 200 dealers selling antiques, collectibles, crafts, furniture, garage sale goodies, cards, old coins, and new merchandise. A snack bar feeds the famished. And handicapped-accessible restrooms are most welcome.

**DEALER RATES:** $17 per 16' × 16' space. First come, first served. If you wish to reserve space, it costs $25 more per month, daily $5. Electricity is available; bring your own setup.

**CONTACT:** Santa Barbara Swap Meet, 907 S Kellogg, Goleta CA 93117. Tel: (805) 964-9050 for tape information, (805) 967-4591 on Sunday. Fax: (805) 683-3601.

# HUNTINGTON BEACH — near Irvine & Santa Ana (Ben)
## Golden West College Swap Meet

**DATES:** Saturday and Sunday, year round. Rain or shine.

**TIMES:** 8:00 AM-3:00 PM.

**ADMISSION:** Free. Parking is free.

**LOCATION:** Golden West College Campus. Between Golden West St and Edinger Ave.

**DESCRIPTION:** This 17-plus-year-old market operates to benefit the college programs and operations. The Saturday market is strictly old goods, antiques, collectibles and whatever. Sunday's market is old and new merchandise. Some of the 600-800 dealers sell fresh produce, records and music memorabilia, as well as the usual flea market goodies. My market visitor was impressed with this market saying you can still get good deals.

**DEALER RATES:** $20 per space reserved. $25 for same day (i.e. grabbing space at the last minute). Cash only. To reserve space call the office at (714) 898-2BUY (2289) Wednesday between 8:30 AM-11:00 AM and 1:00 PM-4:00 PM.

**CONTACT:** Golden West College Swap Meet, 15744 Golden West St, Huntington Beach CA 92647-3197. Tel: (714) 898-SWAP (7927) for tape message, or (714) 895-8737 Tuesday-Friday during office hours 8:00 AM-11:00 AM.

# INDIO — post Palm Springs
## Maclin's Indio Open Air Market

**DATES:** Every Wednesday and Saturday night.
**TIMES:** 4:00 PM-10:00 PM.
**ADMISSION:** $.50, children under 12 free. Saturday is free. Parking is free.
**LOCATION:** 46-350 Arabia St. From Hwy 111 take Monroe south, then east on Dr. Carreon to Arabia.
**DESCRIPTION:** Unlike any of their other markets, this Maclin's Market is open evenings. There is plenty of "locally grown and nationally famous" produce and baked goods, music, handcrafted arts and jewelry and just about anything and everything for your home, family, pets, or car. This place is described as one big fair, especially on Wednesdays. Night shopping here is a treat as it is much cooler in the evenings.
**DEALER RATES:** Wednesday $17 per space, Saturday $15. Just show up the day of the market by 4:00 PM to get your space. Gates open at 2:30 PM for set up. Get there early if you want a space; it goes quickly.
**CONTACT:** Maclin's, 7407 Riverside Dr, Ontario CA 91761. Tel: (909) 984-5131 or 1-800-222-7467 in California. Fax: (909) 988-8041. Email: info@maclinmarkets.com. Web: maclinmarkets.com.

# KING CITY
## King City Rotary Flea Market

**DATES:** First Sunday in April. Rain or shine.
**TIMES:** 7:00 AM-4:00 PM.
**ADMISSION:** $2 for adults. $1 for children age 12 and under. Parking is free.
**LOCATION:** Salinas Valley Fairgrounds. Take Hwy 101 to Canal St, then follow signs to Fairgrounds.
**DESCRIPTION:** This show began in 1969 and is both an indoor and outdoor market that accommodates approximately 150 dealers selling new merchandise as well as some antiques, crafts, collectibles, and fresh produce. There is also a variety of foods available, including Mexican, American, and Oriental. Handicapped-accessible restrooms come in handy.
**DEALER RATES:** $15 for 10' × 15' space. $10 for each additional space. Reservations are required.
**CONTACT:** Chris Davis, King City Rotary, PO Box 611, King City CA 93930-0611. Tel: (831) 385-0414. Day of show call the fairgrounds at (831) 385-3243.

# LANCASTER
## Lancaster Chamber of Commerce
## Semi-Annual Flea Market

**DATES**: First Sunday in May; first Sunday in October. Rain or shine. (They say it always shines.)

**TIMES**: 9:00 AM-4:00 PM.

**ADMISSION**: $4 per adult, $2 seniors and military, children 12 and under free. Parking fee is $2. Handicapped parking is free.

**LOCATION**: Antelope Valley Fairgrounds. 155 E Ave I. Take the 14 Fwy (Palmdale/Lancaster) to Ave I exit and head east approximately 2 miles to the intersection of Ave I and Division St.

**DESCRIPTION**: This indoor/outdoor market has been operating since May 1966 as *the* fundraiser for the local Chamber of Commerce. From 300 to 400 dealers from four states are attracted to this well-organized market selling antiques, arts and crafts, collectibles, jewelry, and new merchandise, with a large yard sale area. Available food goodies: Mexican, Thai, Oriental, Italian, barbeques, and American. Handicapped-accessible restrooms are available. When this market first opened, vendors would wait impatiently until the gates were thrown open, then race for whatever spot they could get. Now it is a finely tuned event run by 300 volunteers.

**DEALER RATES**: $70 for 10' × 10' space inside; $60 per 10' × 10' first choice or $50 per 20' × 20' second choice outside space; yard sale location $20 per 20' × 20' space.

**CONTACT**: Special Event Coordinator, Lancaster Chamber of Commerce, 554 W Lancaster Blvd, Lancaster CA 93534-2534. Tel: (661) 948-4518 or fax: (661) 949-1212.

# LODI
## Lodi Street Faire

**DATES**: First Sunday in May and October. Rain or shine.

**TIMES**: 8:00 AM-4:00 PM.

**ADMISSION**: Free. Parking is free.

**LOCATION**: Downtown Lodi on School St, between Lodi Ave and Lockeford St.

**DESCRIPTION**: This semi-annual fundraiser attracts over 550 dealers selling antiques, collectibles, arts and crafts, and new merchandise. Food vendors sell a variety of treats in two Food Alleys. One parking lot is devoted to tables and chairs for those eating or resting. Over 40,000 attend this fair. There are volunteers roaming the fair in golf carts waiting to be flagged down by weary or overloaded shoppers looking for a lift. Roving entertainment is provided.

**DEALER RATES**: $75 for 13' × 13' space, $110 for 13' × 13' corner space. Reservations are required.

**CONTACT**: Lodi District Chamber of Commerce, 35 S School St, Lodi CA 95240. Tel: (209) 367-7840. Day of show contact workers in on-site information booth.

---

### Cover Your Cup?

One vendor spray paints pictures while you wait. Buyers appreciated her more *after* she was moved away from their line of fire. Apparently, she's quite good at painting too.

---

# LONG BEACH (L.A.)
## Outdoor Antique and Collectible Market

**DATES**: Third Sunday of every month. Rain or shine. Special holiday show first Sunday in November.

**TIMES**: 8:00 AM-3:00 PM.

**ADMISSION**: $4.50 for adults. No fee for children under 12. Free parking.

**LOCATION**: Veterans Stadium at Lakewood Blvd and Conant St. Take Lakewood Blvd N exit from Fwy 405, turn right onto Lakewood Blvd, go north approximately 2 miles, turn right on Conant St.

**DESCRIPTION**: This outdoor market opened in 1982 and is the largest regularly scheduled antique and collectible show in the west. It draws over 800 dealers. Please note that only antiques and collectibles may be sold here. Because of its proximity to Hollywood, it attracts quite a few celebrities. You never know!

**DEALER RATES**: Booths measure 19' × 16' and range in cost from $50, $60, and $70, with corners at $90. Advance reservations are required.

**CONTACT**: Americana Enterprises Inc, PO Box 69219, Los Angeles CA 90069. Tel: (323) 655-5703.

**Don't You Wish**

Recently a customer bought a 1960's battery-operated Japanese-made toy robot for $300. It was listed and sold for $60,000 at a toy auction about the same time. Lucky, lucky!

 (near S.F.?)

# LOS ALTOS HILLS
## Foothill College Flea Market

**DATES:** Third Saturday of each month, year round.
**TIMES:** 8:00 AM-3:00 PM.
**ADMISSION:** Free. Parking is $2.
**LOCATION:** 12345 El Monte Rd at the college, parking lot F.
**DESCRIPTION:** Since 1980 this market, located in the foothills and surrounded by eucalyptus trees, has been a fundraiser for the well-known Foothill College Theatre Guild. The food concession benefits students. The 200 or so dealers enjoy a terrific reputation for their antiques, collectibles, fine art items, great crafts, books, vintage clothing and jewelry, and affluent garage sale items—from affluent shoppers, of course.
**DEALER RATES:** $18 for a single space of 16' × 16', with corner spots available for $25 (no discounts and quite limited). Vendor spaces available for Seniors, Foothill College students and staff rent for $15. Reservations definitely suggested though some standby space is available the day of the market.
**CONTACT:** Foothill College Flea Market, 12345 El Monte Rd, Los Altos Hills CA 94022. Tel: (650) 948-6417.

# MARYSVILLE
## Marysville Flea Market

**DATES:** Sundays.
**TIMES:** 5:30 AM-4:00 PM.
**ADMISSION:** Free. Parking is free.
**LOCATION:** 1468 Simpson Ln.
**DESCRIPTION:** Billed as "one of California's oldest flea markets," this outdoor, but under cover, market of 100-200 dealers (depending on the season) sells antiques, collectibles, fishing supplies, jewelry, stereos, clothing, cards, furniture, produce, and new merchandise. One snack bar and handicapped-accessible restrooms relieve the necessaries. As the management describes this market, "we are small enough to be well traveled, large enough to hunt for bargains with friendly management and vendors."

**DEALER RATES:** $10 per 16' × 18' with 2 tables, or $10 per 20' × 20' with no tables; $15 under cover. Reservations are suggested.
**CONTACT:** Betty Foster, Marysville Flea Market, 1468 Simpson Ln, Marysville CA 95901. Tel: (530) 743-8713. Fax: (520) 742-2124.

# MORGAN HILL
## Morgan Hill Flea Market

**DATES:** Every Saturday and Sunday, year round.
**TIMES:** 7:30 AM-6:00 PM.
**ADMISSION:** Free. Parking is also free.
**LOCATION:** 140 E Main St in Morgan Hill, 25 miles south of San Jose.
**DESCRIPTION:** This show first began in 1964. The market is held outdoors and consists of over 200 dealers selling under shade trees. Shoppers may find antiques and collectibles, as well as new and used merchandise and fresh produce. Food is served on the premises.
**DEALER RATES:** $12 for 3' × 10' table on Saturdays and $15 on Sundays. Reservations are not required.
**CONTACT:** Morgan Hill Flea Market, 140 E Main St, Morgan Hill CA 95037. Tel: (408) 779-3809.

# NILES
## Niles Antique Fair and Flea Market

**DATES:** Last Sunday in August.
**TIMES:** 4:00 AM-4:00 PM. Flashlight shopping allowed!
**ADMISSION:** Free. Parking is $6 and is run as a Boy Scout fundraiser. Some free parking is available early.
**LOCATION:** In the Niles Business District. Take Hwy 680 to Mission Blvd north to Niles Blvd; or take Hwy 880 to Alvarado/Niles Blvd east.
**DESCRIPTION:** This one-day event has been a successful fundraiser for many local non-profit organizations since 1925. Most of Niles Blvd and side streets are closed as over 500 dealers turn Niles into antique heaven. Buyers may start arriving as early as 4:00 AM and continue to shop throughout the day. Antiques, arts and crafts, and a variety of collectibles can be found. Niles itself is an historic landmark, home of the former Essanay Studios (of Charlie Chaplin, Ben Turpin fame), Vallejo's Mill (the first flouring mill) and its Railroad Depot Museum with a large railroad layout. Non-profit organizations run the many food concessions as their fundraiser.

**DEALER RATES:** $145 for 10' × 12' space with early reservations, $175 for later reservations. Reservations are suggested. First come, first served.
**CONTACT:** Niles Main Street Association, PO Box 2038, Fremont CA 94536-2038. Tel: (510) 742-9868. Email: info@niles.org. Web: www.niles.org.

# NIPOMO
## Nipomo Swap Meet and Flea Market

**DATES:** Every Friday, Saturday, and Sunday. Indoors year round, outdoors weather permitting.
**TIMES:** 6:00 AM-6:00 PM.
**ADMISSION:** Free. Parking is $1 Saturday and $2 Sunday.
**LOCATION:** 263 N Frontage Rd, 101 Fwy, off-ramp is Tefft St.
**DESCRIPTION:** Open since 1974 and rejuvenated under new ownership since 1997, this market's 300 or so dealers sell lots of antiques and collectibles (try Dean Wright's Collectibles), clothing, jewelry, crafts, GT wireless, hot tubs, new and used furniture, new and used merchandise, and tons of fresh produce. There are seven food vendors and plenty of handicapped-accessible restrooms. There are 100 indoor spaces in buildings that comprise the flea market area; outdoors is the swap meet with tons of garage sale goodies.
**DEALER RATES:** $3 on Friday, $6 Saturday, $9 Sunday, $15 for all three. $75 monthly, guaranteed in your place. Flea market buildings $125-$175 for 14' × 20' building monthly.
**CONTACT:** Nipomo Swap Meet and Flea Market, 263 N Frontage Rd, Nipomo CA 93444. Tel: (805) 929-7000. Fax: (805) 929-7007. Email: swapmeet@calcoast.com.

---

**Say What?**
There is on-site security for vendors, but one night the guard dog took off with an unsecured $300 cowboy boot. The vendor admitted it was his fault. It was found gnawed and buried.

---

# NORTHRIDGE
## Northridge Antique Swap Meet

**DATES:** The fourth Sunday of every month, as well as the fifth Sunday when there is one—and there are four a year.
**TIMES:** General admission 8:00 AM-2:00 PM. Early birds from 5:00 AM.

**ADMISSION:** $5 before 8:00 AM, $3 after. Parking is free.

**LOCATION:** Cal State Northridge University. Take 5 or 405 to 118 Simi Valley W, exit Reseda Blvd, follow signs to California State University, Northridge. Located on the north parking lot.

**DESCRIPTION:** This open-air market is described by a reader as a "very nice antique market with only old stuff, collectibles, many garage sales and very positive dealing." The 150-330 dealers sell, among the other things: antique furniture, paintings, rugs, bronzes, lighting, pottery, clocks and watches, postcards, stamps, coins, fishing equipment, dishes, crystals, toys and whatever. Food is available on site. The fifth Sunday market is huge and quite popular and as an added attraction includes a hot rod and classic car show.

**DEALER RATES:** $50 per 25' × 17' space, corner spaces $70. Reservations are suggested.

**CONTACT:** Daryll Fisher, Antique Attractions, 17041 Lakewood Blvd, Bellflower CA 90706. Tel: (562) 633-3836. Fax: (562) 408-0496. Web: www.antiqueattractions.com.

# OAKHURST
## Mountain Peddler's Show

**DATES:** The Saturdays and Sundays of Memorial Day and Labor Day weekends. Rain or shine.

**TIMES:** Saturday 8:00 AM-8:00 PM, Sunday 8:00 AM-4:00 PM.

**ADMISSION:** Free admission. Free parking.

**LOCATION:** State Hwy 41 and County Rd 426. Oakhurst is located in the Sierra Nevada foothills on California State Hwy 41, 36 miles north of Fresno, and 16 miles south of Yosemite National Park.

**DESCRIPTION:** Initiated as a revenue source for the Chamber of Commerce, the first flea market was held in 1978. There were 186 booths and a crowd of 10,000. Today, there are 350 booths selling antiques, collector's items, high-quality antique furnishings, glassware, pottery, clocks, porcelain, vintage, estate and costume jewelry, and arts and crafts. Food vendors offer everything from "tri-tip" to deli sandwiches and beer for the visitors. Live entertainment, free to the public, is provided. Handicapped-accessible toilets are available around the market.

**DEALER RATES:** $110-$150 per booth of various depths (8-12' or 14-18') with 20' frontage. Set-up varies depending upon booth location. Some set-up (tables, tents, tarps, but no merchandise) starting Friday at 6:00 PM. Remainder of set-up Saturday 6:00 AM-8:00 AM. Security is on premises.

**CONTACT**: Eastern Madera County Chamber of Commerce, 49015 RD 425, Oakhurst CA 93644. Tel: (559) 683-7766. Fax: (559) 683-0784.

# OAKLAND
## Coliseum Swap Meet

**DATES**: Tuesday through Sunday.

**TIMES**: 6:30 AM to whenever the dealers pack up.

**ADMISSION**: Tuesday and Thursday $.50, Friday $.75, Saturday and Sunday $1. Parking is free.

**LOCATION**: 5401 Coliseum Way. At I-880 and Coliseum Way, ½ mile south of the Oakland Coliseum.

**DESCRIPTION**: Next door to the Oakland "A's," this market averages 400 dealers on weekends, much less during the week, selling "everything" including loads of antiques and collectibles, fruits, vegetables, used and new merchandise, and craft items during the holidays. This place is known for the antiques with many antique dealers prowling the place first thing every day, just to nab the good stuff! (Get there early if you like antiques.) More antiques dealers are selling on weekends than weekdays. Plenty of south-of-the-border fruits are sold here. Food is served on the premises.

**DEALER RATES**: $5 on Tuesday, $10 Wednesday through Friday, $15 on Saturday, $18 on Sunday. They only handle monthly or yearly reservations. You must come in person to make your reservations.

**CONTACT**: Coliseum Swap Meet, 5401 Coliseum Way, Oakland CA 94601-5021. Tel: (510) 534-0325 for a recording or (510) 533-1601 to speak to someone. Web: www.centurytheater.com.

# OCEANSIDE
## Oceanside Drive-In Swap Meet

**DATES**: Every Saturday, and Sunday, and holiday Mondays. Rain or shine.

**TIMES**: 6:00 AM-3:00 PM.

**ADMISSION**: Mondays and Saturdays $.50 fee; Sundays $.75. Parking is free.

**LOCATION**: 3480 Mission Ave, 2 miles east of IF-5.

**DESCRIPTION**: This show started in 1971. There are now more than 1,000 dealers featured in this outdoor market. All types of new, used, and collectible merchandise are sold on approximately 40 acres of land, which includes places to purchase food.

**DEALER RATES**: Saturday $14; Sunday $18; Monday $8 for 18' × 24' space. Reservations are not required. Monthly reservations are available.
**CONTACT**: Greg Crowder, 635 W Mission Ave, Escondido CA 92025. Tel: (760) 745-3100. Fax: (760) 741-5748. Day of show call Gil Cadena at (760) 757-5286, Saturday and Sunday.

# ONTARIO
## Maclin's Chino Open Air Market

**DATES**: Every Tuesday, Saturday and Sunday.
**TIMES**: 7:30 AM-3:00 PM.
**ADMISSION**: $.50, children under 12 free. Free on Saturdays. Parking is free.
**LOCATION**: 7407 Riverside Dr. From points west, take Fwy 60 east to Euclid south, then east on Riverside Dr. From points east, take Fwy 60 west to Grove south, then west on Riverside Drive.
**DESCRIPTION**: This unique place to sell and shop has been serving the public since 1936. It is a cross between a swap meet, a mall, and a country fair, with not just dealers but exotic foods and children's attractions. There is a genuine livestock auction on Tuesdays and a restaurant with a 40s' beer and wine bar and a wide-screen TV. Between 350 to 500 dealers sell everything from antiques and collectibles to clothing and gold jewelry, as well as new merchandise. One area has only used and collectible goodies. There are even children's pony rides. There is also a fish market on the premises. Live entertainment is provided by musicians who come to entertain and sell their music. Handicapped-accessible restrooms are available.
**DEALER RATES**: Rates are from $7 to $25. We suggest dealers come between 7:00 AM-7:30 AM to get a space.
**CONTACT**: Maclin's, 7407 Riverside Dr, Ontario CA 91761. Tel: (909) 984-5131. Or toll-free in California 1-800-222-7467. Fax: (909) 988-8041. Email: info@maclinmarkets.com. Web: maclinmarkets.com.

# PALMDALE
## Antelope Valley Swap Meet at Four Points

**DATES**: Saturday and Sunday, year round.
**TIMES**: Saturday 7:00 AM-4:00 PM; Sunday 6:00 AM-4:00 PM.
**ADMISSION**: $1; parking is free.
**LOCATION**: 5550 Pearblossom Hwy. Intersection of Hwy 138 and Pearblossom Hwy. Five miles east of Palmdale.

**DESCRIPTION**: "Everything under the sun!" describes this swap meet opened in 1977. About 350 dealers sell antiques, collectibles, crafts, garage sale goods, old and new merchandise, tools, fresh produce and "soup to nuts." Great food is easily found including homemade tamales and corn dogs, authentic Mexican food, buffalo burgers, three beer gardens, and biscuits and gravy to mention a mouth-watering few. This market, with its country/western atmosphere, live country and Mexican music every Sunday and pony rides for the kids, seems to offer more than something for everyone. In 1997 they upgraded their facilities for the comfort of their patrons and dealers.

**DEALER RATES**: Saturday: $10 per 20' × 20' booth; Sunday $15 per booth. $20 for both days. Storage sheds are available. Reservations are not required; first come, first served. RV'ers are welcome to stay overnight.

**CONTACT**: Joyce Bruce, Antelope Valley Swap Meet, PO Box 901807, Palmdale CA 93590. Tel: (661) 273-0456. Email: info@swapmeetat4points.com. Web: www.swapmeetat4points.com.

# PANORAMA CITY
## Valley Indoor Swap Meet

**DATES**: Wednesday through Monday.

**TIMES**: Weekdays 11:00 AM-7:00 PM, weekends 10:00 AM-6:00 PM.

**ADMISSION**: Free. Parking is free.

**LOCATION**: 14650 Parthenia St. Take 101 Fwy to Van Nuys Blvd, go north 4 miles to Parthenia St.

**DESCRIPTION**: Started in 1986 and the only major retailing center to survive the Northridge earthquake, this indoor market of 250 dealers sells collectibles, crafts, furniture, produce, and lots of clothing. Three snack bars and a bakery quell the munchies and handicapped-accessible restrooms are on site. They hold promotional events every month including: health fairs, carnivals, circus, Halloween costume contests, bands, and more.

**DEALER RATES**: $500 monthly for a 9' × 13' space. Reservations are required.

**CONTACT**: Dena Weingardt, Valley Indoor Swap Meet, 14650 Parthenia St, Panorama City CA 91402. Tel: (818) 893-8234 or fax: (818) 894-5676. Email: info@indoorswap.com. Web: www.indoorswap.com.

# PASADENA
## Rose Bowl Flea Market

**DATES**: Second Sunday of each month. Rain or shine.

**TIMES**: 9:00 AM-3:00 PM.

**ADMISSION**: $5 per person, children under 12 free with an adult. Free parking, and VIP parking for a fee. Early admission for $10 from 7:30 AM-9:00 AM, and very early VIP admission is $15 from 6:00 AM-7:30 AM.

**LOCATION**: Pasadena Rose Bowl, at the corner of Rosemont Ave and Aroyo Blvd. Well marked. Close to the freeway junctions of 210 Foothill, 134 Ventura and 110 Pasadena Fwys.

**DESCRIPTION**: This monthly market ranks among the largest and best known in the country. It has operated outdoors on the grounds of the Rose Bowl Stadium since 1968 and currently hosts over 2,200 sellers and approximately 20,000 shoppers at each sale. Virtually anything under the sun can be found here, from antiques and collectibles to new merchandise and arts and crafts. Buyers often include Hollywood celebrities. Vendors may not sell food, animals, drug-related items or ammunition. Food and beverages and handicapped-accessible restrooms complete the amenities.

**DEALER RATES**: $40-$90 per 10' × 20' space per day depending upon location. Advance reservations strongly suggested.

**CONTACT**: RG Canning Enterprises, PO Box 400, Maywood CA 90270. Tel: (323) 560-7469 ext 11. Office hours Mondays and Wednesdays 10:00 AM-12:00 PM and 1:00 PM-5:00 PM. Fax: (323) 560-5924. Email: rgc@rgcshows.com or website: www.rgcshows.com.

# POMONA
## Valley Indoor Swap Meet

**DATES**: Daily except Tuesday.

**TIMES**: 10:00 AM-6:00 PM. Summer weekday evenings to 7:00 PM.

**ADMISSION**: Free. Parking is free.

**LOCATION**: 1600 East Holt Blvd. Take San Bernardino Fwy (10) to Indian Hill Blvd, go south 1 mile to Holt Blvd. Indian Hill ends at the swap meet.

**DESCRIPTION**: Started in 1986, this air-conditioned indoor market of 400 dealers and services offers ethnic crafts, furniture, a pet store, one-hour photo service, electronics, an optometrist, a dentist, new merchandise, porcelain, and loads of the last fashion clothing, shoes and accessories. This is considered the largest indoor swap meet in the Inland Empire with unique displays of Mexican and American merchandise. A snack bar quells the munchies and handicapped-accessible restrooms ease the other necessities. There are giveaways for children, live entertainment on weekends, and other fun things to do. On the third Saturday of every month there is a free food giveaway for needy families (the No More Empty Shelf program). You can literally buy or do anything business-wise under this roof.

**DEALER RATES:** $470 monthly for a 10' × 10' space. Reservations are required. There is a multiple space discount after 2 spaces, i.e. first 2 are $470 each, the third and beyond are $370 each space.

**CONTACT:** Valley Indoor Swap Meet, 1600 E Holt Blvd, Pomona CA 91767. Tel: (909) 620-1449 or 620-5083; for taped information 620-4792. Fax: (909) 620-5790. Email: info@indoorswap.com. Web: www.indoorswap.com.

## PORTERVILLE
### Porterville College Swap Meet

**DATES:** Every Saturday, weather permitting.

**TIMES:** 5:00 AM-4:00 PM.

**ADMISSION:** $.50. Parking is also free.

**LOCATION:** From Bakersfield: Go north on Hwy 99 to Hwy 65. Then 50 miles to Hwy 190, then east 1 mile to college. From Fresno, go south on Hwy 99 to Hwy 190, then go east 17 miles to college.

**DESCRIPTION:** Started in 1981, this market has an average of 300 dealers attending. There is always plenty of elegant junk available along with an ample supply of antiques, arts and crafts, collectibles, jewelry, the occasional snake, and music tapes, along with new merchandise and fresh produce. This market is run for the benefit of the student scholarship fund and is a Foundation function. There is always plenty of food available on the premises, as well as handicapped-accessible restrooms.

**DEALER RATES:** $13 for 24' × 36' space (electricity costs an additional $1). Reservations are advised but not necessary.

**CONTACT:** Bill Goucher, Porterville College Swap Meet, 150 E College Ave, Porterville CA 93257-5901. Tel: (209) 791-2200 (college) or Mr Goucher at (209) 784-9161.

## REDDING
### Epperson Brothers Auction and Flea Market

**DATES:** Saturday and Sunday, year round. Rain or shine.

**TIMES:** Sunup to sundown. Also, auctions are held at 6:30 PM every Wednesday and at 1:00 PM every Sunday.

**ADMISSION:** $1 per carload Sundays; Saturdays admission is free.

**LOCATION**: 5091 Fig Tree Ln, 1 mile south of Redding International Airport, off Airport Rd.

**DESCRIPTION**: The market, located on 20 acres of trees, first opened in 1962 and now consists of 100 to 150 dealers selling their goods both indoors and outdoors. Antiques, collectibles, arts and crafts, and new and used furniture can be purchased. Food, beer (had to mention that!), plenty of parking and handicapped-accessible restrooms are available on the premises.

**DEALER RATES**: $5 for 4' × 8' table (plus space for vehicle) on Saturday. $10 per space on Sunday.

**CONTACT**: Jack L Epperson, 5091 Fig Tree Ln, Redding CA 96002. Tel: (530) 365-7242 or Karen Bloom. Fax: (530) 365-3159.

# ROSEVILLE
## Denio's Roseville Farmers' Market and Auction, Inc

**DATES**: Every Friday through Sunday. Rain or shine.

**TIMES**: Friday 8:00 AM-4:00 PM. Weekends 7:00 AM-5:00 PM.

**ADMISSION**: $.50 walk-ins or parking is $2 per car.

**LOCATION**: 1551 Vineyard Rd. Take I-80 to Roseville/Riverside exit, turn left on Cirby Way, right on Foothill Blvd to Vineyard, right on Vineyard Rd.

**DESCRIPTION**: Denio's is a family owned and operated business in the same location since 1947, serving northern California, southern Oregon, and western Nevada. It averages 1,500 to 2,000 dealers selling everything imaginable—antiques, collectibles, comics, clothing, rugs, electronics, motor homes and vans, hats, toys, handmade/craft items, fresh produce and new merchandise. About 50% of the market is old stuff and garage sale goodies. Delicious corn dogs and international foods, provided by a popular Mexican restaurant (there for 31 years) or the Chinese buffet, are available on the premises. Just in case of need, there are handicapped-accessible restrooms.

**DEALER RATES**: Start at $15 per space, about 15' × 20'. Reservations are not required. The rental office is open seven days a week from 8:00 AM-5:00 PM.

**CONTACT**: Rental Office, 1551 Vineyard Rd, Roseville CA 95678. Tel: (916) 782-2704.

# SACRAMENTO
## Auction City and Flea Market

**DATES**: Every Saturday and Sunday. Rain or shine.

**TIMES**: 7:00 AM-5:00 PM.

**ADMISSION**: Free. Parking is free.

**LOCATION**: 8521 Folsom Blvd. Use Hwy 50 going to Lake Tahoe, take Watt Ave south to Folsom Blvd, turn right, go .8 miles to market on right.

**DESCRIPTION**: This show first opened in 1966. It accommodates 250-300 dealers in both an indoor and outdoor market. Four barns house fresh produce, antiques and collectibles in permanent space. This is said to be the longest-operating flea market within the city limits of Sacramento. Several restaurants, including Mexican, Chinese and a deli, operate on the premises. Handicapped-accessible restrooms add to the amenities.

**DEALER RATES**: $20 for one 4' × 8' table. $15 for each additional table. Reservations are accepted Wednesday through Friday 9:00 AM-5:00 PM.

**CONTACT**: Emil, Jr and John Magovac, Owners, Auction City and Flea Market, 8521 Folsom Blvd, Sacramento CA 95826. Tel: (916) 383-0880 or (916) 383-0950. Day of show call Harold Hennessey, Manager, at the above number.

## Forty-Niner (49er) Drive-In Swap Meet

**DATES**: Thursday through Sunday.

**TIMES**: 7:00 AM-4:00 PM.

**ADMISSION**: $.25. Parking is free.

**LOCATION**: At the 49er Drive-In Theater. I-80 at Raley Blvd Exit, 2 miles west of McClellan Air Force Base.

**DESCRIPTION**: Now open about 10 years, this outdoor market draws from 100 dealers (except on Thursday to 250) selling garage- and attic-found treasures including old clothes, t-shirts, household cleaning supplies, some antiques and collectibles and "a little bit of everything." Because so much of the stuff coming in is from "Auntie's attic" there are a lot of "great finds" waiting to be discovered. A hot dog cart serves the starved.

**DEALER RATES**: Thursday $5, other days $8 per 15' × 15' space. However, if you come for Thursday, it's $5 for Thursday, then $4 for each consecutive day after, that weekend. Reservations are required for monthly; otherwise, first come, first served.

**CONTACT**: Bill Brancamp, 49er Swap Meet, 4450 Marysville Blvd, Sacramento CA 95838. Tel: (916) 920-3530. Web: www.centurytheater.com.

# SAN BERNADINO
## San Bernadino Outdoor Market

**DATES**: Every Sunday. Rain or shine.

**TIMES**: 6:00 AM-2:00 PM.

**ADMISSION**: $1, children under 13 are free with an adult. Free and paid parking is available.

**LOCATION**: National Orange Showgrounds. Directly off the 215 Fwy. Take the Orange Show Road exit and follow the signs.

**DESCRIPTION**: There are almost 800 dealers attending this, the area's largest, weekly outdoor show. An enormous selection of merchandise can be found, about half new and half used. Antiques, collectibles, crafts and new merchandise are just some of the items to be ferreted out. Many sellers are "the average guy cleaning out his garage." From one reader: "Worth visiting every several months to keep in touch." For your convenience, food is also available on the premises.

**DEALER RATES**: $7 to $35 depending on location of space. Reservations are suggested. They claim to never turn anyone away. If you are more than a one-time seller, you need a Sales Tax Permit from the State Board of Equalization.

**CONTACT**: RG Canning, PO Box 400, Maywood CA 90270-0400. Tel: (909) 888-0394 Monday or Wednesday between 10:30 AM-4:30 PM. Email: rgc@rgcshows.com or website: www.rgcshows.com.

## SAN DIEGO
### Kobey's Swap Meet at the San Diego Sports Arena

**DATES:** Thursday through Sunday and every day of the week prior to Christmas.

**TIMES:** 7:00 AM-3:00 PM.

**ADMISSION:** Thursday and Friday $.50 per person, weekends $1, seniors 75¢, children under 12 free. Parking is free.

**LOCATION:** Sports Arena at 3500 Sports Arena Blvd.

**DESCRIPTION:** Opened in 1976, this outdoor market of 1,000 spaces hosts 700 vendors selling antiques, collectibles, crafts, produce, coins, stamps, cards, garage sale finds, furniture and new merchandise. Food kiosks and restrooms are available.

**DEALER RATES:** Weekends $25 and up for a 16' × 18' space ($20 unreserved); $6-$8 for Thursday and Friday. Reservations are recommended during holiday or peak seasons. Reservations must be made in person Wednesday through Sunday; Wednesday at the office, Thursday through Sunday at the main entrance at 3500 Sports Area Blvd.

**CONTACT:** Kobey Swap Meet, 3350 Sports Area Blvd #K, San Diego CA 92110. Tel: (619) 226-0650 (24-hour information) or (619) 523-2700 Monday through Friday from 9:00 AM-5:00 PM. Fax: (619) 523-2715. Web: www.kobeyswap.com.

# SAN FRANCISCO
## "America's Largest" Antique & Collectible Shows

**DATES**: 2000 dates: February 12-13, May 20-21, August 19-20, November 11-12. Call for 2001 dates.

**TIMES**: Saturday 8:00 AM-7:00 PM; Sunday 9:00 AM-5:00 PM.

**ADMISSION**: $5, $2.50 under 17, free under 12. Parking is $5.

**LOCATION**: Cow Palace. Cow Palace exit off Hwy 101, San Francisco.

**DESCRIPTION**: This indoor market opened in 1988 and attracts over 500 dealers selling antiques and collectibles only to over 8,000 shoppers. Food and restrooms are available on the premises.

**DEALER RATES**: $140 per 10' × 10' booth. Reservations are required.

**CONTACT**: Chuck or Christine Palmer, Palmer/Wirfs & Associates, 4001 NE Halsey Ste 5, Portland OR 97232. Tel: (503) 282-0877. Fax: (503) 282-2953.

## The San Francisco Flea Market, Inc

**DATES:** Saturday and Sunday, year round.

**TIMES:** 6:00 AM-4:30 PM.

**ADMISSION:** $.50. Children under 12 free. Parking is free.

**LOCATION:** 140 S Van Ness. From 101, exit at Mission St. To the right. The market is located at the corner of Mission and South Van Ness.

**DESCRIPTION:** This popular market attracts over 100 dealers and thousands of shoppers. The dealers sell antiques, collectibles, tools, new merchandise and garage sale goodies.

**DEALER RATES:** $25 per space for the weekend; first come, first served. Monthly reservations now accepted for a $30 fee. Setup starts at 7:00 AM on Saturday, 7:30 AM on Sunday.

**CONTACT:** San Francisco Flea Market, Inc, 140 S Van Ness, San Francisco CA 94103. Tel: (415) 646-0544.

# SAN JACINTO
## Maclin's San Jacinto Open-Air Market

**DATES:** Saturday, year round.

**TIMES:** 6:00 AM-2:30 PM.

**ADMISSION:** Free. Parking is free.

**LOCATION:** 789 N Lyon Ave. From the I-215 exit onto the Ramona Expwy eastbound, continue to Potter Rd. Turn right. At the end of the road, turn left onto De Anza. Turn right onto Lyon Ave.

**DESCRIPTION:** Originally started here in 1936 and closed for several years, this family oriented market reopened in 1998 after the city asked them to come back. Their market has 100-150 dealers selling collectibles and new and used merchandise. Food and restrooms deal with other issues.
**DEALER RATES:** $16 for 20' × 20' space includes city fee. Covered and enclosed spaces are slightly higher. Office hours 6:00 AM-7:30 AM for same-day reservations.
**CONTACT:** Maclin's, 7407 Riverside Dr, Ontario CA 91761. Tel: (909) 984-5131. Or toll-free in California 1-800-222-7467. Fax: (909) 988-8041. Email: info@maclinmarkets.com. Web: maclinmarkets.com.

# SAN JOSE
## Capitol Flea Market

**DATES:** Thursday through Sunday.
**TIMES:** 6:00 AM-5:30 PM.
**LOCATION:** Capitol Expwy at Monterey Hwy.
**ADMISSION:** 50¢ on Thursday, Friday free, Saturday $1.25, Sunday $1.50. Children under 12 free. Parking is free.
**DESCRIPTION:** This outdoor market, in business since 1982, hosts from 500 to 900 dealers depending on the season. They sell mostly antiques, collectibles, and garage sale specials (self-billed as the "World's Largest Garage Sale"). Very little new merchandise is sold here. They describe themselves as an "old-fashioned" flea market in the best sense of the word. Covering 35 acres in a drive-in theater, they park from 4,000 to 12,000 cars a day! "We are crammed!" says their manager. He advises you to "Come *early* for the bargains." They cater to families. There is a gigantic used car and truck sale every weekend selling vehicles at $12 a set of wheels! They've added a huge farmers' market produce area (with 40-50 vendors here alone) featuring farm fresh fruits and vegetables at bargain prices. Live music and free raffles liven the weekends. There are restaurants and snack bars on site with a wide range of food available.
**DEALER RATES:** $14 on Thursday, $10 on Friday, $15 on Saturday, $20 on Sunday. Although spaces may vary, they all accommodate a car or truck and ample selling space. Reservations are not required. Monthly reservations are available.
**CONTACT:** Dwight Price, Capitol Flea Market, 3630 Hillcap Ave, San Jose CA 95136. Tel: (408) 225-5800. Web: www.centurytheater.com.

## The Flea Market, Inc

**DATES**: Wednesday through Sunday, year round.

**TIMES**: Dawn to dusk.

**ADMISSION**: Free. Parking is $5 Saturday and Sunday; $1 Wednesday through Friday.

**LOCATION**: 1590 Berryessa Rd between Hwys 680 and 101.

**DESCRIPTION**: Started in 1960, this humongous market is billed as the "Original Flea Market" and is probably the world's largest covering 120 acres with well over 2,000 dealers selling everything—from antique and collectible, to abused and garage sale. They have a quarter-mile-long produce row, 8 miles of aisles, 25 snack bars, clean, well-attended restrooms and an average of 80,000 visitors each weekend. Watch for their special events: the Salsa Festival including contest (you can eat yourself to death on the sauces and chips!), Octoberfest, Cinque de Mayo, Holiday Crafters Fair (just before Thanksgiving), Bicycle Fairs, whatever! Wednesdays are good days for mid-week bargains, Thursday and Friday for the neighborhood swap meet atmosphere.

**DEALER RATES**: Per 17' × 20' space per day: Wednesday $15; Thursday and Friday $10; Saturday and Sunday $25. No reservations are necessary, but suggested if you have a preference for a space. For a garage sale special: $10 for the first Saturday of the month. There are monthly rates; ask at the office.

**CONTACT**: Reservations Manager, The Flea Market Inc, 1590 Berryessa Rd, San Jose CA 95133-1003. Tel: (408) 453-1110 or (800) BIG-FLEA. Fax: (408) 437-9011. Email: john@sjfm.com. Web: www.sjfm.com.

# SAN JUAN BAUTISTA
## San Juan Bautista Annual Flea Market

**DATES**: First Sunday in August. Rain or shine.

**TIMES**: 8:00 AM-5:00 PM.

**ADMISSION**: Free. Some parking lots nearby are free, some aren't.

**LOCATION**: In downtown San Juan Bautista, 40 miles south of San Jose on Hwy 101.

**DESCRIPTION**: This show first began in 1963, and nowadays over 400 vendors from 9 states and 165 California cities come to participate in this event, all conducting their business outdoors on the main streets of the town. Antiques and collectibles, and fine art can be purchased. This market claims to be the oldest and largest one-day street show in California and has been named one of the top four flea markets in California by *Good Housekeeping* magazine. There are 12 restaurants and plenty of street vendors providing food.

**DEALER RATES**: $185 for 10' × 14' space. Reservations are required. Dealers start arriving as early as 4:00 AM.

**CONTACT**: Chamber of Commerce, PO Box 1037, San Juan Bautista CA 95045. Tel: (831) 623-2454. Fax: (831) 623-0674.

## SANTA CLARITA (SAUGAS)
### Saugus Swap Meet

**DATES**: Every Sunday and Tuesday. Rain or shine.

**TIMES**: 7:00 AM-3:00 PM.

**ADMISSION**: $1 for adults on Sunday only, children under 12 are admitted free. Parking is free.

**LOCATION**: 22500 Soledad Canyon Rd. From Los Angeles, take I-5 to Valencia Blvd exit, turn right on Valencia Blvd, go 3¼ miles. Market is on the right.

**DESCRIPTION**: This show originally began in 1965. There are approximately 650 dealers conducting their business outdoors and selling everything from antiques and collectibles to new merchandise and fresh produce. The market is held on the grounds of movie star Hoot Gibson's former ranch, and formerly the Saugas Speedway. Food is available on the premises. From one reader: "...garage sales were good quality, good dealing available. About 60/40 percent new/collectibles. Many businesses come to advertise." There is pottery, carpets, home repair, remodeling, florals, electronics collectibles; and live entertainment.

**DEALER RATES**: $30 for 20' × 16' space. Assigned location space is available from $25-$60 a day. Reservations are not required. Park on space. Setup starts at 6:00 AM. Tuesdays $10 any space.

**CONTACT**: Saugus Swap Meet, Box 901, Santa Clarita CA 91380-9001. For information contact office Tuesday through Friday 8:00 AM-3:00 PM. Tel: (818) 716-6010 or (661) 259-3886. Web: www.scvpages.com.

## SANTA FE SPRINGS
### Santa Fe Springs Swap Meet

**DATES**: Every Wednesday, Thursday, Saturday, and Sunday. Tuesday and Friday nights April through October. Weather permitting.

**TIMES**: 5:30 AM-3:30 PM all four days. Night hours 5:00 PM-10:00 PM.

**ADMISSION**: $.50 on Tuesday and Wednesday; free on Thursday; $.75 on Friday, Saturday and Sunday. Parking is free. Admission on Harley nights: $6.

**LOCATION**: 13963 Alondra Blvd. Take Valley View exit off I-5.

**DESCRIPTION**: This market first began in 1960 and is said to be the first swap meet in Southern California. Held at a drive-in theater, this market averages 700 dealers on weekends and 500-plus during the week selling arts and crafts, pop collectibles, fine art, new merchandise, and fresh produce. There are kiddie rides and a video arcade to keep children busy. Food, from a snack bar and catering trucks, is served on the premises and there are handicapped-accessible restrooms. On the third Thursday of each month, from 5:00 PM to 10:30 PM, they host a giant Harley Davidson Swap Meet.

**DEALER RATES**: $10 for approximately 15' × 20' space on Wednesday; free on Thursday; $25-$30 per space on Saturday and Sunday; $35 Friday nights; Tuesday $20. Reservations are required, although non-reserved space is available at the higher rate. Monthly rates are available. Advance shopping hours for dealers begins at 5:30 AM. They have a garage sale special: $5 on Saturday and $10 Friday night and Sunday, subject to available space.

**CONTACT**: Santa Fe Springs Swap Meet, 13963 Alondra Blvd, Santa Fe Springs CA 90670. Tel: (562) 921-4359 or (562) 921-9996 for tape message. Fax: (562) 921-1706. Email: info@sfsswapmeet.com. Web: www.sfsswapmeet.com.

## SANTEE
### Santee Swap Meet

**DATES**: Saturday and Sunday. Rain or shine.

**TIMES**: 6:30 AM-2:00 PM.

**ADMISSION**: $.50. Parking is free.

**LOCATION**: 10990 Woodside Ave N. Take 67 north to Riverford Rd exit. Turn left at exit, then left at Riverford Rd, left at Woodside Ave N. Market is on the right side at the drive-in theater.

**DESCRIPTION**: Open since 1984, this outdoor market draws large crowds of buyers as well as sellers. Many a garage is cleaned out here and there are vendors selling new merchandise, antiques, collectibles, crafts and produce. This is a fast growing market which now holds special events on Saturdays. The second Saturday special event is strictly antiques and collectibles. It is held next to the main swap meet. A snack bar serves a wide variety of sandwiches, snacks and breakfasts.

**DEALER RATES**: Saturday $10 per 20' × 20' booth, Sunday $12 per 20' × 20' booth. Reservations are not required; it's a first-come, first-served market.

**CONTACT**: Joe Crowder, 635 W Mission Ave, Escondido CA 92025. Tel: (760) 745-3100. Day of show or tape information (619) 449-7927.

# SEBASTOPOL
## Midgley's Country Flea Market

**DATES**: Every Saturday and Sunday year round. Closed only when there is a "downpour."

**TIMES**: 6:30 AM-4:30 PM.

**ADMISSION**: Free. Parking is free.

**LOCATION**: 2200 Gravenstein Hwy S. Off Hwy 101 to Gravenstein Hwy or Hwy 116. Market is about 5 miles down the road. Only 50 miles north of San Francisco.

**DESCRIPTION**: This family friendly outdoor market, run by the same family, has been open since 1972. There are up to 250 dealers filling 500 spaces during the summer and anywhere from 150 to 200 dealers selling their goods during the winter months. At least 50% of this market is still "bonafide flea market" goodies. There is a large variety of antiques, collectibles, crafts, new merchandise and even fresh produce available. Basically anything new or used is sold including clothes, books, pictures, jewelry, tires, and furniture, just to name a few. Two snack bars and handicapped-accessible restrooms deal with issues other than browsing.

**DEALER RATES**: Currently $13 for 4' × 8' table and parking for one vehicle. Weekly, monthly and seasonal rates available. Reservations are not required.

**CONTACT**: Midgley's Country Flea Market, 2200 Gravenstein Hwy S, Sebastopol CA 95472. Tel: (707) 823-7874 or 1-800-800-FLEA in California.

---

### Lost and Found

Years ago, a rather strange piece of denture was turned into the office as lost. The odd piece sat in the Lost and Found box for months, but the owners couldn't imagine that this curious piece could actually fit anyone. Sure enough, one day a man asked if anyone had turned in any dentures. Well, they said, yes... is this what you are looking for? The fellow took the proffered piece and fitted them in his mouth perfectly.

---

# STANTON

## International Market Place (Indoor Swapmeet of Stanton)

**DATES:** Daily except Tuesday.

**TIMES:** Weekends 10:00 AM-6:00 PM; weekdays 10:00 AM-7:00 PM.

**ADMISSION:** Free. Parking is free.

**LOCATION:** 10401 Beach Blvd, 2 miles south of Knott's Berry Farm.

**DESCRIPTION:** This two-story indoor market has 200 spaces with 70 vendors selling crafts, new merchandise, jewelry, perfumes, sportswear, athletic shoes, luggage, clothing, computer stuff, electronic appliances, gifts, nail and beauty salon, groceries, caps, embroidering, silk flowers and more. One snack bar, a restaurant, and handicapped-accessible restrooms are on site.

**DEALER RATES:** $250-$600 for 4 weeks or 28 days depending on the location for a 8' × 12' space. Reservations are not required.

**CONTACT:** Jila Ilami, Manager, Indoor Swapmeet of Stanton, 10401 Beach Blvd, Stanton CA 90680. Tel: (714) 527-1112 or (714) 527-1234 or fax: (714) 527-1595.

# TORRANCE

## Roadium Open Air Market

**DATES:** Daily, except Christmas and New Year's Day.

**TIMES:** 7:00 AM-4:00 PM.

**ADMISSION:** $1.50 per car and driver, plus $.50 per person up to $3.50 maximum. Children are free.

**LOCATION:** 2500 Redondo Beach Blvd. From Long Beach and the south, take the San Diego Fwy (405) to Crenshaw. Go right to Redondo Beach Blvd, turn right into the market. From the north, take 405 to the Redondo Beach Blvd Exit and go east to the market.

**DESCRIPTION:** For over 40 years the Roadium has been a fixture in Torrance with 470 dealers, spread over 15 acres, offering antiques, collectibles, fresh produce, and plenty of new and pre-owned merchandise. There is a snack bar, roving snack carts, restrooms, and an ATM.

**DEALER RATES:** $14-$55 per space depending on location and day of week; reservations requested. Office hours: 5:30 AM-3:00 PM.

**CONTACT:** John Schoen, Roadium Open Air Market, 2500 Redondo Beach Blvd, Torrance CA 90504. Tel: (213) 321-3709. Fax: (213) 321-0114. Email: roadium@earthlink.com. Web: www.Roadium.com.

# TURLOCK
## Turlock Sales Yard Flea Market

**DATES:** Tuesdays only. Weather permitting.
**TIMES:** 4:00 AM-dark.
**ADMISSION:** Free. Parking is free.
**LOCATION:** At the corner of East Ave and N Johnson Rd.
**DESCRIPTION:** This historic, real old-time flea market on 10 acres of selling space and 15 acres of parking evolved into a hugely popular hit with 400-500 dealers nabbing all 750 spaces selling 5 acres of antiques, collectibles, and just used stuff; 2½ acres of produce; and 2½ acres of new merchandise. This is a great place to buy "used" treasures for resale. In case of famishment, there is a small restaurant doing the burger thing, plus 12 food wagons (selling tacos, Chinese) roaming the market quelling thirsts as well. Handicapped-accessible restrooms come in handy if you sample too much.
**DEALER RATES:** $15 per 12' × 24' space, take as many as you need. No reservations taken. For regular dealers with a preference for a space, they will only hold it until 6:30 AM.
**CONTACT:** Turlock Sales Yard Flea Market, PO Box 25, Turlock CA 95380-0025. Tel: (209) 667-4441.

---

### The Beginnings

In 1938, Scott's grandfather sold horses off a street corner. Gradually, others came to buy and auction off their livestock, then boxed household items. This market exploded into a flea market in the 1970s, the livestock market was sold off and the whole shebang was moved to its current location.

Recently three paintings were purchased for $80, taken to the San Francisco area, sold around there until some savvy seller got them and sold them through Butterfields—for $80,000.

---

# VALLEJO
## Napa-Vallejo Flea Market and Auction

**DATES:** Every Sunday. Rain or shine.
**TIMES:** 6:00 AM-5:00 PM.
**ADMISSION:** Free. $2 parking fee.
**LOCATION:** 303 Kelly Rd, off Hwy 29, halfway between Napa and Vallejo.

**DESCRIPTION**: This show began in 1947. It is both an indoor and outdoor market situated on 20 acres of land. The market accommodates approximately 600 dealers who sell antiques and collectibles, arts and crafts, jewelry, books, sporting goods, and tools, to name a few. In addition, there is a produce market and several permanent businesses located here. For 40 years, one family has owned and operated the snack bar and there are vendors selling Mexican and Chinese food.

**DEALER RATES**: $20 for 3' × 8' table on a 10' × 20' space; vehicle space is included. No reservations are accepted. Sellers should arrive and set up between 6:00 AM-9:00 AM.

**CONTACT**: Nelson or Tom Harding, 303 Kelly Rd, Vallejo CA 94590. Tel: (707) 226-8862.

## VENTURA
### Ventura Flea Market

**DATES**: 2000: Jan 30, Feb 27, April 30.

**TIMES**: 9:00 AM-2:00 PM, although you can shop while the vendors pack up until 4:30 PM. Advice: come early for the best parking.

**ADMISSION**: $4, children under 12 are free with an adult. Parking is free. Early dealer and collector's hours start at 6:00 AM for an $8 admission.

**LOCATION**: Ventura County Fairgrounds, aka Seaside Park at 10 W Harbor in Ventura, just off the 101 Ventura Fwy at California St.

**DESCRIPTION**: There are over 800 dealers attending this outdoor show. Everything from antiques to collectibles to crafts and new merchandise to garage specials can be found here. It is one of California's most popular markets with approximately 8,000 buyers. For your convenience, there are also food and restrooms available on the premises. As one shopper describes this market: "95% collectibles and garage sales, only 5% new stuff. Very good dealers who want to make a deal. Bargains can still be found here."

**DEALER RATES**: $30, $40, or $50 per 20' × 20' space. Reservations are suggested.

**CONTACT**: RG Canning, PO Box 400, Maywood CA 90270-0400. Tel: (323) 560-7469. Office hours are Monday and Wednesday 10:00 AM-12:00 PM and 1:00 PM-5:00 PM. Email: rgc@rgcshows.com or website: www.rgcshows.com.

## VICTORVILLE
### Maclin's Victorville Open-Air Market

**DATES**: Every Saturday and Sunday.

**TIMES**: 6:00 AM-2:30 PM.
**ADMISSION**: $1, children 12 and under free. Seniors $.75. Parking is free.
**LOCATION**: San Bernardino County Fairgrounds, 14800 Seventh St. Located off the 15 Fwy on Roy Rogers exit.
**DESCRIPTION**: Opened in 1998, this Maclin's market has 70-100 dealers selling household goods, clothing, new and used merchandise, collectible and specialty items. There is "great on-site" food service. Live entertainment is provide by local musicians.
**DEALER RATES**: Saturday $15 for any space; Sunday $12 for everything. Spaces are 20' × 20'. Bring your own setup. You can prepay Friday evening from 3:00 PM-5:00 PM.
**CONTACT**: Maclin's, 7407 Riverside Dr, Ontario CA 91761. Tel: (909) 984-5131. Or toll-free in California 1-800-222-7467. Fax: (909) 988-8041. Email: info@maclinmarkets.com. Web: maclinmarkets.com.

# VISALIA
## Visalia Sales Yard, Inc
**DATES**: Thursday and Sunday, year round.
**TIMES**: 6:00 AM-3:00 PM.
**ADMISSION**: Free. Parking is also free.
**LOCATION**: 29660 RD 152, 1½ miles east of Visalia.
**DESCRIPTION**: This show began in 1948 and is currently an all-outdoor market that accommodates approximately 300 dealers. Among the items to be found here are antiques and collectibles, new merchandise, and fresh produce. A snack bar serves hot dogs, burritos, breakfasts and other delights, and handicapped-accessible restrooms take care of other needs.
**DEALER RATES**: $8 per 10' × 10' space. Monthly reservations are available, otherwise first come, first served.
**CONTACT**: Karen Green, Visalia Sales Yard Inc, 29660 Rd 152, Visalia CA 93291. Tel: (209) 734-9092.

# WOODLAND HILLS
## Valley Indoor Swap Meet
**DATES:** Friday through Sunday.
**TIMES:** 10:00 AM-6:00 PM.
**ADMISSION:** Free. Parking is free.
**LOCATION:** 6701 Variel Ave. Take 101 Fwy to Desoto Ave, go north 1½ miles to Kittridge St, left 2 blocks.

**DESCRIPTION:** Opened in 1983, this is the first of three Valley Indoor Swap Meets in California (see Pomona and Panorama City). Housed in two buildings, their 500 dealers sell new merchandise and specialize in clothing and accessories. These markets are huge and sell just about anything you can think of. One of the buildings is open weekends only, the other from Friday through Sunday. Claimed to be "the most famous, well-known indoor swap meet in southern California. Selling high-end merchandise. Many movie and TV celebrities can be seen attending on almost any weekend." Handicapped-accessible restrooms alleviate the load from too many stops at the many snack bars offering all the usual goodies.

**DEALER RATES:** $360 in the 2-day building, $475 in the 3-day building, monthly for a 10' × 10' space. Reservations are required.

**CONTACT:** Jeff Kaplan, Valley Indoor Swap Meet, 6701 Variel Ave, Woodland Hills CA 91367. Tel: (818) 340-9120 or 340-9123. Fax: (818) 340-5413. Email: info@indoorswap.com. Web: www.indoorswap.com.

# YUCCA VALLEY
## Sky Village Outdoor Marketplace

**DATES:** Saturday and Sunday, year round.

**TIMES:** 5:30 AM-2:00 PM.

**ADMISSION:** Free. Parking is free.

**LOCATION:** 7028 Theater Rd, near the intersection of S Hwys 62 and 247.

**DESCRIPTION:** This family owned, still old-fashioned, "not overly commercialized" swap meet's 200 dealers sell a mix of antiques and collectibles, old tools, and new and used merchandise—described as from "junk to gems." As it is so easy to rent and set up here, many locals bring in tons of garage sale goodies. In fact, many items you might be looking for elsewhere and can't find are probably here! The Sky Cafe serves homemade breakfast and lunch. Clean restrooms are on site.

**DEALER RATES:** Saturday: $9 for a 20' space, Sunday $8. Reservations are not required.

**CONTACT:** Bob and Elizabeth Carr, Sky Village Outdoor Marketplace, PO Box 1808, Yucca Valley CA 92288-1808. Tel: (760) 365-2104. Web: www.desertgold.com.

# OTHER FLEA MARKETS

We know or have heard about these markets, but have not personally contacted each one, as we have the markets with descriptions. If you plan to visit one of these markets listed below, *please call first* to make sure they are still open. Flea markets do come and go. While they were open when we went to press, they may not be later. We can't be responsible. *Call first!*

**Alameda:** Norcal Swap Meet, 1150 Ballena Blvd. Tel: (510) 769-7266.

**American Canyon:** Flea Market & Auction, 303 S Kelly Rd. Tel: (707) 226-8862.

**Anderson:** Happy Valley Flea Mart, 17820 Strawberry Ln. Tel: (530) 365-1466.

**Aromas:** Red Barn Flea Market, 1000 Hwy 101. Tel: (831) 726-3101.

**Brentwood:** Brentwood Flea Market, 6715 Brentwood Blvd. Tel: (925) 634-3767.

**Chico:** Silverdollar Swap Meet, Silver Dollar Fair Grounds. Tel: (530) 892-9205.

**Clearlake:** Clearlake Flea Market, 16080 Davis St. Tel: (707) 995-2304.

**Corning:** North State Flea & Produce Market, 7445 State Hwy 99W. Tel: (530) 824-0602.

**Crescent City:** Crescent City Fleamarket, 1075 Pacific Ave. Tel: (707) 464-6384 or (707) 458-4114 or euqinu@gte.net.

**Fresno:** Fresno Flea Market & Swap Meet, 1641 S Chance Ave. Tel: (559) 268-3646.

**Gerber:** Gerber Flea Market, 8795 San Benito Ave. Tel: (530) 385-2919.

**Hesperia:** Crafty Flea Mart, 8125 I Ave. Tel: (760) 947-3333.

**Kerman:** Whitesbridge Auction's Fair, 14443 W Whitesbridge Ave. Tel: (559) 846-9172.

**Los Banos:** World's Faire, 1725 W Pacheco Blvd. Tel: (209) 826-6779.

**McKinleyville:** Redwood Flea Market. Tel: (707) 839-3049.

**Modesto:** Crows Landing Flea Market, 3113 Crows Landing Rd. Tel: (209) 538-3363.

**North Highlands:** Trader Village, 5621 Watt Ave #105. Tel: (916) 344-1507.

**Oakland:** San Pablo Flea Market II, 6100 San Pablo Ave. Tel: (510) 420-1468.

**Orland:** Old Town, 424 Colusa St. Tel: (530) 865-3347.

**Red Bluff:** Red Bluff Market Place Inc, 235 S Main St. Tel: (530) 528-0522.

**San Francisco:** Far East Flea Market, 729 Grant Ave. Tel: (415) 989-8588.

**Santa Rosa:** John Patterson Enterprises, 232 Aileen Ave. Tel: (707) 528-2093.

**Soquel:** Skyview Flea-Market, 2260 Soquel Dr. Tel: (831) 462-4442.

**Stockton:** Stockton Flea Market, 2542 S El Dorado St. Tel: (209) 465-9933.

**Stockton:** Stockton Open Air Mall, 3550 N Wilson Way. Tel: (209) 465-1544.

# COLORADO

## COLORADO SPRINGS
### The Flea Market

**DATES:** Saturday and Sunday, year round.

**TIMES:** 7:00 AM-4:00 PM.

**ADMISSION:** $1, children are free. Parking is free.

**LOCATION:** 5225 E Platte Ave. On Platte Ave 1 mile east of Academy Blvd.

**DESCRIPTION:** Started in 1965, this "super clean" outdoor market has 400 dealers in summer and 200 dealers in winter selling antiques, collectibles, crafts, produce, coins, stamps, cards, garage sale finds, furniture, and new merchandise. There is a farmers' market every Friday from June until October, and they have a great view of Pikes Peak to boot! Five service carts, an outdoor patio snack bar, a walk-up bar, one restaurant (I'm told "great food" and open for breakfast and lunches) and handicapped-accessible restrooms complete the amenities.

**DEALER RATES:** $17 per 20' × 20' space. Reservations are first come, first served or reservations can be made in the summer only, Friday (12:00 PM-4:00 PM), Saturday and Sunday during market hours. No trailer drop-offs.

**CONTACT:** Bob Zifel, The Flea Market, PO Box 7229, Colorado Springs CO 80933-7229. Tel: (719) 380-8599. Fax: (719) 380-8585.

## DENVER
### The Ballpark Market

**DATES:** The last Saturday of the month, May through October.

**TIMES:** 8:00 AM-2:30 PM.

**ADMISSION:** Free. Metered, pay lots and free parking, where you can find it.

**LOCATION:** At the corner of 22nd and Larimer Sts. Just 2 blocks from Coors Field in the Ballpark Neighborhood. Easy access from I-25 and I-70.

**DESCRIPTION:** Started in 1998 with just two dates, and billing itself as "an urban" flea market, after those in New York and Washington DC, this market has dealers selling everything "from fold art to furniture, antiques to vintage clothing.

**DEALER RATES:** $35 for 6' × 8', $45 or 10' × 10', $80 for car access 10' × 20' spaces. Discounted rates for multiple event signups.

**CONTACT:** The Ballpark Market, 1307 22 St, Denver CO 80205. Tel: (303) 295-7059. Fax: (303) 298-9240. Email: ballparkmkt@hotmail.com.

## Mile High Flea Market, Inc

**DATES:** Every Wednesday, Saturday and Sunday, year round.

**TIMES:** 7:00 AM-5:00 PM.

**ADMISSION:** $2 per person weekends, $1 per person Wednesdays, under 12 free.

**LOCATION:** I-76 and 88th Ave.

**DESCRIPTION:** This indoor/outdoor flea market started in 1977 and is currently America's third largest flea market and Colorado's largest flea market. It brings over 1.5 million bargain hunters to 80 paved acres of brand name, close-out, garage sale and seasonal merchandise. It features from 1,800 dealers in summer to 1,500 in winter selling antiques, fine art, collectibles, new merchandise, sports shoes, socks and underwear, clothing, silk plants, crystals, sunglasses, tires, auto parts, tools, luggage, furniture, bicycles, fishing tackle, cowboy boots, baby clothes, army surplus, antique train bells, hog greasers, steam ship whistles, one left mannequin leg, bowling balls, jackalopes, and seasonal merchandise, including bedding plants, Christmas trees, pumpkins and farm fresh produce. About 800 of the dealers are cleaning out their garages, and 700 to 1,000 vendors are regulars. A new family midway features rides for children and adults alike. This is billed as a family event with plenty of parking for motor homes and tour buses. A restaurant, 5 food stands, 2 beer tents, corn roasters, outdoor grills and a fleet of 15 mobile food carts provide ample food and beverage. You can also rent shopping carts, wheelchairs and wagons.

**DEALER RATES:** $20 per 12' × 25' space per day for Saturday and Sundays; $10 per day on Wednesday. There is a $3 per space per day advanced reservations fee. Reservations taken all week beginning Monday afternoons for the following Wednesday and/or weekend (by phone with MasterCard or Visa). Monthly reservations are also available. Tables and storage containers are available for rental.

**CONTACT:** Jim Hurrell, Marketing Director, 7007 E 88 Ave, Henderson CO 80640. Tel: (303) 289-4656 or 1-800-861-9900. Fax: (303) 286-1922.

# FORT COLLINS
## Foothills Indoor Flea Markets

**DATES:** Daily.

**TIMES:** 10:00 AM-6:00 PM.

**ADMISSION:** Free. Free parking is available.

**LOCATION:** Just off I-25, between Fort Collins and Loveland on Hwy 287.

**DESCRIPTION:** Both these shows opened in 1982. They accommodate approximately 100 dealers each. These indoor markets contain over 500,000 different items stashed in 26,000 square feet of space. Sold here are antiques, arts and crafts, and collectibles. There is no food available on the premises aside from popcorn; however, we're told there is a great restaurant next door. There are three more markets in this area—DJs, Itchy's, and Sidekick.

**DEALER RATES:** $140 plus a 7% fee per 100-square-foot space, per month. Reservations are required; monthly rates only are available.

**CONTACT:** Foothills Indoor Flea Market, 6300 S College, Fort Collins CO 80525-4044. Tel: (970) 223-9069.

## Fort Collins Flea Market

**DATES:** Daily.

**TIMES:** 10:00 AM-6:00 PM.

**ADMISSION:** Free. Free parking is available.

**LOCATION:** Just off I-25, between Fort Collins and Loveland on Hwy 287.

**DESCRIPTION:** This market opened in 1985. They accommodate approximately 85 dealers selling antiques, arts and crafts, collectibles, furniture, collectible glassware, clothing, groceries, and more. There is also a selection of new merchandise.

**DEALER RATES:** $140 plus a 6% fee per 100-square-foot space, per month. Reservations are required; monthly rates only are available.

**CONTACT:** Vince and Joy Barnhart, Fort Collins Flea Market, 6200 S College, Fort Collins CO 80525-4046. Tel: (970) 223-6502.

# LAFAYETTE
## Lafayette Flea Market

**DATES:** Daily, year round.

**TIMES:** 10:00 AM-6:00 PM.

**ADMISSION:** Free. Parking is free.

**LOCATION:** 130 E Spaulding, just behind the Conoco gas station on the corner of South Public Rd and Spaulding St.

**DESCRIPTION:** This market opened April 1, 1990 with 20,000 square feet in a climate controlled, heated and cooled former bowling alley. They were ranked 12th out of 50 of the "Biggest and Best" Flea Markets in the US in the March 1994 issue of *Good Housekeeping* magazine. Antique stores are two blocks away. There are 116 dealer spaces, with 90 dealers specializing in glassware, hobbies, stamps, coins, antique furniture, collectibles, sports cards, secondhand items, jewelry, and consignments.

**DEALER RATES:** $1.50 per square foot per month or $150 per month for a 10' × 10' booth. Reservations are required.

**CONTACT:** Bill Hopkins, Lafayette Collectibles & Flea Market, 130 E Spaulding, Lafayette CO 80026. Tel: (303) 665-0433.

# LONGMONT
## Front Range Flea Market

**DATES:** Daily.

**TIMES:** 10:00 AM-6:00 PM. Sunday 12:00 PM-5:00 PM.

**ADMISSION:** Free. Parking is also free.

**LOCATION:** 1420 Nelson Rd. West off US 287 on Colorado Rt 119.

**DESCRIPTION:** This growing market opened in 1989 and currently has over 60 dealers. Housed in a 28,000-square-foot building, these dealers sell new merchandise, collectibles, antiques, jewelry, furniture, sports cards, clothing, and "a lot of everything." No food is available, but restrooms are on site.

**DEALER RATES:** $1.75 per square foot plus 10%. Reservations are required as there is a waiting list.

**CONTACT:** Vicky Andrew or Marj Sater, Front Range Flea Market, 1420 Nelson Rd, Longmont CO 80501. Tel: (303) 776-6605.

# OTHER FLEA MARKETS

We know or have heard about these markets, but have not personally contacted each one, as we have the markets with descriptions. If you plan to visit one of these markets listed below, *please call first* to make sure they are still open. Flea markets do come and go. While they were open when we went to press, they may not be later. We can't be responsible. *Call first!*

**Colorado Springs:** The Flea Market, 5225 E Platte. Tel: (719) 380-8599. Sat, Sun 7 AM-4 PM. Year round.

**Fountain:** Jesse's Seven Day Flea Market, 6346 S Hwy 83 & 87. Tel: (719) 392-8359.

**Pueblo:** Sunset Flea Market, 2641 I-25 N Exit 104. Tel: (719) 584-2000 or 583-8039. Fri, Sat, Sun. 7 AM-4 PM. Year round.

# CONNECTICUT

## COVENTRY
### Coventry Indoor Outdoor Flea Market

**DATES:** Every Sunday, year round except Christmas Sundays.
**TIMES:** 9:00 AM-4:00 PM.
**ADMISSION:** Free. Parking is free.
**LOCATION:** 44 Lake St. Junctions of Rts 31 and 275.
**DESCRIPTION:** Open since October 1990, this indoor/outdoor market of approximately 80 dealers sells sports cards, comics, antiques and collectibles with dealers specializing in jewelry, furniture, records (40 feet worth!), military items, paper, linens, glass, coins, books and bugs—really, beautifully displayed along with his clock repair business. "We will always have dealers with the latest collectibles, tag sale items, fine antique furniture and just plain junk." In 1993, they opened the Coventry General Store selling Coventry-made products: vinegars, dried flowers, furniture, and Westerwald pottery from Pennsylvania with the Coventry pattern. There is a "great clean snack bar with more than hot dogs" as well as handicapped-accessible, clean restrooms.
**DEALER RATES:** $12 to $25 depending on size and location. Reservations are requested.
**CONTACT:** Joseph and Rose Fowler, Coventry Flea Market, 110 Wall St, Coventry CT 06238. Tel: (860) 742-9362. Day of market call: (860) 742-1993.

## EAST HARTFORD
### Connecticut Comic Book Flea Market

**DATES:** Sundays, monthly except January.
**TIMES:** 11:00 AM-5:00 PM.
**ADMISSION:** $.99 fee. Parking is free.
**LOCATION:** Elks Hall at 148 Roberts St. Take Exit 58 from I-84, follow the signs.
**DESCRIPTION:** This show started in 1974 and has approximately 30 dealers. It is an indoor market that sells collectibles, antiques, new merchandise, as well as pulp magazines, science fiction, collectibles, gum cards, and movie items, but they specialize in comic books for collectors. Food is served on the premises.
**DEALER RATES:** $45 for an 8' table. Advance reservations are required.

**CONTACT:** Harold E. Kinney, c/o The Bookies Bookstore, 206 Burnside Ave, E Hartford CT 06108. Tel: (860) 289-1208 in afternoons. Email: hal2000@freewwweb.com.

# FARMINGTON
## Farmington Antiques Weekend

**DATES:** Second weekend in June and Labor Day weekend. 2000: June 10-11, September 2-3. 2001: June 9-10, September 1-2.

**TIMES:** 10:00 AM-5:00 PM. Early admission 7:00 AM.

**ADMISSION:** $5 for adults. Parking is free. Early admission fee $25.

**LOCATION:** At the Farmington Polo Grounds, 10 miles west of Hartford and 3 miles from Exit 39 off I-84.

**DESCRIPTION:** This national antiques event opened in 1980 and is held both outdoors and under tents. There are around 600 dealers at each show selling antiques, fine art, and collectibles, but this market specializes in antiques from rural America. This claims to be the #1 large antiques and better collectibles event in the United States, and it draws approximately 30,000 people per show. All merchandise is guaranteed to be as represented: no new merchandise, no reproductions. Good home-cooked food is available on premises.

**DEALER RATES:** $275 on the lawns, $350 and up under the tents. Reservations are required well in advance as there is a long waiting list. Write for map and motel list.

**CONTACT:** Abby or Bob McInnis, Revival Promotions Inc, PO Box 388, Grafton MA 01519-0388. Tel: (508) 839-9735. Week of show call (860) 677-7862. Email: showinfo@farmington-antiques.com. Web: www.farmington-antiques.com.

# JEWETT CITY
## College Mart Flea Market

**DATES:** Every Sunday.

**TIMES:** 9:00 AM-4:00 PM.

**ADMISSION:** Free. Parking is free.

**LOCATION:** Wedgewood Dr. Exits 84 and 85 off I-395.

**DESCRIPTION:** Started in 1982 in the old Slater Textile Mill, this market now hosts 140 vendors indoors and outdoors selling antiques, glassware, clothing, collectibles, toys, crafts, furniture, all types of old and new jewelry, gold, silver, and new merchandise. Food is available on the premises.

**DEALER RATES:** $15 for a half space (5' × 10') to $30 for a full space (10' × 10'). Outdoor space is $20. Reservations are strongly recommended.
**CONTACT:** Bob Leone, College Mart Flea Market, Wedgewood Dr, Jewett City CT 06351. Tel: (203) 376-3935 or (203) 642-6248.

# MANSFIELD
## Eastern Connecticut Flea Market

**DATES:** Sundays, third Sunday in March (first Sunday in Spring) until Thanksgiving, weather permitting.
**TIMES:** 9:00 AM-3:00 PM.
**ADMISSION:** Free. Parking is $2 from 8:00 AM-9:00 AM; $1 after that.
**LOCATION:** Mansfield Drive-In Theatre at 228 Stafford Rd. At the junction of Rts 31 and 32.
**DESCRIPTION:** Operating since 1975, and one of the first markets in Connecticut, this outdoor market's 200-plus dealers sell antiques, clothes, collectibles, new and used books, tools, toys and more—from "antiques to high tech" with a computer vendor on site. Breakfast and lunch are served at the market, or bring your own. This market is held at a thriving three-screen drive-in theater and its concession is open during the market.
**DEALER RATES:** $20 for a 14' × 14' space weekly; or $17.50 per week on a monthly basis. Rental tables (32" × 7') are $3-$4 a day, if you need one. Reservations are taken on a monthly basis only; otherwise, first come, first served. Setup starts at 7:30 AM and no sales (by local law) before 8:00 AM.
**CONTACT:** Michael Jungden, Eastern Connecticut Flea Market, 228 Stafford Rd, Mansfield CT 06250. Tel: (860) 456-2578. Web: mansfielddi.hollywood.com (click on About Us).

# NAUGATUCK
## Peddlers Market

**DATES:** Every Sunday from the first Sunday in April to the end of November. Weather permitting.
**TIMES:** Dawn to dusk.
**ADMISSION:** Free. Parking is $1 per car.
**LOCATION:** On Rt 63 (New Haven Rd) between Waterbury and New Haven.
**DESCRIPTION:** This market began operation in 1969 on 9 hilly, beautiful acres. There are anywhere from 75 to 80 dealers at this family oriented outdoor market. You can find most anything here from antiques and col-

lectibles to new merchandise and fresh produce, including fishing equipment, furniture, and household items. It is located in a beautiful setting near the highway. This clean market has four food vendors selling delicious egg sandwiches, fried dough, Italian sausage and mushroom sandwichs, and other special foods that are so popular people come for the food alone! There are clean, modern portable toilet facilities on the premises. As a civic service, non-profits are allowed to set up and sale for fundraisers.

**DEALER RATES:** $25 for up to 30' front per day. These are quite generous spaces as there is plenty of room. Reservations are not required.

**CONTACT:** Thomas Murray, Gunntown Rd, Naugatuck CT 06770. Tel: (203) 729-6339; or Gerald Garceau, 33 Hazel Ave, Naugatuck CT 06770. Tel: (203) 729-7762.

---

### You Never Know What It's Worth

Mr. Murray bought a lovely piece of cherrywood furniture for $30 off a dealer's truck. It would make a lovely gift for his wife. Shortly, another dealer approached him and offered him $100 for it. No, not for sale. A few hours later the dealer approached him again offering $200. No, not for sale. A few hours later, Mr. Murray was again approached with a $300 offer. No, that's final. *Really!*

---

# NEW HAVEN
## Boulevard Flea Market

**DATES:** Saturday and Sunday, year round.

**TIMES:** 7:00 AM-4:00 PM.

**ADMISSION:** Free. Parking is $1.

**LOCATION:** 500 Ella T Grasso Blvd. Northbound: I-95, take Exit 44 Kimberly Ave. Bear right off exit, go left at traffic light at ET Grasso Blvd (Rt 10). Market is ¾ mile on the left. Southbound: I-95, Exit 45 Rt 10, bear right down ramp, go straight, market is still ¾ mile on left.

**DESCRIPTION:** Opened in 1949, this outdoor market has to be the oldest in Connecticut. Depending on the weather (if it's raining, the market is open but not overwhelmed) their 100-plus dealers sell about 80% new merchandise including clothes, tapes, produce (in season), and loads of "tag sale" or garage finds. Although not many antiques appear, plenty of collectibles do find their way here. On a good day up to 15-18,000 customers roam and buy. Several snack carts and vendors feed the famished.

**DEALER RATES:** $25 Saturday, $50 for Sunday per 20' space, with plenty of vehicle space. There is always space for dealers. Reservations are not required.

**CONTACT:** Chuck, Boulevard Flea Market, 500 Ella T Grasso Blvd, New Haven CT 06519. Tel: (203) 772-1447 or toll-free (877) 228-7554. Email: info@fleact.com. Web: www.fleact.com.

# NEW MILFORD
## Elephant's Trunk Flea Market

**DATES:** Sundays only, April through Sunday before Christmas, except Easter Sunday.

**TIMES:** 6:00 AM-2:00 PM.

**ADMISSION:** $1 adults, children 13 and under free. Parking is free and plentiful. No pets allowed!

**LOCATION:** Rt 7. Exit 7 from I-84, 7 miles north of Danbury.

**DESCRIPTION:** This market started in 1977. The 300-plus dealers break down their sales as approximately 30% antiques and collectibles; 30% general line merchandise; 20% new items: tools and jewelry etc., and 20% anything and everything else. There are dealers who have been with this market since the beginning and buyers who return the same time every weekend and have, over the years, become friends. There are 55 acres with room for 500 dealer spaces. Food is available on the premises.

**DEALER RATES:** $30 per 25' × 20' space. All dealers are urged to have a Connecticut Tax number. Reservations are not required.

**CONTACT:** Contact Greg Baecker by telephone: (860) 355-1448.

## Maplewood Flea Market

**DATES:** Saturday and Sunday.

**TIMES:** 8:30 AM-4:00 PM.

**ADMISSION:** Free. Parking is free.

**LOCATION:** 458 Danbury Rd, Rt 7 N.

**DESCRIPTION:** Opened in 1991, this indoor market of 100-plus dealers (in a 25,000-square-foot building with dealers usually hogging more than one space) offers antiques, collectibles, glass, antique jewelry, used furniture, and new merchandise. One snack bar with handicapped-accessible restrooms serves the famished in its own food court. This market is especially handicapped-accessible and visited by the busload.

**DEALER RATES:** $55 per 12' × 6' single space per weekend, $95 per double space. Double-space vendors can leave their merchandise overnight. There is complete security on the premises. Reservations are suggested for the "winter" season as they get "crammed."
**CONTACT:** Sandy Modzelewski, Maplewood Flea Market, 458 Danbury Rd, New Milford CT 06776. Tel: (860) 350-0454.

---

**Don't Even Think of It!**

Occasionally, someone has dropped off furniture in their parking lot. Dumb idea. The market dragged it in—and sold it! Of course, they kept the profits for themselves, as the "gift" was anonymous.

Then again, there was a painting purchased here, as well as a table, that when offered through Sotheby's in New York brought in quite a lot of money!

---

# NIANTIC
## Between the Bridges Antique and Collectibles Flea Market

**DATES:** Thursday through Tuesday, year round.
**TIMES:** 10:00 AM-5:00 PM.
**ADMISSION:** Free. Parking is free.
**LOCATION:** 65 Pennsylvania Ave. Take Exit 74 off I-95, turn right, 3 miles.
**DESCRIPTION:** Opened in May 1991, this new market (ok, it's really a store) has 60 dealers and a waiting list selling just antiques, collectibles and used furniture. No new merchandise or crafts. There is an antique radio and television restorer next door.
**DEALER RATES:** $25 for 65 square feet of space. You don't have to be there to sell. There is a waiting list, so call first.
**CONTACT:** John and Diane Deer, 65 Pennsylvania Ave, Niantic CT 06357. Tel: (860) 691-0170.

# OLD MYSTIC
## Old Mystic Antique Flea Market

**DATES:** Every Sunday, weather permitting.
**TIMES:** 8:00 AM-5:00 PM.
**ADMISSION:** Free. Parking is free.
**LOCATION:** Rt 27 in Old Mystic. Across from the southern entrance to I-95, at the Mystic Visitor and Transportation Center.

**DESCRIPTION:** This market, in business since 1974, has co-op dealers in winter, to 25 dealers in the summer. While the market deals mostly in antiques, there is some new merchandise sold as well, including toys. One dealer specializes in antique Matchbox cars. Mystic Seaport is less than one mile away. Breakfast, lunch and snacks are available on the premises.
**DEALER RATES:** $25 per Sunday for 14' × 22' space. Reservations are strongly recommended.
**CONTACT:** Sonny Hendel, 6 Hendel Dr, Old Mystic CT 06372. Tel: (860) 536-0646.

# TORRINGTON
## Wright's Barn and Flea Market
**DATES:** Saturday and Sunday, year round.
**TIMES:** 10:00 AM-4:30 PM.
**ADMISSION:** Free. Parking is free.
**LOCATION:** Wright Rd off Rt 4, between Torrington and Goshen. Follow the large signs on Rt 4.
**DESCRIPTION:** This indoor market opened in 1981 in a huge 10,000-square-foot dairy barn with 40 dealers selling mostly antiques and some collectibles. Most of their dealers are permanent (12 dealers have been there over 17 years) and come from over 20 miles away. There is a snack bar and a fireplace to keep you warm in winter.
**DEALER RATES:** $20 for 10' × 14' booth, Saturday and Sunday. Reservations are required.
**CONTACT:** Milly Wright, Wright's Barn, 149 Wright Rd, Torrington CT 06790. Tel: (860) 482-0095.

# WALLINGFORD
## Redwood Country Flea Market
**DATES:** Every Saturday and Sunday, and some holidays, year round, weather permitting (even in snow!).
**TIMES:** 8:00 AM-4:00 PM.
**ADMISSION:** Free. Parking is also free.
**LOCATION:** At 170 Hartford Tnpk in Wallingford. Take Exit 13 off I-91, or take Exit 64 off Wilbur Cross Pkwy.
**DESCRIPTION:** This show began in 1973. There are approximately 75 to 90 dealers at this outdoor market selling almost anything from antiques and collectibles to new merchandise and fresh produce. They do extensive

advertising in area papers and trade magazines. The Dubars have a restaurant on the premises that is well known to the rich and famous whose pictures cover the walls. Walter Dubar, the original founder of this market, has retired, leaving his son and grandsons to run this unique place. However, if you can find Walter, he has some wonderful stories to tell! Hi, Walter!

**DEALER RATES:** Spaces measure 20' × 10', but it's best to call for their reasonable rates as they vary. Reservations are suggested.

**CONTACT:** Ken Dubar and Steven Hugo, Redwood Country Flea Market, 170 Hartford Tnpk, Wallingford CT 06492. Tel: (203) 269-3500 between 1:00 PM-7:00 PM weekdays or all day Saturday and Sunday.

---

**They Aren't Kidding**

It isn't unheard of to have large snowstorms in Connecticut. Out come the snowplows and the market continues.

---

# WESTBROOK
## Westbrook Flea Market

**DATES:** Saturday and Sunday, April to October.

**TIMES:** 8:00 AM-4:00 PM.

**ADMISSION:** Free. Parking is free.

**LOCATION:** Boston Post Rd. Take I-95 to Exit 64 to Boston Post Rd.

**DESCRIPTION:** Open since 1980, this outdoor market of 50 dealers sells antiques, collectibles, crafts, coins, stamps, cards, garage sale goodies, furniture, choice junk, and new merchandise. According to the owner, 90% of the vendors display collectibles, while the remaining 10% display "choice junk" reclaimed from the town dump! Surprisingly, he says, these sell the best. One restaurant feeds the famished and handicapped-accessible restrooms deal with other necessities.

**DEALER RATES:** Saturday $10 per space, Sunday $15. Reservations are not required.

**CONTACT:** Westbrook Flea Market, 110 Boston Post Rd (PO Box 1065), Westbrook CT 06498-1065. Tel: (860) 664-1737.

# WOODBURY
## Woodbury Antiques and Flea Market

**DATES:** Every Saturday, year round, weather permitting.

**TIMES:** 7:00 AM-1:00 PM.

**ADMISSION:** Free. Parking is free.

**LOCATION:** Junction of Rts 6 and 64. Off I-84, take Exit 15, go 3½ miles on Rt 6E to market.

**DESCRIPTION:** For over 32 years this outdoor market has been considered one of the best antiques markets in Connecticut. Located in a beautiful country setting, their 90 to 140 dealers sell primarily antiques, collectibles, furniture, memorabilia, coins, antique tools, jewelry, books, military items, art and a constantly changing assortment of fascinating items. New merchandise includes tools, jewelry, clothes, household goods, over-the-counter products, plants and new surprises every week. It is described as the "#1 Saturday market in Connecticut" with "great browsing and buying in Woodbury, the Antiques Capital of Connecticut." This market has a strong following because of the quality of the goods sold and its pleasant setting. Food is available on the premises.

**DEALER RATES:** $30 for a 25' × 20' space. Reservations are not required, but recommended.

**CONTACT:** Don and Diane Heavens, PO Box 184, Woodbury CT 06798. Tel: (203) 263-2841. Email: wdbyflea@aol.com. Web: www.woodburyfleamarket.com.

## OTHER FLEA MARKETS

We know or have heard about these markets, but have not personally contacted each one, as we have the markets with descriptions. If you plan to visit one of these markets listed below, *please call first* to make sure they are still open. Flea markets do come and go. While they were open when we went to press, they may not be later. We can't be responsible. *Call first!*

**Bristol**: CP'S Flea Market, 331 Park St. Tel: (860) 585-8450

**Bristol**: Main St Flea Market, 245 Main St. Tel: (860) 589-9912.

**Danielson:** Risom Mill Antiques & Flea Market, 43 Connecticut Mills Ave. Tel: (860) 774-4973.

**East Hartford:** International Flea Market, 663 Burnside Ave. Tel: (860) 610-0126.

**Terryville:** This & That Flea Market, 181 Main St. Tel: (860) 584-1324.

**Thomaston:** Quality Flea Market, 102 E Main St. Tel: (860) 283-8433.

**West Haven:** Flea Mart, 897 Orange Ave. Tel: (203) 931-7473.

# DELAWARE

## DOVER

### Spence's Bazaar and Auction and Flea Market

**DATES:** Every Tuesday and Friday. Rain or shine.

**TIMES:** 8:00 AM-8:00 PM.

**ADMISSION:** Free. Parking is free.

**LOCATION:** 550 S New St, 2 blocks west of Kent General Hospital.

**DESCRIPTION:** This indoor/outdoor market first began in 1933. With a variety of shops on site and 200 dealer tables, a shopper can find antiques, collectibles, household and secondhand items. Also on the premises are a farmers' market selling cheeses, meats, produce, pizza, ice cream and loads more, as well as a restaurant and restrooms.

**DEALER RATES:** $15 for a 3-table setup. Reservations are not necessary.

**CONTACT:** Gregory Spence or Jack Scott, Spence's Bazaar, 550 S New St, Dover DE 19904-3536. Tel: (302) 734-3441.

## LAUREL

### Bargain Bill Indoor/Outdoor Flea Market

**DATES:** Every Friday, Saturday and Sunday. Rain or shine.

**TIMES:** Friday 8:00 AM-4:00 PM; Saturday and Sunday 6:00 AM-5:00 PM. January through March hours on weekends 8:00 AM-5:00 PM.

**ADMISSION:** Free. Free parking is provided.

**LOCATION:** At the intersection of US 13 Dual and Rt 9 E, 14 miles north of Salisbury. From Washington DC, take Rt 50 W to Rt 404 E, then Rt 13 south.

**DESCRIPTION:** This indoor/outdoor show began in 1978 and is located just 30 minutes from the Atlantic Ocean and listed as a Delaware tourist attraction. People come from all over the United States to buy from the 200 (in winter) to 500 dealers (in summer) who sell everything from antiques to new merchandise, from collectibles to fresh produce—all tax free! Other items to be found are: large selection of depression glass, electronics, books, air-brush artist, baked goods, records, jewelry, vacuums, new and used clothing and tools, wicker, doors, portable buildings, and groceries among others. For all you biker fans, Wild Bill's Wheels, in the East building, builds custom Harleys. There's a unique covered market with skylights to illuminate the merchandise where vendors can park next to their treasures. When this market first opened, vendors laid their merchandise on the ground. Now they have a 400' air-conditioned/heated indoor market with over 800 tables. Talk about having everything—in December 1992, they had a wedding here complete with wedding gown, tuxedo, minister, cake and music. A restaurant serves breakfast and lunch.

**DEALER RATES**: $18.75 per 8' × 10' indoor space. $13 per 16' frontage outdoor space, includes two 8' tables. Reservations are not required. Overnight camping with electric hookups and air-conditioned and heated restrooms with showers are available.

**CONTACT**: Bill & Leslie Brown, RD 4 Box 547, Laurel DE 19956. Tel: (302) 875-9958 or (302) 875-2478. Fax: (302) 875-1830. Email: fleamkt@magpage.com. Website: www.bwci.com/bbfmlg.htm.

## Route 13 Outlet Market

**DATES**: Friday, Saturday and Sunday, year round.
**TIMES**: Friday and Saturday 9:00 AM-7:00 PM; Sunday 9:00 AM-6:00 PM.
**ADMISSION**: Free. Parking is also free.
**LOCATION**: Rt 13 at SR 462.
**DESCRIPTION**: Started in 1985, they now have over 100 vendors selling collectibles, as well as items ranging from clothing to jewelry in this 84,000-square-foot building. There are plenty of collectibles. One vendor has loads of new tools that are "priced less than Wal-Mart." Another sells all sorts of electronics: stereos, telephones, car radios and accouterments. Thirty-two vendors sell sportswear and clothing, others jewelry. You can't possibly starve—15 restaurants, including Thai, Chinese, several down-home country, pizza and Italian, and some hot dog purveyors feed the famished. Their huge Amish market and restaurant is one of the big draws of the market selling fresh cheeses, meats, deli and baked goods. Ninety-five percent of the merchandise is new and 80% of the vendors have been with this market from the beginning. Over the last year much of the merchandise has become even more high-end, top quality goods. If an item fails to satisfy, it is quite common to be able to return it to the original vendor.

**DEALER RATES**: $65 per 12' × 18' space per weekend and up. Reservations are not required.

**CONTACT**: Merrill Gravener, Route 13 Outlet Market, PO Box 32, Laurel DE 19956-0032. Tel: (302) 875-4800. Fax: (302) 875-2640.

# NEW CASTLE
## New Castle Farmers' Market

**DATES**: Friday, Saturday and Sunday, year round.

**TIMES**: Friday and Saturday 10:00 AM-10:00 PM; Sunday 10:00 AM-6:00 PM.

**ADMISSION**: Free. Parking is also free.

**LOCATION**: Rt 13 and Hares Corner.

**DESCRIPTION**: Started in 1954, this indoor/outdoor market is really two markets in one. The outside is the flea market for antiques and collectibles, and restricted to used items only; the inside market is the farmers' market with over 60 merchants. This is said to be one of the premier markets on the East Coast with genuine Pennsylvania Dutch merchants selling outstanding quality beef, pork, poultry, cheeses and homemade baked goods. The produce stands are works of art. Food is available on the premises. Handicapped-accessible throughout.

**DEALER RATES**: Friday $12 per day; Saturday and Sunday $16 per day. First come, first served.

**CONTACT**: Steven Stein, New Castle Farmers' Market, 110 N DuPont Hwy, New Castle DE 19720. Tel: (302) 328-4102 or fax (302) 328-9525.

# DISTRICT OF COLUMBIA

## Capitol Hill Flea Market at Eastern Market

**DATES:** Sundays, March to Sunday before Christmas.

**TIMES:** 10:00 AM-5:00 PM.

**ADMISSION:** Free. Parking is where you find it.

**LOCATION:** 7th and N Carolina Aves SE, only ½ block from the Metro Eastern Market station.

**DESCRIPTION:** This outdoor market of up to 175 dealers sells antiques, collectibles, arts and crafts, imports, and produce in season. Started in 1983, and adding farmer's row in 1987, this is a continuation of the selling along these streets that has been going on for a century. There is plenty of food nearby, if not at the market, as this is right on Capitol Hill. The management advertises in *The Washington Post, Maine Antique Digest* and other selected publications.

**DEALER RATES:** $15 per table space, $20 for two 6' tables (½ spaces), $30 per four 6' tables or roughly 100 square feet, $45 in double spaces of eight to nine 6' table space (about 200 square feet), or super spaces—larger than doubles—for $15 more per 100 square feet. Setup begins at 8:30 AM. Prepayment is required; call about cancellation policies. BYOT and setup. Be prepared for lousy weather.

**CONTACT:** Tom Rall, The Flea Market at Eastern Market, 1101 N Kentucky St, Arlington VA 22205. Tel: (703) 534-7612. Email: marketflea@aol.com.

## Georgetown Flea Market

**DATES:** Every Sunday, year round.

**TIMES:** 9:00 AM-5:00 PM.

**ADMISSION:** Free. Limited street parking is free.

**LOCATION:** Parking lot of Hardy Middle School on Wisconsin Ave across from the Safeway, between S and T Sts NW.

**DESCRIPTION:** Started in 1971, this outdoor market has become a legend since its inception. Author Larry McMurty (of *Lonesome Dove* fame) based his novel *Cadillac Jack* on this market. The owner, Michael Sussman, describes his market's wares as "good, solid, middle-class stuff," with many a great bargain. His 70-plus *good* exhibitors, many of whom are regulars, sell fine antiques, collectibles, vintage clothing, antique silver, crafts, homemade furniture, and other fine items. Don't worry about food; there are plenty of places to chow down in Georgetown, and a snack bar on site. Mary Randolph Carter, an avid collector, Ralph Lauren ad exec and author of *American Junk*, loves this market and raids it occasionally. Diane Keaton comes to buy vintage clothing. The local papers (i.e. *The Washington Post*) is forever writing this place up. Restroom facilities are at the north side of the market. If you find Michael at the market, say "Hi" and tell him "we still miss the Phoenix"; he'll understand.

**DEALER RATES:** $15-$45 depending on space and if you have your vehicle with you. Reservations are an excellent idea, but Michael will try to squeeze you in, if necessary. No reservations will be made by phone. Setup starts at 6:00 AM.

**CONTACT:** Michael Sussman, 2109 N St NW, Washington DC 20037. Tel/fax: (202) 223-0289. Web: www.gflea.com.

---

### Great Shopping

Someone bought a painting here for $300 that was worth $9,000. Stickley chairs have gone for $15. Marsten Luce started here as a dealer and is now an antique shop owner. Well-known antiques dealer, Guy Bush, who just purchased former Supreme Court Justice Abe Fortas' Georgetown home, shops here every Sunday morning.

This market is written up all the time in the "big" rags for being "one of *the* places to be in Washington on weekends."

---

## Georgetown Flea Market at U Street

**DATES:** Saturday and Sunday.

**TIMES:** 9:00 AM-5:00 PM.

**ADMISSION:** Free. Parking is free where you can find it.

**LOCATION:** 1345 U St in the Shaw area of DC, between 13th and 14th Sts on U. Next to the Cardosa Metro station.

**DESCRIPTION:** This new market, opened in 1999 when the Georgetown market site was being repaved, was so successful that it will continue here. Eighty vendors sell antiques, collectibles, and some new merchandise. Food vendors will keep you energized and the handicapped-accessible restrooms just may come in handy.

**DEALER RATES:** $25-$50 depending on space and if you have your vehicle with you. Reservations are an excellent idea, but Michael will try to squeeze you in, if necessary. No reservations will be made by phone. Setup starts at 6:00 AM.

**CONTACT:** Michael Sussman, 2109 N St NW, Washington DC 20037. Tel/fax: (202) 223-0289. Web: www.gflea.com.

# FLORIDA

## APOPKA
### Three Star Flea Market
**DATES:** Every Saturday and Sunday. Rain or shine.
**TIMES:** Dawn to dusk.
**ADMISSION:** Free. Free parking is available.
**LOCATION:** 2930 S Orange Blossom Trail. Hwy 441.
**DESCRIPTION:** This market began in 1966. About 60 dealers sell their antiques, collectibles, handicrafts, garage sale items and produce from covered stalls outdoors. They are only 18 miles from Disney World. There is a food wagon on the premises.
**DEALER RATES:** $10.80 per space and parking per day. They provide tables and clothes racks. Reservations are required.
**CONTACT:** Mary C Markeson, Owner, c/o Three Star Flea Market, 2390 S Orange Blossom Trail, Apopka FL 32703-1870. Tel: (407) 293-2722.

## AUBURNDALE
### International Market World
**DATES:** Every Friday, Saturday, and Sunday. Rain or shine.
**TIMES:** 8:00 AM-5:00 PM.
**ADMISSION:** Free. Free parking is available on 30 acres.
**LOCATION:** 1052 Hwy 92 W Auburndale. Between Orlando and Tampa, just east of Lakeland. Near Cypress Gardens.
**DESCRIPTION:** This market opened in 1981 and currently attracts anywhere from 750 (summer) to 1,000-plus (winter) dealers in indoor or outdoor spaces. A new building was added in 1991 adding another 200 stalls. As one of Florida's largest markets, Market World attracts customers from throughout Central Florida as it is only a short 45-minute drive from either Tampa or Orlando down I-4. There is an endless variety of merchandise from antiques and collectibles to new merchandise and fresh produce. Several attractions include karaoke Saturday and Sunday afternoons, a fishing pond, a 1909 antique carousel, alligator display, buffalo farm, and exotic animal rehab-zoo featuring Florida panthers to name a few. There is a delightful country atmosphere and an eager-to-please management. There are numerous concessions serving a variety of foods on the premises. Handicapped-accessible restrooms are available.

**DEALER RATES:** Friday $10, Saturday or Sunday $17 per space or $40.00 per 8' × 10' space per three-day weekend; $155.00 monthly. Reservations are not required, but can be made Wednesday or Thursday between 9:00 AM-5:00 PM. Dealers may start setting up shop at 7:00 AM.

**CONTACT:** International Market World, 1052 Hwy 92 W, Auburndale FL 33823. Tel: (941) 665-0062. Fax: (941) 666-5726. Email: IMW98@hotemail.com. Web: www.angelfire.com/biz/marketworld.

# BONITA SPRINGS
## Flamingo Island Flea Market

**DATES:** Friday through Sunday.

**TIMES:** 8:00 AM-4:00 PM.

**ADMISSION:** Free. Parking is free.

**LOCATION:** 11902 Bonita Beach Rd. Take I-75 to Exit 18W. Go $2/10$ mile west, the market is on the north side.

**DESCRIPTION:** This new market opened in 1999 with up to 200 dealers selling antiques, collectibles, crafts, produce, meats, coins, stamps, cards, garage sale goodies, furniture, manmade waterfalls, jewelry (14k-18k gold, estate, and costume), and new merchandise. In case of hunger, there are seven restaurants and three snack bars. If needed, there are handicapped-accessible restrooms.

**DEALER RATES:** Per month: $177 per 8' × 32' aisle space, $240 per 10' × 10' space, $360 per 10' × 20' space. Reservations are not required—yet.

**CONTACT:** Doralyn Trulson or Glenda Farrow, Flamingo Island Flea Market, 11902 Bonita Beach Rd, Bonita Springs FL 34135. Tel: (941) 948-7799 or 495-9500. Fax: (941) 947-7882. Web: flamingoisland.com.

# BRADENTON
## Red Barn Flea Market Plaza

**DATES:** Entire market Wednesday, Saturday and Sunday; plaza area Tuesday through Sunday.

**TIMES:** Wednesday, Saturday and Sunday 8:00 AM-4:00 PM; Tuesday, Thursday and Friday 10:00 AM-4:00 PM.

**ADMISSION:** Free. Parking is free.

**LOCATION:** 1707 1st St E. Located on US 41 and US 301 at 17th Ave. From I-75 take Exit 42 W on SR 4 to US 41. Take a left on US 41, go approximately 2 miles.

**DESCRIPTION**: The original market opened in May 1981 followed by the plaza in May 1985. On October 21, 1996, the entire market was destroyed by a devastating fire. It reopened July 1998 with 23 retail stores and approximately 400 covered, and over 200 uncovered booths with a variety of new and used merchandise including antiques, collectibles, crafts, clothing, produce, meats, coins, cards, garage sale goodies, and furniture. Over 100,000 square feet under roof shelter a bike shop, tackle store, communications store, beauty store, video games, tool store, art gallery and tons more. They are crammed with a variety of goods and services. There are courtesy carts to and from the parking lots. When the munchies strike, pick from four restaurants and an ice cream stand. Handicapped-accessible restrooms provide relief. A popular, clean, high-traffic market located near the Gulf Coast, it has over 50 peacocks in the trees on the hill. Security patrolled by uniformed off-duty deputies.

**DEALER RATES**: All spaces are approximately 10' × 10'. Inside booths are $25 plus tax per day, outside covered booths $18 and tax per day, and outside uncovered booths are $20-$22 plus tax per day.

**CONTACT**: Red Barn Rental Office, 1707 1 St E, Bradenton FL 34208. Tel: (941) 747-3794 or 1-800-274-FLEA. Fax: (941) 747-6539. Email: redbarn@bhip.infi.net. Web: www.redbarnfleamarket.net.

---

### Pets and Mascots

The Red Barn has very unique mascots in their beautiful peacocks roaming the grounds. Many customers have their pictures taken with the tame birds. Occasionally, when the market is closed, the peacocks roam the aisles playing "customer" until gently ushered back into their "home" among the giant oaks and oleanders. During these strolls, they can be caught admiring themselves in the glass doors. Among the flock is a rare white peacock.

---

# BROOKSVILLE
## Airport Flea Market and Farmers' Market

**DATES**: Every Saturday and Sunday. Rain or shine.

**TIMES**: 8:00 AM-3:00 PM.

**ADMISSION**: Free. Parking is also free.

**LOCATION**: 17375 Spring Hill Dr. Six miles south of Brooksville, just off US 41.

**DESCRIPTION:** This market started in 1977. A new owner took over the market in 1998, repaved it, added a new pole barn with 105 new spaces, upgraded the facilities and cleaned the place up. The market accommodates approximately 400 dealers and is held both indoors and outdoors. There are no specialties but rather a large assortment of goods is offered including antiques, fine art, arts and crafts, collectibles, new merchandise, used household items, and tools. The farmers' market is open daily. Food concessions offer breakfasts and lunches, including Italian and barbecue, and the handicapped-accessible restrooms just may come in handy.

**DEALER RATES:** $73 for 8' × 12' space indoors, per month: $10 for Saturday, $9 for Sunday or $17 for the weekend for three table set-up under covered space outdoors, per day. Reservations are required except during the summer.

**CONTACT:** Bob Murch, Airport Flea Market, 17375 Spring Hill Dr, Brooksville FL 34609. Tel: (352) 796-0268. Fax: (352) 796-1099.

# CHIEFLAND
## McCormack Flea Market, Inc

**DATES:** Friday through Sunday, year round. Rain or shine.

**TIMES:** 7:00 AM-3:30 PM.

**ADMISSION:** Free. Parking is free.

**LOCATION:** US Hwy 19 and 98, Alt 27 N. Market located across from ABC Pizza and Best Western Motel.

**DESCRIPTION:** Since 1983, this indoor flea market has expanded four times on its 23 acres and is in the Suwannee River area, in the center of town, near motels. There are a total of 310 selling spaces, all under one roof, with concrete floors and screens. Water and electricity are available to each booth, as well as RV electricity. Dealers can park their RV next to their booth. Currently the market attracts approximately 55 dealers in the summer and 100 in the winter selling antiques, collectibles, handmade crafts, vegetables, meats, cheeses, dairy products, plants, flowers, nuts, birds and new merchandise among other treats. In addition, there is a small grocery store, glassware, tools, tape store, leather craft shop, Indian shop, RV parts, laundry, cabinet shop and carpet and vinyl store. Two restaurants feed the hungry.

**DEALER RATES:** $7 per 10' × 10' booth on Friday and $8 on Sunday; $10 on Saturday; $22.50 for three days. Reservations are suggested.

**CONTACT:** Jack McCormack, McCormack Flea Market Inc, PO Box 1970, Chiefland FL 32644-1970. Tel: (352) 493-1493 or 493-1491. Fax: (352) 493-9907.

# DAYTONA
## Daytona Flea Market

**DATES:** Friday, Saturday, and Sunday, year round.

**TIMES:** 8:00 AM-5:00 PM.

**ADMISSION:** Free. Parking is free.

**LOCATION:** Southwest corner of I-95 and US 92.

**DESCRIPTION:** This indoor/outdoor market opened in 1981 just five miles from the "World's Most Famous Beach" attracting 2.5 million visitors. Over 1,000 booths on 40 acres sell antiques, collectibles, home furnishings, clothes, jewelry, used and new merchandise, produce, plants and just about everything imaginable. Two sections of the market are fully air-conditioned. Two sit-down restaurants and nine snack bars provide ample food for the hungry.

**DEALER RATES:** For a booth with 10' frontage, $15 and up for Saturday and Sunday, $8 on Friday. Ninety percent of this market is under roof. Reservations are suggested, in some cases required.

**CONTACT:** John Schnebly, Manager or Lisa, Rental Agent, 2987 Bellevue Rd, Daytona Beach FL 32115. Tel: (904) 252-1999. Email: mcnolty@bellsouth.net. Web: www.daytonafleamarket.net.

# DELRAY BEACH
## Delray Swap Shop

**DATES:** Always Friday through Monday. Seasonally Thursdays, December through April.

**TIMES:** 8:00 AM-4:00 PM.

**ADMISSION:** Free. Parking is $1.

**LOCATION:** 2001 N Federal Hwy. Take I-95 to Atlantic Ave in Delray Beach to N Federal Hwy, north 3 miles to Swap Shop.

**DESCRIPTION:** This market has been open since 1976 with 430 dealer spaces mostly outdoors. They have just added 124 indoor spaces with a huge renovation in 1999. Items for sale are mostly new merchandise including: health and beauty aids, clothing, jewelry, hats, pictures and frames, household goods, and vegetables in season. In November 1993, they opened a special antique section of this market. Several snack bars serve the hungry. Handicapped-accessible restrooms are on site.

**DEALER RATES:** Monday and Thursday $10 per space, Friday $15; Saturday and Sunday from $25 to $100 for 11' × 15' spaces. For the antique mall: Monday, Thursday, and Friday $5; $8 Saturday and Sundays, each

day. Reservations are required. There is a waitlist for no-shows, at $25 for space at the last minute with no guarantees. Watch for their website.
**CONTACT:** Loretta Shaw, Manager, Delray Swap Shop, 2001 N Federal Hwy, Delray FL 33444. Tel: (561) 276-4012. Fax: (561) 276-9019.

# FORT LAUDERDALE
## Oakland Park Boulevard Flea Market

**DATES:** Every Wednesday through Sunday, year round.
**TIMES:** Thursday through Saturday 10:00 AM-9:00 PM; Wednesday and Sunday 10:00 AM-7:00 PM.
**ADMISSION:** Free. Parking is plentiful and free.
**LOCATION:** 1½ miles west of I-95, and ½ mile east of SR 7, at 3161 W Oakland Park Blvd.
**DESCRIPTION:** This popular market has been a landmark in Fort Lauderdale since 1971. "This is the place where the neighborhood shops," as well as Fort Lauderdale's original indoor flea market. Over 200 dealers sell only all-new merchandise although antiques and collectibles can be found. There are many clothing and fine jewelry merchants in this modern, clean and air-conditioned facility. Local residents and tourists alike make frequent visits to this market located near major highways, airports and cruise-ports. It is a bit of southern charm that makes this flea market such a success. Handicapped-accessible restrooms, two snack bars and a restaurant serving home-cooked fare add to the amenities.
**DEALER RATES:** $600 and up per space per month includes utilities, advertising and plenty more. Reservations are required. Currently they are accepting applications for the waiting list.
**CONTACT:** Leonard Bennis, Manager, Oakland Park Boulevard Flea Market Inc, 3161 W Oakland Park Blvd, Ft Lauderdale FL 33311. Tel: (954) 733-4617. Fax: (954) 731-1150.

## Swap Shop of Ft. Lauderdale

**DATES:** Everyday including holidays, year round. Rain or shine.
**TIMES:** 6:00 AM-5:00 PM.
**ADMISSION:** Free. Free parking is available. Preferred parking Saturday and Sunday is $1 and $2, free in the south lot.
**LOCATION:** 3291 W Sunrise Blvd, between I-95 and the Turnpike.
**DESCRIPTION:** This well-known show began in 1967. Over 2,000 dealers sell both indoors and out on 88 acres of grounds. All sorts of things can be found here—antiques, crafts and collectibles, new and used items, pro-

duce, watches, electronics, clothing, plants—you name it! All new merchandise comes with a full guarantee. They say they are "the largest flea market in the Eastern United States." Free circus shows are presented daily, and they feature 17 international restaurants in their air-conditioned 180,000-square-foot entertainment center. At night they have the world's largest 13-screen drive-in showing first-run movies nightly.

**DEALER RATES:** Call for current rates. Reservations are advised during the winter season. Reservations are open daily from 9:00 AM-5:00 PM.

**CONTACT:** Reservation Office, c/o Swap Shop, 3501 W Sunrise Blvd, Fort Lauderdale FL 33311. Tel: (954) 791-SWAP (7927). Fax: (954) 583-8920.

# FORT MYERS
## Fleamasters Fleamarket

**DATES:** Friday, Saturday and Sunday, year around.

**TIMES:** 8:00 AM-4:00 PM.

**LOCATION:** 4135 Dr Martin Luther King Jr Blvd.

**ADMISSION:** Free. Parking is free.

**DESCRIPTION:** Opened in 1985, this completely undercover outdoor market, billed "as the largest market in southwest Florida," hosts an average of 1,200 dealers year round. It is still growing—they added another 200 stalls in 1993. Their dealers sell everything "from fruit to nuts," including antiques, collectibles, clothing, wheelchair rentals and more. The food courts provide an ample feast from pizza to ice cream, Mexican, Oriental and good-old-USA fast food. In fact, this market is so popular it has become a tourist attraction in its own right with over 1 million visitors annually.

**DEALER RATES:** $48-$61, plus tax and license, per 10' × 12' booth for a 3-day weekend, depending on location. Reservations are not required—first come, first served—although dealers can continue to hold the same spot week after week.

**CONTACT:** Donna Matthew, Fleamasters Fleamarket, 4135 Dr Martin Luther King Jr Blvd, Ft Myers FL 33916. Tel: (941) 334-7001. Fax: (941) 334-2087. Email: Fleakeeper@aol.com. Web: www.fleamall.com.

# FRONTENAC
## Frontenac Flea Market

**DATES:** Friday, Saturday and Sunday.

**TIMES:** 8:00 AM-4:00 PM.

**LOCATION:** 5605 N US Hwy 1, midway between Cocoa and Titusville, right on US 1.
**ADMISSION:** Free. Parking is free.
**DESCRIPTION:** In operation since 1976, this market has an average of 450 dealers selling antiques, collectibles, new and used merchandise, silk flowers, and a farmers market selling fresh fruits and vegetables. One of the several food concessions sells a "famous quarter-pound hot dog." Just in case you need them, there are handicapped-accessible restrooms. This market is close to the Kennedy Space Center and beaches so you can see the shuttles take off.
**DEALER RATES:** $18.02 per day for a 10' × 8' space indoors; $13.78 for a 10' × 20' space outdoors. First come, first served.
**CONTACT:** Ronnie Christian, Frontenac Flea Market, PO Box 10, Sharpes FL 32959-0010. Tel: (407) 631-0241. Fax: (407) 631-0246.

# HOMOSASSA SPRINGS
## Howard's Flea Market

**DATES:** Friday, Saturday and Sunday, year round.
**TIMES:** 7:00 AM-3:00 PM.
**ADMISSION:** Free. Parking is free.
**LOCATION:** Hwy 19, 3 miles south of Homosassa.
**DESCRIPTION:** Open since 1969, this market of 700 to 800 dealers occupies 50 acres full of antiques, collectibles, some new merchandise, clothes, typical flea market fare, produce and occasionally dairy products (cheeses), and one aisle devoted to garage sale goodies. A polebarn structure houses many of the dealers while the rest are outdoors. Their many concession stands are "excellent" the office assures me. They hold special events with the proceeds used to raise funds for local children's charities. At Christmas, they hold "Adopt-a-Baby" where the dealers "adopt" a needy child for Christmas to give the needy children a good Christmas. Like their sister market in Webster, they hold car shows.
**DEALER RATES:** Daily including tax: Covered $12.72 per 10' × 12' space with 3 tables. Outside $8.48 per 10' × 10' space, or $11 to $14 per 10' × 30' space depending on location. Reservations are suggested, although, if you do show up they will manage to find you a spot somehow. The office is open for reservations on Thursday and Friday.
**CONTACT:** Teri Davis, Howard's Flea Market, 6373 S Suncoast Blvd, Homosassa FL 34446. Tel: (352) 628-4656 (office) or (352) 628-3532.

# JACKSONVILLE
## Beach Boulevard Flea Market

**DATES:** Saturday and Sunday.

**TIMES:** 7:00 AM-6:00 PM.

**ADMISSION:** Free. Parking is free.

**LOCATION:** 11041 Beach Blvd.

**DESCRIPTION:** This market averages 550 dealers selling antiques, collectibles, crafts, clothes, shoes, oriental goods, garage sale goodies, new and used furniture, fresh produce, and plenty of new merchandise. There are four snack bars, a restaurant and handicapped-accessible restrooms on site. Twenty vendors are open daily including a printing setup, a computer dealer, and an embroiderer.

**DEALER RATES:** Outdoors: $15 per 10' × 9' open space, $25 with cover. $102 and $175 respectively monthly. Table space only: $10 per 3' × 8' space with table daily, $51 monthly. They don't take reservations.

**CONTACT:** Beach Boulevard Flea Market, 11041 Beach Blvd, Jacksonville FL 32246. Tel: (904) 645-5961.

## Ramona Flea Market

**DATES:** Saturday and Sunday, year round.

**TIMES:** 8:00 AM-5:00 PM.

**ADMISSION:** $.50 per adult. Parking is free.

**LOCATION:** 7059 Ramona Blvd. From I-295 take I-10 east to first Exit 54, Lane Ave, go south. The first intersection is Ramona Blvd. Turn right. They are 3 blocks down the road on the right.

**DESCRIPTION:** Started in 1971, this indoor/outdoor market has 600 to 800 dealers (depending on the season) selling crafts, produce, coins, new merchandise, garage sale goodies, and furniture. Three snack bars and three restaurants, including a beer garden and an ice cream parlor, fill the famished. And yes, handicapped-accessible restrooms are available.

**DEALER RATES:** $7.52 to $14.91 (includes tax) depending on the location of the 10' × 7' space. They have open or under cover with 2 tables, electricity for inside spaces at $2 per day. The office is open for reservations Wednesday and Thursday from 9:00 AM-5:00 PM and Friday from 9:00 AM-6:00 PM. They recommend reserving space at least 2 weeks in advance. They open for vendors to set up at 6:30 AM.

**CONTACT:** Rick Waller, General Manager, or Joan Wade, Reservation Manager, 7059 Ramona Blvd, Jacksonville FL 32205. Tel: (904) 786-3532 or 1-800-583-3532 (FLEA). Fax: (904) 783-1661. Email: fleaman@jax-inter.net.

# KEY LARGO
## Key Largo Warehouse Market

**DATES:** Saturday and Sunday.

**TIMES:** 8:00 AM-5:00 PM.

**ADMISSION:** Free. Free parking is available.

**LOCATION:** On US Rt l, at Mile Marker 103.5.

**DESCRIPTION:** This small, selective but excellent market has 60 dealers selling "everything you could want," with an emphasis on antiques and collectibles. Charlie's vegetables are said to be "the best on the Keys." A sampling of some of their dealers' specialties are baskets, bathing suits, marine and fishing gear, orchids and exotic plants, ceramic goods and bikes. A snack bar serves American dishes to the hungry. This is the only market open all year long on the Keys. They place a high value on "treating our people right."

**DEALER RATES:** $357 monthly for a front row 10' × 40' space if you are lucky enough to get one; $210.05 for a second row 10' × 30' space; and $123.19 for a 10' × 10' space. Reservations are most necessary.

**CONTACT:** Key Largo Warehouse Market, Key Largo Storage, 103530 Overseas Hwy, Key Largo FL 33037. Tel: (305) 451-0677.

# KISSIMMEE
## Osceola Flea and Farmers' Market

**DATES:** Friday through Sunday. Rain or shine.

**TIMES:** 8:00 AM-5:00 PM.

**ADMISSION:** Free. Parking is free.

**LOCATION:** 2801 E Irlo Bronson Memorial Hwy.

**DESCRIPTION:** Started in 1987, this market averages 900-plus vendors selling antiques, collectibles, jewelry, new merchandise, new and used furniture, tools, produce, garage sale goodies, sports equipment, clothing, shoes, pets, household and DIY goods, and whatever else shows up. There is one restaurant, three snack bars, handicapped-accessible restrooms, and live entertainment to keep you busy between shopping forays.

**DEALER RATES:** $17.50 daily per 10' × 10' under roof. Other rates available; call or hit the website for more information. The office is open Wednesday and Thursday 9:00 AM-3:00 PM, and during regular flea market hours. No, they don't take reservations, but you can call about space availability.

**CONTACT:** Osceola Flea & Farmers' Market, 2801 E Irlo Bronson Hwy, Kissimmee FL 34744. Tel: (407) 846-2811. Fax: (407) 846-3392. Email: osceola@fleaamerica.com or USAFlea@aol.com. Web: www.fleaamerica.com.

# LAKE CITY
## Lake City Flea Market

**DATES:** Every Saturday and Sunday. Rain or shine. Closed from mid-October to mid-November for Columbia County Fair.

**TIMES:** 7:00 AM-4:00 PM.

**ADMISSION:** Free. Free parking is available.

**LOCATION:** Columbia County Fairgrounds, 1 mile east of I-75 on US 90 at SR 247 (Branford Hwy).

**DESCRIPTION:** This indoor/outdoor market opened in 1980 and now accommodates approximately 100 to 150 dealers selling everything from antiques and collectibles to new merchandise and fresh produce. There are 1,500 motel rooms available at reasonable rates located within a half mile of the flea market. There is a snack bar serving flea market "fare" and handicapped-accessible restrooms.

**DEALER RATES:** $9 per 10' × 10' space indoors, per day; $6 and up per day outdoors. Reservations for space indoors are required and all reservations must be prepaid. No reservations are taken by phone.

**CONTACT:** Ralph Tiner, Lake City Flea Market, 2640 Montgomery St, Lake City FL 32025. Tel: (904) 752-1999.

# LAKELAND
## Lakeland Farmers' Market

**DATES:** Saturday and Sunday. Rain or shine.

**TIMES:** 7:00 AM-3:00 PM.

**ADMISSION:** Free. Free parking is available.

**LOCATION:** 2701 Swindell Rd. Take I-4 to W Memorial Blvd exit, then go 1 mile. At the intersection of Swindell Rd and W Memorial Blvd at Kathleen High School.

**DESCRIPTION:** This market, originally a "Curb Market" in the 1930s, moved to its present location in 1971 where local farmers and craftsmen could sell their goods; some of these original sellers still work here. The market now accommodates from 225 to 350 dealers that sell collectibles, arts and crafts, new merchandise, used items, clothing, tools, household necessities, used farm- and work-related items and fresh produce and meats. This is a rustic, down-to-earth flea market with a museum, free of charge, on the premises. There are five restaurants and snack bars to choose from.

**DEALER RATES:** Saturday $11 per 10' × 10' space under cover, Sunday $14. Rates in the open field are $7 per 25' × 15' space. Reservations are advised.

**CONTACT:** Jim Wilbanks, 2701 Swindell Rd, Lakeland FL 33805. Tel: (941) 682-4809.

# LAKE WORTH
## Lake Worth High School Flea Market

**DATES:** Saturday and Sunday, year round. Rain or shine.
**TIMES:** 4:00 AM-3:00 PM. Really.
**ADMISSION:** Free. Parking is free.
**LOCATION:** 1701 Lake Worth Rd at Lake Worth High School parking lot. At I-95 and Lake Worth Rd, under the I-95 overpass next to the Tri-Rail Station. From Florida Tnpk: Exit 93E 6 miles. From I-95: Exit 6th Ave S, right to "A" St to Lake Worth Rd or Exit 10th Ave N, left to "A" St, right to Lake Worth Rd.
**DESCRIPTION:** So how does a high school raise funds for scholarships for needy students and other necessaries? Hold a flea market! Since the mid-'80s this market has contributed more than $1 million dollars to student scholarships. Not bad. In fact the market is so popular it has been repeatedly written up in Florida papers. Every weekend, their 300 dealers spread out across the school parking lot selling wonderful books, antiques, collectibles, produce, new and used merchandise, rugs, luggage, garage sale goodies, and discount groceries. This place is the local "weekend mall" for locals.
**DEALER RATES:** $10 per spot. First come, first served.
**CONTACT:** Betty and Ralph Milone, Lake Worth High School Flea Market, PO Box 6592, Lake Worth FL 33466-6592. Tel: (561) 439-1539. Fax: (561) 439-8742. Email: LWHSFlea@aol.com

# MARGATE
## Margate Swap Shop

**DATES:** Saturday, Sunday, and Tuesday.
**TIMES:** 5:00 AM-2:30 PM.
**ADMISSION:** Free. Parking is $1.
**LOCATION:** 1000 N SR 7 (US 441). West of Pompano Beach; west of Florida Tnpk and I-95 (Atlantic Blvd to Rt 441 then north several blocks).
**DESCRIPTION:** This family type indoor/outdoor market opened in 1976 and has grown to 300 to 550 dealers selling collectibles, new and used merchandise, garage sale goodies, glassware, crystal, clothing, vitamins, t-shirts, and fresh produce. This flea market has one of the largest produce sections

around. The Lake Shore Motel is on the property as well. Two snack bars and handicapped-accessible restrooms are on site. Look for Barbara and say, Hi!

**DEALER RATES:** $8 per 10' × 20' space. Reservations are required for monthly, daily—first come, first served.

**CONTACT:** Manager, Margate Swap Shop, 1000 N SR 7, Margate FL 33063. Tel: (954) 971-7927. Fax: (954) 979-3729.

# MELBOURNE
## Super Flea and Farmers' Market

**DATES:** Friday, Saturday and Sunday.

**TIMES:** 8:00 AM-4:00 PM.

**ADMISSION:** Free. Parking is free.

**LOCATION:** 4835 W Eau Gallie Blvd. At the corner of I-95 and Eau Gallie Blvd, Exit 72.

**DESCRIPTION:** Opened in 1987, this indoor market of 200-350 dealers sells antiques, collectibles, cars, crafts, produce, coins, cards, garage sale goodies, new merchandise, furniture (new and used), quality 14K and silver jewelry, ruby and gem mining, and a huge selection of professional chef and restaurant supplies. Hungry? Their food courts include Gyros, Buffalo-style wings, New York-style pizza, homemade donuts, whatever. Get this: the weekend before Thanksgiving Day they hold their Annual Turkey Bowl. People actually bowl frozen turkeys down a bowling lane to win a free turkey, sodas and other prizes. They have been told that their handicapped-accessible restrooms are the cleanest of any flea market.

**DEALER RATES:** $5 per day and up for 10' × 8' space; $139 and up monthly. Enclosed units are available. Reservations are suggested.

**CONTACT:** Susan Jerome, Manager, Super Flea, 4835 W Eau Gallie Blvd, Melbourne FL 32934. Tel: (407) 242-9124 Thursday through Saturday. Web: www.SUPERFLEAMARKET.com.

# MIAMI
## Opa Locka/Hialeah Flea Market

**DATES:** Daily.

**TIMES:** 5:00 AM-7:00 PM.

**ADMISSION:** Free and $1 plus parking available Saturday and Sunday.

**LOCATION:** 12705 NW 42nd Ave. Take I-75 south to Opa Locka exit. I-95 to NW 103st St, Exit west 4 miles to NW 42nd Ave and north 1 mile, market is on both sides. The market is just 15 minutes north of Miami International Airport on Le Jeune Rd (NW 42nd Ave) at 127th St.

**DESCRIPTION:** Opened in 1985, this indoor/outdoor market boosts 1,000-plus dealers selling collectibles, new merchandise, produce, meats, garage sale goodies, furniture, clothing, you name it. Thirteen restaurants and handicapped-accessible restrooms add to the amenities.

**DEALER RATES:** $30 and up per 20' × 20' space per week. Reservations are not required.

**CONTACT:** Scott Miller, Opa Locka/Hialeah Flea Market, 12705 NW 42 Ave, Miami FL 33054. Tel: (305) 688-0500. Fax: (305) 687-8312.

# MIAMI BEACH
## "World's Largest" Indoor Flea Market

**DATES:** For 2000: December 13-17. 2001: Call, but check around the same weekend.

**TIMES:** Wednesday and Thursday 11:00 AM-10:00 PM; Friday and Saturday 11:00 AM-11:00 PM; Sunday 11:00 AM-8:00 PM.

**ADMISSION:** $3.50 for adults, $1 for children (6-12 years); or $5 for a five-day unlimited pass. Parking costs $.75 per hour for city meters or $1 per hour for use of the parking lot/garage. Valet parking is also available.

**LOCATION:** At the Miami Beach Convention Center, 1901 Convention Center Dr. Take I-95 to I-195, then east to Alton Rd; follow signs to Convention Center.

**DESCRIPTION:** Started in 1979 and celebrating their 65th phenomenally successful edition of this event. This market of over 1,000 booths has something for everyone. Exhibitors include nationally prominent firms, hundreds of local companies, individual dealers, importers, wholesalers, manufacturers, artists and craftsmen from throughout the United States and overseas. Used merchandise is not permitted, but there is a large selection of antiques, collectibles, and fine art. *The New York Times* reported this event as "a one stop (Christmas) shopping spree." It was voted #1 for "most amazing bargains by *South Florida Magazine*. There are many special attractions as well as guest lecturers and well-known celebrities. There are continuous broadcasts from the show's "celebrity corner" where a prize machine promotion, operated by *The Miami Herald* newspaper, is a favorite treat for visitors. This market is widely advertised and is known as "the flea market tradition brought to an outrageously exalted level."

**DEALER RATES:** $575 per 10' × 10' space plus 6½% sales tax. Reservations are required as most shows are sold out before the show date. Larger spaces are available.

**CONTACT:** IBS Flea Markets Inc, 190 NE 199 St Ste 203, N Miami Beach FL 33179-2918. Call Shirley Tralins, Sales Director, at (305) 651-9530, Monday-Friday 9:00 AM-5:00 PM. Fax: (305) 652-2568.

---

### How's That Again?

Years ago, a dealer brought in and set up a little antique hand-carved wooden circus complete with animals, people, the works. It wasn't long after that an official from the Department of Natural Resources showed up saying someone had lodged a complaint against the market for abusing the lions.

---

# MOUNT DORA
## Florida Twin Markets

**DATES:** Saturday and Sunday, except for the 3-day extravaganzas held the third full Friday through Sunday of November, January and February.

**TIMES:** Flea market 8:00 AM-4:00 PM; antique market 9:00 AM-5:00 PM. Extravaganza Fridays 10:00 AM-5:00 PM.

**ADMISSION:** Free on regular dates. Extravaganzas: $10 on Friday, $5 on Saturday, $3 on Sunday. Parking is free.

**LOCATION:** East of Mt. Dora, 25 miles north of Orlando on new Hwy 441, just past intersection of Hwy 441 over Hwy 46 at the bottom of the hill on the right.

**DESCRIPTION:** These markets, started in 1983, are sister markets to the highly successful Pennsylvania Renninger's markets. Sitting on 115 acres, they are actually two distinct and separate markets about 900 feet apart. One is devoted to antiques with over 150 dealers, the other is a farmers and flea market with over 500 dealers. However, during Extravaganzas the antique dealers numbers swell to over 1,200. In addition, they have eight Antique Fairs from March through October on the third full Saturday and Sunday. As you can imagine, they sell just about anything and everything at these two markets. Four restaurants and handicapped-accessible restrooms add to the amenities.

**DEALER RATES:** Flea Market: $13.50 per 10' × 10' space under roof, $7 per 15' × 25' space outside. Extravaganza rates run from $130 and up depending on where the space is. Reservations are required.
**CONTACT:** Florida Twin Markets Inc, PO Box 1699, Mt Dora FL 32757-1699. Tel: (352) 383-8393 Antiques or (352) 383-3141 Flea Market. Email: flatwinmkt@aol.com. Web: www.renningers.com.

# NAPLES
## Naples Drive-In Flea Market

**DATES:** Saturday and Sunday, year round; also Fridays October through April.
**TIMES:** 7:00 AM-3:00 PM.
**ADMISSION:** Free. Parking is free.
**LOCATION:** 7700 E Davis Blvd. Off Exit 15 from I-75.
**DESCRIPTION:** Open since 1975, and under new ownership/management, this outdoor market of 200-350 dealers is half flea market, half farmers' market, with loads of produce and loads of garage sale goodies. Antiques, collectibles, souvenirs, furniture and new merchandise can be found here. One big restaurant and handicapped-accessible restrooms add to the amenities.
**DEALER RATES:** Summer, May through October, $6 or $10 per 10' × 20' space; winter, November through April, $10 or $15 per space. Reservations are first come, first served. Canopies and tables are available from the market.
**CONTACT:** Jack, Naples Drive-In Flea Market, 7700 E Davis Blvd, Naples FL 33942. Tel: (941) 774-2900.

# NORTH FORT MYERS
## North Side Drive-In Flea Market

**DATES:** Wednesday, Friday through Sunday, weather permitting.
**TIMES:** 5:00 AM-2:00 PM.
**ADMISSION:** Free. Free parking is available.
**LOCATION:** 2521 N Tamiami Trail. On Old Rt 41 N, in the old business district. Off Exit 26 from I-75.
**DESCRIPTION:** This outdoor market began before 1980. Wednesday is their *big* day as it is the only Wednesday market around. It accommodates approximately 250-350 (they did *squeeeeze* 396 dealers in one Wednesday) dealers selling antiques, glass, arts and crafts, collectibles, fresh produce, and both new and used merchandise. One snack bar (trust me, you won't starve) serves homemade cooked-to-order breakfast. After that you may

need their handicapped-accessible restrooms. Occasionally, Octagon, a local animal rescue group, brings in animals for show and collects donations for their work.

**DEALER RATES:** Wednesday $10; Friday free; Saturday and Sunday $8. Reservations are not required. Do reserve for Wednesday—it fills quickly!

**CONTACT:** Art, North Side Drive-In and Flea Market, 2521 N Tamiami Trail, N Ft Myers FL 33903. Tel: (941) 995-2254.

# NORTH FORT PIERCE
## Biz-E-Flea Market

**DATES:** Saturday and Sunday, year round.

**TIMES:** 7:00 AM-closing (up to 3:00 PM).

**ADMISSION:** Free. Parking is also free.

**LOCATION:** 3252 N US 1, 1 mile north of St. Lucie Blvd (Airport Rd) and 11 miles south of Olso Rd, Vero Beach.

**DESCRIPTION:** This covered outdoor market first opened in 1980. There are anywhere from 50 dealers during the summer to 90 dealers during the winter selling antiques, collectibles, crafts, tools, electronic equipment, carpeting and new and good used merchandise. Fresh vegetables are also sold. This is a family style market boasting sidewalks for easy walking. One complete concession with seating and restrooms add to the amenities.

**DEALER RATES:** For a 10' × 10' space daily: $8 uncovered with 3 tables, no electric; $10 or $12 covered with electric and 3 tables. Weekly and monthly rates are available. Reservations are not necessary, but suggested.

**CONTACT:** Irma Partridge, 1000 SW 27 Ave Lot 61, Vero Beach FL 32968. Tel: (561) 466-3063.

# NORTH MIAMI
## North Miami Flea Market

**DATES:** Every Wednesday through Sunday; open daily Thanksgiving through Christmas.

**TIMES:** Wednesday and Sunday 10:00 AM-7:00 PM; Thursday-Saturday; 10:00 AM-9:00 PM.

**ADMISSION:** Free. Free parking is available.

**LOCATION:** 14135 NW 7th Ave, 1 block west of I-95 off N 135th St. (The Blue Building.)

**DESCRIPTION:** This is South Florida's original indoor flea market, and it all began in 1967. Between 70-80 (formerly up to 200) dealers sell a variety of goods including antiques as well as new merchandise, fine art, and fresh produce. There is also clothing for the entire family, housewares, electronics, toys—the list goes on. The indoor market is clean and air-conditioned and features deluxe snack bars, a new ice cream shop and a restaurant.

**DEALER RATES:** $250 and up (plus tax) for 10' × 15' space monthly with annual lease preferred. Includes telephone service, advertising, security service, electric and maintenance.

**CONTACT:** Market Manager, North Miami Flea Market, 14135 NW 7 Ave, N Miami FL 33168. Tel: (305) 685-7721.

## OAK HILL
### Oak Hill Flea Market

**DATES:** Tuesday, Friday, Saturday, and Sunday.

**TIMES:** 7:00 AM till around 1:00-3:00 PM.

**ADMISSION:** Free. Parking is free.

**LOCATION:** 351 US 1, 28 miles south of Daytona and 40 miles north of Cocoa. Via I-95: From Daytona, take the Edgewater Exit and go south 8 miles on US 1; From Cocoa, take the Oak Hill Scottsmoor Exit and go north 8 miles on US 1.

**DESCRIPTION:** Opened in 1986, and surrounded by palm trees and sand, this indoor/outdoor market of 70-250 dealers, depending on the season (winter is higher and often sells out of space), sells antiques, collectibles, plants, canned goods, household items, clothing, toys, tools, hardware, produce, appliances, and new merchandise. The ratio of sale items is only 20% new, 10% produce, and the rest is garage sale goodies, and antiques and collectibles. During the winter months, a food concession trailer is set up on the grounds to join the Back to the '50s Restaurant. Baby Boomers, take note— a '50s joint with hand-dipped ice cream, shakes, sundaes, breakfast. Bring back memories? They hold special events during the year: Antique Radio Collectors Annual Meet and Flea Market, Antique Tool Collectors Meet and Flea Market, and the New Car Show and Sale.

**DEALER RATES:** Per 8' table: Tuesday $3, Friday $5, Saturday $7, Sunday $7. Same price for inside or outside tables, or 10' wide spaces outside with no table. Reservations are recommended, particularly from September thru May. There are 180 spaces inside under roof, 100 spaces available outside and 5 enclosed permanent stalls.

**CONTACT:** Ken Glance, Flea Market Manager, PO Box 116, Oak Hill FL 32759-0116. Tel: (904) 345-3570. Fax: (904) 257-9531. Email:

roaringtwnties@ns.gemlink.com. Web: members.tripod.com/ ~roaring_twenties/index-6.html or maxpages.com/maxpage.cgi/roaringtwnties.

---

**Local History**

Oak Hill Flea Market and Back to the '50s Restaurant was originally a busy truck stop and restaurant back in the 1950s and '60s when the Kennedy Space Center was being built. In those pre-I-95 days, US 1 was the main route for travelers and workers. It is still a preferred route for many folks going to Spacecoast to see a lift-off.

---

# OCALA
## Ocala Drive-In Flea Market

**DATES:** Saturday and Sunday, year round. Rain or shine.
**TIMES:** 6:00 AM-4:00 PM.
**ADMISSION:** Free admission and free parking.
**LOCATION:** 4850 S Pine Ave (South 441-301-27).
**DESCRIPTION:** Started in 1979, the Ocala Flea Market is located at the only drive-in theater in the county, which is open on Friday, Saturday, and Sunday. Approximately 300 dealers occupy selling space in the summer and 450 in the winter, offering antiques, collectibles, handmade crafts, vegetables, tools, clothes, plants, birds, and new merchandise. There is a pawn shop on the premises. Food is available.
**DEALER RATES:** $10.50 per day for a 10' × 10' booth under roof; $8 per day for a 10' × 10' booth outside. Reservations are suggested.
**CONTACT:** Sheri Williams, 4850 S Pine Ave, Ocala FL 34480. Tel: (904) 629-1325.

# OKEECHOBEE
## The Market Place Flea Market

**DATES:** Saturday and Sunday, year round.
**TIMES:** 8:00 AM-4:00 PM.
**ADMISSION:** Free. Parking is free.
**LOCATION:** 3600 Hwy 441 S. From I-95: go west on Hwy 710, then west on Hwy 70, then south on Hwy 441. They are approximately 3 miles down the road on the left across from Scotty's.
**DESCRIPTION:** This family owned and operated market has been filling the need of "everything and anything" market for the locals as well as the

transient workers from this area. Their 550 dealers (in season) sell some antiques and collectibles, tons of fresh produce (just picked) and loads of new merchandise (tends towards the flashy stuff, electronics, jewelry, hair decorations). The entire market is under cover on pavement. There are six snack bars, just in case you can't wait to eat. Local advice: "Bring your fishing gear!" They are located on the north end of Lake Okeechobee.

**DEALER RATES:** Winter: $22.50 per 10' × 10' space and table per weekend. Summer: $16 per 10' × 10' space and table per weekend. Reservations are strongly recommended, especially in winter as they get full quickly. Dealers may stay overnight in self-contained rigs as water, electric and a dump station are available on site. A huge KOA Campground is next door.

**CONTACT:** The Market Place Flea Market, 3600 Hwy 441 S, Okeechobee FL 34974. Tel: (941) 467-6639.

# OLDSMAR
## Oldsmar Flea Market

**DATES:** Saturday and Sunday, year round.

**TIMES:** 9:00 AM-5:00 PM.

**ADMISSION:** Free. Free parking available.

**LOCATION:** 180 N Racetrack Rd, at the corner of Hillsboro Ave and Racetrack Rd.

**DESCRIPTION:** This market began in 1980. About 1,100 dealers sell to the public. Ninety-five percent of them are indoors and offer antiques, collectibles, handmade and craft items, produce, meats, and cheeses. New merchandise is also sold. In addition, there are two bakeries, two nurseries, and even beauticians, as well as handicapped-accessible restrooms on the premises. Ten snack bars provide plenty of food and refreshment.

**DEALER RATES:** Prices vary from $10.70 daily with one table and parking; rented on a first-come, first-served basis. Their office is open Wednesday through Friday 9:00 AM-3:00 PM, and weekends 7:00 AM-5:00 PM. They take reservations only one week in advance provided you show up in person.

**CONTACT:** Oldsmar Flea Market, PO Box 439, Oldsmar FL 34677-0439. Tel: (813) 855-5306 (during market days) or (813) 855-2587 office. Fax: (813) 855-1263. Web: home.att.net/~ad-man/oldsmar.htm.

# PALMETTO
## Midway Flea Market

**DATES:** Friday, Saturday and Sunday, year round.

**TIMES:** 8:00 AM-4:00 PM.

**ADMISSION:** Free. Parking is free.

**LOCATION:** 10816 US 41 N. Take Exit 45 from I-75. Market is midway between Tampa and Sarasota, near Sun City.

**DESCRIPTION:** Since 1987 this indoor/outdoor market's 250 to 450 dealers have been selling antiques, collectibles, produce, coins, cards, new merchandise, clothes, furniture, crafts and garage sale goodies. When the munchies strike pick from two restaurants, two snack bars, or beer garden. And yes, there are handicapped-accessible restrooms. The outdoor vendors are under cover, so don't worry about any stray rain. This market is busy from October through May. The management maintains an exceptionally clean market and prides itself on its friendliness.

**DEALER RATES:** $10 and up per 10' × 10' space under cover, or around $150 per month per 10' × 10' space indoors monthly, depending on location. Reservations are necessary for indoors, recommended for outdoors.

**CONTACT:** Ian, Midway Flea Market, 10816 US 41 N, Palmetto FL 34221. Tel: (941) 723-6000. Fax: (941) 723-9093.

# PENSACOLA
## T & W Flea Market

**DATES:** Saturday and Sunday. Rain or shine.

**TIMES:** Dawn to dusk.

**ADMISSION:** Free. Free parking is available.

**LOCATION:** 1717 N T St, on the west side of Pensacola.

**DESCRIPTION:** This indoor/outdoor market started in 1979. There are 400 dealers per weekend selling a variety of objects including antiques, fine art, arts and crafts, new merchandise, fresh produce, etc.—it's all here. They have made many improvements in this market including concrete aisles. Four snack bars provide food for the hungry. Handicapped-accessible restrooms complete the amenities.

**DEALER RATES:** $10 and up. Reservations are required for the more desirable spaces.

**CONTACT:** Red Cotton, 1717 N T St, Pensacola FL 32505. Tel: (850) 433-4315 or 433-7030.

# PINELLAS PARK
## Wagonwheel Flea Market

**DATES:** Saturday and Sunday.
**TIMES:** 7:30 AM-4:00 PM.
**ADMISSION:** Free. Parking is $1.
**LOCATION:** 7801 Park Blvd, at 74th Ave, between Belcher and Starkey Rds. Off I-275 Exit 15W.
**DESCRIPTION:** Opened in 1967, this market of 1200-1800 vendors sells a few antiques and collectibles, crafts, fresh produce, but mostly new merchandise. There is a food court, 30 snack concessions, handicapped-accessible restrooms, a courtesy tram, stroller and wheelchair rentals among other amenities.
**DEALER RATES:** $6 per 10' × 10' open space, $9.50 under cover. Reservations are not taken; first come, first served.
**CONTACT:** Wagonwheel Flea Market, 7801 Park Blvd, Pinellas Park FL 33781-3708. Tel: (727) 544-5319. Fax: (727) 541-4005. Web: zipmall.com/wagonwheel.htm.

---

### Dolphin Watch!

This market is located five miles inland from the Gulf of Mexico, but on the Intercoastal Waterway. Awhile ago, three dolphins ambled into their lake and hung around. Eventually, two decided it wasn't big enough and left. The third fellow is still there, enjoying his personal lake and audience.

---

# PLANT CITY
## Country Village Flea Market

**DATES:** Every Wednesday, Saturday, and Sunday. Rain or shine.
**TIMES:** 7:00 AM-2:00 PM.
**ADMISSION:** Free. Free and paid ($1) parking is available.
**LOCATION:** On corner of State Rd 39 and Sam Allen Rd, 1 mile north of I-4. (Tampa area.)
**DESCRIPTION:** This market began in 1979 and currently ranks among the largest Wednesday markets. It accommodates dealers both indoors and outdoors, selling plenty of used goods. Also available are antiques, collectibles, and fresh produce. Food is served on the premises. Their Wednesday market

is so popular that they have turned away dealers for lack of room! There is a wholesale produce market seven days a week from 6:00 AM to whenever. **DEALER RATES:** $7 and up for 6' × 9' indoor space. $7 for 24' outdoor space. No reservations are required and there are no advance shopping hours for dealers.
**CONTACT:** Sylvia Utter, Country Village Flea Market, 3301 Paul Buchman Hwy 39 N, Plant City FL 33565-5051. Tel: (813) 752-4670.

# PORT RICHEY
## USA Fleamarket
**DATES:** Friday, Saturday and Sunday.
**TIMES:** 8:00 AM-4:00 PM.
**ADMISSION:** Free. Parking is free.
**LOCATION:** 11721 US Hwy 19, 200 yards south of SR 52 on US Hwy 19.
**DESCRIPTION:** Started in 1980, this market, now completely under cover, runs from 600 dealers in summer to crammed full in winter. Their dealers sell antiques, collectibles, crafts, produce, jewelry, western wear, records, tapes, hobby supplies, tools, clothing, perfumes, pewter, scrubs, purses, clocks, art, appliances, silk flowers, sneakers, lamps and other new and used merchandise. There is a dollar shop, an automotive shop, a beauty salon, hobby shop, and seven snack bars as well. Look for their humongous electronic sign at the entrance ("you can't miss it!")—"One of the best flea markets on the west coast (of Florida)."
**DEALER RATES:** From $13 and up daily for booths from 9' × 12' to 12' × 36'. There are weekly and monthly rates available as well as shed rentals. Vendors set up at 7:00 AM, vacate by 5:00 PM.
**CONTACT:** Marie Bruno, USA Fleamarket Inc, 11721 US Hwy 19, Port Richey FL 34668. Tel: (727) 862-3583. Fax: (727) 862-5724.

# ST AUGUSTINE
## St Johns Flea Market
**DATES:** Saturday and Sunday.
**TIMES:** 9:00 AM-5:00 PM.
**ADMISSION:** Free. Parking is free.
**LOCATION:** I-95 and SR 207, Exit 94.
**DESCRIPTION:** This market opened in 1985 and has 500 spaces indoors and out with dealers selling "everything"; antiques, collectibles, new and used merchandise, produce, plants, and more. It is all under roof. Located in

historic St Augustine, the country's oldest city and a major tourist attraction. Food is available on the premises as are clean handicapped-accessible restrooms and RV facilities.

**DEALER RATES:** $11 per day, or depending on dealer's needs. Reservations are suggested.

**CONTACT:** St Johns Flea Market, PO Box 1284, St Augustine FL 32085-1284. Tel: (904) 824-4210. Fax: (904) 824-9287.

# SANFORD
## Flea World

**DATES:** Every Friday, Saturday, and Sunday. Rain or shine.

**TIMES:** 9:00 AM-6:00 PM.

**ADMISSION:** Free. Free parking is available for 4,000 cars.

**LOCATION:** 4311 Hwy 17-92. From I-4, take Exit 50 east to Hwy 17-92, turn right 1 mile.

**DESCRIPTION:** This market started on May 20, 1982, with just a 12-acre tract. It has now grown to accommodate 1,700 dealers on 104 acres of land. There is an "all-under-one-roof" building with 1,700 booths and three other air-conditioned buildings. Shoppers really can get it all here from antiques and collectibles to the unusual: a lawyer, an optometrist, a barber and beauty shop, and an exotic pet shop. The Friday market features $5 garage sales free before 9:00 AM. Fifteen fun food stops quell hunger and a Family Fun Park is located next door. Bingo and other events are held every weekend including circus acts and Elvis impersonators.

**DEALER RATES:** $14.50-$15.50 per space and up. Reservations are required and must be made in person.

**CONTACT:** Alice Butcher, Rental Manager, Flea World, 4311 Hwy 17-92, Sanford FL 32773. Tel: (407) 330-1792 ext. 224.

# STUART
## B & A Flea Market

**DATES:** Saturday and Sunday. Rain or shine.

**TIMES:** 8:00 AM-3:00 PM.

**ADMISSION:** Free. Parking $1.

**LOCATION:** South US Highway 1, just north of Indian Street, across from Martin Square Mall.

**DESCRIPTION:** This market first opened in 1975. It accommodates over 500 dealers both indoors and outdoors who assemble to sell just about everything including antiques, collectibles, fine art, arts and crafts, new merchandise, and everything else imaginable. A farmers' market sells fresh produce. Hot dog carts roam the market and with a deli and other concessions quell hunger. Handicapped-accessible restrooms are on site.

**DEALER RATES:** Starting at $12 daily for an uncovered space, $20 for a covered space. Spaces are 10' × 10' to 10' × 20'. Reservations must be made in person and paid for by 7:00 AM the day of the market.

**CONTACT:** Mary Sue Davis, Flea Market Manager, B & A Flea Market, 2201 SE Indian St, Stuart FL 34997. Tel: (561) 288-4915. Fax: (561) 288-2140. Email: info@bafleamarket.com. Web: www.bafleamarket.com.

# TAMPA
## Big Top Flea Market

**DATES:** Saturday and Sunday, year round.

**TIMES:** 9:00 AM-4:30 PM.

**ADMISSION:** Free. Parking is free.

**LOCATION:** Take I-75 south to Fowler Ave (SR 582), Exit 54, heading east. Market is 500 yards east of I-75.

**DESCRIPTION:** The Big Top Flea Market, opened in October 1990, was built in a unique hub and spoke design so that every booth is well traveled and easily accessible. The market is named after the 27,000-square-foot center core that resembles a huge circus tent. It houses 620 booths with 160,000 square feet of both covered and enclosed spaces. Eventually the Market will have over 1,100 spaces. While there is a wide variety of merchandise including produce, fine jewelry, antiques, collectibles and crafts, this market is keeping the true spirit of a flea market: value, bargains and fun. A full food court and handicapped-accessible restrooms add to the amenities.

**DEALER RATES:** Daily rates from $11-$25 per space depending on location and season (lower in summer). Monthly and weekend rates are available. Office is open Monday 1:00 PM-4:00 PM, Friday 9:00 AM-4:00 PM.

**CONTACT:** Big Top Flea Market, 9250 E Fowler Ave, Thonotosassa FL 33592. Tel: (813) 986-4004. Fax: (813) 986-6296. Email: karnich@aol.com. Web: home.att.net/~ad-man/bigtop.htm.

## Floriland Flea and Farmers' Market

**DATES:** Saturday and Sunday.

**TIMES:** 9:00 AM-5:00 PM.

**ADMISSION:** Free. Parking is free.
**LOCATION:** 9309 N Florida Ave. In Tampa I-275 to Exit 33 (Busch Blvd). Then west 1 block to Florida Ave. Not quite 1 mile west of Busch Gardens.
**DESCRIPTION:** Opened in 1992, this air-conditioned market of 800 spaces filled with 300 dealers sells mostly new merchandise including clothing, produce, groceries, socks, and general merchandise. The antiques and collectibles are in the market next door. One kitchen and two concessions feed the famished and handicapped-accessible restrooms do come in handy.
**DEALER RATES:** $24.22 per day for 10' × 10' space, $44.41 for the weekend. First come, first served.
**CONTACT:** Floriland Flea and Farmers' Market, 9309 N Florida Ave, Tampa FL 33612. Tel: (813) 932-4319. Fax: (813) 935-5558. Web: home.att.net/~ad-man/floriland.htm.

# THONOTOSASSA
## 301 North Flea Market

**DATES:** Tuesday through Sunday.
**TIMES:** 9:00 AM TO 5:00 PM.
**ADMISSION:** Free. Parking is free.
**LOCATION:** 11802 N 301. Just take I-75 to Fowler Ave. Exit and head east or travel east on Fowler from 56th St. Turn left (north) on Hwy 301. You can't miss them: they are just past the Machinery Auction on the left-hand side of the road.
**DESCRIPTION:** Opened in 1980 (the oldest flea market in Hillsborough County), this market has 100 booths, full on weekends, with dealers selling antiques, collectibles, pets, birds, glassware, vacuums, books, furniture, videos, electronics, and lots of new merchandise. There is a snack bar run by Jim, who retired from 35 years in the fast-food business, and restrooms. During the week, only the shops are really open (video, appliance, and book shops).
**DEALER RATES:** Outside: $5 for Saturday and Sunday, free weekdays. Inside rates start at $100 per month. Reservations are not needed for outside, they are for inside.
**CONTACT:** Jim Shafer, North 301 Flea Market, 11802 N 301 Hwy, Thonotosassa FL 33592. Tel: (813) 986-1023. Office hours: Tuesday-Sunday 9:00 AM-7:00 PM. Fax: (813) 986-1023.

# WALDO
## Waldo Farmers' and Flea Market

**DATES:** Every Saturday and Sunday. Rain or shine.

**TIMES:** 7:30 AM-4:30 PM.

**ADMISSION:** Free. Free parking available.

**LOCATION:** Located on Hwy 301 N, north of Waldo on both sides of the road—at the traffic light.

**DESCRIPTION:** This Farmers' and Flea Market attracts an average of 750 dealers in the summer and 900 dealers during the winter selling antiques, collectibles, handmade craft items, vegetables, tools, new merchandise and "much more." The market has been running since 1973 and bought out Smiley's flea market across the street. There is a huge antique mall here, open every day. The majority of spaces are under covered sheds, however outside space and lock-up stalls are also available. Dealers may stay overnight and no county or city licenses are required. There is a snack bar on the premises and camping nearby. "Look for the big chair, windmill and the Big Horse." They describe themselves as: "Country market with big city crowds. Friendly folks."

**DEALER RATES:** $7 and up per 10' × 10' space. The office is open Thursday through Sunday.

**CONTACT:** Waldo Farmer's and Flea Market, 17805 NE US Hwy 301, Waldo FL 32694. Tel: (352) 468-2255.

# WEBSTER
## Sumter County Farmers' Market, Inc

**DATES:** Every Monday year round, except Christmas Day. Rain or shine.

**TIMES:** 8:00 AM-3:00 PM.

**ADMISSION:** Free. Free parking is provided on market grounds.

**LOCATION:** On Hwy 471 in Webster. Accessible from Hwy 50, Hwy 301, or Hwy 98.

**DESCRIPTION:** This market opened in 1937 and currently attracts between 1,200 (summer) and 2,000 (winter) dealers who sell a range of antiques, collectibles, craft items, new and used merchandise, and fresh produce, including citrus and flower plants. This market is well known for its selection of antique items and locally grown vegetables. There is a large wholesale area on site as well. Snack food, as well as a sit-down restaurant, are available on the premises.

**DEALER RATES:** $9 per 10' × 10' booth, covered with 2 tables; $7 per 12' × 12' booth, open with 2 tables. Cancellations are done by a lottery system at 7:00 AM. All dealers must have city and county licenses, available at office every Monday between 7:30 AM and 9:30 AM, for $7 per day or $35 for the year.
**CONTACT:** Margie Hayes, Office Manager, PO Box 62, Webster FL 33597-0062. Tel: (352) 793-3551. Fax: (352) 793-9474. Web: www.websterfleamarket.com.

## Webster Westside Flea Market

**DATES:** Mondays, year round.
**TIMES:** 5:00 AM until the last dealer leaves, literally.
**ADMISSION:** Free. Parking is $2.
**LOCATION:** 516 NW 3rd St. On Hwy 478 at NW 3rd St. On the west side of town.
**DESCRIPTION:** Considered the oldest flea market in the state, they opened as an outdoor market in 1931. Many of the dealers are under cover although, not really indoors. Also known as "Antique Alley" for their quality antiques and collectibles, this market's 800 or so dealers also sell some new merchandise, produce and whatever. They hold Car Shows the first Sunday of the month, with a three-day Extravaganza in February. They tried an antiques-only show one weekend in 1997 and found it was so successful that they were doing them on the first Sunday of the month. Watch for the advertisements as to the dates. Plenty of concessions dot the market. Howard's Flea Market in Homosassa is their sister market and headquarters.
**DEALER RATES:** Daily including tax: Covered with 2 tables: $14.98 per 10' × 10' space. Small field: $9.63 per 10' × 10' with 1 table. Big field: $25 per 30' × 15' space, no tables. Reservations are suggested, although if you do show up they will manage to find you a spot somehow. The office is open for reservations on Thursday and Friday.
**CONTACT:** Teri Davis, Howard's Flea Market, 6373 S Suncoast Blvd, Homosassa FL 34446. Tel: (352) 628-4656 for HQ or (352) 568-0494 or 793-9877 for the market. For a tape of Webster-only information and their voicemail, call 1-800-832-7396.

# WEST PALM BEACH
## Beach Swap Shop

**DATES:** Wednesday, Friday, Saturday, and Sunday.

**TIMES:** 6:00 AM-2:00 PM.

**ADMISSION:** Saturday and Sunday $.50 per car. Free parking too.

**LOCATION:** 1301 Old Dixie Hwy. Between I-95 and US 1.

**DESCRIPTION:** This outdoor market started in 1965 and attracts up to 100 dealers selling mostly used and new merchandise and fresh produce. "All kinds of goodies," according to the manager. There is a nice snack bar with restrooms on premises.

**DEALER RATES:** Wednesday $3, Friday $4; Saturday and Sunday $7-$10 depending on season (winter higher). Reservations are not required. Monthly reservations are available.

**CONTACT:** Beach Swap Shop, 1301 Old Dixie Hwy, Riviera Beach FL 33404. Tel: (561) 844-5836.

# ZEPHYRHILLS
## Zephyrhills Flea Market

**DATES:** Friday, Saturday, and Sunday, September through May. Weekends in the summer.

**TIMES:** 8:00 AM-3:00 PM.

**ADMISSION:** Free. Parking is free.

**LOCATION:** 39336 Chancey Rd. Follow Rt 301 to the south side of Zephyrhills, turn east on Chancey Rd. Go about 1½ miles; the market is on the right.

**DESCRIPTION:** Started in 1991, this indoor/outdoor market has 340 or so spaces with 100 or more dealers depending on who takes up how much room. The outdoor sellers are under roof on concrete paths. They sell antiques, collectibles, baked goods, ceramics, watches, coins, plants, household goods, yard sale items, oldies music, and from one dealer, motorized scooters for the handicapped. Food wagons quell hunger. This market has been noted for its cleanliness and friendly people.

**DEALER RATES:** Outside: $16 for a proper space, special rates for yard sales. Indoors: $160-$180 per month (there are 64 spaces).

**CONTACT:** Zephyrhills Flea Market, 39336 Chancey Rd, Zephyrhills FL 33540. Tel: (813) 782-1483 or 1-800-932-9674.

## OTHER FLEA MARKETS

We know or have heard about these markets, but have not personally contacted each one, as we have the markets with descriptions. If you plan to visit one of these markets listed below, *please call first* to make sure they are still open. Flea markets do come and go. While they were open when we went to press, they may not be later. We can't be responsible. *Call first!*

**Belleview:** Antique Shop & Flea Market, 12180 SE US Hwy 441. Tel: (352) 245-3532.

**Belleview:** Market of Marion, 12888 SE US Hwy 441. Tel: (352) 245-6766.

**Big Pine Key:** Big Pine Key Flea Market, US Hwy 1 MM 30½. Tel: (305) 872-4103.

**Bradenton:** Roma Flea Market, 5715 15 St E. Tel: (941) 756-9036.

**Bradenton:** Bayshore High Flea Market, 703 65 Ave Dr W. Tel: (941) 755-6339.

**Brooksville:** Victory Flea Market, 908 Cedar Dr. Tel: (352) 754-8977.

**Bushnell:** Bushnell Flea Market, 5845 CR 313. Tel: (352) 793-6515.

**Bushnell:** Sumter Flea Market, 7368 SR 471. Tel: (352) 793-3581.

**Callahan:** Bargain Mart Flea Market, 1098 N Kings Rd. Tel: (904) 845-2889.

**Clearwater:** 49er Flea Market, 10525 49 St N. Tel: (727) 573-3367.

**Cocoa:** Jumping Flea Market, 2507 N Cocoa Blvd. Tel: (407) 636-9664.

**Crawfordville:** Wakulla Flea Market, 3016 Crawfordville Hwy. Tel: (850) 926-6466.

**Crestview:** Super Flea, 300 Rasberry Rd. Tel: (850) 683-1117.

**Daytona Beach:** Daytona Flea & Farmers' Market, 2987 Bellevue Ave. Tel: (904) 253-3330.

**Daytona Beach:** Dennis Robertson Flea Market, 325 N Peninsula Ave. Tel: (904) 253-1903.

**Daytona Beach:** Franklin E Gheen Flea Market, 3213 Vail View Dr. Tel: (904) 322-1054.

**De Bary:** Donna P Beske Flea Market, 257 Bayou Vista St. Tel: (407) 668-6617.

**De Funiak Springs:** De Funiak Flea Market, Hwy 90E. Tel: (850) 892-3668.

**De Land:** Albert T Brooks Flea Market, 4380 Robinette Ln. Tel: (904) 736-4488.

**De Land:** Deland Flea Market, 1570 7 Ave. Tel: (904) 740-9432.

**Delray Beach:** Carnival Flea Market at Delray, 5283 W Atlantic Ave. Tel: (561) 499-9935.

**Edgewater:** George Balasko Flea Market, 803 Masthead Ln. Tel: (904) 428-8743.

**Eustis:** Bill Cox Flea Market, 510 E Washington Ave. Tel: (352) 483-0105.

**Florida City:** Florida City Flea Market, 450 W Davis Pkwy. Tel: (305) 247-2287.

**Fort Lauderdale:** Mall 441 Flea Market, 2928 N SR 7. Tel: (954) 717-3090.

**Fort Myers:** Flea Market of Ortiz Avenue, 1501 Ortiz Ave. Tel: (941) 694-5019.

**Gulf Breeze:** Midway Center & Market, 6088 Gulf Breeze Pkwy. Tel: (850) 932-4433.

**Gulf Breeze:** Flea Market, 5760 Gulf Breeze Pkwy. Tel: (850) 934-1971.

**Hallandale:** Hollywood Dog Track Flea Market, 831 N Federal Hwy. Tel: (954) 454-8666.

**Hialeah:** International Market Place, 8000 NW 95 St. Tel: (305) 556-6362.

**Hudson:** Hudson Flea Market, 9411 Denton Ave. Tel: (727) 869-0650.

**Hudson:** New York Avenue Flea Market, 8026 New York Ave. Tel: (727) 868-5929.

**Interlachen:** Rodriguez Flea Market, 1300 Hwy 20. Tel: (904) 684-4969.

**Jacksonville:** ABC Flea Market, 10135 Beach Blvd. Tel: (904) 642-2717.

**Jacksonville:** Beach Blvd Flea & Farmers, 11041 Beach Blvd. Tel: (904) 645-5961.

**Jacksonville:** Golfair Flea Market, 813 Golfair Blvd. Tel: (904) 765-8744.

**Jacksonville:** Liberty Street Flea Market, 3805 Whitehall St. Tel: (904) 634-8824.

**Kissimmee:** Flea & Farmers' Market-Osceola, 2801 E Irlo Bronson Mem Hwy. Tel: (407) 846-2811 or (407) 238-1296.

**Lake Alfred:** Crossroads Flea Market, 1405 S Lake Shore Way. Tel: (941) 956-5166.

**Lecanto:** Stokes Flea Market, 5220 West Gulf to Lake Hwy. Tel: (352) 746-7200.

**Leesburg:** North Lake Flea Market, 2557 US Hwy 441. Tel: (352) 326-9335.

**Miami:** Flagler Flea Market, 401 NW 38 Ct. Tel: (305) 649-3000.

**Miami:** Flea Market On 7th Avenue, 13995 NW 7 Ave. Tel: (305) 681-9973.

**Miami:** Flea Market USA, 3015 NW 79 St. Tel: (305) 836-3677.

**Miami:** International 54th St Flea Market, 1100 NW 54 St. Tel: (305) 758-4822.

**Miami:** Liberty Flea Market, 7900 NW 27 Ave. Tel: (305) 836-9848.

**Miami:** North Miami Flea Market, 14135 NW 7 Ave. Tel: (305) 685-7721.

**Miami:** Robert T Lewis Flea Market, 5895 SW 50 Terr. Tel: (305) 666-6054.

**Miami:** Tropicaire Drive-In Flea Market, 9769 S Dixie Hwy 103. Tel: (305) 663-6570.

**Miami:** US 1 America's Indoor Market, 18901 S Dixie Hwy. Tel: (305) 234-2828.

**Naples:** Bass & Bass Flea Mart, 230 Industrial Blvd. Tel: (941) 643-4424.

**New Port Richey:** Indoor Fleas, 3621 US Hwy 19. Tel: (727) 842-3665.

**New Smyrna Beach:** Alice Hutchinson Flea Market, 533 Mill Dr. Tel: (904) 428-6450.

**Niceville:** Open Air Market, 1032 Bayshore Dr. Tel: (850) 678-8775.

**Ocala:** I-75 Super Flea Market, 4121 NW 44 Ave. Tel: (352) 351-9220.

**Ocala:** Ocala-Gainesville Flea Market, 4121 NW 44 Ave. Tel: (352) 351-9220.

**Odessa:** Gunn Hwy Flea Market, 2317 Gunn Hwy. Tel: (813) 920-3181.

**Okeechobee:** Cypress Hut Flea Market, 4701 Hwy 441 SE. Tel: (941) 763-5104.

**Okeechobee:** Trading Post Flea Market, 3100 Hwy 441S. Tel: (941) 763-4114.

**Opa Locka:** 183rd Street Flea Market, 18200 NW 27 Ave. Tel: (305) 624-1756.

**Orange City:** Eleanor B Riley Flea Market, 360 S Carpenter Ave. Tel: (904) 775-8489.

**Orange Park:** Mine Adcock Flea Market, 1342 Jefferson Ave C. Tel: (904) 272-2676.

**Orlando:** Three Star Flea Market, 2390 N Orange Blossom Trail. Tel: (407) 293-2722.

**Orlando:** KK Flea Market, 1325 W Washington St 2. Tel: (407) 841-0736.

**Orlando:** Orlando Flea Market, 5022 S Orange Blossom Trail. Tel: (407) 857-0048.

**Pace:** Pea Ridge Flea Market, 5186 Hwy 90. Tel: (850) 994-8056.

**Panama City:** 15th Street Flea Market, 2233 E 15 St. Tel: (850) 769-0137.

**Panama City:** 11th Street Flea Market, 1517 E 11 St. Tel: (850) 872-9290.

**Panama City:** Laguna Flea Market, 19987 Back Beach Rd. Tel: (850) 230-8687.

**Pensacola:** I-10 Flea Market, 3205 E Olive Rd 141. Tel: (850) 478-0107.

**Pensacola:** Chicken Nest Flea Market, 1316 N New Warrington Rd. Tel: (850) 456-3226.

**Pensacola:** Apple Flea Market, 1241 W Nine Mile Rd. Tel: (850) 857-1800.

**Perry:** Perry Flea Market, 3609 S US Hwy 19. Tel: (850) 838-1422.

**Plant City:** Frenchmen's Flea Market, 102 N Collins St. Tel: (813) 754-8388.

**Port Charlotte:** Rainbow Flea Market, 4628 Tamiami Trail. Tel: (941) 629-1223.

**Port Charlotte:** Sun Flea Market, 18505 Paulson Dr. Tel: (941) 255-3532.

**Port St Joe:** Big Barn, 412 Monument Ave. Tel: (850) 227-7410.

**Princeton:** Bargain Town Flea Market, 24420 S Dixie Hwy. Tel: (305) 257-4335.

**Southport:** Southport Flea Market, 7435 Hwy 77. Tel: (850) 271-4107.

**St Augustine:** St Johns County Flea & Farmers, 2495 SR 207. Tel: (904) 824-4210.

**St Petersburg:** Peddler's Flea Market, 9401 Bay Pines Blvd. Tel: (727) 392-2198.

**St Petersburg:** Stadium Flea Market & Garage, 1400 Central Ave. Tel: (727) 894-5856.

**Tallahassee:** Tallahassee Flea Market, 200 Capital Circle SW. Tel: (850) 877-3811.

**Thonotosassa:** Big Top Flea Market, 9250 Fowler Ave. Tel: (813) 986-4004.

**Thonotosassa:** Smith's Flea Mart, 9250 E Fowler Ave.Tel: (813) 986-0891.

**Titusville:** Robert H Blakely Flea Market, 3430 Worsham Pl. Tel: (407) 269-9288.

**Titusville:** Antoinett Lewis Flea Market, 890 Allendale St. Tel: (407) 264-4984.

**Umatilla:** Umatilla Markets, 811 N Central Hwy 19. Tel: (352) 669-3202.

**Waldo:** Trading Post Flea Market, 17500 NE Waldo Rd. Tel: (352) 468-2622.

**Wauchula:** Hilltop Flea & Farmers' Market, North Hwy 17. Tel: (941) 773-6148.

**West Palm Beach:** 45th Street Flea Market, 1710 45 St. Tel: (561) 863-6424.

**West Palm Beach:** Beach Drive-In Theater, 1301 Old Dixie Hwy. Tel: (561) 844-0330.

**West Palm Beach:** Driss Zerrouk Flea Market, 401 Executive Center Drive E111. Tel: (561) 687-3091.

**West Palm Beach:** Harry Trent Flea Market, 3107 Palm Rd. Tel: (561) 697-1821.

**West Palm Beach:** Uptown-Downtown Flea Market, 5700 Okeechobee Blvd. Tel: (561) 684-5700.

# GEORGIA

## ACWORTH
### Highway 41 Flea Market

**DATES:** Saturday and Sunday.

**TIMES:** 5:30 AM-5:30 PM.

**ADMISSION:** Free. Parking is free.

**LOCATION:** 3352 N Cobb Pkwy. Take I-75 N to Barrett Pkwy. Turn left. Go down to Hwy 41. Then turn right. Go exactly 6 miles to the market.

**DESCRIPTION:** Opened in 1975, this market averages 450-500 dealers selling antiques, collectibles, garage sale goodies, produce, and lots of new and used merchandise. It's a clean market with four concession stands, two lemonade stands, two boiled peanut stands, and when needed handicapped-accessible restrooms. There are 19 buildings with 1,400 tables here, covering about 42 acres.

**DEALER RATES:** $10 per day for a 8' × 8' space with table. Reservations are suggested and you can go in on Friday during office hours to reserve. Otherwise, first come, first served.

**CONTACT:** Robert Davenport, Highway 41 Flea Market, 3352 N Cobb Pkwy, Acworth GA 30101. Tel: (770) 975-0100.

### Lake Acworth Antique and Flea Market

**DATES:** Every Saturday and Sunday.

**TIMES:** 8:00 AM-5:00 PM.

**ADMISSION:** Free. Parking is free.

**LOCATION:** 4375 Cobb Pkwy NW, approximately 35 miles north of Atlanta and 5 miles west of I-75, off Hwy 92 Exit. Follow Hwy 92 to Cobb, turn right, go approximately 1 mile. Market is on the left.

**DESCRIPTION:** Started in 1978, this flea market was formerly known as Delight's. It is held indoors, in the open air, and under cover. There are 400 dealers exhibiting antiques, arts and crafts, fresh produce, collectibles, and new merchandise. Located near Allatoona Lake on Lake Acworth, the average daily attendance ranges between 5,000 and 6,000 people. Here you will find something for everyone. Three concession stands feed the famished.

**DEALER RATES:** $5 for outside space with 1 table. Inside space with lock-up is charged at $50 per month per 100 square feet of space. Reservations are necessary for inside. No vendors license required.

**CONTACT:** James Little, Lake Acworth Antique and Flea Market, 4375 Cobb Pkwy N, Acworth GA 30102. Tel: (770) 974-5896 (Saturday and Sunday only).

# ALBANY
## Kitty's Flea Market

**DATES:** Friday, Saturday, and Sunday, year round.
**TIMES:** 7:00 AM-6:00 PM.
**ADMISSION:** Free. Parking is also free.
**LOCATION:** 3331 Sylvester Rd. On US 82, 3 miles north of Albany.
**DESCRIPTION:** This market opened in 1985 in the middle of a pecan orchard and accommodates 320 regular dealers under roof and another 350 in the open or under shade, adding new tables all the time. "Anything you can think of" is sold here, including produce, furniture, clothes and jewelry. It is described by one regular as real "country, very laid back" and agreeable. This market is doing a booming business. If you love pecans, you can even pick your own! Four concession stands quell the screaming munchies, handicapped-accessible restrooms provide relief and a new 42-spot RV park provides camping facilities for dealers.
**DEALER RATES:** $6 per table under the shed, $4 outside space. Reservations are required under the shed only. Outside dealers can set up outside with no reservation.
**CONTACT:** Jim Andrews, Kitty's Flea Market, PO Box 51324, Albany GA 31703. Tel: (912) 432-0007.

# ATLANTA
## Lakewood Antiques Market

**DATES:** Second weekend of every month, Friday-Sunday, year round. Extravaganzas held in April for four days and November for five days.
**TIMES:** Friday 9:00 AM-6:00 PM; Saturday 9:00 AM-6:00 PM; Sunday 10:00 AM-5:00 PM.
**ADMISSION:** $3. Parking is free. Thursday is early buyers day for $5.
**LOCATION:** 2000 Lakewood Way. Take I-75-85 S, Exit 88 E and follow the signs.
**DESCRIPTION:** Since 1969, this market has been hosting from 800 to 1,200 dealers selling at least 75% antiques and collectibles. Their historic buildings are situated on 117 acres of land with a fully equipped bar and restaurant and dealer camping stops on site. They have added new air-conditioned and heated buildings.

**DEALER RATES:** $95 per 8' × 10' booth inside space; $70 per 14' × 15' outside space. After advance reservations are filled, then it is first come, first served.
**CONTACT:** Ed Spivia, PO Box 6826, Atlanta GA 30315. Tel: (404) 622-4488. Day of show contact Diane Dominick at above number.

## Scott Antique Market
### Antiques & Collectibles Show

**DATES:** Second weekend of every month.
**TIMES:** Friday and Saturday 9:00 AM-6:00 PM, Sunday 10:00 AM-4:00 PM.
**ADMISSION:** Free. Parking is $3.
**LOCATION:** Atlanta Exposition Centers, North and South Facilities at 3650 Jonesboro Rd. Take Exit 40 (Jonesboro Rd) off I-285, 3 miles east of Atlanta Airport.
**DESCRIPTION:** Since 1986 this indoor/outdoor market has 2,400 dealers selling the finest in antique and collectibles only. Exhibitors from all over the US feature fine antique furniture, jewelry, time pieces, china, pottery, books, coins, silver, glassware, textiles, linens, advertising items, military items, paintings, and much more. Four snack bars and one restaurant supply the energy to keep you browsing. Restrooms are on site.
**DEALER RATES:** Indoors: $115 for a 8' × 10' space; outdoors: $85 for a covered or uncovered space. There is an open field space for $45 for a 15' × 20' space to park and display. Reservations are required. Tables, chairs, pegboards, showcases, and safes are available for rent.
**CONTACT:** Scott Antique Markets, PO Box 60, Bremen OH 43107-0060. Tel: (740) 569-4112. Fax: (740) 569-7595. During the show call (404) 361-2000.

# AUGUSTA
## South Augusta Flea Market

**DATES:** Saturday and Sunday.
**TIMES:** 7:30 AM-6:00 PM.
**ADMISSION:** Free. Parking is free.
**LOCATION:** 1562 New Savannah Rd (Hwy 56). Follow Bobby Jones South to the end. Turn left, follow 1 mile. Market is on the right.
**DESCRIPTION:** It would be hard to miss this market of "only" 1,700 dealers. Their roughly 1,000 permanent and 700 temporary dealers sell everything from antiques, collectibles, Avon, produce, loads of yard sale good-

ies, produce, pets, animals, and whatever else comes in. Their restaurant opens at 7:30 AM serving a breakfast buffet, there are two snack bars, lemonade stands, and handicapped-accessible restrooms to handle all necessities. This is a clean, friendly, very successful market.

**DEALER RATES:** $5 per space, $1 per table. First come, first served. Gates open at 6:00 PM on Friday (but you have to sleep with your stuff on Friday night to hold your space if you come then), or line up the next morning.

**CONTACT:** South Augusta Flea Market, 1562 New Savannah Rd, Augusta GA 30906. Tel: (706) 798-5500.

# CARROLLTON
## West Georgia Flea Market

**DATES:** Saturday and Sunday.

**TIMES:** 8:00 AM-4:30 PM.

**ADMISSION:** Free. Parking is free.

**LOCATION:** 3947 Hwy 27N, I-20W Exit 3 and go south 2.4 miles.

**DESCRIPTION:** This "old time" flea market is one of the oldest and largest in Georgia. There are approximately 400 dealers in 550 spaces selling about half old and half new merchandise—"a good mix" says the manager. Plenty of garage sale goodies make it here, as well as collectibles, crafts, new and used furniture, fresh produce, new and used merchandise. The market consists of buildings, a pole barn and all spaces are under cover. Three snack bars with full menus and handicapped-accessible restrooms take care of essential shopping needs.

**DEALER RATES:** $9 per 10' × 8' outside space (dirt floor) with table, $11 inside with concrete floor. Reservations are highly recommended for the better spaces.

**CONTACT:** West Georgia Flea Market, 3947 Hwy 27N, Carrollton GA 30017. Tel: (770) 832-6551.

# CLEVELAND
## Charlie's Red, White and Blue Flea Market

**DATES:** Every weekend, plus holidays, from April through the weekend before Christmas.

**TIMES:** 8:00 AM-5:00 PM.

**ADMISSION:** Free. Parking is free.

**LOCATION:** 1612 Hwy 129, 1 mile south of Cleveland.

**DESCRIPTION:** Under new management since 1998, this market of 45 or so dealers sells antiques, collectibles, books, new and used merchandise, tools, clothing, western gear, vacuums, jewelry, and fresh produce. There is a snack bar as well as handicapped-accessible restrooms.

**DEALER RATES:** $7 per table per day. Monthly rates available. Reservations are required. Camping facilities are available for dealers; please call.

**CONTACT:** Genie and Charlie, Charlie's Red, White and Blue Flea Market, 1612 Hwy 129, Cleveland GA 30518. Tel: (888) 451-CAMP (toll free). Email: zoec@ngweb.net.

# DARIEN
## Ya'll Come Flea Market

**DATES:** Saturday and Sunday.

**TIMES:** Saturday 8:00 AM-6:00 PM. Auctions on Saturday at 7:00 PM. Sunday 8:00 AM-5:00 PM.

**ADMISSION:** Free. Parking is free.

**LOCATION:** I-95 and Hwy 251, Exit 10 (Darian Exit), 1 mile west of Exit 10 on Hwy 251, on the right side of road.

**DESCRIPTION:** Admittedly small, this rural indoor/outdoor market, opened in 1997, has from 8 (during the worst of the heat) to 23 vendors in 75 booths selling used merchandise, books, pottery, crafts, produce, furniture, garage sale goodies, flowers, and whatever shows up. There is a snack bar serving cool food and drink in the summer and hot homemade meals in the winter; and in case you need them, handicapped-accessible restrooms. Saturday's auction features callers from all over the South, selling new, old stuff, furniture, and more whatevers. Find Laverne in the snack bar and say "Hi!"

**DEALER RATES:** $14 inside 10' × 10' space, $10 outside per day. Friday is setup day 10:00 AM-4:00 PM.

**CONTACT:** Laverne, Ya'll Come Flea Market, Rt 3 Box 3599, Townsend GA 31331. Tel: (912) 437-5650. Fax: (912) 437-3504.

# DECATUR
## Kudzu Antique Flea Market

**DATES:** Friday, Saturday, and Sunday.

**TIMES:** Friday and Saturday 10:30 AM-5:30 PM; Sunday 12:30 PM-5:30 PM.

**ADMISSION:** Free. Parking is also free.

**LOCATION:** 2874 E Ponce de Leon. Off I-285, Exit 31.

**DESCRIPTION:** This dealer's paradise opened in October 1980. Their 27 dealers, in 27,000-square-foot barn-like building, sell mostly American antiques, collectibles, and furniture. There is very little new merchandise sold here and what comes in is exceptionally good. No food available on premises.

**DEALER RATES:** Rarely any vacancies; call for information.

**CONTACT:** Emily Campbell, 178 Lamont Dr, Decatur GA 30030. Tel: (404) 373-6498 or (404) 378-3909.

# EAST POINT
## Greenbriar Flea Market

**DATES:** Thursday through Monday, year round.

**TIMES:** Monday and Thursday 11:00 AM-8:00 PM; Friday and Saturday 10:00 AM-9:00 PM; Sunday 12:00 PM-7:00 PM.

**ADMISSION:** Free. Parking is also free.

**LOCATION:** 2925 Headland Dr. Across from the Greenbriar Mall.

**DESCRIPTION:** Opened in 1983, this friendly market hosts 136 dealers selling all new merchandise including jewelry, clothes, hats, fragrance, shoes, photos, and endless amounts of more at very reasonable prices. They remodeled the entire market in 1993 adding 10,000 square feet, a few retail stores and a little restaurant to handle all your hunger problems; handicapped-accessible restrooms handle other needs.

**DEALER RATES:** $225 and up per month. Reservations are suggested especially around the holidays. They can accommodate traveling dealers passing through. Just ask.

**CONTACT:** Greenbriar Flea Market, 2925 Headland Dr, East Point GA 30344-1908. Tel: (404) 349-3994.

# FLOWER BRANCH
## Gainesville Antique Flea Market

**DATES:** First weekend of each month and preceding Friday. Rain or shine.

**TIMES:** Friday and Saturday 9:00 AM-6:00 PM; Sunday 9:00 AM-5:00 PM.

**ADMISSION:** Free. Free parking is available.

**LOCATION:** 5540 Atlanta Hwy, on Hwy 13S, just 10 miles south of Gainesville.

**DESCRIPTION:** Known for its friendliness and courtesy, many of the 90 dealers have been with this flea market since it opened in 1978. The whole market moved in 1999 just 10 miles down the road where it can offer just antiques and collectibles indoors. The concession is excellent, serving home-cooked food that includes home-baked cakes and cookies. In case you need them, handicapped-accessible restrooms are on site. This is a good place for dealers to stock up.

**DEALER RATES:** A 3-day weekend fee of $50 for space measuring 10' × 12' including 2 tables. Reservations are preferred.

**CONTACT:** Johnny and Barbara Benefield, 3064 Poplar Springs Dr, Gainesville GA 30507-8627. Tel: (770) 536-8068.

# MACON
## Smiley's Flea Market

**DATES:** Saturday and Sunday.

**TIMES:** 7:00 AM-5:00 PM.

**ADMISSION:** Free. Parking is free.

**LOCATION:** On US 129/GA 247, 4 miles south of Macon.

**DESCRIPTION:** Opened in 1985, this indoor/outdoor market's several hundred dealers sell everything from "antiques to zebras" and everything in between, new and pre-owned. Plenty of yard sale stuff comes in as well. There are snack bars to satisfy the munchies, and clean handicapped-accessible restrooms. RV parking is available. By 2000, there will be two new buildings adding 20,000 square feet of selling space with a full sit-down restaurant.

**DEALER RATES:** $7 for 9' × 9' outside space with table in parking lot area, inside the fence with a 10' × 10' space and one table $11 per day. Lock-up buildings are available by the month. Reservations are recommended. Office hours are Thursday and Friday 9:00 AM-5:00 PM; Saturday and Sunday 7:00 AM-5:00 PM.

**CONTACT:** Cynthia Woody, 6717 Hawkinsville Rd, Macon GA 31206. Tel: (912) 788-3700. Fax: (912) 788-5344.

# MCDONOUGH
## Peachtree Peddler's Flea Market

**DATES:** Saturday and Sunday, year round. Also Fridays from Thanksgiving to Christmas.

**TIMES:** Saturday 9:00 AM-6:00 PM; Sunday 10:00 AM-6:00 PM. Friday 10:00 AM-5:00 PM.

**ADMISSION:** Free. Parking is free.

**LOCATION:** 155 Mill Rd. Off I-75, Exit 71.

**DESCRIPTION:** This market of approximately 250 dealers inside and 50 or so outside during good weather sells antiques, crafts, collectibles, leather, fine to cheap art, ethnic goods, garage sale goodies, used and new clothes, fishing and sports gear, and used and new merchandise. They bill themselves as "The largest indoor flea market, in the heart of Georgia" with 70,000 square feet of climate-controlled shopping, outside selling, three snack bars and handicapped-accessible restrooms. There is a special Free Flea Fridays where locals can bring their yard sale stuff and sell it for free on Friday, generally from May through September (weather permitting).

**DEALER RATES:** $65 for a 10' × 12' space per weekend inside, $15 per 10' × 20' space outside per day. Reservations are required for inside space, outside is first come, first served.

**CONTACT:** Peachtree Peddler's Flea Market, 155 Mill Rd, McDonough GA 30253. Tel: (770) 914-2269 or 1-888-661-3532 toll-free. Email: henrycomktplace@mindspring.com. Web: www.smartfleamarkets.com/html/shopping.html.

# PENDERGRASS
## Pendergrass Flea Market

**DATES:** Saturday and Sunday.

**TIMES:** 9:00 AM-5:00 PM.

**ADMISSION:** Free. Parking is free.

**LOCATION:** At I-85 Exit 50. Midway between Atlanta, Gainesville, and Athens.

**DESCRIPTION:** Opened in 1988, this indoor/outdoor market of 300-plus dealers sells antiques, collectibles, new and used furniture, books, crafts, garage sale goodies, fresh produce, watches, and new merchandise. The building is 250,000 square feet, the outdoor selling area is 50,000 square feet. There is a food court as well as handicapped-accessible restrooms on site.

**DEALER RATES:** $10-$80 per space depending on how much and where. Reservations are suggested.

**CONTACT:** Pendergrass Flea Market, 5641 Hwy 129, N Pendergrass GA 30567. Tel: (706) 693-4466 or (770) 945-1900. Fax: (706) 693-4506.

# SAVANNAH
## Keller's Flea Market

**DATES:** Saturday and Sunday, year round.

**TIMES:** 8:00 AM-6:00 PM.

**ADMISSION:** Free. Parking is free.

**LOCATION:** 5901 Ogeechee Rd. From I-95 take Exit 16 for 1 mile east towards Savannah. Take Hwy 17 exit off 204.

**DESCRIPTION:** This outdoor market hosts 300-400 dealers selling antiques, collectibles, garage sale goodies, produce, plants and new merchandise either under cover or in enclosed buildings. Janie Arkwright's Kitchen feeds the famished.

**DEALER RATES:** $15 or $20 depending on where, per day. Setup starts Friday between 8:00 AM-6:00 PM. The office is open the same hours Friday through Sunday. Reservations are not accepted; first come, first served.

**CONTACT:** Keller's Flea Market, 5901 Ogeechee Rd, Savannah GA 31419-8905. Tel: (912) 927-4848. Fax: (912) 925-2638.

## OTHER FLEA MARKETS

We know or have heard about these markets, but have not personally contacted each one, as we have the markets with descriptions. If you plan to visit one of these markets listed below, *please call first* to make sure they are still open. Flea markets do come and go. While they were open when we went to press, they may not be later. We can't be responsible. *Call first!*

**Athens:** J & J Flea Market, 11661 Commerce Rd. Tel: (706) 613-2410.

**Atlanta:** Dill Avenue Flea Traders, 883 Dill Ave SW. Tel: (404) 752-9180.

**Atlanta:** Flea Market USA, 1919 Stewart Ave SW. Tel: (404) 763-3078.

**Atlanta:** Five Points Flea Market, 82 Peachtree St SW. Tel: (404) 681-9439.

**Atlanta:** Johnson's Flea Market, 279 Candler Rd SE. Tel: (404) 284-7478.

**Atlanta:** People Flea Market, 2649 ML King Jr Dr NW. Tel: (404) 699-2405.

**Atlanta:** Scavenger Hunt, 3438 Clairmont Rd NE. Tel: (404) 634-4948.

**Augusta:** Butler's Flea Market, 1772 Broad St. Tel: (706) 737-3100.

**Augusta:** Judy's Flea Market, 3678 Peach Orchard Rd. Tel: (706) 771-0039.

**Augusta:** King's Flea Market, 3035 Milledgeville Rd. Tel: (706) 738-9555.

**Augusta:** Pioneer Junction Flea Market, 3201 Milledgeville Rd. Tel: (706) 667-0903.

**Bainbridge:** Joe's Flea Market, 1329 3 St. Tel: (912) 243-9585.

**Blakely:** Blakely Flea Market, 556 N Main St. Tel: (912) 723-6056.

**Bonaire:** Bonaire Flea Market, 409 GA Hwy 96. Tel: (912) 329-9865.

**Bowdon Junction:** Georgia Flea Market, Hwy 27. Tel: (770) 832-6551.

**Bowman:** Bomart, 89 E Church St. Tel: (706) 245-5557.

**Brunswick:** Brunswick Flea & Farmers' Market, 204 Old Jesup Rd. Tel: (912) 267-6787.

**Cairo:** C & C Flea Market, 221 1 Ave NE. Tel: (912) 377-8906.

**Calhoun:** Old South Flea Market, 1419 N Hwy 41. Tel: (706) 624-0602.

**Canton:** Guffey's Trading Post, 2484 Marietta Hwy. Tel: (770) 479-9201.

**Cartersville:** Brock's Flea Market, Joe Frank Harris Pkwy NW. Tel: (770) 386-4731.

**Cedartown:** Cedar Creek Flea Market, 591 West Ave. Tel: (770) 748-6916.

**Cedartown:** R & M Flea Market, 1573 Buchanan Hwy. Tel: (770) 748-0467.

**Centerville:** Snay's Flea Market, 2806 Watson Blvd. Tel: (912) 953-7245.

**Chamblee:** Buford Highway Flea Market, 5000 Buford Hwy NE 224. Tel: (770) 452-7140.

**Clarkston:** Clarkston Flea Market, 4222 E Ponce de Leon Ave. Tel: (404) 292-0059.

**Cleveland:** Henry's Mountain Flea Market, Hwy 129 S. Tel: (706) 865-1716.

**Cochran:** Rainbow's End Flea Market, 100 Mendal Ln SW. Tel: (912) 934-1221.

**Colquitt:** Collins, 167 S Cuthbert St. Tel: (912) 758-5055.

**Commerce:** Banks Crossing Flea Market, 884 E Ridgeway Rd. Tel: (706) 335-6541.

**Conyers:** Rockdale Flea Market, 2574 Old Covington Hwy SW. Tel: (770) 860-0204.

**Cornelia:** 365 Flea Market, 3399 State Hwy 365. Tel: (706) 776-9262.

**Crawford:** Willis Flea Market, Hutchinson Rd. Tel: (706) 743-8965.

**Cumming:** Another Flea Market, 3850 Georgia Hwy 400. Tel: (770) 887-0959.

**Cumming:** Cumming Antique & Flea Market, 337 Dahlonega Rd. Tel: (770) 844-7059.

**Cumming:** Dixie 400 Flea Market, 4750 Settingdown Cir. Tel: (770) 889-5895.

**Dahlonega:** Seabolt's Flea Market, Hwy 19 N. Tel: (706) 864-1007.

**Dalton:** N Georgia Farmers' Market, 310 Legion Dr. Tel: (706) 278-6369.

**Dalton:** North Hills Flea Market, 2208 Cleveland Hwy. Tel: (706) 259-1875.

**Dalton:** Walnut Grove Flea Market, 2815 Airport Rd. Tel: (706) 278-2277.

**Danielsville:** All American Flea Market, RR 1. Tel: (706) 795-5550.

**Dawsonville:** T & L Flea Market, 236 Hwy 53 W. Tel: (706) 265-3566.

**Decatur:** Flea Mart-Candler, 1954 Candler Rd. Tel: (404) 289-0804.

**Decatur:** Glenwood Flea Mart, 3900 Glenwood Rd. Tel: (404) 284-9139.

**Decatur:** 285 Flea Market, 4525 Glenwood Rd. Tel: (404) 289-4747.

**Dillard:** Rabun Flea Market, Hwy 441 N. Tel: (706) 746-2837.

**Eatonton:** J & B Flea Market, 288 Milledgeville Rd. Tel: (706) 484-0058.

**Edison:** Saul's Flea Market. Tel: (912) 835-3172.

**Elberton:** OK Flea Market, 1784 Fortson Dr. Tel: (706) 283-7333.

**Forest Park:** New South Atlanta Flea Market, 4140 Jonesboro Rd. Tel: (404) 363-6694.

**Geneva:** Dixie Flea Market, Hwy 80. Tel: (706) 269-2567.

**Gray:** 49 Flea Market, 1867 Hwy 49. Tel: (912) 986-4810.

**Greensboro:** Greensboro Flea Market, 1281 E Broad St. Tel: (706) 453-9424.

**Hampton:** Sweeties Flea Market, 2316 Hwy 19-41. Tel: (770) 946-4721.

**Hazlehurst:** Drucie's Flea Market, 106 Hinson St. Tel: (912) 375-9485.

**Jackson:** High Falls Flea Market, 4917 High Falls Rd. Tel: (912) 994-9770.

**Jesup:** Back Yonder Flea Market, 3343 Odum Hwy. Tel: (912) 588-0143.

**La Grange:** Bailey's Flea Market, 1308 Hogansville Rd. Tel: (706) 883-7902.

**La Grange:** Rockville Flea Market, 2266 Westpoint Rd. Tel: (706) 845-0507.

**Lake Park:** Bargainville Flea Market, 5465 Mill Store Rd. Tel: (912) 559-0141.

**Lawrenceville:** Action Point Flea Market, 524 Hwy 20 N. Tel: (770) 995-6781.

**Lawrenceville:** Stella's Flea Market, 524 Buford Dr. Tel: (770) 963-5943.

**Lithia Springs:** Bill's Flea Market, 4205 Bankhead Hwy. Tel: (770) 949-1188.

**Lithonia:** Lithonia Flea Mart, 6933 Main St. Tel: (770) 482-5263.

**Loganville:** Georgia Belle Flea Market, 524 Hwy 78. Tel: (770) 554-0072.

**Loganville:** Loganville Flea Market, Hwy 78. Tel: (770) 466-4223.

**Midville:** Midville Flea Market, 138 S Jones St. Tel: (912) 589-7681.

**Milledgeville:** Old World Flea Market, 2813 Irwinton Rd. Tel: (912) 453-1136.

**Moreland:** M & M Flea Market, 3481 S Hwy 29. Tel: (770) 254-1584.

**Oglethorpe:** Warehouse Flea Market, 131 Sumter St. Tel: (912) 472-8683.

**Oxford:** Brenda's Flea Market, 5503 Old Georgia Hwy 138 SW. Tel: (770) 787-8173.

**Rayle:** Rayle Flea Market, 5278 Lexington Rd. Tel: (706) 274-3594.

**Red Oak:** Reeves Flea Market, 3435 Roosevelt Hwy 2B. Tel: (404) 969-4089.

**Ringgold:** Great New York Flea Market, 143 Park Industrial Blvd. Tel: (706) 858-0188.

**Rutledge:** Bruceville Trading Post Flea, 7170 Atlanta Hwy. Tel: (706) 557-1800.

**Savannah:** John's Barn & Flea Market, 103 Sunshine Ave. Tel: (912) 238-3532.

**Smyrna:** New Windy Hill Flea Market, 1000 Windy Hill Rd SE. Tel: (770) 319-0444.

**Stone Mountain:** Stone Mountain Flea Market, 5615 Memorial Dr. Tel: (404) 294-8806.

**Stone Mountain:** Village Flea Market, 791 Main St. Tel: (770) 413-6436.

**Thomson:** Swap N Shop, 585 Augusta Hwy. Tel: (706) 595-8882.

**Thomaston:** Cecil's Flea Market, 3131 Barnesville Hwy. Tel: (706) 647-2258.

**Toccoa:** Carol's Flea Market, 5178 Williams Cir. Tel: (706) 779-5136.

**Tybee Island:** Tybee Flea Market, 802 1 St. Tel: (912) 786-9244.

**Valdosta:** Valdosta Flea Market, 407 N St Augustine Rd. Tel: (912) 333-0330.

**Warner Robins:** Crossroads, 101 Elberta Rd. Tel: (912) 918-0440.

**Washington:** Flea Market, 324 Hospital Dr. Tel: (706) 678-7195.

**Waycross:** Chrystal's Fleamarket, 1631 Genoa St. Tel: (912) 283-9808.

**West Point:** Hood's Flea Market, 710 3 Ave. Tel: (706) 643-4771.

**Winder:** B & B Flea Market, 186 W May St. Tel: (770) 868-8310.

**Woodbine:** Eudell's Flea Market, 300 Bedell Ave Hwy 17. Tel: (912) 576-3600.

# HAWAII

## AIEA
### Kam Super Swap Meet

**DATES:** Wednesday, Saturday, Sunday, and most holidays. Rain or shine.

**TIMES:** 5:00 AM-3:00 PM.

**ADMISSION:** $.25, children under 12 free. Parking is free.

**LOCATION:** 98-850 Moanalua Rd, across from the Pearlridge Shopping Center.

**DESCRIPTION:** This outdoor meet started in 1966. There are hundreds of dealers in Polynesian and Hawaiian crafts and collectibles, new items, slightly used items, fresh produce, milk caps, ethnic delicacies, fresh island fish, and much more. You will also find a varied assortment of clothes and Polynesian-made arts and crafts. Food is available on the premises.

**DEALER RATES:**

**Unreserved Sellers:** $10 per stall Saturday and Sunday, $9 Wednesday and weekday holidays.

**Reserved Sellers:** Monthly reservations are $19 per stall per day of the week, for an entire month (i.e. a month of Sundays, a month of Wednesdays). Holidays are free to reserved sellers. There is also a daily charge for reserved sellers: $8 per Saturday and Sunday, $7 per Wednesday and weekday holiday.

**Marketplace Sellers:** $75 per stall per day per month (i.e. a month of Sundays, etc.) for Saturdays and Sundays; $60 per stall per day per month for Wednesdays.

**CONTACT:** Kam Super Swap Meet, Kam Drive-In Theatre, PO Box 1359, Aiea HI 96701-1359. Tel: (808) 483-5933 recorded message and instructions or (808) 483-5535 between 7:30 AM-1:30 PM to speak to someone. Fax: (808) 847-9270.

## HONOLULU
### Aloha Flea Market

**DATES:** Wednesday, Saturday, Sunday and some holidays. The week before Christmas open every day.

**TIMES:** 6:00 AM-3:00 PM.

**ADMISSION:** $.50 per person. Children 12 and under are free. Parking is free.

**LOCATION:** Aloha Stadium. Right across the street from the Arizona Memorial in Pearl Harbor. Fifteen minutes from Waikiki.

**DESCRIPTION:** This market opened in 1979 and averages 1,200 vendors selling shirts, antiques, collectibles, diving gear, tools, sporting goods, shoes, and new and used merchandise. During the holiday season, the dealer ranks swell to monumental proportions. Rows of shade trees line the market, so it stays cool. Of course, it offers the ideal weather. No flammables are allowed. Food and restrooms are on the premises. This is the largest market in the state of Hawaii and "on a per capita basis, the largest in the US."

**DEALER RATES:** Wednesday $10-$42.75 per space; Saturday $10.75-$42.75; Sunday $12.75-$42.75 per stall. One of the four stall sizes is 18' × 20'. Reservations are not required.

**CONTACT:** Aloha Flea Market, 3472 Walalae Ave, Honolulu HI 96816. Tel: (808) 486-1529 or (808) 732-9611. Web: www.thisweek.com/AlohaFleaMarket.html.

# IDAHO

## BOISE
### Spectra's Flea Market

**DATES:** Saturday and Sunday, usually the second or third week of September through March. Do call, as the dates depend on the availability of the Fairgrounds buildings. 2000: January 15-16, February 26-27, April 15-16 for starters.

**TIMES:** Saturday 9:00 AM-6:00 PM. Sunday 10:00 AM-4:00 PM.

**ADMISSION:** $1. Parking is free.

**LOCATION:** West Idaho Fairgrounds. From Chinden Blvd to the corner of Glenwood and Chinden. Look for the market.

**DESCRIPTION:** This exceptionally clean indoor market has been around for "15-20" years with 130-180 dealers selling mostly antiques, collectibles, memorabilia, candy, jerky, furniture, Tupper Ware and some new merchandise. There are snack bars and handicapped-accessible restrooms on site as well as special access.

**DEALER RATES:** $50 per 10' × 10' "in-line" space, $60 for a corner space. Reservations are required, as well as a 50% deposit. Table and electric are available.

**CONTACT:** Sam Jones, Spectra Productions, PO Box 333, 4149 W State St, Eagle ID 83616-4439. Tel: (208) 939-6426 or 1-800-635-2274. Fax: (208) 939-6437.

## CASCADE
### Cascade Flea Market

**DATES:** Daily if the dealers want to, mid-May through the first weekend in October. But mainly Friday through Sunday.

**TIMES:** 9:00 AM-6:00 PM.

**ADMISSION:** Free. Parking is free.

**LOCATION:** In front of the Cascade Airport, Hwy 55. Out of Boise north on Hwy 55 to Cascade. Watch for the all the state flags flying!

**DESCRIPTION:** Opened in 1992, this small growing market of 25-35 vendors is held outdoors next to an airport. They have a nice, clean, family oriented market with vendors selling antiques, collectibles, Indian crafts and jewelry, old license plates and bumper stickers, clothes, music tapes and CDs, and whatever. Most of their vendors return every year, bringing pals along. When the necessaries are needed, there are handicapped-accessible restrooms on site as well as a snack bar. Located in a tourist's paradise of hunting, fishing (serious trout fishing here, folks), hiking—the usual extraordinary mountain pleasures—this market has plenty of new faces visiting all the time.

**DEALER RATES:** $25 per 20' × 40' space outside for Friday through Sunday, plus $3 per day electric if needed. $8 per day with electric if the dealer wants to stay all week. Reservations are suggested if you wish to use electric. Thursday is a free day, used for set up. There are RV facilities nearby for dealers who wish to stay all week, but only if selling during the entire stay.

**CONTACT:** Ron and Glenna Young, Cascade Flea Market, PO Box 399, Cascade ID 83611-0399. Tel: (208) 382-4894 (Young's home) or 382-3600 during the season.

---

**Mushies!!**

Note: You may find that a dealer isn't at his or her post—as the Morell mushrooms hide around here. Many have been known to bug-out in search of the delicacies. So, if you see dealers sneaking off, you have an idea where they are going.

---

# KETCHUM-SUN VALLEY—WARM SPRINGS VILLAGE
## Antique Peddler's Fair Antique Show

**DATES:** July 4th weekend and Labor Day weekend, each year. Rain or shine.

**TIMES:** 9:00 AM-7:00 PM.

**ADMISSION:** Free. Free parking is available.

**LOCATION:** In Warm Springs Village, Ketchum-Sun Valley. On world-famous Picaboo St at the base of the ski lift.

**DESCRIPTION:** This show first opened in 1970 in the heart of Wood River Valley, Ketchum and Sun Valley. It is Idaho's largest antique market with over 125 dealers coming from Maine to California bringing wonderful antiques, Oriental carpets, rare books and fine art. There is always a large selection of furniture, Indian and Oriental collectibles, china, high-end jewelry, loads of silver, and vintage clothes, to name a few. Their Labor Day Weekend show is "Wagon Days Celebration" with parades of wagons, rodeo, "shoot-em outs" and plenty to keep everyone busy (including buying awesome goodies).

Because of its extraordinary natural beauty, this area has become a summer playground offering guided pack and river trips, hiking, swimming, fantastic fishing and ice shows featuring the champions. These shows attract many famous people including Olympic athletes and some Hollywood stars who have homes in the area. Food is served on the premises.

**DEALER RATES:** $185 per 10' × 12' space, for all three days. Reservations are required. Bring your own canopy and booth setup.

**CONTACT:** Jan Perkins or Jeffrey, 2902 Breneman St, Boise ID 83703. Tel: (208) 345-0755 or 368-9759.

---

**Interesting Note**

Jan wants you to know that "Sun Valley is the first destination ski resort in the country, started by the Union Pacific Railroad and Averill Harriman—and had the first chair lifts in the world." (Betcha Mad River Glen has the oldest still-running original chair lift in the world... and Heaven help the person who tries to change it!)

---

# SAGLE
## Sagle Flea Market

**DATES:** Saturday, Sunday, and holidays, May through September.

**TIMES:** Whenever, but at least 8:00 AM to dark.

**ADMISSION:** Free. Parking is free.

**LOCATION:** 130 Algoma Spur Rd. Just 40 miles north of Coeur d'Alene in the panhandle of Idaho.

**DESCRIPTION:** Opened in 1979, this market has 100 dealer spaces full of dealers (some hog more than one space) selling "anything used," including garage sale goodies, livestock (not too badly worn), crafts, and produce. When they say "livestock" they aren't kidding—llamas were the big thing in 1999. There is a snack bar and handicapped-accessible restrooms on site. Occasionally, antique donkey engines show up, as well as a "Wilfred Brimley" look-alike dealer selling tools who threatens to charge for the autographs, he gets so much attention.

**DEALER RATES:** $10 for open 10' × 12' space per day, $12 per 12' × 12' space covered per day. Reservations are required.

**CONTACT:** Allen or Sonny, Sagle Flea Market, 130 Algoma Rd, Sagle ID 83860. Tel: (208) 263-2244. Email: asbono@sisna.com.

---

### Hot Doggity

Several years ago, the owners purchased a new batch and type of hot dog from the local meat packing plant for their snack bar. It was so popular that locals started calling the plant looking for the "Sagle" hot dog. The packing plant hadn't a clue—at first.

---

# ILLINOIS

## ALSIP
### Tri-State Swap O Rama

**DATES:** Every Saturday and Sunday. Rain or shine.

**TIMES:** 7:00 AM-4:00 PM.

**ADMISSION:** $.75 per person. Free parking available for 3,500 cars.

**LOCATION:** 4350 W 129th St. Take I-294 to Cicero Avenue (Rt 50) south to 131st, east to Door or Pulaski Rd to 129th west.

**DESCRIPTION:** The Tri-State Swap O Rama is held both indoors and outdoors. Started in 1979, there are now 700 to 900 dealers selling antiques, fresh produce, meats, collectibles, and new merchandise. In 1997, they added another 1,000 parking spaces and a new wing accommodating 200 more dealers. Food is served on the premises.

**DEALER RATES:** $20 for space that measures 8' × 12' indoors or $18 per 12' × 24' outdoor booth. Advance reservations are suggested.

**CONTACT:** Jim Pierski, Swap O Rama, 4600 W Lake St, Melrose Park IL 60160. Tel: (708) 344-7300.

## BLOOMINGTON
### 3rd Sunday Market

**DATES:** Third Sunday May through November.

**TIMES:** 8:00 AM-4:00 PM.

**ADMISSION:** $4.50, children under 13 free. Parking is free. Early-bird Saturday admission: $25 for one, $40 for two people.

**LOCATION:** Interstate Center at the McLean County Fairgrounds. Take Exit 160B off I-39, or I-74, or I-55.

**DESCRIPTION:** Started in 1987, this market of 450 dealers sells only antiques and collectibles. There are 275 antiques dealers inside an Expo Center that is 2½ acres under roof, the rest either under a polebarn or in the open. There is plenty of food available and handicapped-accessible restrooms. Because Don and Carol are experts on antiques and collectibles themselves, the market is consistent in its quality of goods.

**DEALER RATES:** Expo Center: $95-$240 per space. Polebarn: $110-$125. Outside: $75-$120. Reservations are suggested.

**CONTACT:** Don and Carol Raycraft, PO Box 396, Bloomington IL 61761-0369. Tel: (309) 452-7926.

## Serendipity

One cold, miserable, market day, an older man approached Don carrying a paper bag, looking quite stunned. Don, noticing his demeanor, asked him what happened. The gentleman explained that he collected tobacco tins. For 40 years he had searched for the elusive yellow one. He had heard about them, read about them, but had never seen one, much less owned one. Tobacco tins come in red, green, and the elusive yellow. The yellow ones are rare and worth $1,500 according to the gent. And he had plenty of red and green ones. It was that yellow prize that eluded him.

Until that day. He had come into the market on early-bird admission, just to see what was there. As he turned to look at something else—a yellow spot caught his eye.

*Yes!* His heart pounding, he reached for the prized yellow tin. Quite prepared to lay out $1,500 for this gem, he turned the tin over and marked on the bottom was $12.95. *Huh?*

Trembling, he inquired of the dealer as to how much the dealer *really* wanted.

The dealer took back the tin and turned it over—"$11 bucks."

Sold.

## Authors Note

Don and Carol have written 55 books on antiques and collectibles. Have any questions? And yes, some of the book dealers at the market sell their books. Their latest, published by Wallace Homestead, is *Price Guide to American Country Antiques*. It just came out in November 1999.

# CHICAGO
## Ashland Avenue Swap-O-Rama

**DATES:** Thursday, Saturday and Sunday.
**TIMES:** Thursday 8:00 AM-7:00 PM; Saturday and Sunday 7:00 AM-4:00 PM.
**ADMISSION:** $.50 per person; free parking.
**LOCATION:** 4100 S Ashland Ave, 1 mile west of I-94, near White Sox Park.
**DESCRIPTION:** Started in 1990, there are now 800 to 1,000 indoor and outdoor dealers exhibiting fresh produce and new and used merchandise.

Described as "very ethnic and cosmopolitan," this market now claims to be the largest in the Chicago area. Three restaurants serve the hungry.

**DEALER RATES:** $20 per 12' × 8' inside space; $18 per 24' × 12' outside space. Reservations are suggested.

**CONTACT:** Jim Pierski, Swap O Rama, 4600 W Lake St, Melrose Park IL 60160. Tel: (708) 344-7300.

## New Maxwell Street Market

**DATES:** Sundays, year round.

**TIMES:** 7:00 AM-3:00 PM.

**ADMISSION:** Free. Parking is free where you can find it. Or there is $3 parking on Clinton and 14th Pl.

**LOCATION:** Canal and Roosevelt Sts on Canal between Taylor St and Depot Pl.

**DESCRIPTION:** The New Maxwell Street Market is a continuation of the former one started blocks away in the early 1900s. From 350 to 500 dealers sell just about anything you could imagine. However, if you love antiques and fine collectibles, get there especially early and follow or race ahead of the other dealers scarfing up the real treasures. There is plenty of clothing, Mexican and African art and crafts, tons of food including the famous Maxwell Street Polish sausages, tools, toys, household necessities—just about anything. There are the appropriate relief facilities dotted around the market, as well as security. Plenty of great music from renowned blues artists adds to the festivities.

**DEALER RATES:** $10 for a table and table-sized space, if lucky enough to get one. $30 for a selling space with place for a vehicle. *You must have a license before you can sell.* Reservations are mandatory. This is how they are done: The first Thursday of the month the fax line is used only for "alternate" dealers (non-permanent, or those without assigned spaces) to call in and get put on the Alternate List for the month. When a permanent dealer doesn't take the assigned spot that weekend, then the alternates are called in order. Keeps people from lining up for 12 hours just to get a space. The office is open to get your license Wednesday through Friday 10:00 AM-6:00 PM; Saturday 7:00 AM-1:00 PM; Sunday 5:00 AM-2:00 PM.

**CONTACT:** Job Menchaca, New Maxwell Street Market, 548 W Roosevelt Rd, Chicago IL 60607. Tel: (312) 922-3100. Fax: (312) 922-3169 (also used solely for reservations the first Thursday of the month). Web: www.openair.org/maxwell/newmax.html.

# DIXON
## Sauk Valley Community College Flea Market

**DATES:** Third Sunday in January.

**TIMES:** 9:00 AM-4:00 PM.

**ADMISSION:** $1.50, parking is free.

**LOCATION:** Sauk Valley Community College on Rt 2 between Dixon and Sterling.

**DESCRIPTION:** Started in 1987 as a fundraiser for the college, this market boasts 75-100 dealers selling primarily antiques, collectibles and more. There are special guests and special collections to view. The proceeds from this market are used to benefit the sports program at the college. The college athletes run the food concessions as part of the fundraising effort.

**DEALER RATES:** $45 for a 3-table setup; $65 for 5-table setup. Reservations are required. Note: these were the prices in 1998. They can't seem to make up their minds.

**CONTACT:** Sauk Valley Community College, 173 IL Rt 2, Dixon IL 61021-9188. Tel: (815) 288-5511.

# MELROSE PARK
## Melrose Park Swap-O-Rama

**DATES:** Every Friday, Saturday and Sunday.

**TIMES:** 7:00 AM-4:00 PM Saturday and Sunday; Fridays 8:00 AM-3:00 PM.

**ADMISSION:** $.50 per person. Free parking is available for 1,000 cars.

**LOCATION:** 4600 W Lake St, at corner of Lake St (Rt 20) and Mannheim Rd (Rt 45).

**DESCRIPTION:** Started in 1975, 450 dealers both indoors and outdoors offer antiques, fine art, arts and crafts, fresh produce, collectibles, and new merchandise. Food is served on the premises.

**DEALER RATES:** $20 per 12' × 8' space inside, and $17 per 12' × 24' space outside. Reservations are suggested.

**CONTACT:** Jim Pierski, Swap O Rama, 4600 W Lake St, Melrose Park IL 60160. Tel: (708) 344-7300.

# PECATONICA
## The "Pec-Thing" Antique and Flea Market

**DATES:** Third Sunday weekend in May and September.

**TIMES:** 8:00 AM-5:00 PM.

**ADMISSION:** $2 per person. Plenty of free parking is available.

**LOCATION:** Winnebago County Fairgrounds, 7th and 4th St entrances. One mile north of US Rt 20 on Pecatonica Rd.

**DESCRIPTION:** Started in 1980, this market operates both indoors and out. Over 400 dealers sell antiques, collectibles, handmade crafts, and new and used items. All food must pass Fair Board approval. Several local homes are listed in the National Registry. Breakfast and lunch are served on the premises by one restaurant and six snack bars. Just in case, there are handicapped-accessible restrooms.

**DEALER RATES:** Outside Spaces: $25 (20' × 25' frontage by 10' × 15' deep). Open Shed Spaces: $35 (24' × 8', roof over top, dirt floor). Inside Spaces: $50 (average 16' × 10', cement floor). Table Rental: $7 (8' tables, advanced rental only). Vendor setup on Friday before show from 9:00 AM until 9:00 PM. Gates open to vendors at 6:00 AM Saturday and Sunday. Full payment is required to reserve space. Space may be available at the gate during setup hours on a first-come, first-serve basis. Cash only at the gate. Visa/Mastercard accepted.

**CONTACT:** Manager, PO Box K, Pecatonica IL 61063. Tel: (815) 239-1641 or 1-800-238-3587. Fax: 815-239-1653. Web: www.winnebagocountyfair.com.

## ROCKFORD
### Sandy Hollow Antique and Flea Market

**DATES:** Every Saturday and Sunday. Rain or shine.

**TIMES:** 8:00 AM-5:00 PM.

**ADMISSION:** Free admission and parking.

**LOCATION:** Alpine/Sandy Hollow Rd at 3913 Sandy Hollow Rd. Take Hwy 20 to Alpine exit, go north to Sandy Hollow, then west 1½ blocks.

**DESCRIPTION:** Started in 1976 at Alpine Village. At the current location, this market has room for 200 dealers outside and 60 indoors, offering antiques, fresh produce, collectibles (books, records, coins, baseball cards, etc.), and new merchandise. A food grill serves the famished, and just in case there are handicapped-accessible restrooms.

**DEALER RATES:** $25 per weekend for space measuring 10' × 12' inside (dealers must furnish own tables). Reservations are required in advance for indoor space only. $10.00 setup fee outdoors.

**CONTACT:** Carol A. Fritsch, 6350 Canyon Wood Dr, Rockford IL 61109. Tel: (815) 397-6683.

# ROSEMONT
## Wolff's Flea Market
**DATES:** Sundays, April through October.

**TIMES:** 7:00 AM-3:00 PM.

**ADMISSION:** $1 adults, $.50 seniors and children 6-12, under 6 free. Parking is free.

**LOCATION:** Allstate Arena (formerly the Rosemont Horizon), 6920 N Mannheim. Take I-90 west to Lee St Exit near intersection of I-90 and I-294. Literally on the Chicago city line, just 2 miles from Chicago (in the O'Hare flight path—watch the planes!).

**DESCRIPTION:** This outdoor summer market started in 1991 and has over 400 dealers selling antiques, collectibles, crafts, produce, coins, stamps, cards, garage sale goodies, furniture, and new merchandise. Two snack bars and handicapped-accessible restrooms add to the amenities.

**DEALER RATES:** $25 per 25' × 18' space. Reservations are not required. Monthly reservations available for an additional $15.

**CONTACT:** David Wolff, 970 Arkansas, Elk Grove IL 60007. Tel: (847) 524-9590 or (630) 833-7469. Fax: (630) 932-1129.

---

**Pricey Fads**

Someone sold a Peanuts Royal Blue Elephant Beanie Baby here for over $5,000!

---

# SANDWICH
## Sandwich Antiques Market
**DATES:** Held six times each summer, May through October. 2000: May 21 (3rd Sunday), June 18, July 23, August 20, September 24, October 22. Check for the same Sundays each year.

**TIMES:** 8:00 AM-4:00 PM.

**ADMISSION:** $5 per person. Parking is free.

**LOCATION:** The Fairgrounds, SR 34. From I-88, Sugar Grove Exit to Rt 30 to Hinckley. Follow signs on west side of Hinckley. Just 60 miles west of Chicago.

**DESCRIPTION:** Started in 1988, this 160-acre shaded indoor-outdoor market attracts 550 dealers selling only top-quality antiques and collectibles. It is the only market in Illinois where dealers must give a 10-day money-back guarantee that the merchandise is as represented. There is a furniture delivery service available. A cafeteria and several snack concessions recharge the shopping batteries making handicapped-accessible restrooms welcome.

**DEALER RATES:** $100 per 25' × 25' outside booth: $95 per 10' × 10' inside booth. Reservations are required.

**CONTACT:** Robert C Lawler, Show Manager, Sandwich Antiques Market, 1510 N Hoyne, Chicago IL 60622-1804. Tel: (773) 227-4464. Day of show call: (815) 786-3337. Fax: (773) 227-6322. Email: robert@antiquemarkets.com. Web: www.antiquemarkets.com.

# ST CHARLES
## Kane County Flea Market

**DATES:** First Sunday of every month and preceding Saturday afternoon. Unless the Sunday falls on Easter or New Year's Day, then it is the following weekend. Rain or shine. 2000: January 8-9, February 5-6, March 4-5, April 1-2, May 6-7, June 3-4, July 1-2, August 5-6, September 2-3, 30, October 1, November 4-5, December 2-3.

**TIMES:** Saturday 12:00 PM-5:00 PM; Sunday 7:00 AM-4:00 PM.

**ADMISSION:** $5, children under 12 are free. Free parking is available.

**LOCATION:** Kane County Fairgrounds (Randall Rd); west side of St Charles between Rt 64 and Rt 38.

**DESCRIPTION:** Having started with a humble 35 dealers in 1967, there are currently as many as 1,400 dealers (average 1,200 in summer, 800 in winter) selling antiques, fine art, collectibles, coins, fancy "junque" and the occasional new merchandise. Dealers, shoppers and collectors have come from as far away as Korea and all over the United States to shop here. "If you can't find it at Kane County, it was probably never made." There are four indoor buildings for winter months, and nine indoor buildings and seven sheds for summer months. This market has been listed in *Good Housekeeping* as one of the top 25 markets in the United States. So popular is this market, it prompted a local minister to ask: "Would Jesus skip church to shop at the Kane County Flea Market?" Plenty of good food, served by two restaurants and several snack bars, including country-style breakfast, is served on the premises.

**DEALER RATES:** Shed space at $105, North Main building $125, Stripe Buildings at $105 per space; $115 per weekend for a 10' × 20' space outdoors (cash only). Advance reservations are required for space under cover only; outside space is first come, first served. Setup Saturday at 9:00 AM. There is a parking lot in back for dealers.

**CONTACT:** Helen Robinson, Kane County Flea Market Inc, PO Box 549, St Charles IL 60174-0549. Tel: (630) 377-2252. Fax: (630) 377-2989. Web: www2.pair.com/kaneflea.

# SYCAMORE
## Antique, Craft, and Flea Market

**DATES:** The last full weekend in October.

**TIMES:** 9:00 AM-5:00 PM.

**ADMISSION:** $2 for adults; $1 senior citizens and students K-12; under 5 free. Free parking is available.

**LOCATION:** At the Sycamore High School. Take Rt 23 south through downtown Sycamore to the south edge of town. Turn onto Spartan Trail at stop light on Rt 23. Sycamore is only 65 miles northwest of Chicago on Rt 64.

**DESCRIPTION:** This indoor craft fair and flea market, started in 1973 and currently consisting of 155 dealer booths, is operated by the Sycamore Music Boosters. It is run in conjunction with Sycamore's Annual Pumpkin Festival, which includes a variety of activities on that weekend, such as carved and decorated pumpkins on the Court House lawn (approximately 1,000), 10K race on Sunday, food booths, carnival, craft shows, and a giant parade Sunday afternoon. Proceeds from all activities associated with the weekend are used to support non-profit organizations in the community. It is estimated that approximately 100,000 people visit the community over Pumpkin Festival weekend. The Antique, Craft and Flea Market is a juried show which in the past has had handcrafted items, candies, handcarved wood products and other non-commercial goods produced by artists. There are antiques and collectibles as well as the usual flea market fare. Food is available on the grounds. A shuttle bus provides transportation between the school and the downtown area for $.50 per person. A "stroller park" is available, with attendants, as strollers are not allowed in the market.

**DEALER RATES:** $80 for a 9' × 12' or 10' × 12' booth; reservations required.

**CONTACT:** Sycamore Music Boosters, PO Box 432, Sycamore IL 60178-0432. (Show chairmen change yearly.) Day of show call Beverly Smith at (815) 895-6750.

# TOWANDA
## Towanda Antique Flea Market

**DATES:** Every July 4th. Rain or shine.

**TIMES:** 9:00 AM-5:00 PM.

**ADMISSION:** Free. Free parking is available.

**LOCATION:** Northwest of Bloomington, Illinois, on I-55. Take Exit 171.

**DESCRIPTION:** Started in 1968, the show has grown larger every year and currently features 250 dealers outdoors selling antiques, arts and crafts, collectibles, and new merchandise. This market has become known as a buyer's market because of the fair prices. Food is available on the premises. Since this is a July 4th activity, expect the usual festivities and fireworks.

**DEALER RATES:** $30 per 12' × 12' space. Reservations are required.

**CONTACT:** Lyle and Mary Merritt, PO Box 97, Towanda IL 61776. Tel: the Merritts at (309) 728-2810 or Linda Potts at (309) 728-2384.


# WHEATON
## All-Night Flea Market

**DATES:** The weekend after the 3rd Sunday in August. 2000: the overnight of August 26-27, 2001: 25-26.

**TIMES:** 5:00 PM-9:00 AM.

**ADMISSION:** $5. Parking is free.

**LOCATION:** 2015 Manchester Rd. I-88 west to Naperville Rd, north to Rt 38, west to County Farm Rd, north to Manchester.

**DESCRIPTION:** This is the original outdoor overnight flea market. Hundreds of dealers come to sell whatever they can, from old to new stuff. Many concessions will refill you for more shopping, and handicapped-accessible restrooms provide relief. As they say, "Come for dinner, shop until breakfast."

**DEALER RATES:** $90-$130 for a 20' × 25' space. Reservations are necessary.

**CONTACT:** Faith Sugarman, All-Night Flea Market, PO Box 32, Itasca IL 60143-0032. Tel: (847) 455-6090. Email: lovesoldstuff@prodigy.net.


## DuPage Antique & Collectible Market

**DATES:** Third weekend of every month, except no show in July.

**TIMES:** 5:00 AM-3:00 PM.

**ADMISSION:** $3. Parking is free.

**LOCATION:** 2015 Manchester Rd. From O'Hare Airport, take 294 south to I-88 west to Naperville Rd. North to Rt 38 or Roosevelt Rd. West to County Farm Rd. North to Manchester Rd to the fairgrounds.

**DESCRIPTION:** This 28-year-old indoor/outdoor market has 200 dealers selling antiques and collectibles and whatever. There are handicapped-accessible restrooms and a food concession on site.

**DEALER RATES:** $50-$75 per space depending on location.

**CONTACT:** Faith J Sugarman, DuPage Antique & Collectible Market, PO Box 32, Itasca IL 60143-0032. Tel: (847) 455-6090. Email: lovesoldstuff@prodigy.net.

---

**Just Stepping Off**
The market butts up to the railroad line heading into Chicago. A couple of years ago during the market they noticed the conductor, after taking the coal train into Chicago, had hopped another train back to the market to go shopping!

---

## OTHER FLEA MARKETS

We know or have heard about these markets, but have not personally contacted each one, as we have the markets with descriptions. If you plan to visit one of these markets listed below, *please call first* to make sure they are still open. Flea markets do come and go. While they were open when we went to press, they may not be later. We can't be responsible. *Call first!*

**Belleville:** Fairgrounds Exposition Building, 200 S Belt E. Tel: (618) 235-0666.

**Belleville:** West Main Flea Market, 2615 W Main St. Tel: (618) 239-6038.

**Centralia:** Don's Flea Market & NASCAR, 3846 SR 161. Tel: (618) 533-2778.

**Chester:** River City Flea Market & Craft, 111 Market St. Tel: (618) 826-2460.

**Chicago:** 45th Arena Shoppers & Farmers' Market, 4545 S Western Blvd. Tel: (773) 843-0400.

**Chicago:** Buyer's Flea Market, 4545 W Division St. Tel: (773) 227-1889.

**Chicago:** Double Drive-In Flea Market, 2800 W Columbus Ave. Tel: (773) 925-9602.

**Chicago:** M P Flea Market, 7 S Pulaski Rd. Tel: (773) 826-1020.

**Chicago:** Morgan Kinzie Flea Market, 375 N Morgan St. Tel: (312) 455-8900.

**Chicago:** North Side Flea Market, 5906 N Clark St. Tel: (773) 334-8982.

**Chicago:** SMW Flea Market, 3850 S Indiana Ave. Tel: (773) 624-4172.

**Chillicothe:** Olde Tyme 4th of July, PO Box 321. Tel: (309) 274-2353. July 4 only.

**East St Louis:** Fairmont Flea Market, 5410 Collinsville Rd. Tel: (618) 271-9885.

**Elgin:** Elgin Flea Market, 840 N State St. Tel: (847) 622-9696.

**Franklin Park:** Galante, 2727 Mannheim Rd. Tel: (847) 455-6807.

**Gifford:** Gordyville Flea Market, Rt 136 E. Tel: (217) 568-7117. 2nd weekend monthly.

**Grafton:** Jacob's Flea Market, 126 & 128 E Main St. Tel: (618) 786-3689.

**Harvey:** Chicago/South Expo, 17040 S Halsted. Tel: (815) 469-1983.

**Itasca:** Itascafest Antique & Flea Market, PO Box 37. Tel: (630) 773-2697. 3rd weekend in July annually.

**Joliet:** Derald's Indoor Flea Market, 219 Maple St. Tel: (815) 723-0700.

**Joliet:** Preachers Flea Market, 1615 Maple Rd. Tel: (815) 726-0858.

**Joliet:** Save-A-Buck Flea Market, 379 S Chicago St. Tel: (815) 722-4918.

**Marengo:** Marengo Flea Market, 20023 E Grant Hwy. Tel: (815) 568-3532.

**Marion:** Williamson County Flea Market, 1701 E Main St. Tel: (618) 993-6721.

**Springfield:** Grandpa's Flea Market, 2719 S 11 St. Tel: (217) 544-7624.

**Tinley Park:** I-80 Flea Market, 19100 Oak Park Ave. Tel: (708) 532-8238.

**Waukegan:** Waukegan Flea Market, 1700 N Lewis Ave. Tel: (847) 662-9665.

**Wheeling:** Twin Flea Market, 1 E Hintz Rd. Tel: (847) 229-0909.

# INDIANA

## BROOKVILLE
### White Farmers' Market

**DATES:** Every Wednesday. Rain or shine.

**TIMES:** Daylight (really) to noon.

**ADMISSION:** Free. Free parking is available.

**LOCATION:** White's Farm on Holland Rd, 3 miles southeast of town on Hwy 52, 30 miles northwest of Cincinnati, Ohio.

**DESCRIPTION:** A combination flea market and livestock auction, this market was originally started by the present owner's grandfather in 1937. Currently there are between 350 and 400 dealers in summer and between 50 and 75 dealers in the winter selling antiques, arts and crafts, fresh produce and fruits, collectibles and new merchandise on a 160-acre farm. Amish baked goods are offered as well as farm fresh eggs and small animals such as ducks, rabbits and chickens. Don't miss the Chicken Man—he is amazing—as is his flock of creatures. Look for the fellow with a head full of feathers. Next door to the farm one can see and visit the oldest church in Indiana on its original foundation. The market is located in the scenic Whitewater Valley. Indoor setups are located in the farm's original granary and tobacco barns. The buildings have been refurbished in the original antique atmosphere. They have added more storage buildings for inside setups. Special events are held throughout the year.

**DEALER RATES:** $10 per 20' × 22' space outdoors. Reservations are not necessary for outside space, but are required for inside space. Inside spaces from $10 to $18, depending on size and location.

**CONTACT:** Dave or Paula White, 6119 Little Cedar Rd, Brookville IN 47012. Tel: (317) 647-3574 (business) or (317) 647-5360 if desperate.

## CANAAN
### Canaan Fall Festival

**DATES:** Second weekend in September. Rain or shine.

**TIMES:** Friday and Saturday 9:00 AM-10:00 PM; Sunday 9:00 PM-5:00 PM.

**ADMISSION:** Free. Free parking is available.

**LOCATION:** On the Canaan Village Square.

**DESCRIPTION:** Publicized as an old-fashioned event, this outdoor festival draws a very large crowd to this small village. Approximately 160 dealers sell a range of items from antiques and collectibles to craft items, fresh produce, and some new merchandise. Highlights include the longest-running annual Pony Express in the United States, plus many games, contests (including frog jumping and largest/smallest contest), and stage entertainment. On Saturday, the old-fashioned parade starts at 10:30 AM and features floats, bands, horses, a Postal Representative swearing in the Pony Express rider, and other events. The Fire Department's food concession does something special with its fish dish, it's a perennial favorite. The Kremer House Museum with three generations of furnishings was donated to the town in 1980 and is open to the public during this festival.

For those of you who need more exercise, they have added the 6K Yellow Britches Valley/Indian Trails Run/Walk. Enjoy!

**DEALER RATES:** $35 per 20' × 20' space outside for the entire weekend plus $5 for electric.

**CONTACT:** Gale H Ferris, President, Canaan Restoration Council Inc, 9713 N SR 62, Canaan IN 47224. Tel: (812) 839-4770.

---

### Wandering Pets

Years ago, a buffalo got loose from Rising Sun, a town in Ohio County, and wandered across two more counties and through the Canaan Fall Festival. He didn't seem to be a problem, just visiting, but he really had people wondering. By the time the wanderer got to the Proving Grounds, he was deemed a hazard to population and killed. But the people of Canaan haven't forgotten their buffalo visitor.

Ask Mr. Ferris about his rare poultry. He has been raising these special birds for 43 years. Hi, Gale!

---

# CEDAR LAKE
## Barn and Field Flea Market

**DATES:** Saturday and Sunday. Indoors year round, and outdoors weather permitting, usually just the summer.
**TIMES:** 8:00 AM-4:00 PM.
**ADMISSION:** Free. Parking is free.
**LOCATION:** 15049 Parrish Ave. W 151st Ave at corner of Parrish Ave, 1 mile east of Rt 41.

**DESCRIPTION:** Opened well over 20 years ago and housed in a 100-plus-year-old barn with permanent dealers, this country market specializes in antiques and collectibles, used merchandise, used furniture, glassware, lamps, and garage sale goodies. It's a great place for dealers to stock up for their travels. The number of dealers ranges from 20-150 or so, depending on the weather.

**DEALER RATES:** $10 per day for whatever space is needed outside and $15 per weekend. Just roll on in! Inside space is permanently rented, but they do have the occasional vacancy. If you wish to rent inside, call Pat for more information. There is overnight camping for dealers.

**CONTACT:** Pat, Barn and Field Flea Market, PO Box 411, Cedar Lake IN 46303-0411. Tel: (219) 696-7368.

## Uncle John's Flea Market

**DATES:** Saturday and Sunday, year round. Outdoors, weather permitting.
**TIMES:** 8:00 AM-4:00 PM.
**ADMISSION:** Free. Parking is free.
**LOCATION:** 15205 Wicker Ave, Rt 41, 9 mi south of Rt 30. Approximately 20-25 miles south of I-80-94 on Hwy 41 (Indianapolis Blvd) and approximately 10 miles west of I-65, between Rt 30 and SR 2.
**DESCRIPTION:** This market averages 150 dealers in 10 buildings (more in summer when the outdoor area is open) selling antiques, collectibles, garage sale goodies, new and used furniture, jewelry, books, produce, clothing, crafts, and new merchandise. When you get peckish, try the restaurant or snack bar and later the handicapped-accessible restrooms.
**DEALER RATES:** $10-$15 per 15' × something outdoor space. $60 and up per month per 12' × 12' for indoor space. Reservations are not required.
**CONTACT:** Uncle John's Flea Market, 15205 Wicker Ave, Cedar Lake IN 46303. Tel: (219) 696-7911.

# CENTERVILLE
## Big Bear Flea Market

**DATES:** Saturday and Sunday, April through October.
**TIMES:** 8:00 AM-4:00 PM.
**ADMISSION:** Free. Parking is free.
**LOCATION:** On I-70 at Centerville, Exit 145 at the southeast corner, 4 miles west of Richmond, Indiana, 45 miles west of Dayton, Ohio and 62 miles east of Indianapolis.

**DESCRIPTION:** Opened in July 1993, this market has plenty of space on 17 acres with 60 spaces under canopies. Their dealers sell everything from antiques and collectibles, crafts, and new merchandise to secondhand merchandise and produce. A concession stand, convenience store, a complete campground with RV hookups and restrooms add to the amenities.
**DEALER RATES:** $10 a day or $16 for 2 days. Reservations are not required.
**CONTACT:** Ed or Shelby Newman, 2131 N Centerville Rd, Centerville IN 47330. Tel: (765) 855-3912.

---

### Hey, Ladies

Ed tells of one lonely dealer who sells ladies' jewelry, a "very nice man" who wanted to put up a sign, "Looking for a wife who likes to travel and do flea markets." No problem with the Newmans. At last check, he still hadn't found his mate. Ladies, if you're interested, check in with the Newmans. Apparently they do keep an eye on him, just in case. If you happen to run into this chap, please update the Newmans.

Update 2000 — he's still looking, gals!

---

# FRANKLIN
## Gray Goose Collector's Fair

**DATES:** Second Saturday and Sunday, September through May.
**TIMES:** 9:00 AM-4:00 PM.
**ADMISSION:** Free admission and free parking.
**LOCATION:** At the Johnson County Fairgrounds on Fairgrounds St. Take I-65, Exit 90 (Rt 44), go west to Fairgrounds St, turn right.
**DESCRIPTION:** This indoor show began operation in 1966 and was sold to the present owners in 1994. It is southern Indiana's largest. Although a small market with 48-52 dealers, they carry a variety of strictly antiques and collectibles. This is a very friendly market with good dealers who are willing to go out of their way to help their customers. Concessions and a full kitchen provide food on the premises.
**DEALER RATES:** $65 for a 12' × 10' area and two tables inside; outside is $15. Reservations are required.
**CONTACT:** Doris Hubbell or Vicki Jordal, 753 Hillcrest Dr, Greenwood IN 46142. Tel: (317) 881-5719 (Doris) or Vicki at 888-6783.

# FRIENDSHIP
## Friendship Flea Market

**DATES:** Two nine-day shows. 2000: June 10-18; September 9-17. Call for 2001 dates. Generally, starting the second Saturday through the following Sunday a week later. Rain or shine.

**TIMES:** All day and night, really. At least by 9:00 AM.

**ADMISSION:** Free admission. Parking is available at $3 per vehicle.

**LOCATION:** On Hwy 62, 6 miles west of Dillsboro.

**DESCRIPTION:** Started in 1968, this indoor/outdoor market consists of approximately 500 dealers selling antiques, arts and crafts, fresh produce, collectibles such as guns, knives, and beads, and new merchandise. It is located on the grounds adjoining the National Muzzle Loading Rifle Association. Up to 100,000 people attend this event. Food is served on the premises. In 1984, this market was listed by *Good Housekeeping* magazine as one of the 25 best flea markets in the United States. It is the largest of the four markets within a half mile of each other. Every night of the market, a campfire is crackling with country music entertainment. They really mean it is open day and night!

**DEALER RATES:** $150 for nine days per 10' × 10' space indoors or a 20' × 20' space outdoors. Advance reservations are required.

**CONTACT:** Tom Kerr or Jan Hopkins, 654 Wayskin Dr, Covington KY 41015. Tel: (606) 356-7114. Days of the show call the flea market at (812) 667-5645.

# FT WAYNE
## Ft Wayne Flea Market

**DATES:** Friday, Saturday and Sunday, year round. Rain or shine.

**TIMES:** Friday 11:00 PM-7:00 PM, Saturday 10:00 AM-7:00 PM, Sunday 10:00 AM-6:00 PM.

**ADMISSION:** Free. Free parking is available.

**LOCATION:** Hwy 27 and S Hanna St.

**DESCRIPTION:** Opened on August 1, 1990, this already successful market has 153 dealers in an air-conditioned and heated building selling typical flea market fare including: t-shirts, tools, coins and quite a bit of new merchandise. For your convenience, a food concession is on the premises.

**DEALER RATES:** $45 for 15' × 10' or $65 for 15' × 20' per weekend. Reservations are suggested.

**CONTACT:** Kap Lee, Ft Wayne Flea Market, 6901 S Hanna St, Ft Wayne IN 46816. Tel: (219) 447-0081 Friday through Monday.

## Indiana Flea Market at Ft Wayne

**DATES:** 2000 dates: January 14-16, February 25-27, March 31-April 2, and November 10-12. Call for 2001 dates.
**TIMES:** Friday 3:00 PM-9:00 PM; Saturday 10:00 AM-7:00 PM; Sunday 11:00 AM-5:00 PM.
**ADMISSION:** $1. Parking is $2.
**LOCATION:** Allen County War Memorial Coliseum. Corner of Coliseum and Parnell Aves.
**DESCRIPTION:** This new market started in 1991 with 400 dealers selling antiques, collectibles, and the usual flea market everything. Already it is quite successful. Food is available on the premises.
**DEALER RATES:** $75 per 14' × 8' space; $113 per 21' × 8' space; $150 per 28' × 8' space. Reservations are required.
**CONTACT:** Stewart Promotions, 2950 Breckinridge Ln Ste 4A, Louisville KY 40220. Tel: (502) 456-2244 except Tuesday and Friday. Email: sp2950@earthlink.net. Web: www.stewartpromotions.com.

# GARY
## Market City

**DATES:** Friday, Saturday, and Sunday.
**TIMES:** 9:00 AM-5:00 PM.
**ADMISSION:** Free. Parking is free.
**LOCATION:** 4121 Cleveland St at 41st St.
**DESCRIPTION:** This market opened in 1990 and has been full ever since with all 250 inside booths filled. There is plenty of room outside for dealers with at least 20 hanging around through snow and good weather. In good weather, they average 60-100 dealers outside. Inside dealers sell about 80% new merchandise to 20% old, including electronics, clothing, shoes, jewelry, leather, and other new items. Outside is a grab-bag of garage sale goodies, clean-outs, and whatever happens by. Their inside kitchen serves meals and snacks, and just in case, there are handicapped-accessible restrooms.
**DEALER RATES:** Outside: $6 per day in the open area, $12 per day under roof. $35 and up per day inside—if they have room. Reservations are suggested only if you want to be under cover outside. If you are interested in the inside space, call Bill.

**CONTACT:** Bill House, Market City, 4121 Cleveland St, Gary IN 46408. Tel: (219) 887-3522.

# INDIANAPOLIS
## Indiana Flea Market

**DATES:** 2000: January 21-23, 23-25, February 18-20, March 10-12, April 14-16, June 16-18, July 14-16, September 22-24, October 27-29, November 24-26, December 8-10, 29-31. Three-day show monthly except for August during State Fair. Usually the second weekend each month, depending on availability of the fairgrounds.

**TIMES:** Friday noon to 7:00 PM; Saturday 10:00 AM-7:00 PM; Sunday 11:00 AM-5:00 PM. New Year's: Friday and Saturday 10:00 AM-7:00 PM; Sunday 11:00 AM-5:00 PM.

**ADMISSION:** Free. Parking $2.

**LOCATION:** Indianapolis State Fairgrounds.

**DESCRIPTION:** This indoor market opened in 1976 and hosts between 400 to 1,000 dealers depending on the seasons. There are special Antique and Country Craft shows scattered throughout their schedule in addition to the flea markets. Some of these scheduled events fill three buildings! The dealers sell mostly antiques, collectibles and flea market treasures. Food is available on the premises.

**DEALER RATES:** $75 ($85 New Year's) per 14' × 8' space; $113 ($128 New Year's) per 21' × 8' space; $150 ($170 New Year's) per 28' × 8' space depending on the building the show is housed in. Reservations are required and there is a waiting list.

**CONTACT:** Stewart Promotions, 2950 Breckinridge Ln Ste 4A, Louisville KY 40220. Tel: (502) 456-2244 (except Tuesday and Friday). Email: sp2950@earthlink.net. Web: www.stewartpromotions.com.

## Liberty Bell Flea Market

**DATES:** Friday through Sunday, year round.

**TIMES:** Friday 12:00 PM-8:00 PM; Saturday 10:00 AM-7:00 PM; Sunday 10:00 AM-6:00 PM.

**ADMISSION:** Free. Free parking is available.

**LOCATION:** 8949 E Washington St (US 40).

**DESCRIPTION:** This indoor/outdoor show has been operating for over 25 years. Over 88 dealers spread over 200 spaces (they like this market!) sell everything and anything from antiques, collectibles, carpet, furniture, a delightful fellow making leather goods, and new merchandise to produce (in season), meats, cheese, and handmade items. There is a snack bar on the grounds.

**DEALER RATES:** $45 per 12' × 14' booth per weekend. No advance reservations required, but call to make sure there is space. Inside in the winter gets pretty full, so call.

**CONTACT:** Noble Hall, Liberty Bell Flea Market, 8949 E Washington St, Indianapolis IN 46219. Tel: (317) 898-3180.

# LAPORTE
## Wildwood Park Flea Market

**DATES:** Saturday and Sunday, April 1st through October.
**TIMES:** 9:00 AM to whenever.
**ADMISSION:** Free. Parking is free.
**LOCATION:** At the junction of I-94—Hwy 20 and Hwy 35, Exit 40A, off I-94.
**DESCRIPTION:** Opened in 1978, this outdoor summer market, on lovely park-like grounds covered with oak and maple trees, hosts 120 dealers selling basically antiques, collectibles, produce and coins. There is an indoor antique mall on the grounds. A snack bar and restrooms are on site.
**DEALER RATES:** $10 per 20' × 25' space. Reservations are not required.
**CONTACT:** Wildwood Flea Market, 4938 W US 20 NE, LaPorte IN 46350. Tel: (219) 879-5660. Fax: (219) 879-0297.

# LAWRENCEBURG
## Tri-State Antique Market

**DATES:** Always the first Sunday of the month, from May through October.
**TIMES:** 7:00 AM-3:00 PM DST.
**ADMISSION:** $2 per adult. Free parking is available.
**LOCATION:** On Rt 50, 1 mile west from Exit 16, off I-275.
**DESCRIPTION:** Started in 1986, this indoor/outdoor market now draws 300 dealers from three surrounding states. The promoter of this show has said that this is where many shop owners come to stock their shelves and floor space, buying both furniture and small items. "Lots of good treasures." Only antiques and old collectibles are sold. Food is served on the premises.
**DEALER RATES:** $40 per 25' × 25' outside space paid in advance or $40 at site if available; $40 per 10' × 15' space indoors. Advance reservations are suggested. Early birds are admitted for advance shopping at 5:00 AM.
**CONTACT:** Bruce Metzger, PO Box 35, Shandon OH 45063-0035. Tel: (513) 738-7256. Web: www.queencityshows.com.

---

### Classic Market Tales

In 1989, there was a "dust devil" during the show. Hypnotized, the vendors and buyers watched this little mini-tornado form at the end of the fairgrounds. Slowly, it moved down the midway street of the market flipping tables, toppling cupboards, lifting cast-iron ware and dropping it through glass showcases, scattering the "smalls" and light-weight merchandise. After traveling about 100 feet, the twister stood still, lifted off the ground and retreated back to the rear of the grounds, leaving choking dust in the air and wreckage marking its route.

An editor of *Antique Week* was there holding down a table full of smalls to keep them from being sucked up in the twister. Unfortunately for him, protecting the smalls prevented him from shooting pictures of the incredible event!

Says Bruce Metzger, the promoter of this show: "No one was injured in this occurrence, although some merchandise sustained damage and some was just plain lost. It's a hell of a thing to be remembered for, but people still like to talk about the dust devil at Lawrenceburg."

---

## METAMORA
### Canal Days Flea Market

**DATES:** The first full weekend in October, Friday through Sunday. Rain or shine.

**TIMES:** All day Saturday and Sunday.

**ADMISSION:** Free. Parking is available at $3 to $5 per vehicle.

**LOCATION:** From Indianapolis, take US 52 east. From Cincinnati, go west on I-74 to Exit 169, then west on US 52, and then go 8 miles west of Brookville.

**DESCRIPTION:** An estimated 175,000 people attend this October weekend initiated as a continuation of the time, in the 1800s, when local farmers would set up along Main Street to unload their farm surplus. In 1969 a couple of guys got together and thought they'd restart an old tradition by setting up a few card tables next to the canal. The idea took over and grew. Obviously, its time had come. Currently over 700 dealers set up to sell antiques, fine art, arts and crafts, collectibles, and a little bit of new merchandise. Metamora is a lovely old town with a canal and canal boat pulled by horses, and there is an old grist mill which still operates. There are over 130 shops open May until December, and a passenger train runs on the weekends. There is a handicapped-accessible port-a-potty on site.

**DEALER RATES:** From $150 per 10' × 10' space for the three-day weekend and up depending on size space. Reservations are required. Setup on Thursday, but you can't conduct business until Friday.

**CONTACT:** Al and Pat Rogers, PO Box 76, Metamora IN 47030. Tel: (765) 647-2194.

---

**Historical Note**

A local gift shop was once the Farmers Merchants Bank, robbed by John Dillinger who left a bullet hole on an inside wall. Go look for it.

---

# MUNCIE
## Greenwalt's Flea Market

**DATES:** First weekend of every month September through May, except when September's first weekend falls on Labor Day, then it is the second weekend.

**TIMES:** 9:00 AM-5:00 PM on Saturday; 9:00 AM-4:00 PM on Sunday.

**ADMISSION:** Free admission and free parking.

**LOCATION:** At Delaware Fairgrounds-Memorial Building. Take I-69 to Muncie/Frankton Exit 332. Go approximately 7 miles (becomes McGalliard Avenue) to Wheeling Avenue, then turn south and go 7 blocks to the Fairgrounds.

**DESCRIPTION:** This indoor market, which opened in 1976, houses approximately 65-70 dealers selling antiques, collectibles, handmade/craft items, toys, jewelry, baseball cards and new merchandise. Food is available on the premises.

**DEALER RATES:** $35 a weekend for a 10' × 10' booth. Advance reservations are required.

**CONTACT:** Mary Greenwalt, 604 N Kettner Dr, Muncie IN 47304. Tel: (765) 289-0194.

# NASHVILLE
## Westward Ho! Flea Market

**DATES:** Saturday and Sunday, April through October. Three day weekends on Memorial Day, July 4th and Labor Day.

**TIMES:** 9:00 AM-5:00 PM.

**ADMISSION:** Free. Parking is free.

**LOCATION:** 4469 SR 46 E. Located 4½ miles east of Nashville on SR 46.

**DESCRIPTION:** This market features eight acres of shopping both in 100 shops or under roof on concrete floors. Priding themselves on being completely handicapped accessible, their dealers sell antiques, collectibles, leather, lace, hardware goods, ball cards, belts, buckles, paper goods, custom t-shirts, sweats, wicker baskets, perfumes, concrete lawn ornaments, jewelry, crocheted doilies, western wear, ribbons, craft supplies, spices and flavorings and more. There is plenty of food served by Larry under shady trellis' or in the open.

**DEALER RATES:** $9.50 per day per 9' × 10' space, electric included. Reservations would be nice.

**CONTACT:** Phyllis J Thompson, Westward Ho! Flea Market, PO Box 1167, Nashville IN 47448-1167. Tel: (812) 988-0750. Email: westwardhofm@hotmail.com. Web: www.gnawboneindiana.com/westwardhofleamarket.

# SCOTTSBURG
## Saw Mill Hill Flea Market

**DATES:** Wednesday through Sunday, year round.

**TIMES:** 8:00 AM-5:00 PM.

**ADMISSION:** Free. Parking is free.

**LOCATION:** Hwy 56 W. From I-65 take Exit 29 to Hwy 56 W about ¼ mile off the interstate.

**DESCRIPTION:** Opened in 1990, this indoor/outdoor market hosts 65 dealers inside year round and, weather permitting, lots outside. The dealers sell a fair amount of antiques and collectibles, groceries, tools, musical instruments, loads of household goods and whatever comes in. Their motto is: "If we ain't got it, it ain't worth having."

**DEALER RATES:** $21 per weekend inside, $5 per day outside. Reservations are suggested.

**CONTACT:** Michael E Davisson, Saw Mill Hill Flea Market, 1621 McClain Ave, Scottsburg IN 47170. Tel: 812-752-3551.

# SHIPSHEWANA
## Shipshewana Auction and Flea Market

**DATES:** Every Tuesday and Wednesday, May through October. Rain or shine.

**TIMES:** Tuesday 7:00 AM-5:00 PM, Wednesday 7:00 AM-3:00 PM.

**ADMISSION:** Free. $2 per car parking during June, July and August.

**LOCATION:** On SR 5 on the southern edge of Shipshewana, 160 miles north of Indianapolis, 50 miles east of South Bend and 100 miles south of Grand Rapids.

**DESCRIPTION:** This show first opened in 1922 selling six pigs, seven cows, and several head of young cattle. It moved to its present location in 1947. It is held both indoors and outdoors and accommodates approximately 800 dealers (fewer in winter) and has room for more. Just about anything you might want can be found at this market, from antiques and collectibles, to fine art, arts and crafts, to new merchandise, to fresh produce. There is also a Miscellaneous and Antique Auction every Wednesday at 8:00 AM, and a livestock auction at 11:00 AM. The widely known Horse and Tack Sale is held on Fridays at 9:00 AM and always draws a full house of spectators. One full-service and three fast-food restaurants, one snack bar and four drink stands take care of any possible hungers.

**DEALER RATES:** Approximately $36 per 20' × 25' space outdoors, for two days; $45 per 8½' × 10' space indoors, for two days. Reservations are required.

**CONTACT:** Kevin Lambright, PO Box 185, Shipshewana IN 46565-0185. Tel: (219) 768-4129. Fax: (219) 768-7041. Email: tradingplace@shipshenet.com. Web: www.tradingplaceamerica.com.

# TERRE HAUTE
## Terre Haute Flea Market

**DATES:** 2000: May 6-7, June 3-4, August 5-6 and September 9-10. Generally the same weekends every year, but check first.

**TIMES:** Saturday 8:00 AM-6:00 PM, Sunday 9:00 AM-5:00 PM.

**ADMISSION:** Free. Parking $2.

**LOCATION:** Wabash County Fairgrounds.

**DESCRIPTION:** This market, one of several run by Stewart Promotions in Indiana and Kentucky, has over 200 dealers inside selling about 60% antiques and collectibles and 40% crafts and new items. Generally the collectible dealers prefer to set up under the shed area.

**DEALER RATES:** $15 daily outside; indoor $55 for a 14' × 8' space; sheds $55 for a 12' × 12' space.
**CONTACT:** Stewart Promotions, 2950 Breckenridge Ln Ste 4A, Louisville KY 40220. Tel: (502) 456-2244 except Tuesdays and Fridays. Email: sp2950@earthlink.net. Web: www.stewartpromotions.com.

## OTHER FLEA MARKETS

We know or have heard about these markets, but have not personally contacted each one, as we have the markets with descriptions. If you plan to visit one of these markets listed below, *please call first* to make sure they are still open. Flea markets do come and go. While they were open when we went to press, they may not be later. We can't be responsible. *Call first!*

**Evansville:** Diamond Flea Market, 1250 E Diamond Ave. Tel: (812) 464-2675.
**Evansville:** Giant Flea Market, 2600 S Kentucky Ave. Tel: (812) 421-8274.
**Friendship:** Friendship Downtown Flea Market, 5874 Friendship Main St. Tel: (812) 667-5322.
**Gary:** Dunes Plaza Flea Market, 8000 Melton Rd. Tel: (219) 938-6937.
**Gary:** Market City Flea Market, 4121 Cleveland St. Tel: (219) 887-3522.
**Gas City:** Mick's Flea Market, 212 E Main St. Tel: (765) 677-0281.
**Indianapolis:** East INDY Flea Market, 8101 Pendleton Pike. Tel: (317) 898-4322.
**Indianapolis:** Irvington Flea Market, 6301 E Washington St. Tel: (317) 375-1885.
**Laurel:** Pioneer Flea Market, 22211 US Hwy 52. Tel: (765) 698-1210.
**Madison:** Craig Flea Market, 243 Clifty Dr. Tel: (812) 273-0044
**Marion:** Deer Creek Flea Market, 5137 S Adams St. Tel: (765) 674-5620.
**Marion:** Marion Flea Market, 3316 S Nebraska St. Tel: (765) 674-7083.
**Milton:** Old Milton School, 207 N Central Ave. Tel: (765) 478-6245.
**Montgomery:** Montgomery Flea Market, Cty Rd 650 E. Tel: (812) 486-3354.
**Nashville:** Flea Market Enterprises, 4469 SR 46 E. Tel: (812) 988-0964.
**Nashville:** Olde Time Flea Market, 5400 SR 46 E. Tel: (812) 988-2346.
**New Albany:** Pine Ridge Flea Market, 3328 Corydon Pike. Tel: (812) 941-1111.

**North Vernon:** Green Meadows Flea Market, N Hwy 7. Tel: (812) 346-9945.

**Paoli:** Mellie's Flea Market, 201 College Ave. Tel: (812) 723-5666.

**Reelsville:** Croy Creek Trading Post, 8504 W Cty Rd 1000 S. Tel: (812) 986-2836.

**San Pierre:** San Pierre Flea Market, 208 N Fisher St. Tel: (219) 828-3171.

**Washington:** Hometown Flea Market, 401 E Main St. Tel: (812) 257-1043.

# IOWA

## AMANA COLONIES
### Collector's Paradise Flea Market

**DATES:** Last full weekend in June. For 2000: June 24-25. Another the weekend of October 21-22.

**TIMES:** 7:00 AM to whenever.

**LOCATION:** Amana Colonies Outdoor Convention Facility. At Exit 225 off I-80, 12 miles north. Across from the Visitors Center.

**ADMISSION:** $1 per day, 12 and under free with an adult. Parking is free. Early bird admission $2 per day before Saturday.

**DESCRIPTION:** Opened in 1991, this indoor/outdoor market hosts 200 dealers selling antiques, collectibles, old tools, primitives, coins, furniture, glassware, jewelry, stamps, postcards, baseball cards and new merchandise. If this market is as successful as their What Cheer markets, buyers and sellers are in for a treat. Food is available at the market. Amana Colonies is a top tourist attraction in Iowa. See their companion market at What Cheer three times a year.

**DEALER RATES:** $35 with or without electric. Dealer setup starts Friday at 7:00 AM. No reservations taken; first come, first served.

**CONTACT:** Larry D Nicholson, Collector's Paradise Inc, PO Box 413, What Cheer IA 50268-0413. Tel: (515) 634-2109.

## DUBUQUE
### Dubuque Flea Market

**DATES:** Three times yearly, call for dates. Generally Sundays the middle of February, April and October. Do call to check first.

**TIMES:** 8:00 AM-4:00 PM.

**ADMISSION:** $1 for 12 and over, 11 and under free. Parking is free.

**LOCATION:** Dubuque County Fairgrounds, 5 miles west of town on Hwy 20.

**DESCRIPTION:** This indoor/outdoor market began in 1970. Approximately 100 to 140 dealers sell a variety of antiques, collectibles, art objects, music, furniture, stamps, trains, coins, and crafts. Among the local attractions are a dog track and river boats. There is food available on the premises.

**DEALER RATES:** $14 per 8' space inside including a table; wall space is $16; $10 per 20' × 20' space outside with no table. Reservations are required for inside space. Outside is first come, first served.

**CONTACT:** Jerome F Koppen, 260 Copper Kettle Ln, E Dubuque IL 61025. Tel: (815) 747-7745.

# LAKE OKOBOJI AT MILFORD
## Treasure Village Flea Market and Antiques Shows
**DATES:** Memorial Day Weekend (Saturday through Monday); July 4th weekend; Labor Day weekend (Saturday through Monday); and first weekend in August (Saturday and Sunday). Call for specific dates as July 4th falls on different days each year.
**TIMES:** 8:00 AM-6:00 PM.
**ADMISSION:** Free. Parking is also free.
**LOCATION:** Treasure Village, 2033 Hwy 86, 3 miles northwest of Milford.
**DESCRIPTION:** Held outdoors under the trees, this market generally limits its dealers to about 80. They show a variety of toys, coins, collectibles, primitives, antiques, sports cards, crafts, tools, and novelties, among other treasures. To amuse the children there is a children's theatre and for everyone miniature golf. Hand-dipped ice cream, sandwiches, and the usual concession fare are available. This is a real family affair and social gathering for tourists and the local residents. Lake Okoboji is one of only three "bluewater lakes" in the world; the others are Lake Geneva in Switzerland and Lake Louise in Canada. It is also the number-one tourist attraction in Iowa.
**DEALER RATES:** $85 for a 20' × 20' space Memorial Day, Labor Day and July 4th; August first weekend $45. Reservations are required. Prepaid reservations are allowed a discount.
**CONTACT:** Garth Neisess, Manager, 2033 Hwy 86, Milford, IA 51351-7348. Tel: (712) 337-3730.

# OTTUMWA
## Collector's Fair
**DATES:** Third full weekend in January, March and November.
**TIMES:** 9:00 AM-4:00 PM.
**ADMISSION:** $1. Parking is free.
**LOCATION:** Ottumwa Coliseum basement, between Hwys 34 and 63.
**DESCRIPTION:** This indoor market began in 1970. It attracts approximately 40 dealers selling only antiques and collectibles. Some of the items sold are fine furniture, glassware, cookie jars, collectible coins and stamps, and cards. Food is served on the premises.
**DEALER RATES:** $16 per 8' table. Reservations are required.

**CONTACT:** Frosti Chicchelly, 3636 Clark Rd SE, Cedar Rapids IA 52403. Tel: (319) 362-7360.

# SPIRIT LAKE
## Annual Antique Show and Flea Market at Vick's Corner
**DATES:** Memorial Day, July 4th, and Labor Day weekends. For 2000: May 27-29, July 1-4, September 2-4.
**TIMES:** 8:00 AM-6:00 PM.
**ADMISSION:** Free. Parking is also free.
**LOCATION:** Junction of Hwys 9 and 86 at Vick's Corner.
**DESCRIPTION:** This market started the Spirit Lake market corner in 1966. Ninety dealers from 10 different states sell antiques, collectibles and primitives. Absolutely no junk is allowed. People plan their vacations around these market days as the dealers who come here are famous throughout the country for the quality of their goods. This is a 10-acre grove area all grassed and kept up like a golf course. Vick's Corner is a general store established in 1930 and a well-known landmark in the area. Food concessions and restrooms are on site.
**DEALER RATES:** $85 per booth for one show. Reservations are highly recommended.
**CONTACT:** LW Vick, Vick's Corner, RR Box 9131, Spirit Lake IA 51360. Tel/fax: (712) 336-1912 or (712) 336-1496 or 336-5602. Email: vicksno1@ncn.net or vickscorner@lakescable.com.

# WHAT CHEER
## Collectors Paradise Flea Market
**DATES:** First Sunday and preceding Saturday in May, August, and October. 2000 dates: May 6-7, August 5-6, September 30-October 1.
**TIMES:** 7:00 AM to whenever.
**ADMISSION:** $1 per person per day, 12 and under free with adult. Free parking is available. Early bird admission $2 per day before Saturday.
**LOCATION:** At the Keokuk County Fairgrounds in What Cheer. Take Exit 201 off I-80 and drive south 20 miles on Hwy 21.
**DESCRIPTION:** According to local shoppers, Larry Nicholson's Collectors Paradise is well named. Having started this indoor/outdoor market in 1977, Mr Nicholson has raised dealer attendance up to around 500, with some dealers showing up for setup as early as the Wednesday before the show. Dealers come from all of the Midwest states. This market is one of

the major antique and collectible markets in the Midwest. Shoppers, who can number as high as 7,000, are invited to get an early chance to browse through the innumerable bargains on the Saturday preceding the main sale day for the same early bird $2 fee. Antiques and collectibles of every shape and size are to be found here including glassware, toys, tools, coins, jewelry, stamps, baseball cards, postcards, primitives, furniture, and more. Among the foods served is funnel cake, a favorite among local flea marketeers. Lunch is available.

**DEALER RATES:** $35 for outside space for the weekend. Reservations are required.

**CONTACT:** Larry D Nicholson, Collectors Paradise Inc, PO Box 413, What Cheer IA 50268-0413. Tel: (515) 634-2109.

# OTHER FLEA MARKETS

We know or have heard about these markets, but have not personally contacted each one, as we have the markets with descriptions. If you plan to visit one of these markets listed below, *please call first* to make sure they are still open. Flea markets do come and go. While they were open when we went to press, they may not be later. We can't be responsible. *Call first!*

**Cherokee:** B & M's Old Creamery, 301 W Locust St. Tel: (712) 225-6229.

**Clinton:** Cooper's Flea Market, 130 N 4 St. Tel: (319) 243-5279.

**Crystal Lake:** Crystal Lake Flea Market, 150 S State Ave. Tel: (515) 565-3010.

**Des Moines:** Euclid Fleamarket, 1212 Euclid Ave. Tel: (515) 237-8293.

**Des Moines:** Fleamart, 606 E Army Post Rd 2. Tel: (515) 285-0025.

**Des Moines:** SE 14th Street Flea Market, 5912 SE 14 St. Tel: (515) 285-8761.

**Dubuque:** Store Front Flea Market, 1105 University Ave. Tel: (319) 582-9880.

**Oskaloosa:** Trade Station, 214 A Ave E. Tel: (515) 673-6641.

**Sioux City:** Downtown Flea Market, 417 Nebraska St. Tel: (712) 234-0589.

# KANSAS

## HUTCHINSON
### Mid-America Flea Markets

**DATES:** First Sunday of each month, October through June. (Except February 2000, it's the 20th. Slight scheduling snafu.)

**TIMES:** 9:00 AM-4:00 PM.

**ADMISSION:** $.50 per person. Free parking is available.

**LOCATION:** At the Kansas State Fairgrounds, well marked in Hutchinson.

**DESCRIPTION:** This indoor market first opened its doors in 1964. Currently there are approximately 200 dealers that specialize in a variety of types of antiques and collectibles, exhibiting miscellaneous items at a wide range of prices. A concession stand and handicapped-accessible restrooms are available on the premises.

**DEALER RATES:** $17 per 10' × 12' space. Reservations are required.

**CONTACT:** Av Hardesty, Mid-America Markets, PO Box 1585, Hutchinson KS 67504-1585. Tel: (316) 663-5626. Day of show call: (316) 663-9000. Web: midamericamarkets.com.

## OPOLIS
### Opolis Flea Market

*Note: Louie Kukovich had serious health problems in 1997, but is expected to be hale and healthy again and working in the market by 2000. Call first to make sure the market is open.*

**DATES:** Most Saturdays and Sundays, and by chance; year round.

**TIMES:** Daylight hours.

**ADMISSION:** Free, with free parking.

**LOCATION:** On the Kansas-Missouri State Line; junction of US 171 and 57.

**DESCRIPTION:** Since 1978 this relatively small flea market has only antiques and collectibles, including miscellaneous Volkswagen autos and parts, all of it collected by two antique fanatics. This collection of treasures is housed in several warehouses and is a haunt of dealers looking to replenish their stocks. They have had other dealers with them in the past, but the whole situation is in flux. Call first.

**DEALER RATES:** Call for availability, as there wasn't any space available as we went to press. But you never know.

**CONTACT:** Louie and Norma Kukovich, Box 42, Opolis KS 66760. Tel: (316) 231-2543.

# SPARKS
## Sparks Flea Market & Antique Show

**DATES**: Three shows a year: 1) the first Sunday in May plus the preceding three days for a 4-day show; 2) the second weekend in July, Friday through Sunday for a 3-day show; 3) Labor Day and the preceding four days for a 5-day show.

**TIMES**: Most dealers open between 7:00-8:00 AM and close up by 6:00 PM.

**ADMISSION**: Free. Parking is free on 4 acres next to the market as well as around town.

**LOCATION**: K-7 Hwy and old US 36, now known as Mission Rd. Just 23 miles west of St. Joseph, MO or 19 miles east of Hiawatha, KS on Old US 36 Hwy or 24 miles north of Atchison, KS or 11 miles south of White Cloud, KS on K-7 Hwy.

**DESCRIPTION**: Of this market's over 400 dealers, 325 sell antiques. You can count on plenty of quality antiques and collectibles. Started in 1982, this market is on the way to several other markets held the same weekend and together they draw 75,000 people trolling for treasures—this, in a town population of 14 the rest of the year. As the other markets aren't open on Labor Day itself, this market's dealers (and customers) make out like bandits. Plenty of food is available either at the market or around town, including treats from the Sparks Flea Circus Cafe (formerly the Road Kill Cafe) and Granny's Old Fashioned Lemonade. You can't starve. There are 16 food vendors including the cafe serving Mexican, German, Indian, and barbecue among the myriad choices.

**DEALER RATES**: $55-$70 for 20' × 30' outside space or $75-$90 for 10' × 15' inside space for the week. There are larger spaces available. Electricity is $5 a day extra. Table rental is $5 per table for the entire show. Setup starts on Wednesday, Thursday is dealer day. Don't miss it! The Cafe is open to dealers from 6:00 AM-9:00 PM.

**CONTACT**: Ray Tackett, PO Box 223, Troy KS 66087-0223. Tel: (785) 985-2411 except during market hours when Ray can be reached at the market: (785) 442-5555. Web: members.tripod.com/~Sparks_Flea_Market.

## If You Can Find Ray, Say "Hi" For Me!

Ray is a one-man Sparks clean-up crew. His latest effort to clean up three buildings in Sparks just may get the buildings on the Historic Register—as well as keep the town on the map. He has been building this market into the huge success it is today by plowing vendor fees back into enlarging it. At the latest reading of his newsletter, there isn't any more room to grow!

# WELDA
## Old School Flea Market

**DATES:** Daily, except Tuesday.
**TIMES:** Sunday 12:00 PM-6:00 PM, otherwise 10:30 AM-6:00 PM.
**ADMISSION:** Free. Parking is free.
**LOCATION:** 511 Commercial St.
**DESCRIPTION:** Opened in an old high school in 1995, this market of 50 dealers sells lots of old, used, and collectible stuff, including estate sale finds. About 75% of the merchandise is old. No food here, but plenty of restrooms! This is quite a place for filling up your trunk with treasures.
**DEALER RATES:** Inside: $5 for shelves, up to $50 for 8' × 8' space per month. For visiting vendors, setup outside is free. Inside reservations are needed to find space.
**CONTACT:** Old School Flea Market, 511 Commercial St, Welda KS 66091. Tel: 785-448-3367.

# WICHITA
## Village Flea Market

**DATES:** Every Friday, Saturday, and Sunday. Rain or shine.
**TIMES:** 9:00 AM-5:30 PM.
**ADMISSION:** Free. Parking is also free.
**LOCATION:** 2301 S Meridian.
**DESCRIPTION:** This indoor/outdoor market first opened in 1974. Their 125 to 150 dealers sell everything from antiques and collectibles to handmade craft items, vegetables, tools, toys, clothing, and jewelry. An interesting variety of garage items are also available. For your comfort the building is heated as well as air-conditioned. It is also equipped with a modern security system. Food is available on the premises.

**DEALER RATES:** $39 per 10' × 10' booth. Space is rented on a first-come, first-served basis.
**CONTACT:** Dale Cooper, 2301 S Meridian, Wichita KS 67213. Tel: (316) 942-8263.

## Mid-America Flea Markets

**DATES:** Irregular Sunday dates, one per month, except for July and August. 2000: January 23, February 6, March 26, April 16, May 21, June 18, September 17, October 15, November 19, December 17.
**TIMES:** 9:00 AM-4:00 PM.
**ADMISSION:** $1 per person. Free parking is available.
**LOCATION:** At the Kansas Coliseum, at the intersection of 85th St and I-135 N, Exit 17.
**DESCRIPTION:** This indoor market opened in 1978 and accommodates approximately 650 dealers. Visitors come to view the large selection of antiques and collectibles; there is always a wide variety to choose from, at a wide range of prices. A concession stand and handicapped-accessible restrooms are on the premises.
**DEALER RATES:** $17 per 8' × 10' space. Reservations are required.
**CONTACT:** Av Hardesty, Mid-America Markets, PO Box 1585, Hutchinson KS 67504-1585. Tel: (316) 663-5626. Show date phone: (316) 755-2560. Web: midamericamarkets.com.

## OTHER FLEA MARKETS

We know or have heard about these markets, but have not personally contacted each one, as we have the markets with descriptions. If you plan to visit one of these markets listed below, *please call first* to make sure they are still open. Flea markets do come and go. While they were open when we went to press, they may not be later. We can't be responsible. *Call first!*

**Chanute:** Proctors Flea Market, 227 W 7 St. Tel: (316) 431-7655.
**Chetopa:** Pecan Tree, 903 SW Hwy 166. Tel: (316) 597-2991.
**Coffeyville:** B & K Pecans & Flea Market, 802 E 11 St. Tel: (316) 251-6887.
**Dodge City:** Happy Trail Flea Market, 317 W Trail St. Tel: (316) 227-2168.
**Emporia:** Flea Market, 312 Commercial St. Tel: (316) 342-5333.

**Eudora:** Eudora Main Street Fleamarket, 714 Main St. Tel: (785) 542-3934

**Fredonia:** Valley Flea Market, RR4 Box 196F. Tel: (316) 378-4479.

**Garden City:** Sanjuan Flea Market. Tel: (316) 276-6049.

**Independence:** Out West Antiques & Flea Market, 1625 W Main St. Tel: (316) 331-5703.

**Iola:** A & L Flea Market, 401 S State St. Tel: (316) 365-2444.

**Junction City:** Junction City Flea Market, 607 N Washington St. Tel: (785) 762-2321.

**Kansas City:** Merriam Lane Flea Market, 1270 Merriam Ln. Tel: (913) 677-0833.

**La Cygne:** Lucky Penny Flea Market. Tel: (913) 757-2675.

**Linwood:** Linwood Flea Market, 314 Main St. Tel: (913) 723-3230.

**Osawatomie:** Old Country Store Flea Market, 510 Main St. Tel: (913) 755-6595.

**Pittsburg:** Mel's Old Mill, 307 N Elm St. Tel: (316) 231-9442.

**Pittsburg:** Pittsburg Flea Market, 312 N Elm St. Tel: (316) 235-1840.

**Pleasanton:** Big G's Flea Market, 6 & Main. Tel: (913) 352-6113.

**Topeka:** Rollaway Flea Market, 2305 SE 10 Ave. Tel: (785) 234-4420.

**Topeka:** Joyland Flea Market, 2901 SE Adams St. Tel: (785) 266-5401.

**Wichita:** Village Flea Market, 2301 S Meridian Ave. Tel: (316) 942-8263.

**Wichita:** Midtown Flea Market, 509 E Harry St. Tel: (316) 262-7150.

# KENTUCKY

## ASHLAND
### Hillbilly Flea Market

**DATES:** Thursday, Friday, Saturday, and Sunday.

**TIMES:** 8:00 AM-5:00 PM.

**ADMISSION:** Free. Parking is free.

**LOCATION:** Russell Rd, Rt 23, north of Ashland.

**DESCRIPTION:** Opened in 1985, this indoor/outdoor market of 100-150 dealers sells antiques, collectibles, clothing, crafts, jewelry, fresh produce, new and used merchandise. The 21,000-square-foot building is heated and air-conditioned. Their restaurant serves up home-cooked meals and when needed there are handicapped-accessible restrooms.

**DEALER RATES:** Thursday and Friday: $5 per 10' × 25' space, Saturday and Sunday $6 per space, inside depends on square footage.

**CONTACT:** Elwood Gibbs, Hillbilly Flea Market, 100 W Main St, Greenup KY 41144. Tel: (606) 329-1058 or 1-800-357-1058.

## CORBIN
### Cumberland Parkway Flea Market

**DATES:** Saturday and Sunday.

**TIMES:** 9:00 AM-5:00 PM.

**ADMISSION:** Free. Parking is free.

**LOCATION:** 305 W Cumberland Gap Pkwy. Take Exit 29 off I-75.

**DESCRIPTION:** Opened in 1996, this market of 150-160 dealers sells collectibles, crafts, stamps, cards, coins, produce, furniture, garage sale goodies, appliances, TVs, and new merchandise. There is one snack bar and handicapped-accessible restrooms on site.

**DEALER RATES:** $36 per weekend for 10' × 15' space. Reservations are not required.

**CONTACT:** Cumberland Pkwy Flea Market, PO Box 999, Corbin KY 40702-0999. Tel: (606) 526-9712. Fax: (606) 526-1629.

## ELIZABETHTOWN
### Bowling Lanes Flea Market

**DATES:** Saturday and Sunday.

**TIMES:** 8:00 AM-5:00 PM.

**ADMISSION:** Free. Parking is free.

**LOCATION:** 4547 N Dixie, US 31W; 35 miles south of Louisville on I-65 and 8 miles south of Fort Knox.

**DESCRIPTION:** This indoor/outdoor market of 300-500 dealers sells antiques, collectibles, new and used merchandise, clothing, jewelry, furniture, crafts, and fresh produce. There are two booths of antiques in one of the two buildings, handicapped-accessible restrooms, a snack concession, shed space and hundreds in open-air spaces, depending on the weather. Garage sale goodies are mostly outside with loads of new stuff every weekend. Inside is mostly newer merchandise.

**DEALER RATES:** $7 per 10' × 12' in the open per day, $8 for either inside 8' × 8' space, or under shed per 10' × 10' space per day. Reservations are needed for shed or inside space, not for outside. Do check in with the market just in case. They do fill up.

**CONTACT:** Bowling Lanes Flea Market, 4547 N Dixie Hwy, Elizabethtown KY 42701-8857. Tel: (502) 737-5755 or the bowling alley at (502) 737-7171.

# FLEMINGSBURG

## Annual Old-Fashioned Court Day

**DATES:** Second Monday and preceding weekend of October, rain or shine. (Essentially Columbus Day weekend and Monday.)

**TIMES:** Saturday, sunup to whenever; Sunday at noon until Monday whenever.

**ADMISSION:** Free. Parking is wherever you find it; some is free, some isn't.

**LOCATION:** The entire town of Flemingsburg! In the center of town, on Main St.

**DESCRIPTION:** Started in 1969 to continue the tradition of the circuit judge plying his trade (trials and hangings), this town turns into a huge market centered in downtown Flemingsburg. From 450 to 600 outside vendors sell everything and anything you can imagine—old, new and otherwise. They do try to have a booth or two of unusual things like games and rides for kids, clogging, and live entertainment. This shebang ends with a good old-fashioned square-dance on Monday night. See also Maysville and Mt Sterling for the first and third Monday Court Days markets and you, too, can follow the judge's historical "necktie" circuit. This huge event is *the* fundraiser for the local Rescue Squad who sponsors this market.

**DEALER RATES:** Setup anytime after 6:00 PM Friday. $75 per 10' × 10' space for three days. Reservations are strongly recommended.

**CONTACT:** Mr Kim Brewer, Annual Old-Fashioned Court Day, Rt 3 Lot 3 Crestview, Flemingsburg KY 41041-0126. Tel: (606) 849-4797. Email: kimjb@kih.net.

# FREDONIA
## Old Fredonia School Flea Market

**DATES:** Friday through Sunday, year round.

**TIMES:** Friday and Saturday 8:00 AM-5:00 PM. Sunday 1:00 PM-5:00 PM.

**ADMISSION:** Free. Parking is free.

**LOCATION:** Fredonia School on Hwy 641.

**DESCRIPTION:** Located in an old school building on a major highway, this market opened in 1994. There are 15 dealers spread around 11 rooms and all hallways of the old school selling antiques, collectibles (Barbies have a special spot), crafts, cards, stamps, garage sale goodies, clothing, ceramics, pictures, furniture, horse tack, horse-drawn equipment, antique tools, vintage car parts, memorabilia and some new merchandise. No food, but handicapped-accessible restrooms are in the school.

**DEALER RATES:** $100 per month for a 22' × 27' room and Mary will sell for you if you can't be there, no commissions. For transient dealers, there is room to set up outside, weather permitting. Give Mary a call. There is a waiting list for inside space.

**CONTACT:** Mary Boone, Old Fredonia School Flea Market, 306 Cassidy Ave, Fredonia KY 42411. Tel: (270) 545-9115 or 545-3982.

---

### Hysterical Note

What would you do with an old school put up for auction? Buy it. Then what? Turn it into a flea market. That's what Malcolm Boone bought, and Mary did with it. Not only does it have items for sale, but displays of local history. There is an old still (no you can't have it, and doesn't make stuff anymore), a broom-making setup and all sorts of odds and ends tucked everywhere. If you want to hold a really big event there, rent the gym!

---

# GREENVILLE
## Luke's Town and Country Flea Market

**DATES:** Monday and Tuesday, year round, weather permitting.

**TIMES:** 8:00 AM-dark Monday; 6:00 AM-2:00 PM Tuesday.

**ADMISSION:** Free, with some free parking; $1 parking is available nearby.

**LOCATION:** Hwy 62 W, 1 mile from Greenville city limits.

**DESCRIPTION:** This outdoor market has been operating since May 1979. On Monday about 25 to 100 dealers show. Tuesdays are busier, with between 200 and 400 dealers selling antiques, collectibles, crafts, new merchandise, and produce, as well as poultry and livestock. The surrounding area is rustically scenic, with Lake Malone and many other state parks nearby. There is a real family atmosphere here and a large antique display and collection to view (but not for sale) and several antique shops nearby. Food is available on the grounds.

**DEALER RATES:** $3 and up per 8' × 10' space per day Tuesdays and Monday holidays; $2 on non-holiday Mondays. Reservations are appreciated but not necessary.

**CONTACT:** Wayne and Judy Rice, Managers, Luke's Town and Country Flea Market, 2006 US Hwy 62 W, Greenville KY 42345. Tel: (270) 338-4920 or (270) 338-6284.

# HENDERSON
## Ellis Park Flea Market

*This market is closed for renovations through 2000. If you are interested in 2001, contact the market.*

**CONTACT:** Bob Jackson, Ellis Park Office, PO Box 33, Henderson KY 42420. Tel: (812) 826-0608 or 1-800-333-8110.

# HIGHWAY 127
## Highway 127 Corridor Sale

**DATES:** August, from the Thursday before the 3rd Sunday through Sunday for 4 days.

**TIMES:** Whenever.

**ADMISSION:** Free. Park in designated parking areas along the route. Call the Kentucky Office of Public Affairs, Tel: (502) 564-4890 for locations. Or check their website: www.kytc.state.ky.us.

**LOCATION:** All along US Hwy 127 through three states: Kentucky, Tennessee, and Alabama. When you see a collection of sellers, it's there.

**DESCRIPTION:** Started in 1987 as a way to get travelers off the interstate and back onto the country roads by Fentress (TN) County's former County Executive Mike Walker and some of his friends, this market of thousands of dealers in "oddities and antiques," yard sale unloaders, and whoever and whatever else shows up sells everything old and/or crafty. If you wish to travel the entire 450-mile route, start in Covington KY and work your way down to around Gadsden AL. There are plenty of food vendors. This has to be "the World's Longest Outdoor Sale."

**Rules of the road:** 1) *Drive Cautiously*—then you won't hit pedestrians or miss that goody you've been looking for. 2) Be *extremely* careful crossing the road! 3) Use your turn signals and don't stop suddenly for that goody (have a lookout who can give you ample warning). Otherwise, you may be dealing with insurance companies and wreckers rather than rare Ming.

**DEALER RATES:** Whatever the local landowner charges. Check out the website for a list of contacts in each state (it's huge) or call.

**CONTACT:** Wanda, Fentress County Chamber of Commerce, PO Box 1294, Jamestown TN 38556-1294. Tel: (800) 327-3945. Web: jamestowntn.org.

# LEITCHFIELD
## Bratcher's Flea Market

**DATES:** Wednesday and Saturday, year round, weather permitting.

**TIMES:** Dawn to 2:00 PM.

**ADMISSION:** Free admission and parking, including overnight before show days.

**LOCATION:** On Hwy 62, 1 mile east of Leitchfield.

**DESCRIPTION:** This market opened over 30 years ago and is now run by the granddaughter of the founder. Approximately 150 dealers sell their antiques and collectibles outdoors. Handicrafts, new merchandise, and produce in season are also for sale. This is a well-managed, well-run market. There is a food concession at the market.

**DEALER RATES:** $7-$8 per 8' × 10' space per day. Reservations for the month are suggested.

**CONTACT:** Carol Heffley, Bratcher's Flea Market, PO Box 396, Leitchfield KY 42754-0396. Tel: (502) 259-5948.

# LEXINGTON
## Antique and Flea Market

**DATES:** 2000: January 7-8, February 4-6, July 21-23, October 6-8, December 1-3. Call for 2001 dates as these vary considerably.

**TIMES:** Friday and Saturday 11:00 AM-7:00 PM; Sunday 11:00 AM-5:00 PM.

**ADMISSION:** Free. Parking is free.

**LOCATION:** Lexington Center. Downtown Main and Patterson.

**DESCRIPTION:** Started in 1980 this market has about 250 dealers selling antiques, collectibles, flea market fare and everything else but food or weapons. This is considered a fine antique market. Food is available on the premises.

**DEALER RATES:** $75 per 14' × 8' space; $113 per 21' × 8' space; $150 per 28' × 8' space. Reservations are required. Tables available at $8 each inside.

**CONTACT:** Stewart Promotions, 2950 Breckinridge Ln Ste 4A, Louisville KY 40220. Tel: (502) 456-2244 except Tuesday. Email: sp2950@earthlink.net. Web: www.stewartpromotions.com.

# LONDON
## Flea Land Flea Market

**DATES**: Saturday and Sunday, year round.

**TIMES**: 9:00 AM-5:00 PM. Extended holiday shopping days Thanksgiving through Christmas.

**ADMISSION**: Free. Parking is free.

**LOCATION**: Take London Exit 38 off I-75, 2 miles east. Follow the signs.

**DESCRIPTION**: Opened in 1990, this indoor/outdoor market of 400 dealers sells antiques, collectibles, crafts, produce, coins, cards, garage sale goodies, furniture, gold, jewelry, all sorts of home furnishings, rugs, NASCAR items, and new merchandise. Their building is a heated and cooled 80,000 square feet of selling space with one restaurant, a concession stand, and handicapped-accessible restrooms—"the largest in the state of Kentucky." They say they are "known as one of the cleanest and best."

**DEALER RATES**: $38.50 per 10' × 15' space weekly; $43.50 per 10' × 19' space weekly; or $12 per 10' × 10' outside space. Reservations are required.

**CONTACT**: Brenda Hail, Flea Land Flea Market, PO Box 862, London KY 40741. Tel: (606) 864-3532.

## London Tobacco Warehouse Flea Market
**DATES:** Friday, Saturday and Sunday, year round.

**TIMES:** 9:00 AM-5:00 PM.

**ADMISSION:** Free. Parking is free.

**LOCATION:** 420 Tobacco Rd. Off the London Bypass. Watch for the signs.

**DESCRIPTION:** For 17 years, this market's 80 dealers have been selling antiques, collectibles, garage sale goodies, some new merchandise, and produce in season. There are handicapped-accessible restrooms and a concession stand on site.

**DEALER RATES:** $30 per weekend or $10 per day for a 12' × 16' space. Reservations are an excellent idea as the market is usually full.

**CONTACT:** Carl Tuttle, London Tobacco Warehouse Flea Market, 420 Tobacco Rd, London KY 40741-2311. Tel: (606) 878-7726.

# LOUISVILLE
## Derby Park Trader's Circle
**DATES:** Saturday and Sunday, year round. Rain or shine.

**TIMES:** 8:00 AM-5:00 PM.

**ADMISSION:** Free. Free parking for public.

**LOCATION:** I-264 to Taylor Blvd N exit. Turn right on Taylor and go 2 stoplights. Turn left on Arcade. At light make a left onto 7th St Rd and the market is on the right at 2900 7th St Rd.

**DESCRIPTION:** Located 7/10 of a mile from Churchill Downs, this indoor air-conditioned 100,000-square-foot market with 150 outside booths has been operating since 1985. They have dealers in approximately 400 indoor spaces selling antiques, collectibles, handmade crafts, vegetables, furniture, clothing, knives, guns, toys, carpet, baseball cards and new merchandise. They had an "Outrageous Giveaway Promotion" culminating with the winner driving off in a 1969 Rolls Royce Silver Shadow. Wonder what they'll do next time? Four snack bars provide food on the premises and handicapped-accessible restrooms complete the amenities.

**DEALER RATES:** $34 per 6' × 20' or 10' × 12' indoor booth for the weekend; $49 per weekend for 18' × 10' booth; $10 per outdoor booth per day or $25 for the weekend. Reservations are first come, first served.

**CONTACT:** Art Henoch, Derby Park Traders Circle, 2900 7 St Rd, Louisville KY 40216-4126. Tel: (502) 636-3532. Fax: (502) 634-0094.

## Kentucky Flea Market

**DATES:** 2000: January 28-30, March 3-5, April 7-9, 28-30, May 26-28, July 1-4, 28-30, September 1-4, October 20-22, December 29 through January 1, 2001. Rain or shine.

**TIMES:** Friday 12:00 PM-7:00 PM; Saturday 10:00 AM-7:00 PM; Sunday 11:00 AM-5:00 PM. Memorial Day: Friday 12:00 PM-7:00 PM; Saturday 10:00 AM-7:00 PM; Sunday 11:00 AM-6:00 PM; Monday 10:00 AM-5:00 PM. July 4th: Thursday 12:00 PM-7:00 PM; Friday 10:00 AM-7:00 PM; Saturday 10:00 AM-6:00 PM; Sunday 11:00 AM-5:00 PM.

**ADMISSION:** Free. $3 for parking in 15,000 spaces.

**LOCATION:** Kentucky Fair and Exposition Center. Junctions of I-264 and 65. Follow the signs.

**DESCRIPTION:** Started in 1972, and housed in a 250,000-square-foot climate-controlled building, this market consists of 1,000 to 2,000 dealers selling antiques, fine arts, arts and crafts, collectibles, and new merchandise. It is promoted as one of the largest indoor flea markets in the United States, in one of this country's finest facilities. On regular show days the market draws between 30,000 and 50,000 shoppers; on holidays, the crowds can swell to 100,000 or more. Food is served on the premises.

**DEALER RATES:** $85 ($100-$110 holidays) per 14' × 8' space per show; $128 ($150-$165 holidays) per 21' × 8' space; $170 ($200-$220 holidays) per 28' × 8' space. Larger spaces are available. Higher holiday rates. Reservations are required well in advance.

**CONTACT:** Stewart Promotions, 2950 Breckinridge Ln Ste 4A, Louisville KY 40220. Tel: (502) 456-2244 (except Tuesday and Friday). Email: sp2950@earthlink.net. Web: www.stewartpromotions.com.

# MAYSVILLE
## Maysville's Old-Fashioned Court Days

**DATES:** First weekend in October. Rain or shine.

**TIMES:** 9:00 AM-10:00 PM.

**ADMISSION:** Free. Parking is also free.

**LOCATION:** The streets of Market St, Sutton St, and McDonald Pkwy.

**DESCRIPTION:** Started in the horse and buggy days of 1870 when the circuit judge would ride from town to town in Kentucky, then try and hang offenders, this series of Court Days (including Flemingsburg and Mt Sterling) blossomed from the trading that naturally happened when people were brought together from outlying districts for a common gathering once a year.

"If you can't find it on one of those trading days, then it doesn't exist, from jewelry to bent hinges (and bent nails!), even dogs!" Apples, crafts, wooden tool handles, at one time—goldfish, sorghum molasses, collectibles, new merchandise, parts of kitchen sinks, furniture and anything. Food is available on the premises and run by local charity and fraternal groups. Country ham and cheese sandwiches are one of the specialties sold in the special food court area. "The best beef and country ham you ever put in your mouth."

Party! Along with the flea market is a rousing festival with bands, shows, contests, carnival, sternwheeler trips on the Ohio River (Maysville lies along the river) and whatever they can do for fun. Not to be missed!

**DEALER RATES:** $50 each booth up to 3 booths, 4th and more $25 each. Some electric available. Reservations are a must. Setup begins Friday at 6:00 PM.

**CONTACT:** Ms Duff Giffen, Maysville Special Events Committee, PO Box 326, Maysville KY 41056-0326. Tel: (606) 564-9419. Fax: (606) 564-9416. Email: maysville@ntr.net.

---

### Recycling

A dealer in window and doors went to a local tavern, bought two green bottles of Coke, drank them, and put them on his table. Along came a woman from Dayton, OH and asked the price of the bottles. "$1 each," replied the dealer. Remarking that she hadn't seen the green Coke bottles in ages, she bought them.

---

### Entrepreneur in the Making

A small boy carrying a bucket of bent nails was stopped by dealer. He asked the boy how much he wanted for the bucket of nails? The child answered "Thirty-five cents."

"I'll give you twenty-five."

"No, thirty-five." After a bit of this haggling, the child got his thirty-five cents and watched the man go off with the bucket. But then the man put the bucket down on a nearby table and walked off into the crowd. The boy snatched his bucket from the table and went the opposite direction and sold the bucket again.

---

# MT STERLING
## October Court Days

**DATES:** The weekend of and including the third Monday in October, annually.

**TIMES:** 6:00 AM Saturday through 12:00 midnight Monday, non-stop.

**ADMISSION:** Free admission; parking from $5 per day or wherever you can find it.

**LOCATION:** The entire town of Mt Sterling! Take Exit 110 off I-64, 35 miles east of Lexington; or take Exit 113 off I-64, 100 miles west of Ashland, KY.

**DESCRIPTION:** Mt Sterling has always been a big trading center. Around 1796, it was traditional for the local county judge to hang convicted offenders on the third Monday in October, which naturally started people trading over the entire weekend. People came from miles away to buy and sell cows, horses, dogs, produce, tools, and other farm goods. This market attracts 2,000 dealers officially and averages 175,000 shoppers. Even now, during Court Days, people bring objects of all shapes and sizes for sale or trade—more dogs and other farm animals (to Preston), guns, axe handles, hammer handles, and antiques of all kinds that defy cataloging. Among the various foods for sale are corn meal and real Kentucky sorghum molasses, which is still made right in this mountain area. See also Flemingsburg and Maysville Court Days and follow the judge's hanging circuit.

**DEALER RATES:** Average rate is $200 plus $20 for city license per 20' × 20' space for three days. Reservations are required in advance.

**CONTACT:** October Court Days, Montgomery County Tourism Dept, 51 N Maysville, Mt Sterling KY 40353. Tel: (606) 498-8732. Fax: (606) 498-3947. Email: gatkinso@mis.net. Web: mountsterling-ky.com.

---

### Historical Notes

Mt Sterling Court Days are so popular that the market has a life of its own. While the official market is an eight-block area in the center of town—having started at the court house originally, then moved to the street, then to the stock yards (now in Preston)—they have since just plain spread all over town, much of it quite independent of the official function.

When the city fathers decided that having lots of animals in the center of town wasn't healthy, neighboring Preston, in Bath County, took over that part of the market and started their own Preston Court Days, about 15 miles east of Mt Sterling.

One section along the creek is just for trading guns and knives. Visitors to that area are rather startled to feel that they have stepped back in time about 200 years with local mountaineers walking around with several shotguns parked on their shoulders. Yet never has a shot been fired or any injury happened.

# RICHWOOD
## Richwood Flea Market

**DATES:** Tuesday, Saturday, and Sunday, year round.

**TIMES:** Saturday and Sunday 9:00 AM-5:00 PM; Tuesday outdoors, daybreak to 1:00 PM, weather permitting.

**ADMISSION:** Free. $1 per car for parking.

**LOCATION:** 10915 US 25, Richwood exit. I-75 to Exit 175, north on US 25, 15 minutes south of Cincinnati.

**DESCRIPTION:** Opened in 1980, this market has about 300 indoor and 100 outdoor sellers. The indoor sellers are housed in a former tobacco warehouse over three acres *big*. There are many antiques, collectibles, craft items, sporting goods, tools, guns and knives, shoes, general merchandise as well as farm goods, jewelry, and new merchandise to be found. The Tuesday market is a genuine old-fashioned flea and farmers' market with loads of in-season produce and used stuff.

Newly remodeled in 1997, they added two food courts with a big screen television and local entertainment. Their fried chicken is considered the best around and they added a meat smoker and feature fresh pork and chicken barbecue every weekend. Handicapped-accessible restrooms add to the amenities.

**DEALER RATES:** $70 per 16' × 15' space per weekend, or $40 per 8' × 15' space. Reservations are suggested. $12 for a 3-car parking space outdoors on Tuesday; $25 for weekends.

**CONTACT:** Mike Stallings, PO Box 153, Florence KY 41022-0153. Tel: (606) 371-5800. Fax: (606) 371-5680. Email: richflea10@aol.com. Web: www.richwoodfleamarket.com.

# SIMPSONVILLE
## Shelby County Flea Market

**DATES:** Saturday and Sunday.

**TIMES:** 9:00 AM-5:00 PM.

**ADMISSION:** Free. Parking is free.

**LOCATION:** 820 Buck Creek Rd. I-64, exit 28; west of Lexington.

**DESCRIPTION:** Since 1985, this market of 350 inside vendors and up to 150 outside vendors (depending on the weather) sells antiques, collectibles, garage sale goodies, clothing, furniture, jewelry, books, crafts, fresh produce, used and new merchandise. The merchandise mix is generally 70% new to 30% old on the inside, and mostly old and garage sale goodies on the outside. There is a major concession stand with several satellite stands nearby (ice cream, Chester's fried chicken, and more) as well as handicapped-accessible restrooms. This is probably the largest weekly flea market in Kentucky.

**DEALER RATES:** $43.50 per 10' × 12' space inside per weekend, $12 per 10' × 20' space outside per day. Reservations are required inside, as they fill up quickly and generally have a waiting list after the summer season. Outside is first come, first served.

**CONTACT:** Dana Smith, Shelby County Flea Market, 820 Buck Creek Rd, Simpsonville KY 40067-6629. Tel: 502-722-8883. Fax: (502) 722-8881.

# SOMERSET
## Lake Cumberland Flea Market

**DATES:** Saturday and Sunday, year round.

**TIMES:** Saturday 9:00 AM-6:00 PM, Sunday 10:00 AM-6:00 PM. Extra hours during Christmas season.

**ADMISSION:** Free. Parking is free.

**LOCATION:** 95 Super Service Dr. Right off 914, aka New Southern By-Pass or Veterans Memorial Hwy.

**DESCRIPTION:** Opened in 1993, this indoor market's dealers sell antiques, collectibles, crafts, produce, furniture, garage sale goodies, books, herbs and oils, clothes, tools, and new merchandise. There is one restaurant on the premises with handicapped-accessible restrooms. They pride themselves on their clean market.

**DEALER RATES:** $34 per 10' × 15' space per weekend, $68 per 20' × 15' space. First come, first served.

**CONTACT:** Anna Gutting or Vertrees Warner, Lake Cumberland Flea Market, 95 Super Service Dr, Somerset KY 42501-6146. Tel: 606-678-0250. Fax: (606) 678-0250.

# SUWANEE
## Country Village Flea Market

**DATES**: Weekends, year round. Rain or shine.

**TIMES**: 8:00 AM-5:00 PM.

**ADMISSION**: Free with free parking.

**LOCATION**: On Hwy 62, 3 miles west of Exit 40 off I-24 and east of Barkley and Kentucky Dams.

**DESCRIPTION**: There are several indoor and outdoor markets on both sides of the road with approximately 50 vendors. Some of the vendors have been selling here for 20 years. You can find almost anything here such as antiques, glassware, knives, guns, tools, toys, in-season produce, and all kinds of collectibles. This is "a very pleasant shopping experience. One you'll want to tell your friends about."

**DEALER RATES**: Setup fees vary a little between the different markets, but are approximately $4 per 8' × 10' space.

**CONTACT**: Tom Strack, 625 SR 810 N, Kuttawa KY 42055. Tel: (270) 388-7824. Fax: (270) 640-0984. Email: tjstrack@dynasty.net.

# WINCHESTER
## Winchester Flea Market

**DATES:** Saturday and Sunday.

**TIMES:** 9:00 AM-5:00 PM.

**ADMISSION:** Free. Parking is free.

**LOCATION:** 4400 Relivo Rd, I-64 exit 94.

**DESCRIPTION:** Open since 1986, this indoor/outdoor market of 50 dealers sells antiques, collectibles, crafts, coins, cards, garage sale goodies, furniture, records, books, glassware, skillets, hardware, and new merchandise. There is a snack bar and handicapped-accessible restrooms on site.

**DEALER RATES:** $22 per 12' × 12' space; first come, first served.

**CONTACT:** Raymond C Huls, Winchester Flea Market, 1417 W Lexington Ave, Winchester KY 40391. Tel: 606-745-4332.

# OTHER FLEA MARKETS

We know or have heard about these markets, but have not personally contacted each one, as we have the markets with descriptions. If you plan to visit one of these markets listed below, *please call first* to make sure they are still open. Flea markets do come and go. While they were open when we went to press, they may not be later. We can't be responsible. *Call first!*

**Albany:** Highway 127 Flea Market, Hwy 127 S. Tel: (606) 387-9021.

**Barbourville:** Cumberland Gap Parkway, Hwy 25 E. Tel: (606) 546-9906.

**Bowling Green:** Flea Land, 1100 Three Springs Rd. Tel: (502) 843-1978.

**Brandenburg:** T & T SVC Flea Market, 2434 Old Mill Rd. Tel: (502) 422-5558.

**Burnside:** Trader's Paradise Flea Market, 6320 S Hwy 27. Tel: (606) 561-8688.

**Butler:** Crossroads Flea Market, 2105 Hwy 27. Tel: (606) 472-6952

**Campbellsville:** Campbellsville Flea Market, 426 Woodlawn Ave. Tel: (502) 789-0708.

**Clay City:** Industrial Park Flea Market, Hwy 15W. Tel: (606) 663-9297.

**Corydon:** Highway 60 West Flea Market, 12401 US Hwy 60W (PO Box 281). Tel: (502) 533-9912.

**Georgetown:** Georgetown Flea Market, 150 Edwards Ave. Tel: (502) 868-0858.

**Greensburg:** Summerville Flea Market. Tel: (502) 932-3260.

**Hagerhill:** Super Flea Market, 7280 S US Hwy 23. Tel: (606) 789-9799.

**Hazard:** East Main Trade Center, 409 E Main St. Tel: (606) 436-9871.

**Hazard:** Hazard Village Flea Market, 368 Dawahare Dr. Tel: (606) 439-2529.

**Lexington:** Lexington Flea Market, 1059 Industry Rd. Tel: (606) 252-1076.

**Maceo:** Hog Heaven Flea Market, 8424 US Hwy 60 E. Tel: (502) 264-4420.

**Madisonville:** Madisonville Flea Market, 4195 Anton Rd. Tel: (502) 825-9038.

**Manchester:** Mel's Flea Market, N Hwy 421. Tel: (606) 598-6939.

**Morehead:** Great Flea Market, 530 Fraley Dr. Tel: (606) 784-2444.

**Murray:** Gray's Flea Market, 609 S 4 St. Tel: (502) 753-7047.

**Owensboro:** Bob's Flea Market, 1418 E 18 St. Tel: (502) 683-6533.

**Owensboro:** Melba's Flea Market, 1218 Hall St. Tel: (502) 686-7904.

**Paducah:** Traders Mall Flea Market, 6900 Benton Rd. Tel: (502) 898-3144.

**Somerset:** Sunset Flea Market, 375 Sunset Blvd. Tel: (606) 676-9366.

**Stanford:** Stanford Drive-In Flea Market, 1645 Hustonville Rd. Tel: (606) 365-1317.

**Vine Grove:** Ahrdin County Indoor Flea Market, PO Box 332. Tel: (502) 351-0200.

**West Paducah:** Pirates Cove Flea Market, 8940 US Hwy 60W. Tel: (502) 744-6873.

**Wickliffe:** Tri-State Flea Market. 558 4 St. Tel: (502) 851-4442. Open Friday and Saturday.

**Winchester:** Goff's Corner Flea Market, 12449 Ironworks Rd. Tel: (606) 842-3803.

# LOUISIANA

## ARCADIA
### Bonnie & Clyde Trade Days, Inc

**DATES:** The weekend before the third Monday of each month, Friday through Sunday.
**TIMES:** Dawn to dark.
**ADMISSION:** Free. Parking is $3.
**LOCATION:** Take Exit 69 off I-20 in Arcadia and go south 3½ miles to market.
**DESCRIPTION:** Since its opening in September 1990, this show has grown from the original 635 dealers to over 800 dealer spaces. The grounds feature three stocked lakes for free fishing, a restaurant, amphitheater and stage, 100 RV hookups and facilities. There are dozens of concessions and dealers selling just about anything and everything. They have added both a washateria and free shower facilities.
**DEALER RATES:** $40 per 12' × 20' booth. Reservations are suggested.
**CONTACT:** Bonnie & Clyde Trade Days Inc, PO Box 243, Arcadia LA 71001-0243. Tel: (318) 263-2437 or 1-800-835-6112.

## BATON ROUGE
### Deep South Flea Market

**DATES:** Every Friday, Saturday, and Sunday. Rain or shine.
**TIMES:** 10:00 AM-6:00 PM.
**ADMISSION:** Free. Parking is also free.
**LOCATION:** 5905 Florida Blvd.
**DESCRIPTION:** This indoor market began in 1974. Approximately 275 dealers sell everything from antiques and collectibles, to a variety of crafts and art work, to secondhand merchandise and produce. A restaurant and handicapped-accessible restrooms add to the amenities.
**DEALER RATES:** $60 per 8' × 10' space, per weekend. Reservations are not required.
**CONTACT:** Bill Vallery, 5905 Florida Blvd, Baton Rouge LA 70806. Tel: (504) 923-0142 or 923-0333 for a tape.

# GREENWOOD/SHREVEPORT
## Greenwood Flea Market

**DATES:** Saturday and Sunday, year round.
**TIMES:** 10:00 AM-6:00 PM.
**ADMISSION:** Free. Parking is free.
**LOCATION:** 9249 Jefferson-Paige Rd. I-20, Exit 5.
**DESCRIPTION:** This unusual market started in 1982, with 150 dealer spaces inside, 25 railroad boxcars and numerous outside setups. Their dealers sell antiques, collectibles, primitives, baseball cards, glassware, furniture, jewelry, and everything old and new. One of the owners saw the railroad boxcars sitting around a Texas siding and decided they would be fun and brought them over to Louisiana. Handicapped-accessible restrooms and a snack bar are available on the premises.
**DEALER RATES:** $30 per weekend; $110 per month. $110 per railroad car plus electric. $7.50 per day outside. Reservations are required.
**CONTACT:** Larry Milligan, Greenwood Flea Market, 9249 Jefferson-Paige Rd, Greenwood LA 71033. Tel: (318) 938-7201.

# JEFFERSON
## Jefferson Flea Market

**DATES:** Friday through Sunday, year round.
**TIMES:** 10:00 AM-6:00 PM.
**ADMISSION:** Free. Parking is free.
**LOCATION:** 5501 Jefferson Hwy. Three blocks west of Clearview, off the Huey P Long Bridge.
**DESCRIPTION:** This market, opened in 1978, occupies an old 90,000-square-foot building supply warehouse with 70-75 dealers specializing in antiques, collectibles and awesome old stuff. Very little is new. (Maybe some reproductions? They do make furniture here.) Some of their dealers are nationally known for their expertise. "Chef Tommy" holds court in the snack bar serving the "finest hot dogs in the South." The loading dock area is used by the locals for their garage sale goodies and for transient dealers.
**DEALER RATES:** Permanent dealers: $200-$250 for an average-sized space. Daily is $15 in the dock area.
**CONTACT:** Jim and Beverly Russell, Jefferson Flea Market, PO Box 23223, Harahan LA 70183. Tel: (504) 734-0087. Fax: (504) 734-0304.

# LACOMBE
## 190 Trading Post Flea Market
**DATES:** Every Saturday and Sunday. Rain or shine.
**TIMES:** From 9:00 AM until 5:00 PM.
**ADMISSION:** Free. Free parking is available.
**LOCATION:** On Hwy 190, 4 miles east of Lacombe and 6 miles west of Slidell.
**DESCRIPTION:** Started in 1958, this indoor/outdoor market is said to be the oldest in Louisiana, having been in continuous operation since that time. There are 20 dealers selling antiques, fine art, arts and crafts, fresh produce, collectibles, new merchandise, appliances, and furniture, as well as unusual items such as farm equipment, American-made tools, etc. One can find anything and everything here, even hard-to-find items. Food is available nearby.
**DEALER RATES:** From $6 to $40 depending upon size of space.
**CONTACT:** Mary and Harold Fayard, 31160 Hwy 190 W, Lacombe LA 70445. Tel: (504) 882-6442.

# NEW ORLEANS
## French Market Community Flea Market
**DATES:** Daily.
**TIMES:** 7:00 AM-7:00 PM.
**ADMISSION:** Free. Parking is where you find it, or in paid lots.
**LOCATION:** 1235 N Peters St. Located on the riverfront behind the old US Mint (yes, coins were minted here) between the Mint and Café du Monde. It is quite the tourist attraction.
**DESCRIPTION:** This has got to be the great-grandaddy of all flea markets, started in 1791! Located in a historic part of New Orleans, this market (and the adjoining markets that sort of just run together) has around 300 dealers selling just about everything: African clothes and artifacts, antiques, collectibles, quilts, Guatemalan clothes, tie-dye clothing, t-shirts, stained glass, purses, dolls, toys, ceramics, glasses, masks, furniture, stones and rocks, jewelry, plenty of produce, seafood and whatever. Many of the dealers are permanent fixtures, some are seasonal.
**DEALER RATES:** Weekdays: $7-$23 a space; weekends: $12-$40 a space, depending on what is available. Spaces are given out by tenure on a weekly basis. All vendors must have city and state licenses and current photo ID and social security number.

**CONTACT:** Antoinette Guiton, French Market Office, 1008 N Peters St, New Orleans LA 70116. Tel: (504) 522-2621 or (504) 596-3420 or fax (504) 596-3427. Web: www.frenchmarket.org.

# OTHER FLEA MARKETS

We know or have heard about these markets, but have not personally contacted each one, as we have the markets with descriptions. If you plan to visit one of these markets listed below, *please call first* to make sure they are still open. Flea markets do come and go. While they were open when we went to press, they may not be later. We can't be responsible. *Call first!*

**Alexandria:** Dantzler's Flea Market, 5416 Masonic Dr. Tel: (318) 443-1589.

**Baton Rouge:** Flea Market, 5905 Florida Blvd. Tel: (225) 923-0333.

**Baton Rouge:** Merchants Landing Flea Market, 9800 Florida Blvd. Tel: (504) 925-1664.

**Bossier City:** USA Flea Mart, 6201 E Texas St. Tel: (318) 741-0055.

**Cut Off:** Mary's Flea Market, 15091 E Main St. Tel: (504) 632-2705.

**De Ridder:** Southwest Flea Market, 2975 Hwy 171. Tel: (318) 462-0555.

**Dubach:** Hilly Junction Flea Market, 3171 Hwy 167. Tel: (318) 777-3424.

**Eunice:** Cajun Flea Market, 1051 W Laurel Ave. Tel: (318) 457-7274.

**Gretna:** Gretna Flea Market, 225 5 St. Tel: (504) 368-6898.

**Hammond:** Habitat For Humanity, 302 N Cate St. Tel: (504) 543-0216.

**Hammond:** Tri-Parish Flea Market, 101 Alida St. Tel: (504) 542-0911.

**Harrisonburg:** Harrisonburg Flea Market. Tel: (318) 744-5994.

**Iowa:** Cormier's Flea Market, 15311 Hwy 165. Tel: (318) 582-6752.

**Jennings:** B & F Flea Market, 202 S Cutting Ave. Tel: (318) 824-2722.

**Kenner:** Sante Fe Flea Market, 623 Maria St. Tel: (504) 463-5701.

**Labadieville:** Trash & Treasures Flea Market, 2707 Hwy 1010. Tel: (504) 526-3869.

**Lafayette:** Common Market, 2510 Ambassador Caffery Pkwy. Tel: (318) 981-4428.

**Lafayette:** Dud Arnaud Flea Markets, 1016 Cameron St. Tel: (318) 235-4345.

**Lafayette:** Pinhook Flea Market, 3131 W Pinhook Rd. Tel: (318) 234-1538.

**Lake Charles:** Bee & Bee Flea Market, 109 Widgeon St. Tel: (318) 439-0101.

**Lake Charles:** Rainbow Flea Market, 2913 Ryan St. Tel: (318) 439-2575.

**Leesville:** Little Willie's Flea Market, 14004 Lake Charles Hwy. Tel: (318) 537-3000.

**Leesville:** Pickering Flea Market, Hwy 171 S. Tel: (318) 537-0342.

**Metairie:** Veterans Trading Bazaar & Flea Market, 4032 Veterans Memorial Blvd. Tel: (504) 887-2969.

**Natalbany:** Doug's Flea Market, 15054 Hwy 1064. Tel: (504) 345-8277.

**Natalbany:** Natalbany Flea Market, Hwy 51. Tel: (504) 542-7018.

**New Iberia:** Cajun Market, 5205 Hwy 90 E. Tel: (318) 367-1383.

**New Orleans:** Paul's Flea Market, 1834 N Claiborne Ave. Tel: (504) 943-5115.

**Pineville:** 28 E Flea Market and Antiques, 5625 Hwy 28 E. Tel: (318) 443-9966.

**Prairieville:** Greater Baton Rouge Flea Market, 15545 Airline Hwy. Tel: (504) 673-2682.

**Shreveport:** Dunn's Flea Market. Tel: (318) 687-1501.

**Shreveport:** Dunn Robby & Marabella Flea Mkt, 1854 S Brookwood Dr. Tel: (318) 687-1840.

**Zachary:** Zachary Crossroads Flea Market, 20130 Plank Rd. Tel: (225) 658-9566.

# MAINE

## BRUNSWICK
### Waterfront Flea Market

**DATES:** Saturday and Sunday, year round.

**TIMES:** 8:00 AM-5:00 PM.

**ADMISSION:** Free. Parking is free.

**LOCATION:** 14 Maine St. It's the huge 4-story brick mill building down by the Androscoggin River Bridge. You really can't miss this one.

**DESCRIPTION:** Opened in 1996 in a very old 1830s' textile mill, this building houses 70 dealers selling literally everything from antiques and collectibles, cards, and books, to produce and new merchandise. Their snack bar is so popular that people come to the snack bar for the food, and then to shop. Next door is a 140-dealer antique mall, a candle factory and outlet store as well as other shops. (Lock up your wallet!)

**DEALER RATES:** $10 per day for 10' × 10' space including 1 table. Reservations are necessary as there is a waiting list for space.

**CONTACT:** Arthur Young, Waterfront Flea Market, 14 Maine St, Brunswick ME 04011. Tel: (207) 729-0378. Fax: (207) 725-9500.

## FREEPORT
### Red Wheel Flea Market

**DATES:** Saturdays, Sundays, and holidays, from April through October. Rain or shine.

**TIMES:** 9:00 AM-4:00 PM.

**ADMISSION:** Free. Free parking is available.

**LOCATION:** US Rt 1 in Freeport on the south side.

**DESCRIPTION:** This market is in its 31st year, with space for 120 dealers (averages 50) selling both indoors and out. About 70% of the show is collectibles and used merchandise; the rest is new and/or more modern. Right in town is the Freeport Mall with over 90 new outlet stores (LL Bean, included). Food is served from a snack bar serving all home-cooked food.

**DEALER RATES:** Outside: $7 per 8' table with parking frontage on Saturday; $10 on Sunday. Inside: $10 on Saturday, $12 on Sunday. $25 for permanent space per weekend. Reservations are suggested.

**CONTACT:** Ed Collett, 291 US Rt 1 S, Freeport ME 04032. Tel: (207) 865-6492.

# NORTH VASSALBORO
## North Vassalboro Flea Market

**DATES:** Thursday through Sunday, weather permitting.
**TIMES:** 10:00 AM-5:00 PM.
**ADMISSION:** Free. Parking is free.
**LOCATION:** Rt 32.
**DESCRIPTION:** This little indoor/outdoor market sells mostly garage sale goodies and colletibles. The inside market is new merchandise sold by year-round dealers. No food, but there is a restroom on site.
**DEALER RATES:** $5 per day per table. Inside selling only new merchandise by the month. Outside, first come, first served. Just get there by 9:00 AM and see the manager.
**CONTACT:** Richard DeRosby, North Vassalboro Flea Market, Rt 32, N Vassalboro ME 04962. Tel: (207) 872-9253.

# OXFORD
## Undercover Antiques

**DATES:** Daily.
**TIMES:** 8:00 AM to last customer.
**ADMISSION:** Free. Parking is also free.
**LOCATION:** Rt 26. One-half mile north of Oxford Plains Speedway on left. Only 30 minutes from I-95 Gray exit and 45 minutes from Conway.
**DESCRIPTION:** Under new ownership since June 1997, this market originally opened in 1984. There are 65 dealers inside, year round, selling antiques, collectibles, sports cards, primitives, advertising items, videos and paperbacks (40,000 of them!).
**DEALER RATES:** $100-$140 a month for a 8' × 10' booth, tables $60 a month and the market does the selling.
**CONTACT:** Bert Morin, Undercover Flea Market, 960 Main St, Oxford ME 04270. Tel: (207) 539-4149.

# PORTLAND
## Portland Expo Flea Market

**DATES:** Every Sunday except "other scheduled show" Sundays when they can't hold the flea market. Please call to double-check the Sunday in question as they have regular "other" shows scheduled. Check their website for competing shows, including antique expos.
**TIMES:** 9:00 AM-4:00 PM.

**ADMISSION:** Free. Free parking is also available.

**LOCATION:** Portland Exposition Building, 239 Park Ave. From Maine Tnpk Exit 6A or Exit 7, follow I-295 to Exit 5 Congress St exit (Maine Rt 22). At the first set of lights, take a left onto St John St, then at the next set of lights take a right onto Park Ave. Expo is on the left.

**DESCRIPTION:** Started in 1981, this is Maine's largest indoor flea market located in the historic Portland Exposition Building, the second oldest arena in continuous operation in the United States. It is heated, clean, and friendly. There is an average of 150 dealers selling antiques, fine art, arts and crafts, used videos (from video stores), Avon, baseball cards, depression glass, old books, collectibles, new merchandise, and "junque." Full-service concessions provide home-style food on the premises, and handicapped-accessible restrooms come in handy.

**DEALER RATES:** $20 for regular space and table; $26 for bleacher space (includes table); $32 for corner space (includes 2 tables in "L" formation). Reservations are advised.

**CONTACT:** Flea Market, Public Assembly Facilities, 239 Park Ave, Portland ME 04102. Tel: (207) 874-8200. Fax: (207) 874-8130. Email: dennis@ci.portland.me.us. Web: www.portlandevents.com.

# SACO
## Cascade Flea Market

**DATES:** Weekends, May through October. Daily from mid-June through Labor Day.

**TIMES:** 7:00 AM-5:00 PM, or as late as the customers hang around.

**ADMISSION:** Free. Parking is free.

**LOCATION:** Rt 1. Take Exit 5 off Maine Tnpk. After the toll take Exit 2B; sign will read Rt 1N, Portland Rd. Take that exit, go approximately 2 miles north on Rt 1. On the right-hand side at the corner of Rt 1 and Cascade Rd.

**DESCRIPTION:** This outdoor market has been operating since 1979 near Old Orchard Beach and Funtown-Splashtown USA. The dealers, numbering anywhere from 100 to 350 (depending on who hogs how much space), sell plenty of antiques, collectibles, crafts, produce and new merchandise. Two snack concessions serve the hungry. Restrooms are on site.

**DEALER RATES:** Spaces, 15' frontage (with tables): Monday through Friday $8, Saturday $18, Sunday $20. Tables and their little spaces, each: Monday through Friday $4, Saturday $9, Sunday $10. Reservations are suggested as they are usually full.

CONTACT: Betty O'Donnell, Cascade Flea Market, 885 Portland Rd. Saco ME 04072. Tel: (207) 282-8875. Fax: (207) 883-9033.

# SCARBOROUGH
## Scarborough Downs Flea Market & Craft Show
**DATES:** Saturday & Sunday.
**TIMES:** 8:00 AM-4:00 PM.
**ADMISSION:** Free. Parking is free.
**LOCATION:** Scarborough Downs Race Track. Exit 6, Maine Tnpk or Rt 1.
**DESCRIPTION:** This indoor market, opened in 1997, hosts from 20 dealers in summer (face it, the beach market beckons) to 300 tables, worth in winter (i.e. full, when the beach is cold and the tourists are gone). They sell antiques, collectibles, occasional produce (some from Florida), some garage sale goodies, used vacuums and TVs, and new merchandise. There is a concession stand as well as handicapped-accessible restrooms on site.
**DEALER RATES:** Summer: $10 per table per day, winter: $20 per table per day. Reservations are required.
**CONTACT:** Scarborough Downs Flea Market & Craft Show, PO Box 248, Gray ME 04039-0248. Tel: (207) 657-2962 or security at the track at (207) 883-4331. Fax: (207) 657-2965.

# SEARSPORT
## Hobby Horse Flea Market
**DATES:** Every Saturday and Sunday from May through mid-October. Every day but Tuesday, some of the dealers are open anyway.
**TIMES:** 8:00 AM-5:00 PM.
**ADMISSION:** Free. Parking is free.
**LOCATION:** Rt 1, Bangor Rd, 3 miles north of Searsport.
**DESCRIPTION:** This indoor/outdoor market of 30 dealers sells mostly antiques and collectibles including Fiesta ware, coins, loads of old books, plenty of used goods, some furniture, jewelry, crafts, clothing, even Native American stuff from Arizona, gas pumps, cans and auto stuff, as well as a little new merchandise. The dealers are housed in 16 small buildings, one larger building shared by two dealers and tables under canopies for the outdoor dealers. There is a lunch wagon on weekends and a restroom. They have been written up in several papers.

**DEALER RATES:** $6 per table. There are 40 tables to choose from. The indoor spaces are rented by the season. Only charge for Saturday, Sunday and holidays; the rest of the time it's free.
**CONTACT:** Mary Harriman, Hobby Horse Flea Market, PO Box 215, Stockton Springs ME 04981. Tel: (207) 548-2981.

---

**Movie Goodies**
  One of the coffins from Stephen King's movie *Pet Sematary*, was sold here, along with other items from the movie set. A local cemetery was used for the shoot.

---

# TRENTON
## Bargain Barn Flea Market
**DATES:** Saturday, Sunday and holidays, Memorial Day through September, weather permitting.
**TIMES:** 7:00 AM-5:00 PM.
**ADMISSION:** Free. Parking is free if you can find a place. Hint: Look behind the building, there is plenty of room there.
**LOCATION:** Rt 3, between Ellsworth and Bar Harbor, ¼ mile from the bridge entering Acadia National Park and Mt Desert Island.
**DESCRIPTION:** Over 20 years old, this market has between 40 and 50 dealers with room for more. Everything from collectibles to new merchandise, expensive collectibles, good old "stuff," to good new stuff, "quite a mixture," including some crafts. Snacks are available on the premises, but there is a restaurant next door.
**DEALER RATES:** $10 per space per day; seasonal rates available. First come, first served, except for the seasonal
**CONTACT:** George Wallace, Bargain Barn Flea Market, RR1 Box 176, Trenton ME 04605-9717. Tel: (207) 667-5022.

# WOOLWICH
## Montsweag Flea Market
**DATES:** Wednesday, Saturday and Sunday, May through October. Also, Friday, June through August.
**TIMES:** 6:30 AM-3:00 PM.
**ADMISSION:** Free. Free parking is available.
**LOCATION:** On Rt 1 in Woolwich, 5 miles north of Bath.

**DESCRIPTION:** The promoter tells us that this market, started in 1977, is rated number one in Maine and number three in New England. It is pictured in the book *Coastal Maine, A State of Mind*. There are about 100 dealers selling antiques, arts and crafts, fresh produce, collectibles, new merchandise, tools, plants and seedlings, early primitives, and fine jewelry. This market mainly deals with antiques and collectibles. The market is held outdoors and there is food served on the premises.

**DEALER RATES:** $8 and $10 for 3' × 8' tables, depending on market day. Advance reservations are requested.

**CONTACT:** Norma Scopino, 6 Hunnewell Ln, Woolwich ME 04579-4852. Tel: (207) 443-2809. Email: fleamkt@gwi.net.

# OTHER FLEA MARKETS

We know or have heard about these markets, but have not personally contacted each one, as we have the markets with descriptions. If you plan to visit one of these markets listed below, *please call first* to make sure they are still open. Flea markets do come and go. While they were open when we went to press, they may not be later. We can't be responsible. *Call first!*

**Caribou:** Caribou Flea Market, Old Agway Building. Tel: (207) 764-3000.

**Hampden:** Hampden Flea Market & Antiques, 376 Meadow Rd. Tel: (207) 862-3211.

**Lebanon:** Jumping Flea Market, Creamery Hill Rd. Tel: (207) 457-1037.

**Madison:** Madelyn's Fleamarket, Hwy 201. Tel: (207) 474-2705.

**Portland:** Morrill's Corner Flea Market, 33 Allen Ave Rear. Tel: (207) 878-0238.

**Westbrook:** Westbrook Flea-Mart, 1399 Bridgton Rd. Tel: (207) 854-5623.

**Woodland:** Airline Flea Market, RR 1 Box 96. Tel: (207) 454-3862.

# MARYLAND

## BALTIMORE

### North Point Drive-In Outdoor/Indoor Flea Market

**DATES:** Every Saturday and Sunday. Rain or shine.

**TIMES:** 7:00 AM-2:00 PM.

**ADMISSION:** $.25 per person. Parking for 800 cars is free.

**LOCATION:** 4001 N Point Blvd. Take the Baltimore Beltway 695, off at Exit 41, bear left, go to the McDonald's; they are across the street on the right.

**DESCRIPTION:** Started in 1971, this indoor/outdoor market runs year round in a 24,000-square-foot building next to a drive-in theater. It is claimed to be the oldest and one of the largest flea markets in the area. On Saturdays, 150-200 dealers (300 on Sunday) sell antiques, arts and crafts, fresh produce, collectibles, new merchandise, used items, junk, plants, furniture, etc. One snack bar inside, a hot dog stand outside and handicapped-accessible restrooms add to the amenities.

**DEALER RATES:** $10 on Saturday inside or out, $10 inside per table, $15 per space outside on Sundays. Please call for information. Reservations are helpful. Sundays, the back opens at 4:00 AM.

**CONTACT:** Dottie Stevens, North Point Drive-In Flea Market, 7721 Old Battlegrove Rd, Baltimore MD 21222. Tel: (410) 477-1337.

### Patapsco Flea Market

**DATES:** Saturday and Sunday. Rain or shine.

**TIMES:** 8:00 AM-5:00 PM.

**ADMISSION:** $.25. Parking is free.

**LOCATION:** Corner of 1400 W Patapsco Ave and Annapolis Blvd.

**DESCRIPTION:** Started in 1982 in a former "strip mall," this market has 700 dealers indoors (140,000 square feet) and outdoors selling "everything"— a few antiques, new and used merchandise, collectibles, garage sale goodies, and more. They are growing constantly, adding buildings as needed. There are weekly bingo games, an international food court, deli, ice cream parlor, carry-out lunch counters, barbecue pit, hot dog stand, handicapped-accessible restrooms, and more.

**DEALER RATES:** $10 and up for large outdoor space; $15 and up table space inside; $75 and up for a large store. Reservations are not required. Office hours and vendor stocking hours are 9:00 AM-2:00 PM Thursday and Friday.

**CONTACT:** Bob Lomonico, Patapsco Flea Market, 1400 W Patapsco Ave, Baltimore MD 21230. Tel: (410) 354-5262 or 354-3040 or office at 354-3041. Fax: (410) 354-3876.

# BETHESDA
## Farmer's Flea Market

*Note: I was not able to reach Mr. Bonfils; I am making the presumption that the market is still running.*

**DATES:** Every Sunday, April through November.
**TIMES:** 9:00 AM-5:00 PM.
**ADMISSION:** Free. Free parking is available.
**LOCATION:** Two miles south of I-495 at 7155 Wisconsin Ave in Bethesda (northwest Washington DC area).
**DESCRIPTION:** Started in 1974, 50 to 60 outside dealers now sell antiques, collectibles, and furniture. Great sales are available at the Montgomery County Farm Women's Market. Food is served on the premises.
**DEALER RATES:** $15 per 10' × 20' space. Reservations are not required.
**CONTACT:** James R Bonfils, 4530 Alton Pl NW, Washington DC 20016. No phone available.

# COLUMBIA
## The Columbia Market

**DATES:** Every Sunday, March through October. Rain or shine.
**TIMES:** 8:00 AM-3:00 PM.
**ADMISSION:** Free. Parking is available and is also free.
**LOCATION:** Between Baltimore and Washington DC. Off I-95, Exit 41 W to Rt 175, at the mall on the JCPenney's side.
**DESCRIPTION:** This market first opened in 1972. It is held outdoors, but protected from weather, and accommodates up to 300 dealers—200 undercover and 100 in the open. There is a huge variety of antiques, collectibles, and crafts for sale under a double-deck parking lot. Food is available at the mall.
**DEALER RATES:** $50 per 16' × 16' space undercover pre-paid, $45 per space unprotected, pre-paid. Call for more rates. Reservations are suggested.
**CONTACT:** Bellman Promotions Inc, 11959 Philadelphia Rd, Bradshaw MD 21021. Tel: (410) 679-2288. Fax: (410) 679-6919.

# DUNDALK (BALTIMORE)
## Plaza Flea Market

**DATES:** Friday through Sunday.

**TIMES:** Friday 10:00 AM-7:00 PM, Saturday-Sunday 7:00 AM-4:00 PM.

**ADMISSION:** Free. Parking is free.

**LOCATION:** 2401 N Point Blvd. Exit 40 off I-695.

**DESCRIPTION:** Opened in 1987, this market of 310-390 dealers (depending on season) sells antiques, collectibles, crafts, produce, meats, coins, stamps, clothing, cards, electronics, garage sale goodies, new merchandise, furniture, and even has various home-improvement contractors on site. In case you need them, there are eight snack bars, two other food outlets, and handicapped-accessible restrooms. In 12 years, they grew from 10,000 to 112,000 square feet. Not bad at all!

**DEALER RATES:** $65-$70 per week per 10' × 15' space, or $10-$15 per space with table per day.

**CONTACT:** Joe or Mike Miller, Plaza Flea Market, 2401 N Point Blvd, Dundalk MD 21222-1624. Tel: 410-285-4504 or 288-3554. Email: jmille1420@aol.com.

# EDGEWOOD
## Bonnie Brae Flea Market

**DATES:** Every Sunday, weather permitting.

**TIMES:** 7:00 AM-until.

**ADMISSION:** Free. Free parking is available.

**LOCATION:** 1301 Pulaski Hwy in Edgewood, Harford County, Company grounds. Take Rt 40 (Pulaski Hwy), 20 miles NE of Baltimore, between Joppa and Aberdeen; Exit 74 off I-95.

**DESCRIPTION:** Opened in 1974, this indoor/outdoor flea market was at one time (during the '50s and '60s) one of the largest truck stops on the East Coast built and operated by the Merritt family. When I-95 was built the traffic left. Now it's coming back. Their dealers are selling antiques, fine art, arts and crafts, Depression glass (many patterns), some Flo-blue and Carnival, oyster cans, dolls, Roseville and other pottery, some furniture, marbles, clocks, record players, china dishes, collectibles, new merchandise, baseball cards, and much more. The market specializes in Depression and Carnival glass.

**DEALER RATES:** $5 per 12' × 10' space per day. No advance reservations required.

**CONTACT:** Juanita Merritt, 1003 Magnolia Rd, Joppa MD 21085. Tel: (410) 679-2210 or (410) 679-6895.

# ELDERSBURG
## Freedom Lions Club Flea Market

**DATES:** Annually on the last Saturday of April. For 2000: April 29, 2001: April 28.

**TIMES:** 8:00 AM-3:00 PM.

**ADMISSION:** Free and parking is free.

**LOCATION:** In Carroll County, 2 miles south of Eldersburg at the Freedom District Fire Company Carnival Grounds. Only 20 minutes NW of Baltimore and about 8 miles north of I-70.

**DESCRIPTION:** Limited to 150 quality dealers, this market is the fundraiser for the Freedom District Lions Club and benefits the Wilmer Eye Institute at Johns Hopkins Hospital. Among the treasures sold are: antiques, collectibles, baseball cards, homemade dolls, tools, and spring flowers. There is a variety of food to please everyone.

**DEALER RATES:** $15 for a 24' × 24' space outdoors. Reservations are required.

**CONTACT:** Ruth Howsden, 6111 Oklahoma Rd, Eldersburg MD 21784. Tel: (410) 795-0984.

# FORESTVILLE
## Uncle Jack's Flea Market

**DATES:** Friday through Sunday.

**TIMES:** Friday and Sunday 12:00 PM-6:00 PM, Saturday 9:00 AM-6:00 PM.

**ADMISSION:** Free. Parking is free.

**LOCATION:** 7756 Marlboro Pk. Take the Beltway (I-495), Exit 11B, turn right at the first light, right at the second light, quick left into the shopping center.

**DESCRIPTION:** This indoor/outdoor market features 35-40 dealers year round selling antiques, collectibles, crafts, coins, stamps, cards, new merchandise and brand new furniture "at flea market prices." No food, but handicapped-accessible restrooms are on site.

**DEALER RATES:** $15 per table. Reservations are not required.

**CONTACT:** Jack Kalin, Uncle Jack's Flea Market, 7756 Marlboro Pike, Forestville MD 20747-4410. Tel: (301) 736-JACK (5225). Fax: (301) 736-4778.

# INDIAN HEAD
## Village Green Flea Market

**DATES:** Saturdays April through October except July 4th. Rain or shine.

**TIMES:** 7:00 AM-1:00 PM.

**ADMISSION:** Free. Parking is also free.

**LOCATION:** On the Village Green. From out of town take Indian Head Hwy S (formerly known as I-210 S) to the very end. Village Green is located on the right just outside the main entrance to the Naval Surface Warfare Center, off Lackey Dr and Pye St.

**DESCRIPTION:** Started in 1987 by the Town of Indian Head as a way for local residents to have a flea market and a place to have yard sales, this market usually has about 30-35 dealers and residents selling flea market goods, yard sale items, some new merchandise, wood crafts, and local fresh produce.

**DEALER RATES:** $7 per space, collected on site. Reservations are not required. Local permit required for food sales (excludes produce). Pet sales/give-aways not permitted. Pre-packaged food sales allowed by permit only.

**CONTACT:** Town of Indian Head Community Affairs, Attn: Karen L-Williams, 4195 Indian Head Hwy, Indian Head MD 20640. Tel: (301) 753-6633 or (301) 743-5574. Fax: (301) 743-9008.

# NORTH EAST
## North East Auction Galleries and Flea Market

**DATES:** Every day. Rain or shine.

**TIMES:** 8:00 AM-dusk.

**ADMISSION:** Free. Ample free parking is provided.

**LOCATION:** Off I-95, on the corner of Rt 40 and Mechanics Valley Rd.

**DESCRIPTION:** This market has been in operation since 1973, and currently attracts between 50 dealers in winter and 150 in summer who sell a variety of goods including antiques, collectibles, craft items, new merchandise, auto parts, furniture, household goods, appliances, baseball cards, oriental rugs and fresh produce. The market is located at the head of the picturesque Chesapeake Bay, in a high traffic area near state parks, marinas, campgrounds, yacht clubs, and other local attractions. In addition, a consignment auction is held every Tuesday evening and an automobile auction is held every Thursday evening. Food is available on the premises.

**DEALER RATES:** $15 per 8' × 10' table inside; outside tables are $10. Reservations are suggested for inside; outside first come, first served.

**CONTACT:** R C Burkheimer, North East Auction Galleries, PO Box 551, North East MD 21901-0551. Tel: 1-800-233-4169. In Maryland, call (410) 287-5588. Fax: (410) 287-2029.

# RISING SUN
## Hunter's Sale Barn, Inc

**DATES:** Every Monday. Rain or shine.
**TIMES:** 3:00 PM-9:00 PM, auction at 6:00 PM.
**ADMISSION:** Free. Free parking is available.
**LOCATION:** Take Exit 93 off I-95, then go north 2½ miles to a dead end, turn right on Rt 276; market is 2½ miles down on the right.
**DESCRIPTION:** Originally this business was a livestock market. The flea and farmers' market started in 1975, and the livestock sales stopped in 1985. This indoor/outdoor market has 120 dealers selling antiques, arts and crafts, fresh produce, collectibles, and new merchandise. This is a family oriented market kept clean and very pleasant. In addition, an auction is also conducted at the market at 6:00 PM selling eggs, produce and general merchandise. Monday night is Sale Barn Auction Night for the county. There is a full restaurant on the premises. This is a well-attended market drawing 300-plus people to the auction alone. As a result of a nasty Easter Sunday fire burning down their auction house, they have built a new state-of-the-art heated/air-conditioned 17,500-square-foot building to replace the old one.
**DEALER RATES:** $15 per 4' × 8' space, $25 for a 16' × 16' space. First come, first served.
**CONTACT:** Norman E Hunter and Carol A or Ronda L Hunter, PO Box 427, Rising Sun MD 21911. Tel: (410) 658-6400 or fax: (410) 658-3864.

# UPPER MARLBORO
## American Heritage Antique Jubilee — Spring

**DATES:** For 2000: June 10-11. Rain or shine.
**TIMES:** Saturday 10:00 PM-5:00 PM; Sunday 12:00 PM-5:00 PM.
**ADMISSION:** Friday $20 (Early Buyers Pass for 3 days); Saturday and Sunday $5 per day. Parking is free.
**LOCATION:** Prince Georges Equestrian Center. Off Rt 4, midway between Washington DC and Baltimore MD.
**DESCRIPTION:** An annual, multi-dimensional show featuring indoor and outdoor spaces. Over 1,000 dealers come from 35 states. This is an antique

and collectible show only with entertainment and specialty food vendors. Handicapped-accessible restrooms add to the amenities.

**DEALER RATES:** $110 per heated space. $70 for unheated space, $70 per outdoor space. Tents are available for outdoor vendors at affordable rates. Reservations and pre-payment are required.

**CONTACT:** D'Amore Promotions, 2125 McComas Way Ste 102, Virginia Beach VA 23454. Tel: (757) 427-7717. Fax: (757) 427-8888. Web: www.bigfleamarket.com.

## OTHER FLEA MARKETS:

We know or have heard about these markets, but have not personally contacted each one, as we have the markets with descriptions. If you plan to visit one of these markets listed below, *please call first* to make sure they are still open. Flea markets do come and go. While they were open when we went to press, they may not be later. We can't be responsible. *Call first!*

**Baltimore:** Hilltop Indoor Flea Market, 5504 Park Heights Ave. Tel: (410) 358-5870.

**Baltimore:** M & M Flea Market, 700 N Linwood Ave. Tel: (410) 327-4052.

**Boonsboro:** Boonsboro Flea Market, 7700 Old National Pike. Tel: (301) 416-2788.

**Boonsboro:** Rt 65, 7445 Sharpsburg Pike. Tel: (301) 432-7793.

**Hagerstown:** First Inner-City Flea Market, 13617 Pennsylvania Ave. Tel: (301) 791-6408.

**Joppa:** Pulaski Flea Market, 12420 Pulaski Hwy. Tel: (410) 679-3206.

**Laurel:** Teen Challenge Flea Market, 13919 Baltimore Ave. Tel: (301) 490-1667.

**Temple Hills:** Yard Sale & Stuff, 5911 Lambert Dr. Tel: (301) 894-3834.

# MASSACHUSETTS

## AUBURN

### Auburn Antique and Flea Market, Inc

**DATES:** Every Sunday indoors and outdoors, year round. Rain or shine. April through November, Saturdays outdoors, weather permitting.

**TIMES:** 7:00 AM-4:00 PM.

**ADMISSION:** $.50 for adults, children free during winter. Free during summer months.

**LOCATION:** 773 Southbridge St, Rt 12. From Massachusetts Tnpk take Exit 10, follow Rt 12 south for ½ mile. From I-290 take Exit 8, follow Rt 12 south for ½ mile. From I-395 take Exit 7, follow Rt 12 south ½ mile.

**DESCRIPTION:** This indoor/outdoor market has been open since 1975. It accommodates approximately 100 dealers indoors, and 75 dealers outdoors. Many items such as antiques, arts and crafts, collectibles, new merchandise, and even fresh produce can be found. Many dealers also sell a variety of stamps, coins, and baseball cards. One snack bar feeds the wilting, and during the summer, there are handicapped-accessible restrooms on site outside. The inside facilities are upstairs.

**DEALER RATES:** $30 per 9' × 9' space, indoors. $15 per space outdoors on Sundays, $10 on Saturdays. Reservations are required for indoor space during the winter season only.

**CONTACT:** Auburn Antique & Flea Market Inc, 773 Southbridge St, PO Box 33, Auburn MA 01501-0033. Tel: (508) 832-2763.

## BRIMFIELD

*Brimfield always opens the second Tuesday in May, first Tuesdays after July 4 and Labor Day, and runs through the following Sunday. The only exception is when a Jewish holiday falls during the week after Labor Day, then it is pushed back a week.*

*Brimfield, a small town in Massachusetts, turns into a huge and justly famous antiques- and collectibles-only show three times a year.*

### Crystal Brook Antique Show

**DATES:** 2000 dates: May 9-13, July 11-15, and September 5-9. This market is open for the whole Brimfield show.

**TIMES:** 6:00 AM-5:00 PM.

**ADMISSION**: Free. However, they don't have any parking area as they are so small.

**LOCATION**: On Rt 20. Take the Palmer exit off the Massachusetts Tnpk, to Rt 20, then 10 miles east to Brimfield. Or Sturbridge exit on Massachusetts Tnpk, then 10 miles west of Sturbridge on Rt 20.

**DESCRIPTION**: It is an outdoor market that accommodates approximately 35 dealers. This is considered a relatively small market, but there are many quality antiques and collectibles sold.

**DEALER RATES**: Call for current rates.

**CONTACT**: Maureen Ethier, Rt 20, Brimfield MA 01010. Tel: (413) 245-7647.

## J & J Promotions Antiques and Collectibles Shows

**DATES**: 2000: May 12-13, July 14-15, September 8-9. Rain or shine. 2001: May 11-12, July 13-14, September 7-8. Generally, the same Friday and Saturday of each Brimfield show.

**TIMES**: Friday 6:00 AM-5:00 PM; Saturday 9:00 AM-5:00 PM.

**ADMISSION**: Friday $5 per person, Saturday $3. $5 parking fee. Oversized vehicles are $10.

**LOCATION**: From Boston: take Massachusetts Tnpk west to Exit 9 at Sturbridge; follow Rt 20 west to Brimfield for approximately 7 miles to Auction Acres. From New York City: take I-95 north to I-91 north. Go through Hartford to I-84 east to Sturbridge and Rt 20 west for about 6 miles. Or, I-95 north to I-91 through Hartford to Springfield to I-291 east to I-90 (Massachusetts Tnpk) east to Exit 8 at Palmer, go beyond exit booth and turn right at stop light, then left to Rt 20 east for approximately 6 miles. Look for tan colonial house with red shutters and a big red barn located on southern side of Rt. 20.

**DESCRIPTION**: This outdoor show first opened in 1959. Auction Acres is the home of Gordon Reid's original Antique Market. Now owned by his two daughters, this prestigious property covers 40 acres at the center of Brimfield. Today, antiques and collectibles enthusiasts from all over the world continue to visit this famous market. Dealers and exhibitors alike have, year after year, relied on the experience and quality in the organization and presentation of these shows of antiques and collectibles. Food is served on the premises.

**DEALER RATES**: Space size and prices vary. Please call for more information.

**CONTACT:** Jill Reid Lukesh and Judith Reid Mathieu, J & J Promotions, Auction Acres, PO Box 385, Brimfield MA 01010-0385. Tel: (413) 245-3436 or (978) 597-8155. Email: info@jandj-brimfield.com. Web: www.jandj-brimfield.com.

---

### For Sale

One Push-Me-Pull-You from Dr Doolittle fame.

---

### Angus, Where Are You?

During one market, Angus went missing. This little white male dog got "lost" at the market and his prim Scottish owner put out a $500 reward for his safe return. Reports came flying in from all corners of tiny Brimfield that Angus was seen with this female dog, then that one, then another—*for 2½ days!* All the time, she, the owner, would wail in her brogue, that "wee Angus wouldn't be doing *that*." Naturally, the market personnel were frantically trying to deal with the market while trying to help alleviate Mommy Angus' worst fears.

Looking for the reward, streams of people came in with dogs on leashes, none of which fitted Angus's tiny white-bodied description. To top that off, there is a no-pets and animals policy here, for fairly obvious reasons.

Finally, Angus wandered back to Mama, looking extremely worse for wear—filthy, mud-spattered, lumpy coat—just awful looking. "Ah, me Angus," brogued Mommy, "Angus had a *dirrrrty* weekend."

Now, when things go awry at Brimfield, it's known as an "Angus" day.

---

## New England Motel Antiques Market, Inc

**DATES:** This market operates Wednesday through Sunday of Brimfield week. 2000 dates: May 10-14, July 12-16, September 6-10.

**TIMES:** Wednesday opening days 6:00 AM-dusk; other days, 8:00 AM to dusk.

**ADMISSION:** $5, opening day only. Parking is $5.

**LOCATION:** Rt 20, Palmer Rd in the center of the Mart.

**DESCRIPTION:** This show started in 1986 and is said "to have the finest and freshest merchandise in the Brimfield's." About 400 reputable dealers from the United States, Canada and Europe sell quality antiques and collectibles in the center of the Northeast's greatest outdoor show. There is a food court on the premises.

**DEALER RATES:** $230 for a 20' × 24' booth. Reservations are required. Parking is also available.

**CONTACT:** Marie Doldoorian, PO Box 186, Sturbridge MA 01566. Tel: (508) 347-2179. Day of show call: (413) 245-3348. Email: kikdanjo@aol.com. Web: www.antiques-brimfield.com.

## Shelton Antique Shows

**DATES:** 2000 dates: May 9-14, July 11-16, and September 5-10. 2001: May 8-13, July 10-15, September 4-9. This market is open for the entire Brimfield show.

**TIMES:** Daybreak on.

**LOCATION:** 34 Main St aka Rt 20 (aka Palmer Rd). Between Exit 9 Sturbridge or Exit 8 Palmer off Massachusetts Tnpk. Exit Sturbridge Rt 86 from Connecticut.

**ADMISSION:** Free. Parking is $4-6 a day.

**DESCRIPTION:** This market started in 1975 and is located on 1-mile strip of the largest outdoor antique event in the United States. Approximately 175 dealers sell antiques and collectibles. There are dealer showers, food service, and table rentals available. Pets are welcome.

**DEALER RATES:** From $250 per 20' × 20' booth. Reservations are required. One-day rates offered after opening day.

**CONTACT:** Lois J Shelton, PO Box 124, Brimfield MA 01010-0124. Tel: (413) 245-3591. Fax: (413) 245-7905.

---

**Weird**

An antique hearse was sold here after a hot bidding war. It was the only item brought in by the dealer.

---

# EAST DOUGLAS

## Douglas Flea Market, Antiques, and Collectibles

**DATES:** Saturday, Sunday and some holidays.

**TIMES:** Saturday 10:00 AM-4:00 PM; Sunday 8:00 AM-4:00 PM.

**ADMISSION:** Free. Parking is free.

**LOCATION:** Northeast Main St. From Providence or Worcester: take Rt 146 to Rt 16, Douglas exit, go west 3 miles to flashing light, make sharp right turn. Market is ¼ mile on left.

**DESCRIPTION:** This indoor/outdoor market is housed in an historic dairy barn on 50 acres. Dealer tables replace the cows and the silo houses the Snack Bar serving all homemade foods including breakfast, snacks and meals, homemade ice cream. Furniture is sold in the hayloft. Other treasures sold include antiques, memorabilia, glassware, antique toys, country goods, cards, and garage sale goodies. Handicapped-accessible restrooms add to the amenities of this unique and friendly market.

**DEALER RATES:** Outside: $2 per car length, with table $5 = $7. Inside: $10 per week. Reservations are required for inside only.

**CONTACT:** Marlene Bosma, PO Box 634, E Douglas MA 01516. Tel: (508) 278-6027 or weekends at (508) 476-3298.

# GRAFTON
## Grafton Flea Market, Inc

**DATES:** Every Sunday. Rain or shine.

**TIMES:** 6:00 AM-4:00 PM.

**ADMISSION:** $.50 for an adult, children free. Free parking is available.

**LOCATION:** On Rt 140 near the Grafton-Upton town line. Take the Massachusetts Tnpk to Rt 495 south, then take Upton Exit 21B to Rt 140.

**DESCRIPTION:** This show first opened in 1970. There are approximately 200 to 250 dealers attending this market, which is held both indoors and outdoors. A variety of items such as antiques, collectibles, arts and crafts, new merchandise, and fresh produce can be found. There is also a selection of baseball cards, stamps, and coins. There is catered food available on the premises.

**DEALER RATES:** $20 per space, outdoors. $30 per space, indoors. Reservations are required for indoor space only.

**CONTACT:** Harry Peters, PO Box 206, Grafton MA 01519-0206. Tel: (508) 839-2217.

# HADLEY
## Olde Hadley Flea Market

**DATES:** Every Sunday from the third Sunday in April through the first Sunday in November, weather permitting.

**TIMES:** 6:00 AM-4:00 PM.

**ADMISSION:** Free. Free parking is available.

**LOCATION:** On Rt 47 S, Lawrence Plain Rd. Take Exit 19 off Rt 91 north. Or, take Exit 20 off Rt 91 south. Follow Rt 9 east to center of Hadley, then 2 miles south on Rt 47.

**DESCRIPTION:** This show opened in 1980. There are 200-plus dealers selling their goods at this outdoor market. There is everything from antiques and collectibles, from new merchandise to fresh produce sold here including maple sugar, honey and plants. Excellent catered food is available on the premises. This flea market has a beautiful country setting at the foot of the Mount Holyoke Range. Special features of this flea market include antique auto viewing and the Silver Eagle Hot Air Balloon lift-off. There is also the Old Hadley Museum, Skinner State Park, Mitch's Marina, as well as shopping malls and many fine restaurants nearby. Do say "Hi" to Ray and his border collie, Jessie, as they travel around the market in his golfcart.

**DEALER RATES:** $20 per 25' × 25' space. Reservations are not required. First come, first served. There are advance shopping hours for dealers starting at 6:00 AM.

**CONTACT:** Raymond and Marion Szala, 45 Lawrence Plain Rd, Hadley MA 01035. Tel: (413) 586-0352.

# HUBBARDSTON
## Rietta Ranch Flea Market

**DATES:** Sundays, April through October. Rain or shine.

**TIMES:** 6:00 AM-til.

**ADMISSION:** Free admission and free parking.

**LOCATION:** On Rt 68.

**DESCRIPTION:** Opened in 1967, this market attracts 600 dealers who offer antiques, collectibles, handmade/craft items, vegetables, and new merchandise. They offer a full concession with indoor and outdoor dining offering fried dough, hamburgers, hot dogs, and they even have a liquor license. Plenty of handicapped-accessible restrooms and 20 acres of parking make this an easy place to spend the day. They are in the process of restoring a complete antique train with a 1915 steam engine for display.

**DEALER RATES:** Dealers are charged $15 for outside space about the size of a large car including one table. $15 for two tables on the inside. First come, first served or reserve for the season only.

**CONTACT:** Raylene, Rietta Ranch Flea Market, PO Box 35, Hubbardston MA 01452-0035. Tel: (978) 632-0559.

# LEOMINSTER
## Four Seasons Flea Market

**DATES:** Saturday and Sunday, year round.

**TIMES:** 8:30 AM-4:00 PM; except in July and August 10:00 AM-4:00 PM.

**ADMISSION:** Free. Parking is free.

**LOCATION:** 38 Spruce St. Only minutes from Rt 2, I-100 and Rt 12 and Rt 13 off Mechanic St. Just 2 blocks from the center of town.

**DESCRIPTION:** Opened in 1994, this indoor market of 30 dealers in summer (vacation time, doncha know) and 80-90 dealers in winter (now, we're down to business!) sells antiques, collectibles, coins, stamps, cards, garage sale goodies, furniture, and new merchandise. One snack bar with handicapped-accessible restrooms add to the amenities.

**DEALER RATES:** $20 per 10' × 6' space per weekend. Reservations are suggested. There are special rates for multiple spaces.

**CONTACT:** Joe Sans, Four Seasons Flea Market, 38 Spruce St, Leominster MA 01453-3233. Tel: (978) 534-3890 or 1-800-926-9997.

# RAYNHAM
## Raynham Flea Mart

**DATES:** Every Sunday, and Saturdays Thanksgiving through Christmas.

**TIMES:** 8:00 AM-6:00 PM.

**ADMISSION:** $1. Free parking is available.

**LOCATION:** At junction of Rt 24 and Rt 44.

**DESCRIPTION:** This show began in 1974. There are 500 dealers indoors in a 60,000-square-foot one-story building and over 400 dealers outdoors on 10 acres of land. This market screens its dealers to ensure variety and quality of items. These include antiques, arts and crafts, collectibles, jewelry, new merchandise, fresh produce and more. There are six snack bars, a full restaurant and parking for thousands of cars.

**DEALER RATES:** Call for rates as they vary according to location and size. Reservations are recommended.

**CONTACT:** J Mann, Raynham Flea Market, Judson and South St, Raynham MA 02767. Tel: (508) 823-8923. Email: raynhmflea@aol.com. Web: www.raynhamflea.com.

# ROWLEY
## Todd's Farm Famous Old-Fashioned Flea Market

**DATES:** Sundays, mid-April through the Sunday preceding Thanksgiving.

**TIMES:** 5:00 AM to whenever. Flashlights welcome.

**ADMISSION:** Free. Parking is free.

**LOCATION:** Rt 1A. I-95 Exit 54, go east on Rt 133. Then north on Rt 1A 1 mile.

**DESCRIPTION:** This classic flea market, opened in 1973, features up to 240 dealers, depending on the month, selling mostly antiques, collectibles, and especially furniture. There are a number of antique shops in the barn and at the farmhouse. One snack bar inside and one out. Restrooms are available.

**DEALER RATES:** $25 per generous 30' × 20' space per day. First come, first served.

**CONTACT:** Todd's Farm, PO Box 342, Rowley MA 01969-0342. Tel: (978) 948-3300. Email: toddfarm@toddfarm.com. Web: www.toddfarm.com.

## TAUNTON
### Taunton Expo Center Flea Market

**DATES:** Saturday and Sunday, plus some holiday Mondays.

**TIMES:** Saturday 8:00 AM-4:00 PM, Sunday 7:00 AM-5:00 PM.

**ADMISSION:** $1 per adult. Parking is free.

**LOCATION:** 93 Williams St, Taunton Expo Center, Rt 44.

**DESCRIPTION:** Opened under management and enlarged in 1987, this market attracts 500-800 dealers selling antiques, collectibles, crafts, jewelry, clothing, coins, fresh produce, seafood, furniture, garage sale goodies, and new merchandise. There are plenty of food outlets as well as handicapped-accessible restrooms on site.

**DEALER RATES:** Outside: $30 per weekend. Inside: $250 and up monthly. Reservations are required for inside space, not for outside.

**CONTACT:** Armand Gagne, Taunton Expo Center Flea Market, PO Box 68, Taunton MA 02780-0068. Tel: (508) 880-3800. Fax: (508) 880-5100.

## WELLFLEET
### Wellfleet Drive-In Flea Market

**DATES:** Every Saturday, Sunday and holiday Mondays, April through October. Also open every Wednesday and Thursday during July and August. Rain or shine.

**TIMES:** 8:00 AM-4:00 PM.

**ADMISSION:** $1 per carload. $2 per carload during Sundays in high season.

**LOCATION:** On Rt 6 towards Provincetown, on Wellfleet-Eastham line. Once you are on Cape Cod, just follow the road to Provincetown.

**DESCRIPTION:** This show started about 28 years ago in the Cape Cod National Seashore at Wellfleet. They have 26 acres of family entertainment. Depending upon the season, there can be anywhere from 50 to 250 dealers at this outdoor market. They specialize in antiques, collectibles, local shellfish, furniture and new merchandise. There are also arts and crafts vendors, tarot readers, artists, and anything else that is legal. For your convenience, food is available on the premises. The owners of this market pride themselves on running a very clean market with a very fine reputation.

**DEALER RATES:** $20 per 18' × 22' space. Reservations are not required.

**CONTACT:** Eleanor Hazen, Wellfleet Drive-In Flea Market, PO Box 811 Wellfleet MA 02667-0811. Tel: (508) 349-2520 or in Eastern MA 1-800-696-3532. Fax: (508) 349-2902.

## OTHER FLEA MARKETS

We know or have heard about these markets, but have not personally contacted each one, as we have the markets with descriptions. If you plan to visit one of these markets listed below, *please call first* to make sure they are still open. Flea markets do come and go. While they were open when we went to press, they may not be later. We can't be responsible. *Call first!*

**Brockton:** Cary Hill Flea Market, 220 E Ashland St. Tel: (508) 583-3100.

**Dracut:** Big Flea, 1 Mill St. Tel: (978) 957-4242.

**Fitchburg:** Dugout Flea Market, 551 Electric Ave. Tel: (978) 345-2769.

**Fitchburg:** Caron's Flea Market, 11 Summer St. Tel: (978) 345-5682.

**Lawrence:** Jolly Flea, 73 Winthrop Ave. Tel: (978) 682-2020.

**Lynn:** Massachusetts Merchandise Mart, 800 Lynnway. Tel: (617) 598-5450. Open Wed, Sat, Sun, 10 AM-6 PM, Thur-Fri 10 AM-9 PM.

**Malden:** Malden Flea Market, 42 Ferry St. Tel: (781) 324-9113.

**Middleboro:** Middleboro Flea Market, 15 Spruce St. Tel: (508) 946-1900.

**Monson:** Tri-Town Flea Market, 3341 Boston Rd. Tel: (413) 284-0313.

**Plymouth:** Plymouth Flea Market, 377 Court St. Tel: (508) 747-2266.

**Revere:** Revere Swap & Shop, 565 Squire Rd. Tel: (617) 289-7100.

**Tewkesbury:** The Olde & Golden Flea Market, 540 Main St. Tel: (508) 640-1198.

# MICHIGAN

## ARMADA
### Armada Flea Market
**DATES:** Tuesday and Sunday, mid-April through October.
**TIMES:** 6:00 AM-2:00 PM, or total exhaustion, whichever comes first.
**ADMISSION:** Free. Parking is free.
**LOCATION:** 25381 Armada Ridge Rd. Take M97 (Groesbeck Hwy aka North Ave) north to Village of Armada. Turn right at the four-way stop; they are approximately 1 mile down the road.
**DESCRIPTION:** Started in a stockyard in the 1940s, this outdoor market gradually became a flea market in the 1960s. Depending on the weather, they will have up to 300 dealers selling mostly antiques and collectibles, a few crafts, produce in season and some new merchandise. There is a snack bar when the munchies hit, and handicapped-accessible restrooms when needed.
**DEALER RATES:** $10 and up for a single space, $15 and up for a double space. And no, they don't take reservations. Just come on down!
**CONTACT:** Armada Flea Market, PO Box 525, Armada MI 48005-0525. Tel: (810) 784-9604.

## CENTREVILLE
### Centreville Antiques Market
**DATES:** Held five times each summer. May through August and October. Call for exact dates.
**TIMES:** 7:00 AM-4:00 PM EST.
**ADMISSION:** $5. Handicapped-accessible parking is available.
**LOCATION:** At St Joseph's County Fairgrounds on M-86. In the heart of Michigan's Amish area, halfway between Chicago and Detroit, 150 miles from either city.
**DESCRIPTION:** This show opened in 1973. It is both an indoor and outdoor market that accommodates approximately 60 dealers. This show is limited to antiques, fine art, and select collectibles. There is also plenty of food available on the premises. This show provides a chance to "slip back in time and visit a part of small-town America." One can stroll around the 174 acres on the fairgrounds and recheck the merchandise, or walk to the fence near the viewing stand and watch a driver take a practice run around the

track. This show is well thought out and well planned. Although this is a rather large market, Robert Lawler, the show manager, has done his very best to maintain a cozy, family like environment.

**DEALER RATES:** $100 per 25' × 25' space. Inside space for $95 for 10' × 10' space. Reservations are required.

**CONTACT:** Robert C Lawler, Show Manager, 1510 N Hoyne, Chicago IL 60622-1804. Tel: (773) 227-4464.

## COPEMISH
### Timberline Outlets

**DATES:** Every Friday, Saturday, and Sunday from May through October.
**TIMES:** Dawn to dark.
**ADMISSION:** Free. Parking is free.
**LOCATION:** On M-115, 10 miles west of Mesick on M-115, 10 miles east of Benzie and US 31 on M-115.
**DESCRIPTION:** Started in 1940, and formerly the Copemish Flea Market, this outdoor market of 25 dealers sells antiques, collectibles, crafts, produce, coins, stamps, cards, garage sale goodies, furniture, and new merchandise. One snack bar and handicapped-accessible restrooms complete the amenities.
**DEALER RATES:** $8 per day for a 20' × 25' space. First come, first served.
**CONTACT:** John Dillingham, PO Box 116, Copemish MI 49625-0116. Tel: (231) 378-2430. Fax: (231) 378-2430.

## FLAT ROCK
### Flat Rock Historical Society Antique and Flea Market

**DATES:** First Sundays in May and October. Rain or shine.
**TIMES:** 8:00 AM-5:00 PM.
**ADMISSION:** Free. Parking is free.
**LOCATION:** At the Flat Rock Speedway, 1 mile south of Flat Rock on Telegraph Rd.
**DESCRIPTION:** This outdoor market opened in 1973 and accommodates about 350 dealers. There are a variety of antiques, arts and crafts, and collectibles. The money from this show is used to support the Flat Rock Historical Society Museum. Food is served on the premises.
**DEALER RATES:** $25 for a 20' × 20' space. Reservations are not required.
**CONTACT:** Flat Rock Historical Society, PO Box 337, Flat Rock MI 48134-0337. Tel: (734) 782-5220.

# LEXINGTON
## Lexington Harbor Bazaar
**DATES:** Saturday and Sunday.

**TIMES:** 10:00 AM-6:00 PM.

**ADMISSION:** Free. Parking is free.

**LOCATION:** 5590 Main St, 2 blocks south of stop light on US 25 (Main St).

**DESCRIPTION:** Open since 1987, this indoor market of 50 dealers sells antiques, collectibles, fine arts and crafts, furniture and new merchandise. One Mexican cafe and handicapped-accessible restrooms add to the amenities.

**DEALER RATES:** $27 per booth. Reservations are required.

**CONTACT:** Main Office, Lexington Harbor Bazaar, 5590 Main St, Lexington MI 48450. Tel: (810) 359-5333 from 10:00 AM-5:00 PM daily. Fax: (810) 359-5333.

# MT CLEMENS
## Gibraltar Trade Center North
**DATES:** Friday through Sunday, year round.

**TIMES:** Friday 12:00 PM-9:00 PM, Saturday 9:00 AM-9:00 PM, Sunday 10:00 AM-6:00 PM.

**ADMISSION:** $2 a carload.

**LOCATION:** I-94 to Exit 237 N River Rd, go 1 mile down on right-hand side.

**DESCRIPTION:** Opened in 1990, this market has 1,200 dealer spaces and 250,000 square feet of selling space indoors. Dealers sell through special shows: Sports Cards, Sportsman, Computer, Antiques, Home Improvement, Boat & Fishing, Arts and Crafts, etc. Watch for the ads with the listing as to what show is on for the weekend. There is plenty of food available in snack bars and restaurants, and clean, handicapped-accessible restrooms.

**DEALER RATES:** Starting at $75 for a 12' × 6' space, $85-$120 for 12' × 8' space, $175 for 12' × 10', and $275 for 12' × 16'. Outdoors for a 10' × 8' booth under canopy April through October only: to sell new merchandise spaces are $10 a day; used items, produce, plants, antiques or collectibles—$5 per day.

**CONTACT:** Gibraltar Trade Center North Inc, 237 N River Rd, Mt Clemens MI 48043. Tel: (810) 465-6440. Fax: (810) 465-0458. Web: www.gilbraltartrade.com.

# MUSKEGON
## Golden Token Flea Market

**DATES:** Saturdays.

**TIMES:** 6:00 AM-2:00 PM.

**ADMISSION:** Free. Parking is also free.

**LOCATION:** 1300 E Laketon Ave. One block west of US 31 on Laketon Ave.

**DESCRIPTION:** Started in 1985, this growing market of about 75 dealers fills two rooms selling whatever—from antiques and collectibles to whatever comes in. In summer the market is held outside; it moves inside the first weekend in October. Food, from hot dogs to shrimp dinner, is available on the premises.

**DEALER RATES:** $5-$6 per table. Reservations are not required. Yearly rates are available. There is plenty of room!

**CONTACT:** Golden Token, 1300 E Laketon Ave, Muskegon MI 49442. Tel: (231) 773-1137. Fax: (231) 722-4646.

## Muskegon Flea Market

**DATES:** Wednesdays, mid-May through mid-October. They are hoping to expand into November, weather permitting.

**TIMES:** 5:00 AM-3:00 PM.

**ADMISSION:** Free. Parking is free.

**LOCATION:** Seaway Dr at Eastern Ave, ½ mile north of downtown Muskegon; take US 31 Bus N/Seaway Dr to Eastern Ave.

**DESCRIPTION:** This outdoor market of 300 dealers started in 1965. Antiques, collectibles, produce, cards, garage sale finds, ethnic clothing and music as well as new merchandise is sold. Two snack bars and handicapped-accessible restrooms add to the amenities.

**DEALER RATES:** $7 per 10' × 15' covered space; $6 per 10' × 30' asphalt space; $5 per 10' × 40' field space. Overflow area is available if usual space is filled. Reservations are required.

**CONTACT:** Cheri Burdick, Manager, c/o City of Muskegon, 933 Terrace St, Muskegon MI 49443. Tel: (231) 722-3251.

## Select Auditorium Flea Market

**DATES:** Saturday, year round.

**TIMES:** 6:00 AM-2:00 PM.

**ADMISSION:** Free. Parking is free.

**LOCATION:** 1445 East Laketon Ave. At US 31 and Laketon Exit; easy on and off crossway.

DESCRIPTION: Opened in 1975, this indoor/outdoor market of 75-100 dealers sells antiques, collectibles, crafts, coins, stamps, cards, garage sale finds, some furniture, new merchandise and bingo supplies. They hold bingo games after the market. One snack bar and handicapped-accessible restrooms add to the amenities. The market is held outdoors in summer, indoors in winter.

DEALER RATES: $6 for 2 parking spaces outdoors, or $7 per 4' × 8' table inside. Reservations are required for inside only.

CONTACT: Terry Durham, Select Auditorium, 1445 E Laketon Ave, Muskegon MI 49442. Tel: (231) 726-5707.

# PAW PAW
## Reits Flea Market

DATES: Saturdays, Sundays, and summer holidays, from April through October. Rain or shine.

TIMES: 8:00 AM-4:00 PM.

ADMISSION: Free. Free parking is available.

LOCATION: Five miles west of Paw Paw on Red Arrow Hwy, Exit 56 off I-94.

DESCRIPTION: This indoor/outdoor market opened in 1965 and currently accommodates approximately 550 dealers. There are many garage sale items along with antiques, toys, tools, household items, jewelry, collectibles, art, and much more. This is a clean and well-managed family market with events all summer long including a wine feast. Food is available on the premises as well as handicapped-accessible restrooms.

DEALER RATES: $10 per 22' × 20' space per day, outdoors; $9 per space indoors. Reservations are not required. New dealers welcome.

CONTACT: Bob Hixenbaugh and Dene Broadwater, Reits Flea Market, 45146 Red Arrow Hwy, Paw Paw MI 49079. Tel: (616) 657-3428.

# PIERSON
## B & K Storage and Flea Market

DATES: Saturday and Sunday, May through October.

TIMES: 8:30 AM-3:00 PM.

ADMISSION: Free. Parking is free.

LOCATION: 4833 Maple Hill Rd. 131 Hwy, north of Grand Rapids to Exit 114 (Cannonsville Rd), turn right to Federal Rd, turn left, go 1½ mile to Kendaville Rd, turn left and go to the first road on the left, Maple Hill Rd.

DESCRIPTION: This tiny indoor/outdoor market of 3 dealers started in 1996 selling antiques, collectibles, crafts, coins, cards, garage sale goodies, books, automotive bits and pieces, appliances, loads of pictures, and new merchandise. No food, but there are restrooms available.

**DEALER RATES:** $10 per 12' × 16' space per day. Reservations are suggested.

**CONTACT:** Karon Miesiaczek, B & K Storage & Flea Market, 4833 Maple Hill Rd, Pierson MI 49339-9504. Tel: (231) 937-9255 or 937-9256. Email: bkflea@pathwaynet.com.

---

### Lost and Found Again

An elderly woman haunted the market for three weeks looking for a specific book from her childhood. There was a poem in the book she couldn't remember completely. On her third visit, the book was located. With her new treasure, she stood in front of the building and recited the entire poem. Many shoppers stopped to listen to her recitation. She told her audience that "this was the best thing that had happened to her."

She hasn't been seen since.

---

# SAGINAW
## Giant Public Market

**DATES:** Friday, Saturday, and Sunday.
**TIMES:** Saturday 10:00 AM-7:00 PM; Sunday 10:00 AM-6:00 PM.
**ADMISSION:** Free. Parking is free.
**LOCATION:** 3435 Sheridan Ave, I-75 exit 144B, then right onto State St, then left onto Williamson, then right about 3 miles to the market.
**DESCRIPTION:** This market averages 80 to 100 indoor dealers selling antiques, collectibles, new furniture, tools, sports, electronics, games, clothing, garage sale goodies, and new merchandise. Their snack bar makes one heck of a burrito; the handicapped-accessible restrooms could come in handy.
**DEALER RATES:** $36 weekend for 100 square feet. No reservations taken.
**CONTACT:** Bob, Giant Public Market, 3435 Sheridan Ave, Saginaw MI 48601-4458. Tel: (517) 754-9090. Fax: (517) 754-7465.

# TAYLOR
## Gibraltar Trade Center

**DATES:** Friday through Sunday, year round.

**TIMES:** Friday 12:00 PM-9:00 PM, Saturday 10:00 AM-9:00 PM, Sunday 10:00 AM-6:00 PM.

**ADMISSION:** $2 a carload.

**LOCATION:** I-75 and Eureka Rd (Exit 36).

**DESCRIPTION:** Opened in 1980, this market has 1,200 dealer spaces (occupied by 500 or so dealers) and 50,000 square feet of selling space indoors. Regular dealers sell mostly new merchandise, clothes, electronics, shoes, leather goods, and so forth. There are special shows every weekend: Sports Cards, Antiques, Home Improvement, Boat & Fishing, Arts and Crafts, etc. There is plenty of food available in snack bars and restaurants, and clean, handicapped-accessible restrooms.

**DEALER RATES:** Starting at $78 for a 12' × 6' space for the weekend, $104 for 12' × 10', $260 for 20' × 16', and $240 for 18' × 13'. Outdoors for a 10' × 8' booth under canopy April through October only: to sell new merchandise spaces are $15 a day—no used items can be sold outside anymore.

**CONTACT:** Gibraltar Trade Center Inc, 15525 Racho Rd, Taylor MI 48180-5213. Tel: (734) 287-2000. Fax: (734) 287-8330. Web: www.gilbraltartrade.com.

## WARREN
### Country Fair Flea Market

**DATES:** Every Friday, Saturday, and Sunday, year round.

**TIMES:** Friday 4:00 PM-9:00 PM, Saturday and Sunday 10:00 AM-6:00 PM.

**ADMISSION:** Free. Parking is also free.

**LOCATION:** 20900 Dequindre Blvd, 2 blocks north of Eight Mile Rd.

**DESCRIPTION:** This indoor show began in 1978 and currently has about 300 dealers exhibiting antiques, collectibles, produce, crafts, new merchandise, 14-carat gold and silver jewelry, leather, Amish furniture, Hush-Puppy shoes, and brass items. One snack bar and handicapped-accessible restrooms add to the amenities. Watch for their special shows coming in 1998 (Gun, Knife, Barbie and toys, and more). They expanded their sports collection. About 50% of the market is antiques housed in Antique Village. Their dealers take great pride in their merchandise.

**DEALER RATES:** $56 per 5' × 10' space per weekend or $108 for a double-size space. Reservations are suggested.

**CONTACT:** Mike and Katie Holland, Owner, or Terry Bingham, Country Fair Flea Market, 20900 Dequindre, Warren MI 48091. Tel: (810) 757-3740 or 757-3741.

## Michigan Flea Market

**DATES:** Thursday through Sunday.

**TIMES:** Thursday and Friday 4:00 PM-9:00 PM, weekends 10:00 AM-9:00 PM.

**ADMISSION:** Free. Parking is free.

**LOCATION:** 24100 Groesbeck Hwy. Just 1½ miles east of I-696.

**DESCRIPTION:** Opened 13 years ago, this market of 35 dealers sells antiques, collectibles, crafts, coins, stamps, cards, garage sale goodies, furniture, and new merchandise. One snack bar feeds the famished, and handicapped-accessible restrooms come in handy. In the winter, they hold weekly drawings for $50 worth of flea market "dough"—spend it at the market!

**DEALER RATES:** $45 per 8' × 8' space. Reservations are not required.

**CONTACT:** Michigan Flea Market, 24100 Groesbeck Hwy, Warren MI 48089-4716. Tel: (810) 771-3535.

# WATERFORD
## Dixieland Flea Market

**DATES:** Friday, Saturday, and Sunday.

**TIMES:** Friday 4:00 PM-9:00 PM; Saturday and Sunday 10:00 AM-6:00 PM.

**ADMISSION:** Free. Parking is free.

**LOCATION:** On corner of Dixie Hwy and Telegraph Rd.

**DESCRIPTION:** It is nice to discover a market that hangs on to local color. Since 1975 and under its present ownership since 1986 this market has over 200 dealers selling antiques, collectibles, jewelry, glassware, new and used merchandise, and a food court. It has been described as being like a giant outdoor garage sale in summer. Four restaurants across the back of the market create a small food court, making the handicapped-accessible restrooms a necessary visit.

**DEALER RATES:** $45 and up. Reservations are not required.

**CONTACT:** Dixieland Flea Market, 2045 Dixie Hwy, Waterford MI 48328. Tel: (248) 338-3220. Fax: (248) 338-3221.

# OTHER FLEA MARKETS

We know or have heard about these markets, but have not personally contacted each one, as we have the markets with descriptions. If you plan to visit one of these markets listed below, *please call first* to make sure they are still open. Flea markets do come and go. While they were open when we went to press, they may not be later. We can't be responsible. *Call first!*

**Benton Harbor:** Flea Market, 325 Riverview Dr. Tel: (616) 925-8347.

**Cheboygan:** Treasure Hunt Flea Market, 405 Duncan Ave. Tel: (616) 627-6080.

**Detroit:** Metro Flea Market, 6665 W Vernor Hwy. Tel: (313) 841-4890.

**Detroit:** Piquette Trade Center Flea Market, 285 Piquette St. Tel: (313) 872-6080.

**Detroit:** Rosaiah's Flea Market, 11400 Kelly Rd. Tel: (313) 839-4321.

**Fort Gratiot:** Wurzel's Flea Market, 4189 Keewahdin Rd. Tel: (810) 385-4283.

**Grayling:** Ernie's Flea Market, 1499 S Ausable Trl. Tel: (517) 348-5695.

**Harrison:** Parkview Flea Market, 3033 N Clare Ave. Tel: (517) 539-3507.

**Holland:** Unique Flea Market, 5970 136 Ave. Tel: (616) 399-1982.

**Lake City:** Lake City Flea Market, 518 W Union. Tel: (616) 839-3206.

**Lansing:** Bob's Flea Market, 933 W Jolly Rd. Tel: (517) 393-1913.

**Lansing:** Flea Market, 2016 E Michigan Ave. Tel: (517) 372-5356.

**Milan:** Milan Flea Market, 11204 Ann Arbor Rd. Tel: (734) 439-1200.

**Portage:** Mary's Flea Market, 8139 Portage Rd. Tel: (616) 324-4056.

**Portland:** Town of Two Rivers Flea Market, 143 Kent St. Tel: (517) 647-4484.

**Ravenna:** Sullivan Flea Market & Auction, 11851 Heights Ravenna Rd. Tel: (616) 853-2435.

**Warren:** Van Dyke Flea Market, 23524 Van Dyke Ave. Tel: (810) 757-5883.

**Warren:** Seb's Antiques & Flea Market, 24100 Groesbeck Hwy. Tel: (810) 445-2365.

**Warren:** Warren Community Trade Center, 2300 E 10 Mile Rd. Tel: (810) 756-7660.

# MINNESOTA

## ANNANDALE
### Wright County Swap Meet

**DATES:** Saturday and Sunday, from the first Saturday in April until the last of October.

**TIMES:** 8:00 AM-2:00 PM.

**ADMISSION:** Free. Parking is free.

**LOCATION:** 13594 100th St NW. Annandale-West Hwy 55, go 3 miles, turn north on County Rd 136, go 1¾ miles, turn east on 100th St, go ¼ miles to market.

**DESCRIPTION:** Located in the small town of Annandale near lots of lakes, this outdoor, fresh-air market of 150 dealers sells antiques, collectibles, crafts, produce, coins, stamps, cards, garage sale goodies, furniture, and new merchandise. One restaurant and three snack bars feed the famished and there are handicapped-accessible restrooms, just in case.

**DEALER RATES:** $10 per 30' × 20' space. First come, first served.

**CONTACT:** Gladys Miller, Wright County Swap Meet, 13594 100 St NW, South Haven MN 55382-3327. Tel: (320) 274-9005 or 274-8071.

## DETROIT LAKES
### Shady Hollow Flea Market

**DATES:** Sundays from Memorial Day to the Sunday after Labor Day. Three-day shows Saturday through Monday on Memorial Day and Labor Day weekends. Two-day show (Saturday and Sunday) weekend of We-Fest, the first weekend in August, and Labor Day weekend, and a two-day show near July 4th.

**TIMES:** 7:00 AM-5:00 PM.

**ADMISSION:** Free. Parking is free.

**LOCATION:** On Hwy 59, 5 miles south of Detroit Lakes.

**DESCRIPTION:** Started in 1970, this outdoor market averages 75-100 dealers selling antiques, collectibles, furniture, garage sale stuff, junk, crafts, produce, cards, coins, and whatever else. Eighteen cabins are rented for entire season by dealers. Several lunch wagons serve the market.

**DEALER RATES:** $15 and up, depending on size. Reservations are not required.

CONTACT: Ardis Hanson or Monte Jones, Shady Hollow Flea Market, 1760 E Shore Dr, Detroit Lakes MN 56501. Tel: (218) 847-9488 (the Hansons) or 847-5706 (the Jones).

---

**Talk About Success!**

Several years ago a one-shot-a-year vendor called early in the season to request her special, coveted shady spot for Labor Day Sunday. She arrived early with a loaded truck and set up.

Around 8:00 AM she came to the market managers asking for her money back, as she had sold out and was leaving!

---

# DULUTH
## 29th Annual Studebaker Drivers Club
## Swap Meet, Flea Market and Classic Car Show

DATES: Annually, the second Sunday in August. Rain or shine.

TIMES: 8:00 AM-4:00 PM.

ADMISSION: $2 per person, children under 12 and seniors (65 and older) free. $2 parking per car.

LOCATION: Lake Superior College, 2101 Trinity Rd, 2 miles south of Miller Hill Mall.

DESCRIPTION: This show opened in 1972. It is both an indoor and outdoor market that accommodates anywhere from 35 spaces inside to 200 spaces outside. You can buy anything from antiques and collectibles to junk, coins, gifts, crafts, glass, hobbies and new merchandise. Many old and restored antique cars are on display for the Car Show (200 cars). There are also old car parts for all makes and models on sale. Food is served on the premises. There is a car corral with usually 50 cars for sale.

DEALER RATES: $10 per 10' × 20' space outdoors; $10 per 10' × 10' space indoors. Reservations are recommended. There are advance shopping hours for dealers on the Saturday before the show.

CONTACT: North Land Wheels Chapter, PO Box 1004, Duluth MN 55810-1004. Tel: (218) 722-8533, 722-4855, or 624-5932.

# HINCKLEY
## Hinckley Flea Market

DATES: Thursday through Sunday.

TIMES: 8:30 AM-6:00 PM.

**ADMISSION:** Free. Parking is free.

**LOCATION:** Just west of Grand Casino Hinckley. Take 35W north to Hinckley Exit 183. Take a right on Hwy 48. The market is located on the left side of the road about ½ mile down the road.

**DESCRIPTION:** This market is an indoor and outdoor summer market with 40 dealers selling antiques, collectibles, crafts, furniture, cards, garage sale stuff, clothes, and new merchandise. There is some food on the premises, as well as restrooms.

**DEALER RATES:** Outside: $30 per 10' × 15' space with 1 table; inside $37-$45 per 10' × 15' space with 1 table. Reservations are not required.

**CONTACT:** Gus Atrooz, Hinckley Flea Market, 803 Hwy 48, Hinckley MN 55037. Tel: (320) 384-9911. Fax: (320) 384-6589.

---

### Wedding Bells

Two young people working at the market met here, fell in love here, and decided that here was the place to hold their wedding. They did marry here—holding a "shotgun wedding" with their vendor friends dressed in hillbilly attire and their poodle acting ringbearer.

---

# MONTICELLO
## Orchard Fun Market

**DATES:** Every Saturday and Sunday. Rain or shine.

**TIMES:** 9:00 AM-5:00 PM.

**ADMISSION:** Free. Acres of free parking are provided.

**LOCATION:** On Orchard Rd. Take Rt 75 3 miles west from the stoplight in downtown Monticello, then turn at Orchard Rd and go approximately ¼ mile.

**DESCRIPTION:** This indoor/outdoor market began around 1972 and currently attracts between 250 and 500 dealers per market day, depending on the season; the facilities include 250 tables inside and 400 outside. The fare at this market includes antiques, collectibles, and used household items as well as new merchandise and fresh produce. Other attractions include a beer garden and live entertainment on two stages, bumper boat rides, and "slick-rack racers" for the kids. Chicken dinners, bratwurst, hot dogs, funnel cakes, corn dogs and more are served on the premises.

**DEALER RATES:** $10 per 8' table per day. Reservations are not accepted. First come, first served.

**CONTACT:** Orchard Fun Market, 1479 127 St NW, Monticello MN 55362. Tel: (612) 295-2121.

# ORONOCO
## Downtown Oronoco Gold Rush, Inc

**DATES:** Third Saturday and Sunday in August. Rain or shine.
**TIMES:** Sunup to sundown.
**ADMISSION:** Free. Parking is also free. The town provides free outlying parking with bus transportation into town. Parking costs you in town.
**LOCATION:** The entire downtown Oronoco!
**DESCRIPTION:** Started in 1972, the entire town participates in this week-end-long flea market. The main street is closed off to traffic and over 1,500 dealers set up selling antiques, collectibles, flea market goodies, crafts, unfound and refound treasures; as one organizer says "if they don't have it here in those two days, you can't find it!" Some residents sell right out of their garages. Over 40,000 people come through here each day. The money raised is used to help the City of Oronoco finance their First Response system, the fire department, plant new trees, fix the community center, fireworks for July 4th and whatever else is needed. Ample food is available.
**DEALER RATES:** $55 per 15' × 15' space for the weekend. Reservations are required. Many spaces are reserved well in advance.
**CONTACT:** Oronoco Gold Rush, PO Box 266, Oronoco MN 55960-0266. Tel: (507) 367-4405 City Clerk's Office. Fax: (507) 367-4982.

# PARK RAPIDS
## Summerset Market

**DATES:** Thursday and Saturday, from Memorial Day to Labor Day.
**TIMES:** 7:00 AM-4:00 PM.
**ADMISSION:** Free. Parking is free.
**LOCATION:** 3 miles east of Park Rapids on Hwy 34.
**DESCRIPTION:** Opened in 1972, this neat, clean, and friendly market of 50 or so dealers (depending on the weather) sells antiques, garage sale goodies, collectibles, crafts, and some new merchandise. There is a snack bar serving "the best cinnamon buns" in the country, as well as the usual fare. Restrooms are available.
**DEALER RATES:** $10 per 16' × 22' space per day. Reservations are not needed.

**CONTACT:** Summerset Market, Rt 3 Box 1, Park Rapids MN 56470. Tel: (218) 732-5570. Email: denment@wcta.net.

# WABASHA
## Wabasha Indoor/Outdoor Flea Market

**DATES:** Saturday and Sunday, year round.
**TIMES:** 9:00 AM-5:00 PM.
**ADMISSION:** Free. Parking is also free.
**LOCATION:** Hwy 61 and Industrial Ct.
**DESCRIPTION:** Since 1988, this market of 120 tables has been selling new and used merchandise, carpet, furniture, antiques, and collectibles. Coinciding with the arrival of the Mississippi Queen Riverboat, usually in September, the town celebrates Riverboat Days with a parade as well as a huge celebration. Homemade food in their own concession stand is available on the premises. Handicapped-accessible restrooms.
**DEALER RATES:** $10 per table. Reservations are required.
**CONTACT:** Doc Carlson, Wabasha Indoor/Outdoor Flea Market, PO Box 230, Wabasha MN 55981-0230. Tel: (651) 565-4767.

# OTHER FLEA MARKETS

We know or have heard about these markets, but have not personally contacted each one, as we have the markets with descriptions. If you plan to visit one of these markets listed below, *please call first* to make sure they are still open. Flea markets do come and go. While they were open when we went to press, they may not be later. We can't be responsible. *Call first!*

**Eagan:** Marketplace at Cedar Vale, 3920 Sibley Memorial Hwy. Tel: (612) 544-8441.
**Hudson:** Hanley Flea Market, 1830 Hanley Rd. Tel: (715) 386-9767.
**Maplewood:** Amusement City, 1870 Rice St. Tel: (651) 487-1025.
**New Market:** Trader's Market Inc, 16075 260 St E. Tel: (612) 461-2400.
**Pine City:** Indoor Flea Market of Pine City, 805 6 St. Tel: (320) 629-5828.
**St Paul:** Windmill Market, 122 S Wabasha St. Tel: (651) 290-9552.

# MISSISSIPPI

## JACKSON
### Fairgrounds Antique Flea Market

**DATES:** Saturday and Sunday, year round.

**TIMES:** Saturday 8:00 AM-5:00 PM; Sunday 10:00 AM-5:00 PM.

**ADMISSION:** $1 per person. Free parking.

**LOCATION:** 900 High St. Take High St exit off I-55 to 890 Mississippi St at the State Fairgrounds. In the big "steel building."

**DESCRIPTION:** This indoor flea market is in its 15th year and has over 200 dealers in antiques, collectibles, crafts, produce, and new merchandise. There are also some primitives and books. This is a very well-rounded flea market. A little bit of everything, but about 60% antiques and collectibles. A complete concession provides food on the premises and there is a concession area with handicapped-accessible restrooms. Camper electrical hook-ups are available.

**DEALER RATES:** $35 for a wall booth, $45 for an aisle booth, $4 each for tables. Reservations are required one week in advance only.

**CONTACT:** Frank Barnett, Fairgrounds Antique Flea Market, PO Box 23579, Jackson MS 39225. Tel: (601) 353-5327.

---

**Birthday Surprise**

Years ago, a young man was celebrating his 21st birthday with two buddies at the market. Each gave him a present, but he had to guess what was in the box before he was allowed to open it.

As the presenter of the first box handed his over, the birthday-boy guessed candy as the Dad had a candy store. He was right.

As the second box was handed over, the birthday-boy shook it gently, knowing this pal's dad owned a liquor store. Liquid dripped out the bottom, and guessing it was vodka, the kid licked it. No, said the giftor, it's not vodka, try again.

Another wee shake, more liquid, another lick. Champagne!

Wrong again.

It was a puppy.

---

# MCNEIL
## McNeil Flea Market

**DATES:** Thursday through Sunday.

**TIMES:** 8:00 AM to dark.

**ADMISSION:** Free. Parking is free.

**LOCATION:** 2 Cemetery Rd, on Hwy 11 and Cemetery Rd. Only 70 miles from New Orleans.

**DESCRIPTION:** This little market of 25 dealers, housed in a garage and in the parking lot, offers antiques, collectibles, garage sale goodies, and used stuff. This is quite a weekend adventure for the collectors of New Orleans who come here for the treasures. There are snacks available on site as well as handicapped-accessible restrooms.

**DEALER RATES:** $10 per table either under shelter or in the parking lot, per day. Just show up and say Hi to Nita.

**CONTACT:** Nita Alonzo, McNeil Flea Market, 212 Larow Dr, McNeil MS 39426. Tel: 601-798-0350.

# PHILADELPHIA
## Williamsville Flea Market

**DATES:** Friday and Saturday. Rain or shine.

**TIMES:** 6:00 AM-6:00 PM.

**ADMISSION:** Free. Parking is free.

**LOCATION:** 1031 Rd 606. Located at the intersection of Hwy 15 and Hwy 16, across from McDonalds and Key West Inn. Just 5 miles from the Silverstar Casino.

**DESCRIPTION:** This outdoor market averages 35 dealers selling antiques, collectibles, crafts, produce, furniture, garage sale goodies, tools, clothes, Indian jewelry and baskets, rugs and new merchandise. There is a concession stand and restrooms. The best months to visit are July and August as the last weeks of July celebrate the Choctaw Indian Fair and the first week in August is the Neshoba County Fair. Apparently, the entire town shuts down to attend this Fair with concerts every night, horse races, a rodeo, beauty pageant, and the flea market.

**DEALER RATES:** $8 per 10' × 10' or several little 10' × 10' buildings, some with space in front from $135 per month.

**CONTACT:** Lee Harris or Tom McCullough, Williamsville Flea Market, 1031 Rd 606, Philadelphia MS 39350-8601. Tel/fax: (601) 656-8428.

# RIPLEY
## First Monday Trade Days

**DATES:** First Monday and preceding Saturday and Sunday of each month, but primarily on Saturday and Sunday.

**TIMES:** Dawn to dusk.

**ADMISSION:** Free. $1.50 parking fee.

**LOCATION:** 10590 Hwy 15 S, On Hwy 15, 65 miles from Memphis and 45 miles from Tupelo.

**DESCRIPTION:** This outdoor market has operated under present management since the mid-1970s, although local sources claim to be able to trace it back to first Mondays as early as 1893, ranking it among the nation's most venerable. Presently accommodating an average of 500 dealers, there is everything from antiques, collectibles, fresh produce, and new merchandise to a variety of crafts and reproduction oak furniture available. Food, from corn dogs to catfish, is served on the premises. There are handicapped-accessible restrooms as well.

**DEALER RATES:** $25 for a 18' × 18' booth. Reservations are suggested.

**CONTACT:** Ripley First Monday Trade Days, 10590 Hwy 15 S, Ripley MS 38663. Tel: 1-800-4-RIPLEY Monday through Friday, (601) 837-4051 or 837-7442. Fax: (601) 837-7080.

# TUPELO
## Tupelo's Gigantic Flea Market

**DATES:** Friday, Saturday and Sunday, the second full weekend of the month, except February and August.

**TIMES:** Friday evening 6:00 PM-9:00 PM, Saturday 9:00 AM-7:00 PM, Sunday 10:00 AM-5:00 PM.

**ADMISSION:** Free. Parking is free.

**LOCATION:** Tupelo Furniture Market Buildings at 1879 N Coley Rd.

**DESCRIPTION:** This eight-year-old market hosts over 800 dealers selling "everything" (they all say that, and usually mean it!), from antiques and collectibles, to new merchandise. From high-end to low-end—it's all here. Housed in two large heated and cooled buildings with outside spaces as well. Concession stands feed the famished.

**DEALER RATES:** $65 for the full 3-day weekend. Spaces are 9' × 11'. Reservations are preferred.

**CONTACT:** Debbie Griffin-Olive, Tupelo's Gigantic Flea Market, 1879 N Coley Rd, Tupelo MS 38801. Tel: (601) 842-4442. Fax: (601) 844-3665.

**Old Story**

It is said that a picture and frame were sold for $5 at an auction in Mississippi. The new owner took the picture and frame to another auction and sold it for $115 and thought he did real well! The savvy New York buyer took it back to New York and reportedly she sold it for over $50,000.

## OTHER FLEA MARKETS

We know or have heard about these markets, but have not personally contacted each one, as we have the markets with descriptions. If you plan to visit one of these markets listed below, *please call first* to make sure they are still open. Flea markets do come and go. While they were open when we went to press, they may not be later. We can't be responsible. *Call first!*

**Bogue Chitto:** Tucker's Flea Market, 743 Hwy 51 SE. Tel: (601) 833-1802.

**Collins:** Katie's Breezeway Flea Market, 2629 Hwy 49. Tel: (601) 765-6564.

**Florence:** Magnolia Flea Market, 3965 Hwy 49 S. Tel: (601) 845-4655.

**Lucedale:** Tri-County Flea Market, Hwy 98 E. Tel: (601) 947-9699.

**Macon:** Lindley's Flea Market, 105 W Adams St. Tel: (601) 726-9923.

**Mc Comb:** McComb Flea Market Inc, 131 N Front St. Tel: (601) 249-0290.

**Mendenhall:** Mendenhall Flea Market, 142 Main St. Tel: (601) 847-5005.

**Mendenhall:** Tri-State Flea Market, 3452 Simpson Hwy 49. Tel: (601) 847-2055.

**Meridian:** Carol's Flea Market, 2604 State Blvd. Tel: (601) 693-0760.

**Natchez:** Washington Flea Market, 445 Morgantown Rd. Tel: (601) 445-9365.

**Pontotoc:** Pototoc Plea Market, 3498 Hwy 6 E. Tel: (601) 489-7910.

**Poplarville:** Deep South Flea Market & Auction, 3838 Hwy 26 W. Tel: (601) 772-9764.

**Shannon:** Shannon Flea Market, 241 Old Hwy 45. Tel: (601) 767-9050.

**Vicksburg:** Flea Market, 1500 Washington St. Tel: (601) 636-5516.

**Vicksburg:** Flea Market, 5266 Hwy 61 S. Tel: (601) 638-7550.

# MISSOURI

## COLONY
### Colony #1 Flea Market

**DATES:** First weekend of every month from March through November.
**TIMES:** Daylight.
**ADMISSION:** Free. Parking is free.
**LOCATION:** Rt V off Rt K, 1½ miles northwest of town. In the NE corner of Knox County. The closest "big" town is Kirksville about 35 miles west.
**DESCRIPTION:** This 20-year-old market (the one with the row of flags in front, aka the 2$^{nd}$ largest flea market in the area) boasts about 170 dealers hogging 300 spaces selling antiques, collectibles, some crafts, garage sale goodies, tools, trinkets, the occasional emu or other livestock (big and little), produce, fresh baked goods, and new merchandise. They hold auctions on Friday nights at 7:00 PM. There is a snack vendor and restrooms at the market.
**DEALER RATES:** $12 per 20' × 30' space per weekend, $6 extra for electricity. There are hot showers and water available for vendors hanging around. Thursday is setup day. First come, first served.
**CONTACT:** Danny or Dawnetta White, Colony Flea Market, RR1 Box 64A, Rutledge MO 63563. Tel: (660) 434-5504.

## FARMINGTON
### Farmington Flea Market

**DATES:** Friday through Sunday.
**TIMES:** 8:00 AM-4:00 PM.
**ADMISSION:** Free. Parking is free.
**LOCATION:** Hwy 67, 1 mile north of Farmington.
**DESCRIPTION:** This indoor/outdoor market has been operating about 15 years and recently moved from the Fairgrounds to this location next to an antique mall. There are two buildings housing mostly permanent dealers (there is a waiting list), but outside has plenty of space. The 80-100 dealers sell antiques, collectibles, crafts, new and used furniture, books, new merchandise, pottery, tools, household items and garage sale goodies. Snacks are sold on the premises, and there are handicapped-accessible restrooms.

**DEALER RATES:** $5 per day outside, $15 per 10' × 12' space outside, $120 and up for inside 26' × 10' when available. Reservations are a must inside (that waiting list!) but not outside.

**CONTACT:** Farmington Flea Market, 4602 US Hwy 67, Farmington MO 63640-7442. Tel: (573) 756-1691.

# JOPLIN

## Gingerbread House Antique Mall and Flea Market

*Note: For you antique dealers, I know this is more a "store" than a flea market, but it is full of antiques and collectibles! So, say Hi to Nellie for me; she's delightful.*

**DATES:** Daily.

**TIMES:** 9:00 AM-6:00 PM.

**ADMISSION:** Free. Parking is free.

**LOCATION:** Intersection of I-44 and S 43 Hwy on N Outer Rd. Across from the Petro Truck Stop. Take Exit 4 off I-44 to N Outer Rd.

**DESCRIPTION:** Opened in February 1995, this market of 85-90 dealers sells antiques and collectibles including dealers with NASCAR, Hot Wheels, and PEZ among other collectibles. They stress friendly service and will go out of their way to help you find something. Food and drinks are available.

**DEALER RATES:** $1 per square foot of space. Reservations are necessary.

**CONTACT:** Nellie, Gingerbread House, PO Box 3466, Joplin MO 64803. Tel: (417) 623-6690. Email: gingerbread@mail.4state.com.

## Joplin Flea Market

**DATES:** Every Saturday and Sunday, year round. Rain or shine.

**TIMES:** 8:00 AM-5:00 PM.

**ADMISSION:** Free admission and free parking.

**LOCATION:** 1200 block of Virginia Ave in the Old City Market; 1 block east of 12th and Main Sts.

**DESCRIPTION:** This indoor/outdoor show is in its 18th year. It comprises 200 dealers selling all kinds of curios and antiques. There are crafts, collectibles, new and used merchandise, produce, meats and cheeses, primitives, stamps and coins, tools, jewelry, clothing, postcards, and the list goes on. An entire city block, indoors, of flea market space has grown behind this market with new heating units to keep the dealers warm year round. They added another shed with roof in 1996. There is a snack bar and handicapped-accessible restrooms.

**DEALER RATES:** Call for reasonable rates on 10' × 18' space per day outside with parking space by booth or 9' × 20' space inside. There are open butler sheds with asphalt paving, and open space for dealers with their own canopies. Free storage for the following week is provided for inside dealers with advance payment. Reservations are suggested.

**CONTACT:** Laverne Miller, Joplin Flea Market, 2572 Markwardt Ave, Joplin MO 64801. Tel: (417) 623-3743.

---

### A Tad of History

This market was built in the 1930s for the City of Joplin by the WPA to house their produce market. It was the largest watermelon distribution center in the entire United States with trucks parked all around it awaiting their turn. Laverne Miller purchased the property from the city in 1977 to open the area's first flea market. She has since bought up much of the property around here to enlarge her flea market, upgrading the area in the process.

---

# PEVELY
## The Big Pevely Flea Market

**DATES:** Every Saturday and Sunday, year round. Rain or shine.

**TIMES:** 7:00 AM-5:00 PM.

**ADMISSION:** Free admission and free parking.

**LOCATION:** 8773 Commercial Blvd. Take I-55 south from St Louis to Exit 180. Take a left at the bottom of the ramp, go to the third stoplight and turn right for ¼ mile to market.

**DESCRIPTION:** This indoor/outdoor market opened in 1969 in an old drive-in theater. Over the years they have added two buildings housing about 200 dealers each. Altogether, their 500 to 600 dealers in 750 spaces sell antiques, collectibles, crafts, furniture, cards, clothing, garage sale goodies, vegetables, and new merchandise. Snack bars serve the hungry including their "famous farmer's breakfast." There is a special place outdoors for the "garage sale" vendors. One of the buildings is now a Flea Market Mall open daily where the market sells for the vendors. Just in case, there is an ATM machine on site.

**DEALER RATES:** Outside $12 per 10' × 20' per day, covered spaces an additional $5 per day. Inside: $18 per 5' × 12' single space, $40 for a end-cap double space. Reservations are required indoors. Outdoor space can be reserved, or is allocated on a first-come, first-served basis. At the Mall: call for rates, the market does the selling. Open every Friday from 8:00 AM-7:00 PM and Saturday and Sunday at 6:00 AM for vendor setup.

**CONTACT:** Charlie Parker or Lee Douglas, The Big Pevely Flea Market, PO Box 419, Pevely MO 63070-0419. Tel: (636) 479-5400 or 475-3215. Fax: (636) 479-7680. Email: pevelyfleamkt@jcn1.com.

# SAINT LOUIS
## Frison Flea Market

**DATES:** Every Friday, Saturday, and Sunday.

**TIMES:** 9:00 AM-5:00 PM.

**ADMISSION:** Free. Parking is free.

**LOCATION:** 7025 St Charles Rock Rd. Next door to the Metro Link at Rock Rd Station.

**DESCRIPTION:** Opened since 1982, this market has 370 spaces filled with dealers selling some antiques and collectibles, and lots of clothing, jewelry, appliances, and plenty of new merchandise. There is a snack bar, a produce stand, and handicapped-accessible restrooms.

**DEALER RATES:** $15 per 10' × 10' space with out-of-town vendors getting preference. First come, first served.

**CONTACT:** Frison Indoor Flea Market Inc, 7025 St Charles Rock Rd, St Louis MO 63133. Tel: (314) 727-0460 or pager (314) 582-0446.

---

**Recent History**
   To build this Metro Link, the government took away two acres of their parking lot. At least it is convenient!

---

# SIKESTON
## Tradewinds Flea Market

**DATES:** Every Friday through Sunday, rain or shine.

**TIMES:** All day.

**ADMISSION:** Free. Free parking is available.

**LOCATION:** 875 W Malone. Sikeston is 150 miles south of St Louis, 150 miles north of North Memphis.

**DESCRIPTION:** This indoor/outdoor market opened in 1974 and now accommodates approximately 300 dealers. There is everything here from antiques and collectibles to arts and crafts to new merchandise. Tools, toys, fresh produce, as well as chickens, turkeys, guinea pigs, and rabbits are available. The Tradewinds Restaurant is in the middle of the market. This market has been growing steadily since it began, as more and more dealers are coming from all over the United States to sell their goods.

**DEALER RATES:** $7 per 14' × 14' space, per day; Sundays are free. Reservations are first come, first served.

**CONTACT:** Tradewinds Flea Market, 875 W Malone, Sikeston MO 63801. Call the Tradewinds Restaurant at (573) 471-3965 or 471-8419.

# SPRINGFIELD
## I-44 Swap Meet

**DATES:** Saturday and Sunday, March through November, rain or shine.

**TIMES:** Daylight to dark.

**ADMISSION:** $1 per car admission and parking.

**LOCATION:** 2600 E Kearney at Neergard, across from the Bass Pro plant. Then ½ mile north on Neergard.

**DESCRIPTION:** "Sooner or later it's out there, if you want it." Started in 1984, this swap meet has from 200 to 300 dealers selling everything! It is on 30 acres right along I-44. Live bands and 5 snack bars liven things up. Free camping on Friday and weekends.

**DEALER RATES:** For a 30' × 20' space: $8 on Saturday; $10 Sundays. First come, first served.

**CONTACT:** Butch Koonce or Bob Nelson, 2743 W Kearney, Springfield MO 65803. Tel: (417) 866-7493 or (417) 864-4340 or (417) 864-6508.

## Old PO Flea Market

**DATES:** Monday through Saturday.

**TIMES:** 10:00 AM-5:00 PM.

**ADMISSION:** Free. Parking is free.

**LOCATION:** 304 W Commercial St in the old Post Office building.

**DESCRIPTION:** Opened in an old post office building (hence the name), this 13-year-old market is under new management as of November 1996. There are 32 dealers in primarily antiques, collectibles, old books, linens, furniture, old paper or as Dan says, "stuff from 50¢ to $750." There is a big turnover in merchandise as it sells so fast and new goods are always coming in. Another dealer's buying paradise. No food, unless you are a termite.

**DEALER RATES:** $30 per month for a "table section" with shelves, $40 per month for a 8' × 10' booth. There is a large furniture room if you need it. Reservations are a good idea.

CONTACT: Dan, Old PO Flea Market, 304 W Commercial St, Springfield MO 65803-2666. Tel: (417) 865-8444.

# OTHER FLEA MARKETS

We know or have heard about these markets, but have not personally contacted each one, as we have the markets with descriptions. If you plan to visit one of these markets listed below, *please call first* to make sure they are still open. Flea markets do come and go. While they were open when we went to press, they may not be later. We can't be responsible. *Call first!*

**Asbury:** Asbury Flea Market, 101 Main St. Tel: (417) 642-5724.

**Asbury:** State-Line Trade Center & Flea, Hwy 171. Tel: (417) 642-5850. Open every Fri, Sat & Sun. 9 AM-6 PM.

**Aurora:** Houn' Dawg Flea Market, 16 W Olive St. Tel: (417) 678-4555.

**Aurora:** Madison Place Flea Market, 330 S Madison Ave. Tel: (417) 678-6307.

**Barnhart:** Kohler City Flea Market, 7045 US Hwy 61/67. Tel: (314) 464-2322.

**Bertrand:** Bertrand Flea Market, 412 Hwy 62 W. Tel: (573) 683-6345.

**Bolivar:** Super Flea Market, 2869 W Broadway St. Tel: (417) 326-6360.

**Bolivar:** Hidden Treasures Flea Market, 3100 S Morrisville Rd. Tel: (417) 326-4499.

**Bolivar:** Downtown Flea Markets, 110 W Jackson St. Tel: (417) 777-2288.

**Bowling Green:** 3-G Flea Market, 810 N Bus Hwy 61. Tel: (573) 324-2929.

**Branson:** Branson Heights Flea Market, 1139 W Hwy 76. Tel: (417) 335-3165.

**Branson:** Cadwell's Downtown Flea Market, 116 E Main St. Tel: (417) 334-5051.

**Butler:** 3 Mile Junction Flea Market, RR4 Box 203A. Tel: (660) 679-6016.

**Cabool:** Cabool Flea Market, 731 Roberts St. Tel: (417) 962-4258.

**Cape Girardeau:** Doris' Flea Market, 631 Good Hope St. Tel: (573) 651-1665.

**Carl Junction:** Carl Junction Flea Market, 118 S Main St. Tel: (417) 649-7131.

**Cassville:** Hilltop Flea Market, RR 4 Box 4450. Tel: (417) 847-3029.

**Cassville:** Hwy 112 Flea Market, Hwy 112. Tel: (417) 847-5778.

**Cassville:** Peddlers Flea Market, RR4 Box 4040. Tel: (417) 847-4870.

**Cassville:** E & E Flea Market, RR 1. Tel: (417) 847-5301.

**Crane:** Another Darn Flea Market, 208 N Main. Tel: (417) 723-5404.

**Crocker:** Bear Ridge Flea Market, 17984 Hwy 17. Tel: (573) 736-5858.

**De Soto:** Redfield's Flea Market, 500 S Main St. Tel: (314) 586-3456.

**Dexter:** Dexter Flea Market, 1570 W Bus US Hwy 60. Tel: (573) 624-6157.

**Doniphan:** Ripley County Flea Market, RR1 Box 153. Tel: (573) 996-4573.

**Fair Grove:** Old Mill Antique & Flea Market, 99 Main St. Tel: (417) 759-2040.

**Flat River:** Rick's Flea Market, 211 Main St. Tel: (573) 431-9677.

**Flat River:** Jose's Flea Market, 217 W Main St. Tel: (573) 431-7002.

**Fredericktown:** M & M Flea Market, 2564 Madison 220. Tel: (573) 783-8474.

**Fredericktown:** Johnson Trading Post, 8715 Hwy 67. Tel: (573) 783-8069.

**Goodman:** Kelly Springs Flea Market, S 71 Hwy. Tel: (417) 364-7799.

**Granby:** Granby Flea Market, 799 W Valley St. Tel: (417) 472-3532.

**Hardenville:** JU Ju's Flea Market, Hwy 160. Tel: (417) 679-2262.

**Hayti:** Quinn's Flea Market, 305 E Washington St. Tel: (573) 359-2565.

**Hermitage:** Hermitage Flea Market, W Hwy 54. Tel: (417) 745-2200.

**Highlandville:** Eagle's Nest Flea Market, 6922 US Hwy 160 S. Tel: (417) 443-7710.

**Houston:** Echo Flea Market, 7035 Hwy 17. Tel: (417) 967-2456.

**Houston:** Indian Creek Flea Market, 16280 Indian Creek Trail. Tel: (417) 967-5355.

**Imperial:** Beck's Flea Market, 1595 Miller Rd. Tel: (314) 464-4664.

**Imperial:** Barnhart Flea Market, 6850 US Hwy 61/67. Tel: (314) 464-5503.

**Jefferson City:** Van's Flea Market, 4931 Hwy 50 W. Tel: (573) 761-4622.

**Joplin:** Rusty Nail Flea Market, 3004 Silver Creek Rd. Tel: (417) 624-7157.

**Joplin:** Kentucky Street Flea Market, 315 Commercial Alley. Tel: (417) 624-8810.

**Kansas City:** KC Flea Market, 6007 E Truman Rd. Tel: (816) 452-1998.

**Kansas City:** Super Flea, 6200 St John Ave. Tel: (816) 241-5049.

**Kansas City:** Waldo Flea Market, 224 W 75 St. Tel: (816) 363-9938.

**Kennett:** WW Flea Market, 804 Independence Ave. Tel: (573) 888-0078.

**Kimberling City:** Flea World, Hwy 13. Tel: (417) 739-5505.

**Lamar:** Oakton Flea Market, 303 SW 30 Rd. Tel: (417) 682-3217.

**Lincoln:** E & W Flea Market, 138 E Main. Tel: (660) 547-2322.

**Macon:** Huggy Bears Flea Market, 903 US Hwy 63S. Tel: (660) 385-1333.

**Macon:** Colonel Flea Market, 312 S Missouri St. Tel: (660) 385-2497.

**Malden:** Ronnie's Flea Market, 105 E Madison. Tel: (573) 276-3365.

**Malden:** Downtown Flea Market, 113 S Madison St. Tel: (573) 276-3141.

**Mountain Grove:** Mountain View Flea Market, 500 E 7 St. Tel: (417) 934-5505.

**Mountain Grove:** Sunny Slope Flea Market, 1603 Hwy 95. Tel: (417) 926-3307.

**Mountain View:** East Side Flea Market, 215 E 1 St. Tel: (417) 934-6997.

**Neosho:** South Elwood Flea Market, RR5. Tel: (417) 451-5140.

**Neosho:** Vern's Flea Market, Hwy 71 Alt. Tel: (417) 451-9565.

**Nevada:** Nevada Flea Market, RR2 Box 68. Tel: (417) 667-7738.

**Oak Grove:** Oak Grove Flea Market, 1120 S Broadway St. Tel: (816) 690-8885.

**Oak Grove:** Yesterday Treasures Flea Market, 1221 S Broadway.

**Osage Beach:** Osage Beach Flea Market, Hwy 54 & 42. Tel: (573) 348-5454.

**Osage Beach:** Village Flea Market, Poverty Flats. Tel: (573) 348-5616.

**Ozark:** Country Junction Flea Market, 205 E South St. Tel: (417) 581-8116.

**Ozark:** Ozark Flea Market, South Town Center. Tel: (417) 581-8544.

**Pacific:** Old Route 66 Flea Market, 2246 W Osage St. Tel: (314) 271-8325.

**Pineville:** Pineville Flea Market. Tel: (417) 223-7473.

**Poplar Bluff:** Country Junction Flea Market, Hwy 67S. Tel: (573) 686-2275.

**Poplar Bluff:** Fifth Street Flea Market, 1712 S Broadway St. Tel: (573) 686-5852.

**Poplar Bluff:** Flea Market, 522 N G St. Tel: (573) 686-3606.

**Poplar Bluff:** Jordan's Lake Road Flea Market, Cty Rd 556. Tel: (573) 686-4542.

**Poplar Bluff:** Westwood A Flea Market, 2781 N Westwood Blvd. Tel: (573) 686-3184.

**Puxico:** American Way Flea Market, RR1. Tel: (573) 222-8432.

**Reeds Spring:** Old Spring Flea Market, Main St & Hwy 13. Tel: (417) 272-3173.

**Republic:** L & L Flea Market, 340 N Hwy 60. Tel: (417) 732-1110.

**Republic:** West County Flea Market, 336 N US Hwy 60. Tel: (417) 732-8415.

**Rocky Comfort:** Rocky Comfort Flea Market, Hwy 76. Tel: (417) 652-3681.

**Sedalia:** Banks Flea Market, 604 S Ohio Ave. Tel: (660) 826-4140.

**Seligman:** Tom's Flea Market, Hwy 37. Tel: (417) 662-3205.

**Sikeston:** Sikeston Trade Fair Flea Market, 330 H Hwy. Tel: (573) 472-9964.

**Sikeston:** Sikeston Trade Center Flea Market, 2022 E Malone Ave. Tel: (573) 472-9933.

**Springfield:** A & P Super Flea, 6104 Page Blvd. Tel: (314) 721-6693.

**Springfield:** Country Corner Flea Market, 351 N Boonville Ave. Tel: (417) 862-1597.

**Springfield:** Ferguson Flea Market, 7327 E Farm Rd 132. Tel: (417) 863-6699.

**Springfield:** Kountry Korner Flea Market, 6189 N State Hwy H. Tel: (417) 865-9510.

**Springfield:** Standard Flea Market, 505 E Trafficway St. Tel: (417) 831-9110.

**Springfield:** Standard Storage & Flea Market, 651 S Kansas Ave. Tel: (417) 831-6331.

**Springfield:** Standard Storage & Flea Market, 1820 E Trafficway St. Tel: (417) 831-6367.

**Springfield:** Park Central Flea Market, 429 N Boonville Ave. Tel: (417) 831-7516.

**Springfield:** Scenic Hill Flea Market, 605 S Scenic Ave. Tel: (417) 865-1800.

**St Louis:** Bel-Ridge Flea Market, 8943 Natural Bridge Rd. Tel: (314) 426-7848.

**St Louis:** Lou's Flea Market, 8919 Natural Bridge Rd. Tel: (314) 423-6335.

**Stockton:** Indian Treasure Flea Market, 303 W Hwy 32. Tel: (417) 276-2050.

**Sullivan:** Attic Flea Market, 24 Taylor St. Tel: (573) 468-5800.

**Sunrise Beach:** Sam's Flea Mart, Hwy 5. Tel: (573) 374-4101.

**Sweet Springs:** B & N Brickstreet Flea Market, 315 S Miller St A. Tel: (660) 335-6551.

**Ulman:** Ulman Flea Market, SR C. Tel: (573) 369-2730.

**Union:** Mason Dixon Line Flea Market, I-44 & 50. Tel: (314) 583-2014.

**Van Buren:** Riverways Flea Market. Tel: (573) 323-8628.

**Vienna:** Vienna Flea Market & Auction, RR1 Box 51. Tel: (573) 422-3106.

**Walnut Grove:** Cat's Eye Flea Market, 109 N Washington St. Tel: (417) 788-2939.

**Webb City:** Main Street Flea Market, 114 S Main St. Tel: (417) 673-7923.

**Wellsville:** THC Flea Market, 101 N 1 St. Tel: (573) 684-3223.

**West Plains:** Donlo's Flea Mart, 5016 US Hwy 160. Tel: (417) 256-7586.

**Willow Springs:** Traders Village USA, 3649 US Hwy 63. Tel: (417) 469-4494.

# MONTANA

## BILLINGS
### Big Sky Flea Market
**DATES:** Saturday and Sunday, mid-March through mid-October.
**TIMES:** 7:00 AM-5:00 PM.
**ADMISSION:** Free. Parking is free.
**LOCATION:** 2221 Old Hardin Rd. Off I-90 between Exits 452 and 455. Market is on Old Hardin Rd (S Frontage Rd), across from the Tour America RV Center.
**DESCRIPTION:** Opened in 1997, this market of 15 dealers sells antiques, collectibles, produce, furniture, garage sale goodies, tools, knives, and new merchandise. One snack bar feeds the famished and there is a port-a-let when needed.
**DEALER RATES:** $10 per 10' × 20' space. Reservations are not required.
**CONTACT:** Jacque or Tom Moore, PO Box 22732, Billings MT 59104. Tel: (406) 248-2424. Fax: (406) 245-6694.

## GREAT FALLS
### Great Falls Farmers' Market
**DATES:** Every Saturday and Wednesday, from the first Saturday in June through the first Saturday in October.
**TIMES:** Wednesday 4:30 AM-6:00 PM; Saturday 7:45 AM-12:00 PM.
**ADMISSION:** Free. Ample free parking is available.
**LOCATION:** At the Civic Center.
**DESCRIPTION:** This outdoor market hosts about 75 dealers and has been running for 19 years. This traditional farmers' market also features local crafts alongside the traditional meat, dairy, produce and baked goods of local farmers. There is food served on the premises. They have about 2,500 visitors per day.
**DEALER RATES:** $2 minimum or 10% commission up to $30 maximum per 8' × 10' space. Show up and sell.
**CONTACT:** Michael Winters, Great Falls Farmers' Market, 2405 6 St NW, Great Falls MT 59401. Tel: (406) 761-3881.

# NEBRASKA

## BROWNVILLE
### Spring Flea Market/Fall Flea Market

**DATES:** Spring: Memorial Day weekend, Friday through Monday. Fall: Last full weekend in September, Saturday and Sunday.

**TIMES:** 8:00 AM-5:00 PM.

**ADMISSION:** Free. Parking is free.

**LOCATION:** Main St. From I-29, exit for Hwy 136, 5 miles to Brownville. Only 70 miles south of Omaha, 80 miles from Topeka or Kansas City. Brownville is next to the Missouri River.

**DESCRIPTION:** Started in 1957 as a fundraiser for the Town of Brownville to preserve its heritage, this market increases the town population of 148 to 10,000 on market days. Their 260 dealers sell mostly antiques, collectibles, attic finds, some crafts and new merchandise. Several food concessions aid and abet the hungry. Restrooms are available.

**DEALER RATES:** $30 for 22' × 15' space for the each event. Reservations are recommended.

**CONTACT:** The Head Flea, Brownville Historical Society, PO Box 1, Brownville NE 68321-0001. Tel: (402) 825-6001 or 825-4751 (Zac Vice, current Head Flea).

---

**Local History**

Brownville, the oldest town in Nebraska (founded in 1854) and located on the Missouri River, was a starting point for immigrants on the Oregon Trail. Wagons would gather, up to 176 at a time, to await a leader to take them out west. In its heyday, 30 packet boats a day would unload their supplies for the wagon trains and later the Denver Gold Rushers in their quests for new lands and riches. The population would grow to 5,000 until the wagons left, then it shrank until the next train formed.

Most of the town is registered on the National Historic Register and was recently included as one of 25 towns in a book on Historic Towns in America. An excursion boat still operates from spring until mid-summer. To top all this off, think of Brownville along with "sister cities" San Francisco and Rome; all are built on seven hills.

---

# GRAND ISLAND
## Great Exchange Flea Market

**DATES:** Daily, except major holidays.

**TIMES:** 10:00 AM-5:00 PM, except Sundays 12:00 PM-5:00 PM.

**ADMISSION:** Free. Parking is free.

**LOCATION:** 3235 Locust St at intersection with Hwy 34; I-80 Exit 312 onto Rt 281 and go north 5 miles to Hwy 34, then 2 miles east to S Locust.

**DESCRIPTION:** Opened in 1988, this market of 60 dealers sells antiques, collectibles, crafts, sports cards, garage sale goodies furniture, books (through The Paper Route), and new merchandise.

**DEALER RATES:** These are all permanent vendors. Call for vacancies.

**CONTACT:** Great Exchange Flea Market, 3235 S Locust St, Grand Island NE 68801-8816. Tel: (308) 381-4075.

# OMAHA
## Blue Ribbon Flea Market

**DATES:** Daily.

**TIMES:** 9:00 AM-6:00 PM, Fridays until 9:00 PM.

**ADMISSION:** Free. Parking is free.

**LOCATION:** 6606 Grover St. Take I-80 60th St Exit or 72nd St Exit to Grover St. It's the first traffic light north of I-80.

**DESCRIPTION:** Opened in 1994, this indoor market of 175 dealers sells antiques, furniture, cards, garage sale goodies, and a wide selection of new merchandise. There isn't any food in here, but there are handicapped-accessible restrooms.

**DEALER RATES:** $21 per 5' × 5' booth, $37.50 per 10' × 5' medium booth, $50 per 10' × 10' large booth every 2 weeks. There is locked showcase space as well as shelf rentals. Reservations are necessary.

**CONTACT:** Blue Ribbon Flea Market, 6606 Grover St, Omaha NE 68106-3631. Tel: (402) 397-6811. Email: geolapole@infobridge.com.

# WALTHILL
## NE Nebraska's Scenic View Flea Market & Hillbilly Auction

**DATES:** First full weekend of each month.

**TIMES:** Morning to whenever.

**ADMISSION:** Free. Parking is free.

**LOCATION:** South of Winnabago.

**DESCRIPTION:** Open since 1993, this indoor/outdoor market of 50 dealers sells antiques, collectibles, crafts, produce, coins, garage sale goodies, dogs and poultry (do they mix?), and new merchandise. There is food available on the premises as well as restrooms. According to Don, there is plenty to see around here with gorgeous scenery (hills, timber) and horses pulling wagons, stray deer and turkeys roaming... worth a stop.
**DEALER RATES:** $100 yearly for a 30' × 40' or $10 per weekend. Electricity is $5 additional.
**CONTACT:** Don Nottelman, Flea Market, RR 1, Walthill NE 68067-9801. Tel: 402-846-9150 or 349-9320.

# YORK
## Lions Club Antique and Flea Market

**DATES:** April 5, 2000. Watch for 2001 around the same time—usually before Easter.
**TIMES:** 9:00 AM-5:00 PM.
**ADMISSION:** Free. Parking is free.
**LOCATION:** York City Auditorium at the corner of 6th and Nebraska.
**DESCRIPTION:** For 16 years this market has been the main fundraiser of the York Lions Club. Their 65 dealers sell all types of goods, from standard flea market fare to loads of antiques and collectibles and some crafts.
**DEALER RATES:** $32-$35 for upstairs level and $20-$22 for downstairs level. There is an elevator to get downstairs and the Lions Club members are there to help load and unload the treasures. Reservations are most necessary.
**CONTACT:** Gene Mulinix, York Lions Club Flea Market, 137 S Michigan, York NE 68467. Tel: (402) 362-3593 (Gene's home) or (402) 362-4040 (business).

# OTHER FLEA MARKETS

We know or have heard about these markets, but have not personally contacted each one, as we have the markets with descriptions. If you plan to visit one of these markets listed below, *please call first* to make sure they are still open. Flea markets do come and go. While they were open when we went to press, they may not be later. We can't be responsible. *Call first!*

**Hastings:** Big E's Antiques & Flea Market, 212 W 2 St. Tel: (402) 463-0260.

**North Platte:** RJ Flea Market, Hwy 30W. Tel: (308) 534-0138.

**Omaha:** Treasure Trove Flea Mall, 6606 Grover St. Tel: (402) 397-6811.

**South Sioux City**: Siouxland Flea Market, 2111 Dakota Ave. Tel: (402) 494-3221 or (712) 259-0174. Open daily, Monday thru Saturday, 9 AM-6 PM except Sunday, 12-6 PM. Nearly 200 vendors selling antiques and collectibles, crafts, new and used furniture, household items, new merchandise.

# NEVADA

## LAS VEGAS
### Fantastic Indoor Swap Meet

**DATES:** Friday, Saturday and Sunday, year round. Also open additional days during Christmas season.

**TIMES:** 10:00 AM-6:00 PM.

**ADMISSION:** $1, seniors $.50. Children 12 and under free with paying adult. Parking is free on 15 acres.

**LOCATION:** 1717 S Decatur at Oakey Blvd.

**DESCRIPTION:** Opened in 1990, this huge market (200,000 square feet) has dealers in 600 booths selling all new merchandise, crafts, "the most wonderful things" from satellite dishes to more usual fare. There are four restaurants selling Chinese, American, New York City food and a variety of other delectable edibles.

**DEALER RATES:** From $400 and up for four 3-day weekends. Advance reservations are required as there is a two-week waiting period to get a city license. All sellers must have a state tax permit. Office hours: Thursday 10:00 AM-3:00 PM.

**CONTACT:** Berny Krebs or Kandi Roche (Rentals), Fantastic Indoor Swap Meet, 1717 S Decatur, Las Vegas NV 89102. Tel: (702) 877-0087 or fax: (702) 877-3102. Email: fism8888@aol.com. Web: www.fantasticswap.com.

## NORTH LAS VEGAS
### Broadacres Open Air Swap Meet

**DATES:** Friday, Saturday, and Sunday, year round. Rain or shine.

**TIMES:** 6:30 AM to whenever.

**ADMISSION:** $.50 on Friday, otherwise $1 per person weekends, children under 12 free.

**LOCATION:** 2960 Las Vegas Blvd, Las Vegas Blvd N at Pecos. Four miles north of the Union Plaza Hotel on Las Vegas Blvd N.

**DESCRIPTION:** Opened in November 1977, this outdoor market is in its 22nd year of business. Their 700 dealers in the summer attract 18,000 buyers weekly, and 1,500 dealers attract 25,000 buyers during the winter months. Antiques, collectibles, tools, toys, crafts, produce, and new merchandise are available. There are plenty of shade trees and when necessary, clean restrooms.

**DEALER RATES:** The charge for a booth measuring 15' × 30' is $15 on Saturday and Sunday and $8 on Friday. Advance reservations are suggested at least three weeks in advance. Make your reservations during business hours. They have 1,000 reserved spaces and only 500 daily unreserved spaces. Office hours: Friday 6:30 AM-12:30 PM, weekends 6:30 AM-2:00 PM.
**CONTACT:** Jake Bowman, Broadacres Open Air Swap Meet, PO Box 3059, N Las Vegas NV 89030-3059. Tel: (702) 642-3777.

# SPARKS
## El Rancho Flea Market

**DATES:** Saturdays and Sundays, year round, weather permitting.
**TIMES:** Summer from 6:00 AM-4:30 PM: winter from 6:00 AM-whenever.
**ADMISSION:** $.50 per person; children under 12 free, includes parking.
**LOCATION:** 555 El Rancho Dr at the El Rancho Drive-In Theater. Off I-80 at the "G" St exit, go east 2 blocks on Prater then 2 blocks north on El Rancho Dr, turn left on G St. If you are on El Rancho Dr, you can't miss them; they are next to Paradise Park.
**DESCRIPTION:** Located in Sparks, well known for gambling casinos, near Lake Tahoe. Twin city to Reno. Opened in 1978, this outdoor flea market attracts 200-250 dealers selling antiques, collectibles, fresh produce, new merchandise, and garage sale items. There are plenty of food carts roaming the market, a barbecue stand with made-to-order goodies, a beer garden (they do card you) and handicapped-accessible restrooms.
**DEALER RATES:** $16 for booths measuring 10' × 30'; there are other sizes, call for rates. Reservations are not required—first come, first served—although some space is reserved until 8:00 AM.
**CONTACT:** Lance Edwards, El Rancho Swap, 555 El Rancho Dr, Sparks NV 89431. Tel: (775) 331-3227. Fax: (775) 359-2833.

# OTHER FLEA MARKETS

We know or have heard about these markets, but have not personally contacted each one, as we have the markets with descriptions. If you plan to visit one of these markets listed below, *please call first* to make sure they are still open. Flea markets do come and go. While they were open when we went to press, they may not be later. We can't be responsible. *Call first!*

**Carson City:** Carson Valley, 3756 Gross Cr. Bld E Ste D. Tel: (702) 267-0057.

**Las Vegas:** J & R's Outdoors Swap Meet, 3901 Las Vegas Blvd. Tel: (702) 644-SWAP.

**Ruth:** Ruth Swap Meet, 5 Main St. Tel: (702) 289-6032.

# NEW HAMPSHIRE

## DERRY
### Grand View Flea Market

**DATES:** Saturday and Sunday, year round. Rain or shine.

**TIMES:** Saturday 9:00 AM-3:00 PM, Sunday 7:00 AM-4:00 PM.

**ADMISSION:** Sunday only: $.50 for adults; children under 12 free.

**LOCATION:** At the junction of Rt 28 and Bypass 28 S.

**DESCRIPTION:** This show, established more than 30 years ago, is one of northern New England's first and finest. In the center of the market is a pond with a 30-foot-tall Indian totem pole. It also has a strange collection of statuary including two very large elephants, a bear and several genies, purchased from an old amusement park. Two hundred to 400 dealers work indoors and out, selling all sorts of antiques, collectibles, crystals, books, novelties, jewelry, gifts, appliances, fabric and lace, new and used furniture, handmades, and new items. A new addition was added in the fall of 1990 increasing the indoor market by 60 spaces, then another 24,000 square feet was added in 1993. This is an interesting market always trying new things like magic shows to amuse the children. Food and handicapped-accessible restrooms are available on the premises. A golf range is next door.

**DEALER RATES:** $25 per 12' × 8' space indoors per day including 3 tables Sundays, Saturdays are $10; $20 per "large car length" space outdoors per day. Tables are available for rental at $1.50 per day. Reservations are not required.

**CONTACT:** Kathi Taylor, Grand View Flea Market, 34 S Main St, Derry NH 03086. Tel: (603) 432-2326.

## HOLLIS
### Hollis Country Store and Flea Market

**DATES:** Every Sunday, first Sunday of April through the second Sunday of November; plus Memorial Day and Labor Day.

**TIMES:** 7:00 AM-dusk.

**ADMISSION:** Free. $1 parking fee.

**LOCATION:** On Silver Lake Rd (Rt 122). Take Exit 7W off Rt 3 (in Nashua) to 101A west. Go 8 miles, then turn left onto Rt 122S. Market is 2½ miles on the right.

**DESCRIPTION:** Opened in 1965, this outdoor market now attracts over 250 dealers selling antiques and collectibles as well as new merchandise and fresh produce. This is a well-attended, busy market, attracting dealers and customers from all over New England and as far as California. They have an excellent reputation for quality goods at reasonable prices. Food is served on the premises.

**DEALER RATES:** $18 per 15' × 20' space. Reservations are preferred.

**CONTACT:** Alice Prieto, 436 Silver Lake Rd, Hollis NH 03049. Tel: (603) 465-7813. Fax: (603) 882-0927. Email: hollisflea@aol.com.

---

### This'll Get'em Department

A woman brought in a trailer with a shed on it loaded with over $10,000 worth of power tools—and sold it all for $10. She was divorcing her husband.

---

### Just Married

One of their dealers asked if he could hold his wedding and reception at the market. Thinking the wedding itself wasn't appropriate to the market, but a reception was, the reception was held at the market with a neighboring dealer creating a beautiful wedding cake for the event. Other dealers pitched in with punch and ice cream.

Many shoppers that day participated in an unexpected celebration.

---

# LEBANON
## Colonial Antiques and Flea Market

**DATES:** Daily indoors, Sundays outdoors, weather permitting.

**TIMES:** 9:00 AM-5:00 PM. However, Sundays during the dark months the whole market opens at 8:00 AM, and during the light months they open at 6:00 AM.

**ADMISSION:** Free. Parking is free.

**LOCATION:** Rt 12A at Exit 20 off I-89 at Colonial Plaza.

**DESCRIPTION:** Opened in 1976, and under new management since mid-June 1995, this market's over 90 dealers sell antiques, collectibles, estate jewelry, furniture, old books, old clothes, dolls, old tools, postcards, stamps, fine glassware, paintings, bottles, crafts and much more. Many of their dealers are recognized authorities in their field. There are "loads of fine treasures, a bargain hunters paradise," with fine smalls and rare prints among other found prizes. This market strives for the finest quality available. They have a reputation as the "first and oldest and funnest market in New England."

**DEALER RATES:** $27.50 for about 7' × 10' space weekly inside. Outdoors is $14 for 2 parking spaces. Reservations are mandatory for inside as there is a waiting list. No reservations for the outside space.

**CONTACT:** Colonial Antiques and Flea Market, 5 Airport Rd, W Lebanon NH 03784. Tel: (603) 298-7712 or 298-8132.

---

### Okay, I Believe That Department

A woman came in looking for a Christmas present for her doctor husband and "hit" on a 1820 anatomy book published in Edinburgh, Scotland. She leafed through the pages with their copper-plate pictures and found a handsome adult male skeleton. Obviously intrigued she asked, "Who is this?" The dealer, without hesitation, replied, "George Washington." That didn't faze her. Then she happened upon another skeleton picture of an infant. "Who's this?" she asked. Again, without a blink, the dealer replied, "George Washington—as an infant."

She didn't buy the book.

---

# MEREDITH
## Burlwood Antique Center

**DATES:** Daily, May 1-October 31.

**TIMES:** 10:00 AM-5:00 PM.

**ADMISSION:** Free. Free parking is available.

**LOCATION:** 194 Daniel Webster Hwy. On Rt 3. From I-93, take Exit 23, then go east on Rt 104, 9 miles to Rt 3, then turn right to get to Burlwood Antique Center.

**DESCRIPTION:** This indoor market opened in 1983 and currently accommodates over 170 dealers. There is a variety of antiques and collectibles sold and an entire floor of furniture. Fine art and plenty of costume and fine jewelry, smalls, Shaker items and primitives are also available, as well as an antique lighting gallery. Because they are open only six months a year, all the merchandise is fresh each year. This is a great place for dealers to stock up for other markets, as most of their shoppers are dealers.

**DEALER RATES:** $125 per 5' × 3' × 8' space per month. Reservations are required.

**CONTACT:** Mark Diette or Mary Di Maria, 194 Daniel Webster Hwy, Meredith NH 03253. Tel: (603) 279-6387. Web: www.burlwood-antiques.com.

---

### Wonder What They Will Do With That?

One dealer sold a vintage 1880s' portable folding mortician's table. Would you like to try it?

---

## OTHER FLEA MARKETS

We know or have heard about these markets, but have not personally contacted each one, as we have the markets with descriptions. If you plan to visit one of these markets listed below, *please call first* to make sure they are still open. Flea markets do come and go. While they were open when we went to press, they may not be later. We can't be responsible. *Call first!*

**Amherst:** Amherst Outdoor Antique Market, 157 Hollis Rd, Rt 122S. Tel: (603) 673-2093 or (617) 641-0600. Last Sunday of every month from April-October. 6 AM-3 PM. Parking $5/vehicle.

**Amherst:** Howland's Antique Show, Rt 101A. Tel: (603) 673-2737.

**Claremont:** Pee Wee's Flea Market & Antique, 64 Pleasant St. Tel: (603) 542-9331.

**Contoocook:** Davisville Barn Sale & Flea, Rt 103. Tel: (603) 746-4000.

**Gilford:** Lakes Region Flea Market, Rt 11. Tel: (603) 524-2441. Open Sundays 8 AM-3 PM.

**Hampton Falls:** Applecrest Farms Weekly Antiques Market, Rt 88. Tel: (603) 778-8842. Open Saturdays, 7 AM-1 PM.

**Hollis:** Silver Lake Flea Market, Rt 122. Tel: (603) 465-7677. Open Sundays April-November, 7 AM-4 PM.

**Londonderry:** Londonderry Gardens Flea Market, 5 Avery Rd. Tel: (603) 880-9935.

**Nashua:** St Stan's Hall, Rte 3, Exit 6, 2nd left on to Blue Hill Ave. Tel: (781) 329-1192. Open Sunday, 7:30 AM-NOON.

**Rochester:** Mac's Flea Market, 194 Milton Rd. Tel: (603) 330-0177.

**Salem:** Salem NH Flea Market, 18 Hampshire Rd. Tel: (603) 893-8888.

**Woodstock:** Woodstock Flea Market, Woodstock Plz. Tel: (603) 745-2816.

# NEW JERSEY

## ABSECON HIGHLANDS
### L'Erario's Flea Market
**DATES:** Every Saturday and Sunday, weather permitting.
**TIMES:** 7:00 AM-whenever.
**ADMISSION:** Free. Free parking is available.
**LOCATION:** At intersection of Jim Leeds Rd and Pitney Rd, Absecon-Highlands Rt 561. Only minutes from Atlantic City.
**DESCRIPTION:** This outdoor market began in 1968 and currently accommodates approximately 50 to 80 dealers, selling anything from antiques, arts and crafts, and collectibles to new and used merchandise. There is a deli, a restaurant as well as a homemade ice cream and water ice shop on the premises.
**DEALER RATES:** $15 Saturdays; $18 Sundays per 10' × 20' space plus vehicle. Reservations are not required. Bring your own tables.
**CONTACT:** L'Erario's, PO Box 572, Absecon NJ 08201. Tel: (609) 652-0540.

## AUBURN
### Auburn Antique and Flea Market
**DATES:** Outdoors only on Saturday, weather permitting; indoors and outdoors on Sunday, year round.
**TIMES:** 9:00 AM-4:00 PM, although, you can come at 7:00 AM.
**ADMISSION:** Free outdoors, and indoors from May through November. Winter $.50 per person. Parking is free.
**LOCATION:** 773 Southbridge St, Rte 12.
**DESCRIPTION:** Opened in 1974, this market's 100-150 dealers (depending on weather and time of year) sell antiques, collectibles, and new merchandise. There is a snack bar on site, and in the summer there are handicapped-accessible restrooms; in the winter there are the indoor restrooms.
**DEALER RATES:** $10 for outdoor space, plus $3 per table if needed. Indoors: $15-$30, plus $3 per table if rented. Reservations are required for inside space only. Outside, first come, first served.
**CONTACT:** David Adrian, Auburn Antique and Flea Market, PO Box 33, Auburn NJ 01501-0033. Tel: (508) 832-2763. Email: dadrian@allmerica.com.

**Just Try It!**

A dealer came in trying to flog a tombstone he had purchased at a garage sale. It was a great tombstone—very clear names and dates, in great condition. Only trouble was, it's against the law to sell them. It was confiscated by the police, who came to the market to do so!

# BELVIDERE
## Five Acres

**DATES:** Every Saturday and Sunday, year round and holidays.

**TIMES:** 8:00 AM until everyone is gone.

**ADMISSION:** Free. Parking is also free.

**LOCATION:** 421 Rt 46 E. On Rt 80, take Exit 12 south to Rt 46, go east 1,500 feet. Market is on right.

**DESCRIPTION:** This outdoor flea market opened in 1965. There are between 75 and 100 dealers selling anything from antiques and collectibles to arts, crafts and new merchandise. Fresh produce is also available. There are clean restrooms and a bar on premises. They opened a small antiques mall on the premises in the spring of 1999.

**DEALER RATES:** $15 per 10' × 20' space on Sunday, $10 on Saturday. Reservations are not required. If interested in selling in the new antique building, contact Totsy.

**CONTACT:** Totsy Phillips, PO Box 295, Belvidere NJ 07823-0295. Tel: (908) 475-2572.

# BERLIN
## Berlin Farmers' Market

**DATES:** Thursday, Friday, Saturday and Sunday. Rain or shine.

**TIMES:** 8:00 AM-4:00 PM outside flea market Saturday and Sunday only, weather permitting. Farmers' Market Thursday-Friday 11:00 AM-9:30 PM; Saturday 10:00 AM-9:30 PM; Sunday 10:00 AM-6:00 PM inside.

**ADMISSION:** Free. Free parking is available.

**LOCATION:** 41 Clementon Rd. Just off Rt 30, Rt 73 or Rt 42 about 40 minutes from either Atlantic City or Philadelphia.

**DESCRIPTION:** This market started in 1930 as a livestock auction. Today it is located on about 60 acres of land. These spacious accommodations house the outdoor flea market and parking lot. The indoor shopping market is in a building ¼ mile long. Between their indoor and outdoor market, on any given weekend there are anywhere from 700 to 800 dealers. The types of merchandise to be found are unlimited: from antiques to new merchandise, from quality new and used furniture, arts and crafts to fresh produce. Seen and sold: clothing of all kinds, gold stuff, toys, tools, hardware, health and beauty aids, furniture, sports cards, video games and tapes, etc. Once a customer brought in a house on a trailer—and sold it! There are two snack bars and three other food vendors inside, and eight food vendors outside. This flea market is proudly owned and operated by the third generation of the Giberson family.

**DEALER RATES:** For flea market vendors: $20 per 12' × 30' booth—strictly used merchandise for 2 days ($15 for one day); $35 per 12' × 30' booth for all new merchandise. Reservations are suggested. Office is open Thursday and Friday.

**CONTACT:** Stan Giberson, Jr or Ron Smith, 41 Clementon Rd, Berlin NJ 08009. Tel: (856) 767-1284. Fax: (856) 767-1246.

# CHERRY HILL
## Garden State Park Flea Market

**DATES:** Wednesday and Sunday.

**TIMES:** 8:00 AM-3:00 PM

**ADMISSION:** Free. Parking is $1.

**LOCATION:** Garden State Park Race Track. Rt 295 to Rt 70 W exit for Cherry Hill; 3 miles on the right. Use the main entrance on Rt 70.

**DESCRIPTION:** This outdoor market, opened in 1989, consists of 500-1,200 dealers (depending on the season) selling 99% new merchandise. During the winter months, the market moves indoors as well so they have both an indoor and outdoor market. It's considered a good upscale market. They are working on setting up a used and antique section (listen up dealers!). Two food courts with 12-14 vendors at each court and handicapped-accessible restrooms will take care of all your needs. Arthur treats his vendors and customers as human beings, as he has 20 years experience as a vendor. He considers this a fun market. They do a lot of advertising.

**DEALER RATES:** $25 on Wednesday, $35 on Sunday, daily. $115 per month of Sundays. $75 for only Wednesdays, $165 for both days for one month. Reservations are needed. There will be special discounted rates for antiques and used merchandise dealers. Please call Arthur about those.

**CONTACT:** Arthur, Garden State Park Flea Market, PO Box 1024, Somerset NJ 08873-1024. Tel: (856) 665-8558.

# CLIFTON
## Boys' and Girls' Club of Clifton Flea Market

**DATES:** Third Sunday of every month from September through April; additionally there are other shows throughout the year. Call for more information on those.

**TIMES:** 8:00 AM-4:00 PM.

**ADMISSION:** Free admission and free parking available.

**LOCATION:** 802 Clifton Ave at the Boys' and Girls' Club.

**DESCRIPTION:** This annual indoor event has been taking place for 27 years with 85 to 100 dealers selling antiques, collectibles, new merchandise, and craft items. This show is used as a fundraiser for the 1,500 children who use the Club. One snack bar and handicapped-accessible restrooms add to the amenities.

**DEALER RATES:** $20 for the first 8' × 4' table, $10 each additional table. Reservations are required.

**CONTACT:** Joe and Arlene Jiuliani, 46 Potomac Ave, Paterson NJ 07503-1604. Tel/fax: (973) 977-8134.

# COLUMBUS
## Columbus Farmers' Market

**DATES:** Every Thursday, Friday, Saturday and Sunday. Rain or shine.

**TIMES:** Inside hours: Thursday and Saturday 8:00 AM-8:00 PM; Friday 10:00 AM-8:00 PM; Sunday 8:00 AM-5:00 PM. Outside hours: Thursday, Saturday and Sunday dawn to whenever!

**ADMISSION:** Free. Free parking is available.

**LOCATION:** On Rt 206, 5 miles south of Exit 7 off the New Jersey Tnpk.

**DESCRIPTION:** This outdoor market began in 1929. This indoor/outdoor market accommodates from 400 dealers in winter to 1,700 dealers in summer selling antiques and collectibles as well as new merchandise and fresh produce. There are 70 permanent stores including seven restaurants, monogramming, shoe repair, sewing machine repair, a Chinese food shop and all types of specialty shops. Food is served on the premises.

**DEALER RATES:** Thursday $30 per 12' × 30' space; Saturday $10; Sunday $30 per 12' × 30' booth—new items, $15 per 12' × 30' booth—used items. Reservations are not required; spaces are assigned by the management.

**CONTACT:** Columbus Farmers Market, 2919 Rte 206 S, Columbus NJ 08022-0322. Tel: (609) 267-0400.

# DORCHESTER
## Campbell's Flea Market

**DATES:** Saturday and Sunday, March through December. Rain or shine.
**TIMES:** 7:00 AM-5:00 PM.
**ADMISSION:** Free. Parking is also free.
**LOCATION:** Three miles south on Rt 47 from Rt 55.
**DESCRIPTION:** This market opened in 1961 on six acres of century-old trees providing plenty of shade. Rt 47 is the major highway to the beaches making this a terrific spot to attract buyers. Sixty dealers inside and 80 outside sell antiques and crafts to attic treasures, collectibles, glassware, aluminum, and flea market fare. This is a market where social time among dealers and customers is common. Rare finds are still out here. Food is available on the premises. A Texaco station, an ice cream parlor, and deli are next door.
**DEALER RATES:** $10 per table inside; outside $10. Reservations are not required.
**CONTACT:** Terri Campbell, PO Box 131, Dorchester NJ 08316-0131. Tel: (609) 785-2222.

# DOVER
## Dover Marketplace

**DATES:** Sundays, April through December.
**TIMES:** 9:00 AM-5:00 PM.
**ADMISSION:** Free. Parking is free.
**LOCATION:** 18 W Blackwell St. Rt 80 Exit 35A. Near the Chester Lions Club.
**DESCRIPTION:** Opened in 1998, covering 12 city blocks plus an antique center and shops, this market of 200 dealers is a good old-fashioned street fair—"the only continuously operating street fair" according to its owner—as it runs weekly. Averaging 95% new merchandise versus old goodies, and 10-12,000 shoppers, this market also has plenty of food vendors on site, plenty of restaurants nearby, and handicapped-accessible restrooms.
**DEALER RATES:** $50 per Sunday, yearly rate. Daily rate $85. Spaces for the daily rate are very limited so you must call ahead to determine if your merchandise category is open. Reservations are essential.
**CONTACT:** Bob Brumale, Dover Marketplace, 18 W Blackwell St, Dover NJ 07073. Tel: (973) 989-7870. Email: solonpond@aol.com. Web: fleamarketsusa.com (notice the plural, as there is another site with a similar name).

# EAST BRUNSWICK
## Route 18 Flea Market

**DATES:** Every Friday, Saturday, and Sunday.

**TIMES:** Friday 11:00 AM-9:00 PM; Saturday 10:00 AM-9:00 PM; Sunday 11:00 AM-6:00 PM.

**ADMISSION:** Free. Parking is free.

**LOCATION:** At 290 Rt 18; NJ Tnpk Exit 9, take Rt 18 south to Prospect St, make U-turn and go back north 1 block.

**DESCRIPTION:** Described as a "poor man's mall," this indoor market of over 150 vendors sells antiques, collectibles, produce, deli items, coins, cards, furniture, discount groceries, gold jewelry, framing and art galleries, and new merchandise. Ten restaurants in an international food court (Greek, Chinese, Mexican, etc.) feed the famished, and when you need them there are handicapped-accessible restrooms. There is weekly entertainment with live bands, wrestlers, soap stars, car shows and monthly sports card auctions.

**DEALER RATES:** $150 and up per 3-day weekend for a 10' × 10' basic space. Prices range depending on where and how long. Reservations are suggested.

**CONTACT:** Barbara Passwaters, Rt 18 Indoor Market, 290 SR 18, E Brunswick NJ 08816-1905. Tel: (732) 254-5080 or 254-5082. Fax: (732) 254-1761.

# EAST RUTHERFORD
## Meadowlands Marketplace

**DATES:** Every Thursday and Saturday, plus Memorial Day, July 4th and Labor Day; Saturdays only January through March. It will be open on New Years Day, 2000. The Friday after Thanksgiving starts their winter season.

**TIMES:** 9:00 AM-4:00 PM.

**ADMISSION:** Free. Parking is free.

**LOCATION:** At Giants Stadium parking lot 17 on Rt 3 W.

**DESCRIPTION:** This upscale market of 700-800 vendors sells antiques, collectibles, fresh produce, seafood, and used and new merchandise.

**DEALER RATES:** Thursday, $30, Saturday $50-$85 per 18' x 36' space. Antiques $40 per space. Reservations are a good idea.

**CONTACT:** Meadowlands Marketplace, NJ Sports Complex, Giants Stadium, E Rutherford NJ 07073-1405. Tel: (201) 935-5474. Fax: (201) 935-5495. Email: solonpond@aol.com. Web: fleamarketsusa.com (notice the plural).

# EDISON
## New Dover United Methodist Church Flea Market
**DATES:** Every Tuesday, mid-March through December. Rain or shine (unless there is a severe threatening storm).
**TIMES:** 7:00 AM-1:00 PM.
**ADMISSION:** Free. Free parking is available.
**LOCATION:** 687 New Dover Rd. Take Exit 131 on Garden State Parkway, bear right, go to first light (Wood Ave), turn right, go to second light (New Dover Rd), finally, turn left.
**DESCRIPTION:** This indoor/outdoor market began in 1971. Since that time it has grown to accommodate approximately 60 dealers during summer months. Many items such as collectibles, new merchandise, and fresh produce can be purchased. This market is a fundraiser for the church. There are two security guards on the premises. Restrooms are available. The church kitchen, run by volunteers, sells hot homemade food.
**DEALER RATES:** $20 per table, inside with table or outside parking space size. Reservations are required for monthly only. New vendors should arrive by 6:00 AM for space and setup.
**CONTACT:** New Dover United Methodist Church, 687 New Dover Rd, Edison NJ 08820. Tel: (732) 381-7904.

# ENGLISHTOWN
## Englishtown Auction Sales Flea Market
**DATES:** Saturday and Sunday, year round; also open Good Friday, Labor Day, Columbus Day and Friday after Thanksgiving.
**TIMES:** Saturday 7:00 AM-4:00 PM; Sundays and holidays 9:00 AM-4:00 PM.
**ADMISSION:** Free, with free parking available.
**LOCATION:** 90 Wilson Ave; New Jersey Tnpk Exit 9; access from Rt 18 S and Rt 527 S.
**DESCRIPTION:** Since 1929 this market has been known as "shopping at its best for the entire family." This combination indoor/outdoor show is held in five buildings and on 40 acres of outside dealer space. Their hundreds of dealers sell antiques and collectibles, jewelry, hubcaps, clothing, housewares, furniture, as well as new merchandise. Food items are restricted, but three food courts and an air-conditioned tavern as well as handicapped-accessible restrooms add to the amenities. Their mascot Sunny roams the markets on weekends entertaining kids of all ages. Check out their Internet site for specials.

**DEALER RATES:** Spaces start at $5 a day outdoors. $160 and up per month for a single 12' × 15' booth inside. Monthly reservations are suggested. Office hours: Saturday 7:00 AM-4:00 PM, Sunday and holidays 9:00 AM-4:00 PM, and Mondays and Fridays 10:00 AM-2:00 PM.
**CONTACT:** Manager, Englishtown Auction Sales, 90 Wilson Ave, Englishtown NJ 07726. Tel: (732) 446-9644. Fax: (732) 446-1220.
Email: englishtwn@aol.com. Website: www.englishtownauction.com.

# FARMINGDALE/COLLINGWOOD PARK
## Collingwood Auction and Flea Market
**DATES:** Every Friday, Saturday, and Sunday.
**TIMES:** Outside opens every day at 7:00 AM. Inside: Friday 12:00 PM-8:00 PM, Saturday 10:00 AM-8:00 PM, Sunday 10:00 AM-5:00 PM.
**ADMISSION:** Free. Parking is free.
**LOCATION:** On St Hwy 33 and 34, ½ mile west of Collingwood traffic circle, 4 miles south of Colts Neck.
**DESCRIPTION:** Opened around 1950 with 40 acres of selling space, this indoor market of 125 vendors and outdoor market of up to 600 vendors sells antiques, collectibles, crafts, garage sale goodies, jewelry, clothing, furniture, fresh produce, and new and used merchandise—ratio of about 50/50 old to new. Saturday night is Antique Auction night, Friday nights are the tailgate auctions. The last Friday of every month is the car auction, not to forget Saturday's tree and shrub auction which I'm assured is quite popular. There is a snack bar and handicapped-accessible restrooms on site.
**DEALER RATES:** Outside: Friday $2, Saturday $6, Sunday $9 per space. Inside $200 and up monthly with reservations. Outside is first come, first served.
**CONTACT:** Collingwood Auction & Flea Market, 1350 Hwy 33, Farmingdale NJ 07727. Tel: (732) 938-7941. Fax: (732) 938-4652.

# FLEMINGTON
## The Flemington Fair Flea Market
**DATES:** Every Wednesday, April through November.
**TIMES:** 6:00 AM-4:00 PM.
**ADMISSION:** Free. Free parking is available.
**LOCATION:** On Hwy 31, 22 miles north of Trenton; 18 miles north of New Hope, PA; 30 miles southeast of eastern Pennsylvania; 45 miles west of New York City.

**DESCRIPTION:** Started in 1980, this market now accommodates anywhere from 75 to 120 dealers outdoors as well as 16 indoor shops. Although the majority of vendors sell antiques and collectibles, fine art, arts and crafts, new merchandise, plants, clothing, fresh produce and everything under the sun can be found. Situated in the beautiful, historic country setting of the Flemington Fairgrounds, this can be a fun day for the entire family!

**DEALER RATES:** $6 per 8' × 20' space outdoors; $500 per season per 10' × 12' indoor shop which includes 10' × 30' outdoors. Reservations are required for indoor space only. Vendors set up at 6:00 AM on Wednesday.

**CONTACT:** Melissa L Yerkes, 25 Kuhl Rd, Flemington NJ 08822. Tel: (908) 782-7326 after 5:00 PM. Day of show call main office at (908) 782-2413. Email: gourd55@yahoo.com.

# GILLETTE
## Meyersville Grange Antique Flea Mart

**DATES:** Every Sunday, October through March.

**TIMES:** 8:00 AM-2:00 PM.

**ADMISSION:** Free. Free parking is available.

**LOCATION:** On Meyersville Rd, between Rt 78 and Rt 24 in Long Hill Township, in the heart of the Great Swamp Wildlife Preserve in southeast Morris County.

**DESCRIPTION:** This market started in 1970 in the Grange building, built in the early 1900s, in the middle of a swamp. Approximately 35 dealers specialize in antiques, collectibles and handmade craft items. Coffee and food are available and from 10:00 AM-2:00 PM hot dogs, homemade soup, and pastries are served.

**DEALER RATES:** $20-$30 per 8' table, per day. Reservations are required and can be made any evening after 6:00 PM.

**CONTACT:** Ron Miller, Meyersville Grange Antique Flea Mart, 1163 Washington Valley Rd, Basking Ridge NJ 07920. Tel: (908) 306-0231. Day of show call (908) 647-9727.

# JEFFERSON
## Jefferson Township Fire Company #2 Flea Market

**DATES:** Saturday from April through October.

**TIMES:** 6:30 AM to whenever.

**ADMISSION:** Free. Parking is free.

**LOCATION:** Rt 15 S, across from the Pathmark. Take I-80 W to Exit 34B (Rt 15 N), go down 3 traffic lights. Go down Pathmark ramp and cut across through Pathmark.

**DESCRIPTION:** Opened around 1989 as a fundraiser for the Fire Department, this market of 30-50 dealers sells antiques, collectibles, crafts, produce in season, trading cards, Ts and sweats—whatever comes in. The Fire Department runs the food concession.

**DEALER RATES:** $15 for a "oh, car-sized-wide" space daily, $60 monthly, or $300 for a full season. Reservations are suggested and appreciated.

**CONTACT:** Jefferson Township Fire Company, PO Box 5, Lake Hopatcong NJ 07849. Tel: (973) 663-5810.

# LAKEWOOD
## Route 70 Flea Market

**DATES:** Friday, Saturday and Sunday, year round.

**TIMES:** Friday 8:00 AM-2:00 PM. Saturday and Sunday 7:00 AM-4:00 PM.

**ADMISSION:** Free. Parking is free.

**LOCATION:** 117 Rt 70, between Garden State Pkwy and Rt 9. From the South: Take GSP north to Exit 83. Take Rt 9 north to Rt 70 E. Bear right after the golf course, go down to the stop sign, make a left. Go to the traffic light, turn left to the market. From the North: Take GSP south to Exit 88. Pay the toll, turn right onto Rt 70 W. Follow Rt 70 W a few miles and market will be on the right.

**DESCRIPTION:** Opened in 1980, this indoor/outdoor "true flea market" of 700-1,000 dealers sells antiques, collectibles, crafts, fresh produce, meats, seafood, livestock, coins, stamps, cards, clothing, jewelry, garage sale goodies, furniture, and new merchandise. There are snack bars for the hungry and handicapped-accessible restrooms when needed.

**DEALER RATES:** $8 per 8' table on weekends, $4 on Friday. Reservations are not required.

**CONTACT:** Michael Gingrich, General Manager, Rt 70 Flea Market, 117 Hwy 70, Lakewood NJ 08701-5820. Tel: (732) 370-1837. Fax: (732) 840-5684.

# LAMBERTVILLE
## Golden Nugget Antique Flea Market

**DATES:** Every Wednesday, Saturday and Sunday, outdoors, year round. Rain or shine. Indoor shops are open on weekends.

**TIMES:** Outdoors: 6:30 AM-5:00 PM; indoors 8:30 AM-4:00 PM.

**ADMISSION:** Free. Parking is $1 on Sundays, otherwise free.

**LOCATION:** Rt 29, 2 miles south of Lambertville, 5 miles north of Exit 1 on I-95.

**DESCRIPTION:** This indoor/outdoor market began its operation in 1960 and currently accommodates 40 indoor shops and 200 tables outdoors. The main building offers 15,000 square feet of space and is air-conditioned for year-round use. Dealers offer antiques and collectibles such as furniture, glassware and porcelain, craft items, and new merchandise. Friday evenings, weather permitting, they hold tailgate auctions. Food is served on the premises. This market is located within a few miles of several historic sites: Washington Crossing, New Hope-Lahaska and Lambertville.

**DEALER RATES:** $8 for a 8' × 4' table on Wednesday, $15 on Saturday, $25 on Sunday. Reservations are required for Sunday, recommended for Saturday. Please reserve in person or via the tape on the phone number.

**CONTACT:** Tony Rizzello, Manager, Golden Nugget Antique Flea Market, 1850 River Rd, Lambertville NJ 08530. Tel: (609) 397-0811.

---

### Movie News

In September 1997, Dan Rather for *CBS Eye on America* filmed a segment on a falcon figurine sold at the market in 1990. Unusual about the falcon, it had the initials "WB" on the bottom. The purchaser believes it is the figurine used as a prop in the Humphrey Bogart film *Maltese Falcon* filmed by Warner Bros. If true then the falcon, purchased for $8, is estimated to be worth $400,000. Oh, what a return on investment!

---

## Lambertville Antique Flea Market, Inc

**DATES:** Outdoors: every Wednesday, Saturday and Sunday. Rain or shine. Indoors: Wednesday through Sunday.

**TIMES:** Outdoors: 6:00 AM till they leave (closing). Indoors: Thursday and Friday 10:00 AM-4:00 PM, Wednesday and weekends 8:00 AM-4:00 PM.

**ADMISSION:** Free. Free parking is available.

**LOCATION:** On Rt 29, 1 mile south of Lambertville, along the Delaware River.

**DESCRIPTION:** Opened in 1967, this is both an indoor and outdoor market, with a pavilion covering for 49 of its spaces outside. In total, there are close to 150 dealers who attend selling strictly antiques and collectibles. This market was listed in *Good Housekeeping* as one of the 25 best antique markets in the United States. Indoors there are 68 showcases, and three buildings with different dealers selling furniture, pottery, estate jewelry, vintage clothing, sterling, bronzes, and sports memorabilia. The Market Grill serves homemade specials and handicapped-accessible restrooms add to the amenities.

**DEALER RATES:** Wednesdays $12 for a 2-table space under the pavilion, or $7 for a 2-table setup outside. Sundays $48 for a 2-table space under the pavilion and $40 outside; Saturday $32 under the pavilion, $22 outside. Reservations for anything on Sunday, and for Wednesday and Saturday pavilion space are required. Office hours: Wednesday through Friday 10:00 AM-4:00 PM, weekends 8:00 AM-4:00 PM.

**CONTACT:** Heidi, Tom, Rob, or Gwen, 1864 River Rd, Lambertville NJ 08530. Tel: (609) 397-0456.

# MANAHAWKIN
## Manahawkin Flea Mart

**DATES:** Friday, Saturday, and Sunday, year round.
**TIMES:** 9:00 AM-5:00 PM.
**ADMISSION:** Free. Parking is free.
**LOCATION:** 657 E Bay Ave, off Rt 9. Take Garden State Pkwy to Exit 63 Manahawkin Exit. Follow signs to Manahawkin Business District, Bay Ave. Mart is on the right-hand side of the road.
**DESCRIPTION:** This good year-round show started in 1977 and hosts 100 outdoor and 45 indoor dealers featuring antiques, collectibles, produce, meats, new merchandise, and stained glass items. One snack bar and handicapped-accessible restrooms add to the amenities. They are located within 2 miles of Long Beach Island on the Atlantic Ocean, a popular tourist spot.
**DEALER RATES:** $20 per 22' × 19' space per day outdoors; $160 monthly. Inside rates vary. Reservations are not required outdoors, but are for indoors.
**CONTACT:** Warren Petrucci, Manahawkin Flea Mart, PO Box 885, Manahawkin NJ 08050-0885. Tel: (609) 597-1017.

# NESHANIC STATION
## Neshanic Flea Market
**DATES:** Every Sunday, March through December. Rain or shine.
**TIMES:** 6:00 AM-5:00 PM.
**ADMISSION:** Free. $.50 parking donation to the Neshanic Volunteer Fire Company.
**LOCATION:** Midway between Somerville and Flemington, off Hwy 202.
**DESCRIPTION:** This outdoor market opened in 1970 and currently draws approximately 100 dealers. Some of the types of items you can find include antiques and collectibles, fine art, and arts and crafts, as well as new merchandise and fresh produce. There is a snack bar on the premises. This friendly market is family owned and operated, and is located in a beautiful historic village.
**DEALER RATES:** $12 per two 4' × 8' spaces, BYOT (bring your own table). Reservations are not required.
**CONTACT:** Mary and Jack Weiss, Neshanic Flea Market, 100 Elm St, Neshanic Station NJ 08853. Tel/fax: (908) 369-3660.

# NEW EGYPT
## New Egypt Auction and Flea Market Village
**DATES:** Every Wednesday and Sunday, year round.
**TIMES:** 7:00 AM-2:00 PM. (Some vendors leave after noon.)
**ADMISSION:** Free. Free parking is available.
**LOCATION:** On Rt 537 between Rts 528 and 539. Take Exit 7 or 7A off the New Jersey Tnpk. Six miles west of Great Adventure/Six Flags Amusement Park.
**DESCRIPTION:** This "lively, friendly, and unique" indoor/outdoor flea market village has been in existence since 1959. There are approximately 100 dealers in 60 buildings large and small including 12 antique shops or at tables of all sizes buying and selling antiques, collectibles, produce, new and used clothing, tools, hardware, coins, books, furniture, metals recycling, and lots of other used items and oddities. Don't expect all the vendors to be there all the time—this is a unique experience folks. If the weather is iffy, call before going! Food is served on the premises.
**DEALER RATES:** $6 per 5' × 12'-20' table on Wednesday; $7 per table on Sunday. Prices include parking space. Reservations are not required.
**CONTACT:** Les Heller, New Egypt Flea Market Village, 933 Rt 537, Cream Ridge NJ 08514. Tel: (609) 758-2082.

# PALMYRA
## Tacony-Palmyra Swap N' Shop Flea Market

**DATES:** Every Saturday, Sunday, and selected holidays, year round, weather permitting.

**TIMES:** 6:00 AM-3:00 PM.

**ADMISSION:** Free. Free parking is available.

**LOCATION:** On Rt 73. From New Jersey follow Rt 73 to Tacony-Palmyra Bridge. From Pennsylvania take I-95 exit and follow signs to Tacony-Palmyra Bridge.

**DESCRIPTION:** This outdoor market has been open since 1972. There are, on an average, 400 dealers that sell a wide range of objects including antiques, fine art, collectibles, and arts and crafts, along with new merchandise and fresh produce. Food is served on the premises.

**DEALER RATES:** $30 per 18' × 18' space. Additional reserved spaces are available. Reservations are not required. Dealers must have a valid NJ Sales license. There is a reserved line; if interested call.

**CONTACT:** Lauresia Phillips, PO Box 64, Palmyra NJ 08065-0064. Tel: (609) 829-3001. Day of show call the general line at (609) 829-3000. Fax: (609) 768-8419.

# RAHWAY
## Rahway Italian-American Club Flea Market

**DATES:** Wednesday and Friday, year round.

**TIMES:** 7:00 AM-3:00 PM.

**ADMISSION:** Free. Parking is also free.

**LOCATION:** 530 New Brunswick Ave in Rahway. Corner of Inman and New Brunswick Aves.

**DESCRIPTION:** This market has been held for 24 years, featuring up to 35-40 dealers (their space shrank) both indoors and out selling antiques, collectibles, crafts, designer clothes, baseball cards, jewelry, and new merchandise. A snack bar featuring homemade food serves the hungry, and handicapped-accessible restrooms come in handy.

**DEALER RATES:** Wednesday $10, Friday $15 per 12' booth. Reservations are suggested.

**CONTACT:** Angelo, Rahway Italian-American Club Flea Market, 530 New Brunswick Ave, Rahway NJ 07065-2929. Day of show call (732) 574-3840 (the club number).

# RANCOCAS WOODS
## William Spencer's Antique Show

**DATES:** Second Sunday of the month, March through December. Rain date the following Sunday.

**TIMES:** 9:00 AM-4:00 PM.

**ADMISSION:** Free. Free parking is available.

**LOCATION:** On Creek Rd, 1 mile from the Rancocas Woods exit off I-295.

**DESCRIPTION:** This very popular market first opened in 1950. There are over 150 dealers attending this outdoor market set in a beautiful, wooded area. They specialize in antiques and collectibles, and they also have a craft show on the fourth Saturday of every month from March through November. Antique show items include jewelry, glass, vintage clothing, furniture, etc. Craft show items include handicrafts, quilted gifts, handmade toys, etc. They were written up in the *New York Times* in 1993 and people are still coming because of the recommendation. Food is served on the premises.

**DEALER RATES:** They request that you call for more information as there are too many variations on size and show to list here.

**CONTACT:** Isabel Michalski, c/o William Spencer, 118 Creek Rd, Rancocas Woods NJ 08054. Tel: (609) 235-1830.

---

### Local News

During the winter of 1996/97 some locals decided that they had had enough of the "traffic and noise" of this still growing market. When a Zoning Board meeting was held to decide the market's fate, the attendance at the meeting was close to unanimous in favor of continuing the market with slight modifications as to parking and location of stands and how early the vendors can set up. It seems that many local merchants profit from the market's crowds, keeping the area alive and healthy.

---

# VINELAND
## U-Sell Flea Market

**DATES:** Friday, Saturday, and Sunday, year round.

**TIMES:** 6:00 AM-5:00 PM.

**ADMISSION:** Free. Parking is free.

**LOCATION:** 2896 S Delsea Dr. From Philadelphia go south on SR 55 to Sherman Ave exit. Turn left, proceed 2 miles to SR 47 Delsea Dr. Turn right; market is 300 feet down on the right.

**DESCRIPTION:** Opened in 1974, this market hosts up to 350 dealers under steel canopies on a 15-acre blacktop. Some antiques and collectibles, clothing, toys, tools, sports cards, fresh produce, "you name it" are sold here. Three food courts dispense breakfast and lunch, and handicapped-accessible restrooms are available.

**DEALER RATES:** $12 Friday, $17 Saturday and Sunday for a 10' × 26' space and one 8' × 4' table. Reservations are not required.

**CONTACT:** Tim, U-Sell Flea Market, 2896 S Delsea Dr, S Vineland NJ 08361. Tel/fax: (856) 691-1222.

# WARREN
## Washington Valley Fire Company Flea Market

**DATES:** Every Sunday, Easter to Christmas, weather permitting.

**TIMES:** 7:30 AM-4:00 PM.

**ADMISSION:** Free. Free parking is available, although a $1 donation is much appreciated.

**LOCATION:** 140 Washington Valley Rd. Go north from Greenbrook 1½ miles from Rt 22 west on Warrenville Rd to first traffic light, turn left, go 1 mile.

**DESCRIPTION:** Formed in 1971, this outdoor market's 150 to 200 dealers sell antiques and collectibles as well as new merchandise. All this is done by and for the volunteers of the Washington Valley Fire Company so that they can provide their own fire-fighting equipment. Food is served on the premises. They hold a shrub auction twice a year and in 1999 they had a successful psychic reader who plans to return.

**DEALER RATES:** $15 per 10' × 20' space, including a table; additional tables at $7 per table. Reservations are not required. Monthly rates are 25% less.

**CONTACT:** Jerome Boschen, 12 Washington Valley Rd, Warren NJ 07059. Tel: (732) 469-2443.

# WOODSTOWN
## Cowtown Bawl, Inc

**DATES:** Every Tuesday and Saturday, year round.

**TIMES:** 8:00 AM-4:00 PM.

**ADMISSION:** Free. Free parking is available.

**LOCATION:** On Rt 40. From South Delaware Memorial Bridge, take Atlantic City Exit to Rt 40 and go 5 miles to Cowtown. From North 295, take Exit 4 onto Rt 48, go east 5 miles until joining Rt 40. Market is 2 miles on right.
**DESCRIPTION:** This market opened in 1926 in the center of Woodstown and moved to this location in 1940 as they had outgrown their original spot. Nearly 700 dealers sell anything from antiques, arts and crafts, and collectibles to fresh produce, meats, cheeses, and new merchandise. This market is held both indoors and outdoors. Plenty of concession stands and handicapped-accessible restrooms add to the amenities. They draw anywhere from 15,000 to 40,000 people a day. Election Day is very popular here. Maybe it has something to do with the livestock market on Tuesdays. They sell cattle, the occasional buffalo... or as the boss says, "If it walks in here, we'll sell it!" During the summers, there is a professional rodeo every Saturday night.
**DEALER RATES:** $15-$35 per space. Reservations are not required.
**CONTACT:** Robert Becker, Manager, Cowtown Bawl Inc, 780 Rt 40, Pilesgrove NJ 08098-2909. Tel: (856) 769-3000 or 3202.

---

### Keeping It in the Family

The current owner, Grant Harris, is the fourth generation of his family to own and run this market. It grew from the traditional Colonial markets held in New Jersey, officially and legally, on Tuesdays, which, of course, explains the popularity of Tuesdays at the Cowtown Bawl!

The strangest thing sold here was a Chinese wedding bed. No one knew quite what it was, this beautifully carved, gigantic structure, but it did sell.

Not from here, but the news stories were full of the tale of a fellow who, looking through a box of rocks for sale, bought a big chunk of something for about $3. It was later proved to be one of the largest uncut emeralds in the world. The dealer tried to bring a lawsuit against the buyer to get his rock back. No go. The courts ruled that he had sold it, fair and square.

---

# OTHER FLEA MARKETS

We know or have heard about these markets, but have not personally contacted each one, as we have the markets with descriptions. If you plan to visit one of these markets listed below, *please call first* to make sure they are still open. Flea markets do come and go. While they were open when we went to press, they may not be later. We can't be responsible. *Call first!*

**Atlantic City:** Sand Flea Market, Sovereign Ave & Boardwalk. Tel: (609) 449-9415.

**Bayonne:** St Vincent's Flea Market, 28 W 47 St. Tel: (201) 823-3032.

**Camden:** Jerry's Flea Market, 2701 Mt Ephraim Ave. Tel: (609) 338-0088.

**Cherry Hill:** Garden State Park Flea Market, Rt 70 & Cornell Ave. Tel: (609) 665-8558.

**Edison:** Colony Trading Company, 66 Mayfield Ave. Tel: (732) 225-9333.

**Edison:** New Dover Flea Market, 687 New Dover Rd. Tel: (732) 381-7904.

**Florham Park:** Interstate Vendors Market Inc, 1 Quail Run. Tel: (973) 377-5891.

**Howell:** Basics Flea Market. 2301 Hwy 9N. Tel: (201) 308-1105. Open every Fri, Sat & Sun. Fri & Sat 10 AM-9 PM; Sun 10 AM-6 PM.

**Linwood:** Sand Flea, 2021 New Rd 2. Tel: (609) 926-3006.

**Little Ferry:** Victory, 182 Waterside Dr. Tel: (201) 229-1975.

**Newton:** Springdale Farmers Market, 310 Stickles Pond Rd. Tel: (973) 579-3322.

**North Arlington:** J & C Market Place Inc, 117 Prospect Ave. Tel: (201) 998-8331.

**Palmyra:** Tacony Palmyra Flea Market, S Hwy 73. Tel: (609) 829-3000.

**Union:** The Union Market. 2445 Springfield Ave. Tel: (908) 688-6161. Open every Fri, Sat & Sun. Fri & Sat 11 AM-9 PM; Sun 11 AM-6 PM.

**Wildwood:** Market Place, 3410 Boardwalk. Tel: (609) 523-1991.

# NEW MEXICO

## ALAMOGORDO
### Peddler's Village

**DATES:** Saturday and Sunday.

**TIMES:** 7:00 AM-3:00 PM.

**ADMISSION:** Free. Parking is free.

**LOCATION:** 900 Zuni Dr. From Rt 54/70 go north on Le Valle Rd to Zuni Dr, then make a left.

**DESCRIPTION:** Newly opened in 1999, this small but growing indoor/outdoor market features 50 dealers selling antiques, collectibles, crafts, furniture, garage sale goodies, stamps, cards, and new merchandise. There is one snack bar serving a "superb" breakfast and lunch, as well as handicapped-accessible restrooms in this very clean operation.

**DEALER RATES:** $5 per 10' × 15' space. Inside reservations are needed; outside is first come, first served.

**CONTACT:** Art Page, Peddler's Village, 900 Zuni Dr, Alamogordo NM 88310-9041. Tel: (505) 443-8000 or 443-8044. Fax: (505) 443-8045.

## ALBUQUERQUE
### Indoor Mercado

**DATES:** Friday, Saturday and Sunday, year round.

**TIMES:** Friday 12:00 PM-6:00 PM; weekends 10:00 AM-6:00 PM.

**ADMISSION:** Free. Parking is free.

**LOCATION:** 2035 12th St and I-40.

**DESCRIPTION:** This market opened in September 1991 and has 190 to 200 dealers selling mostly new merchandise, some antiques and collectibles, loads of southwestern arts and crafts and jewelry, ceramics, tools, toys, new clothes, books, art and the "usual fare." There are two food courts and handicapped-accessible restrooms just in case.

**DEALER RATES:** $220 to $290 for a 10' × 10' space for 4 weeks depending on length of reservation. Reservations must be made at least 2 weeks in advance. There is some first-come, first-served space.

**CONTACT:** Indoor Mercado, 2035 12 St NW, Albuquerque NM 87104-2301. Tel: (505) 243-8111. Fax: (505) 243-8419.

## New Mexico State Fair Flea Market

**DATES:** Saturday and Sunday, except for September during State Fair.
**TIMES:** 7:00 AM-5:00 PM.
**ADMISSION:** Free. $2 parking fee.
**LOCATION:** New Mexico State Fairgrounds at Louisiana and Central Sts NE, at Gate 9, the main entrance.
**DESCRIPTION:** This market opened in 1979 and currently has between 100-1,200 dealers depending on the weather selling everything: antiques, collectibles, arts and crafts, saddles, tools, boots, iron work, sandpaintings, t-shirts, new merchandise—everything! Probably the largest market in New Mexico. Known for a lengthy jewelry row and one section of Native American arts and crafts. There's a new casino, and occasionally live horse racing next door coincides with the market. Excellent food including American, Italian, barbecue, and Mexican is available on the premises, as well as handicapped-accessible restrooms.
**DEALER RATES:** $12 per space. Reservations are not required. There are monthly rates at a discount.
**CONTACT:** New Mexico State Fair Flea Market, PO Box 8546, Albuquerque NM 87198-8546. Tel: (505) 265-1791 ext 305. Fax: (505) 266-7784.

## North Valley Indoor Flea Market

**DATES:** Monday through Saturday.
**TIMES:** 9:00 AM-5:00 PM.
**ADMISSION:** Free. Parking is free.
**LOCATION:** 1026 Candelaria NW. From I-40, 12th St Exit to Candelaria. Located at 12th and Candelaria.
**DESCRIPTION:** Opened in 1998, this market of 20 vendors sells antiques, collectibles, Native American artifacts, crafts, garage sale goodies, coins, stamps, cards, furniture, and new merchandise. One snack bar relieves the munchies and handicapped-accessible restrooms may come in handy. "Many treasures are found in this market." For that alone, it might be worth the trip.
**DEALER RATES:** $125-$135 per 8' × 10' space per month, $120 per 8' × 8' space per month, consignment items and smaller spaces available. Reservations are required.
**CONTACT:** Gloria or Richard Gould, North Valley Indoor Flea Market, 1026 Candelaria Rd NW, Albuquerque NM 87107-2413. Tel/fax: (505) 344-2130.

## Route 66 Trading Post

**DATES:** Wednesday through Sunday.

**TIMES:** 10:00 AM-5:00 PM.

**ADMISSION:** Free. Parking is free.

**LOCATION:** 5915 Central Ave NE. Between San Mateo and San Pedro Blvds. On US Rt 66.

**DESCRIPTION:** Opened in 1997, there are 30 dealers selling antiques, collectibles, cards, garage sale goodies, furniture, and new merchandise.

**DEALER RATES:** $1.50 per square foot; no reservations required.

**CONTACT:** Jerry or Nette, Route 66 Trading Post, 505 Marquette Ave NW Ste 1212, Albuquerque NM 87102. Tel: (505) 254-9530.

# DEMING

## Traders Village of New Mexico

**DATES:** Friday through Sunday.

**TIMES:** 9:00 AM-3:00 PM.

**ADMISSION:** Free. Parking is free.

**LOCATION:** 4725 Keeler Rd. Take I-10 to Hwy 180, go north approximately 4 miles to Keeler Rd. Turn right and go about 1 mile.

**DESCRIPTION:** Opened in June 1997, this 65-acre indoor/outdoor market of 35-50 dealers sells antiques, collectibles, crafts, coins, stamps, cards, garage sale goodies, furniture, and new merchandise. There is one snack bar and handicapped-accessible restrooms on site; dry camping and RVs are welcome. They also board and train horses here.

**DEALER RATES:** $50 per month for 22' × 16' space indoors, $30 per month outdoors, electricity is extra. First come, first served.

**CONTACT:** Daniel Flores, Traders Village of New Mexico, 1571 N Locus, Las Cruces NM 88001. Tel: (505) 544-7315 or 649-5191.

# FARMINGTON

## Farmington Flea Market

**DATES:** Every Friday through Sunday. Rain or shine.

**TIMES:** 6:00 AM-8:00 PM during summer; 7:00 AM-7:00 PM during winter.

**ADMISSION:** Free. Free parking is available.

**LOCATION:** On Hwy 550, halfway between Farmington and Aztec, at 7701 E Main St.

**DESCRIPTION:** This outdoor market opened in 1970 and currently accommodates up to 300 dealers during peak season. Among the articles available are antiques and collectibles, fine art, crafts, household items, furniture, new merchandise, and fresh produce. A notable feature of this market is that it also offers animals such as horses, goats, pigs, dogs, cats—and a duck or two. One food concession building and handicapped-accessible restrooms add to the amenities.

**DEALER RATES:** $4 per 12' × 26' space Friday and Sunday; $8 per space on Saturday. Reservations are required March through August only. Self-contained trailers may stay on the grounds Friday through Sunday night for no additional fee. Food is served on the premises.

**CONTACT:** Cathey Wright, Owner, 4301 Holiday Dr, Farmington NM 87402. Tel: (505) 325-3129.

# LAS CRUCES
## Big Daddy's Market Place, Inc

**DATES:** Saturday and Sunday, year round.

**TIMES:** 6:30 AM-4:00 PM.

**ADMISSION:** Free. Parking is also free.

**LOCATION:** 7320 N Main (Hwy 70 E).

**DESCRIPTION:** Since 1981 there have been approximately 400 dealers every weekend selling antiques, collectibles, new and used merchandise, anything and everything. A convenience store and laundromat are on premises. To satisfy the munchies, there are two Mexican and one international restaurant on the premises.

**DEALER RATES:** $8 per space under giant metal sheds, outside $6 per space. They supply the tables. Reservations are not required. They do take reservations on Fridays from 8:00 AM-5:00 PM. Motorhomes may stay overnight Friday and Saturday for $5 a night including hookup.

**CONTACT:** Manager, Big Daddy's Market Place Inc, PO Box 1954, Las Cruces NM 88004-1954. Tel: (505) 382-9404 or 382-1055.

# ROSWELL
## Monterey Markets

**DATES:** Daily, except Wednesday.

**TIMES:** 9:00 AM-5:00 PM.

**ADMISSION:** Free. Parking is free.

**LOCATION:** 1400-I W 2nd St.

**DESCRIPTION:** Opened in 1991, this indoor/outdoor market of 40-50 dealers sells antiques, collectibles, crafts, furniture, garage sale goodies, and new merchandise. There is a restaurant, run by the Egg-Roll Queen (a lady from Vietnam), open on weekends only, and handicapped-accessible restrooms. I'm told ERQ's egg rolls are superb. Say Hi to Stormy for me! **DEALER RATES:** $1 per 12' × 12' space outside daily, $15 per month. Inside: $50 plus utilities (runs about $90-$100 total) for a 12' × 12' space. Outside: first come, first served. Inside reservations are required. **CONTACT:** Stormy, Monterey Flea Market, 1400-I W 2 St, Roswell NM 88201-2066. Tel: (505) 622-4430.

---

### Hysterical Note

As to the real fun stuff: Yes, this is the famous (infamous?) Roswell NM where the alleged UFOs landed on July 4, 1947. Find Stormy and ask him about this.

---

## OTHER FLEA MARKETS

We know or have heard about these markets, but have not personally contacted each one, as we have the markets with descriptions. If you plan to visit one of these markets listed below, *please call first* to make sure they are still open. Flea markets do come and go. While they were open when we went to press, they may not be later. We can't be responsible. *Call first!*

**Albuquerque:** Things Etc-The Indoor Flea Market, 1138 San Mateo Blvd SE. Tel: (505) 268-1717.

**Albuquerque:** Star Flea Market, 543 Coors Rd SW. Tel: (505) 831-3106.

**Bosque Farms:** BJ's Flea Market. 1775-A Bosque Farms Blvd. Tel: (505) 869-6995. Every Fri, Sat & Sun during summer. 6:30 AM-4:00 PM. 20-40 vendors. Antiques and collectibles, new and used furniture, clothing, books, used merchandise, crafts.

**Los Lunas:** Leftovers Etc, 604 Main NE. Tel: (505) 865-3300.

**Taos:** Taos Rendezvous. On Paseo del Pueblo Sur, Hwy 522; about 4 miles south of downtown Taos. Every Friday, Saturday & Sunday from May through October. 10:00 AM-5:00 PM. I'm told this market is still running, but can't find out under who's ownership!

# NEW YORK

## BOUCKVILLE
### Bouckville Antique Pavilion

**DATES:** Every Sunday, from the last Sunday of April through the last Sunday of October. Special shows: June Two-Day Show (second weekend in June with antique cars), August Five-Day Show (third weekend in August).

**TIMES:** 7:00 AM-4:00 PM.

**ADMISSION:** Free. Parking is also free.

**LOCATION:** On Rt 20, in the center of Bouckville, 100 miles west of Albany, 35 miles east of Syracuse, 25 miles west of Utica.

**DESCRIPTION:** This market started in 1984 is located "in the heart of antique country." There are 41 shops as well as 6 multi-dealer co-ops included in this show. Close to 200 dealers specialize in antiques and collectibles including furniture, glass, toys, jewelry, paintings, baseball cards, lamps, military items, coins, dishes, dolls, and tools. During the August show, there will be around 2,000 dealers in town for this one show. Whether you are shopping outdoors or under cover, all booths are conveniently protected from the mud if it rains. In 1995, the new owner acquired more land next door making more room for dealers. The June market is a Pre-WWII Antique Car Show. When you need a break from shopping, food is available on the premises.

**DEALER RATES:** $15 for 20' × 25' space outdoors; $20 for 12' × 12' space plus 12' × 20' space for vehicle. Reservations are advised.

**CONTACT:** Steve and Lynda Bono, Rt 20, Bouckville NY 13310. Tel: (315) 893-7483.

## CALLICOON
### Callicoon Flea Market

**DATES:** Weekends May through December; also Monday, Thursday and Friday during June through August.

**TIMES:** Saturdays 9:00 AM-5:00 PM; other days 10:00 AM-3:00 PM.

**ADMISSION:** Free. Parking is also free.

**LOCATION:** 129 Main St, Route 17B W from Monticello, New York. Or Rt 97 from Port Jervis or Hancock, NY.

**DESCRIPTION:** This market began in 1980 in the historical town of Callicoon in sight of the Delaware River. It is privately run with a variety of interesting collectibles, antiques, crafts, lighting fixtures, depression and carnival glass, some new merchandise, furniture, and the occasional railroad and jewelry collectibles. The owner tries to have a bit of something for everyone. Many of the original buildings in town are wonderful examples of 1800s' architecture. There is camping and canoeing nearby, as well as local bed and breakfast inns.

**DEALER RATES:** Not applicable.

**CONTACT:** Carol Kay, Callicoon Flea Market, PO Box 278, Callicoon NY 12723. Tel: (914) 887-5411. Call for seasonal hours.

# CHEEKTOWAGA
## Super Flea and Farmers' Market

**DATES:** Every Saturday and Sunday. Rain or shine.

**TIMES:** 9:00 AM-6:00 PM.

**ADMISSION:** Free. Parking is free.

**LOCATION:** Off New York State Thruway, Exit 52 E, at 2500 Walden Ave.

**DESCRIPTION:** Begun in 1975, this is the largest indoor and outdoor flea market in western New York, with 300 dealers outside in the summer and another 200 inside year round. Offered are a wide range of antiques, collectibles, crafts, new merchandise, as well as fresh produce, meats, and dairy products. The Super Flea and Farmers' Market boasts four fast-food restaurants on the premises.

**DEALER RATES:** $20 per 7½' × 6' booth inside, $30 for a 8' × 8' booth inside per day; $15 per 11' × 22' booth outside per day. Space is available on a first-come, first-served basis.

**CONTACT:** Ronald A Wagner, General Manager, Super Flea and Farmers' Market, 2500 Walden Ave, Cheektowaga NY 14225. Tel: (716) 685-2902. Fax: (716) 685-9605.

# CLARENCE
## Antique World and Marketplace

**DATES:** Every Sunday, year round.

**TIMES:** 8:00 AM-4:00 PM.

**ADMISSION:** Free. $1 parking from May through October, free the rest of the time.

**LOCATION:** 10995 Main St, 15 miles east of Buffalo and 40 miles west of Rochester on Main St (Rt 5).

**DESCRIPTION:** There are approximately 350 dealers in winter and 650 dealers in summer displaying their merchandise. The three buildings on the premises help to separate the various sale items. One building is exclusively for antiques and collectibles (this building went co-op in 1998), one specializes in dealers selling "flea market" merchandise, and the other building also serves as an exhibition center—this one went co-op in 1999 with dealers selling antiques and collectibles as well. There is an enormous variety of items with everything from antiques and collectibles to new merchandise, meats, and cheeses for sale. They hold Great American Garage Sales the first Sunday of each month from June through September. Special shows are scheduled during the year including a Country Harvest antique and crafts show in October, and a twice yearly EXPO featuring 600 of the finest antique and collectible dealers from 22 states and Canada. There are admission charges for these special shows. There are five restaurants and handicapped-accessible restrooms scattered around the market.

**DEALER RATES:** Flea market rates are $20 per 21' × 20' space outdoors; $23-$30 per 9' × 9' booth indoors. Reservations are not required outside but are required for inside space.

**CONTACT:** Katy Toth, Antique World, 10995 Main St, Clarence NY 14031. Tel: (716) 759-8483. Fax: (716) 759-6167. Email: antiques@pcom.net. Web: www.bodnarchuk.com/antique_world.

# LEVITTOWN
## Tri-County Flea Market

**DATES:** Thursday through Sunday.

**TIMES:** Thursday and Friday 12:00 PM-9:00 PM; Saturday and Sunday 10:00 AM-6:00 PM.

**ADMISSION:** Free. Parking is also free.

**LOCATION:** 3041 Hempstead Tnpk.

**DESCRIPTION:** Opened in 1981, this indoor market has 400 dealers selling literally everything—all new merchandise and collectibles including shoes, leather, toys, plants, jewelry, flags, and all sorts of clothing. You could furnish your house and clothe a family from the merchandise sold here. There is one floor containing "America's Largest" Jewelry Exchange, and another at mezzanine level has a collectible card show and a huge wicker furniture display. They have 55,000 square feet of display area loaded with just furniture. A food court provides food to starving patrons. For all merchandise purchased here, there is a seven-day money-back guarantee, except on special orders.

**DEALER RATES:** $800 to $900 for a very large space for 16 working days (about one month). Reservations are required.

**CONTACT:** Barbara Eve, Tri-County Flea Market, 3041 Hempstead Tnpk, Levittown NY 11756. Tel: (516) 579-4500 or fax (516) 579-6715.

# MAYBROOK
## Maybrook Flea Market

**DATES:** Sundays, year round, except holidays like Easter, and the month of January.

**TIMES:** 8:00 AM-4:00 PM.

**ADMISSION:** Free. $.75 per vehicle.

**LOCATION:** Rt 208, 2 miles south of I-84, Exit 5. At the drive-in theater.

**DESCRIPTION:** For over 20 years this market has been hosting from 100 dealers in winter to 500 dealers in summer selling antiques, collectibles, garage sale treasures, new merchandise or what the owner describes as "gems to junk." There is a snack bar on premises as well as clean restrooms. This is the site of a drive-in theater that operated in 1997 and may continue to do so, which leads to funny moments at 2:30 AM when the dealers want to come in to set up and there are still theater patrons occupied.

**DEALER RATES:** Must have NY State Sales Tax ID to sell. $25 for a liberal 18' × 18' space outdoors, $26 for 6' × 10' inside space. Vendor setup starts at 5:30 AM. Don't even think of sleeping in your car after a movie to get in cheap (it has been tried).

**CONTACT:** Nick Perilli, Maybrook Flea Market, Rt 208, Maybrook NY 12543. Tel: (914) 427-2715.

---

**It Can Be Done!**
A vendor told Nick he could sell anything. Nick was skeptical, to say the least. Sure enough, the vendor came back and told Nick he had sold a half used bottle of Listerine!

---

# MONTICELLO
## Alan Finchley's Flea Market at Monticello Raceway

**DATES:** Saturday and Sunday, from July 4th weekend through Labor Day weekend.

**TIMES:** 9:00 AM-5:00 PM, weather permitting.
**ADMISSION:** Free. Parking is free.
**LOCATION:** Just off Rt 17 (future I-86), Exit 104.
**DESCRIPTION:** Established in 1976, this marketplace is New York State's original new-merchandise-only flea market. Local dealers, as well as dealers from up and down the East Coast, offer upscale merchandise sold the old-fashioned way with that friendly personal touch. Average attendance is 10,000 per weekend. Sponsored in part by the Sullivan County Visitors Associate. Food carts and handicapped-accessible restrooms add to the amenities.
**DEALER RATES:** Rentals range from $25-$40 per day depending upon type and size of space. A majority of the vendors may park their vehicle at their space.
**CONTACT:** Alan Finchley, 42 Ohio Ave, Long Beach NY 11561. Tel: (914) 796-1000. Fax: (516) 897-1800.

# NEW YORK CITY
## The Annex Antiques Fair and Flea Market
**DATES:** Every Saturday and Sunday, year round.
**TIMES:** 9:00 AM-5:00 PM.
**ADMISSION:** $1 for antique market. Flea market is free. Ample parking is available, but not free.
**LOCATION:** Avenue of the Americas, between 24th and 27th Sts in Manhattan.
**DESCRIPTION:** This show began over 30 years ago and is claimed to be the longest running outdoor show in the metropolitan area. The market accommodates 600 to 700 dealers who come from all over the United States, Canada, and Europe to sell an amazing variety of merchandise, including antique jewelry, vintage clothing, bronzes, Art Deco, porcelain, and rugs. There are five outdoor selling areas and a new indoor selling area—The Garage—that holds 150 dealers. Restaurants are nearby. In September 1999, *Country Living* magazine held a "What Is It? What is it Worth?" event at this market.
**DEALER RATES:** Saturday: $100 per 10' × 14' booth; $60 per 5' × 14' booth. Sunday: Antique Fair $135 per 10' × 14' booth; $80 per 5' × 14'; Flea Market $100 per 9' × 12' booth; $70 per 4½' × 12' booth. The Garage is $125 for a 9' × 12' space for the weekend. Reservations are preferred. Office hours are Tuesday through Friday 12:00 PM-5:00 PM.

**CONTACT:** Michael, Annex Antique Fair, PO Box 7010, New York NY 10116-4627. Tel: Michael (212) 243-5343 or for the Garage at (212) 647-0707; fax: (212) 463-7099. Day of show call (212) 243-7922.

## GreenFlea at IS 144

**DATES:** Every Sunday, year round. Rain or shine.
**TIMES:** 10:00 AM-4:00 PM.
**ADMISSION:** Free. Parking space is not provided. Garages are available nearby at standard city rates.
**LOCATION:** Columbus Ave at 77th St. Across the street from the Museum of Natural History.
**DESCRIPTION:** This show first opened in 1980 as a benefit for the school. Over 350 dealers attend this market, selling their merchandise both indoors and outdoors. This market is known for its quality antiques, fine art, arts and crafts (many special orders and made-to-orders by metalworkers, wood carvers and the like), vintage clothing and jewelry, and collectibles. Of special interest are the smoked meats, cheeses, and fresh flowers that are available from their farmers' market, an extension of the famous GreenMarket at Union Square. Proceeds are used directly for the benefit of the children, with over $300,000 given to the school each year. This market is unique as one of the first of its kind in the country whose purpose was education and support of the public school system. It is now a community event with a following of many thousands of people attending every Sunday. Beverly Sills, the famous opera diva, said this is one of her favorite places to visit.
**DEALER RATES:** $22 up to $130 for space depending on size. Reservations are required in advance.
**CONTACT:** GreenFlea Inc, 162 W 72nd St, New York NY 10023-3300. Tel: (212) 721-0900. Day of show call: (212) 734-3578.

## Greenflea at PS 183

**DATES:** Every Saturday, year round. Rain or shine.
**TIMES:** 6:00 AM-6:00 PM.
**ADMISSION:** Free. Parking space is not provided. Garages are available nearby at standard city rates.
**LOCATION:** 419 E 66th; or 67th St between First and York Aves.
**DESCRIPTION:** This show first opened on August 12, 1979 as the PS 183 Antique Flea and Farmers' Market. It is now under new management. Over 150 dealers attend this market, selling their merchandise both indoors

and outdoors. One may purchase quality antiques, fine art, arts and crafts, and collectibles; of special interest are the smoked meats, cheeses, and fresh flowers that are available from farmers in the tri-state area. Proceeds are used directly for the benefit of the children, with over $150,000 given to the school each year. This market is unique as one of the first of its kind in the country whose purpose was education and support of the public school system. It is now a community event with a following of 3-5,000 people attending every Saturday.

**DEALER RATES:** $22 up to $130 for space depending on size. Reservations are required in advance.

**CONTACT:** GreenFlea Inc, 162 W 72 St, New York NY 10023-3300. Tel: (212) 721-0900. Day of show call: (212) 734-3578.

## The New Yorkville Antiques and Flea Market

**DATES:** Saturday, year round.

**TIMES:** 6:00 AM-5:00 PM.

**ADMISSION:** Free. Parking is where you can find it.

**LOCATION:** Jan Hus Church, 351 E 74th St between 1st and 2nd Ave in the upper East Side.

**DESCRIPTION:** Under new management, this market is patterned after a quaint and cozy English-style antiques and collectibles market. Over 40 dealers sell antiques, collectibles, jewelry (from Georgian and Victorian eras, and fine estate to retro costume), textiles, laces, vintage clothing, pottery, china, silver, furniture and more. This is a great family place with plenty of homemade foods.

**DEALER RATES:** $50 per table. Reservations are suggested.

**CONTACT:** Bob DiTroia, 98-30 67 Ave, Forest Hills NY 11374. Tel: (718) 897-5992. Fax: (718) 997-8192.

## The Showplace

**DATES:** Saturday and Sunday, year round. An antiques gallery is open daily on the second floor only.

**TIMES:** 8:30 AM-5:30 PM. Upstairs antique gallery weekdays 10:00 AM-6:00 PM.

**ADMISSION:** Free. On weekends, parking around the market is available on the streets.

**LOCATION:** 40 W 25th Street, between Sixth Ave and Broadway.

**DESCRIPTION:** This hugely successful market opened January 23, 1993 and moved to larger quarters. Their 135 dealers on three floors with 31,000 square feet of selling space specialize in antiques and collectibles only. In addition, The Antique Gallery has 32 dealers selling daily on the top floor. They were featured in the *New York Times* two months after their opening when they were the hot topic during the famous 1993 blizzard. If it's old it's probably here: furniture, lamps, jewelry, paintings, silver, toys, clothing, time-pieces, books, comics, whatever. They do plenty of advertising and as a result the market draws in buyers by the thousands each weekend. Lines form here early every weekend before opening looking for the as-yet-unfound bargains. And they have been found here. An espresso bar offers sand-wiches, coffee and teas, and excellent light foods.

**DEALER RATES:** $200 for a 8' × 10' space, $250 for a 10' × 12' space for the weekend. Reservations are required.

**CONTACT:** Amos Balaish, The Showplace, 40 W 25 St, New York, NY 10001. Tel: (212) 633-6063. Fax: (212) 633-6064.

---

**Recognize Anything?**

So popular is this antique emporium that not only are commercials frequently filmed here, but location shots from the movie *The Mirror Has Two Faces* were filmed here too.

---

## Soho Antiques Fair, Collectibles and Crafts

**DATES:** Saturday and Sunday, year round.

**TIMES:** 9:00 AM-5:00 PM.

**ADMISSION:** Free. Parking? Take a bus (#6 on Broadway) or subway (Spring St and Canal St stations Lexington Ave, Broadway, 6th Ave, 7th Ave lines). If you must drive, there are garages and some on-street parking.

**LOCATION:** At the corner of Broadway and Grand St in Soho.

**DESCRIPTION:** This well-known and popular market is a must "do" week-end event in New York. Up to 100 dealers sell the best antiques, memora-bilia and collectibles outdoors. It has been written up as the "best flea market in downtown Manhattan" by the *NY Press* in 1992. Right in the middle of the downtown art scene in Soho and next door to Chinatown and Little Italy, they boast a variety of ethnic diversity in their wares. They draw as many as 10,000 shoppers on any weekend day. Plenty of neighborhood restaurants are nearby.

**DEALER RATES:** For a 8' × 12' space $80; 12' × 12' space $100; 20' × 20' space $135. Reservations are a good idea.

**CONTACT:** Soho Antiques Fair & Collectibles, PO Box 337, Garden City NY 11530. Tel: (212) 682-2000 or fax: (516) 742-4424.

# NORWICH
## 35th Annual Antique Auto Show and Flea Market

**DATES:** Annually, the Saturday and Sunday of Memorial Day. 2000: May 27-28.

**TIMES:** 8:00 AM-5:00 PM.

**ADMISSION:** $4 daily. Shuttle buses run from city parking lots to the site. There is no on-site parking; it's already full of antique cars and dealers. There is parking in the school adjacent to the fairgrounds.

**LOCATION:** Chenango County Fair Grounds, E Main St.

**DESCRIPTION:** This market is a car buff's dream with proud owners and dealers showing and selling antique cars (Sunday), car parts, muscle cars (Saturday), and show cars—and then the regular antique flea market, crafts, and auctions. There were over 700 antique cars on display in 1995, and over 300 muscle cars. They hold two auctions on site: the Car Auction and then the "2+2" Auction, nicknamed the Poor Man's Auction. At the 2+2, the buyer and seller each pay the auctioneer $2 as a fee. All sorts of odds and ends are sold during this auction including "cheap" cars. Naturally, the fabulous cars are sold during the Car Auction.

**DEALER RATES:** All spaces are $30 for two days reserved by May 15; after that all spaces are $40. They do have a few spaces for the unregistered. However, please pre-register for your own peace of mind, and theirs. It's infinitely easier on everyone.

**CONTACT:** Ray Hart, PO Box 168, Norwich NY 13815-0168. Tel: (607) 334-4044.

# PORT CHESTER
## Empire State Flea Market Mall

**DATES:** Friday, Saturday and Sunday, year round. Also Thanksgiving through Christmas, daily with extended hours.

**TIMES:** Friday 12:00 PM-8:00 PM; Saturday, Sunday 10:00 AM-6:00 PM.

**ADMISSION:** Free. Parking is also free.

**LOCATION:** Kohl's Shopping Center at 515 Boston Post Rd.

**DESCRIPTION:** This market started in 1976 and is New York State's original year-round indoor flea market mall. A vast majority of the merchandise offered by the 150 vendors is famous-label quality at obvious savings.

Featured are over 100 new merchandise vendors and the region's only fine jewelry exchange. A uniform cash refund policy is offered by all merchants and supported by on-site management. Handicapped-accessible parking and entrances. One level, climate-controlled shopping with approximately 10,000 shoppers per weekend.

**DEALER RATES:** Space is sold on a monthly basis only. Rentals range from $100 to $1,000 per month depending on size, type, and location of space. A security deposit of one month is required. All vendors must have or acquire a NY State Sales Tax Certificate.

**CONTACT:** Alan Finchley, 515 Boston Post Rd, Port Chester NY 10573. Tel: (914) 939-1800. Fax: (914) 939-5046.

# QUEENS
## Aqueduct Flea Market

**DATES:** Tuesday, Saturday, and Sunday, March through Christmas.

**TIMES:** 9:00 AM-5:00 PM.

**ADMISSION:** $2 per car load. $1 per walk-in.

**LOCATION:** Ozone Park. Take Belt Parkway to Exit 18B Lefferts Blvd, go north to Rockaway Blvd, then a left to 108th St.

**DESCRIPTION:** This outdoor market first opened in 1974 and is now under new management (they used to run Roosevelt Raceway Flea Market for 25 years). There is a wide variety of merchandise to choose from including hardware, electronics, clothing, jewelry, household items, linens and leather to shoes and sneakers. Everything from antiques and collectibles to new merchandise and fresh vegetables can be found. They boast of over 1,000 friendly merchants and thousands of customers from all over the world. There are all types of prepared foods available when you need a break from shopping.

**DEALER RATES:** $50 and up per 12' × 24' booth depending on location. Monthly rates available. Daily vendors can just show up, or make reservations for longer terms.

**CONTACT:** Aqueduct Flea Market, c/o Plain and Fancy Shows, 1550 Old Country Rd, Westbury NY 11590. Tel: 516 222-1530. 516-745-5706. Email: info@aqueductfleamkt.com. Web: www.aqueductfleamkt.com.

# RHINEBECK
## Rhinebeck Antiques Fair

**DATES:** Three shows annually on the Saturday and Sunday of Memorial Day weekend in May, fourth Saturday in July (one-day show) and Columbus Day weekend in October.

**TIMES:** Saturday 10:00 AM-5:00 PM. Sunday 11:00 AM-5:00 PM.

**ADMISSION:** $7 for Memorial and Columbus weekend shows; $6 for the July show. Parking is free.

**LOCATION:** Indoors on the Dutchess County Fairgrounds, on Rt 9 at northern edge of Rhinebeck. From New York Thruway, take Exit 19 to Rhinecliff Bridge, cross bridge and continue 1 mile to Rt 9G, then south 1 mile to Rt 9, and then south to Fairgrounds.

**DESCRIPTION:** 2000 marks the 24th year of this antiques fair. This indoor market attracts approximately 190 (165 for July) dealers exhibiting a wide variety of quality antiques at a variety of prices. Food is served on the premises.

**DEALER RATES:** $400 per space and up. Reservations are required. There is a waiting list from which dealers are first chosen.

**CONTACT:** Jimi Barton, Rhinebeck Antiques Fair, PO Box 838, Rhinebeck NY 12572-0838. Tel: (914) 876-1989.

# SCHENECTADY
## White House Flea Market

**DATES:** Wednesday through Sunday. Rain or shine.

**TIMES:** 9:00 AM-5:00 PM.

**ADMISSION:** Free. Free parking is also available.

**LOCATION:** 950-952 State St.

**DESCRIPTION:** This indoor market has been held every weekend since 1985. Approximately 40 dealers gather in two buildings to sell antiques, collectibles, handmade craft items, furniture, books, records and toys, as well as new merchandise. This is the area's largest indoor, year-round market and an excellent place for dealers to find great treasures.

**DEALER RATES:** Average $27 per week. Advance reservations are required. Permanent dealers usually fill this market.

**CONTACT:** Rudy or Jeanette Fecketter, 952 State St, Schenectady NY 12307. Tel: (518) 346-7851.

# STATEN ISLAND
## Antiques, Arts and Crafts Market

**DATES:** Three shows per year. First Sunday in June; Sunday after Labor Day in September, first Sunday in October. Rain dates: the following Sundays.

**TIMES:** 10:00 AM-5:00 PM.

**ADMISSION:** $1. Parking is free.

**LOCATION:** At the Staten Island Historical Society, Historic Richmond Town, 441 Clarke Ave. From Verrazano Narrows Bridge, follow New Jersey W Rt to Richmond Rd/Clove Rd Exit; proceed to the second light and turn left onto Richmond Rd, about 5 miles ahead turn left onto St. Patricks Place, and finally, turn right on Clarke Ave. From St. George, take bus #74.

**DESCRIPTION:** This show has been in existence since 1970. It is an outdoor market that accommodates approximately 140 dealers from Staten Island, Manhattan, Brooklyn, Long Island, New Jersey, Pennsylvania, and Connecticut. They sell antiques, collectibles, stamps, coins, old photographs, books, baseball cards, oil and water-color paintings, plants, handmade crafts, and much more. Hot dogs, soda, donuts and coffee are available for hungry shoppers. This show attracts crowds of over 3,000 visitors. For an additional fee visitors will also have the opportunity to see the exhibit buildings and museum.

**DEALER RATES:** $40 per 10' × 19' space. Reservations are required.

**CONTACT:** Historic Richmond Town, 441 Clarke Ave, Staten Island NY 10306-1198. Tel: (718) 351-1611 × 280. Fax: (718) 351-6057.

## Yankee Peddler Day

**DATES:** First Sunday in May. Rain date is third Sunday in May.

**TIMES:** 10:00 AM-5:00 PM.

**ADMISSION:** $1. Parking is free.

**LOCATION:** At the Staten Island Historical Society, Historic Richmond Town, 441 Clarke Ave. From Verrazano Narrows Bridge, follow New Jersey W Rt to Richmond Rd/Clove Rd Exit; proceed to the second light and turn left onto Richmond Rd, about 5 miles ahead turn left onto St. Patricks Place, and finally, turn right on Clarke Ave. From St. George, take bus #74.

**DESCRIPTION:** This outdoor market began in 1968. It hosts over 150 dealers from New York, New Jersey, Connecticut, and Pennsylvania who sell antiques, arts and crafts, silver, glass, furniture, jewelry and collectibles. The Women's Auxiliary at the Staten Island Historical Society is responsible for this fundraising event. This is claimed to be the first large outdoor flea market on the Island. This show is always well attended by dealers and buyers alike. Food is served on the premises.

**DEALER RATES:** $40 per 10' × 19' space. Reservations are required.

**CONTACT:** Historic Richmond Town, 441 Clarke Ave, Staten Island NY 10306-1198. Tel: (718) 351-1611 × 280. Fax: (718) 351-6057.

# STORMVILLE
## Stormville Airport Antique Show and Flea Market

**DATES:** Held annually on the last Sunday of April, May (Memorial weekend), first Sundays of July (July 4th weekend), August, September (Labor Day weekend), the second Sunday in October (Columbus weekend) and their Christmas show the first Sunday in November. Rain or shine.

**TIMES:** Dawn to dusk.

**ADMISSION:** Free. Parking is free.

**LOCATION:** At the Airport. On Rt 216 in Stormville.

**DESCRIPTION:** This massive outdoor market began in 1970. Over 700 dealers attend their shows. A variety of purchases can be made, including antiques, arts and crafts, and collectibles. Shopping for new merchandise and fresh produce can also be accomplished at this market. Food is served on the premises. (I'm told by friends who visited here that the goodies go *real* fast early on Saturday. Step lively!)

**DEALER RATES:** $60 pre-paid per 20' × 20' space or $75 at the gate. Reservations are suggested.

**CONTACT:** Pat Carnahan, PO Box 125, Stormville NY 12582-0125. Tel: (914) 221-6561.

# WALTON
## Walton Riverside Open Air Market

**DATES:** Sunday, once a month, Memorial Day through October.

**TIMES:** 8:00 AM-4:00 PM.

**ADMISSION:** Donations accepted. Parking is free.

**LOCATION:** Misty Mountain Produce Stand on Delaware St, in downtown Walton. From NY I-88 (from Albany) take the exit for Rt 28 at Oneonta, follow Rt 28 to Rt 357, turn right on Rt 357, go through the village of Franklin, turn left to Walton. You can't miss it.

**DESCRIPTION:** This outdoor market is run by the Chamber of Commerce and features from 20 to 50 dealers selling most anything: garage sale goodies, antiques, collectibles, produce in season and crafts. This started as a farmers' market and graduated to include flea market fare as well. This place is wild during their County Fair in mid-August.

**DEALER RATES:** $10 per space. Reservations are suggested.

**CONTACT:** Chamber of Commerce, 1 Liberty St, Walton NY 13856-1111. Tel: (607) 865-6656 or 1-800-639-4296.

# YONKERS
## Yonkers Raceway Market

**DATES:** Sundays, last Sunday in March through the Sunday before Christmas.

**TIMES:** 9:00 AM-4:00 PM.

**ADMISSION:** $2 per car.

**LOCATION:** Yonkers Racetrack. Cross the George Washington Bridge, take the Major Deegan Expressway to New York Thruway Exit 2, right there. From the other direction, from the New York Thruway take Exit 4 (Central Ave) to the racetrack.

**DESCRIPTION:** This outdoor market's 400 dealers sell mostly new merchandise, although when there are enough dealers (40 or more) in antiques and collectibles one corner will be put aside for their wares exclusively. There are loads of different foods available: bratwurst, fish and chips, pizza, sausages, and lots more on traveling food trucks and snack bars. Naturally, there are clean restrooms for your convenience.

**DEALER RATES:** $40 for a 9' × 28' space with reservations; $50 without reservations.

**CONTACT:** Marty McGrath, Yonkers Raceway Market Inc, Yonkers Raceway, Yonkers NY 10704. Tel: (914) 963-3898 or 968-4200 ext 216. Fax: (914) 968-1121.

# OTHER FLEA MARKETS

We know or have heard about these markets, but have not personally contacted each one, as we have the markets with descriptions. If you plan to visit one of these markets listed below, *please call first* to make sure they are still open. Flea markets do come and go. While they were open when we went to press, they may not be later. We can't be responsible. *Call first!*

**Belfast:** Belfast Flea Market, Rts 305 & 19. Tel: (716) 365-9989.
**Bridgeport:** South Shore Flea Market, Rt 31. Tel: (315) 633-9766.
**Bronx:** Flea Port USA, 1880 Bartow Ave. Tel: (718) 671-5800.
**Brooklyn:** Amigo Flea Market, 1222 Broadway. Tel: (718) 919-2740.
**Brooklyn:** Brighton Bazaar, 272 Brighton Beach Ave. Tel: (718) 648-1815.
**Brooklyn:** Diana's Flea Market, 379 Rockaway Ave. Tel: (718) 385-1388.
**Brooklyn:** Margarita's Flea Market, 1231 Surf Ave. Tel: (718) 946-5188.
**Brooklyn:** Market Square, 1815 85 St. Tel: (718) 234-8830.
**Brooklyn:** R & J Flea Market, 4119 Church Ave. Tel: (718) 469-7023.
**Flushing:** Genesis Flea Market, 9905 37 Ave.
**Fredonia:** Fredonia Flea Market, 10136 Rt 60. Tel: (716) 679-9848
**Hudson:** PJ'S Flea Market, 348 Warren St. Tel: (518) 828-2271.
**Levittown:** Surinder Arneja Flea Market, 3041 Hempstead Tnpk. Tel: (516) 520-1553.
**Lowman:** Lowman Flea Market, Rt 17. Tel: (607) 734-3670.
**North Tonawanda:** Main Street Flea Market, 140 Main St. Tel: (716) 692-7885.
**Oneonta:** Country Club Flea Market, Country Club Rd. Tel: (607) 436-9171.
**Ontario** Center: Flannagans Flea World, Ontario Center Rd. Tel: (315) 524-6000.
**Orangeburg:** All Star Flea Markets, 9 Helaine Ct. Tel: (914) 359-5131.
**Pottersville:** Dick's Flea Market, Rt 9. Tel: (518) 494-4931.
**Saratoga Springs:** Stan's Flea Market, RR 9. Tel: (518) 584-4339.
**Sayville:** Attias Flea Market, 5750 Sunrise Hwy. Tel: (516) 244-5755.
**Schenectady:** Colonial Flea Market, 1671 Crane St. Tel: (518) 356-7065.
**Schoharie:** Cater's Flea Markets, Grand St. Tel: (518) 295-8057.
**Springwater:** Springwater Flea Market, Mill. Tel: (716) 669-2646.
**Syracuse:** B & V Auction Service, 1105 Wolf St. Tel: (315) 479-7146.
**Syracuse:** Central NY Regional Market, 2100 Park St 101. Tel: (315) 422-8647.

# NORTH CAROLINA

## ALBEMARLE
### Albemarle Flea Market

**DATES:** Friday, Saturday and Sunday, year round.

**TIMES:** Friday and Saturday 9:00 AM-9:00 PM, Sunday 10:00 AM-7:30 PM.

**ADMISSION:** Free. Parking is free.

**LOCATION:** Stony Gap Rd. Take Hwy 52 south from Albemarle, at the former skating rink. Between Hwys 52 and 2427.

**DESCRIPTION:** Located in a former dance hall and skating rink, this market houses 50 dealers selling treasured antiques to yard sale stuff including collectibles, old beer signs and advertisements, depression glass, leather, tools, new merchandise, Avon, army surplus, and crafts. It is said that Fats Domino performed on their stage during the dance hall years. Restrooms and a snack bar are on site.

**DEALER RATES:** $22 for space along the wall with peg boards, $14 for non-wall space. Reservations are required, as there is a waiting list.

**CONTACT:** Lyman Jones, Albemarle Flea Market, 1100 NC Hwy 109S, Mt Gilead NC 27306. Tel: (704) 982-5022.

## CHARLOTTE
### Metrolina Expo

**DATES:** First full weekend based on the first Saturday of the month, Thursday through Sunday.

**TIMES:** Thursday through Saturday 8:00 AM-5:00 PM, Sunday 9:00 AM-5:00 PM.

**ADMISSION:** $3, $10 (Early Buyers Day), $15 (4-day pass) per person for regular shows. Extravaganzas $6, $10, $50 (depending on which day you go) and a four-day pass for $15 per person.

**LOCATION:** 7100 Statesville Rd (Hwy 21).

**DESCRIPTION:** This market, started in 1971, has grown from 800 to 2,000 exhibitors devoted to selling antiques and antique collectibles only. The grounds include 20 buildings, two malls, as well as dealers on the ground. There are restaurant areas, vendors and all sorts of food available, as well as handicapped-accessible restrooms.

**DEALER RATES:** $70-$110 depending on location and size of space. Reservations are required. Contact Metrolina Expo for the latest information.

**CONTACT:** Aileen Lisk, Metrolina Expo, PO Box 26652, Charlotte NC 28226-6652. Tel: (704) 596-4643 or 1-800-824-3770. Email: Info@metrolinaexpo.com. Web: www.metrolinaexpo.com.

# DALLAS
## I-85/321 Flea Market

**DATES:** Saturday and Sunday.

**TIMES:** 8:00 AM-4:00 PM.

**ADMISSION:** Free. Parking is free.

**LOCATION:** 3867 High Shoals Hwy. From I-85 in Gastonia head north on Rt 321 for 3 mi to Cherryville exit, turn right at traffic light and market is 2 miles ahead on right.

**DESCRIPTION:** Operating since 1983, this indoor/outdoor market boasts 500 or so dealers filling 750 spaces and tables. There are 300 indoor booths, 200 outside under cover, and 250 open tables. Items sold include plenty of garage sale goodies, some antiques, collectibles, plenty of fresh produce, new and used furniture, crafts, jewelry, clothing, and loads of new merchandise. There are 10 food outlets and handicapped-accessible restrooms when needed.

**DEALER RATES:** $4 per table outside, $12 per 10' × 10' space outside under cover, and $20 per 12' × 12' space inside daily. Reservations are required for inside and covered spaces. Outside is first come, first served.

**CONTACT:** David Stewart, I-85/321 Flea Market, PO Box 402, Dallas NC 28034-0402. Tel: (704) 922-1416, pager (704) 834-8093. Fax: (704) 922-4525. Email: davidstewart321@prodigy.net. Web: www.321fleamarket.com.

# DEEP GAP
## Wildcat Flea Market

**DATES:** Friday through Sunday, May through October.

**TIMES:** Friday 9:00 AM-5:00 PM; Saturday and Sunday 7:00 AM-6:00 PM. Auction every Saturday at 6:00 PM. Antique auctions one Tuesday a month.

**ADMISSION:** Free. Parking is free.

**LOCATION:** 8156 US Hwy 421 S, 7 miles east of Boone.

**DESCRIPTION:** High in the Blue Ridge Mountains, along the Blue Ridge Pkwy, this family run flea market has been in business since 1972. From 70-80 dealers sell antiques, collectibles, discount groceries, candles, crafts, old and new glassware including depression, old and new gold jewelry, novelties, tools, hardware, new merchandise, coins, cards, furniture, computers and electronics and whatever. From 3,000-5,000 buyers show up in this market every weekend. There is an auction every Saturday night at 6:00 PM, year round. Antique auctions are held as needed on Tuesdays. There is a wonderful restaurant on premises serving full breakfast, lunch and dinner. Large, clean restrooms are on site. Located in the rafters of the main building is a "Hanging Museum," representing 32 years of collecting antiques and primitives, said to make the most diehard collector "envious."

**DEALER RATES:** Outside rates $5 a day for a shed (except free on Friday). Inside and more permanent space available from $60 per month; please call for more information. Reservations are required as most space is reserved for the season.

**CONTACT:** Elaine, Jack or Kevin Richardson, PO Box 163, Deep Gap NC 28607. Tel: (828) 264-7757.

---

**Historical Note**

The original market was built in 1972, and as they were putting the finishing touches on the roof—it collapsed! The builders had to rebuild the entire structure again. Obviously, it stayed up this time. They've used it for 27 years.

A piece of depression glass was purchased here for $5 and later resold for $240.

International Folk recording artist "Doc" Watson makes his home in Deep Gap and can occasionally be found inside the main building "pickin" with his childhood friend and local dealer, Denver Cheek.

---

# FLETCHER
## Smiley's Flea Market and Antique Mall

**DATES:** This market is open every Friday, Saturday, and Sunday, year round. Antique mall is open daily.

**TIMES:** Hours are 7:00 AM-5:00 PM. Antique mall is open 10:00 AM-5:00 PM.

**ADMISSION:** Free with over 10 acres of free parking.

**LOCATION:** Halfway between Asheville and Hendersonville on Rt 25. Take Exit 13 off I-26, then travel north ½ mile on Rt 25.

**DESCRIPTION:** This indoor/outdoor market began in 1984. The market provides over 11,000 square feet of space in the antique mall with 250 shops and over ½ mile of 600 spaces of covered selling spaces and daily spaces under a shed in the flea market. It attracts an average of more than 250 dealers. A large variety of items can be found including antiques, collectibles, handicrafts, fresh produce, and some new merchandise. This place is known as the "Baseball Card and Beanie Baby Capital of Western North Carolina." Two snack bars serve the hungry. RV parking available.

**DEALER RATES:** $11 per 10' × 10' space per day inside the flea market area with two tables. Outside space $7 each. 10' × 25' lockable units are available at $149 per month. $115 per 10' × 12' space per month in the antique mall. Reservations are not required outside.

**CONTACT:** Wade McAbee, Smiley's Flea Market and Antique Mall, PO Box 458, Fletcher NC 28732. (828) 684-3532 or Polly Hickling at the antique mall 684-3515. Fax: (828) 684-5651.

# FOREST CITY
## 74 By-Pass Flea Market

**DATES:** Friday, Saturday, and Sundays, year round.

**TIMES:** 7:00 AM-6:00 PM.

**ADMISSION:** Free. Parking is free.

**LOCATION:** 180 Frontage Rd. Eight miles east of Rutherfordton and 15 miles west of Shelby, exit Forest City off 74 By-Pass.

**DESCRIPTION:** This indoor/outdoor market opened in 1986 and hosts up to 240 dealers in summer and 100 in winter. They sell antiques, ball cards, racing cards, collectibles, electronics, groceries and fresh produce, cheeses, baked goods, clothing, leather goods, tools, jewelry, and new merchandise. The outside tables invite garage sale goodies. Three snack bars and handicapped-accessible restrooms add to the amenities.

**DEALER RATES:** $7 per 10' × 10' inside booth; $6 outside under shed; $3 in the open. Reservations are suggested.

**CONTACT:** Gary Hardin, 180 Frontage Rd, Forest City NC 28043-4348. Tel: (828) 245-7863 anytime.

---

**What a Buy!**

One buyer picked up a 1950s' vintage Buddy L car for $5. When he looked it up in the catalog, it was worth $550. As Gary says, he spent an hour polishing that little thing until it gleamed.

---

# FUQUAY-VARINA
## Fuquay Flea Market

**DATES:** Saturday and Sunday.

**TIMES:** 8:00 AM-5:00 PM.

**ADMISSION:** Free. Parking is free.

**LOCATION:** 6109 NC Hwy 55. Hwy 55E. From Raleigh, take Rt 401S to Hwy 55E, then left on 55E, go ¼ mile and market is on left.

**DESCRIPTION:** This indoor market of 130 dealers sells antiques and collectibles, crafts, new and used furniture, jewelry, and fresh produce. Snack bars feed the famished and handicapped-accessible restrooms are available.

**DEALER RATES:** Call for rates, as reservations are needed.

**CONTACT:** Fuquay Flea Market, 6109 NC Hwy 55, Fuquay Varina NC 27526. Tel: (919) 552-4143.

# GREENSBORO
## "Super Flea" Flea Market

**DATES:** Usually scheduled for the second weekend every month. But call to make sure.

**TIMES:** Saturday 8:00 AM-5:00 PM; Sunday 10:00 AM-5:00 PM.

**ADMISSION:** $2 per person, children under 12 are free. $3 for parking.

**LOCATION:** Greensboro Coliseum Complex, Exhibit Hall. 1921 W Lee St. Follow signs posted in town.

**DESCRIPTION:** This very successful indoor market recently attracted as many as 10,000 shoppers on a weekend, with 500 dealers selling various types of antiques and collectibles, along with arts and crafts and some new merchandise. Food is served on the premises.

**DEALER RATES:** $70 per 8' × 10' space, 1 table and 2 chairs for the weekend, additional tables are $8. Reservations are required in advance.

**CONTACT:** Smith-Tomlinson Co, PO Box 16122, Greensboro NC 27416. Tel: (336) 373-8515. Email: info@superflea.com. Web: www.superflea.com.

# HICKORY
## Hickory Livestock and Flea Market

**DATES:** Every Thursday.

**TIMES:** All day, starting at 5:00 AM.

**ADMISSION:** Free. Parking is $.50 per vehicle.

**LOCATION:** On Sweetwater Rd, 100 yards north of the junction of Hwy 64 and Rt 70. You can see it from the stop.

**DESCRIPTION:** "There's no better Thursday market. Come one, come all and get the bargains while they're here." This outdoor market, which began in 1962 and is probably the oldest in the area, has grown to include approximately 300 dealers selling a selection of antiques and collectibles, craft items, and some new merchandise. There is also a livestock auction, selling everything from cattle to birds, chickens, and rabbits at 1:30 PM every week except during the weeks of Thanksgiving, Christmas, and July 4th. "When you mix animals and cowboys, there's never a dull moment," says Mr. Hahn of the auctions within a flea market. The Stockyard Cafe serves such special meals that people come from all over to eat here, market or not. The cafe also operates a "mobile dealer food cart" taking food to the dealers in their spaces so the dealers don't have to leave their merchandise and miss a sale. What a great idea!

**DEALER RATES:** $7 per 12' space. Reservations are not required for dirt spaces; there's a waiting list for the paved spaces.

**CONTACT:** George E Hahn (father or son), Hickory Livestock and Flea Market, 1958 Kool Park Rd NE, Hickory NC 28601-9260. Tel: (828) 256-5772 (home) or (828) 324-7354 (market).

## Springs Road Flea Market

**DATES:** Saturday and Sundays, year around.

**TIMES:** 8:00 AM-4:00 PM.

**ADMISSION:** Free. Parking is free.

**LOCATION:** 3451 Springs Rd.

**DESCRIPTION:** This indoor/outdoor market opened in the former Springs Road Drive-In Theater in 1981. From 200 to 300 dealers sell anything and everything imaginable including antiques, arts and crafts, collectibles and new merchandise. There is a heated building 500' long for indoor sales which has proved so popular they added 2 outdoor sheds. Two concessions provide food to the hungry.

**DEALER RATES:** $6 per day for a 20' × 20' outdoor space (2 car parking spaces), $7 under a shed with 2 tables, and $10 per day for a 12' × 12' space inside, if available (there is a waiting list). Monthly and yearly rates are available. Reservations are a good idea for the shed spaces; first come, first served for the outside.

**CONTACT:** Jim, Springs Road Flea Market, 3451 Springs Rd, Hickory NC 28601. Tel: (828) 256-7669.

# LEXINGTON

## Davidson Cooperative Farmers' Market and Flea Market

**DATES:** Tuesday and Wednesday, year round. Rain or shine.
**TIMES:** Early (say daybreak?) until everyone drops (usually after dark). Really!
**ADMISSION:** Free. Parking is free.
**LOCATION:** Livestock Market Rd.
**DESCRIPTION:** Since the 1930s this market has been running a livestock and flea market. The flea market has around 400 vendors selling antiques, collectibles, new merchandise, garage sale goodies, lots of produce, clothes, tools and whatever comes in. Wednesday mornings they hold a "Junk Sale Auction" at 9:00 AM. For a 20% commission, they sell the stuff you don't want to! There is a cafe with appropriate restrooms on site.
**DEALER RATES:** $6 per space. Reservations not required.
**CONTACT:** Davidson Farmers Cooperative Inc Office & Sales, PO Box 926, Lexington NC 27292-3402. Tel: (336) 248-2173. Contact Dan York the day of the markets to reserve at (336) 248-5208.

## Farmers' Market and Flea Market

**DATES:** Every Monday, Tuesday and Wednesday of the year. Rain or shine.
**TIMES:** Monday 11:00 AM-7:00 PM (wholesale only—must have a resale license to get in); Tuesday 6:30 AM-2:00 PM (wholesale and retail).
**ADMISSION:** Free. Free parking is available.
**LOCATION:** On Old Hwy 64 W, ¾ mile off of the I-85 business loop.
**DESCRIPTION:** This outdoor market has been in business since 1973 and is run by brothers Tim and Jim Fritts. It attracts 300 to 500 dealers selling a full range of antiques and collectibles, as well as new merchandise, farm produce, and tag sale items. Tim handles the retail end of the market. There is also a wholesale market that operates on Mondays and Tuesdays at this same location. They have over 250 wholesale vendors selling all new merchandise: new clothing, novelties, toys, jewelry, crafts and other assorted goodies. "Wholesale Alley" is not open to the general public and requires a state Sales Tax ID to be able to enter the area. Jim handles the wholesale market. The Wholesale Alley has been a real success story here.
**DEALER RATES:** $15 for a 10' × 10' sheltered booth to $10 per 12' × 16' outside space per day. Wholesale Alley rates are $250 per quarter for a sheltered space. Reservations are suggested.

**CONTACT:** Tim and Jim Fritts, Owners, 224 Berrier Ave, Lexington NC 27292. Tel: (336) 248-2157. Jim handles the Wholesale Alley and Tim handles the rest of the flea market.

---

### Market Toys

Tim bought an empty grenade shell for his young son from an army surplus dealer. Unknown to his mother, Tim's son took it to his kindergarten Show and Tell at school, wrapped in a bag. When his teacher opened the bag, she naturally freaked. "Cleaned the whole school out," says Tim. The sheriff's department was called, and of course, Tim and his wife were summoned. The janitor, fearing for his life I'm sure, carefully took the grenade out to the middle of the playing field and guarded it there. The cops arrived and did their thing. Of course, Tim's son was terribly upset that the officials were taking his favorite toy. Tim duly arrived, went to the field and pocketed the harmless casing. But not before catching a severe lecture from the deputy and the school principal.

---

## MORGANTOWN
### Jamestown Flea and Farmers' Market

**DATES:** Saturday and Sunday, year round. Rain or shine.

**TIMES:** 7:00 AM-5:00 PM.

**ADMISSION:** Free admission and free parking.

**LOCATION:** Jamestown Rd. One half mile off I-40 at Exit 100.

**DESCRIPTION:** This flea market, which attracts 300-400 dealers year round, has been held since 1983. Dealers sell antiques, collectibles, handmade crafts, vegetables, and new merchandise. There are clean restrooms, spacious parking, storage, showers, and security available. Seasonally, up to five restaurants and several snack bars take care of hunger problems (and boost the calorie count).

**DEALER RATES:** $60 for a 10' × 10' booth for 4 weeks; advance reservations are very nice, especially during holiday seasons, but not always necessary.

**CONTACT:** Pete Patton, Manager, Jamestown Flea Market, PO Drawer 764, Morgantown NC 28655-0764. Tel: (704) 584-4038.

**Quite Harmless**

They once had a skunk walk through the market that decided it really didn't want to be there. "It disrupted the equilibrium of quite a few, but did no harm."

# RALEIGH
## North Carolina State Fairgrounds Flea Market

**DATES:** Every Saturday and Sunday, except the month of October during State Fair.

**TIMES:** 9:00 AM-5:00 PM.

**ADMISSION:** Free. Parking is free.

**LOCATION:** North Carolina State Fairgrounds at the intersection of Hillsborough St and Blue Ridge Blvd. Take I-40 to Wade Ave, Exit 289 or 290, Rt 54 east to Hillsborough St.

**DESCRIPTION:** They must be doing something right as they have 500 dealers inside and out in a total of 200,000 square feet of selling space. They particularly welcome antiques and have been known for the quality and quantity of their selection. Among the items sought after by loyal customers are the quality antiques, collectibles, craft items, fresh produce and a huge variety of new merchandise and services (framing, jewelry and bike repairs and more). The 1853 Grill serves up, I'm promised, the best homemade chicken and dumplings, as well as plenty of other homemade soups and sandwiches and awesome Italian pizza. There are outside food vendors, an indoor snack bar and handicapped-accessible restrooms. The park-like fairgrounds boast benches and quiet places. For the kids, the pet dealers have plenty of animals to pet and love.

**DEALER RATES:** $16 per 10' × 20' outside space, including vehicle. There is a waiting list for inside space. Inside space is by the square foot. Outside space is first come, first served.

**CONTACT:** Joan Long, Fairgrounds Flea Market, PO Box 33517, Raleigh NC 27636. Tel: (919) 829-3533.

# SALISBURY
## Webb Road Flea Market

**DATES:** Saturday and Sunday, year round. Rain or shine.

**TIMES:** 8:00 AM-5:00 PM.

**ADMISSION:** Free admission and free parking.

**LOCATION:** Six miles south of Salisbury on I-85 at Webb Rd, Exit 70. Just 30 miles north of Charlotte.

**DESCRIPTION:** This flea market was started in 1985 and attracts 300 to 400 dealers. They sell antiques, collectibles, handmade crafts, vegetables, new merchandise, and coins, and specialize in jewelry, furniture, glass, tools, auto accessories, books and just about anything. Most of the merchandise is new. Food is available on site. There are clean handicapped-accessible restrooms, spacious parking, storage, and 24-hour security.

**DEALER RATES:** $60 per 10' × 10' booth for four weeks inside. Advance reservations are suggested inside. Outside rates: $6 for open 10' × 10' space, $7 for sheltered space.

**CONTACT:** John Nash, Manager, Webb Road Flea Market, 905 Webb Rd, Salisbury NC 28146-8536. Tel: (704) 857-6660.

# WINSTON-SALEM
## Cooks Original Market

**DATES:** Saturday and Sunday.

**TIMES:** Saturday 8:00 AM-5:00 PM; Sunday 9:00 AM-5:00 PM.

**ADMISSION:** Free. Parking is free.

**LOCATION:** 4290 N Patterson Ave.

**DESCRIPTION:** Originally opened 1991, then reopened in 1998, this market has approximately 300-350 dealers selling literally "everything" from antiques and collectibles to loads of new merchandise and garage sale goodies. Snack bars, food vendors and handicapped-accessible restrooms add to the amenities. There is a sister market Cooks Plaza on University Pkwy.

**DEALER RATES:** $25 per 10' × 10' space per weekend. Reservations are a must as there is a waiting list!

**CONTACT:** Cooks Plaza, 5721 University Pkwy, Winston-Salem NC 27105. Tel: (910) 661-0610 or (910) 661-0999.

## Cooks Plaza

**DATES:** Saturday and Sunday.

**TIMES:** Saturday 8:00 AM-5:00 PM; Sunday 9:00 AM-5:00 PM.

**ADMISSION:** Free. Parking is free.

**LOCATION:** 5721 University Pkwy. At Hwy 52 N and University Pkwy.

**DESCRIPTION:** Open since 1990, this market of approximately 400-450 dealers sells literally "everything" from antiques, crafts and collectibles to loads of new merchandise and garage sale goodies. Snack bars, food vendors and handicapped-accessible restrooms add to the amenities. There is a sister market, the Cooks Original Market, in town.

**DEALER RATES:** $34 per 10' × 10' space per weekend. Reservations are a must as there is a waiting list!

**CONTACT:** Cooks Plaza, 5721 University Pkwy, Winston-Salem NC 27105. Tel: (336) 661-0610.

---

**From Former Markets**

Ashland's Dreamland Flea Market

They used to have a part-time deputy sheriff on site just to keep things in order while Dusty and his staff worked inside their office. One day an excited man burst into the office to announce that one of the dealers had brought a lion! Dusty and his partner decided to check this out. After three walks through the market, they still hadn't seen this lion. Then Dusty noticed a school bus taking up three to four spaces with something rather lion-like next to one wheel. Upon closer inspection it proved to be a young male, about 100 pounds, just growing his mane and fortunately on a very short chain. "The deputy pitched a fit!" The dealer put the lion in the school bus for the duration of the market and was never seen again.

It was here that someone bought a WWII artillery shell, took it home, fiddled around with it—and found $400 stashed in the base. You never know what you'll find.

---

# OTHER FLEA MARKETS

We know or have heard about these markets, but have not personally contacted each one, as we have the markets with descriptions. If you plan to visit one of these markets listed below, *please call first* to make sure they are still open. Flea markets do come and go. While they were open when we went to press, they may not be later. We can't be responsible. *Call first!*

**Ahoskie:** Ahoskie Flea Market, 960 S Academy St. Tel: (252) 209-0040.

**Asheboro:** Ramseur Flea & Farmers' Market. Tel: (336) 625-4688.

**Baker's Creek:** Uncle Bill's Flea Market. Rts 441N & 74. Tel: (704) 586-9613. Open Wed through Sun, all day.

**Burlington:** West Webb Flea Market, 1413 W Webb Ave. Tel: (336) 229-9783.

**Charlotte:** Viking Flea Market, 1510 Camp Greene St. Tel: (704) 394-4136.

**Clinton:** Clinton Flea Market, 1555 Turkey Hwy. Tel: (910) 592-3289.

**Clinton:** Sampson County Flea Market, 1480 Hobbton Hwy. Tel: (910) 592-7425.

**Connellys Springs:** I-40 Trade Lot, Connelly Springs Rd, beside I-40 at Exit 113, between Hickory and Morganton. Tel: (704) 879-9970. Open Sat & Sun, 6 AM-5 PM.

**Creswell:** Creswell Flea Market, 105 E Main St. Tel: (252) 797-4183.

**Dillsboro:** 441 Flea Market, Hwy 441. Open Fri, Sat & Sun from daylight to dark. Tel: (704) 586-6768.

**Eden:** Eden Flea Market, 122 N Van Buren Rd. Tel: (336) 627-9440.

**Fayetteville:** A & S Flea Market, 4530 Bragg Blvd. Tel: (910) 860-2309.

**Fayetteville:** Bragg Blvd Flea Market, 3315 Bragg Blvd. Tel: (910) 868-3100.

**Fayetteville:** Great American Market Place, 4909 Raeford Rd. Tel: (910) 423-4440.

**Fayetteville:** Raeford Road Flea Market. 5207 Raeford Rd, Rt 401, off I-95. Tel: (910) 425-8053. Open Fri, Sat & Sun 7:30 AM-5 PM.

**Fayetteville:** Ramsey St Flea Market, 3611 Ramsey St. Tel: (910) 482-3367.

**Franklin:** Franklin Flea & Craft Market, 199 Highlands Rd. Tel: (828) 524-6658.

**Franklinton:** B & W Flea Market, 11 S Main St. Tel: (919) 494-6900.

**Fremont:** Jeffrey's Flea Market, 207 E Main St. Tel: (919) 242-5242.

**Gastonia:** I-85 Flea Market, 1901 Jenkins Dairy Rd. Tel: (704) 867-2317.

**Goldsboro:** Artis Flea Market, 117 W Walnut St. Tel: (919) 736-8590.

**Goldsboro:** Downtown Flea Market & Auction, 217 N Center St. Tel: (919) 734-0641.

**Goldsboro:** Goldsboro Flea Market, 2102 Wayne Memorial Dr. Tel: (919) 736-4422 or 800-282-FLEA. Open Sat & Sun, 10 AM-5 PM.

**Goldsboro:** Olde Antiques & Flea Market, 5552 US Hwy 70E. Tel: (919) 778-4004.

**Goldsboro:** Wayne County Flea Market, 2793 US Hwy 117S. Tel: (919) 731-2854.

**Graham:** Graham Flea Market, 614 W Elm St. Tel: (336) 227-0505.

**Greensboro:** Flea, 3220 N O'Henry Blvd. Tel: (336) 621-9210.

**Greensboro:** Greensboro Flea Market. 4000 McConnell Rd, I-85 Exit 130, 2 mi N of Greensboro, 10 mi S of Burlington. Open Sat & Sun 8 AM-5 PM. Tel: (336) 697-2707.

**Greenville:** 43 South Flea Market, 1906 Fox Trot Ln. Tel: (252) 321-5575.

**Hamptonville:** 421 Flea Market, 3134 US Hwy 421. Tel: (336) 468-2376.

**Hamptonville:** Vintage Village, 2832 US Hwy 421. Tel: (336) 468-8434.

**Hayesville:** Dan's Flea Market, 3998 Old Hwy 64 E. Tel: (828) 389-9725.

**Henderson:** Harris' Flea Market, 48 Allison Cooper Rd. Tel: (252) 438-5816.

**Henderson:** Randy's Flea Mart, 169 Furman Ln. Tel: (252) 492-8062.

**Hertford:** Dail's Flea Market, 405 W Grubb St. Tel: (252) 426-4060.

**High Point:** Westchester Flea Market. 2200 Westchester Dr, Hwy 68. Tel: (910) 884-5063. Open Sat 8 AM-5 PM; Sun 9 AM-5 PM.

**Kill Devil Hills:** Indoor Flea Market, 306 W Lake Dr, W off Rt 158. Open Sat 9 AM-4 PM; Sun 12-4 PM. Tel: (919) 441-8830.

**Lenoir:** Foothills Flea Market, 2330 Blowing Rock Blvd. Tel: (828) 754-1224.

**Linwood:** US Flea & Farmers' Market, 999 7 Oaks Dr. Tel: (336) 853-8449.

**Louisburg:** Perry School Alumni, RR6. Tel: (919) 853-6681.

**Louisburg:** West River Road Flea Market, 44 W River Rd. Tel: (919) 496-1737.

**Lumberton:** Country Flea Market, 1102 Kite Rd. Tel: (910) 738-2823.

**Lumberton:** Lumberton Flea Market, 3651 Lackey St. Tel: (910) 738-4519.

**Lumberton:** Robeson Flea Market, 3551 Fayetteville Rd. Tel: (910) 618-1026.

**Lumberton:** Traders Station Flea Market, Hwy 41E. Tel: (910) 618-0004.

**Lumberton:** T & A Flea Market, US Hwy 74 & I-95 Ext 14. Tel: (910) 739-1885.

**Maysville:** Belgrade Flea Market, 7484 New Bern Hwy. Tel: (910) 743-3143.

**Mebane:** Buckhorn Jockey Lot & Market, 508 Buckhorn Rd. Tel: (919) 563-9420.

**Mocksville:** Mocksville Flea Market. Tel: (704) 751-4676.

**Monroe:** Sweet Union Flea Market, 4420 W Hwy 74. Tel: (704) 283-7985.

**Morehead City:** Trash & Treasure II Flea Market, Hwy 70W. Tel: (252) 240-0005.

**Morganton:** Jamestown Flea & Farmers Market, 709 Jamestown Rd. Tel: (828) 584-4038.

**Mt Airy:** Greyhound Flea Market, 2134 W Pine St. Tel: (336) 789-0417.

**Mt Olive:** Southern Wayne Flea Market, 5460 US Hwy 117 Alt. Tel: (919) 658-8228.

**Murfreesboro:** Inside Outside Flea Market, 904 W Main St. Tel: (252) 398-8198.

**Murphy:** Decker's Flea Market, Jct of Rtes 19 & 129. Open Sat & Sun 7 AM-3 PM. Tel: (704) 837-5753.

**Murphy:** Foster's Flea Market, Hwy 64. Tel: (828) 837-9089.

**Murphy:** Ranger Market, Hwy 19. Tel: (828) 837-8217.

**New Bern:** Cabbage Rose Flea Market, 2403 Trent Rd. Tel: (252) 635-1235.

**New Bern:** Down Home Flea Market, 109 Briarwood Ln. Tel: (252) 745-5891.

**Old Fort:** Catawba Trading Lot, I-40 & Catawba Rd, Exit 73. Open Fri, Sat & Sun, 7:30 AM on. Tel: (704) 668-4737 or 668-4511.

**Raleigh:** Fairgrounds Flea Market, 1025 Blue Ridge Rd. Tel: (919) 829-3533.

**Raleigh:** Watson's Flea Market, 1436 Rock Quarry Rd. Tel: (919) 832-6232.

**Rich Square:** Cecil's Flea Market, 151 N Main St. Tel: (252) 539-2476.

**Roanoke Rapids:** Flea Market, 262 Roanoke Ave. Tel: (252) 537-1258.

**Rockingham:** Airport Road Flea Market, 560 Airport Rd. Tel: (910) 895-0505.

**Rocky Mount:** Pack House Flea Market, Hwy 64E. Tel: (252) 446-6910.

**Rocky Point:** Rocky Point Country Flea, RR2. Tel: (910) 675-0311.

**Rocky Point:** Stallings Flea Market, 12025 US Hwy 117 S. Tel: (910) 675-3023.

**Rolesville:** Rolesville Flea Market, 105 E Young St. Tel: (919) 556-3226.

**Rosman:** Lady Bees Flea Market, HC 1. Tel: (828) 884-2337.

**Sanford:** Kendale Plaza Flea Market, 2726 Industrial Dr. Tel: (919) 774-3807.

**Sanford:** Sanford Flea Market, 405 Wicker St A. Tel: (919) 776-7041.

**Smithfield:** Brightleaf Flea Market, 110 N Bright Leaf Blvd. Tel: (919) 934-9917.

**Smithfield:** Trader's Flea Market, 1505 W Market St. Tel: (919) 989-6026.

**Spring Lake:** 210 Flea Market, 4115 NC Hwy 210 N B. Tel: (910) 960-8112.

**Sylva:** Four-Forty One Flea Market, 1620 US Hwy 441S. Tel: (828) 586-6768.

**Tabor City:** Flea Market Auction, 202 N Wall St. Tel: (910) 653-5033.

**Thomasville:** Eleven Acre Flea Market, 825 Julian Ave. Tel: (336) 472-0244. Open Sat & Sun. 5 AM-12 noon.

**Thomasville:** Westchester Flea & Antique, 713 National Hwy. Tel: (336) 472-7906.

**Union Mills:** Breeze-In Trading Post & Flea, 898 Coney Island Rd. Tel: (828) 287-5411.

**Vanceboro:** Vance Mill Flea Market, 206 1 Ave. Tel: (252) 244-2800.

**Wallace:** Wallace Flea Market, 1562 N Norwood St. Tel: (910) 285-3642.

**Washington:** Poor Man's Flea Market, E Hwy 264. Tel: (252) 975-9956.

**Whittier:** Gateway Flea Market, 8716 W US Hwy 74. Tel: (828) 497-9664.

**Whittier:** Uncle Bill's Flea Market, 5427 Hwy 74 W. Tel: (828) 586-9613.

**Wilkesboro:** Autrey's Flea Market, 4641 W US Hwy 421. Tel: (336) 973-4470.

**Wilmington:** Star Way Flea Market, 2346 Carolina Beach Rd. Tel: (910) 763-5520. Open Fri, Sat & Sun. Fri 7:30 AM-4 PM; Sat 6 AM-4 PM; Sun 7:30 AM-4 PM.

**Wilmington:** Tradewinds Swaparama Inc, Mailing address: 334 Hooker Rd. Tel: (910) 395-6880. Location: 5919 Market St, Hwy 17N, ³/₄ mi off I-40. Open Wed-Sun, 10 AM-5 PM, Sat 9 AM-5 PM.

**Wilson:** Nichol's Big Flea, 1817 US Hwy 301S. Tel: (252) 234-2008.

**Wilson:** Wilson Flea Market, 569 Ward Blvd B. Tel: (252) 243-7762.

# NORTH DAKOTA

## MANDAN
### Dakota Midwest Flea Market and Antique Show

**DATES:** First weekend of every month, except January.

**TIMES:** Saturday 9:00 AM-5:00 PM; Sunday 10:00 AM-4:00 PM.

**ADMISSION:** $1 per person age 10 and older. Free parking.

**LOCATION:** At the Mandan Community Center, 901 Division St. Take Exit 152 off I-94, then travel south on 6th Ave northwest to Division St. Signs are posted.

**DESCRIPTION:** This show has operated indoors since 1984 and currently attracts an average of 80 dealers who sell a wide range of items including antiques and collectibles and fine art works. One snack bar and handicapped-accessible restrooms add to the amenities. The market is close to historic Fort Abraham Lincoln, which was once the home of General Custer and has been restored as a national landmark.

**DEALER RATES:** $10 per 8' × 4' table per day. There are special rates for more tables. Reservations are required.

**CONTACT:** Barb and Bruce Skogen, 2512 93 St SE, Bismarck ND 58504. Tel: (701) 223-6185. Day of show call the Community Center at (701) 667-3260. Fax: (701) 223-9537.

## MINOT
### Magic City Flea Market

**DATES:** Second Saturday and Sunday of every month, except January and July.

**TIMES:** 9:00 AM-4:00 PM.

**ADMISSION:** $1 per person. Free parking is available.

**LOCATION:** On State Fairgrounds. Well marked in downtown Minot.

**DESCRIPTION:** This indoor market first opened in 1967 and currently accommodates an average of 75 dealers. There is a variety of antiques, collectibles, and crafts available at this market. This is an old-fashioned flea market with plenty of treasures dragged out of local attics and basements. Lots of old primitives, crockery and some Victorian treasures are still to be found. There is a concession stand and handicapped-accessible restrooms when needed.

**DEALER RATES:** $24 per 8' × 10' space per weekend, includes table and chairs. Reservations are required.

**CONTACT:** Richard Timboe, Manager, PO Box 1672, Minot ND 58701-1672. Tel: (701) 852-1289 at home or at the antique shop (701) 838-1150.

---

### Drat!

When a former salesman died his family came across loads of his old samples: pipes, combs, sunglasses, condoms, razors and other "stuff" from his cases—stuff that was sold to the likes of cigar shops, billiard halls and barbershops. Three truckloads of this still-in-original-packaging stuff was taken to the local dump. Some was left on the side of the road for anyone to help themselves. Eventually, some of this 1940s' treasure made it to the flea market.

According to Richard, stuff is still turning up!

Another customer bought an old roll-top desk and took it home. Stashed away by one of its former owners: $17,000.

Richard was called to handle an estate sale and found a pristine iron lung, 60 brass fire extinguishers, advertising signs, early time clocks, a copper boiler, and dozens of cream cans among other wild items the former owner of a scrap metal place had stashed. Do ask him about it.

---

# OHIO

## BEACH CITY
### Shady Rest Flea Market

**DATES:** Every Sunday, from the last Sunday in April through the second Sunday in October.

**TIMES:** Dawn to dusk.

**ADMISSION:** Free. The ample parking is free. No dogs or other pets are allowed on the grounds. Please!

**LOCATION:** Rts 250 and 93.

**DESCRIPTION:** Held under the trees, this old-fashioned outdoor market, started in the late 1960s, now averages about 75-100 dealers and offers a range of miscellaneous items including produce, collectibles, new merchandise, and handmade crafts. This is the oldest flea market in Tuscarawas County. In 1997, they considerably updated their facilities. Food and toilet facilities are available. The owner of the market, Mike, is 96 years young and still helps out at the market on Sundays. Stop in and say "Hi, Mike!"

**DEALER RATES:** $7 per day per dealer. Advance reservations not required. There are dumpsters for the leftovers.

**CONTACT:** Mike Vukich or Mildred Dinger Miller, 1762 Johnstown Rd NE, Dover OH 44622. Tel: (330) 343-9508.

## BLOOMFIELD
### Bloomfield Flea and Farm Market

**DATES:** Every Thursday, year round. Rain or shine.

**TIMES:** 7:00 AM-3:00 PM.

**ADMISSION:** Free. Parking is free.

**LOCATION:** One-half mile west of N Bloomfield on Rt 87.

**DESCRIPTION:** Now under new ownership, this market claims to have been in business since 1943, making it one of the oldest markets in the state of Ohio. They are located in the heart of Amish country attracting Amish dealers as well as buyers. There is a buggy parking area away from the car parking. It draws 150-300 dealers who sell both indoors (100) and outdoors (up to 200). Among the offerings are two meat markets (fresh and smoked), a discount cheese outlet, fresh farm products, Amish baker, tools, bulk spices, candles, canned goods, socks, candy, collectibles, lots of garage sale goodies, as well as crafts, new goods and antiques. Food concessions (3-5) and toilet facilities are available. Next door is a cattle barn with auctions.

**DEALER RATES:** $9 per 10' × 12' stall outside; inside, when available, $10. Reservations are required for some stalls.

**CONTACT:** Jo or Bill Herman, PO Box 51, Kinsman OH 44428-0051. Tel: (330) 876-7233. Day of market call (440) 685-9791.

# COLUMBIANA
## Theron's Country Flea Market

**DATES:** Every Sunday, year round.

**TIMES:** 9:00 AM-5:00 PM.

**ADMISSION:** Free. Ample free parking.

**LOCATION:** 1641 Columbiana-Lisbon Rd, 1 mile south of downtown Columbiana, just off I-11.

**DESCRIPTION:** This market has been around since the mid-1960s' and operates both indoors and outdoors. More than 60 dealers sell a variety of items including real antiques, furniture, collectibles, homemade pastries, jewelry, glassware, etc. Annual feast held in October. Auctions every Saturday night at 6:00 PM. Jolinda's Restaurant features home-cooking, open daily 6:30 AM-8:00 PM; Saturday 6:30 AM-10:00 PM, closed on Mondays. Restrooms are available inside.

**DEALER RATES:** $5 outdoor setups for transients. Shops $40-$160. Waiting list for shops.

**CONTACT:** Joann or Linda, Theron's, 1641 Columbiana-Lisbon Rd, Columbiana OH 44408. Tel: (330) 482-4327.

# COLUMBUS
## Amos Indoor Flea Market

**DATES:** Fridays through Sundays, year round.

**TIMES:** 10:00 AM-7:00 PM.

**ADMISSION:** Free. Free parking nearby.

**LOCATION:** 3454 Cleveland Ave at Innis Rd. Take I-71 north to Webber Rd; east on Webber Rd to Cleveland Ave; north about 1 mile on Cleveland Ave.

**DESCRIPTION:** This indoor market has been open since 1980; its dealers, which number approximately 250, sell general flea market merchandise as well as new goods. Food and toilet facilities are available on the premises.

**DEALER RATES:** $18 for a 9' × 8' space per day, $36 per weekend. Advance reservations are suggested.

**CONTACT:** Doug Hott and Paul Gwilym, Rainbow Enterprises, 865 King Ave, Columbus OH 43212. Tel: (614) 291-3133. For information call Paul at the market: (614) 262-0045.

## Livingston Court Indoor Flea Market

**DATES:** Friday, Saturday, and Sunday year round.
**TIMES:** 10:00 AM-7:00 PM.
**ADMISSION:** Free. Parking is also free.
**LOCATION:** 3575 E Livingston Ave. Just west of Courtright Rd.
**DESCRIPTION:** Opened in 1988, this market has about 300 dealers selling antiques, collectibles, arts and crafts, flea market fare and new merchandise. Two snack bars and handicapped-accessible restrooms add to the amenities.
**DEALER RATES:** Starting at $15 per day or $30 per weekend. Reservations are preferred.
**CONTACT:** Bill Marcum, Rainbow Enterprises, 865 King Ave, Columbus OH 43212. Tel: (614) 291-3133. Day of show call Bill Marcum at: (614) 231-7726.

## Scott Antique Market

**DATES:** 2000: January 22-23, February 19-20, March 25-26, April 29-30, May 20-21, June 24-25, November 25-26, December 16-17. Watch for about the same weekends in 2001.
**TIMES:** Saturday 9:00 AM-6:00 PM, Sunday 10:00 AM-4:00 PM.
**ADMISSION:** Free. Parking is $3.
**LOCATION:** Ohio Exposition Center. Off I-71, Exit 111, 17th Ave.
**DESCRIPTION:** This market opened in 1989 with 1,200 dealers (1,600 in November) selling exclusively antiques and collectibles. Considered "a treasure hunter's paradise," their dealers sell antique furniture, jewelry, silver, glassware, textiles, linens, advertising items, military items, paintings and more. There are four snack bars and one restaurant to perk up the weary shopper. Handicapped restrooms are also available. There is a sister market held in Atlanta, Georgia.
**DEALER RATES:** $93 for a 10' × 10' space in the Multi-Purpose and Celeste buildings. Table rental $7.50 per 6' × 30" or 8' × 30" table per weekend.
**CONTACT:** Scott Antique Markets, PO Box 60, Bremen OH 43107-0060. Tel: (740) 569-4112. Fax: (740) 569-7595.

## South Drive-In Theatre Flea Market

**DATES:** Every Wednesday, Saturday, and Sunday, April through October.

**TIMES:** 7:00 AM-2:00 PM.

**ADMISSION:** $.50 per carload includes parking.

**LOCATION:** 3050 S High St. Take I-71 south to Frank Rd; east on Frank Rd to High St; south on High St about 1 mile.

**DESCRIPTION:** In business since 1975, with an average of 350 dealers, outdoors only. Crafts, fresh produce, and new merchandise complement general flea market fare. Food and restrooms are available.

**DEALER RATES:** $5 for a 20' × 20' space, Saturdays and Sundays; $1 on Wednesdays. Reservations not required.

**CONTACT:** Doug Hott, Rainbow Enterprises, 865 King Ave, Columbus OH 43212. Tel: (614) 291-3133 or 491-6771.

## Westland Indoor Flea Market

**DATES:** Friday through Sunday.

**TIMES:** 10:00 AM-7:00 PM.

**ADMISSION:** Free. Parking is free.

**LOCATION:** 4170 W Broad St at Georgesville Rd.

**DESCRIPTION:** This newer market has 400 spaces for dealers selling everything from antiques and collectibles to newer merchandise. It is a sister market to three others in the Columbus area that cover North, East, and South, and this one covers the West Side. Two snack bars and handicapped-accessible restrooms add to the amenities.

**DEALER RATES:** $5 per space per day outdoors. Indoor $17 per day, $33 per weekend. Reservations not recommended.

**CONTACT:** Doug Hott, Rainbow Enterprises, 865 King Ave, Columbus OH 43212. Tel: (614) 291-3133 or 272-5678.

# DAYTON

## Olive Road Flea Market

**DATES:** Saturday and Sunday.

**TIMES:** 9:00 AM-5:00 PM.

**ADMISSION:** Free parking and admission.

**LOCATION:** 2222 N Olive. Approximately 5 miles NW of downtown Dayton. From I-75, take SR 35 W and go about 5 miles to James H McGee Blvd. Go north to Little Richmond, turn left (west) 2 miles south of SR 49 and 2 miles north on SR 35.

**DESCRIPTION:** Opened in 1989, this old-fashioned indoor/outdoor flea market of over 125 vendors sells antiques, collectibles, crafts, garage sale goodies, seasonal produce, and used and new merchandise. Their fully air-conditioned and heated 56,000-square-foot building houses 212 spaces and there is outside space as well. There is a concession stand and handicapped-accessible restrooms when you need them.

**DEALER RATES:** Inside: $35 per 10' × 14' space/booth weekly, $136.50 monthly. 14' × 14' space is $40 weekly, $156 monthly. Outside spaces are $10 per day. Reservations are preferred for inside, outside is first come, first served.

**CONTACT:** Olive Road Flea Market, PO Box 235, Brookville OH 45309-0235. Tel: (937) 837-3084 or (937) 833-3884. Fax: (937) 833-5122. Email: cs228@aol.com. Watch for their website.

## Paris Flea Market

**DATES:** Sunday, mid-April through mid-November.

**TIMES:** 7:00 AM-3:00 PM.

**ADMISSION:** $.50 per walk-in, $1 per car.

**LOCATION:** 6201 N Dixie Dr. Take Needmore Exit W off I-75.

**DESCRIPTION:** There are 60 to 250 dealers in this outdoor market, a fixture here since 1966. There are plenty of antiques for sale, as well as collectibles, arts and crafts, produce in season, and new merchandise. The Air Force Museum is 3 miles down the road. Dayton is the home of the Wright Brothers. Food and restrooms are on the premises.

**DEALER RATES:** $12 per 19' × 25' area (between movie speaker posts). Reservations are not required; first come, first served.

**CONTACT:** Paris Flea Market, c/o Levin Services, 111 W 1 St Ste 848, Dayton OH 45402. Tel: (937) 890-5513 (tape) or headquarters at (937) 223-0222. Fax: (937) 223-0154. Email: turtle848@aol.com.

# DELAWARE

## Kingman Drive-In Theatre Outdoor Flea Market

**DATES:** Every Sunday, April through October.

**TIMES:** 10:00 AM-2:00 PM.

**ADMISSION:** $.50 per carload, includes parking.

**LOCATION:** On Route 23 N at Cheshire Rd, 1 mile south of Delaware and 8 miles north of I-270.

**DESCRIPTION:** This outdoor market began in 1982 and currently attracts about 275 dealers selling a variety of collectibles, as well as fresh produce, handmade goods, and new merchandise. Food and restrooms are available.

**DEALER RATES:** $6 per 20' × 20' space. No advance reservations are required.

**CONTACT:** Dale Zinn, Rainbow Theatres, 865 King Ave, Columbus OH 43212. Tel: (614) 548-4227 or (614) 291-3133.

# HARTVILLE
## Hartville Flea Market

**DATES:** Every Monday and Thursday, year round. Rain or shine.

**TIMES:** 7:00 AM-5:00 PM.

**ADMISSION:** Free. Parking available, $1 per car.

**LOCATION:** 788 Edison St NW; take Rt 77 to Exit 118 (Rt 241) to Rt 619 E. Go east on Rt 619, 6 miles to market.

**DESCRIPTION:** This market began in 1937 as a livestock auction; it currently draws up to 1,200 dealers during the summertime (Mondays tend to draw the largest crowds) and 200 in the winter. Indoor and outdoor selling spaces offer a place to find all sorts of antiques and collectibles, as well as local farm goods, craft items, and new merchandise. Food is available at the Hartville Kitchen; restrooms are also available on the premises.

**DEALER RATES:** $5-$8 per 12' × 30' space depending on location. Advance reservations are suggested.

**CONTACT:** Marion Coblentz, Hartville Flea Market 788 Edison St NW, Hartville OH 44632. Tel: (330) 877-9860. Fax: (330) 877-0961. Email: info@hartvillefleamarket.com. Web: www.hartvillefleamarket.com.

# JOHNSTOWN
## Johnstown Lions Memorial Day Flea Market

**DATES:** Every Memorial Day, rain or shine.

**TIMES:** 6:30 AM-5:00 PM.

**ADMISSION:** Free. Free parking is available.

**LOCATION:** On the public square in Johnstown, at the intersection of Rts 62 and 37.

**DESCRIPTION:** This annual outdoor market has been in operation since 1972 and is now the occasion for 50 or more sellers to show up to offer their collectibles, crafts, and sometimes new merchandise. Food is served on the square on the day of the market. This market is sponsored by the Johnstown Lions Club to raise money for eyeglasses for the needy or eye health care. Some of the dealers have been here since the market began. This tiny town attracts over 3,500 to this event.

**DEALER RATES:** $15 per 10' × 24' space. Reservations are required.

**CONTACT:** Dick Scovell, Johnstown Lions Memorial Day Flea Market, PO Box 428, Johnstown OH 43031-0428. Tel: (740) 967-1279.

# LIMA
## Lima Antique Show and Flea Market

**DATES:** First full weekend, Saturday and Sunday, every month except February, June, July, August, and September.

**TIMES:** 9:00 AM-5:00 PM.

**ADMISSION:** $1 per person; children under 12 enter free. Free parking available.

**LOCATION:** At the Allen County Fairgrounds. Take 309 E Exit, about 1+ miles from I-75 towards Kenton.

**DESCRIPTION:** This indoor market opened in 1976. Antiques and collectibles, new merchandise, and crafts are available from over 50 dealers. One snack bar and handicapped-accessible restrooms add to the amenities.

**DEALER RATES:** $35 per 10½' × 13' space per weekend; $55 per 20' × 10½' space per weekend. Advance reservations are required. Tables are available at $5 each per weekend.

**CONTACT:** Aubrey Martin, Manager, Lima Antique Show and Flea Market, 716 S Main St, Lima OH 45804. Tel: (419) 228-1050, Monday through Friday; weekends and evenings (419) 339-7013.

# MONROE
## Turtle Creek Flea Market

**DATES:** Saturday and Sunday, year round, also Memorial Day and Labor Day, and the Friday after Thanksgiving. Rain or shine.

**TIMES:** 9:00 AM-5:00 PM.

**ADMISSION:** Free. Free parking is available.

**LOCATION:** Just off I-75, Exit 29. Go west on Rt 63, right on Garver Rd. You can see the market from the highway.

**DESCRIPTION:** This flea market opened in 1992. It is held both indoors and outdoors and accommodates approximately 500 dealers during the summer and 300 dealers during the winter. From 7,000 to 11,000 people per weekend come here to shop. Items found here include tools, belts, zippos, furniture, wood products, soaps, gifts, collectibles, craft items, as well as fresh produce. There are a number of food concessions dotted around the market and handicapped-accessible restrooms on site. Wheelchairs and strollers are available in Aisle 3.

**DEALER RATES:** Inside: $35 to $45 for smaller 10' × 13' booths. Outside space: uncovered $12 per 10' × 12' space on the gravel, or $16 per 10' × 14' covered space per day. Reservations are required for indoor space, while outside space is given out on a first-come, first-served basis.

**CONTACT:** Darren Foster, Turtle Creek Flea Market, 320 Garver Rd, Monroe OH 45050. Tel: (513) 539-4497 or the main office (937) 223-0222. Email: turtle848@aol.com. Web: www.turtlecreeks.com.

# PROCTORVILLE
## Proctorville Flea Market

**DATES:** Friday through Sunday.

**TIMES:** 8:00 AM-5:00 PM.

**ADMISSION:** Free. Parking is free.

**LOCATION:** 1 Shade Dr. Near the Huntington East End Bridge, 2 blocks off Rt 7. Follow the signs.

**DESCRIPTION:** Open since February 1991, this market is readily accessible to the many travelers going through three states: West Virginia, Kentucky, and Ohio. It has 185 inside dealer spaces and 60 outdoor spaces. Dealers sell antiques, collectibles, produce, coins, stamps, books, ceramics, crafts and supplies, carpeting, tapes and records, electronics, new and used clothing, tools, lots of new merchandise, garage sale goodies, and more. There is a restaurant with clean restrooms on site. They are adding 40 covered outside spaces (at $3 through Spring 2000). The state is palnning to build a highway by-pass which will bring in more business.

**DEALER RATES:** $10 for a 10' × 14½' space for the weekend in the summer (May through August) and $15 for September through April; or $5 per day inside; $3 a day outside for a 16' × 26' space. Reservations are suggested for inside; outside is first come, first served.

**CONTACT:** Olen Sluder, Proctorville Flea Market, 187 Township Rd 1280, Proctorville OH 45669. Tel: (740) 886-7606.

---

**Mark It Right!**

The story is told here of the dish marked for "40" purchased for $40. The seller thought she did really well as she had marked it for 40 *cents*, not $40. The pleased buyer later told the seller that it was actually a rare dish worth $250!

---

# ROGERS
## Rogers Community Auction and Open-Air Market

**DATES:** Every Friday. Rain or shine.

**TIMES:** 7:30 AM on to midnight? There isn't really a closing time.

**ADMISSION:** Free, with plenty of free parking.

**LOCATION:** On SR 154, 8 miles east of Lisbon.

**DESCRIPTION:** This humongous market and auction has been operating on this site since 1955. A typical, local community-based market, it is mostly outdoors with over 3 miles of outside dealers under lights, and about 300 indoor traders under 90,000 square feet of roof. The 1,200 dealers sell antiques, collectibles, crafts, vegetables, fruit, meats and cheeses, the occasional alpaca or turtle, as well as new merchandise. On mid-summer peak weekends as many as 30,000 shoppers and browsers show up. There is a state park campgrounds nearby, and they have their own small restaurant serving plenty of homemade food, several good stands around the market and handicapped-accessible restrooms. The auction starts at 5:00 PM for eggs, produce, and miscellaneous items, and for poultry at 6:00 PM. You really have to see this one to believe it!

**DEALER RATES:** $13-$14 per 15' × 30' setup space per day. Reservations are required. However, if there is a vacant space available due to a cancellation, then it's first come, first served.

**CONTACT:** Manager, Open-Air Market, 45625 SR 154, Rogers OH 44455. Tel: (330) 227-3233. Fax: (330) 227-2074. Email: rogers@valunet.com. Web: fleamarkets.com/rogers.

# ROSS
## Stricker's Grove Flea Market

**DATES:** Every Thursday, year round. Except Thanksgiving and Christmas.

**TIMES:** 8:00 AM-1:00 PM.

**ADMISSION:** Free. Free parking is available on 25 acres.

**LOCATION:** On Rt 128, 1 mile south of Ross, near Cincinnati.

**DESCRIPTION:** This indoor/outdoor market began July 1977 and hosts 50 to 100 dealers. There are 100 spaces under roof. Among the merchandise for sale are mostly antiques and interesting collectibles, crafts, and fresh produce. In the winter the market is held in a heated hall; in the summer it is held outdoors under covered pavilions, on the grounds of a privately owned amusement park. There is a snack concession open during the market.

**DEALER RATES:** $12 for two tables (furnished) and setup space per day. Reservations are required for indoor selling in winter; first come, first served in summer.

**CONTACT:** Gladys Jordan, 9468 Reading Rd, Cincinnati OH 45215-3420. Tel: (513) 733-5885.

# SOUTH AMHERST
## Jamie's Flea Market

**DATES:** Every Wednesday and Saturday, year round. Rain or shine.

**TIMES:** 8:00 AM-4:00 PM.

**ADMISSION:** Free. Free parking.

**LOCATION:** On Rt 113, ½ mile west of Rt 58, 30 miles west of Cleveland.

**DESCRIPTION:** This market, opened around 1970, has 200 permanent dealers indoors and an average of 400 transient dealers outdoors. All types of goods are available here, both new and used, including books, tools, crystal, china, silver, glassware, jewelry, coins, stamps, handmade goods, baseball cards, floral displays, greenhouse plants and garden supplies, candles, Hummels and Goebbels collector plates, Amish crafts, clocks, lamps, music boxes, clothes, etc. One shopper even reported seeing a kitchen sink here ($50)! Claimed to be the largest and the oldest in Northeast Ohio, average daily attendance has been put at 6,000 in the summer and 2,500 in the winter. An annual Christmas special is held on the first Sunday in December from 10:00 AM-4:00 PM. Fresh farm produce featuring German, Amish, and American specialties are conveniently located for the hungry shopper. More variety of foods is available including bread, health food stands, candy and nuts. Food concessions and restrooms add to the amenities.

**DEALER RATES:** $24-$26 per 10' × 12' space indoors, $10 per 10' × 15' space per day outdoors. There is a waiting list for indoors; outdoors first come, first served.

**CONTACT:** Jamie's Flea Market, PO Box 183, Amherst OH 44001-0183. Day of show call Lolita Mock at: (440) 986-4402.

# SPRINGFIELD
## Springfield Antique Show and Flea Market
**DATES:** Friday through Sunday, usually the third weekend of every month except July. May and September shows are Extravaganzas. Call for specific dates.

**TIMES:** Regular shows Friday 5:00 pm-8:00 pm, Extravaganza Fridays 12:00 PM-6:00 PM. Saturday 8:00 AM-5:00 PM, Sunday 9:00 AM-4:00 PM.

**LOCATION:** Clark County Fairgrounds, next to Exit 59 off I-70.

**ADMISSION:** $2. Extravaganzas $3. Parking is free.

**DESCRIPTION:** Started in 1971, this market attracts 1,500 dealers in summer and 600 indoors in winter selling quality antiques, collectibles, handmade craft items, and new merchandise. Several snack bars and handicapped-accessible restrooms add to the amenities.

**DEALER RATES:** Reserved asphalt spaces 15' × 20' are $30 per weekend; grass spaces 14' × 30' are $45 per weekend. First come, first served spaces $20 per day. Extravaganza rates: asphalt $45, grass $70 per weekend. For other building and long-term rates call. Reservations are required.

**CONTACT:** Steve and Barbara Jenkins, Managers, PO Box 2429, Springfield OH 45501-2429. Tel: (937) 325-0053.

# TIFFIN
## Tiffin Flea Market
**DATES:** Two shows May and October; one weekend each month, June through September. Call for exact dates. Generally the same weekend each time. 2000: May 6-7, 20-21 (first and last weekends), June 17-18 (3rd weekend), July 1-2 (1st weekend), August 19-20 (3rd weekend), September 2-3 (1st weekend), October 7-8, 21-22 ( 1st and 3rd weekends).

**TIMES:** 9:00 AM-4:00 PM.

**ADMISSION:** Free. Plenty of free parking.

**LOCATION:** Seneca County Fairgrounds, Hopewell Ave. Take SR 53 to Euclid Ave, then turn west; or, take SR E18 to Wendy's, then turn right; or, take SR 224 and turn east at Wolohan's.

**DESCRIPTION:** Started in 1977 and sponsored by the Seneca County Jr. Fair Foundation, this market operates from May through October with an average of over 200 dealers selling all types of antiques and collectibles, as well as fresh produce, crafts, tools, clothing, old jewelry, old glassware, and new merchandise. Proceeds go to promoting the welfare of the Seneca County Jr Fair and its activities. Overnight camping is available on the site for $10 per vehicle. Plenty of food concessions (serving breakfast too) and handicapped-accessible restrooms add to the amenities. Sunday shows feature a dinner or barbecue put on by various organizations. July and August Sunday shows have Car and Truck Shows. Pets are discouraged.

The manager of the market, Don Ziegler, is a quadriplegic (from polio) who is around the market all the time. Do stop and say Hi! Without Don, there may not be a market. As June says, "He's the backbone."

**DEALER RATES:** $16 for the weekend, or $10 for the first day for a 10' × 10' space inside, additional day $8 if available, $2 for electric. Outside $8 per day for a 15' × 15' space, $2 for electric. Reservations are required for inside space only. Tables are available for a rental fee of $5 per table period; tables must be reserved in advance. Showers are available for campers.

**CONTACT:** Don and June Ziegler, Tiffin Flea Market, 6627 S TR 173, Bloomville OH 44818. Tel: (419) 983-5084. Email: fleamarket@tiffinohio.com. Web: www.tiffinohio.com/fleamarket.

---

**Pets**

Once a pet snake toured the market draped over his owner's shoulder. As he was upsetting too many people, he had to leave.

---

# URBANA
## Urbana Antiques and Flea Market

**DATES:** Saturday and Sunday, first full weekend monthly. Not in August because of the Fair.

**TIMES:** 9:00 AM-5:00 PM. Winter hours are 9:00 AM-4:00 PM.

**ADMISSION:** $.50 adults, children free. Free parking is available.

**LOCATION:** Champaign County Fairgrounds, Park Ave.

**DESCRIPTION:** This very successful indoor/outdoor market, started in 1971, has a bit of everything available from over 150 indoor dealers alone. Weather permitting, from 100 to 200 dealers sell outside. There are antiques and collectibles, handicrafts and new merchandise, vegetables, meats, and cheeses. Refreshments and food are available on the premises. This is a growing market, full of very good antiques and collectibles. There are three heated buildings full of dealers year round. One of the buildings is air-conditioned for summer.

**DEALER RATES:** $22 and up for a three 8' table setup per weekend. Reservations are required for inside sellers. This market is more than willing to work with their dealers.

**CONTACT:** Elizabeth and Steve Goddard, Urbana Antiques and Flea Market, 934 Amherst Dr, Urbana OH 43078-2212. Tel: (937) 653-6013 or (937) 788-2058.

# WALNUT GROVE
## Holmes Country's Amish Flea Market

**DATES:** Thursday through Saturday, April through December.

**TIMES:** 9:00 AM-5:00 PM.

**ADMISSION:** Free. Parking $1.

**LOCATION:** SR 39, 3 miles east of Berlin. Just about in the dead-center of Ohio, in the heart of Amish country.

**DESCRIPTION:** Opened in 1990, this market of 250 vendors in a 67,000-square-foot building with a paved outside area, sell everything from antiques to Amish woodcrafts, including lace, gifts, ironwork, furniture, jewelry and plenty more. There is a cafeteria which makes its own homemade ice cream in case you want a break from shopping, handicapped-accessible restrooms, and beat this: an escalator from the parking lot up to the market! The owners and manager of this market are quite considerate of their buyers as well as their sellers and plow their profits back into market improvements.

**DEALER RATES:** Outside: $6 per space. Inside: $10 per day or $35 for the weekend for a 10' × 10' space plus $5 for electric.

**CONTACT:** Ben and Laura Mast, PO Box 172, Walnut Grove OH 44687-0172. Tel: (330) 893-2836. Email: amishflea@valkyrie.net. Web: www.fleamasters.com/amish/index.html.

# WILMINGTON
## Caesar Creek Flea Market

**DATES:** Saturday and Sunday, year round, also Memorial Day, Labor Day, and the Friday after Thanksgiving. Rain or shine.

**TIMES:** 9:00 AM-5:00 PM.

**ADMISSION:** $.50 per person or $1 per carload. Free parking is available.

**LOCATION:** 7763 SR 73 W at I-71, Exit 45. Five miles east of Caesar Creek Lake State Park on SR 73. Located only 19 miles north of Kings Island Amusement Park on I-71.

**DESCRIPTION:** This flea market first opened in 1979. It is held both indoors and outdoors and accommodates over 600 dealers. From 12,000 to 14,000 people per weekend come here to shop. Items found here include antiques, collectibles, craft items, dolls, furniture, mattresses, RV equipment, shoes, boots, jewelry, Nascar collectibles, bridal apparel, engraving, tools, kitchen utensils, Indian jewelry, and more. Six indoor restaurants and several concessions outside serve the hungry. Handicapped-accessible restrooms accommodate other needs. Wheelchairs and strollers are available in the office in Aisle 3.

**DEALER RATES:** Inside: $46 to $54 for smaller 10' × 12' booths; $130 per 20' × 25' booth per weekend. Outside space: uncovered $14, sheltered $18. Reservations are required for indoor space, while outside space is first come, first served.

**CONTACT:** Louis Levin, Caesar Creek Flea Market, 7763 SR 73 W, Wilmington OH 45177. Tel: (937) 382-1669 or (937) 223-0222. Fax: (937) 223-0154. Email: turtle848@aol.com. Web: www.caesarcreek.com.

## OTHER FLEA MARKETS

We know or have heard about these markets, but have not personally contacted each one, as we have the markets with descriptions. If you plan to visit one of these markets listed below, *please call first* to make sure they are still open. Flea markets do come and go. While they were open when we went to press, they may not be later. We can't be responsible. *Call first!*

**Alliance**: Carnation Craft & Flea Market, 2025 W State, just off St Rt 62. Tel: (216) 823-1898 or 823-0744. Open Sat & Sun 9 AM-5 PM.

**Amherst:** Johnnie's Flea Market, 46585 Telegraph Rd. Tel: (440) 986-5681. Open Wed, Sat & Sun from May through Oct, 8 AM-5 PM.

**Ashtabula:** Bargain Mart Flea Market, 3729 Jefferson Rd. Tel: (440) 992-9060.

**Ashtabula:** Flea Country USA, 3501 N Ridge Rd W. Tel: (440) 998-3177.

**Ashtabula:** Tannery Hill Flea Market, 3908 Tannery Hill. Tel: (440) 998-6211.

**Barberton:** Fifth Avenue Flea Market, 29 5 St SE. Tel: (330) 753-5530.

**Barnesville:** East Main Flea Market, 511 E Main St. Tel: (740) 425-4310.

**Batavia:** Red Barn Market, 50 W Main St. Tel: (513) 732-0515.

**Bloomfield:** Bloomfield Flea & Farm Market, Rt 87, ½ mile west of N Bloomfield. Tel: (330) 876-7233 or (216) 685-9791. Open Thurs, 7 AM-3 PM.

**Bridgeport:** Chapter Square Flea Market, 68210 Belmont Ave. Tel: (740) 635-0090.

**Brooklyn:** Memphis Flea Market. 10543 Memphis Ave. Tel: (216) 941-5995 or (216) 572-3725. Open Wed, Sat & Sun from April through October, 6 AM-4 PM.

**Canton:** Olde Stark Antique Faire, Stark County Fairgrounds, 305 Wertz Ave. Tel: (330) 794-9100. Several weekends per year. Call for dates. Sat 8 AM-5 PM; Sun 10 AM-4 PM.

**Chesapeake:** Chesapeake Flea Market, 10917 Cty Rd 1. Tel: (740) 867-6355.

**Cincinnati:** Elmwood Trading Post, 6015 Vine St. Tel: (513) 641-4414.

**Cincinnati:** Peddlers Flea Market, 4343 Kellogg Ave. Tel: (513) 871-3700.

**Cincinnati:** Village Flea Market, 2095 Seymour Ave. Tel: (513) 351-3151.

**Cleveland:** Broadway Flea Market, 7640 Broadway Ave. Tel: (216) 341-0007.

**Cleveland:** Cloverleaf Flea Market Center, 7525 Granger Rd. Tel: (216) 524-3020.

**Cleveland:** Don's Garden Valley Flea Market, 7237 Kinsman Rd. Tel: (216) 341-1199.

**Cleveland:** Hopkins Flea Market, 12005 Buckeye Rd. Tel: (216) 752-0683.

**Cleveland:** Kinney Flea Market, 12512 Superior Ave. Tel: (216) 231-7227.

**Cleveland:** Memphis Drive-In Theatre, 10543 Memphis Ave. Tel: (216) 941-2892.

**Cleveland:** Variety Flea Market, 15301 Waterloo Rd. Tel: (216) 692-3532.

**Columbus:** Harvey's Best Little Market, 2697 Sullivant Ave. Tel: (614) 272-0182.

**Columbus:** Hilltop Flea Market, 2006 Sullivant Ave. Tel: (614) 274-3156.

**Columbus:** Southland Expo Center, 3660 S High St. Tel: (614) 497-0200.

**Cuyahoga Falls:** Oakwood Antiques & Collectibles, 3265 Oakwood Dr at Fillmore. Tel: (216) 673-4762. or 923-7745. Open Fri, Sat & Sun, 10 AM-5 PM.

**Dayton:** Berthel Briggs Flea Market, 3200 Oakridge Dr. Tel: (937) 268-7379.

**Dayton:** Brandt Pike Flea Market, 6123 Brandt Pike. Tel: (937) 236-0028.

**Dayton:** Eddie's Flea Market, 3521 Cornell Dr. Tel: (937) 223-8002.

**Dayton:** Forest Park Flea Market, 4444 N Main St. Tel: (937) 274-3983.

**Dayton:** Valley Street Flea Market, 1602 Valley St. Tel: (937) 222-1400.

**Dayton:** West 3rd St Flea Market, 930 W 3 St. Tel: (937) 461-3532.

**Dover:** Dover Flea Market, 120 S Tuscarawas Ave. Tel: (330) 364-3959.

**Franklin:** Schomy's Flea Market, 8862 Dayton Oxford Rd. Tel: (513) 746-0389.

**Fremont:** Fremont Flea Market. 821 Rawson Ave at Fremont Fairgrounds. Tel: (419) 332-1200. Open 2nd weekend of every month. Sat 10 AM-5 PM; Sun 10 AM-4 PM.

**Hartville:** Byler's Flea Market, 900 Edison St NE. Tel: (330) 877-6433.

**Jefferson:** West 40 Flea Market, 4280 US Hwy 40 W. Tel: (614) 879-5801.

**Lancaster:** Dumontville Flea Market, 980 Ginder Rd NW. Tel: (740) 756-4457.

**Lima:** Limaland Flea Market, 117 S Kenilworth Ave. Tel: (419) 999-6640.

**Mansfield:** Lincoln Center Peddler's Market, 995 Ashland Rd. Tel: (419) 589-7785.

**Marietta:** Rinky Dink Flea Market, 404 Fort Harmar Dr. Tel: (740) 373-4797.

**Medina:** Medina Flea Market, 735 Lafayette Rd, Rt 42S. Usually 3rd or 4th Sunday of month. Tel: (330) 723-6083. 9 AM-3:30 PM; early birds 6 AM.

**Navarre:** Navarre Indoor Flea Market, 2 Main St N. Tel: (330) 879-0252.

**Newark:** 11th Street Flea Market, 50 N 11 St. Tel: (740) 349-9179.

**Newark:** Union St Flea Market, 146 Union St. Tel: (740) 344-7774

**North Bloomfield:** Bloomfield Flea Market, 2211 SR 87 NW. Tel: (440) 685-9791.

**North Bloomfield:** Bloomfield Flea Market, Hwy 87, 1 mile W of N Bloomfield. Tel: (216) 876-7233. Open Thurs, 8 AM-3 PM.

**Oberlin:** East Oberlin Flea Market, 43433 Oberlin Elyria Rd. Tel: (440) 774-4312.

**Painesville:** Painesville Flea Market, 1301 Mentor Ave. Tel: (440) 352-7373.

**Perry:** Perry Flea Market, 4650 N Ridge Rd. Tel: (440) 259-2404.

**Piketon:** Southbound Flea Market, 1439 US Hwy 23. Tel: (740) 289-4151.

**Piqua:** Piqua Flea Market, 8225 Looney Rd. Tel: (937) 778-2299.

**Shelby:** Jerry's Flea Market, 209 N Gamble St. Tel: (419) 342-4353.

**Springfield:** Freedom Road Center Flea Market, 1100 Sunset Ave. Tel: (513) 322-5555. Every Fri, Sat & Sun 9 AM-5 PM.

**Strasburg:** Garver's Flea Market, 211 2 St NW. Tel: (330) 878-5664. Open Sun, 8 AM-5 PM.

**Toledo:** Flea Market, 3352 Lagrange St. Tel: (419) 243-1723.

**Toledo:** High-Level Flea Market, 523 Oak St. Tel: (419) 698-4481.

**Toledo:** Tom's Flea Market, 848 E Broadway St. Tel: (419) 697-4744.

**Warren:** Warren Flea Market, 428 Main Ave SW. Tel: (330) 399-8298.

**Washington Court House**: Washington Court House Flea Market, Fayette County Fairgrounds, 213 Fairview Ave. Tel: (614) 335-5856 or 335-5345 evenings until 10 PM. Monthly except July, call for dates. 9 AM-3 PM. Admission - $1/vehicle during summer months, otherwise free.

**Westerville**: 3-C Flea Market, 6950 Chandler Dr. Tel: (614) 882-5076.

**Willoughby**: Indoor Flea Market, 33180 Vine St. Tel: (440) 946-9726.

**Xenia**: Heartland Flea Market. 457 Dayton Ave. Tel: (513) 372-6699. Open Sat & Sun, 10 AM-5 PM.

**Zanesville**: Big Rock Flea Market, 5705 East Pike. Tel: (740) 872-4120.

# OKLAHOMA

## DEL CITY
### Cherokee Flea Market and Swap Meet

**DATES:** Daily, year round.

**TIMES:** 7:00 AM-3:00 PM.

**ADMISSION:** Free. Parking is also free.

**LOCATION:** 3101 SE 15th St, corner of SE 15th and Bryant.

**DESCRIPTION:** Said to be one of the oldest flea markets in Oklahoma, and at the same location for 33 years, this market has over 40 dealers selling everything from antiques and collectibles to garage sale loads, attic finds, furniture, produce, new, used, and old merchandise, VCRs, TVs, and whatever. A snack bar on premises serves breakfast, lunch, and other treats. They invite you to drop in to watch the domino games in the Domino Room of the snack bar.

**DEALER RATES:** $5 per outside table setup; building space starts at $45 and up per space. Reservations are not required. No peddler's license required as they are considered their own 8-block county.

**CONTACT:** KO Jose, 3101 SE 15 St, Del City OK 73115. Tel: (405) 677-4056.

## LOCUST GROVE
### Old Locust Grove Sale Barn Flea Market

**DATES:** Every Thursday. Weather permitting.

**TIMES:** Early morning until mid-day.

**ADMISSION:** Free. Parking is free.

**LOCATION:** East side of the grade school on the east side of Locust Grove. From the junction of Rts 82 and Scenic 412, it's 4 blocks north, 3 blocks west and 1 block south.

**DESCRIPTION:** Starting in the mid-1930s as a outdoor meeting, swapping, and visiting place, this market hosts 25 vendors in winter to 50 in summer selling musical instruments, tools, plants, antiques, collectibles, garage sale goodies, crafts, coins, stamps, cards, furniture, and "just about anything and everything." There are restrooms available, but no mention of food, aside from produce.

**DEALER RATES:** $5-$7.50 for 12' × 24' space outside. Some sheds are available for $6-$8. First come, first served.

**CONTACT:** Jerry Koelseh, HC 64 Box 100, Locust Grove OK 74352. Tel: (918) 479-5960 or 479-8257.

# OKLAHOMA CITY
## AMC Family Flea Market

**DATES:** Saturday and Sunday, year round.
**TIMES:** 9:00 AM-6:00 PM.
**ADMISSION:** Free. Free parking is available.
**LOCATION:** 1001 N Pennsylvania St.
**DESCRIPTION:** This indoor/outdoor market started in 1988 and has 600 booth spaces with over 250 dealers selling antiques, collectibles, baseball cards, coins, stamps, office supplies and furniture, new furniture, Indian art, garage sale treasures, 14-karat gold jewelry, and new merchandise among other things. Housed in a 135,000-square-foot building, with about 50 dealers spaces outside, this is probably the largest flea market in Oklahoma. Four concession stands selling Chinese and American foods and handicapped-accessible restrooms add to the amenities. There is a huge train exhibit taking up 1,000 square feet of space. They produce a TV show called Oklahoma Talent to showcase local talent here at the market. They are expanding their outside area to hold 300 booths on the south end of the parking lot.
**DEALER RATES:** $44 per weekend; $158 per month. Reservations are not required. Daily rates also available: $7 per day outside. New spaces in the outdoor market will be $5 to start with.
**CONTACT:** Nick Adams, AMC Family Flea Market, 1001 N Pennsylvania St, Oklahoma City OK 73107. Tel: (405) 232-5061.

## Mary's Ole Time Swap Meet

**DATES:** Every Saturday and Sunday, year round. Rain or shine.
**TIMES:** Dawn to dusk.
**ADMISSION:** Free admission and parking.
**LOCATION:** Northeast corner of 23rd St and Midwest Blvd.
**DESCRIPTION:** This market started in 1963. There are over 300 dealers selling both indoors and out. Lots of antiques, collectibles, primitives, and western curios complement an assortment of handmade items, produce, as well as new merchandise. Dennis has seen billy-goats to Rolls Royces sold here. One cafe and two concession stands provide eatables; handicapped-accessible restrooms provide relief. There is a Dodge City western town as part of the market where they hold music shows. It has a saloon, authentic old wagons and a jail among other buildings (of course, if the kids get rowdy...).

**DEALER RATES:** $5 and up for 12' × 20' booths, plus electric. No advance reservations are required.

**CONTACT:** Dennis Sizemore, Mary's Ole Time Swap Meet, 7905 NE 23 St, Oklahoma City OK 73141-1430. Tel: (405) 427-0051.

## Old Paris Flea Market

**DATES:** Every Saturday and Sunday, year round. Rain or shine.

**TIMES:** 9:00 AM-6:00 PM.

**ADMISSION:** Free admission and parking.

**LOCATION:** 1111 S Eastern Rd; access from I-40 and I-35.

**DESCRIPTION:** This indoor/outdoor show started January 3, 1976 and hosts 400-plus dealers selling everything from antiques, crafts, and collectibles to produce, meats, cheeses, and new merchandise. Close to a KOA campground and near the Baseball Hall of Fame. Four snack bars and handicapped-accessible restrooms add to the amenities.

**DEALER RATES:** $26.50 per 8' × 15' booth indoors per selling day. $12.50 for 10' × 20' outdoor space daily. Reservations are required by the Monday before the weekend requested. Monthly rate discounts available.

**CONTACT:** Brandi Duncan or Georgie Parker, Old Paris Flea Market, 1111 S Eastern Rd, Oklahoma City OK 73129. Tel: (405) 670-2611 or 670-2612.

# TULSA

## The Great American Flea Market and Antique Mall

**DATES:** Friday, Saturday and Sunday, year round.

**TIMES:** 10:00 AM-6:00 PM.

**ADMISSION:** Free. Parking is also free.

**LOCATION:** 9206-9244 E Admiral Pl.

**DESCRIPTION:** Opened in 1989, this market holds 500 dealers inside and up to 100 outside selling antiques, collectibles, glassware, jewelry, baseball cards, garage sale stuff, and more "from A to Z." There is an electronic message board with advertising messages for dealers! A cafe provides meals. There is a mall and a produce market section adjacent to this market open daily.

**DEALER RATES:** Reasonable rates vary according to location, size and length of rental. Reservations are suggested.

**CONTACT:** Ty Hogan, The Great American Flea Market, 9212 E Admiral Pl, Tulsa OK 74115. Tel: (918) 834-6363 or 492-3476. Web: gamarket.com.

## The Tulsa Flea Market

**DATES:** Saturday, closed during the fair and some holiday weekends.
**TIMES:** 8:00 AM-5:00 PM.
**ADMISSION:** $1. Parking is free.
**LOCATION:** Tulsa Fairgrounds at 21st and Yale.
**DESCRIPTION:** This indoor air-conditioned/heated market has been oper-
ated by the same family for 27 years. From 235 booths, their dealers sell
antiques, primitives and antique collectibles. Very little crafts or new merchandise. This is a dealer's paradise and people come from all over the
country to buy here. One snack bar and handicapped-accessible restrooms
add to the amenities. Described by a lot of dealers as "the best one."
**DEALER RATES:** $30 per space regardless of size; deposit required.
Spaces are approximately 10' × 12' or larger. Table and chairs are available
for rental. Reservations are requested.
**CONTACT:** Tulsa Flea Market, PO Box 4511, Tulsa OK 74159. Tel: (918)
744-1386. Office hours: Wednesday through Friday, 8:00 AM-noon, Saturday 8:00 AM-5:00 PM.

# OTHER FLEA MARKETS

We know or have heard about these markets, but have not personally contacted each one, as we have the markets with descriptions. If you plan to
visit one of these markets listed below, *please call first* to make sure they
are still open. Flea markets do come and go. While they were open when we
went to press, they may not be later. We can't be responsible. *Call first!*

**Adair:** Fleas 4 Sale, Hwys 28 & 69. Tel: (918) 785-4811.
**Adair:** 69 Flea Market, Hwy 69 S. Tel: (918) 785-2903.
**Afton:** Flea Trap, 1 N Main St. Tel: (918) 257-8191.
**Afton:** Shadetree, 102 SE 1. Tel: (918) 257-3428.
**Atoka:** Black Gold Flea Market, 1000½ East Ct. Tel: (580) 889-7113.
**Bartlesville:** Traders, 4017 Price Rd. Tel: (918) 333-8733.
**Eagletown:** Lasch's Flea Market, Hwy 70. Tel: (580) 835-7443.
**Edmond:** Buchanan's Antique Flea Market, 3200 E Memorial Rd. Tel:
   (405) 478-4050.
**Enid:** Enid Flea Market, 1821 S Van Buren St. Tel: (580) 237-5352.
**Fairland:** Fran's Flea Market, 110 N Main. Tel: (918) 676-3400.
**Gore:** Shady Deals Flea Market, PO Box 798. Tel: (918) 489-5345.
**Grove:** Ned's Antique & Flea Market, 3638 Hwy 59 N. Tel:
   (918) 786-4409.

**Grove:** Odds & Ends Flea Market, 5527 Hwy 59 N. Tel: (918) 786-7403.

**Idabel:** American Legion Flea Market, 16 & Indian St. Tel: (580) 286-9418.

**Jay:** Eucha Flea Market. Tel: (918) 253-8460.

**Jay:** Karin's Flea Market, Hwy 1059. Tel: (918) 253-8338.

**Jay:** R-U-Kiddin Flea Market, PO Box 264. Tel: (918) 253-8220.

**Jones:** General Store Flea Market, 204 W Main St. Tel: (405) 399-3532.

**Lawton:** Lawton Flea Market, 3701 SW 11 St. Tel: (580) 355-1292.

**Marietta:** D & V Flea Market, 705 SE 3 Ave. Tel: (580) 276-5594.

**Mead:** Mead Flea Market, State Hwy 70. Tel: (580) 924-7242.

**Moore:** Superflea Fleamarket, 2600 S Service Rd. Tel: (405) 794-2481.

**Muldrow:** Cowboy Red's Flea Market, Hwy 64 W. Tel: (918) 427-3131.

**Muskogee:** Ben's Flea Market, 3301 W 46 St S. Tel: (918) 683-3773.

**Okemah:** Okfuskee Trading Company, 15 W Broadway St. Tel: (918) 623-1510.

**Oklahoma City:** Flea Market Annex, 1015 SE 44 St. Tel: (405) 677-6100.

**Okmulgee:** Arrow Flea Market, 621 E 6 St. Tel: (918) 756-7113.

**Okmulgee:** KC'S Flea Mart, 1303 N Wood Dr. Tel: (918) 756-2715.

**Pauls Valley:** Swap Shop Inside Flea Market, 215 W McClure Ave. Tel: (405) 238-5065.

**Sapulpa:** Sapulpa Flea Market, 804 W Dewey Ave. Tel: (918) 224-4802.

**Shawnee:** Ole Shawnee Town Flea Market, 1 W Main St. Tel: (405) 273-5044.

**Tulsa:** B & C Enterprises, 4118 E 46 Pl. Tel: (918) 744-6523.

**Tulsa:** 21st Street Flea Market, 11666 E 21 St. Tel: (918) 437-6513.

**Tulsa:** Admiral Flea Market, 9401 E Admiral Pl. Tel: (918) 834-9259.

**Tulsa:** Four Corner's Traders Post, 1101 S 193 East Ave. Tel: (918) 266-7355.

**Turpin:** K/O Flea Market, Hwy 83. Tel: (580) 778-3339.

**Tyrone:** D & K Outlet, 102 S Residence St. Tel: (580) 854-6422.

**Wagoner:** Blue Jar Market, Rt 1 Box 237. Tel: (918) 462-3136.

**Wagoner:** Main Street Flea Market, 108 S Main St. Tel: (918) 485-5496.

**Wagoner:** Pestolite Road Flea Market, 1440 S Tyler Ave. Tel: (918) 485-9288.

**Wagoner:** Wagoner Flea Market, 127 S Main St. Tel: (918) 485-9098.

**Wister:** Wister Flea Market, Hwy 271. Tel: (918) 655-3208.

**Wyandotte:** Country Market, Hwy 10. Tel: (918) 678-2442.

# OREGON

## EUGENE
### Picc-A-Dilly Flea Market

**DATES:** Sunday shows throughout the year, generally two per month excluding July and August. Call or write for 1996 dates.

**TIMES:** 10:00 AM-4:00 PM.

**ADMISSION:** $1.50 per adult; children under 10 enter free.

**LOCATION:** Lane County Fairgrounds, 796 West 13th (8 blocks west of city center).

**DESCRIPTION:** Claiming to be "Oregon's First Giant Flea Market," this indoor show has been going strong since February 1970 and draws 400 dealers and 2,000 to 3,000 customers depending on the season, making it one of the largest flea markets in the area. Among the items available are antiques and collectibles, handmade crafts, sports cards, coins, clocks, records, Indian artifacts, plants, gold, silver, toys, new merchandise, and fresh produce when in season. Hot and cold lunches are available.

**DEALER RATES:** $17 per 8' × 2½' table and cloth and 1 chair provided. Reservations are recommended. Setup time begins at 8:00 AM on day of show.

**CONTACT:** Picc-A-Dilly, PO Box 2364, Eugene OR 97402-2364. Tel: (541) 683-5589. Phone open one week prior to each market or leave message. Web: www.fleamarketguide.com/or.htm#eugene.

## FAIRVIEW
### Fairview Flea Market

**DATES:** Saturday and Sunday, year round.

**TIMES:** 9:00 AM-5:00 PM.

**ADMISSION:** Free. Parking is free.

**LOCATION:** 22455 NE Halsey. From I-84, take Fairview Exit (207th St), left at Halsey, head east for about 1 mile, go through 223rd light. They are located on the north side of road.

**DESCRIPTION:** This market of 100-120 dealers fills 250 tables selling collectibles, Disney movies, antiques, primitives, computers and parts, groceries, new clothing, new and used items, as well as vendors selling and trading electronic games. There is an ATM on site, in case you need something badly. The inside concession stand serves "Carol's world famous Biscuits and Gravy," and there are outside vendors, and handicapped-accessible restrooms as well.

**DEALER RATES:** Table rent $10 each table per day. There are discounts for vendors needing lots of tables.

**CONTACT:** Jim Brittan, Owner, Fairview Flea Market, 22455 NE Halsey, Fairview OR 97024. Tel: (503) 618-9119. Email: info@fairviewfleamarket.com. Web: www.fairviewfleamarket.com.

# HILLSBORO
## Banner Flea Market

**DATES:** Fridays, Saturdays, and Sundays.

**TIMES:** 12:00 PM–5:30 PM.

**ADMISSION:** Free. Free parking.

**LOCATION:** 4871 SE Tualatin Valley Hwy, next to Banner Furniture.

**DESCRIPTION:** This indoor/outdoor market is said to be the oldest in Washington County. About 10-30 dealers sell all types of antiques, collectibles, tools, jewelry, and regular flea market fare. Coffee and snacks are available on the premises; restrooms are next door.

**DEALER RATES:** $15 per table per weekend (three days), $5 daily. Reservations are not required.

**CONTACT:** Betty Hansen, Banner Flea Market, 4871 SE Tualatin Valley Hwy, Hillsboro OR 97123. Tel: (503) 640-6755.

# MEDFORD
## The Original Medford Giant Flea Market

**DATES:** Monthly, Sunday only, varies each month.

**TIMES:** 9:00 AM–4:00 PM.

**ADMISSION:** $.50 for anyone over 12. Parking is free.

**LOCATION:** 1701 S Pacific Hwy in the Medford National Guard Armory. Off I-5 Exit 27. Coming from the south turn left on Barnett; coming from the north turn right. Follow Barnett to S Pacific Hwy, turn left. Go 2 blocks; the market will be on your left.

**DESCRIPTION:** Since 1971, this market has been held inside the Armory drawing 130 dealers filling the 184 spaces at the market. They cater to antiques and collectibles, but try to have something for all the 1,000 to 3,000 shoppers. There are concessions and handicapped-accessible restrooms available.

**DEALER RATES:** $15 per table or same size space. Reservations are an excellent idea as they are usually full. Wall spaces have electricity.
**CONTACT:** Dennis & Dee Nelson, The Original Medford Giant Flea Market, 1701 S Pacific Hwy, Medford OR 97504. Tel: (541) 772-8211. Email: nelson@ccountry.net.

---

### Now Who Was That?
Once a dealer tried to sell a coffin with a human skeleton in it, but it caused so many complaints that it was removed.

---

# ONTARIO
## Flea Mart

**DATES:** Friday thru Sunday.
**TIMES:** 9:00 AM-5:00 PM.
**ADMISSION:** Free. Parking is free.
**LOCATION:** 1414 SE 5th Ave. I-84 exit (Ontario) east side of freeway, 1 block from Staples Office Supply, on SE 5th Ave.
**DESCRIPTION:** Opened since 1998, this market is comprised of 20 permanent dealers in buildings and a bunch to 40 dealers outside selling "everything that's legal." Plenty of garage sale goodies, antiques, collectibles, and old merchandise. Food vendors offer sno-cones, tacos and burritos and the usual flea market fare, and there are restrooms when needed. Ladies, Uncle Bud is in need of companionship... Say Hi to Ray and Bud if you can find them.
**DEALER RATES:** Daily spaces $7 per day. 10' × 12' permanent booths with locking capability $100 a month.
**CONTACT:** Ray Miller, Owner, Flea Mart, 550 NW 3 St, Ontario OR 97914. Tel: (541) 889-2795.

# PORTLAND
## #1 Flea Market

**DATES:** Saturday and Sunday.
**TIMES:** 9:00 AM-5:00 PM.
**ADMISSION:** $.50, children under 12 free, seniors $.25. Parking is free.
**LOCATION:** At the D St Corral dance hall, 17119 SE Division St. From I-84 181st Exit, south to Division St, west to 17119 SE Division.

**DESCRIPTION:** Opened in 1989, this market hosts 150 dealers inside and out (in tents) selling antiques, collectibles, garage sale goodies, and some new merchandise. There are three food vendors and handicapped-accessible restrooms.

**DEALER RATES:** $10 per table per day. Reservations are not required for outside tent space. There is a waiting list for inside space. If you want to reserve, you must pre-pay for your space.

**CONTACT:** #1 Flea Market, 17119 SE Division St, Portland OR 97236-1238. Tel: (503) 761-4646.

---

**If I'd Only *Known!***

The owner once sold a painting for $75, only to learn it was worth $3,500.

---

## "America's Largest" Antique & Collectible Sale

**DATES:** 2000 dates: March 4-5, July 15-16, October 28-29. Watch for the same weekends in 2001.

**TIMES:** Saturday 8:00 AM-7:00 PM; Sunday 9:00 AM-5:00 PM.

**ADMISSION:** $5 per person, kids under 12 free, 12-17 $2. Parking is available (4,000 spaces) for $4 per vehicle.

**LOCATION:** Multnomah County Expo Center aka Portland Expo. Take Exit 306B off I-5.

**DESCRIPTION:** This series of shows, which began operation in October 1981, is certainly one of the largest in the country, filling 1,300 dealer booths in March and October, and an additional 500 in July, in an impressive 240,000 square feet of indoor selling space devoted exclusively to antiques and collectibles. It is held three times each year in March, July, and October, and is so successful that the promoter runs similar events in Tacoma and San Francisco. Three snack bars and handicapped-accessible restrooms add to the amenities.

**DEALER RATES:** $140 per 10' × 10' booth. Reservations are required well in advance of shows as they are sold out for the next 4 years in March and October. There is a lottery system to sell remaining spaces for the July show only.

**CONTACT:** Christine or Chuck Palmer, Palmer/Wirfs Associates, 4001 NE Halsey, Portland OR 97232. Tel: (503) 282-0877. Fax: (503) 282-2953.

# "America's Largest" Antique & Collectible Sale

**DATES:** November 18-19, 2000. Watch for the same weekend in 2001.
**TIMES:** Saturday 8:00 AM-7:00 PM, Sunday 9:00 AM-5:00 PM.
**ADMISSION:** $5, kids under 12 are free. Parking is $4.
**LOCATION:** Oregon Convention Center.
**DESCRIPTION:** This is the eleventh show at this facility which began operation in 1990. The Oregon Convention Center is one of the nicest in the country, and filling 800-plus booths you will find an excellent assortment of antiques and collectibles. Food is available on the premises.
**DEALER RATES:** $140 for a 10' × 10' booth. Reservations are required.
**CONTACT:** Chuck Palmer, Palmer/Wirfs & Associates, 4001 NE Halsey, Portland OR 97232. Tel: (503) 282-0877. Fax: (503) 282-2953.

# "America's Largest" Christmas Bazaar

**DATES:** November 24-26, December 1-3, 2000. Generally the same weekends every year.
**TIMES:** Friday and Saturday 10:00 AM-8:00 PM, Sunday 10:00 AM-6:00 PM.
**ADMISSION:** $5 per person, $2.50 under 17, free under 12. Parking available (4,000 spaces) at $4 per vehicle. Friday December 5, admission is 2 cans of donated food for the Oregon Food Bank, or $5.
**LOCATION:** Multnomah County Expo Center. Take Exit 306B off I-5.
**DESCRIPTION:** This annual indoor 6-day show began in 1983 and currently draws around 1,000 dealers selling mostly craft items, gifts, with some new merchandise and some antiques and collectibles. The shows draws over 40,000 shoppers buying stocking stuffers and gifts for the holidays. Food and restrooms are available on the premises.
**DEALER RATES:** $310 per 10' × 10' space for crafters, with one 8' table and 500 watts electricity per 6-day show. Reservations are required.
**CONTACT:** Christine Palmer, Palmer/Wirfs and Associates, 4001 NE Halsey, Portland OR 97219. Tel: (503) 282-0967 or fax: (503) 282-2953.

# Catlin Gabel Rummage Sale

**DATES:** Annually, first weekend in November.
**TIMES:** All day.
**ADMISSION:** Free. Parking is available at $4 per vehicle.
**LOCATION:** Portland Exposition Center. Off I-5, near Jantzen Beach.
**DESCRIPTION:** This indoor 60,000-square-foot "rummage sale" has been held annually since 1943 by the Catlin Gabel School, and certainly ranks

among the largest markets of its type in the state of Oregon, with an average of over 6,000 shoppers attending. Material is donated locally and ranges from antiques and collectibles to books, hardware, furniture and even some new merchandise. In 1998 they sold a car, motorcycle and a 17' sailboat! In the past, they've sold a beer truck and a horse. A most unusual sale. This place is considered a treasure trove of goodies. Imagine, it takes 15-20 semi-trucks to deliver the goods to the Expo Center. Food is served on the premises.

**DEALER RATES:** All merchandise is donated. No independent dealers are admitted.

**CONTACT:** Catlin Gabel School, 8825 SW Barnes Rd, Portland OR 97225-6599. Tel: (503) 297-1894.

## PORTLAND-TUALATIN
### Sandy Barr's Flea Market

**DATES:** Saturday and Sunday, year round.

**TIMES:** 8:00 AM-5:00 PM.

**ADMISSION:** $1; seniors and children $.50. Parking is free.

**LOCATION:** 17942 SW McEwan Rd. Off I-5, Exit 290.

**DESCRIPTION:** Originally opened in March 1969, this market moved in 1999 to its present location. There are up to 75-100 dealers selling everything: antiques, collectibles, office equipment, bulk food, shampoo, electronics, jewelry, dog clothes—you name it! There are Mexican and oriental snack bars, and handicapped-accessible restrooms on site.

**DEALER RATES:** Tables are $15 per day, $25 for the weekend. Booths are $75 per 10' × 10' space per weekend. Reservations are nice.

**CONTACT:** Sandy Barr's Flea Market, PO Box 17202, Portland OR 97217. Tel: (503) 639-3395 or 639-9896. Email: tpsandy@aol.com.

## SUMPTER
### Sumpter Valley Country Fair

**DATES:** Memorial Day, July 4th weekend, and Labor Day, usually Friday afternoon through Monday midday.

**TIMES:** 8:00 AM-5:00 PM.

**ADMISSION:** Free. Free parking is also available.

**LOCATION:** 400 SE Ibex St, the SVD Grounds. From I-84 or US 26, via Hwy 7, take first right and go 3 blocks to the parking lot.

**DESCRIPTION:** Originating in the yard at the Black Market Antiques in 1971, this event has grown to about 400 vendors during the Memorial Day weekend and stretches from one end of town to the other. The SVD Grounds, with modern restrooms and coin-op showers, hosts about 45% of the vendors. Items sold include antiques, collectibles, new merchandise, crafts, and some produce. There are plenty of food vendors selling a variety of goodies. For entertainment, there is Bingo, an old-time Fiddler's show, and tours on the old Sumpter Valley narrow-gauge, steam-powered railroad.

**DEALER RATES:** $2.25 per frontage foot for a space 20' deep/wide, minimum space of 12', plus $20 for City Vendor license. Reservations are required.

**CONTACT:** Leland or Nancy Myers, SVCA, PO Box 213, Sumpter OR 97877-0213. Tel: (541) 894-2264. Fax: (541) 894-2329.

# WALDPORT
## Seamarket

**DATES:** Daily.

**TIMES:** Weekends: 9:00 AM-5:00 PM. Weekdays: 11:00 AM-5:00 PM.

**ADMISSION:** Free. Parking is free.

**LOCATION:** Hwy 101 at 260 SW Arrow. Literally right on the highway.

**DESCRIPTION:** Opened in the winter of 1994, this admittedly little indoor/outdoor market houses 30 dealers inside and as many as want to set up outside. The inside dealers are generally there all the time selling antiques, collectibles, "junk," just about everything, according to Pauline. The garage sale goodies come in mostly during the warmer weather outside. As this market is located right on a major tourist highway running along the Pacific coast, not only do the tourists stop for the market, but the views are "stunningly gorgeous." What an enticement! There are food vendors on the grounds.

**DEALER RATES:** $80 monthly inside. Outside: $5 per day during the week, $10 per day weekends. Reservations are a good idea if you want inside space as there is a waiting list. Otherwise, set up outside!

**CONTACT:** Pauline Gates, 2240 Crestline Dr, Waldport OR 97394. Tel: (541) 563-6436. Email: pgates@harborside.com.

# OTHER FLEA MARKETS

We know or have heard about these markets, but have not personally contacted each one, as we have the markets with descriptions. If you plan to visit one of these markets listed below, *please call first* to make sure they are still open. Flea markets do come and go. While they were open when we went to press, they may not be later. We can't be responsible. *Call first!*

**Central Point:** Country Swap Meet, 5844 Crater Lake Hwy. Tel: (541) 830-3146.

**Cloverdale:** Red Barn Flea Mart, 33920 Hwy 101S. Tel: (503) 392-3973.

**Eagle Point:** Eagle Point Rock Quarry Flea, 125 W Linn Rd. Tel: (541) 826-4477.

**Medford:** Southern Oregon Indoor Swap, 3620 N Pacific Hwy. Tel: (541) 773-9419.

**Ontario:** Flea Market, 1381 N Verde Dr. Tel: (541) 889-4570.

**Portland:** Portland Saturday Market, 108 W Burnside. Tel: (503) 222-6072.

**Sutherlin:** Donna's Flea Market, 116 E Central Ave. Tel: (541) 459-8236.

**Umatilla:** Umatilla Flea Market, 528 6 St. Tel: (541) 922-3013.

# PENNSYLVANIA

## ADAMSTOWN
### Renninger's #1 Antique Market

**DATES:** Every Sunday, year round.
**TIMES:** 7:30 AM-4:00 PM.
**ADMISSION:** Free. Free parking is available.
**LOCATION:** On Rt 272, 1 mile north of Exit 21 on the Pennsylvania Tnpk, between Adamstown and Denver in Lancaster County.
**DESCRIPTION:** This indoor and outdoor market has operated since 1967 and houses up to 500 dealers in a huge, indoor building. They deal in fine antiques and all types of collectibles. No crafts or new merchandise are permitted. In fair weather, outdoor dealers number from 200 to 400. Stands are in a grove and lot behind the main market building.
**DEALER RATES:** $25 per day all Sundays except five special dates, when the fee is somewhat higher. Reservations for indoor stands, if available, are required. No reservations are needed for the outdoor section. Apply at the market office.
**CONTACT:** Renninger's Promotions, 27 Bensinger Dr, Schuylkill Haven PA 17972. Tel: (570) 385-0104 or toll-free (877) 385-0104, Monday through Thursday; Friday through Sunday (717) 336-2177. Web: www.renningers.com.

### Stoudt's Black Angus Antique Mall

**DATES:** Every Sunday, year round.
**TIMES:** 7:30 AM-4:00 PM.
**LOCATION:** Rt 272, 1 mile north of Pennsylvania Tnpk, Exit 21.
**ADMISSION:** Free. Plenty of free parking is available.
**DESCRIPTION:** Over 31 years old, this Sunday market is part of a huge complex including Stoudt's Black Angus Restaurant, brewery, brewery hall, the Stoudtburg Village, and the Clock Tower Antique Mall (open daily except Wednesday 10:00 AM-5:00 PM). They hold a Beer Fest every weekend during August and every Sunday in October. Polka weekend is Labor Day weekend! Only antiques and collectibles are sold at the Antiques Mall by 400 permanent indoor dealers year round, and another 200 dealers set up in four outdoor pavilions in the summer. One source tells me that the Black Angus Restaurant serves the best steak dinner he has ever eaten and this man travels extensively! They built a Bavarian-style German village, called Stoudtsburg, with homes, an antique co-op, and five antique stores. The

downstairs of each unit is a shop, and the owners live above on the second and third floor—like European villages.

**DEALER RATES:** Contact Carl Barto for rates. Reservations are required.

**CONTACT:** Carl Barto, Manager, Stoudt's Black Angus, PO Box 880, Rt 272, Adamstown PA 19501-0880. Tel: (717) 484-4385. Or call Carl directly at (717) 569-3536. Clock Tower tel: (717) 484-2757.

## BENSALEM
### Farmers' Market at Philadelphia Park

**DATES:** Every Friday, March through December.

**TIMES:** 8:00 AM-3:00 PM.

**ADMISSION:** Free. Parking is free.

**LOCATION:** On Street Rd, 3 miles from I-95, or just off Exit 28 of the Pennsylvania Tnpk.

**DESCRIPTION:** Opened in 1982, this outdoor market accommodates 700 dealers selling antiques, collectibles, new merchandise and produce.

**DEALER RATES:** $30 per day for a 12' × 30' space for new goods, $10 per space for used goods. $80 per month for a reserved space. Reservations are suggested.

**CONTACT:** Flea World Inc, PO Box 387, Vorhees NJ 08043-0387. Tel: (609) 795-8393.

## COLLEGEVILLE
### Power House Antique and Flea Market

**DATES:** Every Sunday.

**TIMES:** 9:00 AM-5:00 PM.

**ADMISSION:** Free. Free parking available.

**LOCATION:** On Rt 29 N. From Philadelphia: take Rt 422 west to Collegeville, then north on Rt 29. From Reading: take Rt 422 east to Collegeville, then north on Rt 29.

**DESCRIPTION:** This indoor market has been functioning since 1970 in an old power house, and currently holds approximately 50 dealers who sell many antique items, a range of collectibles including coins, baseball cards, books, and jewelry, as well as new merchandise and crafts. Food is not served on the premises, although restrooms are available.

**DEALER RATES:** $15 for a 9' × 12' space. Reservations are required, and rates for larger spaces are available on request.

**CONTACT:** Janet McDonnell, 45 First Ave, Collegeville PA 19426. Tel: (610) 489-7388.

# DENVER
## Barr's Antique World
**DATES:** Every Saturday and Sunday. Rain or shine.
**TIMES:** Saturday 10:00 AM-5:00 PM; Sunday 8:00 AM-5:00 PM.
**ADMISSION:** Free. Free parking.
**LOCATION:** 2152 Reading Rd. Take Exit 21 off the Pennsylvania Tnpk, take Toll Booth Service Rd to Rt 272 N (¼ mile).
**DESCRIPTION:** This indoor/outdoor market has operated since 1979 and currently attracts around 150 sellers offering a range of items including antiques, Country French furniture and accessories, furniture, paintings, oriental art, cigar labels, clocks, glassware, stamps, primitives, jewelry, quilts, tools, toy trains, postcards, and political memorabilia, as well as crafts. An auction room occupies the rear of the building with regular Monday sales. For items viewed on weekends, you can leave a 25% deposit as an absentee bid. There are special sale dates throughout the year. Food and clean restrooms are available.
**DEALER RATES:** $15 and up depending on number of tables for outdoor space which is unreserved; inside space also available. Call for rates and reservations.
**CONTACT:** Col Bervin L Barr, 2152 N Reading Rd, Denver PA 17517. Tel: (717) 336-2861.

# EDINBURG
## Michaelangelo's
**DATES:** Sunday, year round.
**TIMES:** 7:00 AM-4:00 PM.
**ADMISSION:** Free. Parking is free.
**LOCATION:** On SR 422, 5 miles west of New Castle.
**DESCRIPTION:** This indoor/outdoor market, started in 1971, boasts 200-300 dealers offering antiques, handmades, musical greeting cards, floral arrangements, collectibles, cards, gifts, produce, meats, cheese, and new and used merchandise. Food is always available in ground's concessions, Michaelangelo's Restaurant, and smorgasbord.
**DEALER RATES:** $7 and up for a 14' × 16' space outside; $10 and up for an 8' table plus space indoors. Reservations are not required outdoors, but are required for indoor selling.
**CONTACT:** Michael Carbone, Michaelangelo's, RD 1 Box 211, Edinburg PA 16116. Tel: (724) 654-0382 or 656-8915. Email: melott@icubed.com. Web: www.sbshow.com/PA/MichaelangelosRestaurantAndFleaMarket.

# EPHRATA
## Green Dragon Farmers' Market and Auction

**DATES:** Every Friday (except Christmas). Rain or shine.

**TIMES:** 9:00 AM-10:00 PM.

**ADMISSION:** Free. Thirty acres of free parking.

**LOCATION:** 955 N State St, 1 mile north of Ephrata; also, ¼ mile off Rt 272. Look for the dragon.

**DESCRIPTION:** Green Dragon began in 1932 and now has over 400 merchants weekly, including 250 local growers and craftsmen. Meats, fish, poultry, cheeses, and sweets are among the fresh produce available, and all types of antiques and collectibles may be found at the market. The auction offers a range of products from dry goods to small animals—a real down-home country affair for the whole family. Food is served in five restaurants and seven snack bars; restroom facilities are available.

**DEALER RATES:** $25 per 20' × 20' space, but rates vary by which building and what facilities are available. Advance reservations are required.

**CONTACT:** Larry L Loose, Manager, The Green Dragon, 955 N State St, Ephrata PA 17522. Tel: (717) 738-1117. Email: info@greendragonmarket.com. Web: www.greendragonmarket.com.

# FAYETTEVILLE
## Fayetteville Antique Mall

**DATES:** Daily.

**TIMES:** 9:00 AM-5:00 PM.

**ADMISSION:** Free. Parking is also free.

**LOCATION:** I-81, Exit 6 on Rt 30, 18 miles west of Gettysburg, or 4 miles east of Chambersburg.

**DESCRIPTION:** This market, located in four buildings, has 280 dealers selling mostly antiques, collectibles, cast iron, depression glass, books, toys, dolls, china, tools, postcards, primitives, furniture, and more! A snack bar operates daily. Outside setups are available. There are six to eight smaller buildings rented by individuals selling even more items.

**DEALER RATES:** Call for more information.

**CONTACT:** L L Dymond, Jr, Fayetteville Antique Mall, 3653 Lincoln Way E, Fayetteville PA 17222. Tel: (717) 352-8485 or 352-2515.

## Zern's Farmers' Market and Auction

**DATES:** Every Friday and Saturday, year round. Rain or shine.
**TIMES:** Friday 2:00 PM-10:00 PM; Saturday 11:00 AM-10:00 PM.
**ADMISSION:** Free. Free parking for 5,000 cars is available.
**LOCATION:** On Rt 73, 1 mile east of Boyertown.
**DESCRIPTION:** First opened in 1922, this market is one of the oldest and largest continuous farmers' markets in the country. There are five auctions on Friday and Saturday. Their 400 dealers, both indoors (300) and out (100), sell a vast variety of antiques, collectibles, Amish crafts, and all types of produce, meats and cheeses, seafood, baked goods, poultry, plants, yard sculptures, new and vintage clothing, new and used books, musical instruments, and whatever. You could probably furnish a house and clothe your family from the markets and auctions here—from hearing aids and glasses to kitchens, hats and shoes. There is a livestock auction weekly. Located in the heart of "Amish Country," this market is self-billed as the "World's Largest Dutch Treat." It was once voted "Best of Philly" by *Philadelphia Magazine*. There are food concessions on the premises.

Watch for the festivals, auctions and specials as well as the Garage Sale held the last weekend of the summer months, May through August. Check out their website for future specials as they have one generally every weekend.
**DEALER RATES:** Covered Flea Market: $30 per 8' × 9' outside space with 2 tables for Friday and Saturday. Midway: $25.00 for an 8' × 9' area with 2 tables. The fee covers both Friday and Saturday. Reservations are required. Garage Sale rates: table $20, each additional table $10.
**CONTACT:** Zern's, Rt 73 Box 279, Gilbertsville PA 19525. Tel: (610) 2461. Fax: (610) 367-2403. Web: www.zerns.com.

# GREENSBURG
## Greengate Flea Market

**DATES:** Sundays: April through October outdoors; winter indoors.
**TIMES:** Outdoors 7:00 AM-3:00 PM. Indoors 8:00 AM-3:00 PM.
**ADMISSION:** Free. Parking is free.
**LOCATION:** Rt 30 west of Greensburg, on the upper parking lot next to the Greengate Mall. From the turnpike take Exit 7 (Irwin), go east to market. Winter: basement of the old JCPenney store at the mall.
**DESCRIPTION:** Moved from Latrobe in 1991, this outdoor market has grown with their new space. They can accommodate 150 dealers and have come close in their first year. Their dealers sell antiques, collectibles, crafts,

produce, household goods, garage sale finds, coins, stamps, loads of baseball cards, baked goods, furniture, new merchandise, whatever. I am assured that the snack concession serves the "best hot sausage sandwich in Pennsylvania." People drive from all over just to have a sandwich! Found among the Tupperware and stuff brought in: a hanging salt in blue spongeware (very rare item), and two beautiful handmade quilts. Watch for the opening of the new indoor market in the basement of the old JC Penney store where 70 dealers will operate for the winter until the outdoor market starts again.

**DEALER RATES:** Outdoors: $15 for a 21' × 14' space, $9 for a 11' × 16' space. Spaces always available on Sunday mornings. Indoors: $16-$25 with varied sizes available. Dealers supply their own tables.

**CONTACT:** Carol J Craig, 214 Kenneth St, Greensburg PA 15601-1946. Tel: (724) 837-6881 evenings.

## Hanna's Town

**DATES:** Second weekend Sunday and the previous Saturday afternoon of the month from May through September.

**TIMES:** Daybreak to 4:00 PM.

**ADMISSION:** Free. Parking is $2.

**LOCATION:** Westmoreland County Historical Society, 951 Old Salem Rd. Just 3 miles north of Greensburg between Rts 119 and 819.

**DESCRIPTION:** Founded in 1974, this popular strictly antiques and collectibles market has 275 dealers selling on a wide-open grassy field. This historic site has a recreated 1773 log courthouse tavern, more log buildings, a fort, and an archaeological site. Ten snack bars will keep you energized and raring for more shopping. Their restrooms just may come in handy. Keep an eye out for the hot air balloons from a nearby business; they fly up in the mornings.

**DEALER RATES:** $30 per 24' × 20' space. Reservations are not required. There is a season pass rate for vendors wishing to sell the entire season.

**CONTACT:** Westmoreland County Historical Society, 951 Old Salem Rd, Greensburg PA 15601. Tel: (724) 836-1800. Fax: (724) 836-1653. Email: history@wchspa.com.

**Advance Planning**

When the market was about 10 years old, they had so many cars cramming every available inch of road that it created one serious traffic headache. So bad was it, that the state police flew over the market in a helicopter and through a bullhorn requested the presence immediately of the owners of said event to meet a police car at a specific location. Gulp.

Things were sorted out with the police. Now the traffic runs smoothly and the market has plenty of parking space on two large hillsides.

# HAZEN
## Warsaw Township Volunteer Fire Company Flea Market

**DATES:** First Sunday of the month and preceding Saturday (even if it isn't the same month, i.e. July 31, August 1), May through October.

**TIMES:** Daybreak to around 4:00 PM, depending on weather.

**ADMISSION:** Free. $2 to park.

**LOCATION:** On Rt 28, ½ mile north of Hazen. Take I-80 to Exit 14, then north 6 miles on Rt 28. Located in northwest Pennsylvania near Brookville, Brockway and Dubois. Only 80 miles from the Ohio state line.

**DESCRIPTION:** This extremely successful outdoor market began in the early 1970s as a fundraiser for the fire house. They average 450 dealers selling a majority of antiques and collectibles, as well as farm produce and a few new items, mostly t-shirts and tools. This is truly a great place to find treasures. A violin went for $2,000. One customer was seen walking around with a boa constrictor around her neck. It is quite common for out-of-state dealers to fly to this area several times during the year, stock up on antiques, store them, then return later with a truck to collect their booty. Because of the success of this market, area motels and hotels have expanded to accommodate the influx of traffic. On the day of the flea market, the entire area becomes a giant yard sale. If you are a true-blue hunter of treasures and bargains, come in on Saturday when the dealers start setting up and start hunting. Food and toilet facilities are available.

**DEALER RATES:** $15 for 18' × 24' space outdoors. Call for reservation information. Dealers get discounts at local area hotels and motels. Just ask. All dealers must have a Pennsylvania sales tax number.

**CONTACT:** Warsaw Township Volunteer Fire Co, RD5 Box 146, Brookville PA 15825. Call the Fire Hall at (814) 328-2528 or Clyde at (814) 328-2536.

## Be Specific

An out-of-state dealer asked the price of a butter churn and butter maker dish. "Two-fifty each." Thinking that $250 each was a bit steep, he continued browsing. The next buyer admired the pair and asked the price. "Five bucks for the pair." They were sold on the spot.

Later the dealer told Clyde that he really would have paid $250 each for the items; they were more than worth it.

## Get Smart!

One woman held up a dish she was selling and asked fellow dealers what they thought it was worth, as she had it marked for $10. The others consulted and said it was a very good, expensive dish. The dealer promptly raised the price to $50. No one bought it—yet. When she checked into the matter with experts, she found the dish was worth $1,200!

# HULMEVILLE
## Old Mill Flea Market

**DATES:** Thursday through Sunday, year round. Rain or shine.

**TIMES:** Thursday and Friday 6:00 PM-9:00 PM; Saturday 12:00 PM-9:00 PM; Sunday 12:00 PM-5:00 PM.

**ADMISSION:** Free. Free parking is available.

**LOCATION:** Intersection of Hulmeville Rd/Bellevue and Trenton Aves; 2 miles from Exit 28 on the Pennsylvania Tnpk (US Rt 1); 2 miles from I-95 (US Rt 1) Exit 28 for Penndel/Langhorne.

**DESCRIPTION:** This small, year-round indoor market started in 1971 in a large, 1880s' historic Bucks County grist mill. The market draws several hundred shoppers each weekend. A full range of antiques and collectibles is available, including dolls, books, china, textiles, jewelry, furniture, glassware, advertising, breweriana, photographica, pottery, etc. This place is a "haunt" for dealers and collectors, more so than the general public (who haven't caught on—yet), as the management buys out house contents and estates. No food is available on the premises. Restrooms are provided.

**DEALER RATES:** Currently there is no space available.

**CONTACT:** Kathy Loeffler, Old Mill Flea Market, PO Box 7069, Penndel PA 19047-7069. Tel: (215) 757-1777.

# KUTZTOWN
## Renninger's #2 Antique Market

**DATES:** Antique market every Saturday, year round. Extravaganzas in April, June, and September. Pennsylvania Dutch Farmers' market is open every Friday and Saturday.

**TIMES:** Saturdays 8:00 AM-4:00 PM. Pennsylvania Dutch Farmers' market is open every Friday 10:00 AM-7:00 PM.

**ADMISSION:** Free. There is an admission charge for Extravaganzas. Free parking is provided.

**LOCATION:** 740 Nobel St, 1 mile south from the center of town. Midway between Allentown and Reading on Rt 222.

**DESCRIPTION:** This indoor (outdoor for overflow) market has been in operation since 1955 and now ranks among the most popular markets in the Northeast. The market attracts approximately 300 dealers during regular weekends, and up to 1,500 during the Extravaganzas. A wide range of antiques and collectibles is featured along with craft items, new merchandise, and fresh foods including smoked and fresh meats, poultry, seafood, and baked goods. For the Extravaganzas, dealers are said to arrive from as many as 42 different states, as well as from Canada and Europe. There is no flea market on Extravaganza days.

**DEALER RATES:** $12 per 10' × 25' outdoor pavilion space per day, $10 for special outdoor section, during normal sale days. Call for rates for Extravaganzas. Reservations are required.

**CONTACT:** Renninger's Promotions, 27 Bensinger Dr, Schuylkill Haven PA 17972. Tel: toll-free (877) 385-0104 or (570) 385-0104 Monday through Thursday; Friday and Saturday call (610) 683-6848. Web: www.renningers.com.

# LEEPER
## Leeper Flea Market

**DATES:** Saturday and Sunday, from mid-April to mid-October, plus the holiday Mondays of Memorial Day and Labor Day.

**TIMES:** Dawn to dusk.

**ADMISSION:** Free. Parking is free.

**LOCATION:** At the intersection of Rts 66 and 36, 14 miles north on Rt 66 from Clarion, near Cooks Forest National Recreation Area.

**DESCRIPTION:** Open since 1975, this lively outdoor market averages 60-100 dealers (with 170 available spaces) selling just about everything.

Antiques, garage sale goodies, crafts, and new and used hunting and fishing supplies are among the treasures mentioned by an enthusiastic shopper who sent in this listing of her favorite market. Fresh baked goods are sold by Amish vendors on Saturdays. Fresh produce, mini-donuts, and authentic buffalo burgers are some of the vast variety of foods sold here. They are located near Cooks Forest Recreational Area and the Allegheny National Forest with plenty of camps and weekend getaways around them. On the holiday week July 4th, this market stays open for the entire week and is loaded to capacity with dealers.

**DEALER RATES:** $5 per day for 20' × 20' space, first come, first served. Find Don, the owner, at the Red & White Market located on the upper corner of the market area, daily until 4:00 PM.

**CONTACT:** Don or Helen, Leeper Red & White Market, PO Box 150, Leeper PA 16233. Tel: (814) 744-8811.

---

### The Bear Facts

This market is surrounded by woods. The dumpsters are kept at the lower end of the market away from the crowds. Every fall, black bears come out of the woods to check out the tossed-in goodies. Labor Day 1996 saw a packed market—of shoppers—when the bears decided to pay a visit. "What an audience they had!"

---

# LEESPORT
## Leesport Farmers' Market

**DATES:** The flea market is every Wednesday year round, and the first and third Sunday of each month from April through the first Sunday in December; the farmers' market is held every Wednesday, year round.

**TIMES:** Wednesday flea market from 7:00 AM-close; first and third Sunday 7:00 AM-2:00 PM; farmers' market from 9:00 AM-8:00 PM.

**ADMISSION:** Free admission and free parking.

**LOCATION:** One block east off Rt 61; eight miles north of Reading.

**DESCRIPTION:** This family run market, operating since 1947, currently has over 600 dealers spaces both indoors and out. The complete farmer's market, with a livestock auction on Wednesday, is complemented by the collectibles, jewelry, clothing, crafts and new merchandise available in the flea market. Many items are supplied by neighboring Pennsylvania Dutch merchants. Food is available on the market grounds.

**DEALER RATES:** $10 per 12' × 35' unsheltered space, no tables; $10 per 10' × 10' space with 8' table. Some spaces are reserved for the season. Otherwise, first come, first served.

**CONTACT:** Daniel "Woody" Weist, PO Box 747, Leesport PA 19533. Tel: (610) 926-1307.

# MARSHALLS CREEK
## Pocono Bazaar

**DATES:** Every Saturday and Sunday (except Christmas and New Year's Day if they fall on a weekend), and major holidays (Presidents Day, Memorial Day, July 4th, Labor Day and Thanksgiving Friday).

**TIMES:** 9:00 AM-5:00 PM.

**ADMISSION:** Free. Ample free parking is available.

**LOCATION:** On US Rt 209. Take Exit 52 off I-80 (1 mile west of the Delaware Water Gap toll bridge), then drive 5 miles north on US Rt 209.

**DESCRIPTION:** Located in the Pocono Mountains and started in 1983, this rapidly expanding indoor/outdoor complex currently supports 50 indoor dealers, 140 more under outdoor pavilions, and about 400 more located in an outdoor paved lot. The indoor market is known as the Pocono Bazaar, and the outdoor arrangements trade in a variety of collectibles, crafts, produce, and new merchandise. Food is available at a food court area with a picnic pavilion. Clean, modern restrooms are on site.

**DEALER RATES:** Antique/garage sale outdoor booths (no new merchandise) $10/day. $25-$40 for spaces depending on size and location. No reservations are required. Pennsylvania Sales Tax number required for vendors selling taxable items. Not required for one-time garage sale vendors or non-taxable items (like clothing).

**CONTACT:** Kevin Hoffman, Pocono Bazaar, PO Box 248, Marshalls Creek PA 18335-0248. Tel: (570) 223-8640. Email: office@poconofleamarket.com. Web: www.poconofleamarket.com.

# MECHANICSBURG
## Silver Spring Flea Market

**DATES:** Every Sunday of the year. Rain or shine.

**TIMES:** 6:00 AM-3:00 PM.

**ADMISSION:** Parking and admission are free.

**LOCATION:** 6416 Carlisle Pk, 7 miles west of Harrisburg on US Rt 11.

**DESCRIPTION:** This flea market, founded in 1969, is the largest in the area, with 700 to 1,000 indoor and outdoor dealers attracting thousands of visitors each Sunday. Here you'll find antiques, collectibles, crafts, farm goods, and new merchandise. "You can find anything at this market." Ten restaurants and snack bars quell any screaming munchies.

**DEALER RATES:** $12 per 10' × 10' outside space per day; $45 per 3' × 8' table monthly rental cost. First come, first served. There are some reserved outside spaces.

**CONTACT:** Alan Kreitzer, Silver Spring Flea Market, 6416 Carlisle Pk, Mechanicsburg PA 17055-2393. Tel: (717) 766-7215. Day of market call Anna Smith: (717) 766-9027.

# MENGES MILLS
## Colonial Valley

**DATES:** Every Sunday.

**TIMES:** 8:30 AM-4:30 PM. Special events last longer.

**ADMISSION:** Free. Free parking is available.

**LOCATION:** Colonial Valley Rd. Off Rt 116, 10 minutes west of York and 10 minutes east of Hanover.

**DESCRIPTION:** This market grew from a little flea market into a resort. It has 140 dealers indoors and more outdoors, covering over 140 acres. Antiques, collectibles, craft items, and new merchandise are offered. There is a haunted house for the six weekends up to Halloween. At Christmas, they really light up the whole town with 100,000 lights and have a variety of carriage and sleigh rides! They now have one building devoted to Christmas year round with animated scenes and characters among other goodies. They have a real camel (Bosco), and a petting zoo with white tailed deer for Christmas. Auctions are held occasionally. Bus tours frequently stop here. Handicapped-accessible restrooms are available.

**DEALER RATES:** $10 per table inside; $8 outside. Reservations are required for inside spaces.

**CONTACT:** Judy Phillips or Herb Sterner, Owners, or Betty Staines, Manager, Colonial Valley Resorts, Box 3561 Colonial Valley Rd, Menges Mills PA 17362. Day of show call (717) 225-4811. Fax: (717) 225-4403.

**Quick History Lesson**

This is the site of one of the oldest working post offices. Former President Richard Nixon grew up around here and was at the post office when he got the call to go to China, the first sitting president to do so.

They have over 60 Tennessee walking horses here. Many are trained for police departments all over the country.

## MIDDLETOWN-ELIZABETHTOWN
### Saturday's Market

**DATES:** Every Saturday. Rain or shine.
**TIMES:** Inside 8:00 AM-6:00 PM, but shop early! Outside 5:30 AM until ?—weather permitting.
**ADMISSION:** Free. Ample free parking is available.
**LOCATION:** 3751 E Harrisburg Pk, just off Rt 283, on Rt 230 between Middletown and Elizabethtown PA. Only minutes from Hershey Park and Amish country.
**DESCRIPTION:** This indoor/outdoor market opened in 1984 and claims to be the "largest indoor market in Pennsylvania" and home for 300-plus dealers indoors and hundreds outdoors. Items sold include antiques, arts and crafts and collectibles. New merchandise is also available. At the farmers' market there is always a large supply of fresh produce, bakery snacks, meats, a deli, candies, and sodas, along with the delicacies of 15 other eateries on the premises. They are totally air-conditioned.
**DEALER RATES:** $50 per month for a 10' space inside. Outside special: two spaces for $20. Consult management; reservations are sometimes required.
**CONTACT:** Rod Rose, Saturday's Market, 3751 E Harrisburg Pk, Middletown PA 17057. Tel: (717) 944-2555 or 944-9400. Fax: (717) 944-3232 or 944-1300. Email: info@saturdaysmarket.com. Web: www.saturdaysmarket.com.

## MORGANTOWN
### Clock Tower Plaza Flea Market

**DATES:** Friday and Saturday, April through December. Rain or shine.
**TIMES:** 7:00 AM until exhaustion.
**ADMISSION:** Free. Parking is free.
**LOCATION:** At the junction of Rt 23 and Rt 10 in mid-Morgantown.

**DESCRIPTION:** This market started in 1968 as The Market Place at Morgantown and changed its name in 1997 when the retail stores went independent. The outside flea market is held during the warmer months with dealers selling antiques, collectibles, craft items, and new merchandise. Many of the dealers specialize in antiques and collectibles. Two restaurants, several concession stands and handicapped-accessible restrooms add to the amenities.

**DEALER RATES:** $10 per 10' × 20' space outside. First come, first served for the outside flea market.

**CONTACT:** Clock Tower Plaza Flea Market, 2846-10A Main St, Morgantown PA 19543. Tel: (610) 286-0611.

# NEW HOPE

## New Hope Country Market

**DATES:** Tuesday through Sunday, year round, weather permitting.

**TIMES:** 7:00 AM-5:00 PM.

**ADMISSION:** Free. Parking is free.

**LOCATION:** 463 York Rd. On Rt 202, ½ mile south of New Hope.

**DESCRIPTION:** This outdoor market (formerly Country Host) was formed in 1970 and is now under new management. Their 30-70 dealers sell primarily antiques and collectibles including books, new and vintage clothing, coins, stamps, crafts, fine art, new and used furniture, jewelry and silver, pottery, porcelain, toys, and new and used merchandise. They are located in beautiful Bucks County in "antique" country in the "center of Lambertville, NJ and Lahaska, PA" with buyers from New York City and Philadelphia. There is a diner open during market hours next door and handicapped-accessible restrooms.

**DEALER RATES:** $5 per space with two large tables weekdays, $20 on Saturday; $25 on Sunday. Reservations helpful.

**CONTACT:** Jack Artz, Manager, New Hope Country Market, 463 York Rd Rte 202, New Hope PA 18938. Tel: (215) 862-3111. Fax: (215) 862-9107.

## Rice's Sale and Country Market

**DATES:** Every Tuesday. Rain or shine.

**TIMES:** 6:30 AM-2:00 PM.

**ADMISSION:** Free. Paid parking is available for $1.

**LOCATION:** 6326 Green Hill Rd, between Aquetong and Mechansville Rds, off Rt 263.

**DESCRIPTION:** This market is said to have started in 1857 selling cattle and farm goods, ranking it among the very oldest existing flea markets in the state of Pennsylvania (or in the USA for that matter). There are currently over 1,200 spaces each week at this indoor/outdoor event, selling "everything from A to Z" including antiques, collectibles, and fine art to new merchandise, fresh produce, meats, baked goods, and zucchini. Plenty of snack bars and concession stands feed the hungry; paved walkways and handicapped-accessible restrooms add to the amenities.

**DEALER RATES:** $25 per 8' × 3' table weekly; $100 monthly.

**CONTACT:** Chuck, 6326 Green Hill Rd, New Hope PA 18938. Tel: (215) 297-5993. Fax: (215) 297-8722.

# NEWRY
## Leighty's 29-Acre Indoor/Outdoor Flea Market

**DATES:** Saturday and Sunday, year round.

**TIMES:** Summer: 7:00 AM-5:00 PM. Winter: 8:00 AM-5:00 PM.

**ADMISSION:** Free, with ample free parking.

**LOCATION:** On old Rt 220 (I-99), take Roaring Spring Exit, turn left at light, go 1 mile; 7 miles south of Altoona.

**DESCRIPTION:** This show began 19 years ago and has from 60 dealers in the winter to 350 in the summer both indoor (130 tables) and out (575 tables) exhibiting antiques, collectibles, handmades, and new merchandise, as well as an assortment of yard sale items. Food vendors and a concession are on the property. This is a large, clean, well-managed market for the area and is located near the famous "horseshoe curve." They also have a large farmers' market across the street. There is a new sports shop in an 80,000-square-foot building, a golf range and miniature golf—just for fun.

**DEALER RATES:** $10 and up per 11' × 28' outdoor sales space. Indoor spaces vary in size and price. Reservations are suggested but not necessary. For walk-ins, the earlier you come the better the location for you.

**CONTACT:** Roger Azzarello, Leighty's Flea Market, PO Box 307, Newry PA 16665-0307. Daily information call (814) 695-5151. Weekends at the market call (814) 695-7520. Email: sacbud1@aol.com. Web: www.leightys.com.

# PHILADELPHIA
## Quaker City Flea Market

**DATES:** Every Saturday and Sunday. Rain or shine.

**TIMES:** 8:00 AM-4:00 PM.

**ADMISSION:** Free. Free parking nearby.

**LOCATION:** Tacony and Comly Sts, 3 blocks south of the Tacony-Palmyra Bridge. On I-95 N to Bridge St Exit, right onto Tacony St to 5th traffic light. From I-95 South, take Bridge St Exit, go left 1 block to Tacony St, left to the 3rd light.

**DESCRIPTION:** This market began operation in 1972 and currently attracts between 150 and 175 dealers on indoor and outdoor spaces selling a variety of items including antiques, collectibles, handmade crafts, fresh produce, and new and used merchandise. Quite a few "finds" have come from here (paintings, rare books, furniture, pottery, old jewelry), later to be sold at auction elsewhere for loads of money. Obviously, a good place to haunt. Food is served inside and outside, and restrooms are available.

**DEALER RATES:** Between $20-$25 for an outside space; $50 and up for inside space. Reservations are required in advance for indoors. First come, first served outdoors.

**CONTACT:** Jim or Joan Aiello, Quaker City Flea Market, 5001 Comly St, Philadelphia PA 19135. Tel: (215) 744-2022. Fax: (215) 535-0395.

# PHILADELPHIA/FT WASHINGTON
## Philly Big Flea

**DATES:** For 2000: April 8-9, August 12-13, November 11-12. Call for 2001 dates.

**TIMES:** Saturday 10:00 AM-6:00 PM, Sunday 11:00 AM-5:00 PM.

**ADMISSION:** $5; children under 12 free. Parking is free.

**LOCATION:** Ft Washington Expo Center at 1100 Virginia Dr.

**DESCRIPTION:** This show has over 700 dealers from 20 states selling primarily antiques and collectibles. This market is billed to become the "largest antique market on the East Coast." Food concessions and handicapped-accessible restrooms add to the amenities.

**DEALER RATES:** $90 single space, $180 double space. Reservations are required. This facility does charge $65 for electrical hookup.

**CONTACT:** D'Amore Promotions, 2125 McComas Way Ste 102, Virginia Beach VA 23454. Tel: (757) 427-7717. Fax: (757) 427-8888. Web: www.bigfleamarket.com.

# PITTSBURGH-NORTH VERSAILLES
## SuperFlea Flea Market

**DATES:** Saturday and Sunday.

**TIMES:** 9:00 AM-5:00 PM.

**ADMISSION:** Free. Parking is free.

**LOCATION:** 833 E Pittsburgh-McKeesport Blvd #1. At New Eastland Mall and Marketplace, just off Lincoln Hwy, Rt 30, less than 5 miles east of Pittsburgh.

**DESCRIPTION:** Opened in 1988, this market is part of a chain of markets scattered around the US. Mostly indoors, with 150 outdoor tables, the ratio of old to new is 70/30, making this a great place to cruise for treasures. A lot of garage sale goodies come in, as well as antiques, collectibles, clothing, crafts, new and used merchandise, furniture, jewelry, fresh produce, and even a specialty butcher shop. There are snack bars inside, food vendors outside, and handicapped-accessible restrooms.

**DEALER RATES:** $10 for outside space, $10 for aisle space with table and chair inside; daily $15-$20 depending on size and location, or weekend rates $25-$35. Monthly rates: $80-$200 depending on location and size. You can make phone reservations, however if you are not in your place by 8:00 AM you forfeit the space. Vendors should arrive by 8:00 AM weekends and can come Friday from 9:00 AM-3:00 PM.

**CONTACT:** Ed Williams, SuperFlea Flea Market, 833 E Pittsburgh McKeesport Blvd, North Versailles PA 15137. Tel: (412) 673-3532 or (412) 678-8050. Web: www.americanparknswap.com.

# PITTSBURGH-WILDWOOD
## Wildwood Peddler's Fair

**DATES:** Every Sunday, year round. Rain or shine.

**TIMES:** 6:00 AM-4:00 PM.

**ADMISSION:** Free. Parking on premises is available at $1 per vehicle; free parking is also available nearby.

**LOCATION:** 2330 Wildwood Rd. From Pittsburgh: take Rt 8 to Wildwood Rd towards North Park (Yellow Belt).

**DESCRIPTION:** This indoor/outdoor market has operated year round since 1972 on the site of the Old Wildwood Coal Mine. The mine closed in the 1960s. It currently draws between 350 and 500 dealers in 600 booths, depending on the time of year. A wide variety of merchandise including antiques and collectibles, unique crafts, tools, store close-outs, fresh produce, furniture, jewelry, clothes, baked goods, and sports items is offered here. They have grown substantially, having added 5 new rooms to the one-acre building, making a total of 300 indoor spaces, currently filled to capacity. Additional restrooms and another complete concession stand were added with the addition, making a total of two complete kitchens offering everything from homemade chili to cotton candy. There is a festive family atmosphere at this market.

**DEALER RATES:** Outside: $12 per 14' × 22' space, BYOT (bring your own tables). Inside: $18-$60 per space, with monthly discounts available. Sizes range from 6' × 11' to 20' × 20' in various buildings. Reservations are not required for outdoor space; they are for indoor.

**CONTACT:** Vince Rutledge, President, Peddler's Fair Inc, PO Box 248, Wildwood PA 15091. Tel: (412) 487-2200. Fax: (412) 487-4946. Email: wildwood@usaor.net. Web: www.wildwoodpa.com.

# QUAKERTOWN
## Quakertown Flea and Farmers' Market

**DATES:** Friday, Saturday, and Sunday, year round. Rain or shine.
**TIMES:** Friday and Saturday 9:00 AM-9:00 PM; Sunday 10:00 AM-5:00 PM.
**ADMISSION:** Free. Ample free parking is provided.
**LOCATION:** 201 Station Rd, ¼ mile south of Quakertown, ¾ mile east of Rt 309.
**DESCRIPTION:** Originally established as a farmers' market in 1932, this indoor/outdoor market has been in operation as a flea market since 1970. Things have been moved around in 1999. The flea market is now in a building that can hold 100 permanent vendors with 150,000 square feet of outside selling area for up to 400 dealers. There are several more buildings including a 115,000-square-foot Farmer's Building, a main building, as well as plans to add another 20,000 square feet to the market. Their dealers cover the gamut of antiques and collectibles, crafts, and new merchandise, as well as the traditional farmers' market fare. "Everything you can eat, wear or use!" They have plenty of restaurants, discount grocery stores, butchers/delis, bakeries and produce markets. Yes, they have food! They hold special events throughout the year with special seasonal events. Many of their vendors are second and third generations working the same booths.
**DEALER RATES:** $10 for 2 tables per day, or $15 per 16' × 20' tailgate area. Prime tailgate areas run $20 per day. $45 per 120-square-foot space indoors for three days. Reservations are accepted for outdoor space on a 4-

week advanced pre-pay basis. Discounts on rentals are given for reserved space. Indoor space rents on a week-to-week advanced payment basis and starts at $30 per weekend for a 10' × 10' space. Indoor space is rented on an availability basis and requires a space application to be completed with ID. Vendors are permitted access to the market on Wednesday and Thursday to stock and set up their stands from 8:30 AM-4:30 PM each day. The market is closed Monday and Tuesday.

**CONTACT:** John Chism, Manager, Quakertown Flea and Farmers' Market, 201 Station Rd, Quakertown PA 18951. Tel: (215) 536-4115. Fax: (215) 536-9019. Email: jchiz@prodigy.net.

---

**Whoa!**
This market used to hold auctions of livestock in the barns now housing the flea markets. One regular, Tex, attends this market with his cow. Once, he stopped a President from passing, blocking the road with himself and his companion.

---

# SCIOTA
## Collectors' Cove

**DATES:** Sundays.
**TIMES:** 9:00 AM-5:00 PM.
**ADMISSION:** Free. Parking is free.
**LOCATION:** Rt 33 and 209.
**DESCRIPTION:** Started in 1977 and self-billed as the "Largest Antique and Farmers' Market in NE Pennsylvania," this indoor market's dealers sell antiques, collectibles, garage sale goodies, and whatever else shows up. The market is known as another of those places where dealers scrounge for treasures. The building is 37,000 square feet on 38 acres. There are estate liquidators and dealers in the wholesale warehouses and transient dealers outside. The Country Cafe serves homemade meals and each of the five buildings has handicapped-accessible restrooms.
**DEALER RATES:** $10 to $50 per space.
**CONTACT:** Collectors' Cove, Ltd, Rt 33, Sciota PA 18354-0333. Tel: (570) 992-5110 or 421-7439 (business office). Fax: (570) 421-2783. Email: admin@covemarket.com. Web: www.covemarket.com.

# TARENTUM
## Flea-Tique at Bull Creek

**DATES:** Third Sunday of each month, May through October (and some Saturday afternoon sales, too).

**TIMES:** Daybreak to 4:00 PM.

**ADMISSION:** Free. Parking is $2.

**LOCATION:** 224 E 7th Ave at the Alle Kiski Historical Society.

**DESCRIPTION:** Opened in 1983, this market of 175 outdoor dealers specialize in just antiques and collectibles. Located on a large level field shaded by trees, this market makes a pleasant summer visit with the historic coal mine tours. The specialty of one of the four food booths is homemade perogies. Restrooms are on site.

**DEALER RATES:** $25 per 24' × 20' space. Reservations are not required, but season-long reservations can be made.

**CONTACT:** Alle Kiski Historical Society, 224 E 7 Ave, Tarentum PA 15084. Tel: (724) 224-7666. Fax: (724) 224-7666. Email: akvhs@salsgiver.com.

# WAYNESBORO
## 29th Annual Antiques and Collectibles Market

**DATES:** Annually, second Saturday in June.

**TIMES:** 7:30 AM-4:00 PM.

**ADMISSION:** Free. Free parking is available.

**LOCATION:** On Main St (Rt 16) in downtown Waynesboro, located in Franklin County, just 2 miles from the Mason-Dixon Line or 4.8 miles from I-81.

**DESCRIPTION:** This outdoor market began in 1971 and currently attracts over 35-40 antique dealers from five states, some of whom are said to have attended annually since the market's beginning. This market specializes in antiques and collectibles of varying types and is a great place for dealers to stock up. Food is served on the premises and there are handicapped-accessible restrooms.

**DEALER RATES:** $30 per 22' space along sidewalks. Reservations are required in advance.

**CONTACT:** Greater Waynesboro Chamber of Commerce, 323 E Main St, Waynesboro PA 17268. Tel: (717) 762-7123.

# WEST MIFFLIN
## Woodland Flea Market

**DATES:** Weekends. Rain or shine. Also Memorial Day, July 4<sup>th</sup>, and Labor Day.

**TIMES:** 6:00 AM-2:00 PM.

**ADMISSION:** Free. Parking is free.

**LOCATION:** 526 Thompson Run Rd, 1 mile from the Allegheny County Airport, 1½ miles from Kennywood Park and just 7 miles from downtown Pittsburgh.

**DESCRIPTION:** This indoor/outdoor market has been operating since 1962. It currently attracts between 250 to 500 sellers, and between 10,000 and 15,000 buyers. Antiques, collectibles, handmade and craft items, fresh produce, new merchandise and other items are sold. Food and clean restrooms are available on the premises.

**DEALER RATES:** Outdoors $10 per 10' × 23' space or 2 spaces for $15; indoors $10 per 8' × 3' table or 2 tables for $15; and garage rentals 10' × 25' at $100 per month. Reservations are required for indoor and garage rentals.

**CONTACT:** Bob Kranack, Woodland Flea Market, 526 Thompson Run Rd, West Mifflin PA 15122. Tel: (412) 462-4370. Fax: (412) 462-4334.

# OTHER FLEA MARKETS

We know or have heard about these markets, but have not personally contacted each one, as we have the markets with descriptions. If you plan to visit one of these markets listed below, *please call first* to make sure they are still open. Flea markets do come and go. While they were open when we went to press, they may not be later. We can't be responsible. *Call first!*

**Adamsburg:** Adamsburg & Community Fire Co, PO Box 92. Tel: (724) 523-2797.

**Barto:** Jake's Flea Market, RR3. Tel: (610) 845-8556 or 845-7091

**Beaver Falls:** Indoor Flea Market, 1410 7 Ave. Tel: (724) 847-9650.

**Bird in Hand:** Millcreek Market, 2557 Old Philadelphia Pk. Tel: (717) 299-9625.

**Blairsville:** Jonnet Flea Market, Rt 22W. Tel: (724) 459-0143.

**Carlisle:** Lee's Flea Market, 1446 Holly Pk. Tel: (717) 245-0677.

**Clarion:** Clarion Flea Market, Rt 322. Tel: (814) 764-3532.

**Claysville:** Claysville's Big Flea Market, 24 Varner Dr. Tel: (724) 228-5670.

**Covington:** Wild Turkey Farm Market. Tel: (570) 659-5683.

**Cranberry Twp:** Spot Light 88 Flea Market. Tel: (724) 538-4055.

**Drumore:** Jocky Lot II, 1130 Lancaster Pk. Tel: (717) 284-4965.

**Evans City:** Pioneer Flea Market, 121 Hawk Dr. Tel: (724) 789-9236.

**Honesdale:** Honesdale Farmers' Flea Market, 1839 Fair Ave. Tel: (570) 253-0452.

**Jeannette:** L & L Flea Market, Claridge Rd & Elliott Rd. Tel: (724) 527-2097.

**Johnstown:** West End Flea Market, 79 Fairfield Ave. Tel: (814) 536-1512.

**Jonestown:** Frogs Hollow Flea Market, RR3. Tel: (717) 865-0799.

**Knox:** Elk City Flea Market, RR 208. Tel: (814) 782-3134.

**Kulpsville:** Kulpsville Flea Market, 1375 Forty Foot Rd. Tel: (215) 361-7910.

**Lewisburg:** Route 15 Flea Market, Rt 15N. Tel: (717) 568-8080.

**Limerick:** Limerick Flea Market. Tel: (610) 489-3338.

**Lykens:** Lykens Valley Flea Market, 110 Main St. Tel: (717) 453-7474.

**Mansfield:** Mansfield Flea Market, 763 S Main St. Tel: (570) 662-3624.

**Mechanicsburg:** Silver Spring Antique & Flea, 6416 Carlsle. Tel: (717) 766-9027.

**North Versailles:** Warehouse Flea Mart, 1701 Lincoln Hwy. Tel: (412) 823-4748.

**Paxinos:** Paxinos Flea & Farmers' Market, SR 61. Tel: (570) 648-6232.

**Penns Creek:** Walter's Market. Tel: (570) 837-1050.

**Philadelphia:** Ontario Street Market, 2235 E Ontario St. Tel: (215) 288-7338.

**Philadelphia:** Big T Flea Market, 2600 E Tioga St. Tel: (215) 291-0280.

**Pittsburgh:** Woodland Drive-In Theatre, 526 Thompson Run Rd. Tel: (412) 462-4334.

**Sybertsville:** Hal's Antique Flea Market, Rt 93. Tel: (570) 788-1275.

**Tamaqua:** Tamaqua Indoor Market, 205 W Broad St. Tel: (717) 668-2556.

**Tannersville:** Pocono Peddler's Village, Rt 611. Tel: (717) 629-6366.

**Transfer:** Reynold's Drive-In, 3706 N Hermitage Rd. Tel: (724) 646-2786.

**Wind Gap:** Wind Gap Flea Market, 316 N Broadway. Tel: (610) 863-8534.

# RHODE ISLAND

## CHARLESTOWN
### General Stanton Inn

**DATES:** Saturdays, Sundays and Monday holidays, April through November, weather permitting.

**TIMES:** Saturdays 7:00 AM-3:00 PM, Sundays and holiday Mondays 7:00 AM-4:00 PM.

**ADMISSION:** Free. Parking is $1.

**LOCATION:** 4115A Old Post Rd between Rts 1A and 1. From New York: I-95 N, Exit 92 (Rt 2) 3 miles to Rt 78, 4 miles to Rt 1, go north 12 miles to Charlestown. From Boston: I-95 south, Exit 9 to Rt 1, South Charlestown Beach Exit. They are 35 miles south of Providence and 40 miles northeast of New London CT.

**DESCRIPTION:** There is space for 200 dealers, with Sunday being the big day, at this outdoor market started in 1967. It is located on the property of The General Stanton Inn, one of America's oldest inns. There is everything from antiques and collectibles to handmade crafts, vegetables and new merchandise at this market. There is one restaurant and one snack bar on the premises. They are also conveniently located between Mystic and Newport, so there is plenty to do in the area. They are planning a Christmas in July event. Watch for it.

**DEALER RATES:** $25 for a 15' × 20' space, $35 for a space under tent. Reservations are required. Canopies are available for $10 extra. There is security ($10 extra) for dealers who wish to leave their goods over Saturday night.

**CONTACT:** Janice Falcone, General Stanton Inn, Route 1A Box 222, Charlestown RI 02813. Tel: (401) 364-8888 or fax: (401) 364-3333.

---

**Drool**

One of their dealers found a $450,000 painting and another person found a $55,000 picture here. You never know!

---

## EAST GREENWICH
### Rocky Hill Flea Market

**DATES:** Every Sunday, April through November.

**TIMES:** 5:00 AM-4:00 PM.

**ADMISSION:** Free. Parking is $1.

**LOCATION:** 1408 Division Rd, corner of Division Rd and Rt 2. Take Exit 8A off I-95.

**DESCRIPTION:** This market has been around since 1960 and now attracts approximately 300-400 dealers with virtually all types of merchandise available including crafts, collectibles, fresh produce, and new merchandise. Food is available on the premises.

**DEALER RATES:** $17 per 20' × 25' space, corner spaces go for $22, smaller spaces are available for $12. Advance reservations are not required.

**CONTACT:** Gary Hamilton, Rocky Hill Flea Market, 1408 Division Rd, East Greenwich RI 02818. Tel: (401) 884-4114.

# PROVIDENCE
## Big Top Flea Market

**DATES:** Saturday and Sunday.

**TIMES:** 9:00 AM-5:00 PM.

**ADMISSION:** Saturday free, Sunday $.50. Parking is free.

**LOCATION:** 120 Manton Ave. Just one block from Rt 6, towards Olneyville.

**DESCRIPTION:** Opened in 1976 in a historic 1800s' mill building, this market of 100-150 dealers sells antiques, collectibles, garage sale goodies, produce, used general merchandise, new merchandise, and crafts. There is food on the premises, served by a snack bar.

**DEALER RATES:** $25 per 8' × 10' booth per weekend. Reservations are suggested.

**CONTACT:** Sully or Howard, Big Top Flea Market, 120 Manton Ave, Providence RI 02909. Tel: (401) 274-0060. Fax: (401) 464-8666.

# OTHER FLEA MARKETS

We know or have heard about this market, but have not personally contacted it, as we have the markets with descriptions. If you plan to visit it, *please call first* to make sure they are still open. Flea markets do come and go. While they were open when we went to press, they may not be later. We can't be responsible. *Call first!*

**Central Falls:** Depot Fleamarket, 309 Broad St. Tel: (401) 727-1051.

**Providence:** Flea Market at Eagle Square, 75 Eagle St. Tel: (401) 831-9771.

# SOUTH CAROLINA

## ANDERSON/BELTON
### Anderson Jockey Lot and Farmers' Market

**DATES:** Saturday and Sunday. Rain or shine.

**TIMES:** Saturday 7:00 AM-6:00 PM; Sunday 9:00 AM-6:00 PM.

**ADMISSION:** Free. Parking is free.

**LOCATION:** Hwy 29 between Greenville and Anderson, 10 miles from Anderson.

**DESCRIPTION:** Opened in 1974, this huge market hosts between 1,500 and 2,000-plus dealers selling everything, quite literally. To prove their point, their crowds average 40-60,000! "If we don't have it, you don't need it." Just some of the items sold are: antiques, collectibles, tons of produce, clothing, comics, cleaning supplies, pantyhose, pharmaceuticals, office supplies, cologne, stamps, coins, garage sale goodies, and other new merchandise. There are "lots of restaurants and snack bars" and clean handicapped-accessible restrooms on site. So popular is this place that they once had 40 tour buses at once!

Just as an aside, they have an Anderson exchange telephone at the front of the market, a Williamston exchange telephone at the back of the market and a Belton address. That's what you get for operating at the junction of three separate entities.

**DEALER RATES:** Inside: $10 for one day with a wooden table. Outside, pick a vacant, non-reserved space; one of the owners will tap you for $6 for the space and one concrete table for each day. Reservations are required for inside space only. Those spaces can be hard to get. You must reserve in person. Watch for their website.

**CONTACT:** Anderson Jockey Lot and Farmers' Market, 4530 Hwy 29 N, Belton SC 29627. Tel: (864) 224-2027. Fax: (864) 231-6927.

---

### ¿Que Pasa?

A group of tourists from Poland were visiting the market when one gent was separated from his group and got thoroughly lost. (This *is* a huge place.) One of the group was offered the PA system to call his pal to the office to rejoin the group.

That was cool. It seems there were other Polish visitors who also came to the office looking for their fellow countrymen!

---

# CHARLESTON
## Lowcountry Flea Market and Collectibles Show

**DATES:** Third Saturday and Sunday of each month, year round; except February, the second weekend. 2000: January 15-16, February 12-13, March 18-19, April 15-16, May 20-21 (at a different location), June 17-18, July 15-16, August 19-20, September 16-17, October 21-22, November 11-12, December 16-17. Call for specific dates in 2001.

**TIMES:** Saturday 9:00 AM-6:00 PM, Sunday 10:00 AM-5:00 PM

**ADMISSION:** $2 per person, kids free.

**LOCATION:** At Gaillard Auditorium, 77 Calhoun St, in Charleston, near Meeting and Calhoun Sts.

**DESCRIPTION:** This show has been operating since 1973 in the historic downtown area. Over 50 dealers offer antiques, collectibles, estate merchandise and handcrafts from indoor stalls. This is mostly an antiques and collectibles show. For your convenience food is available on the premises.

**DEALER RATES:** $85 per 10' × 10' booth per weekend. Reservations are required in advance.

**CONTACT:** Donna Garrett Kidd, 605 Johnnie Dodds Blvd, Mount Pleasant SC 29464. Tel: (843) 849-1949.

# COLUMBIA
## Barnyard Flea Market

**DATES:** Friday, Saturday and Sunday. Rain or shine.

**TIMES:** 8:00 AM-5:00 PM and later in summer.

**ADMISSION:** Free. Paved parking is also free.

**LOCATION:** Between Lexington and Columbia on Hwy 1. Just 2.3 miles from Exit 58 off I-20; 3 miles from Exit 111A off I-26.

**DESCRIPTION:** Built as a new market in April 1988, this collection of 12 red-tin-roofed buildings houses 552 spaces for dealers. The number of dealers varies by how many spaces each dealer will rent. They are usually full. The buildings are lit inside and out allowing late evening shopping in summertime. There are 75-100 dealer tables outside without cover. Four restaurants including a brand-new barbecue restaurant take care of hungry shoppers. Among the fares sold are antiques, collectibles, boiled peanuts, car stereos, t-shirts, sunglasses, hardware, fishing supplies, used appliances, fashion jewelry, handbags, clothes new and used, "and the usual generic flea market stuff." Also notable are air-conditioned restrooms and the Barnyard RV park next door. Their sister market is located in Fort Mill.

**DEALER RATES:** $10 per day for 4' × 8' tables undercover in a 10' × 10' space; $5 for 4' × 8' tables outside. Reservations are suggested as they do fill up fast.
**CONTACT:** Manager, Barnyard Flea Market, 4414 Augusta Rd, Lexington SC 29073. Tel: 1-800-628-7496 or (803) 957-6570.

# EDMUND
## Smiley's Edmund Flea Market and Open Air Mall
**DATES:** Thursday, Friday, Saturday, and Sunday.
**TIMES:** 8:00 AM-5:00 PM.
**ADMISSION:** Free. Parking is free.
**LOCATION:** From Columbia, take Hwy 302 south (9 miles south of the airport). From Lexington, off I-20, Exit 55, take Hwy 6 south to Edmund. Only 7 miles north of Pelion on Hwy 302.
**DESCRIPTION:** Opened in November 1996, this is another of Smiley's successful flea markets dotting the South. There are over 500 outside spaces, most with tables and many more under cover. Considering that many dealers take several spaces (and at these prices who wouldn't?) they generally have over 100 dealers outside and 40-60 inside selling almost everything imaginable including lots of garage sale goodies.
**DEALER RATES:** Outside: $3 per table, or 4 for $10. Inside: $5 per space. Reservations are suggested. There is a new full-service RV campground in the back with special deals for dealers who wish to stay. Watch for their website.
**CONTACT:** Tiger and Vikki Mangum, Smiley's Flea Market, 5910 Edmund Hwy, Lexington SC 29073. Tel: (803) 955-9111. Fax: (803) 955-3137.

# FLORENCE
## Florence Flea Market
**DATES:** Saturday and Sunday, year round.
**TIMES:** 7:00 AM-6:00 PM.
**ADMISSION:** Free. Parking is free.
**LOCATION:** Corner of Rts 327 and 76 at 301 N. Exit 170 off I-95; go south 5 miles.
**DESCRIPTION:** Open since 1980, this indoor/outdoor market of 400 dealers sells crafts, produce, new merchandise, and garage sale goodies. Two snack bars and restrooms add to the amenities.

**DEALER RATES:** $8 per 10' × 10' yard space, $10 per 10' × 10' open shed space, $12 per 10' × 10' space in the main building. Reservations are recommended. Office is open Friday for rentals.

**CONTACT:** Florence Flea Market, 4001 E Palmetto St, Florence SC 29506-4205. Tel: (843) 667-9585.

# FORT MILL
## Flea Market at Pineville

**DATES:** Friday, Saturday, and Sunday. Rain or shine.

**TIMES:** Friday 8:00 AM-4:00 PM, Saturday 7:00 AM-5:00 PM, Sunday 8:00 AM-5:00 PM.

**ADMISSION:** Free. Parking is free.

**LOCATION:** 3674 Hwy 51. Exit 90 (Carowinds Exit) off I-77.

**DESCRIPTION:** Built as a new market in June 1995, this collection of red-tin-roofed buildings houses over 416 spaces for dealers. The number of dealers varies by how many spaces each dealer will rent. The buildings are lit inside and out allowing late evening shopping in summertime. There are dealer tables outside without cover. Three restaurants including a deli, pizza place, and canteen take care of hungry shoppers. Among the fares sold are antiques, collectibles, t-shirts, sunglasses, hardware, fishing supplies, used appliances, fashion jewelry, handbags, clothes new and used, "and the usual generic flea market stuff." Handicapped-accessible restrooms add to the amenities. Their sister market is located in Columbia.

**DEALER RATES:** $11 per day per 10' × 10' space inside with electricity, $9 for a covered area. $6 outside for a table per day. Friday is half price. Reservations are required. Permanent warehouse facilities available. Office hours are also Monday 9:00 AM-12:00 PM, Thursday 9:00 AM-4:00 PM, and Friday 8:00 AM-4:00 PM.

**CONTACT:** Manager, Flea Market at Pineville, 3674 Hwy 51, Ft Mill SC 29715. Tel: (803) 548-1817 or 1-800-527-4117.

# GREENVILLE
## Fairgrounds Flea Market

**DATES:** Saturday and Sunday. Rain or shine.

**TIMES:** Saturday 5:00 AM-5:00 PM, Sunday 6:00 AM-5:00 PM.

**ADMISSION:** Free. Parking is also free.

**LOCATION:** 2600 White Horse Rd. From I-85 South, take the White Horse Rd Exit (Exit 44), turn right, go 1 mile to market.

**DESCRIPTION:** This market, opened in March 1990, hosts 800 to 1,000 dealers selling everything: some antiques and collectibles, lots of crafts and produce, garage sale goodies, some new merchandise, racing material, tools, pantyhose, and the occasional goat to chickens, rabbits, dogs and cats. Home-cooking and the usual snack bar fare feed the famished. There are plenty of restrooms, inside and out, just in case.

**DEALER RATES:** $8 under the shed, $6 outdoors, $9 for a 10' × 10' space inside. Reservations are required for all but a few outside spaces set aside for first come, first served.

**CONTACT:** Marvin Kelly or Monika Baker, Fairgrounds Flea Market, 2710 White Horse Rd, Greenville SC 29611. Tel: (864) 295-1183.

# LADSON
## Coastal Carolina Flea Market

**DATES:** Every Saturday and Sunday. Rain or shine.

**TIMES:** 8:00 AM-5:00 PM.

**ADMISSION:** Free. Free parking is available on 15 acres.

**LOCATION:** At the junction of College Park Rd and Hwy 78. Take I-26 to Exit 203 (College Park Rd); or take Hwy 78. Flea market is next door to the local fairgrounds. They are just minutes from the center of historic Charleston.

**DESCRIPTION:** This indoor/outdoor market started in June 1981 and now has over 500 indoor booths and 300 outside spaces available. It usually draws 400 to 450 dealers selling a full range of antiques and collectibles such as tools, jewelry, furniture, old and new clothing, baby items, pets and pet supplies, birds, as well as fresh produce, garage sale items and new merchandise. There are often local airbrush artists on hand for portraits. Computer portraits are also a draw. Their new air-conditioned/heated 100-seat restaurant, "Weekends" at the Flea Market, serves the starving shoppers.

**DEALER RATES:** $12 per 10' × 10' space per day inside. $6 per table outside. Reservations required for inside space; first come, first served outside.

**CONTACT:** Michael W Masterson, Coastal Carolina Flea Market Inc, PO Box 510, Ladson SC 29456-0510. Tel: (843) 797-0540. Fax: (843) 797-0541.

**What a Comeback!**

On Sunday, July 12, 1998, the flea market burned to the ground. Over 100,000 square feet of market and the merchandise of 250 vendors gone. The next day, 95% of their vendors, who had lost everything, as well as the owners pitched in to begin the cleanup. Within a week, they had reopened, filling 300 outdoor spaces.

July 11, 1999 saw their grand reopening in a new state-of-the-art 100,000-square-foot complex. They would like to thank everyone who helped them rebuild, as well as their loyal patrons.

# MYRTLE BEACH
## Myrtle Beach Flea Market

**DATES:** Thursday through Sunday, September through May. Daily, June through Labor Day.

**TIMES:** 9:00 AM-6:00 PM.

**ADMISSION:** Free. Parking is free.

**LOCATION:** 3820 S Kings Hwy, Hwy 17 Bus.

**DESCRIPTION:** This market opened in 1993 with 120 vendors in four buildings selling one building's worth of antiques, some collectibles, garage sale goodies, and lots of used and new merchandise. This is a well-lit, air-conditioned market with wide aisles, and a food court serving full meals with handicapped-accessible restrooms. Plenty of giveaways (vacations and show tickets), magicians strolling the market, loaner wheelchairs and strollers, hourly prize drawings, three times a week auction, a monthly antique auction, free blood pressure screenings every other Thursday, and scary ghosts and goblins (dealers in disguise) on Halloween.

**DEALER RATES:** $10-$25.50 per day depending on location of space. Monthly rates available. Reservations are suggested.

**CONTACT:** Myrtle Beach Flea Market, 3820 S Kings Hwy, Myrtle Beach SC 29577-4833. Tel: (843) 477-1550. Fax: (843) 238-2555.

**Market Notes**

They sell a hot sauce here that is so hot you have to sign a release to try it!

One dealer in '50s-'70s vintage clothing has a size 42 poodle skirt pinned up in her booth. It was used by a local male actor on stage.

# NORTH CHARLESTON
## All New Palmetto State Flea Market

**DATES:** Saturday and Sunday, year round. Rain or shine.

**TIMES:** 9:00 AM-5:00 PM.

**ADMISSION:** Free. Parking is also free.

**LOCATION:** 7225 Rivers Ave. Just off Ashley-Phosphate Rd on Rivers Ave.

**DESCRIPTION:** This market, opened in 1988, has 150 dealers in 300 spaces selling everything that you can ever think of: antiques, collectibles, a carpet outlet, new and used furniture, and typical flea market fare. They have some outside covered spaces. There is a new concession, the Palmetto Grill, on premises. There are handicapped-accessible restrooms as well.

**DEALER RATES:** $10 and up per day per 10' × 10' space with 8' table inside. Outside spaces go for $10 a space with 3 tables on a first-come, first-served basis. Reservations are strongly advised. There is security at the market.

**CONTACT:** All New Palmetto State Flea Market, 7225 Rivers Ave, N Charleston SC 29406-4610. Tel: (843) 553-8030 or 883-3091.

# NORTH MYRTLE BEACH
## North Myrtle Beach Swap Lot and Flea Market

**DATES:** Every Friday, Saturday, and Sunday.

**TIMES:** 9:00 AM-4:00 PM.

**ADMISSION:** Free. Parking is free.

**LOCATION:** Hwy 17 at intersection with Hwy 9.

**DESCRIPTION:** Operating since 1984, this market is full most of the time (it is a tourist area!) with hundreds of dealers filling 350 booths (200 lockable sheds) or under cover. There are several antique dealers, loads of collectibles, crafts, new and used merchandise, tools, and garage sale goodies. The mix is roughly 50/50 old versus new according to management. There is a food court area with handicapped-accessible restrooms.

**DEALER RATES:** $22 for yard sale space outdoors, $200 per month for a lockable shed building. Reservations are required one week in advance.

**CONTACT:** North Myrtle Beach Flea Market, PO Box 3467, N Myrtle Beach SC 29582. Tel: (843) 249-4701.

**Animal Tails**

One season, they had a monkey at the market riding a bike. Another time, a bear got loose and was found behind the market in a wild grapevine.

# PICKENS
## Pickens County Flea Market

**DATES:** Every Wednesday.

**TIMES:** 4:00 AM-2:00 PM.

**ADMISSION:** Free. Parking is free.

**LOCATION:** Hwy 183 W, 2 miles out of town of Pickens on Hwy 183 W.

**DESCRIPTION:** Operating since 1974, this market of 1,000 booths with 500-600 dealers in them sells antiques, collectibles, crafts, animals, new and used merchandise, produce, and almost anything you are looking for. There are food concessions and restrooms on site.

**DEALER RATES:** $5 per 10' × 12' outside space, $6 per 10' × 10' shed and space per day.

**CONTACT:** Pickens County Flea Market, 1427 Wahalla Hwy, Pickens SC 29671. Tel: (864) 878-9646.

# SPRINGFIELD
## Springfield Flea Market

**DATES:** Saturday and Monday. Rain or shine.

**TIMES:** 5:00 AM until afternoon, generally around 2:00 PM. There is no set opening or closing times; however, most people work during these times.

**ADMISSION:** Free. Free parking is available nearby.

**LOCATION:** 9113 Neeses Hwy. At the intersection of Rts 3 and 4, approximately 1 mile east of Springfield.

**DESCRIPTION:** This market evolved from an auction held at a livestock market and has been running as a flea market since 1958. The farmers would often bring along farming tools and "whatever" to auction off as well. Soon, the auctioneer, Oscar Cooper, decided it was time the farmers sold their own stuff and sent them off to the "yard" adjacent to the Stockyard. At first, it was slow going with only ten "dealers," but in the mid-70s this market blossomed turning sleepy Springfield into a lively town one day a week. The market moved to its current 35-acre location in 1983. It now accommodates between 750 and 1,000 dealers inside and outside, selling a varied selection of antiques and collectibles, fresh farm goods, and some new merchandise. According to its current owner, Oscar's son Henry, while there are many regular dealers, the "first-timers" cleaning out their houses generally bring in a wonderful variety of merchandise. Food is served by a concession stand and a convenience store is on the premises. Clean restrooms are available, and law enforcement officers patrol the grounds. It is said that many people come so early they must use flashlights to find their way to the bargains and treasures.

**DEALER RATES:** $5 for an open 12' × 12' space with table outdoors; $7 per 10' × 10' shed space with table. Advance reservations are not required.
**CONTACT:** Henry Cooper, Owner and Manager, PO Box 74, Springfield SC 29146-0074. Tel: (803) 258-3192.

# SUMTER
## The Market at Shaw

**DATES:** Every Friday, Saturday, and Sunday.
**TIMES:** Friday and Sunday 10:00 AM-6:00 PM; Saturday 7:00 AM-6:00 PM.
**ADMISSION:** Free. Parking is free.
**LOCATION:** 5500 Broad St Ext. Hwy 378 E, across from Shaw Air Force Base, 30 mi east of Columbia.
**DESCRIPTION:** Operating since 1988, this market of 63 tables, some under cover and others in the open, and plenty of field space has 50 or so vendors selling antiques, collectibles, crafts, furniture, books, fresh produce, garage sale goodies, all manner of livestock, a woodshop, gifts, and lots of new merchandise.
**DEALER RATES:** Field area, no cover: $2-$3 per space; uncovered tables $5 per day; monthly under cover $173 with electric and security. Reservations are required for monthly space, otherwise first come, first served.
**CONTACT:** Bob, The Market at Shaw, 5500 Broad St Ext, Sumter SC 29154. Tel: (803) 494-5500.

# WEST COLUMBIA
## US #1 Metro Flea Market

**DATES:** Friday, Saturday, and Sunday. Rain or shine. Wednesday wholesale market only.
**TIMES:** Friday 8:00 AM-6:00 PM; Saturday 7:00 AM-6:00 PM; Sunday 9:00 PM-6:00 PM. Wednesday 7:00 AM-12:00 PM.
**ADMISSION:** Free. Free parking is available.

**LOCATION:** 3500 Augusta Rd, on US Hwy 1. From I-26, take US Hwy 1 south to Lexington (Exit 111A South) approximately 1½ miles; from I-20, take US Hwy 1 (Exit 58) to West Columbia, 4½ miles.

**DESCRIPTION:** This show began in March 1980 and currently draws 800 dealers inside (in permanent stalls) and outside peddling antiques, collectibles, crafts, fresh farm produce, and some new merchandise. They are the oldest and "most popular" market in the Columbia area drawing between 5,000-15,000 per weekend depending on weather. There is even a vendor selling medical supplies—one wheelchair went for $2.95! This place is garage-sale heaven! Full of surprises. Food is available on the premises. Wednesday is open for a special wholesalers market only, open from 7:00 AM-12:00 PM. Only 5 miles from the state capitol.

**DEALER RATES:** Fridays are free—no reservations required; Saturday and Sunday $12 per day for covered stalls and $8 per open outdoor stalls. Wednesday wholesale rate is $25 per day or $60 by the month. Advance reservations are recommended for Saturday and Sunday at least a week to two weeks in advance.

**CONTACT:** Richard Hook, US#1 Metro Flea Market, PO Box 1457, Lexington SC 29071-1457. Tel: (803) 796-9294.

# OTHER FLEA MARKETS

We know or have heard about these markets, but have not personally contacted each one, as we have the markets with descriptions. If you plan to visit one of these markets listed below, *please call first* to make sure they are still open. Flea markets do come and go. While they were open when we went to press, they may not be later. We can't be responsible. *Call first!*

**Anderson:** Cricket's Flea Market, 502 Sayre St. Tel: (864) 226-0012.

**Charleston:** Thomas Gaillard Flea Market, 808 Melrose Dr. Tel: (843) 556-2263.

**Columbia:** Thieves Antique Flea Market, 502 Gadsden St. Tel: (803) 254-4997.

**Conway:** Conway East Flea Market, 1080 Hwy 501 Bus. Tel: (843) 347-1414.

**Gaffney:** Highway 18 Flea Market, 905 Shelby Hwy. Tel: (864) 488-1712.

**Greenville:** Fairground Flea Market, 2720 White Horse Rd. Tel: (864) 295-1183.

**Greenwood:** Greenwood Trading Post & Flea, 1428 S Main St. Tel: (864) 229-3791.

**Hartsville:** Open House Flea Market, 1624 S 5 St. Tel: (843) 332-8557.

**Hodges:** Greenwood Flea Market, 123 Dixie Dr. Tel: (864) 223-3045.

**Hollywood:** Hollywood Flea Market, 6325 Hwy 162. Tel: (843) 889-3007.

**Johnston:** Margie's Flea Market, 1194 Hwy 191. Tel: (803) 275-3142.

**Leesville:** Tradewinds, 3967 Hwy 378. Tel: (803) 532-4841.

**Myrtle Beach:** Northgate Flea Market, 4535 Socastee Blvd. Tel: (843) 293-6666.

**Myrtle Beach:** Motiana, 3820 S Kings Hwy. Tel: (843) 238-0825.

**Prosperity:** Prosperity Jockey Lot, 2221 SC Hwy 773. Tel: (803) 276-0084.

**Rock Hill:** Flea World USA, 766 Heckle Bypass. Tel: (803) 324-5333.

**Rock Hill:** I-77 Flea Market, 2697 Cherry Rd. Tel: (803) 329-5114.

**Ruby:** Jewel City Flea Market, 608 W Main St. Tel: (843) 634-6290.

**Santee:** Santee Flea Market, 7655 Five Chop Rd. Tel: (803) 854-3485.

**South Lugoff:** Kershaw County Farmers' Market, IH 20 & US Hwy 601. Tel: (803) 438-5488.

**Spartanburg:** Spartanburg Flea Market, 8010 Asheville Hwy. Tel: (864) 503-9026.

**St Matthews:** St Matthews Flea Market, 151 Bridge St. Tel: (803) 874-4327.

**Sumter:** Sumter County Flea Market, 2277 Myrtle Beach Hwy. Tel: (803) 495-2281.

**Surfside Beach:** Hudson's Surfside Flea Market, 1040 Hwy 17 S. Tel: (843) 238-0372.

**Travelers Rest:** Foothills Flea Market, 1131 N Hwy 25. Tel: (864) 834-2021.

**Walterboro:** Walterboro Flea Market, 415 Sniders Hwy 63. Tel: (843) 538-22664.

**Westminster:** Traders Junction Flea Market, 4265 S Hwy 11. Tel: (864) 638-0100.

# SOUTH DAKOTA

## MADISON
### Memory Lane Flea Market

**DATES:** The weekend before Labor Day, the last Friday, Saturday, and Sunday in August.

**TIMES:** 9:00 AM-dusk.

**ADMISSION:** Free. Parking is free.

**LOCATION:** Madison by-pass curve, south of Pizza Ranch or west of Prostrollo's Auto Mall.

**DESCRIPTION:** Started in 1995 as a revolt against "greedy market-charging," this venture has 27 dealers selling mostly classic antiques, rummage sale junque, collectibles, crafts and a bit of new merchandise. Although small to start with, there are 25,000 visitors attracted to this area as there are other events including a "threshing bee" going on. You can't get into town without passing the market, and the response of the dealers was "well-satisfied." There are food vendors on site as well as plenty of food in the surrounding area.

**DEALER RATES:** $45 plus electricity for 50' × 20' space. Reservations are suggested. A chain-link fence surrounds the grounds for security for dealers who wish to leave their goods overnight.

**CONTACT:** Cheryl and Doc Howard, Box 385, Howard SD 57349. Best time to call is between 9:00 PM and 2:00 AM—really! Don't even think of calling before 10:00 AM. Tel: (605) 772-5376.

---

### Looking Good?

One gal saw her display case and asked about glass eyes. No, Cheryl didn't have one; try the taxidermist. Apparently, she collects glass eyes. I'll bet she cornered the market.

---

### Gotta Have It!

Cheryl saw an old blanket trunk at an auction. It was totally hand-made, but it was obvious the guy couldn't draw a straight line as it was full of wiggly lines trying to match seams. She and Doc bid and won it for $5. She hauled it out to the market, and put $45 on it. A woman saw it across the parking lot while driving by, jumped out of the car and started scribbling a check.

---

# RAPID CITY
## Black Hills Flea Market

**DATES:** Saturday, Sundays and national holidays if on Friday or Monday, May through September. Rain checks given for days completely rained out outdoors.

**TIMES:** 7:00 AM-dusk, both days.

**ADMISSION:** Free. Plenty of easy parking is available.

**LOCATION:** 5500 Mt Rushmore Rd. Take Exit 57 off I-90 on US 16 W south of Rapid City limits.

**DESCRIPTION:** This indoor/outdoor market, which began operation in 1973, is located on the main highway to Mt Rushmore and therefore has high exposure to the many thousands of tourists who visit this national memorial annually. A lovely panoramic view of the Black Hills is among the many attractions of this market. There are currently an average of 150 dealers on hand selling antiques and collectibles, and there is a special arts and crafts section featuring locally made handicrafts. Some new merchandise is available, and among the food for sale is fresh produce when in season. This market operates on the concept that "Flea Markets are Fun!" and has invited the public to "Come out, enjoy the outdoors, and fly your kites" with them.

**DEALER RATES:** $11 per inside table (arts and crafts) per day; $11 per outside tailgate; $13 to $16 for an indoor booth. Tables are furnished. Eight-foot tables are available outside for $2 rental per day. Reservations are recommended for indoor booths.

**CONTACT:** Deborah Cooley, Black Hills Flea Market, 909 Francis, Rapid City SD 57701. Tel: (605) 348-1981 or (605) 343-6477.

## Sioux Falls Flea Market

**DATES:** Saturday and Sunday, first weekend of every month. No shows in June, July or August.

**TIMES:** Saturday 9:00 AM-5:00 PM; Sunday 11:00 AM-4:00 PM.

**ADMISSION:** $1 per person. Ample free parking.

**LOCATION:** Expo Building at 12th and Fairgrounds.

**DESCRIPTION:** This indoor market first opened in 1970. There are 250 dealers selling antiques, collectibles, arts and crafts items, as well as new merchandise. At least 70% of the items shown are antiques. The crowds keep growing every weekend and have more than doubled in size in this good, clean, smoke-free atmosphere. Handicapped access throughout the market is very easy as this is a large well-lit building with wide aisles. Food is available on the premises.

**DEALER RATES:** $30 per 8' table and space per weekend; $95 for 4 tables. Advance reservations are required as there is a waiting list.

**CONTACT:** Ed and Bonnie Benson, PO Box 236, Sioux Falls SD 57101-0236. Tel: (605) 334-1312.

## OTHER FLEA MARKETS

We know or have heard about these markets, but have not personally contacted each one, as we have the markets with descriptions. If you plan to visit one of these markets listed below, *please call first* to make sure they are still open. Flea markets do come and go. While they were open when we went to press, they may not be later. We can't be responsible. *Call first!*

**Belle Fourche**: Belle Fourche Flea Market, Community Hall, 6th Ave. Tel: (605) 892-4006. Usually first Sat & Sun of the month October-April except if Easter falls on first weekend, then it's second weekend. 9 AM-5 PM. 28 dealers inside, some outside. Antiques and collectibles, new and used merchandise.

**Madison:** Four Seasons Flea Market, 223 N Egan Ave. Tel: (605) 256-6696.

**Sioux Falls:** Cliff Avenue Flea Market, 3515 N Cliff Ave. Tel: (605) 338-8975. Open every day except Wednesday, 10 AM-5 PM. About 1½ miles south of Cliff Ave exit off I-90. Around 30 vendors selling antiques and collectibles, used merchandise, jewelry, used furniture, books.

# TENNESSEE

## CROSSVILLE
### Crossville Flea Market
**DATES:** Saturday and Sunday and Memorial Day and Labor Day holiday Mondays and the Friday after Thanksgiving.
**TIMES:** 7:00 AM-3:00 PM.
**ADMISSION:** Free. Parking is free.
**LOCATION:** Hwy 70 N, midway between Knoxville and Nashville. Take I-40, Exit 317 towards Crossville, turn right at 4th traffic light. Right at the next traffic light. Market is about 1½ miles on the right.
**DESCRIPTION:** A flea market in the original sense, operating under covered sheds, this market has been running since 1970. Depending on the season, there are 200 to 400 dealers selling antiques, collectibles, furniture, dogs, coins, cats, cards, chickens, garage sale goodies, livestock, new merchandise, crafts, produce, nursery stock, stamps, and whatever else shows up. Because of the nature of this market, much of the merchandise is old and/or used. Think unfound treasures. There are 4 snack bars and a restaurant as well as handicapped accessible parking and restrooms, and showers. Members of the Tennessee Flea Market Association.
**DEALER RATES:** $8 for a 12' × 14' covered space. Electricity is extra. Reservations are suggested.
**CONTACT:** Mary Gunter or Lois Wilbanks, PO Box 3037, Crossville TN 38557-3037. Tel: (931) 484-9970.

## HIGHWAY 127
### Highway 127 Corridor Sale
**DATES:** August, from the Thursday before the 3rd Sunday through Sunday for 4 days.
**TIMES:** Whenever.
**ADMISSION:** Free. Parking is wherever you can find it—*off* the road.
**LOCATION:** All along US Hwy 127 through three states: Kentucky, Tennessee, and Alabama. When you see a collection of sellers, it's there.
**DESCRIPTION:** Started in 1987 as a way to get travelers off the interstate and back onto the country roads by Fentress County's former County Executive Mike Walker and some of his friends, this market of thousands of dealers in "oddities and antiques," yard sale unloaders, and whoever and

whatever else shows up, selling everything old and/or crafty. If you wish to travel the entire 450-mile route, start in Covington KY and work your way down to around Gadsden AL. There are plenty of food vendors. This has to be "the World's Longest Outdoor Sale."

**Rules of the road:** 1) *Drive Cautiously*—then you won't hit pedestrians or miss that goody you've been looking for. 2) Be *extremely* careful crossing the road! 3) Use your turn signals and don't stop suddenly for that goody (have a lookout who can give you ample warning). Otherwise, you may be dealing with insurance companies and wreckers rather than rare Ming.

**DEALER RATES:** Whatever the local landowner charges. Check out the website for a list of contacts in each state (it's huge) or call.

**CONTACT:** Wanda, Fentress County Chamber of Commerce, PO Box 1294, Jamestown TN 38556-1294. Tel: (800) 327-3945. Web: jamestowntn.org.

# JACKSON
## Friendly Frank's Flea Market

**DATES:** First weekend of every month, except July, from Friday night through Sunday.

**TIMES:** Saturday and Sunday, 9:00 AM-6:00 PM and Friday evenings 6:00 PM-9:00 PM.

**ADMISSION:** Free. Parking is free.

**LOCATION:** Hwy 45 S.

**DESCRIPTION:** Opened in 1983, this indoor/outdoor market's 200-plus dealers sell antiques, collectibles, coins, stamps, cards, furniture, garage sale clean-outs, new merchandise and crafts. Two snack bars serve to quell the munchies. There are clean handicapped-accessible restrooms on site.

**DEALER RATES:** $60 for the weekend for a 9' × 10' space. Reservations are required.

**CONTACT:** Peggy Mullikin, Friendly Frank's Flea Market, PO Box 328, Cordova TN 38088-0328. Tel: (901) 755-6561.

# KNOXVILLE
## Esau's Antique and Collectible Market

**DATES:** Saturday and Sunday, third weekend of each month, except September when it is held the fourth weekend. October is a huge 3-day extravaganza.

**TIMES:** Saturday 9:00 AM-5:00 PM. Sunday 1:00 PM-5:00 PM.

**ADMISSION:** $3 per person for regular markets, $4 for extravaganza. Thirty acres of free parking is provided.

**LOCATION:** Take the Rutledge Pk Exit 392 off I-40 E.

**DESCRIPTION:** This indoor market has run since 1975 and now includes 300 dealers selling a range of antiques and collectibles, craft items, and new articles. (Antiques and collectibles account for about 70% of the merchandise.) Food is available on the premises. Members of the Tennessee Flea Market Association.

**DEALER RATES:** $70 per 9' × 10' space per weekend, plus City and County Business License fee.

**CONTACT:** Cindy Crabtree, Esau Inc, PO Box 50096, Knoxville TN 37950-0096. Tel: (423) 588-1233 or 1-800-588-ESAU (3728). Web: www.esaushows.com.

# KODAK
## Great Smokies Craft Fair/Flea Market

**DATES:** Friday, Saturday, and Sunday, year round.

**TIMES:** Weekdays 10:00 AM-6:00 PM; Saturday and Sunday 9:00 AM-6:00 PM.

**ADMISSION:** Free. Parking is also free.

**LOCATION:** 220 Dumplin Valley Rd W. Off I-40, Exit 407, turn onto Dumplin Valley Rd, about ¼ mile down the road. Sixteen miles from Gatlinburg. Only 12 miles from Dollywood.

**DESCRIPTION:** Ideally situated on 25 acres next to the Interstate, this very successful market opened on August 3, 1990. The dealers are housed in a 230-space air-conditioned building, with unlimited outdoor space. They have a special section of wonderful antiques and collectibles, including player pianos! The dealers are noted for their friendliness, courtesy and helpfulness. They are more than willing to help each other and their customers out. There is a tremendous variety of superb crafts as well as manufacturer-direct booths. There is a food court selling homemade pizzas and corn bread, soup beans, gourmet burgers and regular burgers, hot dogs, and daily specials. A video arcade keeps the kids busy. The market is kept spotlessly clean. They welcome RVs, tour buses, and tractor-trailers. Ninety percent of their dealers are permanent, 80% have been here since they opened. Definitely a family market including vendors with kid's stuff. They choose their vendors to meet the wants and desires of all of their customers. The management strives to be the best market in the business and was chosen as one of the top 10 markets in the state by the Tennessee Flea Market Association. Nearby are 15,000 motels and hotel rooms and plenty of restaurants around the area. Over 71,000 cars go by this market each day! Members of the Tennessee Flea Market Association.

**DEALER RATES:** Winter: $60 per weekend, Friday through Sunday. Outside open spaces $12 a day, covered sheds $12 a day. Tables $2 a day. Summer rates can vary, but within this scale. Reservations are required because of a long waiting list.

**CONTACT:** Charlie Atchley, Great Smokies Craft Fair and Flea Market, 220 Dumplin Valley Rd W, Kodak TN 37764. Tel: (423) 932-FLEA (932-3532). Fax: (432) 932-3534. Watch for their website.

# LEBANON
## Parkland Flea Market
**DATES:** Every Saturday and Sunday, March 1 through December 15.
**TIMES:** 7:00 AM-dark.
**ADMISSION:** Free. Ample free parking is provided.
**LOCATION:** Across the street from the entrance to Cedars of Lebanon State Park. From I-40 take Exit 238, go 6 miles south. Between Lebanon and Murfreesboro on Hwy 231.
**DESCRIPTION:** This indoor/outdoor market has operated since 1977 near the center of the state of Tennessee. It has enjoyed steady growth with a "great group of family type dealers where 90% of the 300 are regulars." They are housed in a complex of seven buildings on ten acres of land, with another 40 acres available for further expansion. Large and small items, both new and used, can be found including boats, trailers, vans, and trucks, as well as the traditional flea market fare. Free weekend camping is available for dealers, and food is available at the site. Another attraction nearby is the Grand Olde Opry and Opryland only 30 miles away. Members of the Tennessee Flea Market Association.
**DEALER RATES:** $10 for 12' × 12' space under shed; $7 per 15' × 15' outside space. Reservations are strongly suggested.
**CONTACT:** Gwynn or Nancy Lanius, Parkland Flea Market, 403 Cambridge, Lebanon TN 37087-4207. Tel:(615) 449-6050.

# LOUISVILLE
## Green Acres Flea Market
**DATES:** Saturday and Sunday, rain or shine.
**TIMES:** 6:30 AM-4:30 PM.

**ADMISSION:** Free. Plenty of free parking is available. Space is also available for vehicles such as motor homes and trailers.

**LOCATION:** On Alcoa Hwy 129 between Knoxville and the Knoxville Airport.

**DESCRIPTION:** Located on 13 acres at the foothills of the Great Smoky Mountains, this indoor/outdoor show has been in operation since 1976. It draws an average of 500 dealers in 400 available spaces outdoors and over 300 indoors selling miscellaneous antiques and collectibles, gold, furniture old and new, as well as new items and farm goods. There is a large restaurant and large breakfast bar on the premises selling yogurt, cotton candy, pork skins and corndogs. Members of the Tennessee Flea Market Association.

**DEALER RATES:** $10 per space, approximately 20' × 20'. Reservations are suggested. Dealers can come on Friday and stay overnight.

**CONTACT:** Green Acres Flea Market, 908 Hillside Dr, Louisville TN 37777. Tel: (423) 681-4433 or fax: (423) 681-1091.

# MEMPHIS
## Memphis Flea Market, The BIG One

**DATES:** Saturday and Sunday, the third weekend of each month.

**TIMES:** 8:00 AM-6:00 PM.

**ADMISSION:** $2 per vehicle.

**LOCATION:** Mid-South Fairgrounds at Central and East Pkwy.

**DESCRIPTION:** Opened in 1969, this indoor/outdoor market of 900 to 1,200 dealers sells anything from antiques, collectibles, crafts, produce, housewares, and clothing to new merchandise. Plenty of food concessions and handicapped-accessible restrooms are on premises.

**DEALER RATES:** $70-$75 for a 10' × 8' inside space per weekend, $40-$50 for a 10' × 12' outside space for the weekend. Covered outside spaces are available. Reservations are needed for inside and covered outside space.

**CONTACT:** Mike Hardage, Memphis Flea Market, 955 Early Maxwell Blvd, Memphis TN 38104. Tel: (901) 276-3532. Fax: (901) 276-0701. Email: memflea@aol.com. Web: www.memphisfleamarket.com.

# NASHVILLE
## The Flea Market at the Nashville Fairgrounds

**DATES:** Weekend of the fourth Saturday of every month except December. One week earlier in December. Rain or shine.

**TIMES:** Saturday 6:00 AM-6:00 PM; Sunday 7:00 AM-5:00 PM.

**ADMISSION:** Free. $2 per car for parking. There is a shuttle bus from the parking lot to the fair.

**LOCATION:** Tennessee State Fairgrounds, at Wedgewood and Nolensville Rd. Easy access from Nashville and middle Tennessee via Interstates 65, 440, and 24.

**DESCRIPTION:** The Flea Market at the Nashville Fairgrounds was established in 1969 and is now run by the Tennessee State Fair. The popular indoor/outdoor market has, on average, about 2,000 booths per month, with the April, May, and October markets being the largest shows of the year. The market contains a large section of antiques and collectible items. Also sold are handmade craft items and some new merchandise. There are a variety of delicious foods available. Member of the Tennessee Flea Market Association.

**DEALER RATES:** $60 for 10' × 10' outside shed space or 12' × 15' parking lot space; $75 for a 10' × 9' inside booth. Reservations and pre-payment are required.

**CONTACT:** Deborah McCanless, Manager, Nashville Fairgrounds Flea Market, PO Box 40208, Nashville TN 37204. Tel: (615) 862-5016. Office is open Monday through Friday 8:00 AM-4:30 PM and during show hours. Watch for the website.

# SWEETWATER
## Fleas Unlimited

**DATES:** Saturday and Sunday, rain or shine.

**TIMES:** 8:00 AM-5:00 PM.

**ADMISSION:** Free. Parking is also free.

**LOCATION:** Directly off I-75 at Exit 60. Between Knoxville and Chattanooga.

**DESCRIPTION:** Opened in December of 1989, this indoor/outdoor market is housed in a 160,000-square-foot building. It attracts 500 dealers inside and there are another 50 spaces outdoors. There is a bit of everything here including plenty of cards, coins, stamps, garage sale finds and some new merchandise. They have an in-house deli, camping facilities with bath house, and a restaurant/candy factory! Members of the Tennessee Flea Market Association.

**DEALER RATES:** Main building: $22 per day per space or $17 a day if paid monthly. North and South buildings: $20 per day per space or $15 per day if paid monthly. Outside spaces $15 per day. Reservations are recommended.

**CONTACT:** Rhonda or Whittney, Fleas Unlimited, 121 County Rd 308, Sweetwater TN 37874. Tel: (423) 337-3532.

## TELFORD (JONESBOROUGH)
### Jonesborough Flea Market

**DATES:** Sunday, year round.

**TIMES:** 6:00 AM-4:00 PM.

**ADMISSION:** Free. Parking is free.

**LOCATION:** Five miles west of Jonesborough on State Hwy 11.

**DESCRIPTION:** This outdoor market boasts 200 dealers in summer and 50 in winter selling antiques, collectibles, crafts, produce, coins, stamps, cards, garage sale finds, furniture and new merchandise. Two snack bars and handicapped-accessible restrooms add to the amenities.

**DEALER RATES:** $8 per 12' × 20' per day, or $7.50 per day if paid by the month. Reservations are not required.

**CONTACT:** John Crawford or Alan Shelton, Jonesborough Flea Market, PO Box 413, Jonesborough TN 37659-0413. Tel: (423) 753-4241 or 753-4115 or 753-4999.

## OTHER FLEA MARKETS

We know or have heard about these markets, but have not personally contacted each one, as we have the markets with descriptions. If you plan to visit one of these markets listed below, *please call first* to make sure they are still open. Flea markets do come and go. While they were open when we went to press, they may not be later. We can't be responsible. *Call first!*

**Arlington:** Galloway Trading Post & Flea, 914 Hwy 70. Tel: (901) 867-7549.

**Arrington:** Triune Flea Market, 7960 Nolensville Rd. Tel: (615) 395-7140.

**Bluff City:** Tri-City Flea Market, 4571 Hwy 11E. Tel: (423) 538-0584.

**Bristol:** Carl's Flea Market, 1120 5 St. Tel: (423) 968-1049.

**Chattanooga:** 23rd Street Indoor Flea Market, 2210 E 21 St. Tel: (423) 624-7017.

**Clarksville:** Carol's Flea Market, 1690 Wilma Rudolph Blvd. Tel: (931) 552-1952.

**Clarksville:** Country Junction, 140 Lafayette Rd. Tel: (931) 645-9349.

**Clarksville:** Davis Depot, 1154 Fort Campbell Blvd. Tel: (931) 552-3038.

**Clarksville:** Dean Drive Flea Market, 135 Dean Dr. Tel: (931) 553-0562.

**Clarksville:** Flea Country II, 739 Madison St. Tel: (931) 645-1607.

**Clarksville:** Gate One Flea Market, Fort Campbell Blvd. Tel: (931) 431-3907.

**Clarksville:** Queen City Flea Market, 1156 Fort Campbell Blvd. Tel: (931) 648-4174.

**Clarksville:** Treasure Chest Flea Market, 200 Providence Blvd. Tel: (931) 553-4414.

**Clarksville:** Two Rivers Flea Market, 690 N Riverside Dr. Tel: (931) 503-0532.

**Clarksville:** Flea World, 1114 Crossland Ave. Tel: (931) 645-6378.

**Cookeville:** Town Plaza Flea Market, 165 S Jefferson Ave. Tel: (931) 520-0463.

**Covington:** A & B Flea Market, 1024 US Hwy 51N. Tel: (901) 476-4525.

**Covington:** Westside Flea Market, 3392 Hwy 59 W. Tel: (901) 476-8995.

**Crump:** Hilltop Flea Market, 3465 US Hwy 64. Tel: (901) 632-0626.

**Dunlap:** Mt Airy Flea Market, RR1 Box 291. Tel: (423) 949-5788.

**Dyersburg:** Dyersburg Trade Fair, 775 US Hwy 51 By-pass N. Tel: (901) 285-2844.

**East Ridge:** East Ridge Flea Market, 6725 Ringgold Rd. Tel: (423) 894-3960.

**Elizabethton:** Street's Flea Market, 1207 19E By-pass. Tel: (423) 543-7515.

**Etowah:** 411 Flea, 1120 Tennessee Ave. Tel: (423) 263-6411.

**Fairview:** Fairview Flea Market, 7258 Anderson Rd. Tel: (615) 799-0509.

**Hohenwald:** J & V'S Flea Market, 115 N Park St. Tel: (931) 796-5303.

**Jacksboro:** Coffey's Craft & Flea Market, 102 West St. Tel: (423) 562-6613.

**Knoxville:** Chapman Hwy Flea Market, 7300 Chapman Hwy. Tel: (423) 573-9143.

**Lebanon:** Gracie T's Flea Market, 1022 Murfreesboro Rd. Tel: (615) 444-5177.

**Louisville:** Green Acres Flea Market, 908 Hillside Dr. Tel: (423) 681-4433.

**Memphis:** A & A Flea Market, 1436 Airways Blvd. Tel: (901) 324-4208.

**Memphis:** A & M Howell Flea Market, 5199 S 3 St. Tel: (901) 789-7650.

**Memphis:** Airways Mini Flea Market, 1426 Airways Blvd. Tel: (901) 323-5505.

**Memphis:** CD Flea Market, 3340 Millington Rd. Tel: (901) 358-4092.

**Memphis:** Flea Market Mall of Memphis, 4389 S 3 St. Tel: (901) 789-7469.

**Memphis:** Frayser Flea Market, 3238 Millington Rd. Tel: (901) 353-3532.

**Memphis:** G & H Flea Market, 1718 Netherwood Ave. Tel: (901) 276-7495.

**Memphis:** JMC Car Wash & Flea Market, 4619 Elvis Presley Blvd. Tel: (901) 345-2271.

**Memphis:** Midtown Flea Market, 2018 Court Ave. Tel: (901) 726-9059.

**Mountain City:** DOE Valley Flea Market, RR3. Tel: (423) 727-4900.

**Nashville:** African Garage Sale, 511 Rosebank Ave. Tel: (615) 262-9311.

**Nashville:** Giant Flea Market, 2917 Nolensville Rd. Tel: (615) 333-8196.

**Parsons:** Tennessee River Flea Market, 545 Pentecostal Campground Rd. Tel: (901) 847-9383.

**Pleasant View:** Pleasant View Flea Market, 6530 Hwy 41A. Tel: (615) 746-9994.

**Powell:** Clinton Hwy Flea Market, 7622 Clinton Hwy. Tel: (423) 947-4232.

**Pulaski:** Tennessee Flea Market & Mall, 9146 Lewisburg Hwy. Tel: (931) 424-897.

**Shelbyville:** Hillis Auction, 2211 N Main St. Tel: (931) 685-9495.

**Sparta:** Cherry Creek Flea Market, 3011 Cherry Creek Rd. Tel: (931) 738-3440.

**Springfield:** Flea Country, 2758 17 Ave E. Tel: (615) 382-7777.

**Sweetwater:** Fleas Unlimited, 121 CR 308. Tel: (423) 337-3532.

**Troy:** Grandma's Flea Market, 406 E Harper St. Tel: (901) 536-0393.

**Union City:** Giant Flea Market of Union, 1700 W Reelfoot Ave. Tel: (901) 885-2377.

**Walland:** Hillbilly Flea Market, 4506 E Lamar Alexander Pkwy. Tel: (423) 983-2410.

**Waverly:** D Daniel Auction & Flea Market, Hwy 13S. Tel: (931) 296-9022.

**White Bluff:** White Bluff Flea Market, 4221 Hwy 70 E.

**Whiteville:** B & G Flea Market, 315 Hwy 100W. Tel: (901) 254-8321.

# TEXAS

## ALAMO
### All Valley Flea Market

**DATES:** Saturday and Sunday. Rain or shine.

**TIMES:** 4:30 AM to dark.

**ADMISSION:** $.25 per person. Parking is free.

**LOCATION:** Intersection of Cesar Chavez (formerly Morningside) Rd and Exp 83.

**DESCRIPTION:** Started in 1969 after a visit to another successful market elsewhere gave Mr Bruns the idea, he opened his first of four markets in Pharr. Also the first in the Valley area. When a highway was built through the market, they moved to Alamo. Now there are around 800 dealers presenting "everything!" And 20,000 to 30,000 buyers coming through every weekend buying everything including antiques, collectibles, used items, and some new merchandise. Food concessions and handicapped-accessible restrooms add to the amenities.

**DEALER RATES:** Saturdays $4.50 for 2 tables and 1 space; Sundays $8 for a 10' × 18' space and 2 tables. Reservations are strongly suggested if you are traveling from far away.

**CONTACT:** David Villegas or Dulce Ruiz, All Valley Flea Markets, 501 N Bridge St Ste 528, Hidalgo TX 78557. Tel: (956) 781-1911.

## AMARILLO
### T-Anchor Flea Market

**DATES:** Every Saturday and Sunday, year round.

**TIMES:** 9:00 AM-5:00 PM.

**ADMISSION:** Free. Free parking is available.

**LOCATION:** 1401 Ross St, off I-40.

**DESCRIPTION:** This indoor market began in 1978. Their 175 vendors in 365 spaces from all over the country sell antiques, collectibles, crafts, produce, and new merchandise. During summer months vendors rent space outdoors. Produce vendors are furnished with a permit. One snack bar and handicapped-accessible restrooms add to the amenities.

**DEALER RATES:** $8 per 10' × 20' space per day outside and $10-$12 inside. Reservations are not required, except during the Christmas season.

**CONTACT:** HD and Claudia Blyth, T-Anchor Flea Market, PO Box 31182, Amarillo TX 79120. Tel: (806) 373-0430.

# AUSTIN
## Austin Country Flea Market

**DATES:** Saturday and Sunday, year round. Rain or shine.

**TIMES:** 10:00 AM-6:00 PM.

**ADMISSION:** $1 per car.

**LOCATION:** 9500 Hwy 290 E.

**DESCRIPTION:** This is central Texas' largest flea market, with over 500 selling spaces. Their dealers sell antiques, collectibles, crafts, vegetables, and new merchandise. Open every weekend, it offers good food, family fun, and big bargains. The entire market is covered.

**DEALER RATES:** $35 per 10' × 8' booth (20' dealer parking directly behind each space if desired, or dealer's vehicle may be moved to an authorized area and parking space can be used as additional selling area). One display table is provided. RV electricity is available in limited areas. Gates are open to dealers at 7:00 AM; gates close at 10:00 PM. Advance reservations required.

**CONTACT:** Buz Cook or David Ritter, Austin Country, 9500 Hwy 290 E, Austin TX 78724. Tel: (512) 928-2795. Office is closed Tuesday-Thursday.

# BLANCO
## Blanco Flea Market

**DATES:** Wednesday through Sunday.

**TIMES:** Wednesday and Thursday 10:00 AM-4:00 PM, Friday and Saturday 9:00 AM-5:00 PM, Sunday 1:00 PM-5:00 PM.

**ADMISSION:** Free. Parking is free.

**LOCATION:** 5th and Pecan Sts. One block north of the Courthouse. Blanco is on Hwy 281, 47 miles southwest of Austin or 47 north of San Antonio.

**DESCRIPTION:** Located in a 6,000-square-foot restored historic mohair warehouse, this market of 3 dealers, including Shandy Hale and his custom knives who can and does play any musical instrument brought in the store (and there are lots of them), sells antiques, collectibles, power tools, manual tools, used or custom-built furniture, musical instruments, and whatever else comes in. There is plenty of outside space available to set up what you will. Say Hi to Shandy and ask for a tune. He'd love to oblige you.

**DEALER RATES:** Inside: $1.15 per square foot, about $138 per month. Outside $15 per day covered or uncovered or how much, or about $85 per month. Outside, reservations are not necessary. Inside is another story—call.

**CONTACT:** Shandy Hale, Manager, Blanco Flea Market, 502 Pecan & 5, Blanco TX 78606. Tel: (830) 833-5640.

# BONHAM
## Bonham Trade Days

**DATES:** Thursday through Sunday the weekend *after* the first Monday, year round.

**TIMES:** 7:00 AM-5:00 PM, mostly daylight to dusk.

**ADMISSION:** Free. Parking is free.

**LOCATION:** Fort Inglish Park. At the intersection of Hwy 56 and Hwys 121 and 82 By-pass.

**DESCRIPTION:** Sponsored by the Kiwanis, this 28-year-old outdoor market is following the Monday Trade Days tradition. There are 300 dealers selling antiques, collectibles, garage sale goodies, produce and new merchandise—"just everything." Plenty of food vendors satisfy the hungry, and there are restrooms when needed.

**DEALER RATES:** $10 per 20' × 30' space per weekend. First come, first served.

**CONTACT:** Jo, Bonham Trade Days, Rt 4 Box 358, Bonham TX 75418. Tel: (903) 583-2367.

# BOWIE
## Second Monday Trade Days

**DATES:** Friday through Sunday before the second Monday of each month.

**TIMES:** 7:00 AM-dark.

**ADMISSION:** Free. Parking is free.

**LOCATION:** Rodeo grounds on E Wise St. Bus Hwy 287 and Hwy 81. Going north from Hwy 287, take the US 81 Waurika exit.

**DESCRIPTION:** Another Monday Court Day market! That judge, he did get around. Now in its second hundred years (started in 1890), this venerable market has approximately 300 dealers (in 470 spots) selling antiques, collectibles, livestock, crafts and whatever comes in. This is the Northern Texas place to be on second Monday. They can easily boast they have 10-15,000 visitors each month. In addition to their current restrooms with showers for dealers, they have expanded their facilities with new paving, more water spouts and electric outlets, awnings on the 50' × 200' shed, a new RV septic dump and a new restroom with showers. Next door to the market is the Palham Park with an RV park, swimming pool, bath house, walking trail and game courts.

**DEALER RATES:** $20 per space; electric is $4 extra per day, per connection. Reservations are recommended.

**CONTACT:** Clyde Johnson, Parks & Recreation Director, Bowie City of Grounds Maintenance Dept, 304 Pecan St, Bowie TX 76230. Tel: (817) 872-1680. Email: 2ndmonday@morgan.net. Web: www.morgan.net/~a2ndmonday.

---

### From Bowie's History

Barter and trade was nothing new in the early days of Bowie. A group of interested livestockmen and dealers across Montague, Clay, and Wise counties conceived the need for a central trade market. In those early years, traders began arriving with their herds Friday evening, before the main trade day, and leaving out the following Tuesday evening. Medicine shows, novelty hawkers and peddlers would ply their "trade"—providing the entertainment. After WWI, commodities were added to the collection of goods.

---

## BUFFALO GAP
### Buffalo Gap Flea Market

**DATES:** Friday, Saturday, and Sunday, third Saturday of each month from February through December (weather permitting in December), except July when it's the fourth Sunday weekend.

**TIMES:** 7:00 AM-10:00 PM.

**ADMISSION:** Free. Parking is available nearby.

**LOCATION:** In Buffalo Gap, 10 miles south of Abilene on Hwy 89.

**DESCRIPTION:** This outdoor market began in 1974 and currently draws around 150 dealers selling a wide range of antiques, collectibles, fresh produce, crafts, and new merchandise. They have well-lit night shopping on Saturday night "under the stars and trees." This market is described by its owner as the "prettiest market in the west." Food and toilet facilities are available. If you see a six-foot Scot with a white ponytail, say Hi to John. He's also the mayor of Buffalo Gap.

**DEALER RATES:** $15 per 12' × 18' space for a three-day weekend, plus electricity, $4 per day, if needed. All electric wiring has been updated. Reservations are required *at least one week in advance*, as they have had to turn away dealers before. A $2 city permit is required to sell.

**CONTACT:** John & Peggy Brolls, Buffalo Gap Flea Market, PO Box 575, Buffalo Gap TX 79508-0575. Tel: (915) 572-3327.

# CANTON
## First Monday Trade Days

**DATES:** Begins on Thursday before the first Monday of each month, and runs Thursday through Sunday and Labor Day Monday. Rain or shine.

**TIMES:** 7:00 AM-dark.

**ADMISSION:** Free. Parking is available for $3 per vehicle. RV spaces are available, with advance reservations and some first come, first served.

**LOCATION:** Two blocks north of downtown square. Easy access on Hwy 19, Hwy 64 and FM Rd 859. From I-20, Exit 526, 2 miles south on left.

**DESCRIPTION:** This is surely one of the most popular and well-known flea markets in the country, if not the world. Originating in 1876 as the town's court day, people at that time began to take care of their trading and purchasing of animals, produce, etc. while waiting for the judge. In 1965, the city of Canton acquired a six-acre plot of land two blocks north of the Court House which is now the Historic District. The dealers selling animals can be found four blocks east of the Court House on the property known as Curry's Trade Grounds or Dog Grounds. Since 1965, the number of available lots has grown from 150 to well over 4,000. The number of visitors is up to 300,000 per month! They now have covered pavilions and an indoor civic center. The heated/air-conditioned civic center is 34,000 square feet with a food concession and handicapped-accessible restrooms. From here all the best antique and collectible dealers sell. First Monday Trade Days began advertising its unique market in 1974, and since then has appeared on NBC's "Today Show," "Good Morning America," the front page of *The Wall St Journal*, in *National Geographic, Smithsonian* and in several other local and national media. All kinds of antiques, collectibles, new merchandise, handmade crafts, and food are available. Restrooms with showers are provided.

**DEALER RATES:** $50 for each lot. Dealer spaces are approximately 12' × 20'. Dealers who reserve in advance may renew for following sale. Unreserved lots are also available. Covered space is limited and ranges from $125-$175.

**CONTACT:** City of Canton, PO Box 245, Canton TX 75103. Tel: (903) 567-6556. Fax: (903) 567-1753. Email: cityhall@vzinet.com. Web: www.firstmondaycanton.com.

---

**Some Canton History**

History relates one incident where a man was hanged for stealing his partner's wagon of goods for trading. He is buried facing south (not east) in Hillcrest Cemetery by the First Monday Park.

# CHANNELVIEW
## White Elephant, Inc

**DATES:** Every Saturday and Sunday. Rain or shine.
**TIMES:** 7:30 AM-5:30 PM.
**ADMISSION:** Free. Parking is free.
**LOCATION:** 15662 I-10 E. Take the Sheldon-Channelview exit; the market is on the Service Rd of I-10.
**DESCRIPTION:** Between 350 and 375 dealers show up each week for this indoor/outdoor market, which has been in operation since 1971. Articles for sale include antiques, collectibles, garage sale items such as tools, furniture, and jewelry, as well as some new items and fresh produce. Food and toilet facilities are available on the premises.
**DEALER RATES:** $13-$17 per space depending on location. Reservations not required.
**CONTACT:** Debby, White Elephant Inc, PO Box 209, Channelview TX 77530-0209. Tel: (281) 452-9022. Office is open Monday-Friday at (281) 452-1701.

# GARLAND
## Vikon Village Flea Market

**DATES:** Saturdays and Sundays, year round. Also the Friday after Thanksgiving and some extra dates in December, usually the Wednesday-Friday before Christmas.
**TIMES:** 10:00 AM-7:00 PM.
**ADMISSION:** Free. Free parking for up to 750 cars is available nearby.
**LOCATION:** 2918 S Jupiter. Near the corner of Kingsley and Jupiter, 2 blocks north of Rt 635.
**DESCRIPTION:** This indoor market began in 1975 and averages around 350 booths with 175 dealers selling such items as books, baseball cards, coins, jewelry, furniture, clothing, and plants, as well as new merchandise. One large snack bar, a popcorn stand and handicapped-accessible restrooms add to the amenities.
**DEALER RATES:** Lease available at $140 and up per month (minimum one month). Weekends are available. Reservations are required. Call for information Thursdays from 10:00 AM-5:00 PM or Fridays 10:00 AM-6:00 PM.
**CONTACT:** Vikon Village Flea Market, 2918 S Jupiter, Garland TX 75041. Tel: (972) 271-0565.

**Great Beginnings**
The chap who started CD Warehouse (selling CDs) began as a vendor here at Vikon Village. Not bad!

# GRAND PRAIRIE
## Traders Village
**DATES:** Every Saturday and Sunday, year round. Rain or shine.
**TIMES:** 8:00 AM-dusk.
**ADMISSION:** Free. Parking for over 7,000 cars is available at $2 per vehicle. Handicapped parking is available.
**LOCATION:** 2602 Mayfield Rd in Grand Prairie. In the heart of the Dallas/Ft Worth area, 5 miles south of Six Flags Over Texas theme park off Hwy 360. Or, take Hwy 360 north 1 mile off I-20.
**DESCRIPTION:** Traders Village is a 106-acre complex, which opened in November 1973. Since that date, over 55 million people have visited this market, roughly 2.5 million a year. The market currently attracts between 1,500 and 1,800 dealers who set up on open, covered, and enclosed spaces. Crowds average 35,000-75,000 per weekend. Special events include a chili cook-off (April), Cajun Fest(May), an Antique Auto Swap Meet (June), Antique Tractor and Farm Implement Show (July), an authentic Indian Powwow (September), a Barbecue Cook-off (October), and more throughout the year. Most of the special events are open to the public for free. Traders Village runs its own food and beverage department, with over 30 stands selling everything from Spanish specialties to pizza by the slice, from chicken-fried steak to funnel cakes. Produce vendors and bulk-food dealers are also on hand. Other features include kiddie rides, an arcade, stroller and wheel-chair rentals, shaded rest areas, two ATM machines and a first-aid room. There is also a sister market in Houston.
**DEALER RATES:** $20 per 14' × 25' open lot per day. $25 per covered space per day. Reservations are required for two-day rentals only.
**CONTACT:** Allan Hughes, Director of General Services, Traders Village, 2602 Mayfield Rd, Grand Prairie TX 75051. Tel: (972) 647-2331. Email: tvgp@flash.net. Web: www.tradersvillage.com.

**Local History**

Traders Village is a continuing extension of the trading that went on between various Indian tribes over the centuries. An historical marker, dedicated in 1980, marks the site of the million-acre "Cross Timbers" area where Shoshone, rooted out by Apaches, in turn chased out by Comanches, traded until white man showed up in 17th and 18th centuries. In the 1840s, white settlers stayed, leading to the Battle of Village Creek on May 24, 1841, marking the end of the Indian domination of the area.

# HOUSTON
## Traders Village

**DATES:** Every Saturday and Sunday, year round. Rain or shine.

**TIMES:** 8:00 AM-dusk.

**ADMISSION:** Free. Parking for over 4,000 cars is available at $2 per vehicle. Handicapped parking is available.

**LOCATION:** 7979 N Eldridge Rd. Off Northwest Fwy (Hwy 290), Eldridge Exit, 3/10 mile south.

**DESCRIPTION:** Traders Village is a 100-acre complex which opened in May 1989. Up to one million people visit each year. The market currently attracts over 600 dealers who set up on covered and enclosed spaces selling imports, antiques, collectibles, crafts, produce, garage sale merchandise, pets, clothes, furniture, auto parts, flowers and plants, electronics and lots more. Crowds average 10,000-15,000 a weekend. Special events are held weekly throughout the year. Most of the special events are open to the public. There are over 30 stands selling everything from Spanish specialties to pizza by the slice, from chicken-fried steak to funnel cakes. Produce vendors and bulk-food dealers are also on hand. Other features include kiddie rides, an arcade, stroller and wheelchair rentals, shaded rest areas, an ATM machine, and a first-aid room. There is also a sister market in Grand Prairie.

**DEALER RATES:** $20 per day, or $41 for the weekend reserved. Reservations are required for two-day rentals only.

**CONTACT:** Michael Baxter or George Esparza, Traders Village—Houston, 7979 N Eldridge Rd, Houston TX 77041. Tel: (281) 890-5500. Fax: (281) 890-6568. Email: tvh@flash.net. Web: www.tradersvillage.com.

## Trading Fair II

**DATES:** Every Friday, Saturday, and Sunday. Rain or shine.

**TIMES:** 10:00 AM-6:00 PM.

**ADMISSION:** Free. Parking $1.

**LOCATION:** 5515 S Loop E. Midway between the Astrodome and the Galveston Fwy on Loop 610. Use the Crestmont Exit either way.

**DESCRIPTION:** This indoor market started in 1974 and currently draws over 400 dealers selling a wide range of antiques and collectibles, as well as craft items. They are possibly the largest indoor market in the Houston area. Their two floors of 60,000 square feet each and an additional 30,000-square-foot annex in the back houses 300 dealers downstairs on a weekly basis. The second floor is now the Lone Star Arena and has been converted to an entertainment center with mostly live shows, with the occasional merchandise shows. Their selection of sale items is described as "some of everything, a lot of some things." Two restaurants and one snack bar take care of hunger problems; handicapped-accessible restrooms provide relief. They do plenty of advertising as well as everything they can to gain the notice, goodwill, and support of the buying public. There's another five acres that will be used for live entertainment when the temperatures fall to reasonable.

**DEALER RATES:** $275 for a 11' × 15' space and up depending on size. Dealer reservations are suggested.

**CONTACT:** Trading Fair II, 5515 S Loop E, Houston TX 77033. Tel: (713) 731-1111. Fax: (713) 731-1121. Watch for their website and email.

# LUBBOCK

## National Flea Market

**DATES:** Every Wednesday through Sunday, except Thanksgiving and Christmas week.

**TIMES:** Wednesday-Friday 9:00 AM-5:00 PM, Saturday and Sunday 9:00 AM-6:00 PM.

**ADMISSION:** Free. Parking is also free.

**LOCATION:** 1808 Clovis Rd. One half block west of Ave Q.

**DESCRIPTION:** This market first opened in 1982. It is both an indoor and outdoor market attracting from 100 to 150 dealers selling everything from antiques and collectibles to crafts and vegetables. New merchandise including clothing, tools and electronics are also available. For your convenience, a snack bar and concession stand are on the premises. The original barn for weekend dealers burned down. They have rebuilt it housing 105 spaces inside with heating, air-conditioning and lovely clean handicapped-accessible restrooms.

**DEALER RATES:** There are two buildings and outdoor space available: weekly rates in the main building start at $43 and up for 10' × 10' booth depending on location; rates in the other building, which usually houses the weekend dealer, vary from $20-$50, while space varies from 10' × 10' to 10' × 20'. Storage sheds that can be sold from are $45 per week or $175 a month.

**CONTACT:** Debie Grant, National Flea Market, 1808 Clovis Rd, Lubbock TX 79415. Tel: (806) 744-4979. Fax: (806) 744-0164.

# MCALLEN-MISSION
## All Valley First Sunday Flea Market

**DATES:** First Sunday of every month.

**TIMES:** 8:00 AM-4:00 PM.

**ADMISSION:** $.50. Parking is free.

**LOCATION:** Villa Real Convention Building. Bentsen Rd, between McAllen and Mission on Exp 83.

**DESCRIPTION:** This market first opened in 1976 as one of three markets in the Valley area. The other markets are in Mercedes and Alamo. This one attracts quantities of tourists to the 285 dealers and their wares. Mostly antiques and collectibles are shown here. One snack bar and handicapped-accessible restrooms add to the amenities.

**DEALER RATES:** $10 per table per day. Reservations are a must!

**CONTACT:** David Villegas or Dulce Ruiz, All Valley Flea Markets, 501 North Bridge St Ste 528, Hidalgo TX 78557. Tel: (956) 781-1911.

# MCKINNEY
## Third Monday Trade Days

**DATES:** Saturday and Sunday preceding the third Monday each month. (It doesn't always fall on the third weekend.)

**TIMES:** 9:00 AM-4:00 PM. The deal is: all dealers must be open during these times. However, they can be open earlier or later. Earlier is the rule.

**ADMISSION:** Free. $2 parking.

**LOCATION:** Hwy 380, 2 miles west of US 75.

**DESCRIPTION:** Another fantastic court day market started when that circuit judge came around and did his job on Mondays (see Kentucky's markets). There are six in Texas: see Canton and Weatherford for First Monday markets, Bowie and Bonham for Second Monday markets and Whitewright for a Fourth Monday market. Although there are 700 spaces here, usually all spaces are filled with at least 500 dealers (some use more space than others). This is a great place to find antiques, collectibles, crafts, produce, animals and new merchandise. There are plenty of food vendors; you won't starve.

**DEALER RATES:** $35 and up for open air, $125 in a building per space per weekend. Reservations are necessary.

**CONTACT:** Darrell Lewis, Third Monday Trade Days, 4550 W University Dr, McKinney TX 75070. Tel: (972) 562-5466 or 542-7174.

# MERCEDES
## Mercedes Flea Market

**DATES:** Saturday and Sunday, year round.

**TIMES:** 4:30 AM to dusk.

**ADMISSION:** $.25. Parking is free.

**LOCATION:** Mile 2 W and Exp 83.

**DESCRIPTION:** Opened in 1973 as the second of the All Valley Flea Markets and now owned by Mr Kim, this market attracts over 600 vendors selling predominately antiques and collectibles, as well as fresh produce, odds and ends, garage sale goodies, tools, plants, used and new merchandise. From 8-10,000 local people come here each weekend. Thirteen concession stands provide a cure for the munchies, and handicapped-accessible restrooms provide relief.

**DEALER RATES:** Saturdays $4.50 outdoors in sun; $6 under shelter per space; Sundays $8 in sun and $9 in shade, plus $.50 per table. Monthly reservations are strongly suggested. Daily, just show up.

**CONTACT:** Tack Kim or Nancy Vargas, Mercedes Flea Market, 501 N Bridge St Ste 528, Hidalgo TX 78557. Tel: (956) 565-2751 market. Or (956) 781-1911 during the week.

# PEARLAND
## Cole's Antique Village and Flea Market

**DATES:** Every Saturday and Sunday. Rain or shine.

**TIMES:** 6:30 AM-6:00 PM.

**ADMISSION:** Free. $1 for parking.

**LOCATION:** 1014-1022 N Main St, 4 miles south of the Hobby Airport on Telephone Rd (Hwy 35).

**DESCRIPTION:** This indoor/outdoor market started in 1969 and currently draws approximately 700 dealers selling a range of antiques and collectibles such as furniture, tools, and glassware; fresh produce and plants, crafts and new items are also sold. Food is available on the premises. They added 50 more new covered tables outside in 1997. The antique co-op is open everyday but Wednesday, as is the office.

**DEALER RATES:** $43 per 10' × 10' space indoors per weekend; $45 per outdoor covered space per weekend. Reservations can be made for these spaces Fridays from 8:00 AM-5:00 PM.

**CONTACT:** Cole's Antique Village and Flea Market, 1014 N Main St, Pearland TX 77581-2208. Tel: (281) 485-2277.

# SAN ANTONIO
## Eisenhauer Road Flea Market

**DATES:** Wednesday through Sunday. Rain or shine.

**TIMES:** Weekends 9:00 AM-7:00 PM; weekdays 12:00 PM-7:00 PM.

**ADMISSION:** Free. Parking is free.

**LOCATION:** 3903 Eisenhauer Rd.

**DESCRIPTION:** This market, started in 1979, operates 90% indoors in an air-conditioned space with over 200 steady dealers plus transients. A variety of antiques and collectibles is sold, along with crafts and new merchandise. Food is served at three snack bars on the premises, and there are restrooms just in case.

**DEALER RATES:** Outdoors: $5 per 8' table per day Saturday and $10 for Sunday. If you rent a table for the weekend, there is no charge for the other three days. Reservations are suggested. Indoors: $8 for Saturday, $17 for Sunday, and other days are free with weekend payment.

**CONTACT:** Harry Weiss or Mrs Pat Walker, Eisenhauer Road Flea Market, 3903 Eisenhauer Rd, San Antonio TX 78218. Tel: (210) 653-7592. Fax: (210) 657-1692.

## Mission Open Air Market

**DATES:** Wednesday, Saturday, and Sunday.

**TIMES:** 6:00 AM-4:00 PM.

**ADMISSION:** $.75 a walk-in or $1 a carload.

**LOCATION:** 207 W Chavaneaux Rd. Between I-35 and 37, Moursund Blvd Exit inside Loop 410 W.

**DESCRIPTION:** Started in 1985, this outdoor "real flea market" consists of 1,500 dealers under covered areas selling 90% used merchandise. They claim to be the "largest outdoor market in South Texas." Some of the items sold include antiques, collectibles, produce, garage sale goodies, furniture, and some new merchandise. When hunger hits, try the snack bar. There are handicapped-accessible restrooms on site. Watch for Swap-O the Clown as he greets visitors during the market. For a touch of excitement, they hold drawings and do cash giveaways every day. During Christmas and Thanksgiving holiday season, the prizes are turkeys or hams. This is not a dull place!

**DEALER RATES:** $17 on Wednesday, $15 on Saturday, $18 on Sunday. Reservations are not required.

**CONTACT:** Mission Open Air Market, 707 Moursund Blvd, San Antonio TX 78221. Tel: (210) 923-8131 (information), 921-1569 (administration). Fax: (210) 923-8004.

## Northwest Flea Market

**DATES:** Saturday and Sunday.

**TIMES:** 7:00 AM-5:00 PM.

**ADMISSION:** Free. Parking is free.

**LOCATION:** 3600 Fredericksburg Rd. Off Loop 410 on north side of town. Go south toward the city 1½ miles to the Northwest Center on Fredericksburg Rd. The market is behind the mall.

**DESCRIPTION:** Open since 1973, this indoor/outdoor market of approximately 250 dealers sells antiques, collectibles, crafts, produce, coins, stamps, cards, garage sale goodies, furniture and new merchandise. "It has not been disputed that this is the first indoor flea market to set up in a modern air-conditioned building for the sole purpose of running a flea market, with permanent tables, storage and lock-up rooms. I have a dealer, Mr and Mrs Linderman, who have rented their tables and left them set up for 26 years 'straight!'" says Mr Markwell.

**DEALER RATES:** Outdoors: $14 per day for 20' × 20' space, table provided for $5 (first come, first served). Inside: $14 per day with 8' table. Rooms starting at $197 per month. Reservations are suggested one week in advance.

**CONTACT:** James C Markwell, Northwest Flea Market, 3600 Fredericksburg Rd, San Antonio TX 78201. Tel: (210) 736-6655.

# SCHERTZ
## Bussey's Flea Market

**DATES:** Saturday and Sunday, year round.

**TIMES:** 7:00 AM to dusk.

**ADMISSION:** Free. $1 per car.
**LOCATION:** 18738 IH-35 N.
**DESCRIPTION:** This outdoor show began in 1979. There are 513 dealer spaces, with most of them filled on the weekends. Anything from antiques and collectibles to very little new merchandise and craft items are available. Generally 90% used, 10% new merchandise. Plenty of garage sale items. There are many Mexican imports and a variety of curios as well. Food is available on the premises with seven fantastic snack bars and plenty of hamburgers, hot dogs, breakfast tacos and special hand-me-down recipes among other delights (sausage on a stick). This is a family operated market. There are handicapped-accessible restrooms on site.
**DEALER RATES:** $10-$12 on Saturday, $18-$25 on Sunday per space. No reservations needed.
**CONTACT:** Harold Smith, General Partner, Bussey's Flea Market, 18738 IH-35 N, Schertz TX 78154. Tel: (210) 651-6830. Fax: (830) 609-0800, yes, the area code is different, but correct.

---

### Tear Your Hair Out

A woman, cleaning out her attic, brought in a crystal punch bowl and cup set and put them out for $25. She was offered $15 by a professional dealer and refused it; another dealer offered her $20 which started a screaming match between the two dealers. Eventually one won and 20 minutes later the victor sold the set for a 900% profit.

---

# WHITEWRIGHT
## Whitewright Trade Days

**DATES:** The weekend before the fourth Monday of every month starting the preceding Friday through Sunday, technically Saturday and Sunday, but some dealers persist in setting up on Thursday and Friday!
**TIMES:** All day Friday through early afternoon Sunday, generally 6:00-7:00 AM until they drop late in the day.
**ADMISSION:** Free. Parking is free.
**LOCATION:** American Legion grounds on Sears St. From Hwy 69, turn right at the Y onto Grant St, then turn right on Sears.
**DESCRIPTION:** This 20-plus-year-old market is another of the judge's famous stops. About 150-plus dealers set up selling antiques, collectibles,

and all manner of items. There are 300 dealer spaces, so drop on down! This market is the fundraiser for the American Legion. Do stop in at Caraway's Exxon and shout a Hi to Jim and Odell!

**DEALER RATES:** $7 per space for the weekend. Reservations are nice.

**CONTACT:** Odell Caraway, Whitewright Trade Days, c/o Caraway Exxon, Box 566, Whitewright TX 75491. Tel: (903) 364-2994.

# WICHITA FALLS
## Holliday Street Flea Market

**DATES:** Every Saturday and Sunday, year round.

**TIMES:** 7:00 AM-dark.

**ADMISSION:** Free, with free parking available.

**LOCATION:** 2820 Holliday St. Near Hwys 281 and 287 on Holliday Rd near Holliday Creek.

**DESCRIPTION:** This market runs both indoors and out. Under the same ownership as before, it began in 1966 and currently hosts 200 to 250 dealers. The property was originally an amusement park, swimming pool and trailer park before becoming a flea market. There are antiques, collectibles, and crafts for sale, alongside produce and new merchandise. In addition, there are Mexican imports, musical instruments, saddles, boots, clothes new and used, t-shirts, furniture, appliances and tack offered. There are 12 acres of selling space (as the city took 5 acres for flood control), including individual buildings with inside lockups. There are food concessions on the premises. As Vivian describes it, "As you know, every Saturday is like Christmas. You never know what will show up."

**DEALER RATES:** $7 per 12' × 30' space uncovered; $10 per 12' × 12' covered shed per day; $85 to $125 per lockup stall indoors per month. Reservations are required for indoor spaces and covered sheds.

**CONTACT:** Jim and Vivian Parish, Owners, 2820 Holliday St, Wichita Falls TX 76301. Tel: (817) 767-1712 or 767-9038.

---

### Is This Maine?
They tell of a dealer couple from Maine who visited several times selling lobster and bear traps—a bit unusual for Texas!

---

# WINNIE
## Old Time Trade Days Flea Market

**DATES:** The weekend following the first Monday, year round.

**TIMES:** Daylight to dusk.

**ADMISSION:** Free. parking is $2 a carload. Tour buses are free.

**LOCATION:** I-10, Exit 829 at Winnie. When you get off the Interstate, you are there. Between Beaumont and Houston.

**DESCRIPTION:** Formerly a part of Larry's Antique Mall and Flea Market in Beaumont, this market opened in 1992, taking the major part of the flea market with it. Housed in permanent shops, covered pavilions, or outdoors, it hosts 500 to 1,000 dealers specializing in antiques, collectibles and crafts. The crafters have their own space showing their wares from the Ozarks to the south Texas coast. Decorators come from all over the country to find those "special somethings" to furnish their jobs. There is a special designated place for garage sales and everyone is invited to use it. With the publicity from the move from Beaumont, this market put the town of Winnie on the Texas map. So much so that all the major fast-food companies have space there including McDonald's, Burger King, Taco Bell, and plenty more. There are clean restrooms available. Very quickly, this market has become "family" to some and a capsule history of Texas in that there have already been at least one wedding, a two-foot flood, tornados, and hurricanes—"some real hair-raisers," says Mrs. Tinkle, one of the owners. "But our customers are loyal, our vendors are loyal, and somehow the market just keeps growing."

**DEALER RATES:** $30 and up depending on location and size: outdoors, covered pavilion, indoors, shop; 20' × 20' to 20' × 50'. Reservations are recommended.

**CONTACT:** Larry and Justine Tinkle, 14902 Hwy 1663, Winnie TX 77665. Tel: (409) 892-4000 or (409) 296-3300. Fax: (409) 296-3301.

---

**Blowing in the Wind**

Well, they had a "big top tent," but that "is somewhere blowing in the wind," according to Justine Tinkle.

---

# OTHER FLEA MARKETS

We know or have heard about these markets, but have not personally contacted each one, as we have the markets with descriptions. If you plan to visit one of these markets listed below, *please call first* to make sure they are still open. Flea markets do come and go. While they were open when we went to press, they may not be later. We can't be responsible. *Call first!*

**Abilene:** Crossing, 1505 S 14 St. Tel: (915) 672-5325.

**Abilene:** Elmdale Flea Market, 5423 E Hwy 80. Tel: (915) 673-8623.

**Abilene:** Old Abilene Town Flea Market, 3300 E I-20. Tel: (915) 675-6588.

**Alvarado:** Johnston's Flea Market, S IH-35 W. Tel: (817) 783-8803.

**Alvin:** Ruth G Rodreguez Flea Market, 118 Elmwood St. Tel: (281) 331-0565.

**Amarillo:** Old ICX Flea Market, 513 Ross St. Tel: (806) 373-3215.

**Amarillo:** Sunset Center Flea Market, 3701 Plains Blvd. Tel: (806) 355-2002.

**Anson:** Old Wagon Wheel Flea Market, 1015 Commercial Ave. Tel: (915) 823-3309.

**Archer City:** Manon Morrow Flea Market, PO Box 633. Tel: (940) 574-4118.

**Athens:** West 31 Flea Market, Hwy 31 W. Tel: (903) 675-8578.

**Austin:** Bergstrom Open Air Market, 917 Bastrop Hwy. Tel: (512) 385-7978.

**Austin:** Oakhill Flea Market, 5526 W Hwy 290. Tel: (512) 892-0402.

**Bay City:** Fiesta Flea Market, 2220 Ave F. Tel: (409) 323-0038.

**Beaumont:** King Mart Flea Market, 2655 S 11 St. Tel: (409) 842-5401.

**Belton:** Bell County Flea Market, George Wilson Rd. Tel: (254) 939-6411.

**Belton:** Centroplex Flea Market, 200 Whitsett St. Tel: (254) 939-5242.

**Bertram:** Traders Paradise Flea Market, 163 Vaughn St. Tel: (512) 355-2141.

**Bridge City:** Gulf Coast Flea Market, 3140 Texas Ave. Tel: (409) 735-5377.

**Brownsville:** Seventy Seven Flea Market, 5955 N Expwy. Tel: (956) 350-9425.

**Burleson:** All American Texas Flea Market, 3004 S I-35 W. Tel: (817) 783-5468.

**Cameron:** Chris & Wayne's Flea Market, 3802 N Travis Ave. Tel: (254) 697-4167.

**Canton:** Mill Creek Trade Ground. Tel: (903) 567-1177.

**Cleburne:** Cleburne Flea Market, 1300 E Henderson St. Tel: (817) 645-9099.

**Cleveland:** Frontier Flea Market, 18431 Hwy 105. Tel: (281) 592-2101.

**Cleveland:** Olde Security Square Flea Market, 20024 Hwy 105. Tel: (281) 592-6017.

**Comfort:** Hwy 87 Flea Market, Hwy 87 N. Tel: (830) 995-2998.

**Corpus Christi:** Casa Linda Flea Market II, 1551 Baldwin Blvd. Tel: (512) 884-2264.

**Corpus Christi:** Corpus Christi Trade Center, 2833 S Padre Island Dr. Tel: (512) 854-4943.

**Corpus Christi:** Flea Market Las Palmas, 4977 Ayers St. Tel: (512) 852-4646.

**Corpus Christi:** Flea Market Mercado Las Palmas, 4951 Ayers St. Tel: (512) 851-0505.

**Corpus Christi:** Swap-A-Rama, 135 S Navigation Blvd. Tel: (512) 887-7135.

**Corsicana:** Cassel Flea Market, 708 S 7 St. Tel: (903) 872-7170.

**Dallas:** Daddy Jack's Flea Market, 2817 S Westmoreland Rd. Tel: (214) 331-6657.

**Dallas:** Ignacia Gomez Flea Market, 9797 Bruton Rd 1009. Tel: (972) 288-3374

**Dallas:** Kleburg Flea Market, 13939 CF Hawn Fwy. Tel: (972) 557-1717.

**Dayton:** County Line Flea Market, FM Rd 1960. Tel: (409) 258-8251.

**Del Rio:** Flores Market, Hwy 277 S Spur 239. Tel: (830) 774-6305.

**Del Rio:** Sal's Flea Market, Spur 239. Tel: (830) 775-9588.

**Denton:** Flea Market 380, 3932 E University Dr. Tel: (940) 566-5060.

**Diboll:** Olde Frontier Town, Hwy 59 S. Tel: (409) 632-8696.

**Dickinson:** Morgan Flea Market, 2802 Hwy 3. Tel: (281) 337-1290.

**Donna:** Valverde Flea Market, Bus 83 & Valverde Rd. Tel: (956) 464-8169.

**Eagle Pass:** Speedy's Flea Market, N Hwy 277. Tel: (830) 773-9783.

**Edinburg:** 281 Flea Market Inc, 3300 N Hwy 281. Tel: (956) 380-2616.

**Edinburg:** Trading Post Flea Market, FM 1426. Tel: (956) 787-9824.

**Elmendorf:** I-37 Flea Market, 14050 Southton Rd. Tel: (210) 633-2220.

**El Paso:** Ascarate Drive-In Swap, 6701 Delta Dr. Tel: (915) 779-2303.

**El Paso:** Bronco Swap Meet, 8408 Alameda Ave. Tel: (915) 858-5555.

**El Paso:** David R Raum Flea Market, 6008 Naples St. Tel: (915) 755-6267.

**El Paso:** Fox Plaza Swap Meet, 5511 Alameda Ave. Tel: (915) 532-2444.

**El Paso:** Montana Flea Market, 9608 McIntosh Dr. Tel: (915) 593-2234.

**Euless:** APNA Bazaar, 102 S Ector Dr. Tel: (817) 545-6786.

**Fort Worth:** Henderson St Bazaar, 1000 N Henderson St. Tel: (817) 877-3021.

**Fort Worth:** Jesus Salvador-Avila Flea Market, 2115 Grayson Ave. Tel: (817) 625-4991.

**Fort Worth:** Little Flea Market, 1100 S Ayers Ave. Tel: (817) 534-1601.

**Fort Worth:** Shady Oaks Trade Days & Market, 7921 Jacksboro Hwy. Tel: (817) 237-3061.

**Fort Worth:** Trader's Market, 4330 Mansfield Hwy. Tel: (817) 535-5284.

**Fort Worth:** Treasure Village, 6250 Old Hemphill Rd. Tel: (817) 293-2898.

**Galveston:** Galveston Flea Market, 5902 Broadway St. Tel: (409) 744-4445.

**Gonzales:** Starnes Family Market, 1619 Hwy 90A By-pass. Tel: (830) 672-3271.

**Granbury:** Old Time Flea Market, 5830 E Hwy 377. Tel: (817) 326-6611.

**Granbury:** Four Seasons Flea Market, 4334 E Hwy 377. Tel: (817) 579-6888.

**Grand Prairie:** Antique Trade Fair, 4601 E Main St. Tel: (972) 264-1378.

**Greenville:** Downtown Tradin' Days, 2801 Lee St. Tel: (903) 454-9908.

**Greenville:** Treasure Chest Flea Market, 3624 Sockwell Blvd. Tel: (903) 455-6811.

**Hallettsville:** Family Resort Flea Market, FM Rd 957. Tel: (512) 798-5028.

**Hereford:** G & W Flea Market, 124 Gough St. Tel: (806) 364-6271.

**Hidalgo:** River Market, 910 S Monterrey St. Tel: (956) 843-9500.

**Houston:** 45 Flea Market Inc, 630 W Little York Rd. Tel: (281) 445-4566.

**Houston:** Airline Flea Market, 8801 Airline Dr. Tel: (281) 445-0126.

**Houston:** Beverly Palms Mini Market, 6061 Beverlyhill St. Tel: (713) 290-5390.

**Houston:** Cheng's Flea Market, 10802 Airline Dr. Tel: (281) 445-5269.

**Houston:** Country Weekend Common Market, 5115 S Shaver St. Tel: (713) 947-8522.

**Houston:** Gulf Freeway Indoor Market, 9820 Gulf Fwy. Tel: (713) 941-3074.

**Houston:** King's Flea Market, 5100 Griggs Rd. Tel: (713) 747-9234.

**Houston:** Northside Flea Market, 1415 Lorraine St. Tel: (713) 223-1030.

**Houston:** New Flea Market, 8315 Long Point Rd. Tel: (713) 722-7122.

**Houston:** Riches Flea Market, 9820 Gulf Fwy. Tel: (713) 944-4390.

**Houston:** San Jacinto Common Market, 630 Uvalde Rd. Tel: (713) 450-4700.

**Houston:** Sin Ta Flea Market, 8813 Airline Dr. Tel: (281) 931-8519.

**Houston:** Star Flea Market, 4412 N Shepherd Dr. Tel: (713) 697-0111.

**Houston:** Sunny Flea Market, 8705 Airline Dr. Tel: (281) 445-1981.

**Houston:** SW Indoor Flea Market, 6116 Windswept Ln. Tel: (713) 266-2785.

**Houston:** TODO Indoor Flea Market, 9429 Kempwood Dr. Tel: (713) 462-3988.`

**Houston:** Westheimer Flea Market, 1733 Westheimer Rd. Tel: (713) 520-6665.

**Irving:** Irving Flea Market, 635 S Belt Line Rd. Tel: (972) 986-2508.

**Jewett:** Flea Market of Jewett, Hwy 79. Tel: (903) 626-5674.

**Kingsville:** Kingsville Flea Market, 2420 E King Ave. Tel: (512) 516-0013.

**Kyle:** Kyle Flea Market, 1119 N Old Hwy 81. Tel: (512) 262-2351.

**Laredo:** Border Town Flea Market, Hwy 359. Tel: (956) 726-1186.

**Livingston:** Boyd Flea Market, 7001 Hwy 190 W. Tel: (409) 967-0547.

**Lubbock:** 50th & D Flea, 410 50 St. Tel: (806) 762-5300.

**Lubbock:** Flea Market, 2323 Ave K. Tel: (806) 747-8281.

**Lubbock:** Interstate Flea Market, 3424 I-27. Tel: (806) 765-7003.

**Lubbock:** Texas Ave Flea Market, 2312 Texas Ave. Tel: (806) 741-1414.

**Mabank:** Gun Barrel City Flea Market, 1307 W Main St. Tel: (903) 887-1000.

**Maud:** Benne Flea Market, 124 Main St. Tel: (903) 585-2392.

**Mauriceville:** Maurceville Flea Market, Hwy 12. Tel: (409) 745-4534.

**Mesquite:** Five Points Flea Market, 2651 S Belt Line Rd. Tel: (972) 329-2130.

**Midland:** Rainbow & Flea Market, 1503 W Industrial Ave. Tel: (915) 570-4408.

**Milam:** Texas Louisiana Flea Market, Hwy 21 W. Tel: (409) 625-3386.

**Mineola:** Co's Flea Market, Hwy 80 W. Tel: (903) 569-9290.

**Mineral Wells:** Mineral Wells Flea Market, 301 Gorgas St. Tel: (940) 325-9153.

**Mission:** Ochoa's Flea Market, N Conway & Four Mile Ln. Tel: (956) 580-1757.

**Mission:** Westown Flea Market, 6 Mile N Conway. Tel: (956) 519-3044.

**Nacogdoches:** Nacogdoches Flea Market, 5904 N St. Tel: (409) 564-3611.

**Nacogdoches:** Nacogdoches Trade Days, 1304 NW Stallings Dr. Tel: (409) 564-2150.

**Nacogdoches:** Twin Cities Flea Market, S Hwy 59. Tel: (409) 560-4366.

**Navasota:** Las Flores Trading Post, 1001 N La Salle St. Tel: (409) 825-8146.

**New Braunfels:** Schumansville Flea Market, FM Rd 725. Tel: (830) 625-0993.

**Odessa:** County Rd Flea Market, 6410 N County Rd W. Tel: (915) 368-4305.

**Odessa:** Henry's Flea Market, 7715 Andrews Hwy. Tel: (915) 366-8189.

**Odessa:** Ramirez Flea Market, 6110 Andrews Hwy 15. Tel: (915) 367-5801.

**Odessa:** VFW Flea Market, 6110 Andrews Hwy. Tel: (915) 367-1530.

**Odessa:** West Texas Flea Market, 4607 Rasco Ave. Tel: (915) 367-5760.

**Onalaska:** Onalaska Flea Market, Hwy 190. Tel: (409) 646-5480.

**Pampa:** B & B Flea Market, 915 Wilks St. Tel: (806) 665-4303.

**Paris:** Gene's Flea Market, 2810 NE Loop 286. Tel: (903) 785-1851.

**Pipe Creek:** Pipe Creek Flea Market, Hwy 16. Tel: (830) 535-4615.

**Pittsburg:** Hometown Flea Market, 800 N Greer Blvd. Tel: (903) 856-7006.

**Port Neches:** Old Towne Flea Market, 1216 Port Neches Ave. Tel: (409) 721-9690.

**Powderly:** Arthur City Flea Market, RR1 Box 297. Tel: (903) 732-4576.

**Quinlan:** Lake Tawakoni Trade Days, 1105 E Hwy 276. Tel: (903) 356-2520.

**San Antonio:** Gibson's Flea Market, 1331 Bandera Rd. Tel: (210) 432-5142.

**San Antonio:** International Flea Market, 1419 Commercial Ave. Tel: (210) 924-9311.

**San Antonio:** Los Gallos Flea Market, 11255 Moursund Blvd. Tel: (210) 628-1149.

**San Antonio:** Marbach Plaza Flea Market, 7014 Marbach Rd. Tel: (210) 674-5030.

**San Antonio:** Maria A Gil Flea Market, 1026 Shadwell Dr. Tel: (210) 735-2636.

**San Antonio:** Northwest Center Flea Market, 3600 Fredericksburg Rd. Tel: (210) 736-6655.

**San Antonio:** Palo Alto Flea Market, 1936 SW Loop 410. Tel: (210) 628-1896.

**San Antonio:** Ralph J Bayer Flea Markets, 126 Tomrob Dr. Tel: (210) 333-4941.

**San Antonio:** WW White Flea Market, 1265 S WW White Rd. Tel: (210) 333-7711.

**San Benito:** San Benito Flea Market, 2450 E Expwy 83. Tel: (956) 399-3690.

**Santa Fe:** 2004 Flea Market, 8935 Baker Rd. Tel: (409) 925-8578.

**Schertz:** County Line Trading Village, 18780 IH-35 N. Tel: (830) 606-1071.

**Seagoville:** KT's Belt Line Village Flea, 4240 S Belt Line Rd. Tel: (972) 287-7440.

**Seven Points:** Big Daddy's Traders Market, Hwy 274. Tel: (903) 432-4911.

**Seven Points:** Cedar Village Flea Market, Hwy 85. Tel: (903) 432-4333.

**Seven Points:** Seven Points Flea Market, Hwy 334 W. Tel: (903) 432-4554.

**Seymour:** Fred Harvey Flea Market, 909 N Main St. Tel: (940) 888-3188.

**Shiro:** Shiro Flea Market. Tel: (409) 874-2749

**Sinton:** Sinton St Flea Market, 200 W Sinton St. Tel: (512) 364-5020.

**Stanton:** Old Sorehead Trade Days, 301 N St Peter St. Tel: (915) 756-2006.

**Stephenville:** 3-Way Flea Market, Hwy 67. Tel: (254) 965-6868.

**Stephenville:** Chicken House Flea Market, Dublin Hwy. Tel: (254) 968-0888.

**Texarkana:** 67 Flea Market, 5605 W 7 St. Tel: (903) 838-4663.

**Texarkana:** Eylau Flea Market, 4112 S Lake Dr. Tel: (903) 832-7964.

**Texarkana:** Flea Market, 2411 W 7 St. Tel: (903) 792-5276.

**Texas City:** Texas City Flea Market, 621 7 Ave N. Tel: (409) 948-9708.

**Tyler:** N Beckham Flea Market, 825 N Beckham Ave. Tel: (903) 593-6693.

**Tyler:** Downtown Flea Market, 302 E Locust St. Tel: (903) 592-7123.

**Tyler:** Tyler Trade Day, Mineola Hwy. Tel: (903) 595-2223.

**Victoria:** Victoria Flea Market, 1402 E Mockingbird Ln. Tel: (512) 576-5924.

**Waco:** Treasure City Flea Market, 2118 La Salle Ave. Tel: (254) 752-5632.

**Waxahachie:** Waxahachie Flea Market, 2004 Howard Rd. Tel: (972) 937-4277.

**West Columbia:** Bridge St Flea Market, 115 Bridge Ave. Tel: (409) 677-3676.

**Wharton:** Lee's Flea Market, 622 E Milam St. Tel: (409) 532-0777.

**Whitesboro:** 82 Flea Market, RR4 Box 157. Tel: (903) 564-5348.

**Whitney:** Hwy 1713 Flea Market, Hwy 1713. Tel: (254) 694-2128.

# UTAH

## SALT LAKE CITY
### Antique Collectors' Fair

**DATES:** 2000: April, June, October. *Do call before going as the Salt Palace is undergoing renovations and the dates are set around their schedule.*
**TIMES:** Saturday 10:00 AM-6:00 PM; Sunday 10:00 AM-5:00 PM.
**ADMISSION:** $4, $3 with ad from local newspaper (in the classified section). Early bird admission for Saturday 9:00 AM-10:00 AM: $10.
**LOCATION:** Salt Palace Convention Center, in the heart of downtown Salt Lake City, 150 SW Temple (1 block from Temple Square).
**DESCRIPTION:** Limited to antiques and collectibles only, this market opened in 1986 and hosts 70 to 100 dealers during its three to four shows per year. Savvy shoppers and other dealers come from all over the west to restock their own inventory buying jewelry, vintage clothing, glassware, a huge variety of oak furniture, primitives, kitchenware, Mormon pine, prints, dolls, postcards, books, old tools, cowboy items, toys and more. Plenty of hotels, motels, and restaurants surround the Center. This is the only market of its type between Denver and the West Coast. Food is available on the premises.
**DEALER RATES:** $150 for a 10' × 13' booth; 10% additional for a wall or aisle end position. Setup Friday 10:00 AM-7:00 PM. Security is provided by the Salt Palace. RV parking within 3 miles of site.
**CONTACT:** James Reece Antique Promotion, PO Box 510432, Salt Lake City UT 84151. Tel: (801) 532-3401. Fax: (801) 364-1898. Email: 110126.2022@compuserve.com. Web: www.utmart.com.

### Redwood Swap Meet

**DATES:** Every Saturday and Sunday.
**TIMES:** Winters 9:00 AM-3:00 PM; summers 8:00 AM-4:00 PM.
**LOCATION:** 3600 S Redwood Rd. Take I-15 to 3300 S. Go west to 1700 W. Go south to Redwood Swap Meet.
**ADMISSION:** $.50 per person. Parking is free.
**DESCRIPTION:** This indoor/outdoor market started in 1972 and currently draws approximately 170 dealers in winter and up to 700 dealers in summer. The merchandise available includes antiques, collectibles, tools, electronics, hundreds of garage sales and new merchandise. Fresh farm goods and craft items are also available. Food is served on the premises. Showers and overnight parking are available on premises.

**DEALER RATES:** $12 per dealer on Saturday; $15 and up per space on Sunday. Reservations are suggested.
**CONTACT:** Redwood Swap Meet, 3688 S Redwood Rd, West Valley UT 84119. Tel: (801) 973-6060. Fax: (801) 973-0644.

## OTHER FLEA MARKETS

We know or have heard about these markets, but have not personally contacted each one, as we have the markets with descriptions. If you plan to visit one of these markets listed below, *please call first* to make sure they are still open. Flea markets do come and go. While they were open when we went to press, they may not be later. We can't be responsible. *Call first!*

**Blanding:** Ol'West Traders, 1949 S Hwy 191. Tel: (435) 678-2568.

# VERMONT

## CHARLOTTE
### Charlotte Flea Market

**DATES:** Saturday and Sunday, April through November, weather permitting.

**TIMES:** 6:00 AM-5:00 PM or later.

**ADMISSION:** Free. Parking is free.

**LOCATION:** Rt 7, just south of the Wildflower Farm, 10 miles south of Burlington. About 5 miles south of the Shelburne Museum.

**DESCRIPTION:** Located next door to the Wildflower Farm and just south of the famous Shelburne Museum, this market enjoys the crowds driving scenic Route 7. One of the oldest (opened in 1970) in Vermont, this market attracts an average of 40 dealers selling literally everything: old tools, books, clothing, garage sale items, paper, jewelry, crafts, glass and bottles, used and antique furniture, "stuff," new merchandise, whatever. A snack bar serves the hungry. This place really is a local flea market in every good sense of the word.

**DEALER RATES:** For a 3-table setup, tables and canopies included: $15 a day. Reservations are not required.

**CONTACT:** Larry Lavalette, PO Box 415, Shelburne VT 05482-0415. Tel: (802) 425-2844.

## CHELSEA
### Chelsea Flea Market

**DATES:** Second Saturday of July.

**TIMES:** 10:00 AM-4:00 PM.

**ADMISSION:** Free. Parking is free.

**LOCATION:** On the North and South Common of Chelsea, on Rt 110, south of Barre.

**DESCRIPTION:** Started in 1971 by the Ladies Service Guild of a local church, this show has grown to include 110-120 vendors from all over New England. Over 3,000 visitors choose from antiques, collectibles, and whatever. The Fish and Game Department runs the famous chicken barbecue (a special Vermont treat); hot dogs and sodas are sold by the Ladies Service Guild. The Chelsea Library holds their annual Book Sale at the Town Hall during this show. Chelsea is another of Vermont's beautiful towns stretched along the back roads. Definitely worth the trip.

**DEALER RATES:** $20 per space. Call for reservations as there is a long waiting list.
**CONTACT:** Elaine Braman, Flea Market Coordinator, 444 VT Rt 110, Chelsea VT 05038. Tel: (802) 685-3392.

---

### History Lesson

Chelsea is stretched out along the picturesque First Branch of the White River and Route 110. Because it is the shire town of Orange County, it is the legal seat of the county with its own courthouse. In the very early years farmers would graze their sheep and livestock in two areas along the main street—the park in front of the courthouse, and the one in front of the church at the other end of town. Thus, Chelsea is one of the few towns (if there are any others) with *two* town commons.

---

# CRAFTSBURY COMMON
## Craftsbury Antique and Unique Festival

**DATES:** Second Saturday in July, come heck or high water!
**TIMES:** 10:00 AM-4:00 PM.
**ADMISSION:** Free. Parking is free.
**LOCATION:** On Craftsbury Common itself. From the south: take Rt 100 heading north through Morrisville to Rt 15 east to Rt 14 north, follow the signs to Craftsbury, then Craftsbury Common. From the north: Rt 14 south from Newport and follow the signs.
**DESCRIPTION:** Set in the picturesque village of Craftsbury Common, this special market, started in 1970, helps raise funds for the Vermont Children's Aid Society. The dealers specialize in antiques, collectibles and unique crafts including stuffed animals, jewelry, handmade wooden clocks and other treasures. Sterling College is next door and the local sports center is home to some wild mountain-bike races. Food is provided by local bakers. The Anderson sisters bring in 15 to 20 home-baked pies and there are lines backed up to buy their mouth-watering specialties before they ever get there! This is considered a "four-plunger day" by the two directors of the Festival. You'd better ask either Judy and Alice about this one. Relief facilities are available, for real now.
**DEALER RATES:** $65 for a 16' frontage and ample space behind. Reservations are a must and should be in by sometime in January as the invitations to sell are sent in February. There is a *long* waiting list for this event.

**CONTACT:** Judith Reiss, VCAS, PO Box 127, Winooski VT 05404-0127. Tel: (802) 655-0006.

# MANCHESTER CENTER
## Manchester Flea Market

**DATES:** Every Saturday and Sunday, May through October, weather permitting.
**TIMES:** 9:00 AM-5:00 PM.
**LOCATION:** Junction of Rts 11 and 30. Take Bromley Mountain Rd 3 miles from the center of Manchester.
**ADMISSION:** Free. Free parking is available.
**DESCRIPTION:** This outdoor show has operated since 1970 in the heart of the Green Mountains and ski country. Stratton, Magic and Bromley ski areas surround Manchester. It currently attracts 35 to 40 dealers of primarily antiques, with collectibles, crafts, with some farm goods also available. There is an exhibit of antique farm machinery here, and this is also the location of a locally well-known Saturday auction. Robert Todd Lincoln's historic home Hildene is nearby and open to the public. Wessners Surplus Store resides here, too. One snack bar and restrooms add to the amenities.
**DEALER RATES:** $15 per 20' × 15' space. Advance reservations are suggested.
**CONTACT:** Albert H Wessner, Box 1960, Manchester Center VT 05255. Tel: (802) 362-1631.

# NEWFANE
## The Original Newfane Flea Market

**DATES:** Every Sunday, May through October. Rain or shine.
**TIMES:** 7:00 AM-5:00 PM.
**ADMISSION:** Free. Ample free parking is available.
**LOCATION:** On Rt 30, 1 mile north of downtown Newfane.
**DESCRIPTION:** This outdoor market has been around since 1963 and is claimed to be the oldest and largest in Vermont. It is well known throughout the state, attracting between 150 and 200 dealers who come from near and far to exhibit such diverse items as antiques, collectibles, craft items, new merchandise, and fresh produce—in a word: "Everything." Three food concessions and an ice cream stand satisfy any hunger pangs you may suffer.
**DEALER RATES:** $20 per space. No reservations period! Dealers may camp free Saturday nights.

**CONTACT:** Bill Morse, The Original Newfane Flea Market, PO Box 55, Newfane VT 05345-0055. Tel: (802) 365-4000.

---

### History Notes

When Teddy Roosevelt was President, he came through Newfane and had dinner at the hotel that was then attached to the local jail. The hotel has since been torn down, but the building's other half, still housing the now discontinued jail, is the Windham Co. Sheriff's office. In any case, when TR heard that the prisoners were fed the same food as the hotel guests, he volunteered to return after his term of office, break some minor law, and retire in bliss to the jail, where he could get the same wonderful meals for free.

*From Archer Mayor*

---

### Some Mysterious Fiction

For those of you who read Archer Mayor's mystery series, starring Joe Gunther of the Brattleboro Police Department, this is just about where all his stories take place, in and around southeastern Vermont.

---

### On the Subject of Breakfast

From Bill Morse, whose wife's grandmother served TR coffee at that hotel, it was TR who coined the phrase, "Good to the last drop," referring to his morning java.

---

## SOUTH HERO
### South Hero Flea Market

**DATES:** Saturday and Sunday and holidays, Memorial Day weekend through the end of September.
**TIMES:** 8:00 AM-4:00 PM.
**ADMISSION:** Free. Parking is free.
**LOCATION:** US Rt 2 in the Champlain Islands, with easy access from Burlington off I-89 Exit 16 or from New York State.
**DESCRIPTION:** This indoor/outdoor market of up to 50 vendors sells a variety of items. Some of the stuff sold is antiques, collectibles, sporting goods (this is the land of sports, folks), books, furniture, crafts, tools, clothes,

and whatever. Don't count on any real new stuff. According to Helena, "If you can't find it here, you don't need it." Getting to this market is a treat as the drive through the islands is quietly gorgeous—especially towards the end of September.

**DEALER RATES:** For 30' × 30' space outside: $7 per day. $1 per round table and $2 for a long. Inside units at $100 per month. Some covered areas $10 per day with electricity. Reservations are not required.

**CONTACT:** Helena Wilder, South Hero Flea Market, 595 Rt 2, S Hero VT 05486. Tel: (802) 372-4769. Or contact Charles Langlois, 21 Curtis Ave, Burlington VT 05401. Tel: (802) 864-5091.

# WAITSFIELD
## Mad River Green Farmers' Market

**DATES:** Saturday, from last weekend in May through first weekend in October.

**TIMES:** 9:30 AM-1:30 PM.

**ADMISSION:** Free. Parking is free.

**LOCATION:** Mad River Green Shopping Center, Rt 100.

**DESCRIPTION:** Started in 1992 as a way for local farmers to sell their rich produce, this outdoor market attracts a chair caner, craftspeople, flowers and herbs, fresh organic produce, cookie mixes, new clothing, baked goods, relishes, jams and jellies, maple syrup, handcrafted furniture and other Vermont-produced goods. A live band of local musicians (different every week) plays during the market in a gazebo constructed for that purpose. There are plenty of home-grown and organic foods as well as home-made snacks available on the green. It is at the far end of a small shopping center which includes a Green Mountain Coffee Roasters coffee shop, a restaurant, hardware store and other businesses. This is quite a tourist attraction in a four-season resort area with three ski areas, golf, horseback riding (and Icelandic pony rides), and soaring, among other activities. Labor Day weekend the Valley Players hold their annual 2-day Craft Fair with over 100 Vermont crafters selling high quality goods.

**DEALER RATES:** $15 per market day for 12' × 14' space. No walk-ins permitted. Reservations are required.

**CONTACT:** Burgy von Trapp, PO Box 269, Waitsfield VT 05673-0269. Tel: (802) 496-5856.

## Some Local History

Waitsfield is located just about in the middle of Vermont. When the founding fathers decided to build a state capital, they reckoned where the middle of the state was—Waitsfield (so they were wrong by 6 miles). They asked Waitsfield's founding father if they could build their capital in this picturesque valley. Henry Wait's reply, "Not in my backyard!" Montpelier was built about 20 miles east on the Winooski River, which is considerably larger than the Mad River that meanders through Waitsfield into the Winooski.

Charles Kuralt wrote an article on his 10 favorite roads in the United States, this section of Route 100, from Granville through Waitsfield, was #7 on the list.

# WATERBURY
## Waterbury Flea Market

**DATES:** Saturday, Sunday, and holidays, weather permitting, May through October.

**TIMES:** Daybreak to exhaustion. Usually 6:00 AM to 6:00 PM, but things slow down in the afternoon.

**ADMISSION:** Free. Parking is free.

**LOCATION:** Rt 2, just north of Waterbury. Exit 10 W off I-89.

**DESCRIPTION:** Opened in 1979, this outdoor market attracts anyone and everyone with up to 100 vendors selling everything from classic antiques, attic treasures, ancient books and old magazines, new merchandise, jewelry, tools new and very old, furniture, yard-sale and house cleanouts, collectibles and "stuff." It's the locals clearing house. Great finds! A snack concession with delicious hot dogs sates hungry appetites. Then again, there is Ben & Jerry's Ice Cream and the Cider Mill around the corner and down Route 100.

**DEALER RATES:** $7 Saturday, $9 Sunday for a 20' × 25' space. Dealers may camp over the weekend for free and setup on Friday. No dogs, please.

**CONTACT:** Waterbury Flea Market, PO Box 178, Waterbury, VT 05676.

## Winter Indoor Flea Markets

**DATES:** They run one Sunday market a month from October through March or April depending on Armory schedule. Call for dates.

**TIMES:** 9:00 AM-3:00 PM.

**ADMISSION:** $1. Parking is free.

**LOCATION:** Waterbury Armory. Take Exit 10 W off I-89 towards Waterbury, at the T-intersection turn left, then left again. Follow the signs to the Armory.

**DESCRIPTION:** These popular shows are used as fundraisers for a variety of local non-profit organizations (Red Cross, library programs, and more). At least 30 dealers come to sell their antiques, collectibles, attic finds, garage sale clean-outs, crafts, trinkets, and what-have-yous to eager patrons. A food concession and restrooms are available on the premises.

**DEALER RATES:** About $25 a table (depends on the Armory's benevolence). Reservations are required.

**CONTACT:** Willis & Willis, PO Box 182, Waterbury Center VT 05677-0182. Tel: (802) 244-5519.

# WATERBURY CENTER
## Stowe Road Flea Market

**DATES:** Saturday and Sundays, June through October's fall foliage season. Weather permitting.

**TIMES:** 9:00 AM-5:00 PM. Could be earlier and later depending on weather, light and dealer inclination.

**ADMISSION:** Free. Parking is free.

**LOCATION:** Rt 100. Only 3.2 miles from I-89, Exit 10 Waterbury Stowe, on the road to Stowe. Not even 3 miles north of Ben & Jerry's Ice Cream Factory.

**DESCRIPTION:** This outdoor market, opened in 1971, has the unique distinction of being surrounded by some of Vermont's biggest attractions: Ben & Jerry's Ice Cream Factory (the largest tourist attraction in the state), the Cold Hollow Cider Mill across the street, and the resort town of Stowe just north on scenic Route 100. They host anywhere from 20 to 50 dealers selling loads of antiques, collectibles, Vermont crafts, glass, furniture, garage sale goodies and whatever turns up. New merchandise is rare and discouraged. If you are hungry, try B&J's or the cider mill. Enjoy! Do find Walter and say Hello.

**DEALER RATES:** $10 for a 25' × 20' space per day, or $18 for the weekend. Reservations are not required. Tents (10' × 20') or 8' tables are available by advance reservation.

**CONTACT:** Col Walter Flatow, CAI, 3579 Waterbury Stowe Rd, Waterbury Center VT 05677. Tel: Walter or Marie at (802) 244-8817 or Barb at (802) 244-8879.

# WILMINGTON
## Wilmington Outdoor Antique and Flea Market

**DATES:** Saturday, Sunday and holiday Mondays, from the weekend before Memorial Day through the weekend after Columbus Day.

**TIMES:** No specific times, really. Say dawn on…

**ADMISSION:** Free. Parking is free.

**LOCATION:** Junction of Rts 9 and 100.

**DESCRIPTION:** Since 1982 this market has been located on a choice 10-acre lot at the junction of two heavily traveled scenic roads through Vermont. They do a lot of advertising and draw crowds. Up to 125 dealers sell antiques, collectibles, garage sale items, all manner of stuff. Food is available from a concession stand.

**DEALER RATES:** $15-$20 per space. Reservations are not required.

**CONTACT:** Peter and Sally Gore, Wilmington Outdoor Antique and Flea Market, PO Box 22, Wilmington VT 05363-0022. Tel: (802) 464-3345.

---

**On TV**

Wilmington Flea Market was mentioned on "Antique Road Show" when someone told the ARS they bought a painting for $50 and it sold for $450.

---

Two dealers met at the market and decided that combining their booths as well as their lives was a pretty good idea. Check them out; they sell handcrafted items.

---

Sign on the Millbrook Store at Willoughby Lake:
FLEE MARKET
INSIDE

---

**Chickens to Chippendale**

If you are on an antique scouring of Vermont, don't miss the markets scattered along Rt 5 that follows the Connecticut River on the east side of Vermont. They are everywhere!

---

# VIRGINIA

## ALTAVISTA
### First Saturday Trade Lot

**DATES:** First Saturday of each month and the preceding Friday, year round.

**TIMES:** Friday noon until 4:00 PM on Saturday.

**ADMISSION:** Free. Parking is free, *but limited*.

**LOCATION:** On Seventh St, 1 block off Bus Hwy 29, between Lynchburg and Danville.

**DESCRIPTION:** This outdoor market first opened in 1911 and is one of the oldest flea markets in the East. There are more than 200 dealers selling mostly antiques, collectibles, crafts, new and secondhand merchandise, as well as some produce. There is also food available on the premises. Don't miss the hot dogs. I am assured they are terrific! The Altavista High School Band Boosters now run this show and man the concession stand to help pay their expenses. Uncle Billy's Day (the first Saturday weekend in June, including the preceding Friday) is a town-wide celebration that lasts three days centered around the Trade Lot. Uncle Billy started the Trade Lot by trading animals at the turn of the century. Fireworks, entertainment and more are featured on this weekend.

**DEALER RATES:** $10 per 9' × 20' space for the weekend. Six-month reservations are $8 per weekend paid in advance. Uncle Billy's Day space is $25 a space unless already reserved for six months. Reservations are strongly suggested, or else. Town permits are required and sold there for $1.50 a year. No telephone reservations are accepted.

**CONTACT:** Altavista Band Boosters, PO Box 333, Altavista VA 24517-0333. Tel: (804) 369-5001 (Town Hall).

## CHANTILLY/WASHINGTON DC
### DC Big Flea

**DATES:** For 2000: January 8-9, March 4-5, July 15-16, September 16-17. Call for 2001 dates.

**TIMES:** Saturday 10:00 AM-6:00 PM, Sunday 11:00 AM-5:00 PM.

**ADMISSION:** $5; children under 12 free. Parking is free.

**LOCATION:** Chantilly Convention Center.

**DESCRIPTION:** This show has over 500 dealers from 20 states in one (two in January) huge building. Their dealers sell primarily antiques and collectibles. It is claimed to be the "fastest growing market on the East

Coast." Food concessions and handicapped-accessible restrooms add to the amenities.

**DEALER RATES:** $90 single space, $180 double space. Reservations are required. This facility does charge $65 for electrical hookup.

**CONTACT:** D'Amore Promotions, 2125 McComas Way Ste 102, Virginia Beach VA 23454. Tel: (757) 427-7717. Fax: (757) 427-8888. Web: www.bigfleamarket.com.

# CHRISTIANBURG
## A-1 Flea Market and Antique Emporium

**DATES:** Saturday and Sunday.

**TIMES:** 8:00 AM-5:00 PM.

**ADMISSION:** Free. Parking is also free.

**LOCATION:** 940 Radford St. Rt 11.

**DESCRIPTION:** Open since 1982, this market houses 20 permanent dealers selling everything including guns, knives, antiques, dolls, tools, vintage glassware (Fenton, Cambridge, Heisey, Fostoria—loads of these treasures), custom-made clothing, sports (race and ball) cards, comics and much more. Every weekend they hold remote-control car races both on paved and off-road track!

**DEALER RATES:** $115 per month for a 12' × 24' space. Reservations are required.

**CONTACT:** Kathryn Minnick, A-1 Flea Market and Antique Emporium, 940 Radford St, Christiansburg VA 24073. Tel: (540) 382-9811.

# FREDERICKSBURG
## Manor Mart Flea Market

**DATES:** Saturday and Sunday, year round.

**TIMES:** 7:00 AM-dusk.

**ADMISSION:** Free. Parking is free.

**LOCATION:** US Hwy 1, just south of Fredericksburg.

**DESCRIPTION:** An indoor/outdoor flea market established in 1983, the Manor Mart offers over 100 dealers selling antiques, collectibles, crafts, and new merchandise, as well as fresh produce. It is located near historic Fredericksburg, scene of much Civil War fighting and near other historic battlefields. Food is available on the premises; motels and campgrounds are nearby.

**DEALER RATES:** $10 per 16' × 10' booth (indoors and out). Reservations are not required. There are monthly rates for buildings; just call.
**CONTACT:** Nick or Jeannie Dommisse, Manor Mart Flea Market, 9040 Jeff Davis Hwy, Fredericksburg VA 22407. Tel: (540) 898-4685.

# HARRISONBURG
## Shenandoah Heritage Farmers' Market
**DATES:** Monday through Saturday.
**TIMES:** 10:00 AM-6:00 PM.
**ADMISSION:** Free. Parking is free and quite ample.
**LOCATION:** 121 Carpenter Ln. Take I-81 Exit 243, go south on Rt 11. Market is on the left.
**DESCRIPTION:** This market's dealers sell antiques, collectibles, garage sale goodies, crafts, home-canned goods, fresh produce, sports equipment, bulk foods, silk flowers, and plenty of new merchandise. There is a full-service restaurant and handicapped-accessible restrooms to satisfy your every need.
**DEALER RATES:** Please call for rates, as their dealers are permanent, but there may be openings.
**CONTACT:** Brenda, Shenandoah Heritage Farmers' Market, 121 Carpenter Ln, Harrisonburg VA 22801. Tel: (540) 433-3929.

# HILLSVILLE
## VFW Labor Day Gun Show and Flea Market
**DATES:** Friday through Monday, Labor Day weekend. Rain or shine.
**TIMES:** 8:00 AM-6:00 PM.
**LOCATION:** At the VFW Complex. On US Rt 58-221 W (Galax Rd), 1 mile east of I-77.
**ADMISSION:** $1 per person; children under 12 admitted free. Parking is $3 a day; $10 a day for RVs.
**DESCRIPTION:** This market is one of the granddaddys of markets! The population of the town of Hillsville expands five-fold during this annual event sponsored by the Grover King Post 1115 Veterans of Foreign Wars. The show has been held each year since 1967, and in 1986 it brought over 250,000 shoppers despite rain and cold weather, according to local police records. There are over 2,400 spaces (they added another 45 new spaces in 1999), but how many dealers depends on how many spaces a dealer nabs. Usually, 950-1,500 dealers set up selling a variety of items that goes beyond

firearms and militaria to encompass all types of antiques and collectibles including coins, jewelry, glassware, tools, toys, and other Americana. For the 1986 show, visitors registered from 40 different states plus four foreign countries, and attendance is growing each year. Food is served on the premises.

**DEALER RATES:** $50 per 9' × 20' space plus vendor license fee, for four days. Dealer reservations are required. Dealers set up Thursday prior to the show.

**CONTACT:** Joseph G Semones, VFW Flea Market, 2421 Airport Rd, Hillsville VA 24343-8581. Tel: (540) 728-7188.

# OAK GROVE
## Red Barn Flea Market

**DATES:** Friday through Sunday. "Absolute" auctions held on the first and third Saturdays. No buyers premium.

**TIMES:** Winter: Friday and Sunday 12:00 PM-4:00 PM, Saturday 9:00 AM-4:00 PM; Summer: Friday and Sunday 12:00 PM-5:00 PM, Saturdays 9:00 AM-5:00 PM.

**ADMISSION:** Free. Parking is also free.

**LOCATION:** Westmoreland County, 36 miles east of Fredericksburg on Rt 3. On left of road, look for the big red barn.

**DESCRIPTION:** This market started in August 1989 as an addition to an auction house, which started originally as a huge horse barn—"the size of a football field." Crammed with 38-plus dealers inside and growing, selling antiques, and baby booties to house trailers, collectibles, glassware, toys, books, TVs, appliances, "everything." Carolyn loves old books and collects them; if you have any old books or stories, stop and chat. This is a friendly, old-fashioned country market the way flea markets used to be. They were written up in the July 1998 issue of *Mademoiselle* as a great place to shop.

**DEALER RATES:** $35 per month inside. $5 a day for outside table space. Reservations are suggested as they have a waiting list.

**CONTACT:** Curtis and Carolyn Bartmess, Red Barn Flea Market, 330 Circle Ln, Colonial Beach VA 22443. Tel: (804) 224-1119.

---

### Don't You Wish

The Bartmess' sold a set of candlesticks with hanging crystals on them for $20, then they saw them for sale at Christie's for $20,000.

# PETERSBURG
## South Side Station Market Place

**DATES:** Daily.

**TIMES:** Weekdays 10:00 AM-5:00 PM. Weekends 8:30 AM-5:00 PM.

**ADMISSION:** Free. Parking is free.

**LOCATION:** 5 River St, off I-95 Exit 52 to Washington St, follow Historic Olde Towne Petersburg signs to Visitor's Center. They are located just behind the farmers' market.

**DESCRIPTION:** Opened in 1993, this indoor/outdoor market's dealers sell antiques, collectibles, crafts, produce, cards, garage sale goodies, furniture, new merchandise, fabric, Old Mansion coffee, teas and spices, ceramics, fine jewelry, toys, and clothing. One coffee shop and handicapped-accessible restrooms add to the amenities.

**DEALER RATES:** Building 1: $.75 per square foot. Building 2: $150 per 13' × 16' space, monthly. First come, first served. Outdoor sales: $5 per day.

**CONTACT:** Gibbons Sloan or Emily, PO Box 2820, Petersburg VA 23804-2820. Tel: (804) 733-5050. Fax: (804) 733-0667.

# RICHMOND
## American Heritage Antique Jubilee

**DATES:** For 2000: October 27-29. Rain or shine.

**TIMES:** Saturday 10:00 PM-5:00 PM; Sunday 12:00 PM-5:00 PM.

**ADMISSION:** Friday $20 (Early Buyers Pass for 3 days); Saturday and Sunday $5 per day. Parking is free.

**LOCATION:** Richmond State Fairgrounds at Strawberry Hill, 600 E Laburnum Ave.

**DESCRIPTION:** An annual, multi-dimensional show featuring indoor and outdoor spaces. Over 1,000 dealers come from 35 states. This is an antique and collectible show only with entertainment and specialty food vendors. Handicapped-accessible restrooms add to the amenities.

**DEALER RATES:** $110 per heated space, $70 for unheated space, $70 per outdoor space. Tents are available for outdoor vendors at affordable rates. Reservations and pre-payment are required.

**CONTACT:** D'Amore Promotions, 2125 McComas Way Ste 102, Virginia Beach VA 23454. Tel: (757) 427-7717. Fax: (757) 427-8888. Web: www.bigfleamarket.com.

## Bellwood Flea Market

**DATES:** Saturday and Sunday, year round. Weather permitting.
**TIMES:** 5:30 AM-4:30 PM.
**ADMISSION:** $1 per person. Free parking.
**LOCATION:** 9201 Jefferson Davis Hwy. Exit 64 off I-95 and Willis Rd, south of Richmond.
**DESCRIPTION:** This market has been run since 1970 outdoors. Between 150 and 400 dealers offer antiques, collectibles, handmades, produce, meats, musical instruments, auto parts, appliances, real estate, furniture, clothing and new merchandise, as well as tools and curios. A large air-conditioned food concession opens early and remains open all day. There are still reminders of the fierce Civil War battle fought on the Bellwood property as people are occasionally finding mini-balls and some trench-works are still visible. Dealers and buyers from as far away as Alaska and Florida come here for goodies!
**DEALER RATES:** $12 per 20' × 20' space. First come, first served.
**CONTACT:** Julie Kline Campbell, c/o Bellwood Flea Market, 9201 Jeff Davis Hwy, Richmond VA 23237. Tel: (804) 275-1187 or 1-800-793-0707.

---

### What a Find

An old ugly wooden chair, with pegs, was purchased for $50 from an elderly couple. The young man knew it was worth something because of the pegs. It was sold in Pennsylvania at a big market for enough to buy a new truck!

---

## The Big Flea Market at the Richmond State Fairgrounds

**DATES:** For 2000: January 29-30, March 18-19, April 15-16, July 8-9, August 5-6, September 2-3, November 25-26. Call for 2001 dates.
**TIMES:** Saturday 10:00 PM-5:00 PM; Sunday 12:00 PM-5:00 PM.
**ADMISSION:** $2; children under 12 free. Parking is free.
**LOCATION:** Richmond State Fairgrounds at Strawberry Hill, 600 E Laburnum Ave.
**DESCRIPTION:** Part of a series of shows started in 1977, this show has between 300 to 600 spaces filled with dealers from 15 states. They sell primarily antiques and collectibles and some new merchandise. This market is considered the largest antique flea market in the Mid-Atlantic region. Food concessions and handicapped-accessible restrooms add to the amenities.

**DEALER RATES:** $75 per space per show. $140 for two spaces per show. Reservations are required.

**CONTACT:** D'Amore Promotions, 2125 McComas Way Ste 102, Virginia Beach VA 23454. Tel: (757) 427-7717. Fax: (757) 427-8888. Web: www.bigfleamarket.com.

## SuperFlea Flea Market

**DATES:** Saturday and Sunday

**TIMES:** 9:00 AM-6:00 PM.

**ADMISSION:** Free. Parking is free.

**LOCATION:** 5501 Midlothian Tnpk, (Rt 60), 1 mile east of Chippenham Pkwy.

**DESCRIPTION:** This 12-year-old indoor/outdoor market houses up to 250 dealers in 300-400 booths in a huge 100,000-square-foot heated and air-conditioned building and has 200 or so outside spaces. The mix is about 50/50 new merchandise to antiques, collectibles, and garage sale goodies. There is a restaurant on site, as well as handicapped-accessible restrooms.

**DEALER RATES:** 10' × 12' booth—$210 per month, 6' × 12' booth—$165 per month, tables—$15 per day or $25 per weekend, sidewalk—$10 per day. Electricity is available in all booths.

**CONTACT:** SuperFlea Flea Market, 5501 Midlothian Tnpk, Richmond VA 23225. Tel: (804) 231-6687. Web: www.americanparknswap.com.

# ROANOKE

## Happy's Flea Market

**DATES:** Tuesday through Sunday, year round.

**TIMES:** Tuesday through Friday 8:00 AM-5:00 PM; Saturday and Sunday 6:30 AM-5:30 PM.

**ADMISSION:** Free. Parking is free.

**LOCATION:** 5411 Williamson Rd NW (Rt 11). Hershberger Rd Exit off Rt 581.

**DESCRIPTION:** Obviously successful, this market has been open since 1978. There are 150 inside dealers, another 300 outside with 100 of those spaces permanently reserved. The dealers sell an endless variety of everything: antiques, batteries, collectibles, used and new merchandise, and much more. A restaurant is on the premises as well as handicapped-accessible restrooms. There are outlet stores as part of the scene.

**DEALER RATES:** $10 Saturday and Sunday; $3 Tuesday; $5 Wednesday through Friday. Monthly and yearly rates available. First come, first served.
**CONTACT:** Bob Meyer, Manager, Happy's Flea Market, 5411 Williamson Rd, Roanoke VA 24012. Tel: (703) 563-4473/4.

# VIRGINIA BEACH
## Virginia Beach Antique and Collectible Expo
**DATES:** May 26-28 and August 25-27, 2000.
**TIMES:** Friday 7:00 PM-10:00 PM; Saturday 10:00 AM-7:00 PM, Sunday 12:00 PM-5:00 PM.
**ADMISSION:** $2; children under 12 are free. Free parking.
**LOCATION:** Virginia Beach Pavilion Convention Center. Take Rt 64 to the end, Rt 44. Follow the signs.
**DESCRIPTION:** For 17 years this show has been attracting up to 300 dealers from 15 states selling only antiques and collectibles, plus assorted crafts and new merchandise. This show is considered one of Virginia's largest antiques and collectibles shows and is part of a series of shows held in Richmond, Hampton, DC and Salem. Food concessions and handicapped-accessible restrooms add to the amenities.
**DEALER RATES:** $75 per single space; $140 per double space per show. Reservations and deposits are required. Dealer space sells out fast.
**CONTACT:** D'Amore Promotions, 2125 McComas Way Ste 102, Virginia Beach VA 23454. Tel: (757) 427-7717. Fax: (757) 427-8888. Web: www.bigfleamarket.com.

# OTHER MARKETS

We know or have heard about these markets, but have not personally contacted each one, as we have the markets with descriptions. If you plan to visit one of these markets listed below, *please call first* to make sure they are still open. Flea markets do come and go. While they were open when we went to press, they may not be later. We can't be responsible. *Call first!*

**Abingdon:** Banner Star Flea Market, 550 Russell Rd NW. Tel: (540) 628-2937.
**Aldie:** Great Aldie Flea Market, 39359 John Mosby Hwy. Tel: (703) 327-4452.

**Boones Mill:** A 1 Flea Market, 21231 Virgil H Goode Hwy N. Tel: (540) 334-2323.

**Boones Mill:** Buckboard Flea Market, Rt 220N.

**Bristol:** Lee Hwy Flea Market, 2671 Lee Hwy. Tel: (540) 669-6366.

**Brookneal:** Bill's Bargain Barn, Hwy 501 N. Tel: (804) 376-5151.

**Chesapeake:** Bypass Flea Market, 1325 Battlefield Blvd S. Tel: (757) 546-1584.

**Chesapeake:** Do Drop In Flea Market, 3020 S Military Hwy Bldg B. Tel: (757) 485-8511.

**Edinburg:** Flea Market, 164 Landfill Rd. Tel: (540) 984-8771.

**Franklin:** A-Z Flea Market, 618 South St. Tel: (757) 562-3955.

**Gainesville:** Park's Flea Market, 14221 Lee Hwy. Tel: (703) 754-4087.

**Gordonsville:** Gordonsville Antique & Flea, Rt 15 & Klockner Rd. Tel: (540) 832-7376.

**Gretna:** Gretna Flea Market, 101 N Main St #A. Tel: (804) 656-6902.

**Hillsville:** Bowman Flea Market, Hwy 221. Tel: (540) 728-2340.

**Hillsville:** Howlett St Flea Market, 1017 W Stuart Dr. Tel: (540) 728-0604.

**Kilmarnock:** Noah's Ark Flea Market, 21 N Main St. Tel: (804) 435-6716.

**Manassas:** Manassas Flea Market, 9608 Grant Ave. Tel: (703) 330-1197.

**Martinsville:** Broad St Flea Market, 226 Broad St. Tel: (540) 632-9873.

**Martinsville:** Martinsville Mega Flea, Rt 220S. Tel: (540) 638-1471.

**Mechanicsville:** Frances's Flea Market, 10211 Chamberlayne Rd. Tel: (804) 730-1230.

**Mechanicsville:** Mechanicsville Flea Market, 8238 Mechanicsville Pike. Tel: (804) 746-4248

**Newport News:** Flea Market, 10171 Jefferson Ave. Tel: (757) 599-5565.

**Norfolk:** Big Top Flea Market, 7600 Sewells Point Rd. Tel: (757) 480-3122.

**Norfolk:** Flea Market of Norfolk, 3416 N Military Hwy. Tel: (757) 857-7824.

**Portsmouth:** J&L Flea Market, 3709 Victory Blvd. Tel: (757) 485-3013.

**Pound:** Mountain Traders Flea Market, 10115 Orby Cantrell Hwy. Tel: (540) 796-9276.

**Richmond:** Azalea Flea Market, 5209 Wilkinson Rd. Tel: (804) 329-8853.

**Richmond:** Best Flea Market, 5400 Midlothian Tnpk. Tel: (804) 232-8828.

**Richmond:** Larry's Flea Mart, 4104 Williamsburg Rd. Tel: (804) 236-9378.

**Richmond:** Super Flea Mart, 5501 Midlothian Tnpk. Tel: (804) 231-6687.

**Roanoke:** Melrose Flea Market & Antique, 4215 Melrose Ave NW. Tel: (540) 362-2201.

**Rustburg:** Big B Flea Market, RR1 Box 195 Lot 1-7. Tel: (804) 821-1326.

**Smithfield:** Smithfield Flea Market, 120 N Church St. Tel: (757) 357-0417.

**South Boston:** Fifty Eight Flea Market, 8216 Philpott Rd. Tel: (804) 753-1637.

**South Boston:** Riverside Flea Market. Tel: (804) 575-6816.

**Suffolk:** Boone's Indoor Flea Market, 226 E Washington St. Tel: (757) 539-4350.

**Temperanceville:** Shore Flea Market, 12085 Lankford Hwy. Tel: (757) 824-3300.

**Virginia Beach:** Bill's Flea Market, 4815 Virginia Beach Blvd. Tel: (757) 340-0233.

**Warsaw:** Warsaw Flea Market, 396 Main St. Tel: (804) 333-4062.

**Waynesboro:** Waynesboro Flea Market, 121 E Broad St. Tel: (540) 943-8933.

**Winchester:** Swap Mart, 134 N Loudoun St. Tel: (540) 665-3146.

**Winchester:** Valley Avenue Flea Market, 1000 Valley Ave. Tel: (540) 722-6768.

**Zuni:** CJ's Yard Sale Heaven, 5358 Windsor Blvd. Tel: (757) 242-3413.

# WASHINGTON

## CLARKSTON
### Bridge Street Marketplace

**DATES:** Friday and Saturday, year round.
**TIMES:** 8:30 AM-2:30 PM.
**ADMISSION:** Free. Parking is free.
**LOCATION:** 1342 Bridge St. Bridge St is on Hwy 12 running through Clarkston from Walla Walla to Lewiston ID.
**DESCRIPTION:** This new flea market, opened in March 1999 with 20-35 indoor and outdoor (the spillover) vendors, offers antiques, collectibles, comics, vintage clothing, yard sale goodies, Budweiser memorabilia, tools, antique toys, car parts, lots of miscellaneous items, and new and used merchandise. There is a Farmers' Market in summer. An antique shop is being added to the structure. There are camping facilities nearby. Other necessary amenities: handicapped-accessible restrooms and an expresso wagon. If you hit their website, you can see some of the goodies for sale: a Mariner's signed baseball (signed by them all!), a Harley-Davidson etched logo, and old Singer sewing machines.
**DEALER RATES:** $10 per table. Reservations would be nice.
**CONTACT:** Lisa, Bridge Street Marketplace, 1342 Bridge St, Clarkston WA 99403. Tel: (509) 751-9939. Email: antique@clarkston.com. Web: www.highway12antiques.com.

---

**Historical Note**

For you history buffs, the Bicentennial of the Lewis & Clark Expedition will be celebrated in these parts in 2003. Highway 12 *is* the Lewis & Clark Trail.

---

## EVERETT
### Puget Park Swap-O-Rama

**DATES:** Saturday and Sunday, April through October. Weather permitting.
**TIMES:** 9:00 AM-3:30 PM.
**ADMISSION:** $1 per person. Free parking is provided.
**LOCATION:** 13020 Meridian Ave S. The 128th St exit off I-5.
**DESCRIPTION:** Started in 1975, this market currently attracts up to 250 dealers who set up to sell a wide range of objects including antiques, col-

lectibles, fine art, crafts, fresh produce, and some new merchandise. A snack bar with a full kitchen feeds the famished. This area is near the marina where the whale-watching boats take off for trips through the spectacular San Juan Islands. Not to be missed.

**DEALER RATES:** $13 for a 20' × 20' space per day; $16 for a 20' × 40' space with electricity. Advance reservations are advised, but not necessary, and can be made in person Fridays from 12:00 PM-5:00 PM or during market hours.

**CONTACT:** Valentine Reyes, Puget Park Swap-O-Rama, PO Box 91723, Bellevue WA 98009. Tel: (425) 337-1435 (market) or call Mike Lancaster at the head office (425) 455-8151. Fax: (425) 455-8165.

# KENNEWICK
## Cable Bridge Flea Market

**DATES:** Daily, except Tuesdays and Sunday mornings.

**TIMES:** 10:00 AM-5:00 PM, except Tuesday and Sunday morning.

**ADMISSION:** Free. Parking is free.

**LOCATION:** 433 E Columbia Dr. Find the cable bridge (it's hard to miss); they are below it.

**DESCRIPTION:** This two-year-old market may have only 12 dealers, but that's all they could stuff into a 4,000-square-foot building. According to Mary, this place is so crammed that first-time visitors stand in awe upon entering. They are especially loaded with collectibles and old jewelry; other items include some antiques, one dealer sells appliances, others housewares. Anyone can set up outside, there's always room. This is the former Kennewick Flea Market moved from its old location. Say Hi to Mary, if you can find her among the treasures.

**DEALER RATES:** Outside: $5 per table, first come, first served. Inside, call first, as it is *stuffed!* However, Mary says she could make room for you. Then you would be charged by the square foot (not cubic foot).

**CONTACT:** Mary Scott, Cable Bridge Flea Market, 210 905E Schuster Rd, Kennewick WA 99337. Tel: (509) 586-7413.

# KENT
## Midway Swap 'N Shop

**DATES:** Saturday and Sunday, year round.

**TIMES:** 8:00 AM-4:00 PM.

**ADMISSION:** $1 adults, children under 12 free. Parking is free.

**LOCATION:** 24050 Pacific Hwy S, 5 miles south of Sea-Tac Airport on Hwy 99.

**DESCRIPTION:** Opened in 1971, this large indoor/outdoor market hosts 200 dealers inside and 500 outside selling plenty of yard sale treasures, appliances, clothes, some antiques and collectibles (culled from the yard sale stuff), produce in season and new merchandise. There is plenty of food available from speed bars and snack bars, as well as a Polish barbecue. Handicapped-accessible restrooms are on site.

**DEALER RATES:** $13.50 per space per day, inside 9' × 9', outside 18' × 18'. Reservations are required in the summer as they get full. Pay in advance for the following weekend, or come in on Friday for that weekend to assure yourself a space.

**CONTACT:** Frank Wilson, Manager, Midway Swap 'N Shop, PO Box 3068, Kent WA 98032-3068. Tel: (206)878-2536.

# PASCO
## Pasco Flea Market

**DATES:** Every Saturday and Sunday, March through November.

**TIMES:** 6:00 AM-4:00 PM.

**ADMISSION:** $1 per carload.

**LOCATION:** Pasco Kahlotus Hwy. Jct of Hwy 12 and E Lewis St.

**DESCRIPTION:** Averages up to 300 vendors with antiques, collectibles, new and used merchandise, cars, crafts, books, clothing, new and used furniture, and lots of fresh produce. Snack bars and concessions feed the famished.

**DEALER RATES:** $7 per space, 20' × 25'. Reservations are nice, but not necessary.

**CONTACT:** Pasco Flea Market, PO Box 3845, Pasco WA 99302. Tel: (509) 547-5035 (market) or 547-7057 (home).

# PROSSER
## Prosser Harvest Festival

**DATES:** Friday through Sunday, the third weekend of September.

**TIMES:** 10:00 AM-5:00 PM or later.

**LOCATION:** At the corner of 6th and Meade in downtown Prosser. Mostly downtown Prosser.

**ADMISSION:** Free. Free parking is available nearby.

**DESCRIPTION:** This outdoor market started in 1972 and is held in conjunction with the annual Great Prosser Balloon Rally. This is the annual Harvest Festival (formerly known as the Prosser Flea Market) that includes the entire town of Prosser. There are sidewalk sales, farmers' market stands and vendors everywhere. It currently attracts a lot of outside dealers selling a large variety of antiques and collectibles, unbelievable arts and crafts "to die for," fresh herbs, new merchandise, and loads of freshly harvested produce. Food is available on the premises. There is entertainment for the children. The balloons go up early Saturday and Sunday morning and Saturday night they light the balloons up in a spectacular "night glow" display.

**DEALER RATES:** $15 per dealer for the whole shebang. Reservations are required.

**CONTACT:** Prosser Chamber of Commerce Harvest Festival Chairman, 1230 Bennett Ave, Prosser WA 99350. Tel: (509) 786-3177 or 1-800-408-1517.

## SEATTLE
### Fremont Sunday Outdoor Flea

**DATES:** Sundays, May through October.

**TIMES:** 10:00 AM-5:00 PM.

**ADMISSION:** Free. Parking is free.

**LOCATION:** At the corner of N 34th St and Fremont Ave near the Fremont Bridge in the central parking lot of the Red Door Tavern. Just 1 mile from the Space Needle.

**DESCRIPTION:** Established in 1989, this popular Sunday market offers 120-150 vendors selling antiques, collectibles, used merchandise, used furniture, crafts, jewelry, fresh farmers' produce, international items, new and used merchandise.

**DEALER RATES:** $26 and up for either 8' × 8' or 10' × 10' space. First come, first served. To set up, come between 7:00 AM-8:30 AM. Tables and chairs can be rented for $5 per day.

**CONTACT:** Fremont Sunday Flea and Farmers Market, 3416 Evanston Ave N, Seattle WA 98103-8604. Tel: (206) 781-6776.

## TACOMA
### "America's Largest" Antique and Collectible Sale

**DATES:** 2000: February 5-6, June 3-4, and September 29-October 1 (this last date is tentative at press time, call first).

**TIMES:** Saturday 8:00 AM-7:00 PM; Sunday 9:00 AM-5:00 PM.

**LOCATION:** Tacoma Dome, Tacoma Dome Exit off I-5.

**ADMISSION:** $5, kids under 12 are free, kids 12-17 are $2. Parking is handled by the Tacoma Dome and costs $4 to $5.

**DESCRIPTION:** The first Tacoma Dome market was held June 1989. This market and its more than 785 booths deal only in high quality antiques and collectibles. Food is available on the premises.

**DEALER RATES:** $140 per 10' × 10' booth. $280 per 10' × 20' booth, $275 per 10' × 30' booth. Reservations are mandatory.

**CONTACT:** Chuck or Christine Palmer, Palmer/Wirfs & Associates, 4001 NE Halsey, Portland OR 97232. Tel: (503) 282-0877 or fax: (503) 282-2953.

## TACOMA
### Star-Lite Swap 'N Shop

**DATES:** Tuesday through Sunday.

**TIMES:** Tuesday-Friday 10:00 AM-7:00 PM inside, 8:30 AM-6:00 PM outside. Weekends 9:00 AM-6:00 PM inside, 8:00 AM-6:00 PM outside.

**ADMISSION:** $1 adults, $.75 seniors and juniors (12-15), under 12 free. Parking is free.

**LOCATION:** The Star-Lite Drive-In Theater, 8327 S Tacoma Way.

**DESCRIPTION:** This huge indoor/outdoor market hosts 200 or so dealers inside year round and 300-400 dealers outside in an old-fashioned flea market. Much of the merchandise is new, although there are some collectibles (beanies) and other items, plenty of produce in season, some furniture, appliances, and clothes. There are a Chinese deli, a cafeteria, and handicapped-accessible restrooms on site.

**DEALER RATES:** Outside: weekdays $8 for space, weekends $10 for 10' × 20', $15 for 20' × 30' space. Inside: $200 per month.

**CONTACT:** Star-Lite Swap 'N Shop, 8327 S Tacoma Way, WA 98499-4577. Tel: (253) 588-8090. Fax: (253) 588-8929.

## OTHER FLEA MARKETS

We know or have heard about these markets, but have not personally contacted each one, as we have the markets with descriptions. If you plan to visit one of these markets listed below, *please call first* to make sure they are still open. Flea markets do come and go. While they were open when we went to press, they may not be later. We can't be responsible. *Call first!*

**Blaine:** King's Flea Market & General Store, 2078 Peace Portal Dr. Tel: (360) 332-8278.

**Burlington:** Skagit Valley Market Place, 973 S Burlington Blvd. Tel: (360) 757-2443.

**Ephrata:** Major Flea Market, 1884 Basin St SW. Tel: (509) 754-2788.

**Ferndale:** Grandview Flea Market, 7056 Portal Way M. Tel: (360) 366-0128.

**Hoodsport:** Flea Market Potlatch, 22190 N US Hwy 101. Tel: (360) 877-6686.

**Lynden:** Flea Market Inc, 444 Front St Ste 104. Tel: (360) 354-7576.

**Ocean City:** Ocean City Flea Market, 2615 SR 109. Tel: (360) 289-9635. Open daily 9 AM-5 PM.

**Pe Ell:** Fleamarket, 217 N Main St. Tel: (360) 291-3202.

**Puyallup:** South Hill Trading Post, 6805 112 E. Tel: (253) 435-5653.

**Shelton:** Jackson's Flea Market, 14848 N US Hwy 101. Tel: (360) 426-7282.

**Shelton:** Treasure Cove Flea Market, 1209 Olympic Hwy S. Tel: (360) 426-5577.

# WEST VIRGINIA

## BLUEFIELD
### City of Bluefield Parking Facilities Flea Market

**DATES:** Every Saturday, March through November.

**TIMES:** 6:00 AM-2:00 PM.

**ADMISSION:** Free. Metered parking is available.

**LOCATION:** On Princeton Ave, at the junction of Rts 19 and 460, in the heart of Bluefield.

**DESCRIPTION:** This indoor market began in 1981, and now draws approximately 175 dealers selling a wide range of items including antiques and collectibles, crafts, fresh produce, and new merchandise. Shopping can begin as early as 5:30 AM as people hurry to catch the best bargains. Two snack bars serve the hungry.

**DEALER RATES:** $5 per 14' × 20' space. First come, first served or some reserved.

**CONTACT:** Sharon Leffel, City of Bluefield, Parking Commission, 514 Scott St, Bluefield WV 24701. Tel: (304) 327-2401 ext 272 at City Hall.

## EARNSHAW
### Spring Mountain Park

**DATES:** Friday through Sunday, April through September.

**TIMES:** 10:00 AM-6:00 PM.

**ADMISSION:** Adults $1, seniors $.50, children under 12 free when accompanied by an adult. Parking is free.

**LOCATION:** Wetzel County Rt 64. Between WV SR 7 and Scenic Rt 250. It's the 7th property coming from WV Rt 7 going toward Earnshaw.

**DESCRIPTION:** This new market, opened in 1999 on 105 acres, boasts 600 shops selling crafts, antiques, collectibles, the "most wonderful things," and new merchandise. Various snack vendors are scattered around the market.

**DEALER RATES:** Starting at $120 and up for four 3-day weekends. Self-contained camping is available for dealers. Advance pre-paid reservations are required, as is a West Virginia State Tax Permit. Office hours: Thursday 10:00 AM-3:00 PM.

**CONTACT:** Jonathan Barnes, Rentals or Kandi Roche, PO Box 99, Mail Rt 1, Earnshaw (Metz) WV 26585. Tel: (304) 775-5396. Main Office: (702) 804-8788. Fax: (702) 804-8807. Email: KernCo88@aol.com.

# FAYETTEVILLE
## Bridge Day

**DATES:** Third Saturday in October (by state law!).

**TIMES:** 10:00 AM–4:00 PM.

**ADMISSION:** Free. Parking along roadway and in Fayetteville.

**LOCATION:** New River Gorge Bridge, US 19 between Fayetteville and Lansing.

**DESCRIPTION:** Remember the TV ad where a "Jimmy" car was shoved over the side of a bridge attached to a bungee cord? This is the bridge; the longest single arch bridge in the world, the second highest in the United States at 876 feet. Bridge Day is the celebration of the building of this bridge. One day a year, since 1980, the police close off the northbound lanes of this four-lane bridge and all traffic is narrowed down to the two remaining lanes. Tourists come from all over to watch the goings on. Last year 42 vendors set up along the north end of the 3,030-foot-long bridge and the rest (total averages 200 vendors) on the south end, selling or performing West Virginia crafts, food, produce, tourism, gospel singing—whatever! Over 100,000 people invade the bridge on foot to participate. Parachutists fling themselves off the bridge trying to land on the "landing pad." Some don't make it onto the dry parts and have to be fished out of the water. The dealers must meet and get organized starting at 6:30 AM and then line up in their assigned order of booth number. At the appointed moment, they charge the bridge to their space, set up and sell like mad until 3:00 PM when the state police come by to tell them it's time to pack up. They must be off the bridge by 4:00 PM, otherwise they will be run over.

**DEALER RATES:** Out-of-state dealer rates: $110 before August 1, $200 for a 25' space after August 1, $150 for WV residents. Reservations are mandatory.

**CONTACT:** Executive Director, Bridge Day, 310 Oyler Ave, Oak Hill WV 25901. Tel: 1-800-927-0263. Email: fayette@citynet.net. Web: www.fayettecounty.com (look under Links).

---

### Market Tales

A couple married on the bridge during one Bridge Day, then "took the plunge" parachuting down the gorge. That year, they had about 210,000 visitors!

Ace Whitewater runs rafting trips with a special on Bridge Day. They stop under the bridge, serve a gourmet meal and watch, from safe river banks, the shenanigans of parachutists and bungee jumpers—plunging into space.

# HARPERS FERRY
## Harpers Ferry Flea Market

**DATES:** Saturday and Sunday, plus Memorial Day and Labor Day, from March to December.

**TIMES:** Dawn to dusk.

**ADMISSION:** Free. Parking is free.

**LOCATION:** On Dual Hwy 340 at Bloomery Rd, about 1 mile from Harpers Ferry Historical Park. Only 60 miles from Washington DC and Baltimore.

**DESCRIPTION:** Started in 1983, this market hosts an average of 200-plus dealers selling collectibles, antiques, crafts, yard sale treasures, a veritable variety of goodies. This is definitely a family market! Funnel cakes, fries, ice cream, and hot dogs as well as breakfast are sold at the various snack bars. Visitors come from all over the East Coast but mainly from Baltimore and Washington DC. Harpers Ferry is located where the Potomac and Shenandoah Rivers converge, where John Brown led his famous raid on the Harpers Ferry Arsenal, with plenty of interesting outdoor activities (hiking, biking, etc.) as well as a National Park, the C&O Canal and a historical museum. It is truly a beautiful area to visit.

**DEALER RATES:** $11 per day per 20' × 24' space with a table. Reservations are not required. First come, first served. A limited number of pavilion spaces are also available.

**CONTACT:** Harpers Ferry Flea Market, 904 Oregon Trail, Harpers Ferry WV 25425. Tel: Ron at (304) 725-4141 or Dan (304) 725-0092. Email: info@harpersferryfleamkt.com. Web: www.harpersferryfleamkt.com.

### Family History

A man from Washington DC, visiting the market and looking at old pictures, found a familiar photo. Taken 35 years before, it showed the fellow as a lad fishing with his father and grandfather, both of whom had since died. He was so excited to see the picture that the kind dealer gave it to him as a gift.

**Just Hanging Around**

Two older couples once asked if they could rent a space. No problem. They picked a nice grassy spot with a great view, laid out their blankets and then a grand picnic. For four hours they sat and watched the market and the view while enjoying their repast. They later thanked the owners for giving them such a lovely observation area.

# MARTINSBURG
## I-81 Flea Market

**DATES:** Friday, Saturday and Sunday, weather permitting, year round.
**TIMES:** 8:00 AM-6:00 PM.
**ADMISSION:** Free. Parking is free.
**LOCATION:** Off Exit 20, off I-81, Spring Mills area.
**DESCRIPTION:** Opened in 1989, this outdoor market has up to 140 outside dealers selling antiques, collectibles, crafts and new merchandise. Their building, housing the inside dealers and farmers' market, burned down on September 3, 1995, but the outside dealers have kept the market alive. A food wagon serves the standard snack bar fare and handicapped-accessible restrooms come in handy.
**DEALER RATES:** $5 Friday, $11 Saturday and Sunday per space, plus tax. Reservations would be nice, but not necessary.
**CONTACT:** Betty Kline, I-81 Flea Market, Rt 2 Box 230, Martinsburg WV 25401. Tel: (304) 274-3387.

# MILTON
## Milton Flea Market

**DATES:** Friday, Saturday and Sunday.
**TIMES:** Friday 8:00 AM-4:00 PM, weekends 8:00 AM-5:00 PM.
**ADMISSION:** Free. Parking is free.
**LOCATION:** Take Exit 28 (Milton WV) off I-64, turn north to junction US 60, turn east ¼ mile. You can't miss it.
**DESCRIPTION:** Open since 1989, this indoor/outdoor market has 500 dealers inside and spaces for 100 outside (number of dealers depends on the weather!) selling "really old antiques," collectibles, crafts, tools, new and used clothing, musical instruments, baseball cards, books (you can trade in the ones you've read), trains, toys, comic books, *fudge*, woodwork, and a

variety of other goods. One restaurant and two snack bars deal with the hunger not quelled by the *fudge*. There are restrooms (handicapped accessible) on the premises. In 1993 they added roofs to the outside spaces as well as 60 new vendor spaces. The local Chamber of Commerce recommended this market and said it was one of the biggest around.

**DEALER RATES:** $30 and up for the weekend indoors (there is a waiting list) for a 10' × 14' space; $8 and up for 10' wide and whatever deep outside space (depends on the location of the space). First come, first served. Reservations are okay.

**CONTACT:** Boyd & Betty Meadows, PO Box 549, Milton WV 25541-0549. Tel: (304) 743-9862 or 743-1123.

# MORGANTOWN
## Blue Horizon Flea Market at the
## Morgantown Auto Auction

**DATES:** Sunday, year round.

**TIMES:** 6:00 AM-1:00 PM (when people drift out).

**ADMISSION:** Free. Parking is $1 per car.

**LOCATION:** Rt 19 north of Morgantown.

**DESCRIPTION:** Opened in 1989, this indoor/outdoor market houses about 100 dealers selling lots of "good old junk" as well as some antiques and collectibles, yard sale stuff, the occasional new merchandise, produce in season, household stuff, some live animals (rabbits), historic old newspapers, and whatever. There is a cafeteria serving breakfast, a hot dog stand, a corner meeting area especially adapted for the handicapped, as well as handicapped-accessible restrooms.

**DEALER RATES:** $7 per table inside, outside $2-$3 per space, depending on size. Reservations are needed inside (some dealers have been there for ages and reserve "their" spot). Outside is first come, first served.

**CONTACT:** Morgantown Auto Auction, Box 2118, Morgantown WV 26505-2118. Tel: (304) 328-5851 or 1-800-443-7702. Fax: (304) 328-5854.

---

**I Didn't Know That!**

One of the owners of the Auto Auction found a 1948 phone book among the piles of stuff sold. It listed his then phone number as 3217. Weren't those the easy-to-remember days.

---

# OTHER MARKETS

We know or have heard about these markets, but have not personally contacted each one, as we have the markets with descriptions. If you plan to visit one of these markets listed below, *please call first* to make sure they are still open. Flea markets do come and go. While they were open when we went to press, they may not be later. We can't be responsible. *Call first!*

**Belle:** Witcher Flea Market, 2211 E Dupont Ave. Tel: (304) 949-5480.

**Center Point:** Center Point Market. Tel: (304) 782-4417.

**Chapmanville:** Traders Town Flea Market, Corridor G. Tel: (304) 855-4259.

**Charleston:** Capitol Flea Market, 24 Meadowbrook Shopping Plz. Tel: (304) 342-1626. Open every Friday, Saturday and Sunday, 8AM-5PM.

**Charleston:** Rt 21 Flea Market, 2388 Sissonville Dr. Tel: (304) 345-4603.

**Charleston:** Bill's Flea Market, 1457 Washington St W. Tel: (304) 344-4337.

**Elkins:** Elkins Flea Market, 110 Poplar St. Tel: (304) 636-5823 or 636-0175.

**Fairmont:** Baxter Volunteer Fire Department Flea Market, Auburn & Belt St. Tel: (304) 366-7201.

**Falling Waters:** I-81 Flea Market Inc, 1721 Robin Ln. Tel: (304) 274-3387.

**Glen Dale:** Glen Dale Drive-In Theatre. Tel: (304) 845-2064.

**Kermit:** Corner Flea Market, Rt 52 Eastgate Mall. Tel: (304) 393-3643.

**Kingwood:** Price Street Flea Market, 146 South Price St. Tel: (304) 329-3679.

**Masontown:** Valley Trading Center, RR 1 Box 316. Tel: (304) 864-9915.

**Moorefield:** Tony's Flea Market, 231 S Main St. Tel: (304) 538-7680.

**Morgantown:** Walnut Street Indoor Flea Market, 218 Walnut St. 26505-5402. Tel: (304) 292-9278.

**Mt Clare:** Suds Run Flea Market, 126 Suds Run Rd #A. Tel: (304) 622-1032.

**Parkersburg:** Sundowner, 1025 Gihon Rd. Tel: (304) 422-8935.

**Ripley:** Fort Ripley Flea Market, Ripley Shopping Ctr, 108 Academy Dr. Tel: (304) 372-3532.

**Shinnston:** The Sunset Flea Market, Rt 19. Tel: (304) 592-0405.

**White Sulphur Springs:** Valley Barn, Rt 92. Tel: (304) 536-1028.

**Yawkey:** Midge's Flea Market, RR 3. Tel: (304) 524-7639.

# WISCONSIN

## ADAMS
### Adams Flea Market

**DATES:** Every Saturday and Sunday, May through October; also open Memorial Day, July 4th, and Labor Day.
**TIMES:** 6:00 AM-4:00 PM.
**ADMISSION:** Free. Free parking available.
**LOCATION:** 556 S Main St, by the railroad tracks in Adams.
**DESCRIPTION:** This market has been operating since 1980 and growing each year. There are 57 permanent indoor dealers and 100 outdoors, with 15 acres of grounds on which to expand. This is a country market with plenty of trees, grass, wildflowers, birds and small animals around to awe the newcomers. There's a bit of everything here, from antiques, collectibles, and handcrafted items, to farm produce and a good mix of old and new merchandise. One dealer deals with sports cards, another is one of the largest suppliers of canopies around. For your convenience, there is a lunch wagon on the premises. A note: no dogs are allowed on the grounds; please leave them in your car if you bring them.
**DEALER RATES:** $7 or $10 per day for each table. There is reserved table space for the whole year, should you need it. No advance reservations are taken. No overnight camping.
**CONTACT:** Ms Irene Steffen, 2151 Hwy 13, Adams WI 53910. Tel/Fax: (608) 339-3079. Day of show call (608) 339-9223.

## CALEDONIA
### 7 Mile Fair/Market Square

**DATES:** Saturday and Sunday, year round.
**TIMES:** April-October 7:00 AM-5:00 PM; November-March 9:00 AM-5:00 PM.
**ADMISSION:** $1.25 for adults, senior citizens $1. Children 11 and under free with parents. Free parking is provided.
**LOCATION:** 2720 W 7 Mile Rd. At the intersection of I-94 and 7 Mile Rd, Exit at 7 Mile Rd. It is 15 miles south of Milwaukee and 25 miles north of the Illinois-Wisconsin state line.
**DESCRIPTION:** This indoor/outdoor market began in 1961, added a 45,000-square-foot building in 1989 and another 60,000-square-foot building in 1994. There are now approximately 1,000 dealers in summer and 300 in

winter marketing a wide variety of antiques, crafts, collectibles, and new merchandise. The outdoor farmers' market sells fresh vegetables, fruits and flowers. Permanent food concessions and handicapped-accessible restrooms are on the premises.

**DEALER RATES:** $25 per 12' × 24' space per weekend outside, first come, first served; $50-$80 per 8' × 10' booth inside per weekend, reservations required. Office hours are Monday through Friday 8:00 AM-4:00 PM.

**CONTACT:** Scott T Niles, 7 Mile Fair Inc, PO Box 7, Caledonia WI 53108-0007. Tel: (414) 835-2177. Email: sevenmf@execpc.com. Web: www.fleamarkets.com/7milefair.

# CEDARBURG
## Maxwell Street Days

**DATES:** Four shows a year. Always the last Sunday in May and July, Labor Day Monday, first Sunday in October. Rain or shine.

**TIMES:** 6:00 AM to between 2:00-3:30 PM.

**ADMISSION:** Free. Parking $3 on the Park grounds.

**LOCATION:** Firemen's Park. 796 N Washington Ave. Follow the cars (or pedestrians) and if you find an empty parking space—*grab it!*

**DESCRIPTION:** This is an all-volunteer non-paid firemen-run market and the main fundraiser for the Cedarburg Fire Department. (The American Legion gets the parking money as their fundraiser.) Opened in the 1960s, it is one of the largest markets in the Midwest. There are over 1,100 spaces for dealers. Representative of what is sold includes: lots of antiques and collectibles, junk, flea market goodies, fresh produce, garage sales, a sign-maker, a construction company selling gazebos, and a siding company plying their trade. No animals, firearms or fireworks allowed. They are encouraging mostly antiques, collectibles, and used items rather than new. Some spaces have been property settlements in divorce cases! The firemen handle all the food concessions, including specialties like bratwurst, sauerkraut, pizza (okay, this is the local Booster Club's effort), health food, ice cream, and the usual fare.

**DEALER RATES:** $30 and up per space per event. Reservations are absolutely necessary. Call the number and follow instructions on the tape message.

**CONTACT:** Cedarburg Firemen's Park, PO Box 344, Cedarburg WI 53012-0344. Tel: (414) 377-8412.

# DELAVAN

## Geneva Lakes Greyhound Track Flea Market

**DATES:** Saturday and Sunday, from the first weekend in May through the first weekend in October.

**TIMES:** 8:00 AM-5:00 PM.

**ADMISSION:** Free. Parking is free.

**LOCATION:** Hwy 50 and I-43, located right off I-43 at Delavan.

**DESCRIPTION:** Started in 1999, this new market of 16 dealers and growing sells antiques, collectibles, crafts, books, fresh produce, and new merchandise. There isn't any food at the market, but there is at the track, as are potties. Located on beautiful grounds in the Heart of Vacation Land. Two thousand vehicles are there for the dog races on Friday evening, Saturday matinee, Saturday evening and Sunday matinee. There are special events held on the grounds several weekends in the summer, including one of the best fireworks displays in the area. This is a great resort area with several major resorts within a five-mile radius.

**DEALER RATES:** $30 per 16' × 24' space. Bring your own setup. There isn't any electricity. No early breakdowns and weekends can be split up as long as Sally knows ahead of time. Setup starts at 6:00 AM Saturday, and 7:00 AM Sunday morning. If you pre-pay and get rained out, Sally will honor rain dates.

**CONTACT:** Sally Yungerman, Geneva Lakes Greyhound Track, 1600 E Geneva St Hwy 50, Delavan WI 53115. Tel: 1-800-477-4552 ext 510. Email: sjkb@elknet.net.

# EAGLE RIVER

## ERRA Flea Market

**DATES:** Sunday of Labor Day Weekend.

**TIMES:** 8:00 AM-4:00 PM.

**ADMISSION:** $1. Parking is free.

**LOCATION:** Eagle River Recreation Arena. One mile east of Eagle River on Rt 70.

**DESCRIPTION:** Started in 1989 to celebrate the last weekend of the summer season, this market of 100-plus vendors sells antiques, collectibles, new merchandise, junk, tools, crafts and whatever. This area is a summer resort attracting thousands of visitors from all over the country. They close out the season having a field day checking out and buying new "finds." Food is available on the premises.

**DEALER RATES:** $29.50 per space. Reservations are suggested.
**CONTACT:** Zurko's Midwest Promotions, 211 W Green Bay St, Shawano WI 54166. Call Eileen Potasnik or Bob Zurko at (715) 526-9769. Fax: (715) 524-5675.

# ELKHORN
## Antique Flea Market

**DATES:** 2000: May 21, June 25, July 16, August 13, September 24.
**TIMES:** 7:00 AM to whenever.
**ADMISSION:** $2 per adult, children free. Parking is free.
**LOCATION:** Walworth County Fairgrounds, Hwy 11 E.
**DESCRIPTION:** Started in 1989, this indoor/outdoor market hosts 700-plus dealers selling almost entirely old stuff. The requirement is pre-1970. Ladies, here's your chance to unload your hot pants and poodle skirts. Plenty of garage sale goodies and attic clean-outs show up here making it a good place to raid. There is plenty of good food and handicapped-accessible restrooms when the need strikes.
**DEALER RATES:** $40 per outside space, $50 per inside space, sizes vary. Reservations are a darned good idea.
**CONTACT:** Nona, NL Promotions LLC, PO Box 544, Elkhorn WI 53121-0544. Tel: (262) 723-5651.

# HATFIELD
## Giant Flea Market and Crafts at Thunderbird Village

**DATES:** Memorial weekend, July 4th weekend, the second weekend in August, and Labor Day weekend. The holiday weekends are all three days.
**TIMES:** Sunup to sundown.
**ADMISSION:** Free. Parking is free.
**LOCATION:** N9517 Thunderbird Ln. Thunderbird Village behind the Museum in downtown Hatfield. Just 12 miles NE of Black River Falls on County Trunk E or 6 miles SE of Merrillan on County Trunk K.
**DESCRIPTION:** For more than 30 years the Thunderbird Museum has held this market for approximately 180 dealers on the grounds of their museum. Amid towering pines, shoppers can browse through loads of antiques, collectibles, crafts, in-season produce, garage sale goodies and some new merchandise. The Thunderbird Eatery, Brenda's Fry Bread and several other food concessions satisfy the hunger pangs. Restrooms add to the amenities.

This market is in a summer resort area next to Lake Arbutus with plenty of camping, restaurants and an Indian casino nearby.

**DEALER RATES:** $10 and up depending on lot size (depends on the number of trees on the space and vehicle size), maximum 25' long. Electricity is available at $4 per day. Reservations are requested.

**CONTACT:** Jerry Miller, Thunderbird Museum, 7621 Hwy 13N, Pittsville WI 54466. Tel: summer (715) 676-2838.

# HAYWARD
## Hayward Fame Flea Market

**DATES:** Every Tuesday and Wednesday during June, July and August. They have four special events: Memorial and Labor Day weekends, Log Rolling weekend; and the weekend of July 4th and July 4th itself. Call for dates.

**TIMES:** 7:30 AM-4:00 PM.

**ADMISSION:** Free admission and free parking.

**LOCATION:** Junction of Hwy 27 S and Hwy B.

**DESCRIPTION:** This outdoor flea market, started in 1978, is located across from the National Fishing Hall of Fame. It attracts between 70 and 80 dealers in the summer who sell antiques, collectibles, crafts, and new and used merchandise. A world log rolling contest is held two blocks down the street from this market. Food is available and there are handicapped-accessible restrooms.

**DEALER RATES:** $8 per 12' × 25' booth. Reservations are suggested.

**CONTACT:** Jan Thiry, 10556 N Sunnyside Ave, Hayward WI 54843. Tel: (715) 634-4794.

# KENOSHA
## Kenosha Flea Market

**DATES:** Friday, Saturday and Sunday, year round.

**TIMES:** Friday 10:00 AM-5:00 PM; Saturday and Sunday 9:00 AM-5:00 PM; Christmas season hours are longer.

**ADMISSION:** Free. Parking is also free.

**LOCATION:** 5535 22nd Ave.

**DESCRIPTION:** Started in 1985 this small, but solid, "calm old-fashioned" indoor flea market has 40 vendors selling some antiques, collectibles, handmade decorated dolls and clothing, fresh produce, new appliances, more new merchandise, jewelry, household goods, electronics, junk, and more.

The variety of items changes as dealers leave and are replaced with different dealers and merchandise.

**DEALER RATES:** $20 and up depending on booth, location and size. Reservations are required, as they are currently full.

**CONTACT:** Beth or Don Goll, Kenosha Flea Market, 5535 22nd Ave, Kenosha WI 53140. Tel: (414) 658-3532.

# LADYSMITH
## Van Wey's Community Auction and Flea Market

**DATES:** April 20-something through last weekend in October, plus two-day holiday markets. Now held on either Saturday or Sunday, two or three times a month. Do call or write for the dates.

**TIMES:** 6:30 AM to sundown.

**ADMISSION:** Free. $.50 per vehicle parking.

**LOCATION:** On Hwy 8, 4½ miles west of Ladysmith.

**DESCRIPTION:** Now run by the third generation of the same family, this outdoor market began as a small community consignment auction on April 20, 1926, and had operated until 1996 on the fifth and twentieth of summer months, as these are the farmers' paydays from the local creamery. When the paydays changed, the market did too. Now the market is held on weekends, by popular demand. The flea market originally developed beside the auction and now has grown to attract nearly 200 dealers at peak season, along with thousands of shoppers from all over the country. As far as the range of items available, the managers have commented boldly that, "If you don't find it here you don't need it." Aside from the standard flea market fare, antiques, collectibles, auto parts, farm machinery, used clothing, and fresh farm products are available, along with miscellaneous and new merchandise. An auction starts at 10:00 AM on market days. A lunch stand and restrooms are available.

**DEALER RATES:** $8 or $10 per 14' × 20' space. Reservations are not required.

**CONTACT:** Mark and Judy Van Wey, W10139 Van Wey Ln, Ladysmith WI 54848. Tel: (715) 532-6044. Send a self-addressed stamped envelope for a schedule card of dates. Email: van-weyauction@jrec.com.

# MILWAUKEE
## Rummage-O-Rama

**DATES:** The schedule generally follows these weekends depending on holidays: January 1st weekend, February 1st and 3rd, March 3rd, April 2nd, May 3rd, September 2nd, October 1st and 3rd, November 3rd, December 1st and 3rd. *Please call first!*

**TIMES:** 10:00 AM-5:00 PM.

**ADMISSION:** $2; seniors $1.75; children 12-16 $.50; under 12 is free. Parking is free.

**LOCATION:** Wisconsin State Fair Park in Milwaukee. Off I-94, Exit 306.

**DESCRIPTION:** Started in 1973, classified as the "largest indoor show in the mid-west" and rated "one of the top ten in the USA," this market has 450-750 dealers selling antiques, collectibles, flea market treasures, new clothes, rummage goods, crafts, oak furniture, reproduction furniture, and a bit of everything including a kitchen sink. The dealers must stand behind their products, with a refund or replacement for new goods sold. This is such a family market/local affair that events are planned around these market dates, including weddings! Early birds come and line up their purses and bags to hold their places in line while they go chat and catch up on local gossip. An excellent biergarten restaurant serves luscious meals including sauerkraut and sausages, and there are booths selling homemade sausages and cheeses and low-cholesterol cookies. *Candid Camera* made an appearance here in September 1992 for one of their shows.

**DEALER RATES:** $70-$86 for a 10' × 10' space per weekend. Additional rental fee for table and chairs. Reservations are required.

**CONTACT:** Rummage-O-Rama, PO Box 510619, New Berlin WI 53151-061969. Tel: (414) 521-2111.

---

### There's a Lesson Here Somewhere
One dealer has discovered and purchased, inexpensively from this market, plenty of paintings that he has turned around and sold for over $10,000 each.

---

# OCONTO
## Copperfest 2000 9th Annual Flea Market
**DATES:** The second Saturday and Sunday in June.
**TIMES:** 8:00 AM-4:00 PM.
**ADMISSION:** Free. Parking is free.
**LOCATION:** Copperfest Grounds. Watch for the signs. Oconto is 30 miles north of Green Bay.
**DESCRIPTION:** This market of about 50 dealers is part of the annual Copperfest celebrated by the entire town of Oconto. It is put on by the Business Association and Jaycees with a parade, flea market, and the grand festival which runs from late Thursday through Sunday evening. The town is on Green Bay on the shores of Lake Michigan. Over 12,000 people view the ground parade through downtown Oconto. There's a craft show as part of this festival. A country-music pick-off is sponsored by a local tavern. Dealers sell handmade goods, antiques, collectibles, and garage sale stuff.
**DEALER RATES:** $15 for one day, $25 for two days, for a 20' × 20' space. Reservations are required. This rate will be confirmed by the market managers by market time.
**CONTACT:** Oconto Area Chamber of Commerce, PO Box 174, Oconto WI 54153-0174. Tel: (920) 834-2255.

---

### Great Beginnings
In 1963, Indian burial grounds were found nearby and money was needed to preserve this treasure. The City of Oconto decided to hold a festival to raise funds for this preservation work. The Copperfest has been a tradition since 1982.

---

# SHAWANO
## Shawano County Fairgrounds Flea Market
**DATES:** Every Sunday, April through October, except Labor Day weekend (when they hold their Eagle River ERRA market).
**TIMES:** Dawn-4:00 PM.
**ADMISSION:** $1 per person Sunday. Free parking (200 spaces).
**LOCATION:** Shawano County Fairgrounds. On Hwy 29, 30-minute drive west of Green Bay.
**DESCRIPTION:** This outdoor market has been around since 1972 and attracts over 200-plus dealers, as well as thousands of tourists seeking bar-

gains on such items as folk art, advertising items, antiques, tools, produce, gift items, fresh produce, etc. Special events include a "Super-Special" Memorial Day sale, a "Special Chicken Picnic" in mid-July, a July 4th "Big Bang" annual sale, stock car races every Saturday evening, three Indian casinos and many other attractions. Campgrounds and hotels are available nearby, and there are lots of food sellers, including popcorn and barbecue. Toilets are available.

**DEALER RATES:** $21.50 for a 20' × 15' space. Reservations are not required.

**CONTACT:** Zurko's Midwest Promotions, 211 W Green Bay St, Shawano WI 54166. Call Eileen Potasnik or Bob Zurko at (715) 526-9769. Fax: (715) 524-5675.

---

### Sad, but True Devotion

It was here that an 87-year-old dealer, a long-time fixture at the market, drove in to set up. Instead of his usual routine of driving directly to his spot, he drove around and through the market, everywhere, slowly. When he got to his spot, he stepped out of his car—and died.

---

## ST. CROIX FALLS
### Pea Pickin' Flea Mart

**DATES:** Saturday and Sunday and holidays, starting the third weekend in April through third weekend in October.

**TIMES:** 6:00 AM-5:00 PM.

**ADMISSION:** Free. Free parking is provided.

**LOCATION:** On Hwy 8, 5 miles east of St. Croix Falls near the junction of Rt 35 N.

**DESCRIPTION:** This indoor/outdoor market has been in business since 1968 selling a "good variety of things" including new and used merchandise, fresh produce, and "sophisticated junque." Dealers and shoppers come from all over, and camping space is provided for those who want to come on Friday afternoon and spend the night. There is plenty of food available, including a taco stand and snack bar with mini doughnuts and popcorn. Toilet facilities are available.

**DEALER RATES:** $9 per day. Reservations are suggested.

**CONTACT:** Steve and Judy Hansen, Pea Pickin' Flea Mart, 1938 Little Blake Ln, Luck WI 54853. Tel: (715) 857-5479 or 483-9460.

# OTHER FLEA MARKETS

We know or have heard about these markets, but have not personally contacted each one, as we have the markets with descriptions. If you plan to visit one of these markets listed below, *please call first* to make sure they are still open. Flea markets do come and go. While they were open when we went to press, they may not be later. We can't be responsible. *Call first!*

**Janesville:** Janesville Flea Market, 3029 S CR G. Tel: (608) 755-9830.

**Janesville:** Red Carpet Flea Market, 25 W Milwaukee St. Tel: (608) 756-9878

**Kaukauna:** Greyhound Park-N-Market Inc, 1601 Delenglade. Tel: (920) 766-6613.

**West Allis:** Rummage-O-Rama, 8100 W Greenfield Ave. Tel: (414) 521-2111.

**Wild Rose:** Wild Rose Flea Market & Craft, 350 CR G & H. Tel: (920) 622-4949.

# WYOMING

## CASPER
### Antique Show and Sale

**DATES:** The first full weekend in June and October.
**TIMES:** Saturday 10:00 AM-5:00 PM; Sunday 10:00 AM-4:00 PM.
**ADMISSION:** $1.25 per person. Free parking is provided.
**LOCATION:** Central Wyoming Fairgrounds. Take CY Ave (Hwy 220) from downtown Casper.
**DESCRIPTION:** This indoor show began in 1971 and currently draws a select 40 dealers selling only antiques and collectibles. Run by a non-profit organization, The Casper Antique and Collectors Club, which donates to Wyoming museums and other charities, this show is said to be among the largest in the state. Food is served on the grounds.
**DEALER RATES:** $25 per 8' table, 4-table minimum. Reservations are required. There is a long waiting list.
**CONTACT:** Casper Antique and Collectors Club Inc, c/o Mr Bruce Smith, 1625 S Kenwood, Casper WY 82601-4049. Tel: (307) 234-6663.

### Casper Flea Market

**DATES:** March, August and November. Call for dates.
**TIMES:** Saturday 10:00 AM-5:00 PM; Sunday 10:00 AM-4:00 PM.
**ADMISSION:** $.50. Parking is free.
**LOCATION:** Central Wyoming Fairgrounds. Take CY Ave (Hwy 220) from downtown Casper.
**DESCRIPTION:** Started in 1974, this indoor flea market is sponsored by the Casper Antique and Collectors Club, a non-profit organization. Forty-five dealers gather to trade in antiques, collectibles and miscellaneous items.
**DEALER RATES:** $20 per 8' table. Reservations are required.
**CONTACT:** Casper Antique and Collectors Club Inc, c/o Mr Bruce Smith, 1625 S Kenwood, Casper WY 82601-4049. Tel: (307) 234-6663.

## CHEYENNE
### Avenues Flea Market and Auction

**DATES:** Daily.
**TIMES:** Monday through Saturday 10:00 AM-5:00 PM, Sunday 12:00 PM-5:00 PM.
**ADMISSION:** Free. Parking is free.

**LOCATION:** 315½ E 7th Ave, at Evans Ave.

**DESCRIPTION:** This indoor market opened in 1993 with 50 dealers selling antiques, collectibles, coins, books, clothing, used merchandise, furniture, Western memorabilia, "a great collection of Victorian glassware and estate jewelry," and furniture.

**DEALER RATES:** Call for rates and to check on vacancies.

**CONTACT:** Avenues Flea Market & Auction, 315½ E 7 Ave, Cheyenne WY 82001. Tel: (307) 635-5600.

# JACKSON HOLE
## Mangy Moose Antique Show and Sale

**DATES:** Annually, the second weekend in July. Rain or shine. Call for specific dates. They have added another show, Arts and Antiques at the Mangy Moose, the third weekend in August.

**TIMES:** 9:00 AM-6:00 PM.

**ADMISSION:** Free. Free parking is available.

**LOCATION:** In Teton Village, behind the Mangy Moose Restaurant and the Hostel at the base of the gondola to the Tetons.

**DESCRIPTION:** This outdoor show opened in 1985 and is considered Wyoming's biggest and best antique show. It currently accommodates approximately 95 dealers and is growing fast. This show specializes in fine antiques; dealers display furniture, carpets, jewelry, dolls, accessories, china, silver, Indian items, vintage clothes, books, and much more. All of this is sponsored by the Mangy Moose Restaurant. Food is served on the premises. Jackson Hole, in the heart of the Tetons, offers gondola rides to the top, horseback riding, white water trips, and "the greatest golf in the U.S."

**DEALER RATES:** $185 per 10' × 12' space for all three days. Reservations are required. Bring your own canopy, tables and chairs. If you wish to sell here, and come from far away, the Hostel comes highly recommended.

**CONTACT:** Jan Perkins or Jeffrey, 2902 Breneman St, Boise ID 83703. Tel: (208) 345-0755 or 368-9759. Day of show call (307) 733-4913 at the Hostel; leave a message.

# OTHER FLEA MARKETS

We know or have heard about these markets, but have not personally contacted each one, as we have the markets with descriptions. If you plan to visit one of these markets listed below, *please call first* to make sure they are still open. Flea markets do come and go. While they were open when we went to press, they may not be later. We can't be responsible. *Call first!*

**Cheyenne:** Bargain Barn Flea Market, 2112 Snyder Ave. Tel: (307) 635-2844. Open daily, Mon-Sat 10 AM-5 PM; Sun 12-6 PM.

**Cheyenne:** Bart's Flea Market, 408 E Lincolnway. Tel: (307) 632-0063.

**Cheyenne:** Frontier Wholesale Flea Market, 1515 Carey Ave. Tel: (307) 634-4004. Open Mon-Sat 10 AM-6 PM; Sun 12-5 PM.

**Cheyenne:** Lincolnway Flea Market, 2825 E Lincolnway. Tel: (307) 634-1503.

**Cheyenne:** Stanford & Son Flea Market & Consignment, 715 S Greeley Hwy. Tel: (307) 635-6025. Open daily, 8 AM-8 PM.

**Cheyenne:** Tee Pee Flea Market, 3208 S Greeley Hwy. Tel: (307) 635-8535.

**Riverton:** Flea Market, 524 E Main St. Tel: (307) 857-2487.

# Canada
# and
# International
# Markets

# CANADA

## BRITISH COLUMBIA
### CLEARBROOKE
### Abbottsford Flea Market

**DATES:** Sunday.
**TIMES:** 5:00 AM–4:00 PM.
**LOCATION:** Exhibition Park
**CONTACT:** Tel: (604) 859-7540.

## SURREY
### HiWay 10 Flea Market

**DATES:** Saturday and Sunday.
**TIMES:** 9:00 AM–5:00 PM.
**ADMISSION:** Free. Parking is free.
**LOCATION:** 17790 56th Ave Hwy 10.
**DESCRIPTION:** This market of 300 tables has dealers selling everything including antiques, collectibles, crafts, coins, cards, toys, clothing and new merchandise.
**CONTACT:** Larry Williams, HiWay 10 Flea Market, 17790 56 Ave Hwy 10, Surrey, British Columbia V3S 1E2. Tel and Fax: (740) 594-3808.

# ONTARIO
### BARRIE
### The 400 Market, Inc

**DATES:** Saturday and Sunday.
**TIMES:** 9:00 AM–5:00 PM.
**LOCATION:** Exit 85 Innisfil Beach Road, Hwy 400.
**DESCRIPTION:** This market of 300 dealers, as per others, sells just about everything including antiques, collectibles and new merchandise.
**CONTACT:** The 400 Market, PO Box 1312, Barre, Ontario, L4M 4V3. Tel: (705) 436-1010.

### BROCKVILLE
### The Market

**DATES:** Saturday and Sunday.

**TIMES:** 9:00 AM–4:00 PM.
**ADMISSION:** Free. Parking is free.
**LOCATION:** 175 King St W.
**DESCRIPTION:** This market of 10 vendors specializes in antique and collectibles. It is obviously a tiny but thriving local market. If you stop by, find and say "Hi" to Anna!
**DEALER RATES:** $25 per space.

## Traders Post Flea Market

**DATES:** Saturday and Sunday.
**TIMES:** 9:00 AM–4:00 PM.
**ADMISSION:** Free. Parking is free.
**LOCATION:** 14 Courthouse Ave.
**DESCRIPTION:** This market of 10 vendors specializes in antiques and collectibles. Another thriving local market—Anna comes here, too.
**DEALER RATES:** $25 per space.

---

**Only the Lonely**

Occasionally, a local gent feels lonely. His cure? He puts out a sign reading, "John's Flea Market." Within minutes, someone is bound to stop to chat. If you see the sign—stop and say "Hi!"

---

# MISSISSAUGA
## Fantastic Flea Market

**DATES:** Saturday and Sunday.
**TIMES:** 10:00 AM–5:00 PM.
**ADMISSION:** Free on Saturday, $.25 on Sunday (the money goes to local charity). Parking is free.
**LOCATION:** Dixie Mall, QEW and Dixie Rd.
**DESCRIPTION:** This market of 100 dealers is strictly a flea market in every sense of the word. They sell plenty of old goodies as well as new merchandise. Two small food concessions feed the famished. Its sister market is in North York.
**CONTACT:** Fantastic Flea Market, 1250 S Service Rd, Mississauga, Ontario O5E 1V4, Canada. Tel: (905) 274-9403.

# NORTH YORK
## Fantastic Flea Market
**DATES:** Saturday and Sunday for the flea market.
**TIMES:** 10:00 AM–6:00 PM for the flea market, every day but Monday 10:00 AM–6:00 PM as a regular retail outlet.
**ADMISSION:** Free. Parking is free.
**LOCATION:** 2375 Steels Ave W.
**DESCRIPTION:** On weekends, they open up folding doors and turn the place into a huge flea market with up to 150 dealers selling just about everything you can imagine. During the week they are the Steels West Marketplace.
**CONTACT:** Fantastic Flea Market, 2375 Steels Ave W, North York, Ontario M3J 3A8. Tel: (416) 650-1090.

# STOUFFVILLE
## Stouffville Country Flea Market
**DATES:** Saturday and Sunday.
**TIMES:** Saturday 8:00 AM–4:00 PM, Sunday 9:00 AM–5:00 PM.
**ADMISSION:** Free. Parking is free.
**LOCATION:** 12555 Tenth Line North (Hwy 47 N).
**DESCRIPTION:** This is a flea market in every sense of the word with 300 dealers selling loads of stuff. In 1996 they opened a new building housing a food court and food vendors including a butcher, baker, and deli, selling fresh fruit and other goodies. I'm told the lasagna is superb.
**DEALER RATES:** From $20 per day. Reservations are required for inside, outside is first come, first served.
**CONTACT:** Stouffville Country Flea Market, 12555 Tenth Line N (Hwy 47 N), Stouffville, Ontario L4A 7Z6. Tel: (905) 640-3813.

# TORONTO
## Dr Flea's Hwy 27 and Albion Flea Market
**DATES:** Saturday and Sunday.
**TIMES:** 10:00 AM–5:00 PM.
**ADMISSION:** Free. Parking is free.
**LOCATION:** From Toronto take Hwy 401 to Dixon Rd. Exit (near the airport) to Hwy 27 N. From there it is about a 10-15–minute drive. It would be hard to miss with its 35-foot-tall flea on the top of the building.

**DESCRIPTION:** This market of 400 vendors sells everything including antiques, collectibles and new merchandise.
**DEALER RATES:** $375 per month and up.
**CONTACT:** Dr Flea's Hwy 27 & Albion Flea Market, 8 Westmore Dr, Rexdale, Toronto, Ontario. Tel: (416) 745-FLEA (3532). Fax: (416) 745-7193. Email: drflea@idirect.com.

# QUÉBEC
## BROMONT
### Marché aux Puces de Bromont
**DATES:** First Sunday of May through second Sunday of November.
**TIMES:** 9:00 AM–5:00 PM.
**ADMISSION:** Free. Parking is free.
**LOCATION:** Motorway 10 at Bromont.
**DESCRIPTION:** This indoor market's 350 dealers sell crafts, produce, garage sale finds, furniture, coins, stamps, cards, and new merchandise.

## MONTREAL
### Super Mercado
**DATES:** Thursday through Sunday, year round.
**TIMES:** 9:00 AM–5:00 PM.
**ADMISSION:** Free.
**LOCATION:** Brossard, just south of Montreal.
**DESCRIPTION:** This is the "hot" place to shop around Montreal— which means it is very crowded. While they don't sell antiques, per se, they do sell just about anything else.

## SAINT EUSTACHE
### Marché aux Puces de Saint Eustache
**DATES:** Thursday through Sunday.
**TIMES**: 9:00 AM–5:00 PM.
**ADMISSION:** Free. Parking is free.
**LOCATION:** 640 W. Just north of Montreal, 3 miles before St Eustache.
**DESCRIPTION**: This year-round indoor/outdoor market's dealers sell antiques, collectibles, crafts, produce, garage sale finds, furniture, new merchandise, stamps, coins, and cards among other things. This is one of the biggest markets around and apparently crammed full of customers on Sundays. So beat the crowd and go another day.

# INTERNATIONAL

A note about European markets in the big cities: Generally everyone just walks about the market—no admission fees—and in the cities take the subway and save yourself a lot of aggravation.

In Paris, the market seems to run all daylight hours depending on whether you are visiting shops or wandering among the street vendors.

In England, all the markets I have personally visited or my friends have checked and visited lasted through the mornings only. Most of the fun and excitement was gone after lunch, although there may be a few stragglers.

In the provincal markets, Saturdays are the days—usually a farmers' market in season, like in the small town of Jonquières in Provence with the woman selling homemade goat's cheese out of the back end of a small pickup truck, or the occasional roving market like the one we happened upon in northern Germany.

I haven't put any times and admission information in with the listings, therefore, unless it was pertinent.

# FRANCE
## PARIS
### Marché aux Puces

**DATES:** Saturday through Monday, year round.
**TIMES:** Daylight and then some; just get there.
**LOCATION:** Outside the Porte de Clignancourt Metro station (Line 4—Porte D'Orleans to Porte de Clignancourt). Just about due north at the edge of Paris.
**DESCRIPTION:** This market, started last century when people gathered to sell old clothes, is an institution. Visitors used to eat french fries and dance the polka. In the twenties, masterpiece paintings were found by chance here and made the market famous. Nowadays, it's practically its own village. You can find "anything you want, or don't want, or could ever dream about." You can find the most fabulous antiques and collectibles to the standard flea market t-shirts, bracelets, and whatnots. From food to junque. Vendors are all over the place—on the sidewalks, in shops, filling the streets, wherever. It's a treat. The atmosphere is electric, pulsing, bright, lively, and loud. Hold onto the kids and be prepared to use your elbows.

# ENGLAND
## LONDON
### Bermondsey Market
### (aka New Caledonia Market)

**DATES:** Sundays.

**TIMES:** 5:00 AM–6:00 AM for the serious dealings, but open all day.

**LOCATION:** Walk over Tower Bridge (heading south) to the crossroad (past the vinegar factory), turn right and you are there.

**DESCRIPTION:** This is *the* market in London. The serious antique deals are made here. Just be there very early. If you happen to watch *Lovejoy* on A&E, you'll understand. He mentions this market. It is also the one market where "unauthorized" goods get "legally" traded, according to my source.

### Brick Lane Market

**DATES:** Sundays, year round, 9:00 AM–2:00 PM.

**LOCATION:** Shoreditch tube station, in the East End.

**DESCRIPTION:** Described as "straight out of Dickens," "with the best curry in town" by a London friend of mine, although he also describes the area as "Jack-the-Ripper-type." Everything here is second- to fourth-hand, at least.

### Camden Lock Market

**DATES:** Sundays, year round.

**LOCATION:** Camden Town tube station (Northern Line).

**DESCRIPTION:** This is the current trendy market selling antiques, clothes, and jewelry. It is getting more popular every year. Traffic can get tricky especially during excellent weather. Take the tube.

### Camden Passage (or Walk) Market

**DATES:** Sundays, year round.

**LOCATION:** Outside the Angel tube station, turn right, then turn right again.

**DESCRIPTION:** This outdoor market is mostly shops selling antiques. But they are excellent antiques.

### Petticoat Lane

**DATES:** Sundays, year round.

**TIMES:** Early to noon; after that the excitement is gone.

**LOCATION:** Middlesex Street in East End of London. Take the tube to Liverpool Street (take the road facing the station and the road will take you directly to the market), Aldgate or Aldgate East and follow the noise and crowd.

**DESCRIPTION:** All around the area, vendors are in a garage, on the streets, in shops, wherever. Hold on to anything of yours that you value. Better yet, don't take anything of value with you. This is the granddaddy of markets—full of new merchandise, used stuff, clothing of all sorts, dishes (you have to see the way the vendors display and demonstrate their wares to believe it—spinning, tossing, balancing—it's a performance!), electron-ics, the usual flea stuff, literally whatever. Called Petticoat Lane because petticoats were made here a very long time ago.

In the '70s when I was in London, there was a brass band made up of older gents (doing this to raise money for charity) who would play and entertain here. On Wednesdays they entertained us as we boarded the tube for work from the Earl's Court Station. Their band leader would recognize me from Wednesdays and always dance a little jig and wave to say "Hi." I have him immortalized on film.

## Portobello Road

**DATES:** Saturdays, year round for the big market, daily for the shops.

**TIMES:** Morning is best.

**LOCATION:** West End of London. Take the tube to Notting Hill Gate.

**DESCRIPTION:** This was the classic antique and collectible market of London. If you ever saw the movie *Bedknobs and Broomsticks*, this is where the "market" part was filmed. Saturdays is the open-air market, otherwise the shops are open normal hours. Now it's rather "old hat."

# THE NETHERLANDS
## Queen's Birthday

**DATES:** April 30, every year.

**TIMES:** All day.

**LOCATION:** Everywhere.

**DESCRIPTION:** It's their beloved Queen's birthday, so everywhere and every place is suddenly a flea market, or a huge party or some sort of celebration. This is not to be taken heavily! Enjoy!

# RUSSIA
## MOSCOW
### Ismailovsky Park Market

**DATES:** Saturday and Sunday.
**TIMES:** All day.
**LOCATION:** Ismailovsky Park in northeast Moscow. Take the blue Metro line to Ismailovsky Park station. Get out and follow the long lines ambling towards the market.
**DESCRIPTION:** Another mega market with hundreds and hundreds of vendors at the market, and more poorer vendors lining the way there, all selling everything including nesting dolls, toys, art, Russian everything, wooden spoons and bowls, pins, amber, traditional clothing, and linen among others. Advice: take a Russian-speaking friend if you wish to haggle. And don't attempt to take any ancient religious icons with you; they can't leave the country. From an American who frequents this market, it is worth the trip to Moscow for all the sights, smells and sounds.

A Russian friend gave this sage advice "from a Russian reality" for shopping in big Russian flea markets:

1. Never, ever flash any wads of money around. There are people watching foreigners, waiting for them to do this. When they find a mark—a quick push and the money disappears. It is better to stash small amounts in different pockets. Otherwise, as our friend says, "You'll reach for your key and all that's left will be dust and Moscow air."
2. Don't eat the food in these markets—it isn't always cooked thoroughly. The resulting food poisoning can be a serious problem.
3. If not buying souvenirs keep this in mind: "People do not sell things because they are tired of seeing them, they sell them because something is really wrong with their things. So, keep your eyes open and double-check everything you buy."

# RUSSIAN FAR EAST—MAGADAN
## Street Market of Magadan

**DATES:** Saturday and Sunday.
**TIMES:** Daylight.
**LOCATION:** 1,000 miles west of Anchorage, Alaska.

**DESCRIPTION:** This market of maybe 40-50 dealers is the equivalent of the Super Bowl in Magadan. This is the place to shop. Although originally it was illegal to hold this market, the police patronized it too. Dealers sell clothing, hardware, and stuff you'd expect to find in a supermarket. Much of the wares come from China and Japan. Americans are welcome.

# SPAIN
## MADRID
### Coin and Stamp Market

**DATES:** Sundays.
**TIMES:** Mornings.
**LOCATION:** Plaza Major (the main Plaza of Madrid).
**DESCRIPTION:** If you are looking for any type of coin or stamp, this is the place to come. The columns surrounding the plaza are filled with dealers who have hundreds or more items on display. The collection blows the mind.

### Rastro

**DATES:** Every Sunday, forever.
**TIMES:** Early morning until around 2:00 PM when the place empties.
**LOCATION:** The Rastro secton of Madrid, on the main road to Toledo.
**DESCRIPTION:** This monster market has easily thousands of dealers and even more thousands of shoppers spread over miles of main and side roads, up and down the hilly road. It is quite a sight.

# CAYMAN ISLANDS

In the Cayman Islands, British West Indies, an unofficial national sport—known locally as Garage Sailing—is trolling the "Leaving the Island Sales." You can snag some real bargains. My friends picked up a $70 dive mask for $5. Start out Saturday morning and cruise through George Town, South Sound, and West Bay or grab a copy of the *Caymanian Compass* and check the listings for lawn sales. Trouble is getting the goodies back home, which is why the stuff is being sold in the first place!

# HOW TO BE INCLUDED
# IN THIS DIRECTORY

If you own or operate a flea market and would like to have your market considered for inclusion in the next edition of *The Official® Directory to U.S. Flea Markets*, either write us a letter requesting a questionnaire form or send complete information corresponding to the format currently employed in this directory. Market listings must be complete in order to be considered for publication. For a full explanation of the acceptable format for market listings, refer to the section entitled "How to Use This Book."

Address all mail to:

House of Collectibles
Editorial Department
201 East 50th St
New York NY 10022